DAILY DEVOTIONS FROM

BESIDE STILL WATERS

BARRY STAGNER

THE TRUTH ABOUT GOD

PUBLISHING

BESIDE STILL WATERS

by Barry Stagner

ISBN-13: 978-1-7323808-0-6

Copyright ©2018

The Truth About God Publishing

Printed in the United States of America

For Dad

TABLE OF CONTENTS

INTRODUCTION

Drawing from the Well

—

NOTHING in the history of human literature will ever come remotely close to what you are about to encounter.

Listen to the heartfelt pleas of mankind that arise from the depths of personal pain and despair, and you will hear the ecstatic praise of the same, offered to Him alone who is worthy to receive it.

Together we will read the lyrics to songs that have long since lost their melodies, and we will hear the confessions of a man who has been broken by his own sin.

We will learn how to walk through the valley of the shadow of death and fear no evil. We will discover that we are to bless the Lord *at all times* and let His praise continually be in our mouths—no matter how we are "feeling."

You will soon discover that our study in the Book of Psalms will be much like reaching into a deep well and drawing out untold riches and truth that can we can apply to our everyday lives.

The "Book of Psalms" is actually divided into five smaller books. The first book contains Psalms 1-41, the second, Psalms 42-72, the third book includes Psalms 73-89, the fourth, Psalms 90-106, and the fifth, Psalms 170-150.

Each section, or book, ends with a closing doxology, words of glory to the Lord, and Psalm 150 blesses us with the closing doxology of the entire Psaltery.

The five books included in the Psalms point back to the five books of the Pentateuch—the Law—and include numerous authors along with "the sweet psalmist of Israel," King David, as the primary author.

Books 1 and 2 are Davidic psalms; Book 3 includes the psalms of Asaph and the sons of Korah; Books 4 and 5 are largely anonymous psalms, with a few attributed to King David.

The Book of Psalms has often been called the Hymn Book of Israel, which is a bit of a misnomer, simply because not all psalms are songs.

As a matter of fact, when the Lord gave the children of Israel the Law, it included no instructions for musical worship.

Let's take a look:

Deuteronomy 32:44-47:

So Moses came with Joshua the son of Nun and spoke all the words of this song in the hearing of the people. Moses finished speaking all these words to all Israel, and he said to them: "Set your hearts on all the words which I testify among you today, which you shall command your children to be careful to observe —all the words of this law. For it is not a futile thing for you, because it is your life, and by this word you shall prolong your days in the land which you cross over the Jordan to possess."

The songs of Moses, Miriam, and Deborah were songs of reminder and songs of victory for the nation of Israel, and because of this, some have noted that it was King David who introduced the musical aspect of corporate worship.

Interestingly, the psalms are not all songs. In fact, the five books are interspersed with various types of psalms:

1. The royal psalms are declarations of the greatness of God.

2. The psalms of Zion focus on Jerusalem and the temple as the holy site where they were to worship his name.

3. Penitential psalms are confessions of sin as well as prayers for forgiveness and restoration.

4. The wisdom psalms, including Psalm 1, draw a contrast between the wisdom of God and that of men.

5. The imprecatory psalms call upon God for deliverance and the destruction of Israel's enemies.

6. Prophetic psalms, such as Psalm 2, and Hallel psalms ("Hallel" being a Hebrew word for praise).

There is one more element of the psalms that we need to recognize before we go any further:

Romans 15:4:

> For whatever things were written before were recorded for our learning, that we, through the patience and comfort of the Scriptures, might have hope.

The psalms are very practical when it comes to teaching us patience. It is also from these verses that we find comfort and hope. Let's take the next step and dig a little deeper into the wealth of wisdom, comfort, admonition and practical advice.

Get ready! We are going to examine the psalms a little more deeply. Our text is very down to earth and practical. The title I've chosen is going to bring us down to street level, figuratively, and what we will learn about life from Psalm 1 is twofold: you can choose to live . . . Blessed Up? or Messed Up? (The choice is yours.)

Our journey begins with what is often described as the preface psalm, and there is some evidence of that. Psalms 1 and 2 were actually intended to be a single composition.

As this Davidic psalm prefaces the five books, it will indeed give us an overview of the human condition and the distinctions between the life experience of the godly and the ungodly.

We will find this as a continual theme throughout the five books of the Psalms, including even the imprecatory psalms, where God is not only presented as the one to whom we cry out for deliverance but as the one who actually can, and does, deliver!

The choice is yours. We can live "blessed up" or messed up, and Psalm 1 will tell us why, and how, this is true. Let's begin!

JANUARY

Blessed Up? or Messed Up?

¹Blessed is the man who walks not in the counsel of the ungodly, nor stands in the path of sinners, nor sits in the seat of the scornful; ²But his delight is in the law of the Lord, and in His law he meditates day and night. ³He shall be like a tree planted by the rivers of water, that brings forth its fruit in its season, whose leaf also shall not wither; and whatever he does shall prosper. —*Psalm 1:1-3*

ONE OF the more popular Christian colloquialisms of our day is "*The world needs to know what we are for and not just what we are against.*" Although true, what has come from this is the idea that as Christians we're not supposed to be against anything. Yet here the Holy Spirit inspires David to present the key to living a blessed life in the negative . . .

"Blessed [happy] is the man who does *not* . . ." followed by three idioms for human behavior: "walk," "stand," "sit." We often talk about our "walk with the Lord," and we hear about people "running with the wrong crowd." Those with whom we align ourselves will certainly have an effect on our thinking and behavior. "Standing," as used here, implies taking a position. We may ask where someone "stands" on a particular issue. The progression is clear: those with whom you walk will influence what you stand for and will help to determine your beliefs, morally and spiritually. You will soon find yourself "sitting" with them, i.e, agreeing with their positions.

What's the advice in this, if you want to be a blessed person? Don't listen to the advice of the ungodly! Don't let the world define your course of life or influence your decisions. Above all, never allow yourself to be seated comfortably with worldly people, compromising your beliefs.

To those who take to heart this sound counsel, God offers the beautiful illustration of a tree that is planted by rivers of water, bearing fruit and never withering. In other words, the comparison is to the one who meditates on God's Word day and night, choosing to make Him the focus of their plans and purpose, and who will prosper in all they do.

Psalm 1 shows us the way to be blessed now, and, in the end, receive the reward of eternal life. To follow a different path will ruin one's life and will ultimately lead to eternal death. Blessed up—or messed up? The choice is yours. ("I have set before you life and death; therefore choose life" (Deut 30:19).

January 2

Delightful Living

²But his delight is in the law of the Lord, and in His law he meditates day and night. —Psalm 1:2

WHAT EXACTLY is meant in this verse by "The law of the Lord"? What is it really saying? The Law of God, which the blessed person delights in, some may see as the whole of the Old Testament, but in fact, it seems clear that these verses are talking about the *moral code* of God, which was given to Moses on Mt. Sinai. The book of Romans explains that the law of God does a bit of a role reversal once we are saved. In fact, the same law that condemns all under sin protects all who come to Christ and are saved!

Consider this, for example: "You shall not commit adultery" (Exodus 20:14).

Let me ask you: Who has the more blessed life? The person who is faithful in their marriage? Or is it the one who ravages their spouse, and often their children, by committing adultery, leaving a trail of unbearable grief?

Consider this verse: "You shall not covet your neighbor's house; you shall not covet your neighbor's wife . . . " (Exodus 20:17). What do you think? Is a person more blessed by being content with such things as he has, or by working night and day to obtain the illusive and fleeting riches of this world, which are passing away? Or by dreaming of another partner and growing to despise the one whom you promised to love, honor, and cherish?

It's really pretty simple: God will not force anyone to do things His way. On the other hand, He will not bless disobedience (even though disobedient believers may also enjoy the *common grace* of God, just as the ungodly do, because God is good). But who wants to live hanging onto the edge like that? The dos and don'ts of the Christian faith both lead to *blessings*! There are things that we are to be for and things we are to be against, and both are cause for divine blessing! The peace we gain in our lives by obeying God's good commandments is well worth the effort. Do you delight in the law of the Lord? There is every reason to do just that! ♪

Life or Death?
The Choice Is Yours

> ³He shall be like a tree planted by the rivers of water, that brings forth its fruit in its season, whose leaf also shall not wither; and whatever he does shall prosper. ⁴The ungodly are not so, but are like the chaff which the wind drives away. ⁵Therefore the ungodly shall not stand in the judgment, nor sinners in the congregation of the righteous. ⁶For the Lord knows the way of the righteous, but the way of the ungodly shall perish. —*Psalm 1:3-6*

THE RESULT of delighting in the Law of the Lord is illustrated here by a tree that is planted by a river, bearing fruit and never withering, followed by the interpretation of the metaphor: *Those who meditate on and follow through with the plans and purposes of God and His Word will prosper in whatever they do.*

In Joshua 1:8-9, we read, "This Book of the Law shall not depart from your mouth, but you shall *meditate* in it day and night, that you may observe to do according to all that is written in it. . . . For the Lord your God is with you wherever you go." [Emphasis added]

From studying Joshua's life, we see that prospering and having success are not defined as the *absence* of trials, tribulations, or battles, but rather the attainment of *victory* through them.

Are you interested in victorious living? Here's the ticket: Set your moral compass, your priorities, and your definition of success by the Word of God, and you will be like a tree that is continually being watered. In other words, you will be fruitful in your endeavors, and even the non-spiritual elements of your life (represented by the leaves) will be blessed.

It isn't so for the ungodly! They are described as "chaff driven away by the wind." Many "church-goers" expect the blessings that follow obedience even as they continue to live in *disobedience* to the Word of God.

God has a better plan for you! He desires that you do His will, and to do that you must seek to *know* His will by studying His Word. The glorious result will be joy and peace in our hearts now, no matter what our circumstances may be, and an incredible future in eternity! ⌣

Fear Not!

¹Why do the nations rage, and the people plot a vain thing? ²The kings of the earth set themselves, and the rulers take counsel together, against the Lord and against His Anointed, saying ³"Let us break their bonds in pieces and cast away their cords from us." —Psalm 2:1-3

REGARDING the continual plotting of the nations against Israel and their God, we are in a day where the same concern applies to us! We daily find ourselves in the midst of attacks against Christians and against Christianity in general. The world seems to have turned upside down. What was once right is now considered wrong (Isaiah 5:20). We may find ourselves fearful for our children and the things to which they are daily exposed; we fear for our income, our jobs, our safety, and often for our very lives.

As we listen to the voice of rebellious man around us, there is an eerily familiar tone to what David, writing under the influence of the Holy Spirit, said of the world. He wrote, in essence, "Why do the nations plot against God [referring to Godhead], collectively seeking to break 'their' bonds and cast away their cords?" (Psalm 2:1-3).

"Bonds and cords" represent the Word of God, with its precepts and principles. Don't we see a concerted effort today in our country to disparage the very Word of God that has brought much blessing and prosperity to our land? In fact, the desire of many is to deny that there is a God at all! ⸬

The Apostle Paul wrote, "The coming of the lawless one is according to the working of Satan, with all power, signs, and lying wonders, and . . . deception among those who perish because they did not receive the love of the truth. . . . For this reason, God will send . . . strong delusion, that they should believe the lie . . . " (2 Thessalonians 2:9-11).

This is a chilling warning that should cause us to search our own hearts. Christians (who are commanded by God to love their enemies and also to speak the truth in love) are considered enemies of "progress" who hold to beliefs considered irrelevant in our postmodern culture. Our world is in a condition of Godlessness, which leads to Lawlessness. In the midst of this, how do we maintain an attitude of Fearlessness? By always keeping in mind what we know to be true from Genesis through Revelation: in the end, the nations rage, but God wins!

When God Laughs

⁴He who sits in the heavens shall laugh; the Lord shall hold them in derision.⁵ Then He shall speak to them in His wrath, ⁵And distress them in His deep displeasure: ⁶"Yet I have set My King on My holy hill of Zion."
—Psalm 2:4-6

THERE'S an old adage: "I'm not laughing at you; I'm laughing with you!" In the verse above, however, God says to men, with all of their plots against Him, "I am not laughing with you; I am laughing *at* you." Imagine the scene: The Father sits in the heavens with the Son at His right hand and laughs with derision as He sees the nations raging and plotting against Him! ↖mockery

Remember how God dealt with arrogant men in the past? I think of Nebuchadnezzar and his seven years of madness resulting from his pride (Daniel 4). Or consider Korah and his followers in their rebellion against Moses (who had been called to lead Israel), and they wound up being swallowed by the earth (Numbers 16)!

One of the most notable reminders that God always wins goes back to when Israel was a fledgling nation that was being forced to exist as slaves in Egypt. Pharaoh commanded that every son born to the Jews was to be cast into the river to drown. He feared that the Israelites would become too great, so he wanted all the males to die, lest a deliverer of this slave nation should arise from among them. So where did God hide the future deliverer of Israel? In Pharaoh's own house, eating at Pharaoh's table, after Pharaoh's own daughter rescued the baby Moses from the basket in which his parents had placed him, setting him adrift in the Nile in an attempt to save his life!

The raging and plotting of man against God is laughable. Neither man nor Satan can ever overturn the will of God, try though they may. In Psalm 52, God speaks to mankind: "Why do you boast in evil, O mighty man? . . . Your tongue devises destruction, like a sharp razor, working deceitfully. You love evil more than good, lying rather than speaking righteousness. . . . God shall likewise destroy you forever . . . (Psalm 52:1-7).

In the end, God and His people win and will have the last laugh when the Lord sets His feet on His holy hill in Zion to rule and reign upon the earth. What a glorious day that will be!

Even so, come quickly, Lord Jesus!

Judgment Day Is Coming!

[7]I will declare the decree: The Lord has said to Me, "You are My Son, Today I have begotten You. [8]Ask of Me, and I will give You the nations for Your inheritance, And the ends of the earth for Your possession. [9]You shall break them with a rod of iron; You shall dash them to pieces like a potter's vessel." [10]Now therefore, be wise, O kings; Be instructed, you judges of the earth. [11]Serve the Lord with fear, And rejoice with trembling. [12]Kiss the Son, lest He be angry, And you perish in the way, When His wrath is kindled but a little. <u>Blessed are all those who put their trust in Him</u>. —Psalm 2:7-12

IN PSALM 2:9, the Lord, speaking to His Son, tells Him that He will "break the nations with a rod of iron [and] crush them like pottery." When did that ever happen? Never, to our knowledge. This leaves us with only two options: either the Bible is wrong, or the Son of God is still to return. What must we expect for the future? It is this: *The only way to stop the advance of human evil is final divine judgment.*

Just as the Lord had said to Noah, "I will destroy man whom I have created . . . both man and beast . . . for I am sorry that I have made them" (Genesis 6:6-7). "But Noah found grace in the eyes of the Lord" (Genesis 6:8). And God did as He had said. A flood destroyed the entire planet. Everyone died except for Noah and His family, whom God had promised to save.

Is our world reaching the point of such wickedness that there is no hope of stemming the tide? Some are finding grace yet today when they look to the Lord, but the overall moral condition of the world has brought it to the point of no return. Though we pray for revival, the sad truth is this: *man will only become more evil as he continues to reject the God of the Bible.* There is only one way to stop the downward spiral. Jesus must come and break the nations "with a rod of iron," just as the psalm above indicates.

To believers, the Holy Spirit says, in essence, "Wise up! Repent of the constant rebelling and rejection of the will and plan of God." Remember: God will forgive any and all sins committed against Him except the sin of rejecting Jesus. If Christ is rejected, as the Bible says He will be, there is no hope of reconciliation with God. <u>We must search our own hearts in the days ahead</u>, remembering the Apostle John's plea at the end of the book of Revelation, when Jesus says, "Surely I am coming quickly": *Even so, come, Lord Jesus!*

Be ready!

Lord, Teach Us to Pray

¹Give ear to my words, O Lord, consider my meditation. ²Give heed to the voice of my cry, my King and my God, for to You will I pray. ³My voice shall You hear in the morning, O Lord, in the morning I will direct it to You, and I will look up. —*Psalm 5:1-3*

I BELIEVE I can say with confidence that we all would like to have a more effectual prayer life. Most of us wonder, "If God already knows what's going to happen, and if He's going to do things His way anyway, then why do we even need to pray?"

It's important to understand why God wants us to pray. First of all, does He hear and answer our prayers? Yes! And yet, in the verses above, David asks the Lord to "consider his meditation" and "give heed to the voice of his cry." Notice that he respectfully addresses God the first thing in the morning.

In fact, it's best to *preface* any endeavor or decision with prayer. Don't wait to pray until after you've tried everything else! Give your concerns to the Lord before you jump in and end up messing up and having to start over again or before you ruin something that you had thought was for good.

David prays with reverence, awe, and expectation. It isn't a "work." The *spirit* of prayer is more important than the *practice*. In Matthew, Jesus contrasted the hypocrites, who pray publicly, " . . . that they may be seen by men," to the way we are encouraged to pray: "Go into your room, and when you have shut your door, pray to your Father . . . and your Father who sees in secret will reward you openly. And . . . do not use vain repetitions . . . " (Mt 6:5-7). Sincere, heartfelt prayer is what we see with David. It's the spirit in which we pray that's the most important aspect of our prayer.

In summary, if we want to understand, own, and excel at effective prayer, we must pray *from* our hearts what is *in* our hearts for the things we believe are in the will of God. And God, who hears our hearts' cries from heaven, will respond in love.

(No is also love.)

Lord, Forgive Me for My Sins

⁴For You are not a God who takes pleasure in wickedness, nor shall evil dwell with You. ⁵The boastful shall not stand in Your sight; You hate all workers of iniquity. ⁶You shall destroy those who speak falsehood; the Lord abhors the bloodthirsty and deceitful man. ⁷But as for me, I will come into Your house in the multitude of Your mercy; In fear of You I will worship toward Your holy temple. —Psalm 5:4-7

IN THIS PSALM, David draws a contrast between the unrighteous and the righteous by exalting God in His righteousness, which is what worship songs are supposed to do. David states that God takes no pleasure in wickedness, and that evil does not dwell with Him. He hates all workers of iniquity. In the Hebrew language, "hate" isn't an indication of God's emotion but rather of His reaction. And what is that reaction? The verse goes on to say that He will ultimately destroy the wicked!

Looking within our own hearts as we contemplate these verses, we come to see that we fall under the same categories we see listed in these verses. Are we boastful? Do we ever do the things that God hates? Have we lied? Acted hatefully? Lived dishonestly? It's then that we realize what we really need to pray about: our own sins! We're pretty comfortable asking God to deal with those who have caused harm to us, or those whom we see around us doing things that we know are offensive to the Lord. But when it comes to our having hurt others or sinned against God, we tend come before Him with false humility: "Lord, you know that I am but dust. I am weak, Lord. Have mercy on this small offense, Father. I slipped up, and I didn't mean to."

To take this a little further, let's look at another psalm to see what the writer said in his prayer: "*If I regard iniquity in my heart, the Lord will not hear . . .*" (Psalm 66:18-20). Many people seem to be unable to pray the way the Lord wants them to because sin is bossing them around! The one prayer that God wants to hear from us is that we agree with Him about our sin: that it is evil, and we must repent because it grieves Him. Then, the Bible tells us, "Repent therefore, and be converted, that your sins may be blotted out, so that times of refreshing may come from the presence of the Lord" (Acts 3:19).

And that is how our prayer time may be truly pure before the Lord!

An Honest Look at Our Hearts

⁸Lead me, O Lord, in Your righteousness because of my enemies; Make Your way straight before my face. ⁹For there is no faithfulness in their mouth; Their inward part is destruction; Their throat is an open tomb; They flatter with their tongue. ¹⁰Pronounce them guilty, O God! Let them fall by their own counsels; Cast them out in the multitude of their transgressions, For they have rebelled against You. ¹¹But let all those rejoice who put their trust in You; Let them ever shout for joy, because You defend them; Let those also who love Your name Be joyful in You. ¹²For You, O Lord, will bless the righteous; With favor You will surround him as with a shield. —Psalm 5:8-12

IN THIS PSALM, David continues to contrast the wicked and the righteous. He says that the words of the wicked come from a heart of destruction, but he asks God to lead *him* in the way of *righteousness* and to make His way straight before him. The following two verses show us what this means.

"*The steps of a good man are ordered by the Lord. . . . Though he should fall, he shall not be utterly cast down; for the Lord upholds him with His hand*" (Ps 37:23-24). "*Trust in the Lord with all your heart, and lean not on your own understanding: in all your ways acknowledge Him, and He shall direct your paths*" (Prv 3:5-7).

So, in order to pray the way that God wants us to pray, we must trust that He hears our cries and will answer our prayers, even when we don't see it. Remember: prayer is seeking God for *His* will—not just telling Him *ours*.

David doesn't hesitate in this psalm to call out the enemies of God. <u>Plots against us are plots against God!</u> David prays that God might let the wicked reap what they have sown; that they might experience the consequences of their rebellion. When attacks against God's children come, Satan is the one behind it. <u>Never forget that the battle belongs to the Lord.</u> Jesus is Victor!

Prayer is an expression of trust and confidence in the will and power of God. Why pray if you don't believe that He will answer? Remember: your situations are *never* impossible. And your enemies? They are fighting against God himself, because He is your shield! So, if we can trust Him in that, then we can believe that we also have our requests for other things, like being soul winners, better witnesses, living righteously in a wicked world. That's the meaning of fervent, effectual prayer! Do I hear an "Amen"? AMEN!

[handwritten margin note:] God takes abuse toward us personally!

Lord of All Creation

¹O Lord, our Lord, How excellent is Your name in all the earth, who have set Your glory above the heavens! ²Out of the mouth of babes and nursing infants You have ordained strength, because of Your enemies, that You may silence the enemy and the avenger. —Psalm 8:1-2

NOTHING in the world requires more attention than a human child, yet here David states that from the mouths of babies and nursing infants God has ordained strength and silenced the enemy! Matthew 21:14-16 ends with the chiefs and scribes, who were upset that children were crying out "Hosanna to the Son of David" in the temple, being rebuked by Jesus, who asked, "Have you never read, 'Out of the mouth of babes and nursing infants You have perfected praise'?" (This indicates that praise was being offered to the Lord in the face of God's enemies, as Psalm 8 describes.

In verse 1, David looks all the way back to creation as a source of praise, and we, too, should praise our Creator to silence the enemies of creation who strike out at God and the idea of creation in hatred. In verse 2, David also points to helpless, innocent human babies as a reason for praising God.

Genesis 1:27-28 tells us that "God created man in His own image . . . male and female He created them." Evolution could never have resulted in a human child. Think of it! A baby is far too complex, too needy, to possibly survive without the attention of a mother. And there had to be a mother and a father to produce the child, which would have required two fully formed adult humans—a male and a female—either through science's theory of "punctuated equilibrium," or the miracle of "In the beginning God . . . "

Think about it. Which perspective gives you a greater respect for life: 1) you came from nowhere, your life means nothing, and neither will your death, because you were just part of the evolutionary process without purpose or meaning, or 2) you were fearfully and wonderfully made in the image and likeness of God, who has a purpose for your life and has made a way for you to live in endless perfection with Him forever?

I'm going with the Bible on this one! I don't want to stake my future on a fairy tale. How about you?

How Does God View Man?

3 When I consider Your heavens, the work of Your fingers, the moon and the stars, which You have ordained, 4what is man that You are mindful of him, and the son of man that You visit him? 5For You have made him a little lower than the angels, and You have crowned him with glory and honor. —Psalm 8:3-5

SOMEONE once said, "No one goes to the Grand Canyon to feel better about one's self." When you look at the Grand Canyon, the mighty oceans, or the majesty of the Alps or Himalayas, you don't walk away thinking, *Man, I am awesome!*

David has the proper perspective. He says, "Lord, when I consider your heavens, the work of your fingers, the moon and the stars . . . what am I in the midst of all of this?" He answers his own question: Man was made a "little lower than [lit.] Elohim" ["God," in the original]. The truth is that man will never be equal to God, yet in all of God's creation, man is the highest order of being. Yes, the Bible says that God has made man "a little lower than angels" (Heb 2:6-8) in our subjection to hunger, thirst, pain, and death, all due to the sin of Adam and Eve in the Garden. And yet angels are "spirits sent forth to minister to those who will inherit salvation" (Heb 1:14). We also read "Do you not know that we shall judge angels?" (1 Cor 6:3).

Does the lesser judge the greater? No, man in his restored sinless and glorified state will judge the angels with the Lord, because men, not angels, are created in the image and likeness of God. The highest order of living beings in all of the heavens and the earth is obviously of great value to God.

David says, "Lord, in light of all your vast creation, the magnificent heavens, and the countless stars and planets, what is man that you are mindful of and visit him?" God's answer, in essence: "Man is made in My likeness and image, and human life is therefore sacred above all else." Ignoring that one fact has brought us the world we have today.

That's a lot to ponder. May the Lord continue to draw us and to open our eyes to the wonders of His creation and His incredible plan to include us in His future plans!

Yes we should be good stewards of creation but not at the expense of humans!

How Does Man View God?

⁶You have made him to have dominion over the works of Your hands; You have put all things under his feet, ⁷all sheep and oxen—even the beasts of the field, ⁸the birds of the air, and the fish of the sea, that pass through the paths of the seas. ⁹O Lord, our Lord, how excellent is Your name in all the earth! —Psalm 8:6-9

MANY WHO ATTEND church today believe that "portions" of the Bible are inspired by God, or, as they say, "The Bible *contains* the Word of God." This has left the church without influence in our world today. If the Word of God is not absolute truth, then it is subject to either consensus or regional beliefs, which leaves us to our own ideas about how we *feel* about God and His Word. Here's the thing: *Feelings are not the unit of measure we use when determining truth.*

Man's dominion on Earth is reflective of God's dominion in heaven. Our God is Lord of all creation, which is subject to Him. He has dominion over the stars, planets, angels, and people. And He has set man over all that He made on Earth.

God rules over the universe, but on this one planet, where we *know* there is life, He is mindful of man and visits him, encircling him with the honor of being His stewards over the earth and having dominion over all the works of His hands. The question for us is: Are we living up to the role He has assigned us as His ambassadors and living as salt and light on the earth? Satan has been trying to diminish the role of man by attacking his mind through evolution and the postmodern worldview. Why? Because Satan hates man. Man will have what Satan wanted but could never attain as an angel—to be in God's image and likeness. He has tried to drag man down from the beginning by subverting the Word of God in man's mind.

Compared to the universe, we are pretty insignificant. Yet God is mindful of us and "visits" us. This is why David praises God and declares that His name is excellent in all the earth and His glory greater than the heavens. !

Are you living like you are part of the royal priesthood today? Because you are! Am I?

Overcoming through Praise

¹I will praise You, O Lord, with my whole heart; I will tell of all Your marvelous works. ²I will be glad and rejoice in You; I will sing praise to Your name, O Most High. *—Psalm 9:1-2*

THOSE WHO WAIT upon the Lord shall renew their strength; they shall mount up with wings like eagles . . . (Isaiah 40:30)

Instructions that precede this psalm state that it's to be accompanied by the tune of "Death of the Son." Some believe it's about the death of the son of David and Bathsheba after their sinful encounter, and others claim that it's a song of mourning over the death of his son Absalom.

And yet, David's psalm of lament begins with praise! As Isaiah suggests, he "ascends on high" like an eagle above his enemies even in his despair.

We often think, "I'll never be able to 'soar' again, because this moment is too heavy!" You feel as though you're grounded by your circumstances. But hang in there! Psalm 9 will show us that what Isaiah says is true! When in distress, it's good for us to understand the principles of flight (in a spiritual sense). Simply put, if the upward force is greater than the gravitational force imposed on an object, the object will go up. If the gravitational force is greater, the object will go down or remain on the ground.

But how can we be lifted up when we are at our lowest point, spiritually speaking? Despite his sorrow, David says, "*I will praise you*, O Lord, unreservedly, with my whole heart." Praise, the "greater force," is lifting him up. He then begins to recite God's marvelous works, being glad and rejoicing in the Lord, and singing praise to the "Name above all names."

Just as in physics the greater force wins, so in our spiritual lives praise can be the force that gets us through *anything*! We praise God not because there is an absence of pain or problems, nor because there is an abundance of material blessings. We praise God for *who He is*! God is worthy to be praised for His creative power, His perfection, wisdom, mercy, grace, longsuffering. Even at our lowest points, He deserves our praise and thanksgiving. Praise is what gives us God's power to get through *anything*, even soaring above our problems and distresses when all seems lost.

Don't Let the Devil Drag You Down!

³When my enemies turn back, they shall fall and perish at Your presence. ⁴For You have maintained my right and my cause; You sat on the throne judging in righteousness. ⁵You have rebuked the nations, You have destroyed the wicked; You have blotted out their name forever and ever. ⁶O enemy, destructions are finished forever! And you have destroyed cities; Even their memory has perished. ⁷But the Lord shall endure forever; He has prepared His throne for judgment. —*Psalm 9:3-7*

DOES THE DEVIL ever try to drag you down? Peter wrote: "Do not think it strange concerning the fiery trial which is to try you. . . . But rejoice to the extent that you partake of Christ's sufferings, that when His glory is revealed, you may also be glad . . . " (1 Peter 4:12-16).

In physics, the term "drag coefficient" means the calculation of the amount of *thrust* necessary to overcome the *drag* resistance as an object is being forced through something (e.g., air or water). We can apply the same idea to Satan's attempts to drag us down. Does God have the power to overcome Satan? David believed so. From what he wrote in Psalm 9, we can understand two things: 1) We can insert our own adversaries and struggles into these verses, and 2) he describes what God has done as a "finished work," or already done. That's the omniscient sovereignty of God!

Spiritually speaking, God is able to overcome the "drag coefficient" in your life. God has always known what you would go through, and He knows how to get you through it now (Isaiah 51:7-8). What should be our response? To praise Him! Remember, Satan will try to stifle and stagnate us, in order to keep us from moving forward with God. He wants us to believe that nothing can help, so what's the point of serving God?

Much as the engine on a plane needs to be engaged in order for the second law of the physics of flight to become useful, *praise* must be initiated for us to move forward (see Psalm 34:1). David, in v. 7 above, showed His faith in God as he faced Satan's oppressive tactics by viewing his enemies as *already defeated*. He praised God as if Satan were already finished! As we, too, praise the One who is more powerful than our enemies, we'll begin to experience freedom from fear and oppression when going through fiery trials. Like the Apostle Paul (Philippians 3:12), are you encouraged to "press on"?

When the Pressure's On

*8*He shall judge the world in righteousness, and He shall administer judgment for the peoples in uprightness. *9*The Lord also will be a refuge for the oppressed . . . *10*And those who know Your name will put their trust in You . . . *11*Sing praises to the Lord, who dwells in Zion! Declare His deeds among the people. *12*When He avenges blood, He remembers them; He does not forget the cry of the humble. *13*Have mercy on me, O Lord! . . . *14*that I may tell of all Your praise in the gates. . . . *15*The nations have sunk down in the pit which they made; in the net which they hid, their own foot is caught. *16*The Lord is known by the judgment He executes; ❧The wicked is snared in the work of his own hands. . . . *18*For the needy shall not always be forgotten; the expectation of the poor shall not perish forever. *19*Arise, O Lord . . . let the nations be judged in Your sight. *20* . . . that the nations may know themselves to be but men. Selah
—*Psalm 9:8-20*

ANOTHER PRINCIPLE related to the physics of flight states that an *increase* of a flow results in a *decrease* of pressure. Under some conditions, airflow above the wing [of a plane or a bird] travels faster than the flow below the wing, so the pressure below the wing is higher than that above it. Lift is created that *pushes the wing upward*. How does this apply to us? Although the pressure from below may feel very strong, that is the very force that can lift you up!

David stressed that *public* praise is important (v. 11), and there is *never* a time when praise is powerless. When the pressures of life are exploited by the enemy and he tries to talk you into setting aside the work of God, remind him that God is doing a great work in your life and you are going to use the hard times as a resource to lift yourself up through praising Him.

Praise will raise us up and thrust us forward at all times. Do we allow the presence of our enemies to silence our praise? Or do we long to bring glory to God when things seem to be working against us and the outcome doesn't look good, or even when tragedy has already occurred?

Consider this: we are designed for praising the Lord. Everything in creation will one day bow the knee and acknowledge that Jesus is Lord, but some won't praise Him. The devil and his angels will acknowledge Him, but they won't praise Him. Believers can and must praise Him. So if you have breath this morning, let the pressure from below your "wing" (no matter how intense) lift you above, and praise the Lord! It is what you were created for!

January 16

Godliness Defined

[1]Help, Lord, for the godly man ceases! For the faithful disappear from among the sons of men. They speak idly everyone with his neighbor; [2]With flattering lips and a double heart they speak. [3]As for the saints who are on the earth, "They are the excellent ones, in whom is all my delight." [4]Their sorrows shall be multiplied who hasten after another god; their drink offerings of blood I will not offer, nor take up their names upon my lips. *Psalm 12:1-4]*

Ps 12:1-2
Ps 16:3-4

WHAT'S THE DEFINITION of the word "godliness"? It actually means piety or reverence toward God, and represents a willing submission, acknowledging God as Lord and Master. We need to recognize this, because today many believe that godliness can be whatever they imagine it is.

In Luke 6:46, Jesus, speaking to the multitudes, said, "But why do you call me 'Lord, Lord' and not do the things which I say?" This is what many attempt to do, and the Bible calls it honoring the Lord with one's lips but not with one's heart; in other words, being hypocritical in their faith (Matthew 15:8). Submitting to God doesn't mean to grudgingly obey Him. In fact, submission begins where David did in these verses above, acknowledging God as almighty and the only One in whom we can put our trust. David humbly admits that God is the One who knows what's best, and he wants to willingly submit to Him.

We are definitely living in days where the godly man appears to have ceased and even the faithful have disappeared (v. 1). Wickedness and lies surround us. Even professing Christians have bought into many false ideas about God in the ways that they choose to "honor" and "worship" Him. Man has put himself on the throne in place of God, and many don't even realize it. David, in verses 3 and 4, makes a clear distinction between those who truly honor the Lord and those who believe they have the right to do whatever they please *in the Lord's name*, warning that they are actually going after other gods.

May we, like David, cry out, "Help, Lord! For the godly man ceases." And may we pray with sincere hearts that we will be willing to stand up for His Word and His truth, demonstrating our godliness by showing God's love to any deceived ones whom we may encounter this very day!

Help me, Lord, to be a good and faithful servant.

Are You Seeking to Be Blessed?

⁵O Lord, You are the portion of my inheritance and my cup; You maintain my lot. ⁶The lines have fallen to me in pleasant places; yes, I have a good inheritance. ⁷I will bless the Lord who has given me counsel; my heart also instructs me in the night seasons. ⁸I have set the Lord always before me; because He is at my right hand I shall not be moved. —Psalm 16:5-8

IN THESE VERSES, David acknowledges the blessings of God in his own life, and, as he says, the Lord is his portion and His cup. In other words, the Lord is his *source of blessing*. When he speaks of the "lines" falling to him "in pleasant places," David is saying that God has blessed him greatly.

In Psalm 103, David wrote, "*Bless the Lord, O my soul; and all that is within me, bless His holy name! Bless the Lord, O my soul; and forget not all His benefits; who forgives all your iniquities, who heals all your diseases, who redeems your life from destruction, who crowns you with lovingkindness and tender mercies, who satisfies your mouth with good things, so that your youth is renewed like the eagle's.*"

It would be easy to think, *Well, of course David was thankful and praised the Lord. His "lines fell to him in pleasant places." He was a king. And he was rich.* Although David acknowledges this in Psalms 16 and 103, he also establishes in both psalms that the spiritual blessings of God are the greatest blessings.

It's interesting that those whom the Bible records as being significantly blessed materially are those who didn't seek it. Abraham gave the best land to Lot for his flocks and herds, and God blessed Abraham, while Lot wound up in Sodom. Solomon was given the chance to ask for anything he wanted from God, and he asked God for wisdom to rule God's people. God gave that to him along with great wealth.

Do we demonstrate our godliness by being thankful to God for our material blessings, whether they are much or little, according to the world's measure? We're to live by faith and trust in God no matter what life may bring!

January 18

Can You Believe It?

> ⁹Therefore my heart is glad, and my glory rejoices; my flesh also will rest in hope. ¹⁰For You will not leave my soul in Sheol, nor will You allow Your Holy One to see corruption. ¹¹You will show me the path of life; in Your presence is fullness of joy; at Your right hand are pleasures forevermore. —Psalm 12:9-11

DAVID ends this psalm with praise, expressing his gladness for God's salvation, His faithfulness, and His kindness. This psalm also contains one of the great Messianic verses, establishing for us why there is hope! David says that God's Holy One will not undergo the decay of His flesh in the grave (v.10).

Flash forward to the New Testament book of John. In chapter 11, Jesus has come to the home of Martha and Mary, sorrowing with them over the death of their brother Lazarus. We read in verse 38: "Then Jesus, again groaning in Himself, came to the tomb. It was a cave, and a stone lay against it. Jesus said, 'Take away the stone.' Martha, the sister of him who was dead, said . . . 'Lord, by this time there is a stench, for he has been dead four days. . . .'" Jesus did return life to Lazarus's body, but it had already begun the natural process of decay and would need to be restored by the Lord.

Jesus' human body did *not* go through that decay process, even in the grave, just as the Lord had promised. To believe that Jesus conquered death for all of us is one more factor in proving our own godliness.

Summing up the lessons of these last three days in Psalm 12, when we truly believe all that has been revealed here, what are the wonderful results?

1. We will willingly submit to God as our Lord and Master.
2. We will have a love for the things and people of God.
3. We will live by faith in God, no matter what life brings.

Life has its problems, but the source of our hope and joy is that we, too, will rise one day to immortal incorruptibility and forever be with the Lord! God has shown us the path of life through Jesus Christ, and at the end of that path, we, through faith and trust in God, await fullness of joy and pleasures forevermore! Let's go out today with that promise in our hearts. (v.11)

Fool's Gold

¹The fool has said in his heart, "There is no God." They are corrupt, they have done abominable works, there is none who does good. ²The Lord looks down from heaven upon the children of men, to see if there are any who understand, who seek God. ³They have all turned aside, they have together become corrupt; there is none who does good, no, not one. —Psalm 14:1-3

KING DAVID experienced the same emotional tidal wave that Elijah did and that we often do when he cried out to God: "Help, Lord, for the godly man ceases! For the faithful disappear from among the sons of men" (Psalm 12:1). What a messed up world we live in! But, like David and Elijah, we must remember that the Lord always has His remnant, and in His own sovereign will He allows things to degenerate to the point where we may feel like we're all alone—but we're not. Jesus said the righteous would be relatively few in the last days and even drew a comparison to the days of Noah (2 Peter 4:11). To reiterate: we may be few, but *we are not alone.*

We live in an age where human opinion is exalted above the Word of God. This is fool's gold. It won't stand in the Day of Judgment; it won't prevail over the Word of God.

People today are embracing things that they think are golden—tolerance that rejects the Word of God, morality that denies God's moral code—and because they "feel good" about these things, they think their opinions are *like* gold. And indeed they are. Fool's gold.

Psalm 14 pits the foolishness of man against the contrasting omniscience and perfect wisdom of God. Verse 1 sets the stage and gives us great insight into man's love of fool's gold: "The fool has said *in his heart. . . ."* So we see that this is not a cognitive decision but a moral one. It comes from the heart, not the mind, and is in defense of corrupt, abominable behavior. Saying "no" to God always leads to moral depravity. Man may think that he is evolving beyond the antiquated and outdated mandates of Scripture, but look around, Christian! Is our world getting better? NO!

It is the fool who says "no" to God and chooses instead the way whose end is the way of death. Let's say "yes" to God and all of His Word, for blessed is the man who walks not in the counsel of the ungodly!

Help me, Lord, to have a hearing heart for You only!

Pity the Fool

⁴Have all the workers of iniquity no knowledge, who eat up my people as they eat bread, and do not call on the Lord? ⁵There they are in great fear, for God is with the generation of the righteous. ⁶You shame the counsel of the poor, but the Lord is his refuge. —*Psalm 14:4-6*

DO YOU ever wonder why God's children have to go through abuse and suffering when they're doing their best to serve the Lord out of love for Him? In these verses David takes note of the fact that a very difficult reality is that those who don't acknowledge God or those who hate Him will often abuse those who love Him, sometimes to the point where they fear for their lives. But God knows all about it, and ultimately the ungodly and their actions will be put to shame. Psalm 1:5-6 tells us "...the ungodly shall not stand in the judgment... for the Lord knows the way of the righteous, but the way of the ungodly shall perish."

A hard truth for Christians has always been that no matter in what era one lives, there will always be the Neros, Domitians, Islamic Caliphates, Ottoman Empires, Hitlers, Stalins, etc. Because these hate God, they hate and persecute His people. Jesus said, "*If the world hates you, know that it hated Me before it hated you. If you were of the world, the world would love its own. Yet because you are not of the world, but I chose you out of the world, therefore the world hates you*" (John 15:18-19).

Conversely, the Scriptures tell us that our response to the haters is to love them in return! Whether they're liars, thieves, the sexually immoral, gossips, or even murderers, we are to love them. And there's no greater act of love than to warn someone that there are consequences for sin and the denial of God's moral and spiritual standards. In fact, to condone or minimize sin is the most hateful thing a person can do, knowing full well that the wages of sin is death.

Although most of the ones we will try to reach with the gospel of Jesus will reject you and Him, we must press on. Even if we're separated from the ones we love because we love the Lord, nothing can separate us from His love. Ever! "*Be strong in the Lord, and in the power of His might. Put on the whole armor of God that you may be able to stand against the wiles of the devil ...*" (Ephesians 6:10-11), always keeping in mind that it's not people against whom we wrestle but Satan himself. And the good news is that he has already been defeated.

Don't Be "Fools, and Slow of Heart . . ."

⁷Oh, that the salvation of Israel would come out of Zion! When the Lord brings back the captivity of His people, let Jacob rejoice and Israel be glad. —*Psalm 14:7*

"ZION" is an idiom for Jerusalem. "Salvation" in this verse means deliverance, and, in this case, deliverance from the persecution of the God haters mentioned in yesterday's verses. David longs for the deliverer to arise, speaking prophetically of when God will bring His people back into the land of Israel, never to be uprooted again. In those days, "Jacob" and "Israel" will rejoice and be glad.

In the times in which we live, where fools seem to reign, and good is called evil, and evil is called good, we see the consequences all around us. David ends this psalm on a hopeful note, and we will do the same.

Listen, Christian, in an age where we are belittled and demeaned, where God is mocked, and there is no fear of Him (and therefore no fear of consequences for persecuting His people), where it's popular to say that there is no God and be applauded and respected for doing so, remember: it's all fool's gold. But here's the truth: A permanent change is coming soon! What does that mean?

Never forget that *this world is not our home*, and the Lord will not strive with man forever. Revelation 1:7-8 says, "*Behold, He is coming with clouds, and every eye will see Him, even they who pierced Him. And all the tribes of the earth will mourn because of Him. Even so, Amen. 'I am the Alpha and the Omega, the Beginning and the End,' says the Lord, 'who is and who was and who is to come, the Almighty.'*"

We also read in Philippians, "*Therefore God also has highly exalted Him and given Him the name which is above every name, that at the name of Jesus every knee should bow, of those in heaven, and of those on earth, and of those under the earth, and that every tongue should confess that Jesus Christ is Lord, to the glory of God the Father*" (2:9-11). Stay bold! Deliverance is coming from Zion, and it will be permanent! His kingdom is an everlasting kingdom that has no end. Although fool's gold may be highly valued, even in much of the church, permanent change is coming—and it just might be today!

In truth, we already enjoy this. We've been set free from our captivity to sin, and joy and gladness can be ours right now while we wait for our deliverance. We can rejoice that we've been counted worthy to suffer shame for the name of Christ. Even though fools abound and their foolishness and lack of wisdom may impact us at times, the change that is coming will happen in a moment—in the twinkling of an eye—and you and I will put on immortal incorruptibility and will forever be with the Lord! (1 Corinthians 15:52).

Godliness Defined

¹Preserve me, O God, for in You I put my trust. ²O my soul, you have said to the Lord, "You are my Lord, my goodness is nothing apart from You." —Psalm 16:1-2

WHAT is the Christian life supposed to look like? We often talk of holiness, moral purity, and sanctification, or setting ourselves apart for service to God. But what exactly is godliness?

The word actually means piety, or reverence, toward God. How does David exhibit piety toward his Father? He says to Him, "You are my Lord," using the word "Adonai," which means "master." How well David understood the role of God!

He also contrasts himself with God, saying that apart from God's helping him, his own goodness is nothing. He recognizes that his righteousness is imputed to him from the Lord.

So piety, or godliness, begins with God doing a work *in* us that shows itself *through* us. But as we've seen with Israel, and even with King David himself, even those through whom God has done much don't always do the will of God. Do Christians ever act ungodly at times?

Many people these days believe that godliness can be whatever they want it to be. But in Luke 6:46, we read: "Why do you call Me 'Lord, Lord,' and do not the things which I say?" We can't make up our own definition. Godliness is *willing submission* to our Lord and Master. It isn't begrudging or obligatory submission. It's submission that begins where David did, in essence: "For in you, God, I put my trust. I believe you know what is right, and I willingly submit to your will."

Easier said than done? Do you ever feel like you've blown it and exalted your own will and desires above His? Is that godliness? God's response, as it was with David, is to bring us to the point where we realize that His will is the very best way for us to live after all, and then we are glad to submit to it.

This is where true godliness begins. God does a work in us, and as we grow and walk with Him, we find that His way is *far* better than our own will and desires, and we are thus instilled with a genuine love-based willingness to submit to Him as our Lord and Master, to whom no human master could ever compare!

Living the Good (Godly) Life

³As for the saints who on the earth, "They are the excellent ones, in whom is all my delight." ⁴Their sorrows shall be multiplied who hasten after another god; their drink offerings of blood I will not offer, nor take up their names on my lips. ⁵O Lord, You are the portion of my inheritance and my cup; You maintain my lot. ⁶The lines have fallen to me in pleasant places; yes, I have a good inheritance. ⁷I will bless the Lord who has given me counsel; My heart also instructs me in the night seasons. ⁸I have set the Lord always before me; Because He is at my right hand I shall not be moved. —Psalm 16:3-8

SOMETIMES, it's a good idea to take a closer look at not only how we spend our time but also at those with whom we spend it. David realized that he wanted to surround himself with people who were going in the same direction that he was. He wanted to spend his time with others who willingly submitted to God as Lord and Master. David knew that those who "hasten after" other gods will only wind up with their sorrows multiplied. From this we can understand another element of what it means to live a godly life: We will have a *love* for the practices and people of God.

Nowadays, it's popular to ignore established universal moral standards and ethics and just let everybody decide what's right for them. It's a sad truth that in the last days as we see society yielding to whatever seems right in their own eyes, the world will have more impact on the church than the church will have on the world (2 Timothy 3:1-5). Even so, we are to take the gospel to them.

David calls God's people "excellent ones" and makes it clear that he won't permit idolatrous ways to be a part of his life. He loved the practices and the people of God, so it was natural—or perhaps supernatural—for him to do so as a godly man.

When we can recognize God's blessings in our lives, we, like David, can say that the Lord is our portion and our cup—in other words, God is the source of our blessing. And just as God blessed David, He wants to bless us also in this life. Although some of us may have a hard time understanding or believing that, as we look through the Scriptures, we begin to see a pattern: those whom the Bible records as being significantly blessed materially are those who didn't seek it. Remember how God rewarded Abraham when he permitted his nephew to claim the best land for himself? God blessed him, while Lot wound up in Sodom. Solomon was given the chance to ask for anything he wanted, and he asked for wisdom to rule God's people. God granted that to him, and great wealth as well.

Friends, God knows what we need. Are we thankful to Him for our material blessings, whether they be great or small, according to the world's measure? Remember, godliness *with contentment* is great gain. David has the right idea. In these verses, he is saying, "I will put God first, every day of my life, because He is at my right hand. He is my strength, and I will not be moved." May we do the same! It's a part of living a godly life.

January 24

O Death, Where Is Your Sting?

⁹Therefore my heart is glad, and my glory rejoices; my flesh also will rest in hope. ¹⁰For You will not leave my soul in Sheol, nor will You allow Your Holy One to see corruption. ¹¹You shame the counsel of the poor, but the Lord is his refuge. —Psalm 14:9-11

Ps 16:9-10   v.11 is Ps 14:6

DOES YOUR heart rejoice when you contemplate upon the Lord? David's did, and his faith was strengthened and his heart was made glad. His contemplation resulted in joy and hope and trust. It's the Lord who is David's strength, and he shall not be moved. Therefore, his heart is glad, and he is able to rejoice.

When he mentions that his "flesh will rest in hope," he refers to his death. He takes comfort in the fact that he knows his soul won't be left in "Sheol," the grave. Then, David gives us one of the great Messianic verses in the psalms and establishes for us why this is his great hope: *"You will not allow your Holy One to see corruption."*

What does this mean to David, and also to us? There are several incredible scriptures that help to put this all together. In John 11, we read that Lazarus had been dead within the tomb for four days when Jesus raised him, bringing him out of the grave with his life restored. Jesus himself was in the grave for the same number of days that Jonah was in the belly of the great fish (Jonah 1:17). The book of Daniel gives us an amazing prophecy: "And after sixty-two weeks, *Messiah shall be cut off*, but not for himself.; and the people of the prince who is to come shall destroy the city and the sanctuary . . . " (Daniel 9:26; emphasis added).

Putting this all together: David prophesied the death and resurrection of Christ; Jonah was an Old Testament "picture" of that remarkable event; Daniel also prophesied the Messiah being "cut off," i.e., put to death—not for what He had done, but for others. And then He proved Himself to be the Messiah by rising from the dead and appearing before many.

What is the message here? We can have complete confidence that death has been conquered by Jesus Christ on our behalf. Is this good news? It's incredibly good news! Eternal life—to live forever with the Lord and with believers from all the ages—how wonderful is that! If we can truly grasp what this means, we will gladly submit to God as our Lord and Master. We'll also discover that we have a new love for the truths of God and for the people of God. We can live in faith in who God is and that He is with us, no matter what life may bring.

Even though now we struggle with sorrows and sickness and fears and difficult people, the true source of our joy doesn't come from anything on this earth. David's heart was glad and rejoiced because he knew—he KNEW—that something far better than this life lay ahead for him: fullness of joy and pleasures forevermore! Are you able to have that same outlook? "Seek and you shall find . . ." is what the Scriptures tell us. Even so, come quickly, Lord Jesus!

January 25

I Will Bless the Lord at All Times

¹I will love You, O Lord, my strength. ²The Lord is my rock and my fortress and my deliverer; my God, my strength, in whom I will trust; my shield and the horn of my salvation, my stronghold. ³I will call upon the Lord, who is worthy to be praised; so shall I be saved from my enemies. —Psalm 18:1-3

DAVID SAYS that he spoke this song to God on the day the Lord delivered him from all his enemies . . . and from the hand of Saul. We know from 1 Samuel 24:1-7 that although Saul had previously tried three times to pin David to the wall with his spear, and after three months of David's being on the run from King Saul, sleeping in caves and being hungry and thirsty and in danger because of the enemies of Israel and their king, David does not count King Saul among his enemies! He opens this psalm with praise for the Lord's attributes.

"Blessed are the merciful, for they shall obtain mercy" (Mt 5:7). This was certainly true in David's life, as displayed in his treatment of King Saul, who wanted to kill him. What can we learn from David's life as a friend of God, and one whom God called "a man after God's own heart" (1 Sm 13:14)? There are at least two lessons: We can learn not to fear in the face of adversity, and we can believe that we can bless the Lord at all times.

To begin with, David opens this psalm telling God that he loves Him. Although that may not seem very notable, the word David uses here for "love" speaks of an intimate, familial love as opposed to "love" for what another may have done. Twice David says that God is his strength, his rock, his fortress, his God, one in whom he trusts, his shield, his horn of salvation, his stronghold, one whom he can call upon who is worthy to be praised, and one who saves him from his enemies. Can we begin to fathom the depths of such love for the One who loved us and redeemed us to Himself?

David seems to have understood all of that, and we, too, can take comfort in knowing that we are never without God's divine affection and protection. Although He may chasten those whom He loves, He still loves them and offers His divine protection. Nothing can separate us from the Father's love, and no one can snatch us from His hand. As the hymn writer wrote: "What wondrous love is this, O my soul?"

January 26

The God Who Hears Our Cries

⁴The pangs of death surrounded me, and the floods of ungodliness made me afraid. ⁵The sorrows of Sheol surrounded me; the snares of death confronted me. ⁶In my distress I called upon the Lord and cried out to my God; He heard my voice from His temple, and my cry came before Him, even to His ears. ⁷Then the earth shook and trembled; the foundations of the hills also quaked and were shaken, because He was angry. ⁸Smoke went up from His nostrils, and devouring fire from His mouth; coals were kindled by it. ⁹He bowed the heavens also, and came down with darkness under His feet. ¹⁰And He rode upon a cherub, and flew; He flew upon the wings of the wind. ¹¹He made darkness His secret place; His canopy around Him was dark waters and thick clouds of the skies. ¹²From the brightness before Him, His thick clouds passed with hailstones and coals of fire. —Psalm 18:4-12

WE OFTEN forget that David, like many other individuals in the Scriptures, was a very normal human being even though he was God's chosen king over Israel. We find him describing his fears and desperation in these verses using terms such as "the snares of death," and "the sorrows of Sheol" that were all around him. Yet in faith, he called upon the Lord, and God heard him. In fact, verses 7-12 are filled with magnificent word pictures describing God's heavenly response to David's cry.

The darkness that David mentions in verse 11 refers to the unknowable depths of the majesty and mystery of God, and the brightness before Him speaks of God's holiness and righteousness —all of which points to one amazing fact that we should remember and hold dear: _Nothing can hinder God from being our strength and our deliverer._ The One who heard David's cries will also move heaven and earth to deliver his children. Who can stop God? The Bible says that He is a consuming fire and rides on the wind, and His holiness and righteousness puts all darkness under His feet (See Deuteronomy 33:26-29).

Only my unbelief may hinder You yet I've seen You work anyway! ♡

If you think that God doesn't hear you, you're wrong. He does. If you think the devil is holding God back from helping you, you're wrong. One angel may hinder another, as we read in Daniel, but we aren't reading about an angel here. This is the One before whom the whole creation trembles at His word (v. 7). *God cannot and will not be hindered from being our strength and our deliverer.* Let us go out today remembering that our confidence is in *Him* and not in ourselves. And that's something in which we can truly trust.

January 27

"Hallelujah! What a Savior!"

¹³The Lord thundered from heaven, and the Most High uttered His voice, hailstones and coals of fire! ¹⁴He sent out His arrows and scattered the foe, lightnings in abundance, and He vanquished them. ¹⁵Then the channels of the sea were seen, the foundations of the world were uncovered at Your rebuke, O Lord, . . ¹⁶ He sent from above, He took me; He drew me out of many waters. ¹⁷He delivered me from my strong enemy, . . . For they were too strong for me . . ¹⁸in the day of my calamity, but the Lord was my support . . . ¹⁹He delivered me because He delighted in me. —*Psalm 18:13-19*

"THE WICKED plots against the just, and gnashes at him with his teeth. The Lord laughs at him, for He sees that his day is coming" (Ps 37:12-13). The wicked plot against us and proceed with their plans. But Psalm 18 reassures us that, one day, hailstones and burning coals will scatter the persecutors of His people! David knows that God will move heaven and earth to protect His children. God hears our cries, although we don't always realize it.

"All things are naked and open to the eyes of Him to whom we must give account" (Heb 4:13), i.e., God *always* knows better than we do! We may not like His response, and sometimes things *don't* "turn out for the better," in our minds. Well, remember the story of Job? He had lost everything—his children, his livestock, his possessions, and, finally, his health. But Job trusted in God anyway! His response? *"The Lord gave, and the Lord has taken away. Blessed be the name of the Lord"* (Job 1:21). He understood that everything God does is perfect and every answer to our cries is the right one—even if it's not the one we were hoping to hear.

David, too, understands that this One who thunders from heaven did all these things for *him*! But what about the persecution of Christians today? Where was their protection? I can assure you that every martyr is safe in the arms of Jesus, and they were never separated from His love. Whatever God's response is to my cry, it's the right response in every way.

Christian, it's a fact: God never tires of being our Savior. When we cry out to Him in repentance and ask for deliverance, He never says, "What? You again?" (see 2 Chronicles 16:9a). If you're in a mess, *cry out to God*. If it's your own fault, cry out to God! Call to the Savior, and He will answer! He is our Father, and He loves for us to come to Him in repentance and faith and love.

January 28

Blessed Are the Blessable

[20]The Lord rewarded me according to my righteousness; according to the cleanness of my hands He has recompensed me. [21]For I have kept the ways of the Lord and have not wickedly departed from my God. [22]For all His judgments were before me, and I did not put away His statutes from me. [23]I was also blameless before Him, and I kept myself from my iniquity. [24]Therefore the Lord has recompensed me according to my righteousness, according to the cleanness of my hands in His sight. —*Psalm 18:20-24*

THERE'S a progression as new believers: we begin with the *positional truths* of the Word before we move forward in the *practical application* of the Word. It's often a matter of taking baby steps. The Bible reassures us that what has transpired in our hearts is real: "*If anyone is in Christ, he is a new creation; old things have passed away . . . all things have become new*" (2 Cor 5:17). We all begin the journey in the same *position*: being "in Christ," complete in Him, and made new. But that's only the beginning! As David transitions in our psalm today, we move with him through the meaning of the great positional truths that we believed when we were first saved into the application of those truths. In 2 Corinthians 6:16-7:1 (which begins, "Do not be unequally yoked together with unbelievers"), Paul establishes the promises of God based solely on our *position* in Christ: God will *live* with us, *walk* with us; He will be our God; He will receive us as sons and daughters. Then comes the "therefore": "Let us cleanse ourselves from all filthiness of the flesh and spirit, perfecting holiness in the fear of the God."

Everyone experiences God's grace, but the blessings that God promises to *believers* are conditional. David, whom we saw spared from death from King Saul and others, and who had treated Saul with mercy, now states that his faith in God impacted his behavior and allowed him to live as a "blessable" man rather than as one under the disciplinary hand of God. Why? Because David had cherished God's judgments and precepts even during very dark times, and God responded with blessings. God's affection and eternal protection are always ours in Christ, but obedience is the key to maintaining our bless-ability. "*Love your enemies, do good to those who hate you ...*" (Lk 6:27-33). With God's help, all things are possible. May we begin to apply these truths to our lives today—with the reward of becoming blessable because we have been a blessing.

An Imputed Righteousness

25With the merciful You will show Yourself merciful; with a blameless man You will show Yourself blameless; 26With the pure You will show Yourself pure; and with the devious You will show Yourself shrewd. 27For You will save the humble people, but will bring down haughty looks. 28For You will light my lamp; the Lord will enlighten my darkness.
—*Psalm 18:25-28*

DAVID, understanding that he had remained "blessable" in God's eyes even when his life was a mess, now points us to the character of God. What do we find in these verses about how God deals with people? He tells us that the merciful will receive mercy; the blameless (i.e., those with moral integrity) will be blessed. Those who have kept themselves pure will also reap blessings.

But to the *devious* (crooked or perverted) God will show Himself *shrewd* (severe). "*Do not be deceived, God is not mocked; for whatever a man sows, that he will also reap.*" (Gal 6:7). You can't sow one kind of seed and expect a different kind of plant to grow from it. So those who sow pride will reap pride in their lives, and the Bible tells us that God hates pride. Proverbs 16:5 says, "Everyone proud in heart is an *abomination* to the Lord; [emphasis added]." That's a pretty serious condemnation!

People who struggle with addictions sometimes fall into a similar pattern. They may *desire* the fruit of the Spirit of self-control, but they allow themselves to be put into situations where they know they will be severely tested, and when they fall, they wonder why they "just can't seem to have victory over this." The same goes for those who struggle with pornography, or shopping, or gossip. They permit themselves to get into situations where they are tested and find that they can't resist their urges. Then they wonder why they don't have the power of the Spirit.

Romans 6:1-4 provides much insight to this problem. "*Shall we continue in sin that grace may abound? Certainly not! How shall we who died to sin live any longer in it?...*" Too many Christians are "resurrecting the dead" in their lives—and walking in their old dead flesh. Remember what David wrote: God has lighted the path for us so that we can walk mercifully, blamelessly, and purely in that light, reaping the benefits that such a life brings.

True Power Is in the Word,
Not in the World

29For by You I can run against a troop, by my God I can leap over a wall. 30 . . . His way is perfect; the word of the Lord is proven; He is a shield to all who trust in Him. 31For . . . who is a rock, except our God? 32It Is God who arms me with strength, and makes my way perfect. 33He makes my feet like the feet of deer, and sets me on my high places. 34He teaches my hands to make war. . . . 35You have also given me the shield of Your salvation; Your right hand has held me up, Your gentleness has made me great. 36You enlarged my path . . . , so my feet did not slip. —Psalm 18:29-36

DAVID continues to describe the wisdom and attributes of the Lord as well as the marvelous things He does for His people: He saves the humble (but brings down the haughty); He lightens our darkness; His way is perfect and His Word proven. He protects His children. He is a rock; He gives strength and directs our paths. He has provided His wonderful salvation! *God* is the one who protects, teaches, and holds us through all of our doings.

He gives us the power to live in purity and according to His Word. In this great battle of good vs. evil, those who have been made pure in Christ have the true power of the Word, which is far superior to the power of the world. The Bible makes it very clear that the truly powerful (through Christ) are those who love their enemies, stand for truth, are morally pure, etc.

God's power is revealed when He breaks the chains of darkness and sets the captives free. Drunks are made sober; addicts are made clean. If you want to be blessed with power, seek to live a life that is pure before the Lord, which is only possible by accessing *His* righteousness, which was imputed to us through the death and resurrection of Jesus Christ. The truly powerful are those who love their enemies, who stand for the truth, and who are morally pure.

Real power is to know the truth and be free—to turn from darkness to God's marvelous light. God's power is accessed by living according to His Word and is available only to God's people. If you want to be blessed with power, live a life that is pure before the Lord. You will find that you, too, can "run against a troop" and "leap over a wall" when you're living in God's will.

Pulling Down Strongholds

37I have pursued my enemies and overtaken them; neither did I turn back again till they were destroyed. 38I have wounded them, so that they could not rise; they have fallen under my feet. 39For You have armed me with strength for the battle; You have subdued under me those who rose up against me. 40You have also given me the necks of my enemies, so that I destroyed those who hated me. —Psalm 18:37-40

SOMETIMES there are battles in our lives that seem beyond our power to fight. We may be faced with fierce temptations resulting from past sinful actions or thoughts, and although we believed we'd obtained victory over them, we find that the old struggles are once again raising their ugly heads and we risk falling into the same pit from which the Lord had delivered us.

David acknowledges that God had *armed him with strength* for the battles that he faced, allowing him to wound the opposing armies to the point where they were unable to rise up against him ever again. David wrote: "I have pursued my enemies and overtaken them; neither did I turn back again *till they were destroyed*" (v. 37—emphasis added). Sometimes we have to go on the offense against our enemies, especially when they are returning ones.

James, through the Holy Spirit, wrote, "Submit to God. *Resist the devil* and he will flee from you" (Jas 4:7). James isn't talking about resisting an enemy like you would resist having a second piece of chocolate cake but of an aggressive, pursue-your-enemy-until-it-is-destroyed kind of resistance. David describes this type of battle in the verses in our psalm above. We must *be relentless in our fight against sin.*

Matthew 5:27-30 explains that sin takes place in the mind and heart as well as in our flesh: "I say to you that whoever *looks at a woman* to lust for her has already committed adultery with her in his *heart*. . . ." Jesus continues, noting that we must take drastic action against the things that cause us to stumble: "If your eye causes you to sin, pluck it out . . . ; if your hand causes you to sin, cut it off . . ."! David took drastic action against his enemies. Shouldn't we attack the sin that pursues us with the same fervor? The truth is that we must be relentless in our fight against sin. Whether it is sin of the flesh, the mind, or the heart, we must pursue our enemy and overtake it, trusting that the Lord is on our side, and not letting go until it is destroyed.

FEBRUARY

Slaying Giants

40bI destroyed those who hated me. 41They cried out, but there was none to save; even to the Lord, but He did not answer them. 42Then I beat them as fine as the dust before the wind; I cast them out like dirt in the streets. 43You have delivered me from the strivings of the people; You have made me the head of the nations; A people I have not known shall serve me. 44As soon as they hear of me they obey me; the foreigners submit to me. 45The foreigners fade away, and come frightened from their hideouts. —Psalm 18:40b-45

DAVID isn't saying in these verses that his enemies "cried out in repentance to the Lord, but He did not hear them." They weren't asking God to save them from their sinful ways; they were asking Him to save them from the sword of David! Does God hear everyone's prayers? Psalm 66:18 says, "If I regard iniquity in my heart, the Lord will not hear." Speaking even more harshly, Proverbs 29:1 states, "*He who is often rebuked, and hardens his neck, will suddenly be destroyed, and that without remedy.*" It seems that one can reach a point of no return because their heart becomes so hardened that repentance and salvation is impossible (Ex 5-14).

David, as a young man, was loyal to the Lord from early on. He was willing to face the giant Goliath, saying, "*You come to me with [weapons], but I come to you in the name of the Lord of hosts, the God of the armies of Israel . . . that all the earth may know that there is a God in Israel*" (1 Sam 17).

Likewise, He slays giants in our lives so that the world may know there's a God who is powerful and mighty to save. He heals hearts and minds that psychology can't help so that people can know there's a God in heaven. He delivers addicts and drunks, whom the world's programs can't help, so that we all may know there's a God in heaven who saves and sets free.

When you, with the help of God, pull down strongholds that have held you in bondage, glory is given to Him in the eyes of the world, and there's no enemy that can't be conquered. You *can* control your tongue; you *can* change that bad attitude; you *can* be free from that addiction—because God is with you, and He gets all the glory for it. Don't worry because you feel powerless! You have the God of all power beside you, and He is mighty to save! It's not too late. God can take the most messed-up life and make it magnificent. "Old things pass away, all things are become new."

Live, Think, and Act
Like a Victor, Not Like a Victim

⁴⁶The Lord lives! Blessed be my Rock! Let the God of my salvation be exalted. ⁴⁷It is God who avenges me, and subdues the peoples under me; ⁴⁸He delivers me from my enemies. You also lift me up above those who rise against me; You have delivered me from the violent man. ⁴⁹ . . . I will give thanks to You, O Lord, among the Gentiles, and sing praises to Your name. ⁵⁰Great deliverance He gives to His king, and shows mercy to . . . David and his descendants forevermore. —*Psalm 18:46-50*

IN THE CLOSING verses of this psalm, David hints at the eventual salvation of the Gentiles, which would come through the Jews years later as they began to proclaim everywhere the Good News of the Savior of the world. He mentions God's mercy on His descendants, pointing to one particular descendant of David: the King of kings and Lord of lords, Jesus Christ. He praises God for saving him from "the violent man," referring to King Saul. We don't find David dwelling on the harm that Saul attempted to do to him, or the unfair way that David had been treated and forced to run and hide on more than one occasion. He lives more like a victor than a victim.

From a natural standpoint, many of us fail at doing this. If there are strongholds in your own life—things that hold you back, you're afraid of moving forward in your walk, you struggle with sins or a painful past—remember: it doesn't matter when it started! It may be that you will never understand how or why or when the stronghold began. Don't analyze it. Just *pull* it down! Psychology won't help you, even the so-called Christian variety, with regression therapy falsely packaged as deliverance.

Deliverance *is* real, but it can't be manufactured by digging deeper into why you are the way you are. Are you going to discuss with a drowning person why they fell into the water or what hindered them from learning how to swim as a child? No! You're going to rescue them.

If you think like a victim, you'll act like a victim. When you think like a victor, you'll act like a victor. *"Thanks be to God, who gives us victory through our Lord Jesus Christ"* (1 Cor 15:57-58). Seek to live a victorious life, not a victimized one. Do as David did: give glory to the Lord, even (or especially) in front of non-believers. Be relentless in your fight against sin. Live, think, and act like you're on the winning side, because you are!

In the Beginning . . .

> ¹The heavens declare the glory of God; and the firmament shows His handiwork. —*Psalm 19:1*

WE LIVE in an age where it's popular to disparage and question the Bible regarding its validity both in the area of inspiration and information. Yet it's also true that the Bible made these claims thousands of years ago, and man is only now discovering them.

For example, in Job 26:7 we read, *"He stretches out the north over empty space; He hangs the earth on nothing."* Isaiah 40:22 says, *"It is He who sits above the circle of the earth, and its inhabitants are like grasshoppers; Who stretches out the heavens like a curtain, and spreads them out like tent to dwell in."*

The author of the book of Job isn't known, but significant evidence within the Scriptures reveal that it was written some time after the Iron Age around 1100 BC. The book of Isaiah was authored by a man with that name late in the seventh or early in the eighth century BC.

Why is this important? Virtually every culture in the ancient world had traditions concerning the earth and its placement in the universe—ideas such as that the earth was flat or that it was held up on the back of a great turtle or on the trunk of a huge elephant, or even upon the shoulders of Atlas, a Titan in Greek mythology. Only the Jews stood alone in their belief that the earth was a sphere that hung on nothing in a universe that was expanding and being stretched out like a curtain. Where did they get this information? From the Torah, basically the first five books of the Bible! So, long before Edwin Hubble was able to determine through scientific calculations that the universe is expanding, the Bible had said so more than 2,700 years earlier!

The "theory" that has now replaced the biblical narrative concerning the formation of the universe isn't the result of scientific research but is actually the end result of man's spiritual depravity and desire for a godless creation and existence. And yet Psalm 97:6 proclaims, "*The heavens declare His righteousness, and all the peoples see His glory.*" Just as creation declares the righteousness of God, so does King David in our verse today. So rather than buying into the propositions of the spiritually depraved, let's listen to the creation proclamation this morning and hear the voice of God!

Creation speaks

A Hill to Die On

> ²Day unto day utters speech, and night unto night reveals knowledge; ³There is no speech nor language, where their voice is not heard. ⁴Their line has gone out through all the earth, and their words to the end of the world. —*Psalm 19:2-4*

Not Mother Nature!

THESE VERSES proclaim that the heavens are the work of God's hands, and that He (not undirected natural causes) created the stars, constellations, and galaxies, and that creation itself was His first preacher. Through the magnificence of the design of the cosmos, God is declared to be the Creator behind the order seen in the sun, moon, and stars. Order never happens by chance, and thus man, because of creation (if he is honest), is driven to search for God. In Jeremiah 29:13, God assures us, "You will seek Me and find Me, *when you search for Me with all your heart.*" When we seek after that One whom the heavens declare to be the Creator, He can be found.

Let's consider a few facts related to the proclamation that God is the Creator: 1) The heavens themselves prove what the Bible claims. Creation declares that there is someone or some thing greater than us, especially when we measure ourselves against the innumerable stars. 2) The Bible proclaims that a Triune God created and holds all things together. 3) Scientists can offer no other real evidence for how *anything* began.

In Psalm 19, David points to the continuing night-day cycle that was initiated in the beginning. This agrees with Genesis 1:3-5: "*And God said, 'Let there be light'; and there was light . . . and God divided the light from the darkness. God called the light Day and the darkness He called Night.*"

Scientists fail in their efforts to disprove creation because they have no actual proof of how the universe could have come about through any other means. Yet they persist in their denial of God and cling to their own unproven theories. Sadly, denying the creation of the universe by a loving God is the reason our world is in the moral condition it's in (Romans 1:18-19). If there is no Creator of all that exists to whom we must give an account, then there is nothing to prevent wickedness from having free rein. But the truth is, no one is without divine revelation. The otherwise unexplainable proclamation of creation itself proves that this is so. In fact, the very things that the evolutionist uses to declare that there is no God are what God will use to judge them in the Tribulation (Revelation 6:12-17).

For those who know the truth, this is indeed a hill worth dying on.

February 5

The Mindfulness of God

4bIn them [the heavens] He has set a
tabernacle for the sun — *Psalm 19:4b*

IN THIS VERSE, David points to our own star that warms the entire earth to a life-sustaining temperature and causes plant, animal, and human life to flourish on the only planet among the trillions of heavenly bodies that we know of where life exists.

Regarding this subject, recently deceased Stephen Hawking, the well-known director of research at the Department of Applied Mathematics and Theoretical Physics and founder of the Centre for Theoretical Cosmology at Cambridge, said this regarding our sun and magnificent planet:

> *We are such insignificant creatures on a minor planet of a very average star in the outer suburbs of one of a hundred thousand galaxies. So it is difficult to believe in a God that would care about us or even notice our existence. [From a BBC interview]*

And yet in Psalm 8:3-6, David writes, "*When I consider Your heavens, the work of Your fingers, the moon and the stars, which You have ordained, what is man that You are mindful of him, and the son of man that You visit him? For You have made him a little lower than the angels, and You have crowned him with glory and honor. You have made him to have dominion over the works of Your hands; You have put all things under his feet . . .*"

King David was overwhelmed with the vastness of the universe and the glory of God's creation even though His perspective was only that which could be directly observed through the human eye. Yet even at that, his conclusion was the exact opposite of Hawking's as he considered the immensity of it.

Psalm 8 reminds us that God is mindful of man. He visits him, He doesn't consider him insignificant, and He has ultimately given man dominion over the entire earth. He has custom-made our sun and placed it in our solar system at exactly the right distance from the earth and having a less than one-tenth of one percent fluctuation in radiance—something that is so distinct from all other stars that we can't help but see that God specifically designed it for us. What a great love this is! *Lord, help us to understand that Your mindfulness of all Your creation, whether human, animal, plant, or stars and planets, should draw us ever nearer to You in love and gratitude for all that You have done!*

February 6

Our Wonderful Orderly Creator

4bIn them [the heavens] He has set a tabernacle for the sun, 5which is like a bridegroom coming out of his chamber, and rejoices like a strong man to run its race. 6Its rising is from one end of heaven, and its circuit to the other end; and there is nothing hidden from its heat.
—Psalm 19:4b-6

SPEAKING of the sun, David says that it is so magnificently crafted by the Word of God himself that every sunrise is similar to a bridegroom coming out of his chamber, dressed and ready for his bride. As the sun moves across the sky, David compares it to a seasoned athlete who runs the race and stays the course, day after day, from one end of the heavens to the other, warming the entire earth and proclaiming the Lord each time it completes its circuit.

And how interesting it is that in our own solar system, with all of its moons and planets, only our planet with its one moon, which is 250,000 miles from the earth, and our sun, which is 93 million miles away, appear to be the same size in the sky, allowing for solar and lunar eclipses to mark the times and the seasons.

In the spiral galaxy known as the Milky Way, the earth is placed not in one of the arms of the spiral, where gas and dust would make visibility of the heavens impossible, nor is our solar system on the edge of this huge galaxy where the asteroid presence is far higher and the earth would be much more susceptible to the constant impact of extinction-level asteroid and meteor strikes.

Why would these things be? Was it blind luck that resulted in the design and placement of our planet that permits us to view the wonders of the skies? It makes far more sense (and agrees with the Bible) to realize that the consistency of the cosmos demands an intelligent, orderly Creator.

God did not use evolution to create all that we can now see through our eyes or the lens of a telescope. No matter how far out into universe we may gaze, the fact remains that God has created and ordered the universe for His glory and of His will. There is no evidence to support anything other than the words that David wrote as confirmation of the Genesis record of star, galaxy, and planet formation and the origin of first life.

The answer that seems so elusive is really very simple: *"The heavens declare the glory of God; and the firmament shows His handiwork"* (Psalm 19:1). The heavens demand that there is a God, and the Bible tells us who He is and how we can come to know Him! It really is that simple.

No Experience Required

[10]More to be desired are they than gold, yea, than much fine gold; sweeter also than honey and the honeycomb. [11]Moreover by them Your servant is warned, and in keeping them there is great reward. [12]Who can understand his errors? Cleanse me from secret faults. [13]Keep back Your servant also from presumptuous sins; Let them not have dominion over me. Then I shall be blameless, and I shall be innocent of great transgression. [14]Let the words of my mouth and the meditation of my heart be acceptable in Your sight, O Lord, my strength and my Redeemer.
—Psalm 19:10-14

WE'RE ALL aware of textless sermons, feel-good messages, and the exploitation of the Word of God as a means for gaining wealth and prosperity, which, interestingly, works . . . for those who preach it! But there is another issue that needs to be addressed today, and let me first say this: Nothing is worse than making the Word of God dry and boring, because it is not. It is living and powerful, and the Bible is emotional and experiential. But let me ask you this: Have you ever said or heard said, after returning from a Christian concert or event, a statement like, "That really blessed me." It's not that I'm against Christian concerts, but isn't the purpose of our praise and worship to bless God and not necessarily ourselves?

The reason that experientialism is so rampant in our day is because of the lack of preaching of the Word, which leaves Christians looking for other things to create the experiential aspect that is lacking from the hearing and then doing of the Word.

Have you ever heard or said the phrase "creating an atmosphere of worship"? Since worship means to prostrate oneself and submit to God, there is no "atmosphere" that needs to be created. Worship is a way of life, not just songs and "feelings" that bless you and give you an "experience." Many today are wanting to "feel'" God's power and will go to an event hoping to find it and experience it there, when in fact it is available to them all the time in the specific revelation of God called the Holy Scripture! Yet some are incorporating the Scripture through the practice of *Lectio Divina* today in an attempt to create a "God encounter" by focusing on a single word or verse in Scripture and asking God, "What does this mean to me?"

The fact is that isolating verses or words and asking for meaning outside of the context is how cults are born, and although this Benedictine practice may sound good, it's dangerous at its core.

You may come to church and not "feel" anything, but if you heard or learned more about God and what is acceptable to Him, even if you didn't get any goose bumps or "have a moment," you have benefited greatly no matter how you feel, because there is no experience required in order for the Word of God to be profitable to you!

Some of us need to change our thinking regarding what we're looking for in a church. We need to have our "heresy" filters on, but the real test is if the Word of God in its purity was brought forth or not. You may not like the music or style of preaching, but all that matters is if the truth of the Bible was proclaimed and Christ was held up as King and Lord over all. If so, then God was glorified, and that's the most important thing. Let's all take another inward look and offer our hearts to the Lord once more.

February 8

Repurposed People

Introduction

—

PSALM 22 is one of the most amazing chapters in the Scriptures. It describes the experiences of God's people collectively, it has personal application for those who read it, and it speaks prophetically of the Messiah who was to come.

David wrote this psalm, and although we don't know the details of what he was going through, it's clear that he felt alone, dry, discouraged, and overwhelmed—and he confessed this under the inspiration of the Holy Spirit. Whether he understood that what he was writing was prophetic or not isn't completely clear, but regardless, he was definitely being used of the Lord to write these words, which have incredible prophetic significance (see 2 Peter 1:19-21). He was inspired of the Holy Spirit to describe his own personal experiences that would later be quoted and lived out by Jesus on the cross, confirming them as prophetic. This psalm is cited 27 times in the New Testament, with each reference related to Christ's suffering on the cross.

You've heard of the word "repurposed." It describes taking items that were intended for one use and changing them into an entirely different item. Taking wood from a barn door and turning it into a table, for example, is to repurpose it. It's still barn wood, but it now serves a different purpose.

This is similar to what takes place in this psalm as King David uses figurative language to describe his mindset, emotions, and circumstances. Meanwhile, the Holy Spirit inspired and "repurposed" these figurative expressions and applied them literally to Jesus!

God does much the same with us. He takes people who were once apart from Him and living for themselves but who were then saved. He is able to repurpose them for His own use in the lives of others. As for those who have been repurposed, they now live to glorify and exalt Jesus, giving a new and true meaning to "purpose driven."

And as God uses His newly repurposed children, we can delight in the knowledge that we are fulfilling His ultimate plan. How amazing it is to realize that as David lived his life under the hand of the Lord, God was directing his steps, through good times and bad, and at the same time proclaiming the future Messiah—and David didn't even know it! Let us keep that in mind as we go through this day, realizing that we're being led by our heavenly Father, who is using us for His own wonderful purposes. ♥

February 9

Praise Brings Peace

¹My God, My God, why have You forsaken Me? Why are You so far from helping Me, And from the words of My groaning? ²O My God, I cry in the daytime, but You do not hear; and in the night season, and am not silent. ³But You are holy, enthroned in the praises of Israel. ⁴Our fathers trusted in You; they trusted, and You delivered them. ⁵They cried to You, and were delivered; they trusted in You, and were not ashamed.
—Psalm 22:1-5

ALTHOUGH David wrote these words to the Lord expressing his own anguish, they were actually prophetic, because Jesus later quoted part of this verse as He hung on the cross. At the time that David wrote this, he was crying out to God because he felt that his enemies were gaining the upper hand against him, so he uttered this very honest and heartfelt cry to God.

It's believed that when Jesus cried out these same words, "My God, My God . . . ," He was enduring the greatest agony of all time as he took upon Himself the horror of all the sins of mankind and, at the same time, experienced the separation from His Father, who turned His face away from His Son. The emotional and heartfelt cry of David became the literal experience of Jesus.

We know from the Scriptures that God is holy and is enthroned in (or inhabits) the praises of His people. But as we view the lives of those who served the Lord throughout the Bible, we also see that praise and problems are not mutually exclusive. Both can be present in our lives simultaneously. Remember: praise should not be the result of being problem free, and problems should not result in the silencing of praise.

When we are tempted to fear, we need to remember two beautiful New Testament truths: "For God has not given us a spirit of fear, but of power and of love and of a sound mind" (2 Timothy 1:7); "There is no fear in love; but perfect love casts out fear, because fear involves torment. But he who fears has not been made perfect in love. We love Him because He first loved us" (1 John 4:18-19).

Psalm 22:3 above tells us that God is *enthroned* in the praises of His people, so if we praise Him when life is mean and ugly and filled with people who are, too, our praise brings glory to God, who is far above all this pettiness. And praising God even from the valley of the shadow of death is proof that for "repurposed" people, praise and problems are not mutually exclusive. Let us go out to face this day with praise on our lips and in our hearts, regardless of what may be going on in our lives and minds. We will bring glory to Him and peace to our own troubled hearts.

February 10

Enduring Hatred for His Name's Sake

⁶But I am a worm, and no man; a reproach of men, and despised by the people. ⁷All those who see Me ridicule Me; they shoot out the lip, they shake the head, saying "He trusted in the Lord, let Him rescue Him; let Him deliver Him, since He delights in Him!" ⁹But You are He who took Me out of the womb; You made Me trust while on My mother's breasts. ¹⁰I was cast upon You from birth. From My mother's womb You have been my God. —*Psalm 22:6-10*

THE HOLY SPIRIT is using David's own experience to point to and exalt Jesus! In deep despair David states that he feels subhuman, more like a worm than a man. He considers himself a reproach, despised and ridiculed. Onlookers spew out accusations and insults toward him because of his faith in God. Undaunted, he answers his detractors by citing the faithfulness of God and continues to credit Him as being the very Giver of life.

The Messianic elements in this psalm are apparent. Isaiah 53:3 says: "He [the Messiah] is despised and rejected by men, a Man of sorrows and acquainted with grief. And we hid . . . our faces from Him; . . . we did not esteem Him." Written long before the crucifixion of Christ, how accurate are these verses regarding that future event! Listen to Matthew: "And those who passed by blasphemed Him, wagging their heads and saying, 'You who destroy the temple and build it in three days, save Yourself! If You are the Son of God, come down from the cross.' . . . [T]he chief priests also, mocking . . . said, 'He saved others; Himself He cannot save. If He is the King of Israel, let Him now come down from the cross, and we will believe Him. He trusted in God; let Him deliver Him now if He will have Him; for He said, "I am the Son of God"'" (Matthew 27:39-44).

So we see in Psalm 22 that even as David describes his own suffering, the Holy Spirit inspires him to write things that would become true of Jesus, God in human flesh, in even harsher reality! Through David's words, we look ahead to the suffering of the Messiah, becoming the beneficiaries of having all of this laid out in these verses. And yet, we must always keep in mind that what was true of David will be true for us: If we live for Jesus, we will be treated like Him—and I don't mean that in a "good" way! Luke wrote, "You will be hated by all for My name's sake . . . " (Luke 21:17-19). And in John 15:18-20, we are reminded of that again: "If you were of the world, the world would love its own. Yet because you are not of the world . . . therefore the world hates you." May we learn to regard these insults and attacks as opportunities to reflect Jesus, who cried from the cross, "Father, forgive them, for they know not what they do!"

Onward, Christian Soldiers!

> [11]Be not far from Me, for trouble is near; for there is none to help. [12]Many bulls have surrounded Me; strong bulls of Bashan have encircled Me. [13]They gape at Me with their mouths, like a raging and roaring lion. [14]I am poured out like water, and all My bones are out of joint; My heart is like wax; it has melted within Me. [15]My strength is dried up like a potsherd, and My tongue clings to My jaws; You have brought Me to the dust of death. —*Psalm 22:11-15*

THIS SECTION presents a very graphic picture, prophesied by King David, of some of what Christ went through as He hung on the cross. Jesus endured horrific suffering during those hours. "Poured out like water" predicts the blood and water that flowed from His pierced side. The heart "melted like wax" describes the emotional draining of life that David felt and that Jesus physically endured. Jesus' mouth was so dry that His tongue literally stuck to His jaws when on the brink of death. In John 19:28 we are told that He cried out, "I thirst."

The imagery in this psalm is very graphic, even if poetically presented. And beneath it we see that just as David's life was spent surrounded by enemies, difficulties, discouragement, and heartbreak, so it was with Jesus' life. But it was necessary! And we need to realize this: Our own mission in life is to save God's *enemies*!

Reading the words in this psalm, we can sense the aching emotions behind them. We, too, will experience many of these same feelings, but the purpose has been changed. David's role was to fight and defeat his enemies. Ours is to love and rescue them from death. Jesus himself, as He hung on that cross, cried out, "Father, forgive them, for they know not what they do" (Luke 23:33-34). One of the men being crucified beside Him, hearing His words and seeing His manner, believed in Him as God, and said, "Lord, remember me when you come into your kingdom," and Jesus assured the man that he would be with Him in Paradise that very day (Luke 23:42-43).

Romans 5:10 says that before coming to Christ, *we* were "enemies of God." Whom did Christ come into the world to save? His enemies! And now we are to be of the same mind as Jesus. In fact, 1 Corinthians 2:16 tells us that "we *have* the mind of Christ" already! So we need to squelch our natural human tendency to run away in self-preservation and instead seek to infiltrate the enemy's camp with the love of Christ.

Remember, *our* enemy is Satan, and he is doing his best to deceive and draw to himself as many as he can before it's too late. Our only real mission in life is to save as many of God's enemies as possible. Putting on the armor of God, and in the power of His might, we can. The battle belongs to the Lord! (1 Sam 17:47; 2 Chr 20:15).

February 12

O the Deep, Deep Love of Jesus

16For dogs have surrounded Me; The congregation of the wicked has enclosed Me. They pierced My hands and My feet; 17I can count all My bones. They look and stare at Me. 18They divide My garments among them, and for My clothing they cast lots. 19But You, O Lord, do not be far from Me; O My Strength, hasten to help Me! 20Deliver Me from the sword, My precious life from the power of the dog. 21Save Me from the lion's mouth and from the horns of the wild oxen! You have answered Me . . . —Psalm 22:16-31

THE PROPHETIC nature of this psalm is staggering. Look at Matthew 27:35, written centuries after Psalm 22: "Then they crucified Him, and divided His garments, casting lots, that it might be fulfilled which was spoken by the prophet: "They divided my garments among them, and for my clothing they cast lots." And also Luke 24:39-40: "*[Suddenly] Jesus Himself stood in the midst of them, and said . . . ,*

'Peace to you.' But they were terrified and frightened, and supposed they had seen a spirit. He said . . . 'Why are you troubled? And why do doubts arise in your hearts? Behold My hands and My feet, that it is I Myself. Handle Me and see, for a spirit does not have flesh and bones as you see I have.' . . . He showed them His hands and His feet. . . ." Why did Jesus show them His hands and His feet? Because they still bore the holes where the nails had pierced them.

Crucifixion wasn't practiced in Israel in David's time, making it highly unlikely that he knowingly wrote this psalm with the sufferings of Christ in view. David clearly portrayed the idea of being on the brink of death himself. In the deepest darkness of his soul, he cried out to the Father, "O Lord, do not be far from me; O my Strength, hasten to help me . . . Deliver me . . . Save me." He stated simply, "You have answered me." Then he moved on in the rest of these verses, praising His wonderful Deliverer, who is incapable of indifference to the cries of His children.

He has answered you, too, Christian! If things in your life seem too difficult, do as David did. Cry out to the Lord, but never forget to recall His faithfulness in the past. This is God, who can part the Red Sea, heal the sick, raise the dead, give sight to the blind, set captives free, heal the broken-hearted, make the lame walk, and, most important, save a soul from death. ◁

It's possible that as Christians we may be treated like Jesus and be rejected even by those closest to us. Remember that Christ himself endured all of this patiently. We must never allow persecutions to cause us to cease to praise Him, because He is God, and He is worthy of all praise!

February 13

The Great Shepherd

Introduction to Psalm 23

*[11]*The Lord is my shepherd; I shall not want. (Psalm 23:1) "I am the good shepherd. The good shepherd gives His life for the sheep" *—John 10:11*

IN PSALM 22, we saw that the Holy Spirit, through David, prophesied the undeniable experiences of Jesus, the coming Messiah, as He died for the sins of the world. From His cry on the cross, "My God, My God, Why have You forsaken Me?" to the dividing of His garments, the casting of lots for His robe, and much more, we are reminded that we, too, are to be representatives of Jesus, and through our own lives, point others to Him.

Jesus proved Himself to be the Good Shepherd of the sheep by dying on the cross for our sake. He willingly put Himself between His sheep and the second death that lies ahead for all who refuse to receive His gift of salvation. In John

10:16, Jesus said, "*And other sheep I have which are not of this fold; them also I must bring, and they will hear My voice; and there will be one flock and one shepherd,*" indicating that His death was for more than just the Jews. The Gentiles are to be included as sheep within His fold, thus making all believers, Jew and Gentile, simply "Christians," i.e., "followers of Christ!"

How wonderful that the Good Shepherd proved that He is God by not only dying for the sins of all the world but by rising from the dead! And now He reigns from heaven in His glorified body, seeking to make His sheep complete in every good work, that we may be used to lead others to Him.

Thank you, Lord, for the precious gift of salvation through Your Son! May we this day treasure the picture of our Good Shepherd, and may we seek to follow in His steps as He leads us wherever He would have us to go, knowing that as the good Shepherd, He will never leave us nor forsake us (Hebrews 13:5).

February 14

Follow the Leader

> [1]The Lord is my shepherd; I shall not want. [2]He makes me to lie down in green pastures; He leads me beside the still waters. [3]He restores my soul; He leads me in the paths of righteousness for His name's sake.
> —*Psalm 23:1-3*

SHEEP HAVE many characteristics that make them the perfect animal to describe humans. Since the beginning of human history, sheep have needed a shepherd to survive (see Genesis 4:2). They have no natural defenses. Unlike cattle and other herding animals, sheep cannot be driven. They require a shepherd to *lead* them, and without one, they scatter. King David, who was a shepherd as a boy, recognized the similarity between himself and his flock, and wrote, "The Lord is my shepherd; . . . "

Notice that he didn't write, "The Lord is *our* shepherd." He recognized the fact that, unlike what some claim today, we are not "all God's children." Yes, we're all products of God's creation, but we don't become His children unless "we are made alive" (Ephesians 2:1-3) and adopted into His family. In other words, if you haven't received Christ as Lord and Savior, you can't say, "The Lord is my shepherd" (John 1:12-13).

The shepherd protects the sheep from "want," or "lack." What we want may differ dramatically from what the Lord knows is best, but we must learn to trust Him that He will give us exactly what we need, moment by moment. Sheep must be led because they have a natural tendency to wander. The shepherd goes before them, leading the way, and they follow.

These beautiful verses also describe the shepherd's watchful care over his flock. As grazing animals, sheep need green pastures, but when they eat the grass they pull it up out of the ground rather than eating the top and leaving the roots. Thus they would eat themselves into starvation if they weren't always being led to fresh pastures. They need *still* waters to drink from, being skittish of any stirring of the waters, which would cause them to flee.

David refers to his own Shepherd, saying that He restores his soul and leads him in paths of righteousness. "Restore" here means to turn back. The Good Shepherd has rescued us from being wandering, shepherd-less sheep, heading toward eternal death, and leads us to the still waters and green pastures of a life lacking nothing, having victory over death forever and the grace to walk in the paths of righteousness for His name's sake. Jesus has proven Himself the Great Shepherd, and He is worthy to lead us like sheep.

The Valley of
the Shadow of Death

⁴Yea, though I walk through the valley of the shadow of death, I will fear no evil; for You are with me; Your rod and Your staff, they comfort me. ⁵You prepare a table before me in the presence of my enemies; You anoint my head with oil; My cup runs over. —*Psalm 23:4-5*

DAVID CONTINUES his comparison between people and sheep. Keep in mind that sheep are essentially defenseless creatures. They don't have fangs or claws, they're not fast, they can't fly, and they have been known to run right into their predator's jaws! The Lord sees us in much the same way. Although we may see ourselves as invincible, we are actually traveling through "the valley of the shadow of death." This phrase refers to the deepest darkest times in life, but it also represents one's *entire* life, because we're never really out of danger. Most believers eventually come to realize that we live among what the Bible calls "savage wolves," with doctrines of demons, along with others who seek to steal, kill, and destroy God's sheep.

Although David emphasizes that he "will fear no evil," he explains that His peace comes from the Lord, who is with him, and from His rod and staff that assure him of God's protection! These same weapons are used at times to inflict painful discipline, and yet they were the very implements that brought David comfort because they were in the *Lord's* hands. Can we, too, take the same comfort in realizing that the *Good* Shepherd both defends and disciplines His sheep? Wandering sheep are in danger, whether they be human or animal! The rod is for our good. Has God ever disciplined you in a way that hurt your emotions or ego, and yet, looking back, you see that it was the best thing that could have happened? If not, it's probably coming!

The Lord prepared a table for David before his enemies. We usually see that sheep are prepared for the table—not vice versa! But God uses His Word as a rod and staff to protect His sheep, to restore our souls, and to prepare a "table" before us when enemies are pressing in. In David's culture, an honored guest was anointed with perfume-laced olive oil and given a cup of wine to welcome him. David uses picturesque language to describe this bounteous provision of God through the rod and staff of His Word.

Let's allow God to bless us instead of doing whatever we want. And what blesses Him is to lead His sheep beside the still waters of His Word, lavishing His love, protection, and discipline on us even though we live among wolves in the valley of the shadow of death. May we praise Him today, for, truly, our "cup runs over"!

February 16

The "Shear" Goodness of the Shepherd

⁶Surely goodness and mercy shall follow me all the days of my life; and I will dwell in the house of the Lord forever. —*Psalm 23:6*

OVER THE PAST few days, we saw what the Great Shepherd is to the sheep, and next we saw how He leads the sheep, and now, we'll see where He takes His sheep: to dwell in the house of the Lord!

As we've observed traits about sheep, we've seen that they could never survive without a shepherd. One very important part about taking care of sheep is that they must be shorn. If its wool gets too long, it becomes a haven for fleas and ticks and may become so dense and heavy that if a sheep were to fall down it wouldn't be able to get back on its feet.

We've seen how like sheep we are, but there's another metaphor that is important to understand. Jesus said: *"I am the true vine, and My Father is the vinedresser. Every branch in Me that does not bear fruit He takes away; and every branch that bears fruit He prunes, that it may bear more fruit"* (John 15:4-5). Like branches on the vine, we have been called to produce fruit. In order for that to happen, we need pruning, just as we, being "sheep," need shearing in order to live a blessed life, pleasing to the Lord. David wrote that the Lord *"restores my soul,"* and in Psalm

23:6 he says, "I will *dwell*. . . ." Both words indicate a change of direction in circumstances or situation. And what blessing is available for those who obey Him? They will experience the "goodness and mercy" of the Lord "all the days of [one's] life" and will "dwell in the house of the Lord forever."

Remember this: God always does what is best for His sheep. We may not enjoy the process of pruning or shearing, but without it, there wouldn't be any fruit, and our heavy "wool" would become a danger to our walk in every aspect. John 14:1-3 tells us that Jesus has gone to prepare a place for us. Will we only receive His blessings when things are good, and when we are good? No, as His children, His sheep, "goodness and mercy" will follow us *always*, even when that goodness includes shearing away the evil that we may fall into and pruning unfruitful things from our lives. It may at times include the loving discipline of the rod and staff to keep us from evil. Oh, that we might have a heart to please our Lord and that displeasing Him might be the thing we fear the most!

Our Shepherd has gone to prepare a place for us (John 14:2), and He is now preparing us for that place. Even so, come quickly, Lord Jesus!

February 17

Who Is the King of Glory?
The Lord, Strong and Mighty!

[1]The earth is the Lord's, and all its fullness, the world and those who dwell therein. [2]For He has founded it upon the seas, and established it upon the waters. —*Psalm 24:1-2*

IN PSALM 22, we met the Good Shepherd, who *gave His life* for His sheep. In Psalm 23, the Holy Spirit prompted David to tell us that Yeshua is the Great Shepherd, who *leads* His sheep. In Psalm 24, we'll see that He's the Chief Shepherd, who *rules and reigns* over His sheep.

This psalm was performed by seven choirs of singers and musicians, when David brought the ark into Jerusalem and placed it in the Tabernacle (2 Samuel 6:15). This is important to us today because the temple that housed the presence of "the Lord, strong and mighty" in the form of the Ark of the Covenant prefigured the future home of the presence of God. This psalm predicts the return of the Messiah and His Millennial reign on earth!

In the opening verses, David reaches back to creation as evidence of God's greatness and goodness. The devil and his minions try to deceive people into believing that we came into being through the processes of evolution. Evolutionists can't deny that we're here, but they can't explain how we got here. In other words, "nothing" became "everything" for no reason other than that it happened. This, of course, is impossible. And the first words of the Bible tell us what really happened: God *spoke* everything into existence! There is no scientific explanation that can prove otherwise.

The way we perceive God will determine how we perceive life. The present world shows little respect for human life, and wickedness is increasing. This is directly related to the world's view of God. If we merely evolved—if there is no God—then there's no afterlife. Everyone is free to do what's right in his own eyes. We know that nothing comes from nothing. There must have been a *someone* with knowledge, intellect, power, and love. We have no other explanation. What's your view of God? Is He your buddy? The Man Upstairs? Your higher power? *Or is He the Lord God Almighty*?

The Bible says that the same Spirit of God that raised Jesus from the dead lives in you, if you are a believer! The almighty God, who said, "Let there be light," and there was light, lives in *you*. The One who wrote the information on the spine of a DNA molecule lives in you! The same God who will one day cast the devil, his angels, and all evil into hell forever lives in you! How do you view our God? Is the King of Glory living in you?

A Sin by any Other Name

³Who may ascend into the hill of the Lord? Or who may stand in His holy place? ⁴He who has clean hands and a pure heart, who has not lifted up his soul to an idol, nor sworn deceitfully. ⁵He shall receive blessing from the Lord, and righteousness from the God of his salvation. ⁶This is Jacob, the generation of those who seek Him, who seek Your face. Selah —*Psalm 24:3-6*

THE HEADING of this psalm in the Septuagint reads, "A Psalm of David for the first day of the week." Some refer to it as "The Sunday Psalm." This portion of the psalm was intended to be a "responsive" psalm (in David's day) in which one group of people asked a question and the others gave the response. The first two questions ask who may ascend the hill of the Lord and who may stand before Him. The response of the congregation would be "He who has clean hands and a pure heart." And who might those be who would fit that description? They would be the ones who have received the righteousness of God. And who may stand in His holy place? They who have not lifted up their hearts to idols nor dishonestly made promises.

In these verses, clean hands represent outward moral purity, and the pure heart represents our motives. The two need to go together, because it *is* possible to be an unsaved outwardly "good" person, but to truly worship the Lord, the heart must be changed. No one who knows God will defend the right to sin. No one who knows the Lord, strong and mighty, is going to say that fornication, adultery, idolatry, homosexuality, sodomy, stealing, coveting, drunkenness, partying, and extortion are not sins. In fact, everyone who identifies with Christ will acknowledge these things as sin and repent of them, even if they may still struggle with some of these very things.

In verse 6, David says, "This is Jacob, the generation of those who seek His face." This means that those who bear the title "Chosen by God," whether by birth as a Jew or by faith as a Christian, and who have received the righteousness of God through salvation, are going to agree on God's definition of sin and His command to repent and come away from one's sins and separate oneself from them. Christians may struggle with sin or stumble into sin, sometimes repeatedly, but no *true* believer is ever going to deny or redefine sin. Clean hands come from a purified heart that doesn't worship the things of this world, and according to this "Sunday psalm," these people receive blessings from the Lord. To repeat: No one who truly knows God defends the right to sin.

February 19

Thy Will Be Done

⁷Lift up your heads, O you gates! And be lifted up, you everlasting doors! And the King of glory shall come in. ⁸Who is this King of glory? The Lord strong and mighty, the Lord mighty in battle. ⁹Lift up your heads, O you gates! Lift up, you everlasting doors! And the King of glory shall come in. ¹⁰Who is this King of glory? The Lord of hosts, is the King of glory. Selah —*Psalm 24:7-10*

He

IF OUR PERCEPTION has the power to change our life perspective, then we need to find out all we can about our great and awesome God. Look again at the verses above. Some think that the mentioning of the gates twice represents the human heart and the heavenly gates. Others see this as the foretelling of Jesus' ascension into heaven through the heavenly gates and His return to Jerusalem through the Eastern Gate to rule and reign for a thousand years. Other commentators see this from the perspective of the gates being the judicial center for the cities in David's time and the doors representing the smaller passages through the city walls.

I tend to view the meaning here as symbolic. The doors to a city would hardly be everlasting doors. We could associate the lifting of gates and doors with the gates of heaven and eternity, however. The King of Glory will come through the gates of Jerusalem. He will return to the earth to end the Tribulation, and yes, He will be mighty in battle at the end of the Millennium. But what we need to remember is this: God's will is going to be done, and no one can stop Him! Why? Because He is the LORD! He is the "Lord, mighty in battle. Who is this King of glory?"

Take comfort, Christian! The King of Glory, who is the Lord of Hosts (armies) is going to come back and take full control of the earth and all that is in it, and Satan will be unable to stop Him. Jesus will come against the forces of the enemy at the end of the Millennium, and they don't stand a chance. Satan, who accuses God's people day and night to God himself will be bound for 1,000 years, then loosed for a little while, and finally thrown permanently into the lake of fire. This is the will of God, and nothing, nor anyone, is going to stop Him.

Remember, He keeps His covenant and mercy with all who walk before Him with all their hearts—even when they fail. Even when they do the very things they know sent Christ to the cross. But He only *saves* those who agree with Him about His definition of sin. He doesn't debate. The earth is the Lord's and all its fullness, and all who dwell on it. The Lord of Hosts is His name. Let's give Him all the glory!

February 20

One Direction

> ¹To you O Lord, I lift up my soul. ²O my God, I trust in You; let me not be ashamed; let not my enemies triumph over me. ³Indeed, let no one who waits on You be ashamed; let those be ashamed who deal treacherously without cause. ⁴Show me Your ways, O Lord, teach me Your paths. ⁵Lead me in Your truth and teach me, for You are the God of my salvation; on You I wait all the day. ⁶Remember, O Lord, Your tender mercies and Your lovingkindnesses, for they are from of old. ⁷Do not remember the sins of my youth, nor my transgressions; according to Your mercy remember me, for Your goodness' sake, O Lord. —*Psalm 25:1-7*

THIS PENITENTIAL psalm is filled with reminders of the intimate relationship that God desires to have with His children. The Holy Spirit leads David to write that although such intimacy is available to everyone, it is exclusive only to those who humbly fear the Lord. Psalm 103 expresses this beautifully: "*As a father pities his children, so the Lord pities those who fear Him. . . . He knows our frame; He remembers that we are dust. . . . The mercy of the Lord is from everlasting to everlasting on those who fear Him . . . and to those who [do] His commandments*" (vv 13-18).

In our Scripture reading today, David establishes the contrast between those who are going in one direction and those going the other way, i.e., the friends of

God vs. the enemies of God. Verse 3 indicates that shame is the destiny of those who deal treacherously. Conversely, the contrite, unashamed soul is one who trusts and waits upon the Lord. How can we know that we're on the right path?

One clue is that *the ways and paths of the Lord will lead us and teach us the truth.* Don't listen to the world, which tries to tell you that truth is relative. Many famous people have tried to tell us that there can't be just one way to God, or that we are seeing new "kinds" of Christianity, or that hell isn't real. These people influence millions, and those who follow their teachings are all going in one direction. The wrong one!

Those who are on the right path can be identified by their love of repentance (which reveals the heart) and their hatred for sin, especially in their own lives. We see that David has continued throughout his life to ask God to teach him *His* ways. Those who are going in the right direction can be identified by their attitudes toward the Lord, even when disciplined. *"The sacrifices of God are a broken spirit, a broken and a contrite heart—These, O God, You will not despise"* (Psalm 51:7). ✓ 17 Which path are you on? It's never too late to step onto the right one. May the Lord give us peace in this.

Going Your Way, or the High Way?

> [8] Good and upright is the Lord; therefore He teaches sinners in the way. [9] The humble He guides in justice, and . . . teaches His way. [10] All the paths of the Lord are mercy and truth, to such as keep His covenant and His testimonies. [11] For Your name's sake, O Lord, pardon my iniquity, for it is great. [12] Who is the man that fears the Lord? Him shall He teach in the way He chooses. [13] He . . . shall dwell in prosperity . . . his descendants shall inherit the earth. [14] The secret of the Lord is with those who fear Him, And He will show them His covenant. [15] My eyes are ever toward the Lord, for He shall pluck my feet out of the net. —*Psalm 25:8-15*

GOD WANTS US to know that He loves us even when we fail and falter—but He doesn't love the fact that we do. He is always there to extend mercy, but He also calls us to get up and walk in truth. What a precious thought! The word "sinners" in verse 8 describes all of us. But it's only those who humble themselves who will receive the blessings of His justice, His way, His mercy, and His truth. Learning "His way" involves moving in the direction in which He shows us. Hosea writes, "For the ways of the Lord are right; the righteous walk in them, but transgressors stumble in them" (Hosea 14:9).

It isn't always easy to walk in God's direction! Proverbs 14:12 and 16:25 both say, "There is a way that *seems right* to a man, but its end is the way of death." The danger is very great if we don't allow the Lord to lead us in His direction. And the humble are happy to follow Him. ☺

David mentions those who *fear* the Lord (vv. 12, 14). God will teach them to go in the way He chooses, and His way is far superior to the paths we often choose. How much better to stay on His straight paths, headed in the right direction, building our lives around His Word, not around the world.

David writes of "dwell[ing] in prosperity" if we fear the Lord. This is something far greater than the prosperity the world offers. To have peace in one's heart, to know where we're going when we die, and that we can trust the Lord for *everything*, makes us rich far beyond any material blessings. God promises that the meek shall inherit the earth (Matthew 5:5)!

It's true that those who are going in God's direction in humble fear of Him do so because they have a single source of direction for all things related to life and the Word of God. Remember, if you want to go in God's direction, don't be too proud to follow His ways and His plans. Your ideas are not better than His, and you don't know what tomorrow will bring . . . or if there will even be one.

February 22

The Right Direction

> ¹⁶Turn Yourself to me, and have mercy on me, for I am desolate and afflicted. ¹⁷The troubles of my heart have enlarged; bring me out of my distresses! ¹⁸Look on my affliction and my pain, and forgive all my sins. ¹⁹Consider my enemies, for they are many; and they hate me with cruel hatred. ²⁰Keep my soul, and deliver me; let me not be ashamed, for I put my trust in You. ²¹Let integrity and uprightness preserve me, for I wait for You. ²²Redeem Israel, O God, out of all their troubles! —*Psalm 25:16-22*

NOBODY—whether King David or the Apostle Paul or anyone at any time—can stand before God in his own righteousness, and no one knew that better than David. Listen to his plea to God for mercy, comfort, deliverance, and protection, recognizing that He is a sinner in need of the Lord's love and grace. True integrity and uprightness are solely dependent upon God's mercy, forgiveness, and deliverance. David prays that God will forgive him and keep him going in *one direction*—the direction that pleases Him.

The longer we continue in the right direction, the more we become aware of our own sins, because we are walking in God's paths and growing ever closer to

Him. As painful as the realization of our innate wickedness is, it's also a reason for rejoicing! When we're honest with ourselves about the sin that we know we're *capable* of, the humbler and more obedient to the Lord we'll become. We realize that we need to cling more tightly to Him than ever, thus growing closer and closer to Him! Sadly, among the leaders in many churches, we find statements that are blasphemous and contrary to what God has laid out. These "pastors" see themselves as being above the Word, questioning its authority, denying the Scriptures.

But what do they do with truth? Where is humility? Where is repentance? Are these men and women better than the prophets of old? Better than the apostles? Better than Peter and Paul and John the Baptist—men who willingly gave their lives rather than compromising the Word of God? Better than all of the writers of Scripture, who were led by the Holy Spirit? These false teachers have the audacity to attempt to tear God from His throne, placing themselves there in His stead!

The longer we walk with Jesus and seek to be like Him, the more we realize how *unlike* Him we are and how far we have to go. How wonderful that God chooses to use imperfect people who study to learn more about Him through His Word. There's only one direction that all true Christians should be going—it's God's direction. Let's point our compasses toward the "S" for Son of God, trusting that the Lord will make our paths straight.

February 23

No Fear

> [1]The Lord is my light and my salvation; whom shall I fear? The Lord is the strength of my life; of whom shall I be afraid? [2]When the wicked came against me to eat up my flesh, my enemies and foes, they stumbled and fell. [3]Though an army may encamp against me, my heart shall not fear; though war may rise against me, in this I will be confident. [4]One thing I have desired of the Lord, that will I seek: that I may dwell in the house of the Lord all the days of my life, to behold the beauty of the Lord, and to inquire in His temple. [5]For in the time of trouble He shall hide me in His pavilion; in the secret place of His tabernacle He shall hide me; He shall set me high upon a rock. [6]And now my head shall be lifted up above my enemies all around me; therefore I will offer sacrifices of joy in His tabernacle; I will sing, yes, I will sing praises to the Lord.—*Psalm 27:1-6*

THIS BEAUTIFUL and beloved psalm will sound familiar to many, having been quoted in many songs and sermons throughout all the years of Christianity. The Lord inspired these words, and they've been used in many quotes, such as Spurgeon's: "He who fears God has nothing else to fear."

In the six verses above we find a veritable treasure that God has given to us. Because of Him, we have light, salvation, no fear, confidence, a dwelling place, the joy of beholding His beauty, the opportunity to inquire of Him, a hiding place in time of need, our feet placed upon a rock, and our downcast heads lifted up. All of that, in just these few verses!

David writes, "The Lord is my light and my salvation." He's saying that the Lord is his strength, so fear is defeated. Does this mean that David has unlimited strength? Not physically, although God's strength is limitless. But as Christians, we have everything we need to get through life. If enemies arise, they will stumble and fall. Even if we're surrounded, we have nothing to fear. God will give us confidence in time of war.

Then David gives us the key to unlocking such confidence through the one thing he really desires and seeks of the Lord: to be in His house forever. This is so wonderful in what it means for us! *We* can behold the beauty of the Lord; we can seek His help in times of trouble; a hiding place can be found in Him; our feet can be set upon the Rock, and our head can be lifted up in praise, even if surrounded by enemies. When threatened, we can be sheltered, protected, and provided for in the "pavilion" of God. To be there means that we have everything we need for anything we may go through. He will be our Deliverer, our Provider, and our Defense. Of whom shall we be afraid? Christian, it's all yours. Have you appropriated the promises of God?

When the Going Gets Tougher

> [7]Hear, O Lord, when I cry with my voice! Have mercy also upon me, and answer me. [8]When You said, "Seek My face," my heart said to You, "Your face, Lord, I will seek." [9]Do not hide Your face from me; do not turn Your servant away in anger; You have been my help; do not leave me nor forsake me, O God of my salvation. [10]When my father and my mother forsake me, then the Lord will take care of me. —*Psalm 27:7-10*

HAVE YOU EVER felt like God wasn't hearing your prayer? You've done all that you know how to do—you've cried out to the Lord, claimed His promises, repeated them back to Him—and yet you still feel as though He doesn't hear your cries. Well, take heart. You're in good company!

David appears here to be experiencing a similar situation. He cries out to the Lord, pleading with Him to answer him. He reminds God of His own words to "Seek My face," but he is still experiencing what feels like rejection. What does David do?

He recalls what he knows about the Lord. In verse 9, he says, *"You have been my help."* He *knows* that God has always been faithful to help him in the past.

Let's reason through this: Does God sometimes permit us to endure hard things? Do people ever forsake us? Psalm 34:17-19 says: *"The righteous cry out, and the Lord hears, and delivers them out of all their troubles. The Lord is near to those who have a broken heart, and saves such as have a contrite spirit. Many are the afflictions of the righteous, but the Lord delivers him out of them all."*

We must always remember that we belong to God. No matter what we face, we have every reason to trust Him and to not be afraid, based on God's promises in His Word and even as we look back on our own lives, having seen Him work wonderful things during hard times in the past. He deals differently with His children than we deal with one another, or than the way He deals with those who do evil. The face, countenance, character, and nature of God is against evildoers, but the righteous can *expect* deliverance, salvation, and the nearness of the Lord when life is heartbreaking.

Our Father's love for us makes human love look like hatred by comparison. Circumstances don't change His love. No matter how it may appear, His love never fails. He hears our cries, and even though His answer might be "Wait a little while," we know that we are never alone, and that His eyes are always upon us, watching, testing, protecting us, every moment until that glorious day when we find ourselves safe forever with Him in our eternal home.

February 25

This World Is Not Our Home

[11] Teach me Your way, O Lord, and lead me in a smooth path, because of my enemies [12] Do not deliver me to the will of my adversaries; for false witnesses have risen against me, and such as breathe out violence. [13] I would have lost heart, unless I had believed that I would see the goodness of the Lord In the land of the living. [14] Wait on the Lord, be of good courage, and He shall strengthen your heart; wait, I say, on the Lord! —*Psalm 27:11-14*

MANY TODAY seem blind to the concept of right and wrong. "Christian" leaders scoff at the church's use of "2,000-year-old letters." Abortion is seen as a "right" rather than a hideous crime against our Creator God. People tolerate evil within some religions whose "god" is a monster, and others accept anything (except Christianity) under the guise of "tolerance."

David experienced desperation like what we often feel, but he reminds us that there's a path for believers to follow, and the Lord will show us the way in His Word.

David asks God to lead him in a "smooth path." The Hebrew word for "smooth," *miyshor*, means level or straight, as in "just." David asks God to teach him how to walk the narrow path of justice and equity found in the Word. He writes, "I would have lost heart, *unless....*" As we look back on our lives since becoming believers, we realize, like David, that God was faithful to us *through everything.*

Remember this: In a world that continues to spiral out of control, the Lord is with us! Everything may seem to be falling into irreversible immorality and spiritual chaos, but hold onto these truths: 1) As a Christian, you have victory in Jesus to stay pure and pleasing to the Lord. 2) As a believer, you have victory over drugs and alcohol through Christ. 3) In a world filled with spiritual delusion and deception, we've been promised that true believers can't be deceived because they have the same Spirit who raised Christ from the dead living within them, teaching them all things.

Like David, we're to wait on the Lord and be of good courage! God promises that He will strengthen our hearts through the hardest of times. Even in the worst scenarios taking place, when Christians are being killed for their faith, remember this: these bodies can't inherit eternal life. The soul goes into eternity, where it will never grow old or get ill, and it will never die. *Nothing* can separate us from the love of God nor snatch us out of our Father's hands. The great enemy, Death, has been defeated and is nullified by our faith in Christ. Maintain your hope! Jesus is on the way, and the things He promised that await us in heaven are ours because of Him.

February 26

Revival Fires

Introduction to Psalm 32

³² "Blessed is he whose transgression is forgiven . . ." —*Psalm 32*

THIS HEART-WRENCHING but hope-filled psalm is believed to be King David's response to his confrontation with Nathan the prophet concerning the sin he had committed with Bathsheba against her husband Uriah, resulting in his murder. Nathan comes to David with a list of consequences, including the fact that his own son, who had resulted from his sin with Bathsheba, would die. David, who had thought he'd kept his sin a secret, confessed: "'I have sinned against the Lord.' And Nathan said to David, 'The Lord also has put away your sin; you shall not die'" (2 Samuel 12:13).

We get a behind-the-scenes look at David's life when he lived in unconfessed sin and the horrible consequences that he suffered and then the relief he experienced when he sincerely confessed what he had done before the Lord. This is considered a "wisdom" psalm as well as a "penitential" psalm. The two go together because wisdom tells us to confess our unconfessed sin.

Repentance certainly isn't a popular subject today, but the Lord Jesus warned the churches in the book of Revelation to repent for two reasons: 1) Because they were committing sin, repentance was the *only* solution; 2) The sins in which they were engaging were taking place within the church, thus giving the enemies of God opportunity to blaspheme and rob the church of its power and influence in the world.

What believers need today, and what David needed, as recorded in this psalm, was revival of the heart. In Ezra, we read, *"Since the days of our fathers to this day we have been very guilty, and for our iniquities . . . have been delivered . . . to the sword, to captivity, to plunder, and to humiliation. . . . Now for a little while grace has been shown from the Lord our God . . . to give us a peg in His holy place . . . and give us a measure of revival in our bondage"* (Ezra 9:7-8). The word "revival" here means "to preserve life, to recover ourselves, to renew validity" and was applied to the people of God and the consequences of their fall into great sinfulness.

Just as with David, so with the church today. As we study King David's painful experience with unconfessed sin and its consequences, may the Lord reveal to us the urgency of repentance in re-igniting the fires of revival within our hearts. *Lord, open our hearts to hear Your Word today.*

February 27

Revive Us, O Lord

[1]Blessed is he whose transgression is forgiven, whose sin is covered. [2]Blessed is the man to whom the Lord does not impute iniquity, and in whose spirit there is no deceit. [3]When I kept silent, my bones grew old through my groaning all the day long. [4]For day and night Your hand was heavy upon me; my vitality was turned into the drought of summer. Selah. [5]I acknowledged my sin to You, and my iniquity I have not hidden. I said, "I will confess my transgressions to the Lord," and You forgave the iniquity of my sin. Selah —*Psalm 32:1-5*

DAVID BEGINS this psalm with the astute observation that the blessed life begins with forgiveness, and we sense that he was never far away in his mind from the understanding that he'd been forgiven much. Nor should we! Let's look at some of the blessings of being forgiven: our sins are covered by the blood of Christ; we receive His imputed righteousness; deceitfulness in our hearts has been done away with.

How does one experience the relief that David describes here? In verses 3 and 4 he states that before he confessed his sin, his entire body and soul was consumed with pain. He knew that God's hand was heavily upon him, not letting him experience rest until . . . (verse 5): "I acknowledged my sin to You . . ." and the wonderful, blessed relief of sins having been forgiven and a clear conscience overwhelmed him.

Why do so many ignore or even turn away from the simple solution to the curse of a guilty conscience? Sadly, most people don't like to hear that they're sinners! They want to *feel* "religious" and righteous, and they want pastors to tell them things that will keep them coming back to church—not what will keep them from going to hell.

The pain isn't worth it! David said that when he was silent about his sin, he felt dried up. His guilt ate at him, and he had no vitality in his life. BUT when he acknowledged his sin before His Father, confessing his transgressions, his merciful Lord completely forgave and restored him. How can we experience this same relief and see revival begin? From the verses above, we see that the fires of revival in our hearts will be quenched where sin is left unaddressed. And those who desire to feel "blessed" must hear and believe the information that their sin is keeping them from the life that God desires to give them. May we open our hearts to the Lord, seeking and appropriating His forgiveness and love.

February 28

Set Your Heart on Fire

> ^{6}For this cause everyone who is godly shall pray to You in a time when You may be found; surely in a flood of great waters they shall not come near him. ^{7}You are my hiding place; You shall preserve me from trouble; You shall surround me with songs of deliverance. Selah ^{8}I will instruct you and teach you in the way you should go; I will guide you with My eye. —*Psalm 32:6-8*

HAVING CONFESSED his sins and experiencing the gift of forgiveness from God, David's faith and love for his Lord has been revived and strengthened. God is his hiding place. He promises to instruct and guide him in the ways that He wants him to go. We can learn from this as well. "Everyone who is godly" would also apply to us! We can pray to the Lord in the way that David did and discover that the floodwaters will not come near, the Lord will hide us in times of trouble and surround us with songs of deliverance. Zephaniah 3:17-18 says, "*The Lord your God in your midst, The Mighty One, will save; He will rejoice over you with gladness, He will quiet you with singing. . . .*"

What a precious promise! Both David and Zephaniah describe the Lord *sing-ing*, in one case with songs of deliverance, and in the other, to quiet troubled hearts. And we can share in these promises! The Lord sings over those who are burdened about the condition of the church today. That doesn't necessarily mean that He will save us from literal floodwaters or that there won't be any trouble from any direction. But the precious truth is that we can be quieted with His love instead of being disturbed by His heavy hand on us. It means that He will rejoice over us with gladness, making us glad instead of groaning all day long. It means that instead of the drought of summer (which can also even mean spiritual dryness), He will sing over us of His refreshing love.

David longs to see his people repent that they might experience the blessings of God by confessing their sins, iniquities, and transgressions. That should be our heart as well. The health of our nation depends upon the health of the church. Although the whole nation may enjoy the "common grace" of God, which is given to all, we have also been blessed because of our Christian heritage and the number of Bible-believing Christians within our borders. America's hope is not and never will be the White House or the Houses of Congress or anything else. The hope of America is revival fires sweeping through God's house and God's people, the church. May it begin today!

MARCH

"You May Grow Up to Be a Mule"

⁹Do not be like the horse or like the mule, which have no understanding, which must be harnessed with bit and bridle, else they will not come near you. ¹⁰Many sorrows shall be to the wicked; but he who trusts in the Lord, mercy shall surround him. ¹¹Be glad in the Lord and rejoice, you righteous; and shout for joy, all you upright in heart! —Psalm 32:9-11

WARREN WIERSBE said we have three choices of how God will treat us: like a sponge, with His hand heavy on us, squeezing out the unwanted elements; like a person, protected and hidden in Him, or like an animal, such as a horse—needing forceful guidance to go in the right direction. Here, David also says that we can be guided like the horse or mule, with a bit and bridle, and unable to be led otherwise.

A clear contrast is drawn in these verses between the wicked and the righteous. *God's people are to be remarkably different from worldly people.* Sorrows await the wicked, but mercy, gladness, and joy are reserved for the upright in heart.

> *The blessing of the Lord makes one rich, and He adds no sorrow with it. To do evil is like sport to a fool, but a man of understanding has wisdom. The fear of the wicked will come upon him, and the desire of the righteous will be granted. (Proverbs 10:20-15)*

The lines are being blurred, in this age of tolerance, between the sexes, classes, religions, and just about anything where distinctions between people are made. Sadly, this has made its way into the church as well, both morally and spiritually. All of this is paving the way for the Man of Sin and his False Prophet to come, deceiving the world with a false religion. Romans 1:28-32 issues a strong warning about this very thing. Approving of sin is evidence of one's not retaining God in one's knowledge and being given over to a depraved mind. We live in those times now. Revival is our only hope. God has done His part, giving us all we need by sending His Holy Spirit to fan the flames of revival fire. But they must be true moves of the Spirit. If a "revival" leaves people unchanged, it wasn't of the Lord.

David warned us not to be like a stubborn animal when it comes to repentance having to be forced on us because we won't come to it ourselves. If we love our sin more than we want to please the Lord, we will never see true revival. Do you need revival? Do you want revival? Or "would you rather be a mule?"

Persecution is coming to the church, even in America. It has already begun, targeting our beliefs and then our behaviors. If we believe and behave like Christians, we will soon be the targets of the darkness lovers in our land. The only hope is revival, and it won't begin in a worldly church. It will begin among people who say, like King David, "I can't live like this anymore. I have to go all out and all in for God." What is God saying to you today? It's time to light the revival fires. Jesus is coming soon!

March 2

Nevertheless . . . !

Introduction

¹ᵃA Psalm of David when he pretended madness before Abimelech, who drove him away, and he departed. —*Psalm 34:1a*

ISN'T IT WONDERFUL that God left us such an amazing piece of literature as the Book of Psalms? And of course, it isn't merely literature but historical fact, which makes it all the more remarkable. The background to this psalm, in brief, is that God had appointed David king, and, as everything that's in God's will, nothing and no one could change or halt that fact. That doesn't mean, however, that the enemy stops trying! King Saul repeatedly attempted to kill David, and at the time this psalm was written, David was actually on the run and had arrived at a city called Nob.

His stay was short lived, as he was recognized by one of Saul's servants, and the information was reported to the king, so David was forced to flee. Instead of running back to the wilderness where the Lord had been keeping him safe and providing for him, David headed to Gath, the hometown of Goliath, the giant whom he had killed with the sword after knocking him out with a stone. In fact, he is carrying the giant's sword with him at this time! Once again, he is recognized, and in order to avoid arrest and execution, David feigns insanity.

If we search really hard—well, probably not that hard—we can likely relate to David at this point. I know that I have made poor decisions and put myself in the wrong place and acted like a nut. And yet the Lord delivered me! Nevertheless . . . !

"Nevertheless" what? Nevertheless, we can find encouragement and majestic truths in this psalm of David, even in his disgrace. There are encouraging words of comfort here related to the Lord: *heard, delivered, encamps, near, saves, guards*.

Reading majestic texts like this and understanding the circumstances surrounding them, such as the Exodus from Egypt, the crumbling walls of Jericho, or the manifestations of power through the apostles, we often think those things are exclusively for the "elite" of the faithful.

But the truth is that the *will* of God for you, the *plan* of God for you, and the *power* of God in you, is nevertheless *for* you, and it is always the best. Let's not read these amazing Bible accounts and think, *Wow, look at what God did for and through David!* Let's read them and say, "Wow! Look at what God will do for and through us!"

What God wants and is able to do through us, no matter how helpless we many consider ourselves to be, is the same as the amazing things He does for and through others. And it's always greater that we can imagine. "[He] is able to do exceedingly abundantly above all that we ask or think, according to the power that works in us . . . " (Eph. 3:20).

Let's allow that "nevertheless" reminder to carry us through this and every day when our doubts assail us and fear threatens to bring us down. Our God, who is perfect, is the God of "nevertheless," meaning that through Him all things are possible!

Never-the-less . . . and More!

> [1]I will bless the Lord at all times; His praise shall continually be in my mouth. [2]My soul shall make its boast in the Lord; the humble shall hear of it and be glad. [3]Oh, magnify the Lord with me, and let us exalt His name together. —*Psalm 34:1-3*

IN THE INTRODUCTION to this psalm yesterday, David mentions the situation in which he finds himself and is "forced" to feign madness, but he gives no further details. Instead he begins, "I will bless the Lord . . . " and says that he will praise Him always, even under the worst possible conditions (even the ones in which he presently found himself). He says that he will *continually* praise the Lord! David then invites us to join him in magnifying the Lord, no matter our own situation.

Psalm 145 says, "*The Lord is near to all who call upon Him, to all who call upon Him in truth. He will fulfill the desire of those who fear Him; He also will hear their cry and save them. The Lord preserves all who love Him, but all the wicked He will destroy. My mouth shall speak the praise of the Lord, and all flesh shall bless His holy name forever and ever*" (vv 18-21).

It may seem difficult for us to praise the Lord when we're in dark or heavy or frightening situations. Let's look a little deeper at what was going on in David's life when he wrote these words. He was trapped in Gath; he had to pretend like he'd lost his mind; he was somewhere where he never would have gone if he could have helped it. He was already on the run from Doeg, his enemy, who had identified him in Nob. And now, here he was in Gath with the ironic reminder that he had taken a stand for God when no one else would hanging by his side in the form of Goliath's sword. Things couldn't be any worse, and the mighty David was afraid. Nevertheless, he knew that God is worthy of our praise, and he made the practical decision to give God what was His due, no matter what he himself was facing.

David understood and put into practice what we need to learn and remember: The power of praise is never diminished by feelings and emotions. "But," you may ask, "isn't fear an emotion? Wasn't David afraid?"

Good question. David was afraid. But did he wait to praise God until his fear faded and his confidence rose? No, *he praised God in the face of fear!* We can praise Him in the face of fear also, and in the face of doubt, frustration, sorrow, self-pity. David wrote: "I will bless the Lord *at all times*; His praise will *continually* be in my mouth" (emphasis added).

The power of praise is independent of our circumstance. In fact, praising the Lord is the best way to rise above any situation. And David indicated, as he praised the Lord, that he also would boast in the Lord! How glorifying to God—to put His name, His praise, His honor, before ourselves and our circumstances. And His response is to free us in our hearts and minds, and often even from the situations that hold us bound. Praise Him in truth today, and experience the freedom that comes with putting God ahead of ourselves.

Don't Be Afraid, but Do Fear!

8Oh, taste and see that the Lord is good; blessed is the man who trusts in Him! 9Oh, fear the Lord, you His saints! There is no want to those who fear Him. 10The young lions lack and suffer hunger; but those who seek the Lord shall not lack any good thing. —Psalm 34:8-10

DO YOU EVER FEEL confused about the fact that sometimes the Scriptures, as in our verses today, tell us that if we love and seek the Lord, we won't want for *anything*? Yet as we look at our own lives, we wonder how this applies, considering our circumstances. What David is doing here is drawing a contrast between those worries that occupy our feelings and emotions and the things that really matter, which are the things of God.

I'm not saying that poverty and hunger don't matter, but David is making a personal statement regarding his own experience. I mean, when you wind up in Gath holding Goliath's sword in the city where his family lives, you want to call to mind that the fear of the Lord will help you to deal with the fear of man, in this case, a man named Achish (see 1 Sam 21). Psalm 14:27 says, "The fear of the Lord is a fountain of life, to turn one away from the snares of death." And Proverbs 15:16 reads, "Better is a little with the fear of the Lord, than great treasure with trouble."

In fact, the takeaway from these verses might be that *there is nothing we need more than the fear of the Lord!* Why would that be? "The fear of the Lord is the beginning of knowledge" (Proverbs 1:7); " . . . the beginning of wisdom" (Proverbs 9:10); " . . . a fountain of life"; " . . . better than treasure"; and the list goes on.

But what does it mean to fear the Lord? Some think it means to respect or revere God, but it's more than that. For the believer, a biblical fear of God includes understanding how much He hates sin. It also includes a fear of His judgment on sin—even in the life of a believer.

The word "fear" in these verses means "moral reverence," but it can also have the connotation of being frightened. This simply means that we should have such a reverence of God that it impacts the way we live our lives, and we fear that our own flesh will fail us and disappoint Him. We are to respect Him by obeying Him, submitting to His discipline, and worshiping Him in awe. After all, He's the Creator of the universe! He holds our lives in His hand. He sent His Son to die on the cross for our sins, so that we could spend a glorious eternity with Him! Is it unreasonable to ask that we offer Him our deepest respect and love, and, yes, even our fear of displeasing Him?

So, back to our point, we're to fear the Lord *for our own good* and for His pleasure. I don't know about you, but I long for nothing more than to know that I am pleasing Him. If we fear the Lord, we will lack nothing that is good. That shouldn't be a difficult decision to make. The right kind of fear for God will conquer all circumstances and will defeat all of our enemies. Even when in Gath, with Goliath's sword, acting like a nut—even *then*, David did not lack any good thing, and the Lord delivered him. And that is what we, too, may expect from our perfect, loving Father.

The Art of Living

> *11*Come, you children, listen to me; I will teach you the fear of the Lord. *12*Who is the man who desires life, and loves many days, that he may see good? *13*Keep your tongue from evil, and your lips from speaking deceit. *14*Depart from evil and do good; seek peace and pursue it.
> *—Psalm 34:11-14*

"I WILL BLESS *the Lord at all times; His praise shall continually be in my mouth*" (Ps 34:1). What we've learned through David's writings is that praise is natural and easy when times are good—but it's tactical and *empowering* when times are not! The power of praise is never diminished by negative feelings and emotions. Our merciful Lord "knows our frame; He remembers that we are dust" (Ps 103:14). You may not feel like praising Him in your circumstances, but praising Him will soon lead to boasting in Him for what He has done! Christian, there is power in praise, and even our doubts and fears cannot quench it!

Next David invites the children (which could indicate anyone who needs help understanding these truths) to come, and he will teach them the most important aspect of following the Lord. And what is that? It's the *fear of the Lord*.

Charles Spurgeon described the contents of these verses as "The Art of Living." It occurred to me that when our lives have come to an end, we should leave behind us, for others to see, a portrait of Jesus reflected through the way we've lived. Our lives should have been lived in His goodness, His power, His grace, and His mercy.

David asks, "Who desires life and loves many days, that he may see good?" Well, who doesn't? It's built into us to long to live to a ripe old age and enjoy many good things. But that doesn't always happen, even among the godliest of people. Could it be that David isn't really talking about the quantity of our days but the quality? Psalm 90, attributed to Moses, says, "Teach us to number our days, that *we may gain a heart of wisdom*" (Ps 90:12). So it really doesn't have to do with the *time* on earth we're given, but what we do with that time. Part of the art of living and seeing real goodness manifested through our lives, no matter their length, is to really understand what it means to fear the Lord.

A few things worth considering: Does God allow trials? Can we create our own by sinning? Which is better: a life of integrity, or a life of lies and deceit? Is the life of a peacemaker better than the life of a troublemaker? Most important: can a proper portrait of Christ be painted through an immoral and dishonest life?

The art of living in the fear of the Lord actually limits the trials of life to only those that God has permitted to increase our trust and strengthen our faith. Isn't that a good place to be, even though difficult at times? The Lord is with us and *on our side* through all of these difficulties. The art of living in the fear of the Lord is accomplished by walking in the Spirit and not fulfilling the lusts of the flesh. As Galatians 5:25 says, "If we live in the Spirit, let us also walk in the Spirit." Are you ready?

March 6

Righteousness or Relevance?

> [15]The eyes of the Lord are on the righteous, and His ears are open to their cry. [16]The face of the Lord is against those who do evil, to cut off the remembrance of them from the earth. [17]The righteous cry out, and the Lord hears, and delivers them out of all their troubles. [18]The Lord is near to those who have a broken heart, and saves such as have a contrite spirit. —*Psalm 34:15-18*

THERE SHOULD BE a noticeable difference between the life experience of the righteous and the unrighteous. These verses above make that quite clear. The Lord hears the righteous, but His face is against the unrighteous. He cuts off the remembrance of the evildoer from the face of the earth, but He delivers the righteous from their troubles. He's near to the brokenhearted, and He saves the contrite in heart.

It's important for believers to reflect the joy and peace this brings. Even though some "Christians" will criticize and mock you for living in the light of God's love and His Word, please understand something: if one's mouth, morals, and mindset haven't changed since they raised their hand, walked down an aisle, and prayed a prayer, they haven't really met Christ. If they had, their own heart would convict them!

Be aware that there can also be "this life" consequences for a true Christian who persists in living in sin (1 Thess 4:7-8). We have the Holy Spirit within us to help us avoid the need for God's discipline because of our disobedience.

Listen, Christians, the church will be much more effective in these last days when it gets back to living righteously and quits trying to be relevant. There are comforts and protections that are exclusive to righteousness, and when the world sees the church trapped in the same sins that they are, the church becomes *irrelevant* and unnecessary. But when believers practice the art of living in the fear of the Lord, the world takes notice, recognizing that we not *of* them because we are nothing *like* them.

We need to stop encouraging unbelievers around us to continue as they are through our silence. Do they struggle in relationships? Do they have broken hearts? Do they have worries and concerns? Do they fear death? Do we have the answer? Yes, in every way. The Lord is near to the *broken hearted*! Share His love. Never let your fear of what someone might think of you interfere with the clear command of Christ: "Go and make disciples." Remember that as they are now, you once were—and God was able to reach you, and He probably used an individual or maybe several to draw you to Himself. Allow Him now to work through you so that your righteousness will shine as a light through any "relevant" shadows you may encounter.

The Art of Living in the Fear of the Lord

[19]Many are the afflictions of the righteous, but the Lord delivers him out of them all. [20]He guards all his bones; not one of them is broken. [21]Evil shall slay the wicked, and those who hate the righteous shall be condemned. [22]The Lord redeems the soul of His servants, and none of those who trust in Him shall be condemned. —*Psalm 34:19-22*

THE CHRISTIAN LIFE isn't affliction- or pain-free, but we're promised deliverance from those things, unlike the unrighteous. How can we take comfort in these verses, when we go through situations that often have no solution and may result in death? Jesus said, "*These things I have spoken unto you, that in Me you may have peace. In the world you will have tribulation; but be of good cheer, for I have overcome the world*" (John 16:32-33). In Revelation 21 we read, "*The tabernacle of God is with men, and He will dwell with them, and they shall be His people. God himself will be with them and be their God. And God will wipe away every tear from their eyes; there shall be no more death, nor sorrow, nor crying. There shall be no more pain, for the former things have passed away.*"

Although these verses in John and Revelation were written long after King David had written his inspired words, we know that David had the same mindset when he wrote, "The Lord redeems the soul of His servants, and none . . . who trust in Him shall be condemned." He understood the concept of the saving of the soul. He also understood divine judgment when he said that the wicked will be slain and those who hate the righteous shall be condemned.

What do we tell the lost? Do we tell them comfortingly that they have nothing to fear? Do we say, "God loves you, and has a wonderful plan for your life"? or "God cares for you and will provide for you and take you to heaven"? Do these words of cheer to the lost tell the whole story? What about the fact that God wants to *change you*? He doesn't want you just the way you are. He wants to change your mouth, your morals, and your mindset! Romans 12:1-2 tells us, " . . . *Present your bodies a living sacrifice, holy, acceptable to God, which is your reasonable service. And do not be conformed to this world, but be transformed by the renewing of your mind. . . ."*

Here's food for thought: How can you prove, or test, the Word of God by not doing the will of God? What is His will? *"For this is the will of God, your sanctification: that you should abstain from sexual immorality; that each of you should know how to possess his own vessel in sanctification and honor, not in passion of lust . . . "* (1 Thes 4:3-6). People are being defrauded today by teaching that denounces the fear of the Lord, denies sanctification, and are devoid of any reason to fear God and repent. King David understood it. Was he perfect? No. Did his own sin cost him dearly? Yes. But David knew and taught the fear of the Lord. Can we possibly teach others about the fear of the Lord by removing any reason for people to fear? Hell is real, and the soul that sins will die the second death unless that person become positionally righteous in Christ, which will always be proven by practical righteousness in life. And this is the true art of living in the fear of the Lord.

March 8

No Fear, No Faith

[1]A Psalm of David the servant of the Lord. An oracle within my heart concerning the transgression of the wicked: There is no fear of God before his eyes. [2]For he flatters himself in his own eyes, when he finds out his iniquity and when he hates. [3]The words of his mouth are wickedness and deceit; he has ceased to be wise and to do good. [4]He devises wickedness on his bed; he sets himself in a way that is not good; he does not abhor evil. —*Psalm 36:1-4*

THIS PSALM is an oracle, which means "a divine utterance," or a word from the Lord. The difference between this oracle and his other psalms is that David recognized that God himself was speaking these words through him. He opens this psalm with a description of the wicked man. What are some of his "qualifications"? In Romans 3, Paul gives a list of features that identify the wicked, but he sums it up with this: "There is no fear of God before their eyes"—exactly as David said above. Let's begin by looking at the contrast between God's people and the ungodly.

The first point David makes is that the ungodly man has no fear of God *before his eyes* (like radical atheists today). It could even be said that the wicked person understands the obvious evidence that God exists but flatters himself that he doesn't need Him. As described here, his mouth, his morals, and his mind are wicked, because he has no fear. The *fear* of the Lord is the first step toward saving faith! (It's an important element that shouldn't be ignored as we witness to others.)

Paul describes the behavior of those with saving faith: "Let love be without hypocrisy. Abhor what is evil. Cling to what is good . . . " (Rom 12:9-13). He continues with other phrases describing true believers, but one of the first attributes mentioned is that they will hate evil and cling to what is good. The wicked have no desire to do genuine good because they have *no fear of the Lord*. That doesn't mean they never do anything kind or good, but they never desire the ultimate good, which God says is to abhor evil! Having no fear of the Lord means no salvation.

Each of us was once apart from Christ and perishing in our sins. Hell would be our eternal home. But Christ died on the cross for the sins of the *world*. When we heard and believed this, realizing that we were sinners, we received the faith needed for salvation, which is available to ALL who will receive it! What initiated that faith in us? It wasn't just hearing Bible stories about Jesus healing the sick and loving the little children. It was *the fear of the Lord* as we realized that we were dead in our sins and headed for hell! The Bible tells us that God's judgments are true and righteous—and if you don't fear the Lord, you really don't believe in Him. You may flatter yourself that he'll let you into heaven "as is" (see Revelation 21:8 regarding those who won't see the Lord in heaven but who will experience the "second death"). It's clear that those who have no fear of a mighty God have no saving faith, so the outcome can't possibly be a good one.

As we pray for those who don't know the Lord, let's ask God (who desires that none should perish) to show us how we can be living examples of what it means to have our fear turned into faith and the blessed peace that this brings.

Fear of the Lord
Illuminates God's Mercy and Grace

⁵Your mercy, O Lord, is in the heavens; Your faithfulness reaches to the clouds. ⁶Your righteousness is like the great mountains; Your judgments are a great deep; O Lord, You preserve man and beast. ⁷How precious is Your lovingkindness, O God! Therefore the children of men put their trust under the shadow of Your wings. ⁸They are abundantly satisfied with the fullness of Your house, and You give them drink from the river of Your pleasures. ⁹For with You is the fountain of life; in Your light we see light. —Psalm 36:5-9

YESTERDAY WE SAW the depravity of man. Today we see the overwhelming goodness of God and His mercy. Mercy is the bridge that allows man to cross over from a world of utter wickedness to the domain of a perfect heaven. How wonderful that our all-powerful God, whom Hebrews 12 says is a consuming fire, still saves utterly wicked people because of His loving-kindness! But the hitch is that they must see themselves as He sees them. No one is worthy of being saved. No one can contribute one iota to our salvation. We must see ourselves as lost and sinful apart from God's redeeming love and grace.

He offers what we call "common grace" to all—man and beast alike—through His provision on this earth. The Bible says the rain falls on the just *and* the unjust. He blesses the entire world with beauty and splendor. The majesty of a sunset or a lightning storm is available for all to see and appreciate. That is common grace. But common grace does not save our souls.

There are many who have no fear of God or appreciation for His blessings. Filled with hatred for Him, they actually love wickedness and evil. On the other hand are those who taste of His mercy, faithfulness, righteousness, and His loving-kindness, and there they find their satisfaction as they drink from the river of His pleasures and from the fountain of life, and, in return, receive an upright heart instead one that's dead in trespasses and sins.

How does a sinner get from the first category to the second? Be aware, Christian, that when you share the Lord with unbelievers you must allow them to understand the fear of God and the consequences of unbelief. They must be able to accept the fact that they're sinners and that sin has horrendous eternal consequences. If they don't grasp this, not only will they not fear the Lord, but they'll also be able to rationalize that they have no need for repentance or a Savior.

Many (even professing Christians) fear man and man's opinions more than they fear God. They reason within themselves that if they were to say that God hates sin, they would drive people away. Repentance might sound repugnant to the nonbeliever. The sad result of the church's losing its fear of God has resulted in apathy toward holiness and reverence. People have lost sight of the fact that the fear of the Lord doesn't deny God's mercy and grace. It illuminates it! We must continue to preach God's judgment in order for people to be saved. Without that, we condemn them to eternal damnation, and they will never see and experience the mercy and grace of our loving Father. <u>May God grant us wisdom in all of these things.</u>

Thy Steadfast Love

[10]Oh, continue Your lovingkindness to those who know You, and Your righteousness to the upright in heart. [11]Let not the foot of pride come against me, and let not the hand of the wicked drive me away. [12]There the workers of iniquity have fallen; they have been cast down and are not able to rise. —Psalm 36:10-12

DAVID'S LOVE and trust in the Lord came from the fact that He saw the loving-kindness of God as a treasure greater than anything else. He understood that God's righteousness draws those who long for uprightness, and he asks that the wicked wouldn't keep him away from his Lord. He also asks that his own pride wouldn't cause him to wander from what God had for him to do, and he closes with a statement concerning the finality of the unrepentant fallen, whom he refers to as "the workers of iniquity," who are unable to rise.

This humble fear of the Lord results in love for righteousness and hatred for sin. David prays that Israel would continue to know God's loving-kindness also that he wouldn't fall prey to pride and the wandering from truth that it creates.

One of the things the Lord hates is a "proud look" (Prv 6:16). The word "pride" here means arrogance or haughtiness. In contrast to this, we see God's mercy, faithfulness, and righteousness as well as preservation from final judgment. We also see abundant satisfaction received from God's river of pleasures for all who will come to the fountain of life. How ugly is pride before such a backdrop!

How far should we be removed from the ways of the world? The Apostle John wrote: "Do not love the world or the things of the world. If anyone loves the world, the love of the Father is not in him. For all that is in the world—the lust of the flesh, the lust of the eyes, and the pride of life—is not of the Father but is of the world. And the world is passing away, and the lust of it; but he who does the will of God abides forever" (John 2:15-17).

The fruit of having a proper fear of the Lord is that one will also have a love of righteousness and a hatred of sin. David says, "Lord, please don't let pride have a hold on me so that I waver." He understood the danger of falling into pride.

Those are the words of one who understands that the fear of the Lord illuminates God's mercy and grace, not diminishes it. They're the words of one who seeks to walk always in the fear of the Lord.

There's a horrible thing happening today with the virgin bride of Christ. She has lost her fear of the Lord, and thus much of the church has become apostate—exactly as was prophesied concerning the last days (see Jeremiah 18:11-13). Remember: it isn't our job to present God to the world in a way they will accept. It's our job to present to the world that if they don't accept God on His terms, they'll end up in hell forever. The fear of the Lord is the beginning of everything holy, including the salvation of our souls. To reiterate what we've already come to understand, "No Fear, No Faith"; but "Know Fear, and Know Faith." It really is that simple.

Future-First Thinking

Introduction to Psalm 37

*¹Do not fret because of evil doers, nor be envious of
the workers of iniquity. —Psalm 37:1*

—

PSALM 37 is one of the "Wisdom Psalms," expressing God's wisdom through a king who is now old and well versed in the ebb and flow of life as he shares truths that he was probably unable to see when he was going through them.

As we continue on this journey, we see that although the Holy Spirit guided and inspired every word that David wrote, He also used David's life experiences and personality to teach us how to apply truth and wisdom to our own lives.

The topic of this psalm is "How to Live for the Lord in the Midst of a Wicked and Perverse Generation," which requires some tactical maneuvers if we're going to keep from losing our hope and joy. In Psalm 73, Asaph expressed something that we can relate to: " . . . my feet had almost stumbled; my steps had nearly slipped. For I was envious of the boastful, when I saw the prosperity of the wicked. . . ."

We all wonder at times why bad things happen to "good people," or why good things happen to "bad people." As David looks back on his own life, he shares what he has learned about how to keep one's feet from slipping or getting tripped up. We can learn from him how to deal with those times when evil seems to prosper and "no good deed goes unpunished." Hence the title of this message: "Future-First Thinking."

It's important that we consider the future—especially regarding what happens after this life is finished. When we think about the next life, we often minimize the seriousness of it. Take note: it's not possible to be "too heavenly minded." We should be thinking about eternity all the time! Remember that this life is "but a vapor" and the next is *forever*, regardless of whether yours will be far better or far worse than the one you're living now.

The Bible acknowledges that wickedness is in the world, and it is great. God never condones it, nor does He turn away from it. There are many times when as believers we feel defeated by the wickedness surrounding us. The wicked appear to prosper and flourish when others are suffering real hardships. God wants us to cling to Him during the times when wickedness prospers, remembering that this world is *not* our home, and we have a far better place to go, where wickedness is nonexistent.

Fret and envy are our natural tendencies when evil seems to advance unabated, but trusting and leaning on the faithfulness of God is the way to combat those feelings. King David had a wealth of experience from which to draw as he looked back over his life, and now he can clearly see one thing that shines through: God's faithfulness. Let's press on in our walk with the Lord, looking back at how far we have come, remembering how God brought us through every single trial one way or another, and, above all, looking forward to the glorious future that lies ahead, when every tear shall be wiped away and we'll be able to clearly see and know Jesus Christ, because we shall be like Him (1 John 3:2). Hallelujah!

March 12

Live for the Next Life Now

¹Do not fret because of evildoers, nor be envious of the workers of iniquity. ²For they shall soon be cut down like the grass, and wither as the green herb. ³Trust in the Lord, and do good; dwell in the land, and feed on His faithfulness. —*Psalm 37:1-3*

FRET AND ENVY are our natural responses when evildoers and workers of iniquity seem to advance in life unhindered, but trusting God and feeding on His faithfulness is the secret to peace. We see the contrast here between what our flesh *wants* to do and what we can and *should* do by the power of the Holy Spirit.

David certainly had a wealth of experience to draw from as he reviewed his life. His many encounters with the workers of iniquity and evil over the years had brought him to the place where he could look back and see one thing clearly about them all, and that was God's faithfulness.

The Apostle Paul had much the same experience, as he describes in 2 Corinthians: "*We were burdened beyond measure, above strength, so that we despaired even of life. Yes, we had the sentence of death in ourselves that we should not trust in ourselves but in God who raises the dead, who delivered us from so great a death, and does deliver us; in whom we trust that He will still deliver us*" (vv 8-10). By remembering God's faithfulness in the past, we're encouraged that He is helping us in the present and will help us in the future. God, who has saved us, is still our Deliverer.

That's why David could say, "Don't fret because of evildoers, because one day they'll be cut off. So trust in the Lord, do good, and feed on God's faithfulness." Of course, this may be one of those "easier read than done" scriptures at times! But no matter what we experience, we can heed David's words: "Do not fret." Trust the Lord to show you how to do what is right, and feed on His faithfulness.

We should show our trust in Him by living for the next life during this one. That's future-first living. When was the last time you couldn't sleep because you hadn't told anyone about the Lord that day? Can't remember? On the other hand, have you ever laid awake at night stressing over something that means nothing in eternity? The sad truth is that we sell short biblical principles and apply them to *this* life rather than to the next. But do we believe that evildoers and workers of iniquity will be cut down like grass? If so, does their eternal destiny trouble you? Do your perishing neighbors keep you up at night, as you pray and worry over their souls? Does knowing that they are condemned create a note of urgency in your prayers?

Why are you wasting time fretting about things that mean nothing in eternity or getting angry over the fact that evildoers seem to get away with things unnoticed? They haven't, and they won't. But hearts that are tender toward God should be tender toward lost souls. Trust in the Lord, and do good. Let God's proven faithfulness in the past feed your thinking in the present. He'll never leave us nor forsake us. Can we allow our joy and trust in Him to shine through us even into the lives of the wicked? That's what it means to live for the next life while we're still in this one!

The Desires of Your Heart

√ [4]Delight yourself also in the Lord, and He shall give you the desires of your heart. [5]Commit your way to the Lord, trust also in Him, and He shall bring it to pass. —*Psalm 37:4-5*

DELIGHTING in the Lord is going to lead to committing our ways to Him. If we delight in Him, then the things that delight Him will become our desires! It's a package deal. Philippians 4:19 says, "*And my God shall supply all your need according to His riches in glory by Christ Jesus.*" Let's look a little more closely at this. Is it possible for you to ask God for material things and for Him to say no? On the other hand, is it possible for you to ask God for strength to share His Word and to give words of His love to others and for Him to say no? Which is the better of the two—more money or leading more people to Jesus?

It's evident that God's riches are different from our definitions of them. Are we delighting in that which pleases the Lord? Remember, God's will is a *destiny*. It's not just *disciplines*.

We need to address this from two perspectives, the long and the short term. In Proverbs 10, Solomon wrote, "*The blessing of the Lord makes one rich. And He adds no sorrow with it. To do evil is like sport to a fool, but a man of understanding has wisdom. The fear of the wicked will come upon him, and the desire of the righteous will be granted . . . the righteous has an everlasting foundation.*" And Paul, in 1 Timothy 6:10, wrote, "*For the love of money is a root of all kinds of evil, for which some have strayed from the faith in their greediness, and pierced themselves through with many sorrows.*"

So if there are no sorrows attached to God's blessings, and if many sorrows can be associated with the love of money, then that means that money and material things are not equivalent to blessings! Delighting in the Lord will allow you to experience life at its very best. You may not have all that the world defines as riches, but your life will be rich in the things that money can't buy—things that are exclusive only to those born of God; things that only God can give and that no man can earn or merit: His riches in Jesus Christ.

Friends, Christianity isn't just a list of "*thou shalt nots*" but it is a *better* way. Delight yourself in the Lord, and He will give you the desires of your heart.

An even better promise is the destiny ahead for those who have put God first: heaven! Are you excited about heaven, where we will experience fullness of joy and pleasures forevermore? It's hard for us to even imagine that! But David looks forward to that day, and as we do the same, it helps to keep things in perspective.

The Christian life isn't just a discipline. It's a destiny. It takes you somewhere that others may not go, to a place where peace that passes understanding is possible—no matter what one's going through; a place where we can bear anything that comes to us because we have a far better promise: a city whose Builder and Maker is God. Let's remember to be future-first thinkers, with eyes fixed upon the prize.

Leaning on the Everlasting Arms

6He shall bring forth your righteousness as the light, and your justice as the noonday. 7Rest in the Lord, and wait patiently for Him; Do not fret because of him who prospers in his way, because of the man who brings wicked schemes to pass. —Psalm 37:6-7

"REST IN THE LORD." It sounds wonderful! To spend our days basking in His love, worshiping Him, studying His Word, trusting Him for everything—that's something we all desire. The reality is that we too often camp out on the cares of this life, the fears, the "what ifs"—leaving precious little time for contemplating on and giving glory to the One who gives us life and breath.

There's a lot of wickedness in the world, and sometimes we feel helpless to stem the tide of evil, especially when it enters our own homes. Life is often unfair. Evil people get away with their deeds. Those around you devise wicked schemes and even profit from them. Do you ever look around at the wickedness in the world and wonder, *God, where are You? What can I do?*

Read today's verses again! *"Rest in the Lord, and wait patiently for Him"* . . . to bring righteousness to light once again. It can be difficult to "rest," but as you reflect back and see what God has brought you safely through, even if you may be a bit battle scarred you can have the peace of knowing that He's still taking care of things. Remember the conclusion that Jeremiah came to in the midst of his overwhelming discouragement? *"Ah, Lord God! Behold, You have made the heavens and the earth by Your great power and outstretched arm. There is nothing too hard for You"* (Jer 32:17).

Nothing is too difficult for the Lord! He sees and knows all: the number of hairs on your head, what's in your mind, and the deepest desires of your heart. His love is unending and unchanging. He knows where He's taking you and what He is doing in and through you. Although the wicked seem to prosper, their days are numbered. King David could look back on a myriad of circumstances within his own family and speak with authority that we are to *wait patiently on the Lord*, and

He will bring justice—not only in the end, but also in this life. The key to handling difficulties in our lives is to remember this: our greatest battle is already won!

Jesus encourages us: *"Come to Me, all you who labor and are heavy laden, and I will give you rest. . . . For My yoke is easy and My burden is light"* (Matthew 11:28-30). If you've come to Jesus, rest is yours—"rest" in the sense of the assurance of God's faithfulness. Although He may not move on our timetable, His timing is perfect. Our job is to "wait patiently for Him." We know that He will never, ever fail us (See 2 Tim 2:13). And even though we live in an evil, fallen world, the battle for your soul was already fought and victory attained at the Cross. Satan can try to make you fret and feel anxious, but you can always rest in the fact that God is going to take care of you permanently someday, and in this life, every day. The devil can never snatch you out of the Father's hands.

Our greatest battle is already won, so rest in that fact. Wait patiently for the Lord, trusting and doing good as you wait. You won't be disappointed. And you may even find yourself once again basking in His love!

March 15

Be Still, and Know That I Am God

> *⁸Cease from anger, and forsake wrath; do not fret—it only causes harm. ⁹For evildoers shall be cut off; but those who wait on the Lord, they shall inherit the earth. ¹⁰For yet a little while and the wicked shall be no more; indeed, you will look carefully for his place, but it shall be no more. ¹¹But the meek shall inherit the earth, and shall delight themselves in the abundance of peace. —Psalm 37:8-11*

"DON'T HURT YOURSELF!" It's a warning we hear often from a friend or spouse, or maybe said to our children. David is telling us that anger and wrath, which cause fretting, will turn around and bite us! How? If we allow anger to consume us, it will make its way from our hearts and minds into our actions. Then it becomes *our* sin, as well as that of the individual whose sin "made" us angry to begin with. God wants us to put a halt to our angry feelings. In fact, David is saying that if we fret and get angry, evildoers get the satisfaction they were looking for.

What have we learned about future-first thinking? It certainly applies here. How did Jesus comfort His disciples about His soon departure? *"Let not your hearts be troubled . . . "* (John 14:1-4). How could they do that? Only by clinging to the words that He spoke next: *"In my Father's house are many mansions; . . . I go to prepare a place for you . . . and I will come again and receive you to Myself; that where I am, there you may be also. . . ."* In other words, applying future-first thinking, Jesus says, "Deal with the here-and-now by remembering that I'm coming again to take you to heaven with Me!"

As we consider those who do evil and how much they can hurt us at times, lets see what Solomon wrote in Proverbs 24:16-20: *"A righteous man may fall seven times and rise again, but the wicked shall fall by calamity. Do not rejoice when your enemy falls . . . lest the Lord see it, and it displease Him, and He turn away His wrath from him. Do not fret because of evildoers, nor be envious of the wicked; for . . . the lamp of the wicked will be put out."*

It's not God's will that any should perish but that all would come to repentance (John 3:16). But, sadly, not all will come. So, down to the nitty-gritty: How do we get to this "ceasing from anger" and "not fretting" attitude? Keep this in mind: *there is no injustice in eternity*. No one will be in heaven who doesn't love Christ, and no one will go to hell undeserved. Heaven will be a place absent of injustice, pain, and sorrow. The truth is, friends, we may be abused and betrayed, and the wicked may seem to prosper. Christians may be killed just for being Christians. But eternity lasts a long, long time (to put it mildly), and there will be no such injustice there.

Are you a future-first thinker? Or is your mind consumed with the here-and-now? The better way requires ceasing from anger, wrath, and fretting. All those who bring wicked schemes to pass and don't repent will surely reap the whirlwind of what they have sown. And it's an eternal penalty. But the wonderful news is that no one is prevented from becoming a person who trusts, delights, and rests in the Lord—for eternity!

March 16

The Strong and the Mighty

[12]The wicked plots against the just, and gnashes at him with his teeth. [13]The Lord laughs at him, for He sees that his day is coming. [14]The wicked have drawn the sword and have bent their bow, to cast down the poor and needy, to slay those who are of upright conduct. [15]Their sword shall enter their own heart, and their bows shall be broken.

[16]A little that a righteous man has is better than the riches of many wicked. [17]For the arms of the wicked shall be broken, but the Lord upholds the righteous. [18]The Lord knows the days of the upright, and their inheritance shall be forever. [19]They shall not be ashamed in the evil time, and in the days of famine they shall be satisfied.

²⁰But the wicked shall perish; and the enemies of the Lord, like the splendor of the meadows, shall vanish. Into smoke they shall vanish away. ²¹The wicked borrows and does not repay, but the righteous shows mercy and gives. ²²The steps of a good man are ordered by the Lord, and He delights in his way. *—Psalm 37:12-22*

EVIL SEEMS to be on the rise, and wickedness invades our lives every day. David understood this well, and the Lord has used him and his experiences to show us how to change our attitude from one of fear and worry to resting and delighting in the Lord.

Maybe you're being confronted with a very serious situation and you can't seem to find peace no matter how hard you try or how much you pray. Life has become painful, whether through sickness, poverty, loss, or something else, and you find yourself constantly worrying. It doesn't help to hear, "Don't worry; be happy!", which sounds almost like what David's been telling us in this psalm. But it isn't that at all! It's something much deeper.

Imagine this scenario: you've suddenly been laid off at work. No jobs appear on the horizon, bills are stacking up, and creditors are calling. But one day you receive a certified letter stating that a rich relative has died, leaving you several million dollars. A check for the funds will arrive within 30 days. Would that information about the future change how you handle the present? Would the ringing phone or the "shut-off" notices continue to cause you to fret? No! You would view and handle everything differently now, based on what was going to happen *in the future*. That's the mindset we need to hold on to.

David continues his use of contrast to keep our minds focused on the future, even though for the moment he's still enduring a threatening situation. We seem to forget that God takes the weak and makes them into the strong and the mighty. Need proof? Consider the apostle Peter, who went from being the "thrice-denier" to the bold proclaimer! In the same way, the Bible describes believers as those who can do all things through Christ, who strengthens us, so in reality we become the strong and the mighty!

David makes a very important statement that even though nothing can snatch us from the Father's hand, the enemy plots against us anyway and is sometimes temporarily successful. But God's response (v. 13)? "*The Lord laughs at them, for He sees that his day is coming.*" The key for us to remember is (v. 16) that it's better to have a little now and riches forever than riches now and shame forever.In our times, the extreme wickedness of ISIS or Boko Haram in slaughtering Christians is very hard to comprehend. But remember this as you consider these atrocities: *A Christian is so mighty, that even death can't harm him.*

God takes no pleasure in the death of the wicked (Ezekiel 33:11), but every Muslim "martyr" who blows himself up in hopes of killing Jews or Christians goes straight to Hades to await his final destiny in hell. Every Christian who dies at their hands goes straight into the presence of the Lord, and heaven will be their eternal home.

We're not to respond to the wicked like the wicked, but we're to be merciful and giving. Death has no power over us, and our real enemy is already defeated! Precious truth.

March 17

"I Have a Reservation"

²³The steps of a good man are ordered by the Lord, and He delights in his way. ²⁴Though he fall, he shall not be utterly cast down; for the Lord upholds him with His hand. ²⁵I have been young, and now am old; yet I have not seen the righteous forsaken, nor his descendants begging bread. ²⁶He is ever merciful, and lends; and his descendants are blessed. ²⁷Depart from evil, and do good; and dwell forevermore. ²⁸For the Lord loves justice, and does not forsake His saints; they are preserved forever, but the descendants of the wicked shall be cut off. ²⁹The righteous shall inherit the land, and dwell in it forever. ³⁰The mouth of the righteous speaks wisdom, and his tongue talks of justice. ³¹The law of his God is in his heart; none of his steps shall slide. *—Psalm 37:23-31*

IN OUR VERSES today, David reminds us that God is ever-faithful and then goes on to describe that truth from every angle. He tells us that God *directs our steps*. All of us could probably give wonderful testimonies of how many times the Lord has put us in just the right place at exactly the right time! But then he goes on to list many other assurances we have that God is with us always, overseeing our lives, our relationships, our walk with Him.

As Christians, we should stop and count our blessings now and then. David is doing that in these verses. He says that although we may fall, God will sustain us. He provides for us, He will always be with us, and He has a wonderful future in store for us. This doesn't mean that life will always be a bed of roses (and even that would be full of thorns!). It does mean that He is always with us and in us, and even our children and those around us will be blessed through us as we walk with Him.

Wisdom and justice are two key themes in these verses. David writes that God loves justice, and we should too. Verse 30 says that our mouths should speak wisdom and our tongues proclaim justice. God is pleased with us when we follow His own example in these areas and promises that "none of our steps shall slide."

Do you believe that whatever God asks of us He will also enable us to do? In James 1:21-22 we read, *"Therefore lay aside all filthiness and overflow of wickedness, and receive with meekness the implanted word, which is able to save your souls. But be doers of the word, and not hearers only, deceiving yourselves."*

If we're commanded to lay aside weights and sins, then God empowers us to lay aside weights and sins. By the very fact that He *commands* this of us, we can be assured that the devil cannot *make us* do anything! Sin has no power over the child of God who is leaning on and trusting the Lord to preserve him. If we feel threatened in that area, maybe we need to get our eyes off the moment and back onto the future that God has preserved for us.

When we fail to do what we know is right, or when we do what we know is wrong, Satan tries to drag us down and keep us there, where we are useless in the Kingdom of God. We need to remind the devil—and ourselves—that we have a reservation in heaven, bought and paid for by the precious blood of Jesus, and God has already assured our safe arrival there. Remember that we *can* do all things through Christ, who strengthens us (Philippians 4:3). In Him, the power of sin and darkness cannot hold us. As David looked back on his life, he saw the defeats, but he also saw the victories. And when the Lord had ordered his steps and he didn't take them, even then God did not utterly cast him down but upheld him with His hand. Walk forward, Christian. The best is yet to come!

March 18

"Deliver Us from Evil"

³²The wicked watches the righteous, and seeks to slay him. ³³The Lord will not leave him in his hand, nor condemn him when he is judged. ³⁴Wait on the Lord, and keep His way, and He shall exalt you to inherit the land; when the wicked are cut off, you shall see it. ³⁵I have seen the wicked in great power, and spreading himself like a native green tree. ³⁶Yet he passed away, and behold, he was no more; indeed I sought him, but he could not be found. ³⁷Mark the blameless man, and observe the upright; for the future of that man is peace. ³⁸But the transgressors shall be destroyed together; the future of the wicked shall be cut off. ³⁹But the salvation of the righteous is from the Lord; He is their strength in the time of trouble. ⁴⁰And the Lord shall help them and deliver them; He shall deliver them from the wicked, and save them, because they trust in Him. —*Psalm 37:32-40*

WHAT A BLESSING it is to realize that our future doesn't include the wickedness that we see all around us today and about which David was writing in these verses. Just knowing that a city awaits us whose Builder and Maker is God gives us good cause to press on in Christ!

David writes that he has seen the wicked in places of power, spreading their influence like a shade tree over the land, but they died and eventually the evidence of their existence was nowhere to be found. He tells us that when wicked men rule, we need to pay attention to the blameless and upright ones and follow after them, because the future of the righteous man is peace.

The apostle John wrote: "*We know that whoever is born of God does not sin; but he who has been born of God keeps himself, and the wicked one does not touch him. We know that we are of God, and the whole world lies under the sway of the wicked one. And we know that the Son of God has come and has given us an understanding, that we may know Him who is true; and we are in Him who is true, in His Son Jesus Christ. This is the true God and eternal life. Little children, keep yourselves from idols. Amen*" (1 John 5:18-21).

David says much the same thing as John in the closing lines of this psalm. He reminds us that God is our strength in the time of trouble. He is our Help and our Deliverer. He saves us, David adds, because we trust in Him. How amazing to consider that we have the omniscient and omnipotent God on our side! The devil is no match for the Father, Son, and Holy Spirit. He is a defeated enemy already. His evil plot against the Messiah failed miserably, because even death couldn't harm our Savior!

Sin had no power over Him, but He had power over sin! Do you remember the prophets of Baal in 1 Kings 18? They cried out to their god for hours and cut themselves as they conducted all of their religious rituals in the hope of drawing a response from him. (If you haven't read, or don't remember, this passage be sure to go back and check it out!) What was the result of all this drama? Nothing! Why?

"*All the gods of the people are idols, but the Lord made the heavens. Honor and majesty are before Him; strength and gladness are in His place*" (1 Chronicles 16:26-27). Friends, Islam will not prevail because there is no such god as Allah. Even though the wickedness brought by that religion seems to be winning in our day, remember that it's really the devil who is behind every idol. As for us, we came to Jesus in weakness and human frailty, but when His Spirit came into us, we were transformed into the strong and the mighty over whom the kingdom of darkness can never prevail!

From the Mire to the Choir

Introduction to Psalm 40

¹I waited patiently for the Lord; and He inclined to me, and heard my cry. . . . Let all those who seek You rejoice and be glad in You; let such as love Your salvation say continually "The Lord be magnified!"
—*Psalm 40:1,16*

IT BECOMES very clear that the Holy Spirit is directing David's thoughts and hands, inspiring him to write things that were later fulfilled by the Messiah. But it's also evident that the Spirit allowed plenty of room for David's personal life and personality to show through in his writings. Although there are clearly Messianic verses in this psalm, which is both a psalm of lament and a psalm of praise, we're reminded that King David was merely a mortal like us.

As he moves through this inspired song, he praises God for His faithfulness and petitions Him for deliverance. He soars the heights and roams the depths. In other words, he has good days and bad days, just like the rest of us! He describes God's faithfulness and lovingkindness with expressions filled with joy and/or hope.

In Psalm 30, David wrote these beautiful words: "*You have turned for me my mourning into dancing; You have put off my sackcloth and clothed me with gladness, to the end that my glory may sing praise to You and not be silent. O Lord my God, I will give thanks to You forever*" (vv. 11-12). Dancing with joy and singing when previously mourning indicates a shift in perspective and understanding as well as a remembrance of the proven truth that God is worthy of praise at *all* times. As David is exhorted by his own words from Psalm 34:1, we, too, can "bless the Lord at all times," and His praise can and should be continually in our mouths!

It's important to see in David's psalms that as he writes these verses he sometimes swings back and forth between lament and praise, which we can clearly see comes from his heart and isn't just phony lip service. Nor is it a canned ritualistic response that he's describing when he speaks of "dancing with joy" and "singing to the Lord." It was quite literal for David, and we see in 2 Samuel 6 that he *did* dance before the Lord and was known as the "sweet psalmist of Israel."

He is describing true, heartfelt joy, which we, too, should experience in our lives. Through his words, David is going to teach us about a transition we can all experience in an "Aha!" moment as we move from the mire to choir. It was from this psalm that the great old hymn from 1898 by Henry J. Zelley was written:

He brought me out of the miry clay,
He set my feet upon the Rock to stay;
He puts a song in my soul today,
A song of praise, hallelujah!

Perhaps you realize that you, too, need to transition from the mire to the choir and sing a song of praise. As we continue through this psalm, David will teach us how to do this, while he points to a Divine Reality, a Rightful Reaction, and Confident Rest. Are you ready to sing a song of praise? Hallelujah!

March 20

Wait for It . . .

¹I waited patiently for the Lord; and He inclined to me, and heard my cry. ²He also brought me up out of a horrible pit, out of the miry clay, and set my feet upon a rock, and established my steps. ³He has put a new song in my mouth—Praise to our God; many will see it and fear, and will trust in the Lord. ⁴Blessed is that man who makes the Lord his trust, and does not respect the proud, nor such as turn aside to lies. ⁵Many, O Lord my God, are Your wonderful works which You have done; and Your thoughts toward us cannot be recounted to You in order; if I would declare and speak of them. They are more than can be numbered. —*Psalm 40:1-5*

HAVE YOU ever *not* waited for the Lord but acted first on your own behalf? Have you ever allowed the mire of the world to mess with your mind and then taken matters into your own hands because God's "in due time" wasn't meshing with your schedule? And how'd that work out for you?

David, who has learned from his times of going ahead of God, is writing here of the importance of waiting on the Lord for *His* means of deliverance and finding God completely faithful. Isaiah wrote: "*[T]hose who wait upon the Lord shall renew their strength; they shall mount up with wings like eagles, they shall run and not be weary, they shall walk and not faint*" (Isaiah 40:31).

David's time of waiting wasn't a period of apathy or complacency, because if you read our verses today, you can see a chronology. While he was waiting, David was actively praying, and the Lord inclined His ear and heard. Then God brought him up from horrible circumstances, set his feet upon a rock, established his steps, gave him a direct path, and put a new song in his mouth, "Praise to Our God." Are you beginning to understand why it's so much better to wait on the Lord and let Him direct our steps instead of rushing headlong into a situation that may prove disastrous? David knows that those who choose to trust the Lord and His timing will not make the mistake of listening to scoffers or turning aside to their lies.

Verse 5 of this psalm expresses the idea that God has provided for us through Christ everything of eternal significance. We needed a savior; God sent one in His Son. We needed a deliverer; God sent one in His Son. We needed someone to direct our steps; God's Son came into the world and walked among us, and said to us, "Follow Me."

Christian, we must keep what David said ever in our minds, because what he described is what God has done, is doing, and will do, which is more than you will ever know. What you needed to be done for you was already accomplished through Jesus Christ. And the great news is that since you are complete in Jesus, then heaven is already your home, and a reunion with lost loved ones lies ahead.

There's a force within you that is greater than all the forces in the world. Why? Because you have a friend who sticks closer than a brother and a guaranteed inheritance of riches beyond all that the world has to offer. How and where did you get it? God supplied it through Christ, and, therefore, we can move with David from the mire to the choir and sing a new song of praise. This puts the idea of waiting for the Lord's help and instructions in a whole new and wonderful light!

March 21

Making Melody in Our Hearts

> [6]Sacrifice and offering You did not desire; my ears You have opened. Burnt offering and sin offering You did not require. [7]Then I said, "Behold, I come; in the scroll of the book it is written of me. [8]I delight to do Your will, O my God, and Your law is within my heart." [9]I have proclaimed the good news of righteousness in the great assembly; indeed, I do not restrain my lips, O Lord, You Yourself know. [10]I have not hidden Your righteousness within my heart; I have declared Your faithfulness and Your salvation; I have not concealed Your lovingkindness and Your truth from the great assembly. [11]Do not withhold Your tender mercies from me, O Lord; let Your lovingkindness and Your truth continually preserve me. [12]For innumerable evils have surrounded me; my iniquities have overtaken me, so that I am not able to look up; they are more than the hairs of my head; therefore my heart fails me. [13]Be pleased, O Lord, to deliver me; O Lord, make haste to help me! —Psalm 40:6-13

THESE VERSES contain humbling admissions by David regarding his failed desires to do God's will despite the fact that he wanted to do so. When surrounded by evil, his iniquities took control, and now he cries out to the Lord for deliverance.

Have you ever been there? David pleads from the depths of his heart, and, despite his transgressions, the Holy Spirit leads him to write words that could also apply to the Messiah! (Note: verse 12 could never be applied to Jesus, because our Savior was perfect in every way, including being perfectly sinless.) But these verses do reestablish the truth that everything of eternal significance God has already done for us in Christ.

David affirms that he *delights* to do the Father's will and that he holds God's Word within his heart. This indicates a transformation in David by the Word of God and he is a different person who now loves doing whatever the Lord asks him to do. The fact is that life is Christ should be a glorious anthem, not a dutiful dirge!

Paul, in Ephesians 2:10 tells us, "[*We*] *are His workmanship, created in Christ Jesus for good works, which God prepared beforehand that we should walk in them."* And Peter says that we're to abstain from fleshly lusts, exhibiting instead honorable conduct even in the face of persecution, that nonbelievers will see and, prayerfully, be led to the Lord themselves (See 1 Peter 2:11-12).

There you have it. The Christian life will be a *changed* life that exhibits the love of Christ. Once one truly encounters Jesus, a holy life should be the result. But here's the thing: it won't be a burden or a chore, because when you hide the Word in your heart and the Holy Spirit lives within you, doing the will of God becomes a delight, not a drag! There will still be some tough times, but as we remember that we've moved from the mire to the choir, we'll carry a new song in our hearts.

And now back to where we began this day's reading. Once we become Christians, will we never fail God again? Will our lives be perfect and sinless every day? Sadly, the answer is "probably not." But look again at David's confession and then his humble cry in verses 12-13, asking God to deliver him and help him. This is our loving *Father*, who hears our cries and answers our prayers. Do you need to cry out to Him today? He is waiting patiently, and He will hear you. Listen to these beautiful words: "He will rejoice over you with gladness, He will quiet you with His love, He will rejoice over you with singing" (Zephaniah 3:17). Take heart!

His Eye Is on the Sparrow

[14] Let them be ashamed and brought to mutual confusion who seek to destroy my life; Let them be driven backward and brought to dishonor who wish me evil. [15] Let them be confounded because of their shame, who say to me, "Aha, aha!" [16] Let all those who seek You rejoice and be glad in You; let such as love Your salvation say continually, "The Lord be magnified!" [17] But I am poor and needy; yet the Lord thinks upon me. You are my help and my deliverer; Do not delay, O my God. —Psalm 40:14-17

WHEN WE'RE surrounded by difficulties and it feels like we're being attacked from every direction, even then the Lord wants us to have a confident rest *in Him.* This is not physical rest (although that's waiting for us in eternity) but the sense of assurance that no matter by what means the enemies of God seek to destroy us, the gates of hell will not prevail against God's children (Matthew 16:18). David prays that they will be confounded, driven back, and brought to dishonor, including those who gloat, "Aha! We've got them!" Then we who seek God will rejoice in Him, our Help and our Deliverer, and we can say with full assurance, "The Lord be magnified!"

It's comforting to read this reminder that although he was poor and needy, the Lord was "thinking upon" David. He knew in his heart the same thing that Jeremiah would later write: *"For I know the thoughts that I think toward you, says the Lord, thoughts of peace and not of evil, to give you a future and a hope. . . .And you will seek Me and find Me, when you search for Me with all your heart . . . "* (vv. 11-14). Similarly, in Matthew 10, the Lord reminded His disciples not to fear those who can *"kill the body but cannot kill the soul . . . Are not two sparrows sold for a copper coin? And not one of them falls to the ground apart from your Father's will. . . . Do not fear, therefore; you are of more value than many sparrows"* (vv. 28-31).

Jeremiah reminds us, like the author of Hebrews, that whom the Lord loves, He chastens. Even though we may often bear the consequences of our sin in this life, God says, "I'm thinking about you, and I will restore you." So whether the enemies of God seek to oppress us or due to our own sin the Lord must discipline us, He is always thinking about us and doing what's best. Take heart! Nothing the devil tries to do can stop God.

No matter how bad things get in our lives, we can hold onto this thought: The next life will be nothing like this one! In 1 John 3:2 we read that when we see Him, we'll be like Him, and the power of sin will have no hold on us. In Hebrews 4:15, we're told that Jesus was tempted in all ways that we are and yet was without sin. And that's how we'll be! We'll no longer need to feel sorry or ashamed, because there's no evil or temptation of any kind in heaven, thus no sin or need of repentance. We'll never live under the threat of death again. The devil thought he had dealt with Christ on the cross, but the one who really got nailed was the devil! Satan lost. Death was forever defeated. The devil can't defeat Christians by killing them because they go straight to the presence of the Lord. He can't stop the church, because the Bible says that the kingdom of hell will not prevail against it, but he still tries threatening the church with political correctness, laziness, and biblical illiteracy. Christians, we should delight to do God's will because we know the One who has saved our soul, and His Word is forever implanted in our hearts. May we pray like David, "You are my help and my deliverer. Come quickly, Lord Jesus!"

March 23

Blessed Endurance

[1]Blessed is he who considers the poor; the Lord will deliver him in time of trouble. [2]The Lord will preserve him and keep him alive, and he will be blessed on the earth; You will not deliver him to the will of his enemies. [3]The Lord will strengthen him on his bed of illness; You will sustain him on his sickbed. —*Psalm 41:1-3*

DAVID IS LYING on his sickbed pondering the dichotomy of living a life as a "man after God's own heart." We understand his confidence and trust in the Lord, but we have questions: Why are the good punished for standing for the truth? Shouldn't those who are hurt or sick be given loving attention? Yet here's King David, lying there sick, pondering his own life, feeling like he's getting kicked while he's down.

Have you ever felt like that? Have you ever done something for someone that you meant as a kindness and had it blow up in your face? Listen: what David is describing isn't only his own experience, but it's also prophetic of the Messiah! In John 15:24-25, Jesus said, "If I had not done among them the works which no one else did, they would have no sin; but now they have seen and also *hated* both Me and My Father." He's quoted in Matthew, Mark, and Luke: "We will be *hated* by *all* for His name's sake." It appears that receiving the opposite of what one would expect is the experience of those who desire to live godly in Christ Jesus. Instead of recognition, we get tribulation. Standing up for truth has become despised, and doing what's right is disparaged as foolishness and even evil! If we're going to follow the things of God, we'll need blessed endurance to make it through to the end.

As David lies in his bed, he ponders the key to living a blessed life, which includes having concern for those who are destitute or suffering (Proverbs 22:8-9). He says that those who care for the poor are delivered from trouble, kept alive, blessed, delivered from the enemy's plans, and sustained on their sickbed. It's interesting that God didn't say that they would never have to *lie* in a sickbed, or that their enemies would stop hating them. How unlike what we hear all around us today! Christians, we are told, should experience prosperity and health *all the time*.

Listen, the key to obtaining blessed *endurance* is that one "considers the poor." In the Hebrew, this means "teaches the poor" or "causes to prosper." The church is guilty of what I call "selfish giving," i.e., giving in order to get. Teachers instruct naïve people in the art of sowing "seed money" in order to reap a big harvest of blessings. But is giving in order to get really considering the poor, or is it considering yourself? Can I expect the blessings of the Lord when it's really myself I'm considering? If you tithe, thinking that it's some kind of biblical pyramid scheme, don't expect God to reward you for your "kindness." Generosity is not a get-rich-quick scheme.

Charlatans often misuse the verse: "Give, and it will be given to you: good measure, pressed down, shaken together, and running over will be put into your bosom . . . " (Luke 6:38). But preceding these verses, Jesus said, "Love your enemies, do good, and lend, *hoping for nothing in return*; and your reward will be great . . . " (Luke 6:35). So what is the lesson here? It's the attitude that counts! Love your enemies and lend . . . expecting *nothing in return*. This is the kind of giving that has the greatest returns in the way of deliverance, preservation, and blessing on the earth, and maybe it will include financial blessing too! But trust me, if you give $10 because you think you'll yield $100 from the Lord, you have another "think" coming. If you want to enjoy blessed endurance in this life, learn to look at generosity as a spiritual attribute and not as way to line your pocket.

March 24

A Fly in the Ointment

> [4]I said, "Lord, be merciful to me; heal my soul, for I have sinned against You." [5]My enemies speak evil of me: "When will he die, and his name perish?" [6]And if he comes to see me, he speaks lies; his heart gathers iniquity to itself; when he goes out, he tells it. [7]All who hate me whisper together against me; against me they devise my hurt. [8]"An evil disease," they say, "clings to him. And now that he lies down, he will rise up no more." —*Psalm 41:4-8*

KING DAVID pleads with God, expressing his own trust in Him even as he lies sick in his bed. He confesses his sin and asks for healing. The result? His enemies speak evil of him, claiming that his illness is because of his wickedness! He is attacked and insulted—and this is all happening to one whom the Lord called a man after His own heart.

We've all been through seasons where it seemed like everything was going from bad to worse. There's a wonderful verse that helps to make sense of these times in our lives. Jesus is speaking: "*I am the true vine, and My Father is the vinedresser. Every branch in Me that does not bear fruit He takes away; and every branch that bears fruit He prunes, that it may bear more fruit*" (John 15:1-2). We understand the meaning of "bearing fruit," having the "fruits of the Spirit," or being "fruitful." We also know that the vinedresser must prune the branches that aren't producing fruit. God does this in our own lives as well, and it may be painful!

But let's consider one other aspect of fruit trees or vines. Fruit can attract pests! In the same way, good works will often draw more attacks that they will appreciation. I can prove this point in one word: Jesus. Satan hates those who love Jesus and who seek to honor and serve Him and will do all he can to destroy those good works: "*Your adversary the devil walks about like a roaring lion, seeking whom he may devour*" (1 Peter 5:8).

There's a movement today that is contrary to what Scripture tells us ought to be, and it rots the fruit that we should be bearing. The "Doctrine of Tolerance," which many are promoting, declares that if we want to reach the world, we must change or remove everything "offensive" in the church. It sounds ludicrous, and yet the number of "pests" who attack what should be appreciated is increasing exponentially.

Let me use just one example. The Bible identifies homosexuality as a sin. To warn someone of this, trying to help them to repent of this sin and saving their soul from eternity in the fires of hell, is the most loving and caring thing that you could do. Is this deed appreciated or attacked? Why is it that if you believe that homosexuality is wrong, you are a bigoted homophobe, but if you believe lying is wrong, you're not considered a bigoted liar-a-phobe? The same with stealing, adultery, or murder! We should *all* be sin-a-phobic because sin, which is clearly defined in the Bible, sends people to hell The only preventive is to receive the sacrifice of Christ's blood and to repent of and forsake the sin!

If you love others enough to call them to repentance, then you're not only going to be unappreciated, but you're going to be attacked! Don't expect Satan to lay off because you're having a hard day and feel like you're drowning in difficulties. He doesn't care! He will keep attacking. But our God will deliver, preserve, bless, and strengthen you even as the opposition increases in these last days. Oh yes—if you're going to bear fruit, remember—there will always be fruit flies, whispering against you, laughing when you're hurting, and kicking you when you're down. But when you're down, what should you do? Look up! "*Now when these things begin to happen, look up and lift up your heads, because your redemption draws near*" (Luke 21:28).

Betrayed!

⁹Even my own familiar friend in whom I trusted, who ate my bread, has lifted up his heel against me. ¹⁰But You, O Lord, be merciful to me, and raise me up, that I may repay them. ¹¹By this I know that You are well pleased with me, because my enemy does not triumph over me. ¹²As for me, You uphold me in my integrity, and set me before Your face forever. ¹³Blessed be the Lord God of Israel from everlasting to everlasting! Amen and Amen. —*Psalm 41:9-13*

IT'S AWFUL to realize a loved one has betrayed you, especially one in whom you'd trusted completely. It's somewhat comforting to know that even David, the mighty man of God, endured the same thing. It's possible that in our verses today David is referring to one of his trusted counselors, Ahithophel. "*So David went up by the Ascent of Olives, and wept as he went up; and he had his head covered and went barefoot. . . . Then someone told David, saying, 'Ahithophel is among the conspirators with Absalom' And David said, "O Lord, I pray, turn the counsel of Ahithophel into foolishness!*" (2 Samuel 15:30-31).

What a betrayal this was! One of David's closest friends and advisors, who had eaten bread with him at his table, had aligned himself with David's own son, Absalom, who had betrayed David during his illness. David petitions the Lord from his position as king, asking that God would raise him up so that he could retaliate against his enemies. Although it isn't certain that Ahithophel is the one in view here, whoever it was, it was someone very close to David. When that's the case, it hurts the betrayed more than ever.

David refers, as he petitions the Lord, to his own integrity. We read yesterday in verse 4 of this psalm that David had confessed his sin before the Lord. Take note: without the *confession* of sin there can be no expectation of reaping the benefits of moral innocence, nor can those benefits be expected when there is no *repentance*.

The sentiments of Psalm 41:9 were referenced by Jesus as He spoke with the apostles on the eve of His betrayal, and He even quoted this verse, as recorded by the apostle John: "*I know whom I have chosen; but that the Scripture may be fulfilled, 'He who eats bread with Me has lifted up his heel against Me'*" (John 13:18).

Three things that can be gleaned from Psalm 41 should be brought to our attention: how we are to treat others; how others treat us; how God treats us. And the main takeaway from that third point is that God doesn't treat us like people do. Too often we end up consumed with pain from betrayal by others and forget that God will uphold us!

David begins this psalm with God's blessings on us, and he ends it with us blessing God, the everlasting One. Let's look back for just a moment. Remember Balaam, the prophet-for-hire, whom King Balak of Moab hired to curse Israel? He replied, "God is not a man, that He should lie, nor a son of man, that He should repent. Has He said, and will He not do? Or has He spoken, and will He not make it good? Behold, I have received a command to bless; He has blessed, and I cannot reverse it" (Numbers 23:19-20).

Christian, listen! All the devil's hired hands in the world cannot reverse the will of God for your life You can invite your own disaster through disobedience and lack of integrity, as David had done. But David also knew that God was a forgiver of sins, so he confessed. And having done so, he lived his life in a blessable condition, and therefore had the expectation of his enemies *not* triumphing over him in the end. We can have the same expectation, although it's hard to remember when the enemy is busily kicking you while you're down. But it's still true! Remember: there is none like our God, and in and through Jesus, we, as children of God, are set before the Father's face forever! Amen and Amen!

The Highest Praise

Introduction to Psalm 46

To the Chief Musician. A Psalm of the sons of Korah.
A Song for Alamoth. —*Psalm 46*

AS WE MAKE our way through the Book of Psalms, we're moving into the second of the five divisions in the Book. The first forty-one chapters (Book One) were the Davidic psalms. The thirty chapters that make up Book Two comprise the Psalms of Asaph, Solomon, King David, the sons of Korah, among others, some of whom are anonymous.

The first recorded words of the sons of Korah are familiar to us all and are introduced in the first verse of Psalm 42: "*As the deer pants for the water brooks, so pants my soul for You, O God.*"

A little background is in order: The sons (descendants) of Korah are reminders of the grace and mercy of God and also that the sins of those in the past *do not and cannot rule our present.* Early on, when the children of Israel were spending their days in the wilderness, Korah led a group into rebellion. Numbers 16:1-3 gives us the very interesting story of Korah, of the tribe of Levi, who, along with Dathan and Abiram, descendants of Reuben, took some men with them and led a rebellion against the authority of Moses and Aaron, accusing them of trying to usurp all of the authority over the people (which authority God had given to Moses and Aaron, remember?). Moses responded, *"By this you shall know that the Lord has sent me to do all these works.... If these men die naturally ... then the Lord has not sent me. But if the Lord creates a new thing, and the earth opens its mouth and swallows them . . . then you will understand that these men have rejected the Lord"* (Numbers 16:28-33). As soon as Moses finished speaking, the earth opened up and, yes, it swallowed them, along with their households and all of the men who were with Korah!

Now we see that just as Korah had led a group of people into rebellion and its consequences, the *sons* of Korah were leading people into righteousness and its rewards! Although we all are born sinners, we don't inherit the sins of our fathers, as the sons of Korah demonstrate.

Another beautiful song attributed to them is Psalm 84. Listen to the first two verses: *"How lovely is Your tabernacle, O Lord of hosts! My soul longs, yes, even faints for the courts of the Lord; my heart and my flesh cry out for the living God."* And verses 10-12 give us even more glorious images of the goodness and greatness of our Heavenly Father: *"For a day in Your courts is better than a thousand. I would rather be a doorkeeper in the house of my God than to dwell in the tents of wickedness. For the Lord God is a sun and shield; the Lord will give grace and glory; no good thing will He withhold from those who walk uprightly. O Lord of hosts, blessed is the man who trusts in You."*

Can you sense the excitement that these singers had for their Lord? They *long*; they *cry out*; they would rather be doorkeepers than to dwell among the wicked, participating in their sin. Good things await those who trust in the Lord. May He help us to assimilate some of their joy and delight in Him as we begin this walk through the second book in the Psalms.

March 27

Beautiful Hands

> [1]God is our refuge and strength, a very present help in trouble. [2]Therefore we will not fear, even though the earth be removed, and though the mountains be carried into the midst of the sea; [3]though its waters roar and be troubled, though the mountains shake with its swelling. Selah
> —*Psalm 46:1-3*

An INTERESTING FACT: the Hebrew word for "praise" is *yada*. Its meanings are many. It can mean to use or to hold out the hand; it can mean to throw; it may describe the act of extending the hands during worship, or it can indicate the wringing of the hands in worry. The point is that praise is not limited to singing but includes other actions that we take in response to the wonderfulness of God.

In the opening verses of this psalm, the Sons of Korah establish for us a reminder of the actions of God on our behalf followed by our reaction to His actions. He is our refuge, strength, and present help when trouble comes. And what should be our response? "We will not fear!"

We will not fear? . . . even though . . . even though (worst case scenario!) the earth be removed, and the mountains carried into the midst of the sea? These descriptions could be understood this way: Even though the world around you is falling apart, God is still our refuge, our strength, and our help in times of distress *of any kind*. Even though the waters roar and are troubled, and even though the mountains swell and shake, it is still true that "*God has not given us a spirit of fear, but of power and of love and of a sound mind*" (2 Timothy 1:7). In fact the highest praise often comes during the hardest times in our lives! We can sing to the Lord anywhere, any time. "I will bless the Lord *at all times*; His praise will continually be in my mouth . . . " (Psalm 34:1).

Remember, too, that another definition of *yada* besides singing refers to our actions—our hands uplifted in praise while others are wringing theirs. This exhibits continual steadfastness that won't be shaken no matter what assails us, and reminds us that the highest praise is often exhibited through our actions and not heard from our mouths. The Apostle Paul, in 2 Corinthians 11:22-28, wrote of his labors, beatings, scourgings, imprisonments, stonings, being shipwrecked, being beaten, suffering through inclement weather, and other dangers of every kind. What an example to us of what the highest praise looks like! The earth being moved in our personal lives and other tragedies can tear at our hearts, but moving forward, even at a crawl, is sometimes the highest form of praise, because the natural response of the world would be doubt, fear, and discouragement.

When people around us see us using our hands to love and praise our God while they are wringing theirs, they'll become aware that we have something they don't have. May the Lord show us today how we can shine His light in this very dark world.

Victory in Jesus

⁴There is a river whose streams shall make glad the city of God, the holy place of the tabernacle of the Most High. ⁵God is in the midst of her, she shall not be moved; God shall help her, just at the break of dawn. ⁶The nations raged, the kingdoms were moved; He uttered His voice, the earth melted. ⁷The Lord of hosts is with us; the God of Jacob is our refuge. Selah —*Psalm 46:4-7*

JERUSALEM was one of the few ancient cities not built on a river, so the idea of a river whose streams make the city of God glad would be quite attractive. But beyond that, the subject of the nations raging and the earth moving have pretty significant implications that remind us of Psalm 2: *"Why do the nations rage and the people imagine a vain thing? The kings of the . . . and the rulers take counsel together, against the Lord and against His Anointed . . . Yet I have set My King on My holy hill of Zion. . . . Ask of Me, and I will give You the nations for Your inheritance . . ."* (Psalm 2:1-2,6,8).

What is going on in our world today? It seems that Christianity is under siege and being continually belittled and disparaged. Is it possible for God's ultimate plan to be thwarted? Listen, we must keep in mind that times of trouble for man are no trouble for God. He isn't held back by our troubles. And the highest praise we can give Him is to live by faith and trust in His Word, no matter what's going on around us.

Remember, God is literally living in the midst of His people through the indwelling of the Holy Spirit, and we're the tabernacles of His presence on earth. Thus *we will not be moved . . .* even if threatened with death. Anyone can lift up their hands while singing, but not everyone can hand their Bible to their executioner without fear. That's Holy Spirit power in a life that's been lived in faith and trust in the Word of God!

We need to toughen up. Satan has been trying to weaken the church by diminishing the authority of the Word of God within the church. He won't prevail as long as God's Word is going out because, *"So shall My word be that goes forth from My mouth; it shall not return to Me void, but it shall accomplish what I please, and it shall prosper in the thing for which I sent it"* (Isaiah 55:11). So, whether by handing the Word of God to your executioner, sharing Jesus' sacrificial love with the haters of our day, or standing on the Word of God and living by faith, all are forms of highest praise to God.

Luther's great hymn "A Mighty Fortress Is Our God" is said to have been inspired by Psalm 46, and is often referred to as the Battle Hymn of the Reformation:

A mighty fortress is our God, a bulwark never failing;
Our helper He, amid the flood of mortal ills prevailing:
For still our ancient foe doth seek to work us woe;
His craft and power are great, and, armed with cruel hate,
On earth is not his equal.

Did we in our own strength confide, our striving would be losing;
Were not the right Man on our side, the Man of God's own choosing:
Dost ask who that may be? Christ Jesus, it is He;
Lord Sabaoth, His Name, from age to age the same,
And He must win the battle.

War and Peace

*8*Come, behold the works of the Lord, Who has made desolations in the earth. *9*He makes wars cease to the end of the earth; He breaks the bow and cuts the spear in two; He burns the chariot in the fire. *10*Be still, and know that I am God; I will be exalted among the nations, I will be exalted in the earth! *11*The Lord of hosts is with us; the God of Jacob is our refuge. Selah *—Psalm 46:8-11*

LIKE THIS PSALM by the sons of Korah, Isaiah also wrote of a time when the Lord's House will be established and He will be worshiped above all. People will throng to honor Him on the "Mountain of the Lord." Wars will have ceased. There will be no more weapons. God will be exalted among the nations (See Isaiah 2:2-4).

What kind of wonderful dream is this? Well, it won't happen during the current age. There is much more that must ensue before this beautiful scene will be realized. The time is coming when there will be a great war such as the world has never seen. It will be a time when the armies of the earth will gather in collective revolt against God and fight against the Lord Jesus himself!

We know that Jesus is the Lamb of God, humble, gentle, meek, silent when accused. But it won't be the Lamb against whom they will wage their battle. This time He will meet them as the Lion of Judah on the plains of Megiddo, where they will meet their demise.

Christians make a huge mistake these days in their efforts to make Christianity appealing by catering to the whims of man and adapting the message to his desires. People want the "ends" (meaning peace and prosperity) but not the "means" that will bring that about. They want peace without the Prince of Peace and they want the Millennium without having to repent. They claim that they want a world in which righteousness dwells, but they want righteousness redefined.

Doing the work of the Lord is to bring about a kingdom in which true righteousness dwells, and this can only come about through God bringing disasters unlike anything seen before to this earth (see Zephaniah 1:14-18). When someone believes that wars can cease without God breaking the bow and cutting the spear in two by punishing the wicked, they have essentially dethroned God and taken His place.

Our psalm today tells us that God will be exalted among the nations and exalted in all the earth! People don't want to honor and worship God, because Self has the throne in their hearts. And yet they want to believe that heaven is still in their future someday. Jesus said, "Why do you call me 'Lord, Lord' and do not do the things which I say?" He continues by comparing them to the man who built a house upon the sand without a foundation that was destroyed when the flood came.

We need to search our hearts. We must accept God for who He says He is and believe that He will do what He said He would do. Whether one believes it or not, it will come to pass. Merely saying, "Praise the Lord" but not obeying Him is merely to give lip service to Him. The highest praise is seen, not merely sung. Jesus is coming soon, ready or not, and He will break the bow and cut the spear in two and burn the chariots in fire, then we will have peace. But before that, we need to make certain that when we share this beautiful truth with nonbelievers we also warn them of what will come first and not be afraid of their possible rejection. Those "who have an ear to hear" will hear, and their lives will be changed for much better things than they experienced when their own "self" sat upon the throne that rightfully belongs to our Maker.

From Lameness to Leaping

Introduction

A Psalm of the Sons of Korah—*Psalm 47*

HAVE YOU EVER been so excited about something you heard that you expressed your excitement in a physical reaction? Maybe you jumped up and down, or shouted, or cried, or all of the above. It's generally an unexpected and involuntary reaction. That's what praise is like! If you've just received the best news that anyone could ever receive, praise is the natural reaction.

When the apostles Peter and John went up to the temple at prayer time, they came upon a man who had been lame in his legs since birth lying at the gate of the temple. He was accustomed to begging alms from those who were going into the temple. Peter told the man to look at him and John. The man, expecting to get something from them, waited. Peter said to him, "Silver and gold I do not have, but what I do have I give you: In the name of Jesus of Nazareth rise up and walk." The man rose up with Peter's help, and immediately knew that strength had entered his limbs. The verse continues, "So he, leaping up, stood and walked and entered the temple with them—walking, leaping, and praising God" (Acts 3:1-8).

That is a picture of praise, from lameness to leaping because of what Christ had done for him. I don't believe this man had to *decide* to leap and praise God. It just happened. So it is with us. It's not mechanics or discipline—it's natural and even necessary. There's simply no other way to express our joy.

Over the past few days we've looked at what praise is and how we can praise God in ways other than by singing. As we study Psalm 47, we're going to move from the "what" and "how" of praise to examining the object of our praise. The object of our praise determines the intensity of our praise. You can praise a child for an accomplishment or praise the pizza guy for delivering your pizza on time. But there's One alone who is worthy of the highest praise, and that is the Great King.

The background of this psalm is God's victory over the Assyrian king Sennacherib who had laid siege against the city of Jerusalem. The words in these verses go far beyond the moment, carrying with them a prophetic message that points ahead to the time of Jesus and to our day as well.

The next time the Lord comes, it will be for a purpose other than dying for man's sins. It will be for bringing us to the fullness of our salvation, including our glorified bodies. We know this is true because it's been promised, and we'll find hints of it in these verses.

Let's prepare to learn more about the Object of our praise so that we, too, can go our way leaping and praising God. "To those who eagerly wait for Him, He will appear a second time, apart from sin, for salvation" (Hebrews 9:28). Are you excited?

Praise the Great King!

¹Oh clap your hands, all you peoples! Shout to God with the voice of triumph! ²For the Lord Most High is awesome; He is a great King over all the earth. ³He will subdue the peoples under us, and the nations under our feet. ⁴He will choose our inheritance for us, the excellence of Jacob whom He loves. Selah —*Psalm 47:1-3*

I PERSONALLY THINK it's wrong to cheer like crazy at a sporting event and then come into a church and act like you're at a funeral. Church ought to be the most exciting thing you do all week—not because of the speaker or the music but because the Great King is here! It's in church that we read and study in order to find out what God's plan is for our lives. After visiting a church, don't ask yourself if you "liked" it. Ask yourself if you learned anything more about the Great King and His will for your life. The Lord himself is present within the hearts of the believers with whom you gathered there. Did you learn anything wonderful about Him? Was your faith in Him reconfirmed somehow during your time there? Were you inspired to praise Him as you sang and worshiped and listened to His Word being taught?

The sons of Korah begin this psalm of royal praise with instructions to clap and shout. Then they point to the object of their praise and the reason they clap and shout: because the Lord Most High is awesome, and He is the Great King over all the earth!

God's title in verse 3, Lord Most High, tells us more about the Great King than any other title used in Scripture. We read of *El Shaddai*, which means God Almighty, and He is that. We read of *Jehovah Rapha*, the Lord who heals, and He does that. We read of *Jehovah Jireh*, the Lord who provides, and He is that. He is Almighty, He does heal, and He can provide because He is *El Elyon*, the Supreme God, the only God. Our God is the Great King over all the earth. He is greater than the invading armies of Ezekiel 38-39; He is greater than the god of ISIS and Boko Haram and the Ayatollah, and He is the Great King over *all* the earth! He is *The Lord Most High*!

I believe that the world would be a better place if just one of the Ten Commandments were obeyed by everyone. Just pick one, and imagine the world under those conditions. A world of no murder, or no stealing, or no lying, or no idolatry. It would be a completely different world if everyone obeyed just one of these!

But God didn't give us only one thing that could improve life and the world around us. He gave us *everything* we need to know (2 Peter 1:1-4). Nothing compares to the riches of God's truth. You can be "worldly rich" but poor in the truth, and if you don't know God's truth, you can't be free; and if you're not free, then you can't be His child—and if you're not His child, you can't dwell in His house forever.

The truth is what gains us access to heaven, and the Great King has disclosed to all the earth what is right and true. "If you abide in My word, you are my disciples indeed; and you shall know the truth, and the truth shall make you free" (1 John 8:31-32). Yes, He subdues our enemies, and they'll be under our feet someday, but the greatest thing He has done is to choose our inheritance for us (v. 4)! He has revealed to us what is right and true and how to be reconciled to Him and receive an inheritance incorruptible and undefiled that does not fade away (1 Peter 1:3-5). If that doesn't make you want to clap and shout, you might want to check yourself for a pulse!

APRIL

Sing Like Someone's Listening . . .
Because He Is!

⁵God has gone up with a shout, the Lord with the sound of a trumpet.
⁶Sing praises to God, sing praises! Sing praises to our King, sing praises!
⁷For God is the King of all the earth; sing praises with understanding.
—*Psalm 47:5-7*

"GOD HAS GONE UP . . . with the sound of a trumpet." The setting of this psalm is one in which the Lord has gone up against the Assyrians and miraculously defeated them (2 Kings 19:35; Isaiah 37:36). In Hebrew, verse 5 would read, "God has ascended with acclamations of joy, or a battle cry." Most scholars see this as pointing to a yet future event when not only is a wicked army beaten, but also when man's greatest enemy is defeated: "*Now when He had spoken these things, while they watched . . . a cloud received Him out of their sight. And . . . behold, two men stood by them in white apparel, who also said, 'Men of Galilee, why do you stand gazing up into heaven? This same Jesus, who was taken up from you into heaven, will so come in like manner as you saw Him go into heaven*" (Acts 1:9-11).

There's another prophetic element in view here, because there is a second ascension ahead that is accompanied by a trumpet blast: " . . . *flesh and blood cannot inherit the kingdom of God . . . Behold, I tell you a mystery: We shall not all sleep, but we shall all be changed—in a moment, in the twinkling of an eye, at the last trumpet. For the trumpet will sound, and the dead will be raised incorruptible, and we shall all be changed. . . . Then shall come to pass the saying that is written: 'Death is swallowed up in victory. O Death, where is your sting? O Hades, where is your victory?'*"

Jesus' ascension pictures for us the defeat of a far greater foe than Sennacherib and his army. Understanding His ascension allows us to "sing praises with *understanding*." We could see this as meaning, "In light of what you've come to understand about the Great King and His goodness and truth, sing praises!" Why should we sing praises? Well, for starters, the Great King has proven conclusively that there is life after death! Upon His rising from the dead and ascending into heaven, all questions and doubts about life after death were resolved.

All over the world there are groups who promote unproven propositions about life after death through reaching higher states of consciousness or Nirvana or through reincarnation—and some simply believe that death is the end of everything. But there's one group that has conclusive evidence that all other propositions are false, and that is the true church, the people of God. The proof? In John 14:1-6, Jesus told the disciples that He was going to prepare a place for them in heaven. When the apostle Thomas asked Him, "Lord, we do not know where You are going, and how can we know the way?", Jesus responded, "*I am* the way, the truth, and the life. No one comes to the Father except through Me." So if Jesus had merely said that He was the way to heaven but He was never seen again by anyone after His death, we'd have reason to doubt. But the One who made these claims was crucified publicly, yet seen on many occasions *after* His burial—in some cases by as many as 500 people! You just might want to pay attention to Him, especially since He ascended visibly into heaven in front of many eyewitnesses, proving beyond question that the Bible's proposition concerning life after death stands alone as proven truth!

Our response? Sing praises, live a life of faith and trust in Him, "shout to God with a voice of triumph," for He has defeated the greatest enemy, Death! The Great King has conquered our adversary the devil on a sinner's cross. Sing praise! And strive to live by faith and trust in His Word, which is the highest praise of all.

April 2

Our God Is an Awesome God!

8God reigns over the nations; God sits on His holy throne. 9The princes of the people have gathered together, the people of the God of Abraham. For the shields of the earth belong to God; He is greatly exalted. —Psalm 47:8-9

TODAY WE READ that God is greatly exalted—not "He will be," but He already is. Earthly conditions don't affect that. We exalt Him first of all for *who He is*, because who He is determines everything about what He does and why.

God is *the* Great King who is on His throne and reigns over all the nations, whether they know it, or like it, or want it, or not! In the future, He will end all rebellion everywhere, and the wicked will be cast into the Lake of Fire forever. But all who love the Lord, the people of the God of Abraham, will be gathered together before His throne, for He is their shield and protector. He promises that none of them will be lost. The apostle John quotes Jesus as saying, "*I . . . pray . . . for those whom You [the Father] have given Me, for they are Yours. All Mine are Yours, and Yours are Mine. . . . Those whom You gave Me I have kept; none of them is lost except the son of perdition [Judas], that the Scriptures might be fulfilled*" (John 17:9-10). In John 20-21, Jesus prays for all those in the future who would believe in Him without seeing Him first. So all of these will be safe in the Lord during the terrible days that lie ahead for this world.

The Assyrians were no threat to the Great King, nor is the devil. Not even death posed a threat to the God of all the earth when He came "in the likeness of sinful flesh" as a tiny baby, born, as prophesied, in Bethlehem. And everything else that was prophesied about Him came to fulfillment during His time here on earth except that which is being reserved for God's future judgment against mankind.

Dare anyone doubt that everything God has said He would accomplish will be done? Take heed, doubter! Our God will *always prevail in the end*! When Hezekiah was threatened by King Sennacherib in 2 Chronicles 32, he boldly told the people, "*Be strong and courageous; do not be afraid nor dismayed before the king of Assyria . . . for there are more with us than with him. With him is an arm of flesh; but with us is the Lord our God, to help us and to fight our battles*" (vv. 7-8).

Do you believe this today? By "this" I mean the fact that there are more with us than there are against us? Hezekiah was referring to the armies of heaven, led and ruled by the Great King. The result? "The Lord sent an angel who cut down every mighty man of valor, leader, and captain in the camp of the king of Assyria."

The obvious question to ask would be, "Why did God allow the enemies of Judah to lay a siege against Jerusalem in the first place?" We might wonder about some of our own battles and question why we're allowed to be attacked. Something we need to hold on to, especially at such times, is this: the Great King will always prevail in the end, so our part is to remain faithful until then.

But we should also remember this: a day is coming when not only will all of our enemies be defeated, but we'll be separated from them forever, never to see them again, with all thanks to our Great King. Clap your hands, and shout to God with the voice of triumph, for our God will always prevail, both in the moment and, ultimately, in the end. Praise His holy Name!

Great Expectations

[1]A Song. A Psalm of the sons of Korah. Great is the Lord, and greatly to be praised in the city of our God, in His holy mountain. [2]Beautiful in elevation, the joy of the whole earth, is Mount Zion on the sides of the north, the city of the great King. [3]God is in her palaces; He is known as her refuge. —Psalm 48:1-3

TODAY WE'LL BEGIN to look at this final psalm in the trilogy of praise psalms by the sons of Korah regarding God's victory over the Assyrian king, Sennacherib, and his armies, and also His supernatural protection of Mount Zion and Jerusalem.

"Thus the Lord saved Hezekiah and the inhabitants of Jerusalem from the hand of Sennacherib, the king of Assyria, and from the hand of all others, and guided them on every side" (2 Chronicles 32:22). It's with this in view that our psalm opens with the great anthem of praise: *"Great is the Lord, and greatly to be praised . . . "* Where? *" . . . in the city of our God. . . ."*

When King Solomon had finished building the Temple in Jerusalem, the Lord appeared to him, saying, *"I have heard your prayer and your supplication . . . I have consecrated this house which you have built to put My name there forever, and My eyes and My heart will be there perpetually"* (1 Kings 9:3). With such a magnificent declaration from the Lord regarding Jerusalem and the Temple, should King Hezekiah and Judah have expected anything less than such a divine response as His saving them from the hand of their enemies?

And now, since those who love the Lord are the temple of the Holy Spirit, and since Jerusalem typifies the church (although they are distinct from one another in the covenantal sense) and is presented in these verses as beautiful and the joy of the whole earth, what else could be said of a city where the Lord's name is there perpetually?

But let me ask you this: are we not the joy that was set before the Lord when He hung on the cross (Hebrews 12:2)? Are we not the beautiful bride of Christ made spotless and without blemish by the blood of our Lord and Savior Jesus Christ (Ephesians 5:27)? Is He not our refuge and our strength, our present help in time of need (Psalm 46:1)? Therefore, should we not have great expectations just as Judah should have in the face of the siege of the Assyrians? As God's building, as the temple of the Holy Spirit, we can expect this: God will make Himself known through us!

When David confronted Goliath, he said: *"This day the Lord will deliver you into my hand, and I will strike you and take your head from you. And . . . I will give the carcasses of the camp of the Philistines to the birds of the air and the wild beasts of the earth, that all the earth may know that there is a God in Israel"* (1 Samuel 17:46).

The entire earth was able to see that there was a God in Israel because God was manifested through David's words and corresponding actions. He wants to manifest His power through us to the world as well, so that the world can know that He is the Great King and the Lord of the church. But our responsibility, like that of Moses, Joshua, and David, who were people of action, is to speak and do what God tells us to do, and then others will be able to know that THERE IS A GOD, Who is in Israel and in all the world!

April 4

If God Is for Us . . .

⁴For behold, the kings assembled, they passed by together. ⁵They saw it, and so they marveled; they were troubled, they hastened away. ⁶Fear took hold of them there, and pain, as of a woman in birth pangs, ⁷as when You break the ships of Tarshish with an east wind. ⁸As we have heard, so we have seen in the city of the Lord of hosts, in the city of our God: God will establish it forever. Selah —Psalm 48:4-8

THE BACKGROUND for our verses today is in 2 Kings 18:29-30: *"Then the Rabshakeh stood and called out with a loud voice in Hebrew, hoping to demoralize those who were . . . saying, 'Hear the word of the great king . . . of Assyria! Thus says the king: "Do not let Hezekiah deceive you, for he shall not be able to deliver you from his hand; nor let Hezekiah make you trust in the Lord, saying, 'The Lord will surely deliver us; this city shall not be given into the hand of the king of Assyria.'"'"*

We've already established the fact that the Assyrians had laid siege against the city of Jerusalem, and here we see exactly how close their proximity was: they were within speaking distance. And yet . . . Hezekiah *"tore his clothes, covered himself with sackcloth, and went into the house of the Lord. . . . Then Hezekiah prayed before the Lord, and said: 'O Lord God of Israel, the One who dwells between the cherubim, You are God, You alone, of all the kingdoms of the earth. You have made heaven and earth'"* (2 Kings 19:15).

Christian, keep this in mind: You can praise God with expectancy no matter what you're going through. No battle you encounter will ever be faced alone! This doesn't mean there won't be battles and that we won't see the enemy getting uncomfortably close at times, but God will make Himself known. He made Himself known to the Egyptians through the plagues that came upon them. He made Himself known to Pharaoh, who sent the Egyptians in pursuit of Israel, which resulted in the death of the Egyptians.

Who was it who instructed Moses regarding where to tell the Israelites to camp? It was the Lord. In fact, intricate details of where to camp were given to Moses by God in Exodus 14:1-4. Why were they to camp there? Because the Lord was going to harden Pharaoh's heart and cause him to pursue Israel into that very site so that the Egyptians *may know that He is the Lord.*

In other words, God told Moses, "Tell Israel to camp with their backs to the Red Sea between the Mouth of Gorges, the Well of Bitterness, and the Master of Doom, and I will stir up the Egyptian army to pursue them while they're camped there" (See Exodus 14:10-14). An important point to note is that the fourth side of the campground was the Red Sea itself. *"The people were dismayed, saying, 'It would have been better for us to serve the Egyptians than we should die in the wilderness.' [But] Moses said to the people, 'Do not be afraid. Stand still, and see the salvation of the Lord. . . .'"*

The truth is, the enemies of the church are growing in number and closing in on believers. We need to remember that *we're not the ones in danger.* Our enemies are! We have nothing to fear; they have everything to fear. They are rising up against the blood-bought, Spirit-filled church of the living God! What we have heard, we will see (Psalm 48:8). No battle will ever be faced alone. God is for us and with us! Go forward this day, knowing that if God is for us, who can be against us? (Romans 8:31).

April 5

Thy Lovingkindness Is Better than Life

[9]We have thought, O God, on Your lovingkindness, in the midst of Your temple. [10]According to Your name, O God, So is Your praise to the ends of the earth; Your right hand is full of righteousness. [11]Let Mount Zion rejoice, let the daughters of Judah be glad, because of Your judgments. [12]Walk about Zion, and go all around her. Count her towers; [13]mark well her bulwarks; consider her palaces; that you may tell it to the generation following. [14]For this is God, our God forever and ever; He will be our guide even to death. —*Psalm 48:9-14*

AS THE FOCUS of our psalm now turns from Jerusalem to its inhabitants, and then finally to the Great King, we find much for which to praise Him. The Jews remembered His lovingkindess as displayed in their deliverance. The people of Judah are told to be glad because God's judgments are righteous and true. He can always be trusted.

Why does He love Jerusalem so much? Is it because of its geographic location? No, His love is for the people. It's His people that He loves and upholds with His righteous right hand. In verses 12 and 13 the psalmist invites them to look around and see all that God has done. Then verse 14 brings it back to the center. *It is God who has done this.* He is our God, forever and ever, and He will be our guide even to death, which also means "until we die, and even after that."

The Scriptures tell us that we are God's building and temple! (Ephesians 2:19-22). He loves us, but He hasn't promised us a painless and problem-free existence, and we still make mistakes and even fail Him at times, but here is truth: God's lovingkindess is an expression of His character, not of our deservedness. We may find ourselves under His disciplinary hand, but even then, we are never outside of His watchful care (see Jeremiah 31:1-7). There are wonderful benefits that have come even through God's divine discipline. Consider this: it was from the 70 years that the Jews were in Babylonian captivity that we received the prophetic book of Daniel containing the story of the lions' den and God's faithfulness to these men who stood up for Him under extreme persecution. Also during that disciplinary time, God revealed dreams and interpretations to Daniel, as He had done with Joseph, and by these two men, good came to those who meant evil against them. After the Assyrian siege, God's people were reminded of God's lovingkindness as they looked around and saw a city once under siege now free because of the protective and delivering hand of God.

Believer, you can have those expectations as well, even concerning those who mean harm against you. Evil may present itself, and it may possibly involve persecution or imprisonment for us, but we are still not outside of God's lovingkindness. Even this will work together for good, because all things do for those who love the Lord and are the called according to His purpose (Romans 8:28). We have great cause to praise the Lord always. God has never failed you, and He never will. Count the times that God has been a strong tower for you, and then tell the next generation of the faithful lovingkindness of our God.

The end is at hand, church, and one thing we know for sure is that God's enemies will not prevail because they never have in the past, and we are promised that they will not in the future. Although the enemy is closing in, let's not ever forget the expectant hope that is shown by praising the Lord, because the truth is that even though we're surrounded by enemies, we're safe under the shadow of the Great King's wings, even to death—and beyond.

The Best Things in Life

Introduction to Psalm 49

¹[To the chief Musician. A Psalm of the sons of Korah] Hear this, all peoples; Give ear, all inhabitants of the world. —*Psalm 49:1*

THIS PSALM, attributed to the sons of Korah, has a pretty urgent-sounding opening line. Essentially the author is saying "Hey, everybody! Pay attention! This is a very important message!"

Considered one of the Wisdom Psalms, these verses suggest prophetic undertones. I don't mean prophetic in the sense of predicting the future, but prophetic in the sense that they sound forth a truth that is timeless and without boundaries. The messages in this psalm are true for every season of history or type of culture; they are true for every person, no matter their stature or status in life. They foretell something that is timely and relevant today—maybe even more so than ever.

The wisdom in these verses far surpasses any limits of time. They were written for all people at every point in history, yet they specifically discuss the end of life, i.e., what lies ahead for everyone who now lives or who has ever lived or whoever will live on this earth. Do you see why we had better listen up to what the psalmist has to say?

If you remember from your Bible, the sin of Babylon was self-glorification and wantonness, or extreme extravagance. Don't get the idea, though, that God is anti-wealth. He is anti-*worshiping and trusting* in wealth. God has long blessed many of His own people with great wealth, and He has entrusted earthly riches into the care of many Christians who are faithful stewards today. In fact, without wealthy Christians, or even the nonbelieving rich who nonetheless see virtue in Christianity, we wouldn't have many of the hospitals and universities that we have today. We do, however, see atheists living lives of self-glorification, immorality of all kinds, and promiscuity.

In Luke 12, Jesus said, "*Do not seek what you should eat or what you should drink, nor have an anxious mind. For all these things the nations of the world seek after, and your Father knows that you need these things. But seek the kingdom of God, and all these things shall be added to you . . .*" (vv. 29-34).

In these verses, Jesus was speaking primarily to Jews, who believed that material wealth was an indication that the rich were pleasing to God. Yet in Matthew 19:23, Jesus said that it was hard for the rich to enter the kingdom of God. Warren Wiersbe, writing on this subject, said, "It is not a sin to have the things that money can buy, as long as you don't lose sight of the things that money can't buy."

It's amazing how many people think that certain sayings on this subject come from the Bible, such as "God helps those who help themselves," or "Money is the root of all evil." In fact the Bible states in many places that God lifts up the *humble*, and it is with them that He dwells (Isaiah 57:15). He "resists the proud [self-sufficient], but gives grace to the humble" (James 4:6). And regarding money, the Lord clearly says, "For the *love of money* is the root of all evil"—not that money in and of itself is evil—but a familiar truism honestly reminds us, "You can't take it with you." As we head into the rest of the verses of this psalm, we're going to learn not only the way we are to live, but also the way we are to die. Are you ready to discover, as our title suggests, the best things in life?

April 7

Blessed Are the Poor

¹Hear this, all peoples; Give ear, all inhabitants of the world, ²both low and high, rich and poor together. ³My mouth shall speak wisdom, and the meditation of my heart shall give understanding. ⁴I will incline my ear to a proverb; I will disclose my dark saying on the harp. ⁵Why should I fear in the days of evil, when the iniquity at my heels surrounds me?
—Psalm 49:1-5

—

AS WE SAW yesterday, it's not a sin to be wealthy. Neither is it God's desire that everyone have wealth, in the material sense. Nor is it His desire that the government seize the wealth of some and bestow "financial equality" by taking from the rich to redistribute it to the poor. It is true that the rich have a responsibility to the poor, but the forced equalization movement of our day is not the will of God.

In the Bible, we read that God made Abraham, Jacob, Joseph, Moses, King David, Solomon, and many others very wealthy, but for others, who also loved and served Him, He did not do the same. It would appear that in God's economy, it's okay for some to have more than others materially. In fact, efforts to equalize the material status of everyone by some governments is a precursor to the final governmental control system of all people under the Antichrist.

God doesn't give us things that will harm us and cause us to perish. Although it's true that He gives some the power to get wealthy, He also warns of the power of wealth (see Deuteronomy 8:18-19), which is the very heart of Psalm 49. The psalmist addresses the lyrics of this psalm to *all* people the world over, from all walks of life, the rich as well as the poor. He says that wisdom is found in a proverb and that it is a "dark saying," a conundrum, a riddle, or a puzzle. He is speaking to all people everywhere whose lives have been impacted by abusers of power who see their riches as giving them the right to abuse others. "*When the righteous* are in authority, the people rejoice; but when a wicked man rules, the people groan" (Proverbs 29:2).

Verse 5 gives us the nitty-gritty question that implies a comforting answer: *"Why should I fear in the days of evil, when the iniquity at my heels surrounds me?"* One answer would be that the best things in life can neither be bought nor lost. In 2 Timothy 1:7, we are told that God has not given us a *spirit of fear*. So if a spirit of fear is not what He has given us, then He has given us the gift of fearlessness, and what God gives, Satan cannot take away.

Money can't buy the peace that passes understanding, which comes from the absence of fear. There are no possessions that can "guard your heart and mind" when facing fear. Nothing you own can help you during a season of trauma or tragedy. Having a loving family is a tremendous help when facing life's tragedies, but what God gives is even greater than that. Colossians 3 tells us that during those times, you are to *"set your mind on things above, not on things on earth. For you died, and your life is hidden with Christ in God."* In His Sermon on the Mount, Jesus said to *seek first the kingdom of God* and His righteousness, and let God handle everything else! The psalmist asks, "Why should I fear?" Yes, fortunes can be made and lost, but the Word of the Lord endures forever. The Lord himself promised that He will never leave us nor forsake us. The best things in life cannot be bought or lost, and we can always take comfort in that.

April 8

The Best Things in Life Aren't Things

⁶Those who trust in their wealth and boast in the multitude of their riches, ⁷none of them can by any means redeem his brother, nor give to God a ransom for him— ⁸for the redemption of their souls is costly, and it shall cease forever— ⁹that he should continue to live eternally, and not see the Pit. ¹⁰For he sees wise men die; likewise the fool and the senseless person perish, and leave their wealth to others. ¹¹Their inner thought is that their houses will last forever, their dwelling places to all generations; they call their lands after their own names. ¹²Nevertheless man, though in honor, does not remain; he is like the beasts that perish. ¹³This is the way of those who are foolish, and of their posterity who approve their sayings. Selah —*Psalm 49:1-5*

WHAT THE PSALMIST in today's verses is saying is exactly what Jesus said: Wealth can't bring to your life anything of lasting value. Verses 7-9 tell us that salvation cannot be bought. No one will get into heaven through philanthropy. Building hospitals and orphanages, digging wells in Africa, and even feeding the poor, as good as those acts may be, will not purchase salvation for anyone.

What is salvation? We are saved when trust in the life, death, burial, and resurrection of Jesus. *"For by grace you have been saved through faith, and that not of yourselves; it is the gift of God, not of works, lest anyone should boast. For we are His workmanship, created in Christ Jesus for good works, which God prepared beforehand that we should walk in them"* (Ephesians 1:8-10). Good works don't save you, but they are part of the life of the saved. The best things in life feed the spirit, not the flesh. Verses 6 and 7 above tell us that those who trust in their wealth, thinking they can buy their way into heaven and won't see the Pit, are fools. The buildings named after them and the land holdings in their name—soon no one will even remember those names.

Please remember: There is nothing wrong with having "things." In 3 John 3, he wrote that he prayed for his beloved friend Gaius that he would prosper in all things even as his soul has prospered. But the most precious possession of Gaius, according to the verses, was that *he walked in the truth*. Can we honestly say that that is our most precious possession? Listen, there is nothing wrong with travel and leisure and enjoying life, but having money will do nothing for you when you face that great equalizer, Death. Life is a short opportunity to sow into eternity. There is little time left to reach this lost world before all hell breaks loose on the earth. The danger in our day is that some people get so busy that all of their efforts and resources are dedicated to making a name for themselves instead of exalting the name of the One who saved them.

Are you putting as much effort into building God's kingdom as you do your company or career? When you die, your name might still be on the building, but after you've been dead for a while, no one will remember, the building will sell, and someone else's name will be on it. Did you ever stop to think that it's possible to have a saved soul and a wasted life? That's the heart of Psalm 49, accompanied by a warning to the wealthy about trusting in riches to do what cannot be done with money. What is more important in these last of the last days: the accumulation of wealth, or evangelism? You know the answer to that question. I just think we need a reminder once in a while of what is truly important.

Sowing It Forward

¹⁴Like sheep they are laid in the grave; Death shall feed on them; the upright shall have dominion over them in the morning; and their beauty shall be consumed in the grave, far from their dwelling. ¹⁵But God will redeem my soul from the power of the grave, for He shall receive me. Selah. ¹⁶Do not be afraid when one becomes rich, when the glory of his house is increased; ¹⁷for when he dies he shall carry nothing away; his glory shall not descend after him. ¹⁸Though while he lives he blesses himself (for men will praise you when you do well for yourself), ¹⁹he shall go to the generation of his fathers; they shall never see light. ²⁰A man who is in honor, yet does not understand, is like the beasts that perish. —Psalm 49:14-20

THE PSALMIST compares sheep with the foolish who trust in riches. It isn't a pretty picture! Death feeds upon them, their beauty consumed in the grave. Then the psalmist continues: "But God . . . !" *He will redeem my soul from the power of the grave* (v. 15). Verse 16 continues with *"Do not be afraid when one becomes rich. . . ."* There are those who are rich and abuse their position in life, and we are told not to fear them. But there is another meaning here, and it may be the primary one: "*I was envious of the boastful, when I saw the prosperity of the wicked*" (Psalm 73:3). There is a very important truth here: You may struggle in life as one who has been made rich in Christ but who finds it a real battle to make ends meet. Like the author of Psalm 73, you're tempted to look at those who do wickedly yet live prosperously as a cause for "slipping up" in your own walk. But the psalmist says that *your best life is your next life*, and you've been redeemed from the power of the grave. No one takes his wealth with him!

Both those who bless themselves (v. 18), and those who praise a person just because he has money, shall die like everyone else and not see the morning light (v. 14). Those who are honored in this life with material things but don't understand that the ability to gain wealth comes from God, will find that their lives and their accumulation of wealth will have been a waste. Saints, listen: The best things in life are those we send ahead, not what we leave behind. I'm speaking of sowing into God's kingdom, not physical reaping of wealth. There's nothing wrong with planning ahead or investing for the future. Just make sure that you're also investing in the spiritual long term as well!

Matthew 5:11-12 tells us that we're blessed when reviled and persecuted for the name of Christ. Sadly, in our country no one is going to "revile and persecute"—or even challenge—the disengaged, compromised Christian. As a matter of fact, they will praise him even as many are praising the churches that support marriage equality or anti-Semitism. The Bible refers to our rewards as crowns, but the reward in heaven that will be second only to being in the presence of God forever will be to meet those who are there because of *our* efforts through the Lord to reach them for Christ.

Christian, we're going to be in heaven for a long time. We'll be reunited with lost loved ones, see Jesus face to face, talk to the saints of old, and who knows what else? But the best things in life are those we send ahead, not what we leave behind. It is only what we've done for God's name and glory that will be remembered forevermore. Money isn't evil, but loving it can pierce you through with many sorrows. Let's choose good instead, and remember that we are sowing into eternity by our good works done in Jesus' name!

April 10

Keepin' It Real

Introduction to Psalm 50

¹[A Psalm of Asaph.] The mighty God, even the LORD, hath spoken, and called the earth from the rising of the sun unto the going down thereof. —Psalm 50:1

ALTHOUGH there are several in the Bible who went by the name Asaph, this is the one to whom many of the Davidic psalms are addressed. He had the role of "the chief musician" in David's kingdom. In other words, he was the worship leader for the king.

In Psalm 24, David wrote, *"Who is this King of glory? The Lord strong and mighty, the Lord mighty in battle. Lift up your heads, O you gates! Lift up, you everlasting doors! And the King of glory shall come in. Who is this King of glory? The Lord of hosts, He is the King of glory"* (vv. 8-10).

In our verses today, Asaph does what King David did in Psalm 24. He will take our minds and our hearts to a much-needed place in light of the minimalist teaching that is predominant in our world concerning truth and right. We shouldn't be surprised, because Paul warned us that this would be a sign of the last days: *"Know this, that in the last days perilous times will come: for men will be lovers of themselves, lovers of money, boasters, proud, blasphemers, disobedient to parents, unthankful, unholy, unloving, unforgiving, slanderers, without self-control, brutal, despisers of good, traitors, headstrong, haughty, lovers of pleasure rather than lovers of God, having a form of godliness but denying its power. And from such people, turn away!"* (2 Timothy 3:1-6).

We're told to turn away from such people, yet in Matthew and Mark we're told to go to such ones and preach the gospel to them! Friends, the Bible never contradicts itself. Paul writes, "*I wrote to you in my epistle not to keep company with sexually immoral people. Yet I certainly did not mean with the sexually immoral people of this world, or with the covetous, or extortioners, or idolaters, since then you would need to go out of the world. But now I have written to you not to keep company with . . . a brother, who is sexually immoral, or covetous, or an idolater, or a reviler, or a drunkard, or an extortioner—not even to eat with such a person. For what have I to do with judging those also who are outside? Do you not judge those people who are inside? But those who are outside, God judges. Therefore, 'put away from yourselves the evil person'*" (1 Cor 5:9-11).

Wow! Paul was not describing the world in these verses. He was describing the church! And that is what Asaph is doing also. Both were addressing the behavior of collective groups called the chosen people of God, and they are doing what can only be described as "keepin' it real." I wish that the "grace abusers" of our day would read this chapter, penned by Asaph but inspired by the unchanging Holy Spirit of God! It was an act of divine grace that sent God's Son into the world to purchase salvation through His blood in order that all men might be saved. But only those who will *believe* are saved.

Instead, many of the hyper-grace teachers seem to have forgotten the rest of the story, and grace has become license—or even divine indifference—to the actions of those who count themselves among "the called according to His purpose" (Romans 8:28).

Let's pray that the words of this psalm will help us to cut to the chase as we learn directly from our Father in heaven what He expects from those whom He bought with His own Son's blood.

Working Out Your Salvation

[1]The Mighty One, God the Lord, has spoken and called the earth from the rising of the sun to its going down. [2]Out of Zion, the perfection of beauty, God will shine forth. [3]Our God shall come, and shall not keep silent; a fire shall devour before Him, and it shall be very tempestuous all around Him. [4]He shall call to the heavens from above, and to the earth, that He may judge His people. [5]Gather My saints together to Me, those who have made a covenant with Me by sacrifice. [6]Let the heavens declare His righteousness for God Himself is Judge. —*Psalm 50:1-6*

"THE MIGHTY ONE, God the Lord." These opening words introduce the majesty that lies ahead. In Hebrew it would read, "El, Elohiym, YHWH" has spoken. In other words, the almighty, triune, and eternal God is calling the earth together, "from the rising of the sun to its setting," to witness what is essentially a courtroom scene, with the Father, Son, and Spirit all in attendance—the Son, in His perfection and beauty; the *shekinah* glory of the Holy Spirit, and the Father as the consuming fire and covenant Keeper and Maker. We are warned here of the coming judgment of all the earth by fire.

Peter also wrote of such a time: "*The day of the Lord will come as a thief in the night, in which the heavens will pass away with a great noise, and the elements will melt with fervent heat; both the earth and the works that are in it will be burned up. Therefore, since all these things will be dissolved, what manner of persons ought you to be in holy conduct and godliness . . . ?*" (2 Peter 3:10-11). We will escape the fiery destruction, but believers will be called before God so that He may judge them.

Look at how Asaph presents the Lord as a devouring fire. Please note that the God who is a consuming fire is the same God who also calls for the judgment of *His people* (v. 4), i.e., believers. Peter pointed out the same thing—but he doesn't mean that we need to fear melting away in the fervent heat. He's saying that in light of the fact that our God is powerful enough to destroy the heavens and the earth, we ought to consider our own conduct and godliness, since we bear His Name and are responsible for how we represent Him during our time on earth.

Some day our works will be tested by fire (see 1 Corinthians 3:11-15). Although we don't need to fear the *eternal judgment* of God, we will all stand before the Judgment Seat of Christ (Romans 14:10) to give an account of ourselves to God. Our *works* will be tested by fire to see of what sort they are. And right here, we come to an interesting fact to consider: *rewards* in heaven are earned, not merited! We should already understand that we can't ever earn our salvation. Christ accomplished that on the cross. But rewards in heaven must be earned! What we do after we're saved matters very much to God, as well as our motivation for doing it. If we do nothing for Him while here on earth as believers, then we can expect nothing in the sense of eternal rewards when we arrive in heaven. Keep these two things straight: Heaven is the free gift that results from salvation; rewards are earned in the sense of being deserved. Works done in genuine faith will be rewarded after our arrival in heaven. Paul reminds us to "work out your own salvation with fear and trembling," (Philippians 2:2), not working *for* our salvation, but working it *out* through our deeds, and for those He will reward us! We should all seriously consider how it will go for us on that day, and how much we should be willing to give Him our all, considering all that He has done for us.

April 12

God Didn't Save Us to Serve Us

⁷Hear, O My people, and I will speak, O Israel, and I will testify against you; I am God, your God! ⁸I will not rebuke you for your sacrifices or your burnt offerings, which are continually before Me. ⁹I will not take a bull from your house, nor goats out of your folds. ¹⁰For every beast of the forest is Mine, and the cattle on a thousand hills. ¹¹I know all the birds of the mountains, and the wild beasts of the field are Mine. ¹²If I were hungry, I would not tell you; for the world is Mine, and all its fullness. ¹³Will I eat the flesh of bulls, Or drink the blood of goats? ¹⁴Offer to God thanksgiving, and pay your vows to the Most High. ¹⁵Call upon Me in the day of trouble; I will deliver you, and you shall glorify Me." —*Psalm 50:7-15*

"HEAR YE, HEAR YE!" God is speaking! He calls His people to listen as He testifies against them. He qualifies His position as Judge and says that He will not rebuke them for their sacrifices or burnt offerings but reminds them that they are missing the point. Those weren't intended to be ritualistic we'd-better-do-this-or-else actions. He wants their hearts! He wants them to trust and believe in Him. He wants to be able to reward good works that are done in *faith in Him!* He reminds them that they aren't offering anything to Him that was theirs to begin with, because He already owns everything!

Many pagan religions taught that meat that was offered to idols was actually eaten by the pagan "gods." God straightens them out on that point, and tells them that even if He were ever hungry, He wouldn't come to them, because as the *true* God, He didn't need to!

"Burnt offerings and blood offerings" could be seen as the equivalent of church attendance and tithing now, and God tells them, "I'm not rebuking you for doing what you're supposed to do, but you don't get *rewarded* for doing what you ought to do!" Since we're of Christ, we should live as He did. He died to sanctify us, so let us live a sanctified life. Don't live for this world but for the next one, and don't forsake or ignore sharing with others even if you get hurt, because these are the things that please God.

Remember: God didn't save us to serve us. He saved us to serve Him! And it should be a blessing and a joy when we consider all that He's done for us. To hear some preachers talk you'd think that one day we'll give God a performance review instead of Him giving one to us. They act as if God is sitting on His throne just waiting for us to give Him orders (accompanied by our "faith," of course) that will produce the lifestyle that we feel we're owed. Let's look at this God's way: Hebrews 12:28-29 tells us, "*Since we are receiving a kingdom which cannot be shaken, let us have grace, by which we may serve God acceptably with reverence and godly fear. For our God is a consuming fire.*" And yet, Jesus came to serve and not to be served. This wasn't to set a pattern for how we should expect the Lord to respond to us. It was to be an example of how we are to be servants of God and of one another! We cannot give our orders to God. We're always going to be servants, and servants will never be greater than their master.

And, for the record, going to church is not serving God. Paying tithes is not serving God. These are acts of obedience to God's Word, and we should expect NO reward for doing these things. The works that He *will* reward are described in verses 14-15 of today's reading, and it's more the attitude than the act that is in view. If we give Him thanks, serve Him, trust Him, and watch His deliverance, we will thus glorify Him!

April 13

You Don't Have the Right

[16] But to the wicked God says: "What right have you to declare My statutes, or take My covenant in your mouth, *[17]* seeing you hate instruction and cast My words behind you *[18]* When you saw a thief, you consented with him, and have been a partaker with adulterers. *[19]* You give your mouth to evil, and your tongue frames deceit. *[20]* You sit and speak against your brother; you slander your own mother's son. *[21]* These things you have done, and I kept silent; you thought that I was altogether like you; but I will rebuke you, and set them in order before your eyes. *[22]* "Now consider this, you who forget God, lest I tear you in pieces, and there be none to deliver: *[23]* whoever offers praise glorifies Me; and to him who orders his conduct aright I will show the salvation of God."
—*Psalm 50:16-23*

GOD ASKS, "What right do you have to preach My Word? Who are you to tell other people that you're one of Mine, when you hate my instructions, defy My words, consent with evil, and condone immorality? You talk trash on those who honor their vows to keep My words and condemn others among My chosen people. You've mistaken My silence for indifference, thinking that because judgment wasn't immediate, I think like you do or else I just don't care what you do because you're among my 'chosen.'"

Then the Lord says, "I will rebuke you and set things in order!" Take notice: not all who "attend church" are of the church. Are the Jews God's chosen people? Do all Jews thus go to heaven? Not according to Jesus, who told Nicodemus, the Jew, "You must be born again." God is serious here. "Lest I tear you in pieces" is pretty sobering. He concludes with "Whoever offers praise glorifies Me and conducts himself rightly before Me, that one will see the salvation of God!" Church, listen. God is looking for those whose hearts are loyal to Him, willing to serve Him. He didn't save you so He could serve you, and He doesn't pass out unearned rewards in heaven.

"He who overcomes shall inherit all things, and I will be his God and he shall be My son. But the cowardly, unbelieving, abominable, murderers, sexually immoral, sorcerers, idolaters, and all liars shall have their part in the lake which burns with fire and brimstone, which is the second death" (Revelation 2:7-8). God cares about the way we live, as those who bear His name, and He doesn't tolerate our casting His Word behind our backs and ignoring it. Nor does He allow our consenting with evil, condoning it, or partaking in immorality. Christian, through God's grace we are saved by faith in His Son as Savior. Every saved person is a new creation who

lives in agreement with God's definitions of right and wrong. They may not live up to it all the time, but they never dispute it. Can a Christian commit adultery or fornication and go to heaven? Yes. Will a Christian ever think that adultery or sex outside of marriage is fine? Never. The Holy Spirit will never give a Christian convictions that contradict the Word of God.

God sanctifies every person He saves, because only those who are sanctified can serve Him. Those who are not sanctified (transformed by the renewing of their minds), have no right to declare His statutes or claim to be partakers of His covenant when their life is consenting of and participating in evil. Are you living to serve the living Savior? Or are you still trying to figure out how to better serve yourself? God has a much better plan. He knows your heart and where He wants you to go. Trust and obey Him, and continue to serve Him.

April 14

Exposed!

Introduction to Psalm 51

[1]To the Chief Musician. A Psalm of David when Nathan the prophet went to him, after he had gone in to Bathsheba. —*Psalm 51:1*

DAVID WROTE this psalm after he had fallen deeply into adultery and even murder, as we studied in Psalm 32. Sadly, it's common today to hear about church leaders who engage in adulterous affairs and are discovered. Our first response is often, "How could they do this?" The same could be asked about David. But God is faithful. He doesn't want his children to get away with their sin and sometimes permits painful consequences to insure that it won't happen again. In 2 Samuel 12, we read, "Then the Lord sent Nathan to David" (v. 1a). Nathan bluntly confronts the king with the exact details of his carefully covered-up sin, bringing David to lie on the ground all night in painful remorse.

David wrote: "*When I kept silent, my bones grew old through my groaning all the day long. For day and night Your hand was heavy on me; my vitality was turned into the drought of summer*" (Psalm 32:3-4). His silence about his sin was eating him up, and, in His mercy, the Lord sent Nathan to confront him. David responds by confessing to the Lord. He knows that God is kind and loving. Hebrews 4 tells us that we, too, have access to our loving Father. Through the sacrifice of Christ on the cross, we now have Jesus as our own High Priest, who is able to understand every human frailty though He never sinned. He provides grace for us to "obtain mercy" from our Father in time of need.

Everyone sins. David tried to hide his sin, but he learned "... *be sure your sin will find you out*" (Numbers 32:23)! John wrote, "... *These things I write to you, so that you may not sin. And if anyone sins, we have an Advocate with the Father, Jesus Christ the righteous*" (1 John 2:1). John is talking about our position in Christ and reminding us that our Advocate died for all of our sins, past, present, and future. He's not saying, "Don't worry about having sinned." In fact, John's statement about this is pretty serious: "*And He Himself* [Jesus] *is the propitiation for our sins, and ... for the whole world. Now by this we know that we know Him, if we keep His commandments. He who says, 'I know Him,' and does not keep His commandments, is a liar ... but whoever keeps His word, truly the love of God is perfected in him. By this we know that we are in Him. He who says he abides in Him ought himself also to walk just as He walked*" (1 John 2:2-4).

In other words, the positional righteousness we have in Christ is proved by the practical righteousness we manifest in our lives. If we sin, yes, we are still positionally secure, but we can be rendered ineffective *practically* in the kingdom and lose the joy of our salvation. Those who have been truly born again will keep the Word of God as their guide through life, and if they fall into sin, they will call it what it is. Sin may be kept hidden for a while, but it isn't hidden from God. Sin grieves the Spirit, and when the Spirit is grieved, so is the sinning saint. One's joy is lost or diminished and must be restored through sincere repentance. Don't wait for the Lord to send a Nathan to expose your sin. Confess it now before your Father and enjoy sweet fellowship once again!

April 15

Face First

> [1]Have mercy upon me, O God, according to Your lovingkindness; according to the multitude of Your tender mercies, blot out my transgressions. [2]Wash me thoroughly from my iniquity, and cleanse me from my sin. —*Psalm 51:1-2*

THE TITLE of today's devotional has two meanings. David fell, *face first*, into sin, but in order to restore his joy and usability, there were three things he needed to face first. We'll explore these over the next couple of days. Let's look once more at the situation behind this heart-wrenching psalm. David, the "man after God's own heart" (1 Samuel 13:14; Acts 13:22), had sinned horribly, yet he was trying to act as if nothing had happened. To be honest, what David had done was culturally acceptable to the world, and the world wouldn't judge him, nor should there have been any consequences by their standards. Kings did this kind of thing all the time.

But *God's standards are not the world's standards*, and we must keep our minds centered on His Word and guard against diminishing or doing violence to His commandments. We may *not* adapt or change them to accommodate culture.

Recently, a prominent pastor announced that his position on gay marriage was "evolving." Listen: the Bible doesn't evolve. Absolute truth doesn't evolve. God's Word is absolute and unchanging, and it is the final moral authority over all creation. Yes, we all stumble and even fall face first into things we know better than to do, but as saints, believers in the Living God, we can and should learn how to "face first" the truth and be restored and set free from the weights and sins that so easily beset us. Let's look at the first of three things from David's confession that will help us to understand what we must face first in order to renew our joy and effectiveness.

An important detail about the setting of this event was that David had kept his sin hidden. Or so he thought. Let's look at this again: *"Then the Lord sent Nathan to David"* (2 Samuel 12:1a)!

Isn't our Father faithful? Isn't it awesome how He doesn't allow us to wallow in our sinfulness for too long, even though when, in this case, help arrived through a "Nathan," David surely experienced a moment of horror, realizing that his sin had been found out. The first thing he did, however, which is key, was to immediately confess that he was a sinner and to cry out to the Lord for mercy. Despite the awfulness of the situation, how sweet it is that David knew full well the character and nature of God, in that He is a God of mercy and is loving and kind. God is *approachable*, even to us—even in our sinfulness. How much better it is to go before the Lord in the name of His Son, Jesus, and confess our sin to Him before He has to bring us to the woodshed Himself! Confession is the first thing that we must do if we want our relationship with the Lord restored.

Hebrews 4:14-16 tells us that have a great High Priest, Jesus, who, coming as a Man to earth, understands our weaknesses, being One who was also tempted in all things and yet never once sinned.

And this is where our help lies. As we confess our sin before Him, we can fall face first into His arms because of the mercy and loving kindness of our gracious God.

Have Mercy on Me

³For I acknowledge my transgressions, and my sin is always before me. ⁴Against You, You only, have I sinned, and done this evil in Your sight— that You may be found just when You speak, and blameless when You judge. —*Psalm 51:3-4*

IN YESTERDAY'S reading we saw that David confessed before the Lord, asking Him to blot out his transgressions, to wash him from his iniquity, and to cleanse him from his sin. Now he acknowledges those transgressions before God, indicating that he hadn't been able to get them out of his mind. He confesses that his sin is against God alone—that horrible sin, which had harmed Bathsheba, killed her husband, Uriah, and which ultimately would also result in the death of his infant son. He must confess that he sinned against God because He is our righteous Judge and the only One who can truly forgive our sins. In 1 John 1:9, we read, "*If we confess our sins, He is faithful and just to forgive us our sins and to cleanse us from all unrighteousness.*"

What an amazing thing! The mercy and the lovingkindness of God allow us to approach Him to confess our sins (which means that we agree with Him that we have sinned against *Him*) and repent of them!

God is a God of love. The common grace and mercy of God are experienced by everyone. The rain falls on the just and the unjust under the banner of His common grace. He often gives good things to those who don't deserve them, and He also often withholds from them bad things they do deserve. This is called the "conditional mercy" of God, and it's this mercy that David is seeking. It restores the joy of salvation, blots out sin, delivers from guilt, and renews a steadfast spirit. Listen to this bit of conversation between David and Nathan: "*So David said to Nathan, 'I have sinned against the Lord.' And Nathan said to David, 'The Lord also has put away your sin; you shall not die. However, because . . . you have given great occasion to the enemies of the Lord to blaspheme, the child also who is born to you shall surely die.'*"

Why did God punish the child for David's sin? Listen, this was not punishment. The baby went straight to heaven! He was actually *spared* punishment. David was also spared. Confession and repentance are the keys to unlocking the conditional mercy of God. But there are times when there are still consequences even for forgiven sin. We sometimes pursue God's mercy hoping to avoid His discipline and chastening for unrepentant sin. We can still be eternally secure but must undergo the temporal punishment of God here on earth. What we should never do though is what some try: Let's say someone is committing sexual sin, and he comes to God asking for His mercy and lovingkindness, saying "Forgive me, for I have sinned."

Then he goes back and repeats is sin, and comes back the next day, "Forgive me, for I have sinned," and on and on it goes. What's missing? Repentance! Without repentance, one will receive no mercy and will never change. It's even possible that they aren't really even saved to begin with.

Remember: nothing is hidden from God: *"There is no creature hidden from His sight, but all things are naked and open to the eyes of Him to whom we must give account"* (Hebrews 4:13). It kind of makes you want to think twice before willfully entering into a sinful situation!

April 17

Please Pass the Hyssop

⁵Behold, I was brought forth in iniquity, and in sin my mother conceived me. ⁶Behold, You desire truth in the inward parts, and in the hidden part you will make me to know wisdom. ⁷Purge me with hyssop, and I shall be clean; wash me, and I shall be whiter than snow. ⁸Make me hear joy and gladness, that the bones You have broken may rejoice. ⁹Hide Your face from my sins, and blot out all my iniquities. ¹⁰Create in me a clean heart, O God, and renew a steadfast spirit within me. ¹¹Do not cast me away from Your presence, and do not take Your Holy Spirit from me. ¹²Restore to me the joy of Your salvation, and uphold me by Your generous Spirit. *—Psalm 51:5-12*

GOD HAS a wonderful way of helping us to see who we really are, and it isn't always in the most flattering light. David has reached the point where he sees just who and what he really is, and it's a pretty humbling unveiling for this King of Israel!

He begins by acknowledging that he was conceived and brought forth as a sinner (like all of us). Then he acknowledges that God is the one who initiates change in those who have the same "heart" that He does. You can't get by with committing a sin, coming to the Lord for mercy, sinning again, coming to the Lord *ad nauseam.* You must agree with God that sin is sin and bring a repentant heart that desires to change!

Next he mentions being purged and cleansed with hyssop. A hyssop branch is fuzzy, or hairy, and was used to catch the blood of the Passover lamb in the basin much as a paintbrush grabs paint and is used to paint the door (See Exodus 12:22). David is referring to having his sin purged by blood, and it's the sacrificial blood that's the important thing here, not the instrument with which it was applied. Then he asks the Lord to wash him and make him clean, whiter than snow! He longs to hear the sounds of joy again, which have been stifled due to his unconfessed, unrepentant sin, which he had carried for some time. He even says that it was the Lord who had "broken him" (v.8)!

This brings us to the second key in the restoration process. The first part was to confess (acknowledge) our sin and repent of it. In verse 10, David asks the Lord to *create* in him a clean heart and renewed steadfastness. He has learned a powerful lesson about himself through this heartbreaking experience. He sees himself in all the ugliness and evil of which he is capable. But "Then the Lord sent Nathan to David."

Is God using His Word in your life today? Is He perhaps showing you your sin, of which you haven't repented? Has that been making you feel miserable? Do you want to have the joy of your salvation restored to you? Is there a "Nathan" knocking on your heart? Here's the second key to the door that we must unlock before joy and usability are restored: *God is looking for obedience in the spirit, not apologies from the flesh.* An apology from the flesh is one that is only concerned about the consequences of the sin, not the act of sinning, i.e., "Lord, spare me! Don't let me reap what I've sown!" What the Lord wants to hear is a humble heart saying, "I have sinned against you, God. I know that your judgments are true and righteous altogether, and whatever You do is just."

Saints, God isn't looking for apologies. He's looking for repentance. It's not "to keep you saved"; it's that He wants the saved to repent so they can have joy and be used again! Do you want to "go out with joy and be led out with peace"? You know what you need to do!

April 18

Free Indeed!

¹³Then I will teach transgressors Your ways, and sinners shall be converted to You. ¹⁴Deliver me from the guilt of bloodshed, O God, the God of my salvation, and my tongue shall sing aloud of Your righteousness. ¹⁵O Lord, open my lips, and my mouth shall show forth Your praise. ¹⁶For You do not desire sacrifice, or else I would give it; You do not delight in burnt offering. ¹⁷The sacrifices of God are a broken spirit, a broken and a contrite heart—these, O God, You will not despise. ¹⁸Do good in Your good pleasure to Zion; build the walls of Jerusalem. ¹⁹Then You shall be pleased with the sacrifices of righteousness, with burnt offering and whole burnt offering; then they shall offer bulls on Your altar.
—*Psalm 51:13-19*

TODAY WE'RE GOING to discover the third and final truth we must face as we move forward after repenting of our sin. David describes the importance of confessing and repenting *beyond* our own fleshly desire to avoid embarrassment or punishment (which can nevertheless be useful in preventing future sinful actions). David was guilty of shedding innocent blood when he sent Uriah to the front lines of the battle to be killed. Having confessed his sin to the Lord, he now asks God to deliver him from the awful *guilt* of bloodshed. In truth, God is the only One who can free us from guilt. We'll never be free of our guilt until we're free of our sin. And then we can be truly free indeed in every way.

David knows that God wasn't looking for a ritualistic service as an act of repentance. God can't be bought, nor can restored joy and usability be purchased. He wanted David's heart to be broken over what he had done, of which the greatest consequence was that he'd given God's enemies reason to blaspheme the Lord (2 Samuel 12:14a).

It's sad how seldom we see prominent church leaders and saints who've fallen into sin turn around and face those first difficult steps of restoration. Few seem truly repentant, and even worse is the occasion their sin gives to the enemies of God. Most don't have that broken spirit and contrite heart (v. 17) that David experienced. Instead they seem more ashamed of their personal loss than the fact that they supplied fodder to God's enemies.

David humbly cries to the Lord, "Do good, Lord, for the sake of Your city Zion. Build up what my own actions have torn down." He says, "Then you shall be pleased with the sacrifices and offerings of your servants." Tragically, David's sin had shamed all of Israel as sins of saints today shame the church. This brings us to the final truth we all must "face first" if our joy and restoration after sinning can be made complete, and that is this: *There is nothing more important in life than our witness.* Think about how many families have been devastated by the exposed sin of a prominent church leader. Not only was their own witness destroyed but the lives and witness of their family members has been drastically altered as well. We tend to focus on the embarrassment and consequences for sin, but the most important element of restoring the joy of salvation and the key to removing the guilt is a broken and contrite heart over having given God's enemies the chance to blaspheme (1 Corinthians 9:24-17). Being disqualified for preaching Christ because of our actions is a far greater loss than any other. We all stumble in many things, and sadly, many don't get up after stumbling but repeat the same sin and then ask God for mercy again and again.

God is merciful and loving, but *He is more concerned about His name than yours!* Expecting mercy without confessing and repenting is like covering a huge hole in the floor with a carpet. It might be covered up, but the dangerous hole is still beneath. God is looking for a broken and contrite heart from those who have sinned against Him and disqualified themselves from telling others about Jesus.

We don't have to fall. Every temptation has a way of escape (1 Corinthians 10:13). Find that exit, and get out of there!

Courage Under Fire

Introduction to Psalm 56

[1]To the Chief Musician. Set to "The Silent Dove in Distant Lands." A Michtam of David when the Philistines captured him in Gath.—*Psalm 56:1*

DAVID IS ON THE RUN from King Saul. The four psalms that precede this one bring him to where we find him in our text today. He's experiencing something that we've all struggled with, and that is the dichotomy between the goodness of God and bad things of all sorts. These diametrically opposed realities often occur simultaneously, leading us to situations like David's, where we are filled with discouragement and even fear. Do you remember why David was on the run and is now in the city of Gath to begin with? It was due to betrayal and treachery, even though he had been handpicked by God for the very thing that was causing all of this opposition, which was to be the king of Israel.

It seems that doing God's will is going to bring opposition, which the enemy hopes will morph into *oppression* and its companions, fear and despair. According to 1 Samuel 16:10-13, David was chosen and anointed by God to be king over Israel, but he was opposed and afflicted by man because of that very same calling and choosing. Just to set up the scenario, let's look back a little bit. Psalm 52 records David's contemplation over Doeg the Edomite, who had betrayed him to King Saul in 1 Samuel 22. Psalm 53 is a near-verbatim repeat of Psalm 14, and is the heartfelt lament of a man betrayed by evil men. Psalm 54 is David's contemplation when he was again on the run from King Saul as the Lord's anointed and appointed, and his position was leaked by the people in whose town he was hiding. First Samuel 23 and 26 record the Ziphites' disclosure to King Saul of David's position as he hid in the wilderness. Psalm 55 records the lament of David when his son Absalom rebelled against him, and David's trusted counselor Ahithophel sided with Absalom against David (2 Samuel 15-17). Whew! And you thought you were having a bad day?

King David, this "man after God's own heart," faced external and internal opposition from before he became king until he lay on his deathbed. This psalm and Psalm 34 show that David is in serious physical danger in the capital city of the Philistines. The man of God is on the run in the Goliath's hometown, and whose sword he now carries (1 Samuel 21:10-15).

David fought to maintain courage under fire, even as he struggled under treachery. He was often afraid, and he said so. But he also battled his fears in a way that will help us as we consider that bad things happen to good people, and the enemy has a lot of latitude when it comes to opposing our calling. We must never forget that in Christ we remain more than conquerors, even though we might be afraid sometimes when we find ourselves in the enemy camp where they're saying, "You're a *Christian* and you don't even have victory over the giants in your own life?" Let's learn how to have courage under fire from the exact words of the appointed and anointed of God, who is surrounded by the enemy, who oppose everything that God has called him to do.

April 20

"A Clear and Present Danger"

[1]Be merciful to me, O God, for man would swallow me up; fighting all day he oppresses me. [2]My enemies would hound me all day, for there are many who fight against me, O Most High. [3]Whenever I am afraid, I will trust in You. [4]In God (I will praise His word), in God I have put my trust; I will not fear. What can flesh do to me? *—Psalm 56:1-4*

HERE WE SEE an opportunity to clear up a misconception that if a believer experiences fear it is considered a lapse of faith. According to 2 Timothy 1:7, "*God has not given us a spirit of fear, but of power and of love and of a sound mind.*" This, of course, is true, but it's also true that God has given us a fear *mechanism* for our own safety and wellbeing. The Greek word used in 2 Timothy isn't the word that means terror or fright but it means *cowardice.* You can have fear and not be a coward. Fearing heights isn't a lapse of faith or cowardice. It's a fear of death—not the second death but the first.

Here is King David in Gath, carrying Goliath's sword. He was afraid. But he also battled his primal fear by his faith in God. He's on the run from the man God said he's going to replace. He runs from place to place, only to be betrayed by those who know who he is and what he represents: Saul's replacement.

History has proven over and over that some people are loyal to persons in power simply because they are *in power*, and they hope to gain favor from them. The same thing is true today. God chose David and God chose you. God anointed David, and God has anointed you—maybe not to be king of a nation but to be an heir of the King of kings. Many are they who fight against us. They twist our words and call us "haters" for loving God and respecting His Word. They destroy the businesses and therefore the livelihood of those who, as the called and anointed of God, do not waiver in the truth.

What do we do when we find ourselves in negative circumstances because of our positive stance on the Bible? The first thing to remember is this: Trusting in the truth incapacitates every enemy tactic. David says, "Have mercy, for man would swallow me up. . . . They are many, and I am afraid." In verse three, things turn around, because David says, "In God I have put my trust and will not fear. After all, what can flesh do to me?"

See the transition that began when trust was activated through praise and confidence in God's Word? I'm not saying that trusting in truth incapacitates the enemy, but it does keep the enemy out of your head and emotions, and it incapacitates their ability to create fear. King David seems to have arrived at the conclusion that "Did God not choose me and anoint me, and I have yet to actually be king?" And then he could fall back on what the Lord had promised in Psalm 27:1-4. Listen, no matter what the enemy tries to pull, you're not done until God says you are. The proximity of the enemy and the difficulty of your circumstances might be a clear-and-present danger, but as the called and anointed of God you can trust the outcome into His hands, knowing that it will be His will that is done in your life, and not the enemy's.

If it seems as though a good God and bad things have collided in your life right now, and you need courage under fire, remember this: Trust incapacitates every enemy tactic. That doesn't mean he'll stop trying. It just means his efforts won't succeed in creating fear and spiritual despair. And that's just the news we needed to hear!

April 21

"Facing the Giants"

⁵All day they twist my words; all their thoughts are against me for evil. ⁶They gather together, they hide, they mark my steps, when they lie in wait for my life. ⁷Shall they escape by iniquity? In anger cast down the peoples, O God! ⁸You number my wanderings; put my tears into Your bottle; are they not in Your book? ⁹When I cry out to You, then my enemies will turn back; this I know, because God is for me.
—*Psalm 56:5-9*

IT'S AN AWFUL FEELING to have your words twisted by someone to their own advantage. David is describing just such a situation to the Lord in these verses. He says that his enemies are devising evil against him, setting traps, lying in wait, hoping to hurt and probably even kill him. Even today, those who hate the Lord and

His people continually look for ways to bring them down, discredit them, and lure them into a trap to make them look bad and destroy their ministries.

David cries to the Lord, "Shall they escape the consequences of their wickedness?" He implores God to rise up against them and cast them down in His righteous indignation. David had also written, *"The face of the Lord is against those who do evil. . . . The righteous cry out, and the Lord hears, and delivers them out of all their troubles. The Lord is near to those who have a broken heart, and . . . a contrite spirit. . . . Evil shall slay the wicked. . . . The Lord redeems the soul of His servants, and none . . . who trust in Him shall be condemned"* (Psalm 34:16-22).

We're told to pray for our enemies and do good to those who hate us (Luke 27; Matthew 5:44), but we don't have to pray that our enemies' weapons would prosper against us! We all have enemies. Many of them are enemies of the church and unknown to us individually. It's sad that often the ones who come at us the hardest are people who call themselves Christians. But the Lord knows the thoughts and hearts and motives of all.

David writes that although he'd been frequently on the run, God kept track of his wanderings, both physical and emotional. His tears were numbered and noted by the Lord. Archaeologists have unearthed small "tear bottles" in Israel, in which people would capture their own tears during moments of extreme pressure or grief. In like manner, David is saying that the Lord is grieved by the actions of those who were attacking His anointed one, and that applies to our time as well. Perhaps you've been attacked by loved ones or old friends. They don't approve of the fact that now you're sharing the gospel and people are getting saved. They mock you, twist your words, and hope to take you out of the battle.

There's a somewhat silly expression used today that I can't help but think of when I've experienced situations like this. It causes me to remember the most important thing, and you can use it, too: "Who's your Daddy?" David says to his Father with confidence, "When I cry out to *You,* then my enemies will turn back." He could trust in the divine protection and deliverance from God. And so can we! He is our Abba, our Papa, our Daddy! He watches over our lives with great love and compassion. The Lord said, "I will never leave you nor forsake you" (Hebrews 13:5). Remember, friend, you're not out there facing giants on your own.

There Is a "Happily Ever After"!

¹⁰In God (I will praise His word), in the Lord (I will praise His word), ¹¹In God I have put my trust; I will not be afraid. What can man do to me? ¹²Vows made to You are binding upon me, O God; I will render praises to You, ¹³For You have delivered my soul from death. Have You not kept my feet from falling, that I may walk before God in the light of the living? —Psalm 56:10-13

DAVID'S REVERENCE for the Word of God was obviously a sustaining element in his life, and the same should be said of all of us! He reminds us that ours is a fact-based trust, not a "Fairy Tale trust," as some accuse us of today. David says, "I will praise His word, I will praise His word. In God I have [not "will" but "have"] actively put my trust; I will not be afraid"! On what grounds did David base his faith? He says, "You have delivered my soul from death and kept my feet from falling by giving me a lighted path."

We have to acknowledge the truth that God allows hard things in our lives, but let me add this: Not once has any believer had to face the trials and traumas of life alone. As we continue to look at the topic of Courage under Fire, David's statement about God's deliverance of his soul from death clearly shows us the *eternality* of the human soul. David knew that his soul would not see the Second Death, no matter what the enemy tried to use against him. When it comes to having courage under fire, we need to remember to keep one eye on the enemy and the other on eternity, and in the midst of that, spiritually, to keep both eyes on the Lord.

The apostle Paul, in 2 Corinthians 2 wrote " . . . *if indeed I have forgiven anything, I have forgiven that one for your sakes in the presence of Christ, lest Satan should take advantage of us; for we are not ignorant of his devices*" (vv. 10-11). The opposite of ignorance is awareness, and this negatively stated truth means we are aware of the enemy's devices. We find David here in Gath as the man chosen and anointed of God to be king. There is no way that this could be considered the route to the throne that David would have chosen, just like we, as the chosen and anointed of God, encounter things that we would not expect along the way. So how do we maintain courage under fire?

Trusting in the truth of God will keep the advances of the enemy at bay. Remember who our Almighty God is, and then ask yourself, "Who's your daddy?" Your Daddy is the King of kings and Lord of lords who fights and always wins. Your soul is saved by the blood of His only begotten Son. Since the devil can't rob you of your saved soul, what can flesh or man or Satan actually do to you that is of eternal harm? Nothing! But that doesn't make the enemies around us any less real, although it does make them less threatening.

So how do we handle their presence? By keeping one eye on your enemy and another on eternity. Church, we are under attack, and the enemy is coming in like a flood. We need to have courage under fire, based on faith in the Word of God. Remember who your Daddy is as you keep one eye on your enemies and the other on eternity. It lies before us now. Even so, come quickly, Lord Jesus!

<hr>

April 23

Only God

Introduction to Psalm 62

[To the Chief Musician. To Jeduthun.
A Psalm of David.] —*Psalm 62:1*

WAITING ON THE LORD is often not an easy thing to do. It's entirely different from waiting in line or waiting for a package to arrive. Waiting on the Lord has a much greater element of anticipation involved because the end result is usually expected to be life altering. In this Psalm, David is waiting for divine victory over his enemies. He recognizes that the Lord is going to use him as His instrument in bringing about that victory and trusts that God's working and divine favor will ultimately bring it about.

As we go through this psalm over the next few days, notice that the word "only" appears six times within the twelve verses. In Hebrew, the word can also be translated as "alone" or "surely." There are situations and seasons in life where God is the *only* One who can help us or sustain us or deliver us, and we often find ourselves, like David, waiting for Him to do so.

We see in the introductory notes to this psalm that it is addressed to Jeduthun, one of the choir leaders in the temple, according to 1 Chronicles 16:41-42, and the historical background of the text is unknown (though some have associated it with the rebellion of David's son Absalom, which is likely). Whatever the background, the truth of the message is the same, which is that there are some things that *only God* can do in our lives. Some of them are practical, some are spiritual, and some are emotional, but the common feature among them all is that we must wait for them.

"*But those who wait on the Lord shall renew their strength; they shall mount up with wings like eagles, they shall run and not be weary, they shall walk and not faint*" (Isaiah 40:31). What beautiful, encouraging words! There is much blessing for those who wait patiently upon the Lord to accomplish His will. We have promises from the Father that sometimes we have to wait on Him to accomplish. Our desire, as we wait, should be to develop within our hearts the right attitude during those periods of waiting (which can seem excruciatingly long at times, but we always find that it was well worth the wait).

If you're undergoing a time in which you have no choice but to wait upon the Lord, are you able to wait with eager expectation? The Lord will give us the grace to do just that! Remember these verses from Psalm 34? *"Delight yourself also in the Lord, and He shall give you the desires of your heart. . . . Rest in the Lord, and wait patiently for Him; do not fret because of him who prospers in his way, because of the man who brings wicked schemes to pass. . . . For evildoers shall be cut off; but those who wait on the Lord, they shall inherit the earth. . . . Wait on the Lord, and keep His way, and He shall exalt you to inherit the land. . . ."* (Psalm 37:4, 7, 9, 34).

Let us learn to patiently tarry when only God can do or supply what it is that we need. May He give us wisdom and grace in these things.

April 24

How Long, O Lord?

¹Truly my soul silently waits for God; from Him comes my salvation. ²He only is my rock and my salvation; He is my defense; I shall not be greatly moved. ³How long will you attack a man? You shall be slain, all of you, like a leaning wall and a tottering fence. ⁴They only consult to cast him down from his high position; they delight in lies; they bless with their mouth, but they curse inwardly. Selah —*Psalm 62:1-4*

DAVID OPENS this psalm by describing his current situation of being made to wait upon the Lord. He states that he waits *silently* for God. The word "waits" as translated here describes the attitude of waiting, which incorporates quietness, stillness, or silent trust. It's not always easy (especially for some of us) to wait silently for *anything*! We murmur and complain about the long wait, questioning why this is taking so long. Will there ever even be an answer to our prayer?

David is able to wait silently because he knows his Lord so well, and he remembers that God is his rock, his salvation, and his defense, which enables David to remain immoveable! What is David waiting for? Look at the next verses. He was being attacked and slandered by those who were conspiring to overthrow him as king, a position that the Almighty had given to him. This most likely refers to the Absalom/Ahithophel incident. Listen to the heart and emotions of David as he is faced with these dual betrayals by his son and his trusted counselor: *"Fearfulness and trembling have come upon me, and horror has overwhelmed me. So I said, 'Oh, that I had wings like a dove! I would fly away and be at rest. Indeed, I would wander far off, and remain in the wilderness. I would hasten my escape from the windy storm and tempest.' Destroy, O Lord, and divide their tongues. . . . Day and night they go around [the city] on its walls; iniquity and trouble [and] destruction [are] in its midst; oppression and deceit do not depart from its streets. For it is not an enemy who reproaches me; then I could bear it. Nor is it one who hates me who has exalted himself against me; then I could hide from him. But it was you, a man my equal, my companion and my acquaintance. We took sweet counsel together, and walked to the house of God in the throng"* (Psalm 55:5-14).

You can hear the heartbreak in his words. Have you ever felt like this, where you wanted to just run away and hide until the storm had passed? Sometimes it feels like it's one thing after another and "the hits just keep on comin'!" This brings us to our first reminder that will help to keep our minds and emotions in check when we face a prolonged season of trouble and are waiting on the Lord to tangibly answer our cries. Remember this: *only God* is always perfect in His work *and in His timing.* When you hold onto this, it takes a lot of pressure off of you. God is handling this situation, and you are safe in Him. Sometimes we feel like, "Okay, Lord, I'm pretty sure that this is the right time for you to step in. I'm waiting. . . . Did you hear me?" But God does what is perfect at the perfect time—every time!

David says in our verses today that God only is his rock and salvation. So what is one to do? Peter wrote: "Therefore humble yourselves under the mighty hand of God, that He may exalt you in *due time*, casting all your care upon Him, for He cares for you" (1 Peter 1:6; emphasis added). Only God is always perfect at what He does and when He does it. Wait for God, and see His great salvation, no matter how long it takes.

God Is Not Your Genie

⁵My soul, wait silently for God alone, for my expectation is from Him. ⁶He only is my rock and my salvation; He is my defense; I shall not be moved. ⁷In God is my salvation and my glory; the rock of my strength, and my refuge, is in God. ⁸Trust in Him at all times, you people; pour out your heart before Him; God is a refuge for us. Selah —*Psalm 62:5-8*

YESTERDAY WE SAW in verse one that as David waited on the Lord, he remained in quietness and silent trust. As he moves forward with his song, we again find him encouraging himself to wait silently, only this time the translation for "silence" indicates astonishment, or the inability to even speak. We would say that he is "aghast" at his situation, yet he will wait expectantly for his Lord, knowing that God is his only Rock and salvation and, therefore, David will not be moved. He calls God his salvation and his glory, and refers to Him as his strength and refuge.

What faith David has! Even though he is still stuck in this mode of having no alternative but to wait for the Lord, he has steadfast determination to hold onto what he already knows and believes about his Father. He is able to look back and also to look ahead expectantly, knowing that God *will* do astonishing things on his behalf, as He has before, and so he waits for Him to move.

In Psalm 27 David wrote, "*I would have lost heart, unless I had believed that I would see the goodness of the Lord in the land of the living. Wait on the Lord; be of good courage, and He shall strengthen your heart; wait, I say, on the Lord!*" (vv. 13-14).

Sometimes our thoughts about what God is able to do are too small and we expect too little from Him. We are put in the position of having to wait, but as we wait we think of a million ways that God *could* provide or deliver. "Maybe God wants me to buy a lottery ticket, and I'll win, and all my money problems will be over!"

Don't try to tie God's hands. He created the universe. He doesn't need your assistance! Remember this: *Only God* can see the outcome of all things beforehand. We can't. Can you see beyond this moment in time and know for certain what would happen if God were to act like your personal genie instead of like Jehovah that He is? I would imagine that we've all prayed for things that would have been disastrous down the road had not God, in His loving omniscience, said "NO!" As with David, God is our refuge, our Protector!

Philippians 1:6-7: "*Be anxious for nothing, but in everything by prayer and supplication, with thanksgiving, let your requests be made known to God; and the peace of God, which surpasses all understanding, will guard your hearts and minds through Christ Jesus.*"

Friend, know this: We are to pray with expectancy *and* thanksgiving, knowing that the divine response to our cries and petitions will be perfectly timed and appropriately proportioned and weighed in the light of all the possible outcomes, and God's *best* for your good and His glory will be the end result! Don't get hung up on trying to figure out the "how" and "when" and "what." Only God is perfect and will bring about what is the perfect answer regarding our deliverance, provision, and victory. Trust Him! He is going to astonish us all with what He does. David cried, "God is my refuge." And do you know what? He is ours, too! Praise His name!

Money Can't Buy Me . . . Peace

⁹Surely men of low degree are a vapor, and men of high degree are a lie: if they are weighed on the scales, they are altogether lighter than vapor. ¹⁰Do not trust in oppression, nor vainly hope in robbery; if riches increase, do not set your heart on them. ¹¹God has spoken once, twice I have heard this: that power belongs to God. ¹²Also to You, O lord, belongs mercy; for You render to each one according to his work. —Psalm 62:9-12

WE LEARN HERE that the rich and the poor are equal. In what way? David says that both of them are only vapors! A vapor appears as a mist and evaporates rapidly. He's saying that, likewise, the substance of even rich men who don't know the Lord is of no value in this life. Many of the rich were oppressors of the poor; many of the poor were robbers of the rich. He adds that if you're blessed with riches, don't take credit for that. In fact, beware of putting too much trust in your wealth. You've heard the old adage "Money talks." Indeed it does, and it usually says, "Goodbye!"

David puts the focus back onto the Lord, saying, "Power belongs to God, and He renders to each according to their works." In Psalm 49:6-13, we find a more detailed explanation of this: "*Those who trust in their wealth and boast in the multitude of their riches, none of them can by any means redeem his brother, nor give to God a ransom for him—for the redemption of their souls in costly, and it shall cease forever—that he should continue to live eternally, and not see the Pit. For he sees wise men die; likewise the fool and the senseless person perish, and leave their wealth to others. Their inner thought is that their houses will last forever, their dwelling places to all generations; they call their lands after their own names. Nevertheless man, though in honor, does not remain; he is like the beasts that perish. This is the way of those who are foolish, and of their posterity who approve their sayings.*"

What David is saying here is that money may buy you a house, but it can't make it a home. Money can't do for you what must be done by God. It can't redeem a soul; it can't redeem a relationship; it can't justify one before God, and it's not evidence that you've obtained His favor. Power-hungry Absalom and Ahithophel may indeed be the ones in view here, but the same is true no matter what names we might fill in. Earthly riches fall far short of the riches we have in Christ. Is anything too great or difficult for our God? Philippians tells us, "*My God shall supply all your need according to His riches in glory by Christ Jesus. Now to our God and Father be glory forever and ever. Amen.*" Look at the connection between riches and God's glory. Riches should be something that we realize are from the Father, and all the glory for them should be given to Him! Most people think it's because of their personal achievement and look down on others, forgetting that their ability to earn riches at all comes from the Lord.

Meanwhile, the poor often allow their poverty to justify stealing from or carrying grudging attitudes towards those who have more than they. In truth, both groups need to remember that *only God* has a standard of measure by which He will judge the world. And guess what? Money has nothing to do with it! Even though we'll be judged for what we do with what we have, money is of no value to God! David says it's not the amount of riches that God will judge one for. It is by His own perfect standard of moral purity and what will bring Him glory. The result will be rewards for those who love Him for what He did in dying on the cross for their sins, and eternal judgment for those who refused to accept His gift of salvation, worth more than all the treasures in the world! The Lord gives, and the Lord takes away. Can we, like Job, say, regardless, "Blessed be the name of the Lord?" It's certainly a thought worth considering.

April 27

Streams in the Desert

Introduction to Psalm 63

A Psalm of David when he was in the wilderness of Judah.

AS WE GO through this psalm, David's words will help us to learn how to deal with a particular Christian life experience that's common to believers everywhere. The duration of it may vary from person to person and instance to instance, but we've all experienced it.

King David is writing this when he is in the wilderness of Judah. We could truthfully say that we know where David was, but we don't know exactly why he was there. I'm pretty sure that the same is often true for us. The seasons of life, which we are going to address over the next few days, come without cause many times, but they do come nonetheless. We may find ourselves in a situation similar to David's, and although we may not know why he was in the wilderness, he certainly knew.

The psalmist who wrote Psalm 102 stated it well: *"Hear my prayer, O Lord, and let my cry come to You. Do not hide Your face from me in the day of my trouble; incline Your ear to me; in the day that I call, answer me speedily. For my days are consumed like smoke, and my bones are burned like a hearth. My heart is stricken and withered like grass, so that I forget to eat my bread. Because of the sound of my groaning my bones cling to my skin. I am like a pelican of the wilderness; I am like an owl of the desert. I lie awake, and am like a sparrow alone on the housetop"* (vv. 1-7).

Have you ever felt like that? You're sailing along through life, and then one day, out of nowhere, spiritually you feel like a piece of dried toast. There may or may not be an identifiable cause, leaving you wondering where the Lord is. Does He hear your prayers? You feel discouraged and may not feel like reading the Word, thus abandoning the spiritual food that you so desperately need.

The truth about today's psalm is that it doesn't matter who or what sent David into the wilderness of Judah in the Dead Sea area. The psalm doesn't record his escape or the closing chapter to this trial. Regardless of why he's there, or how he got out of there, the lesson is about *what we are to do when we find ourselves in a dry and thirsty land.*

The title of today's reading and the theme for our study of this psalm is "Streams in the Desert," like the popular devotional book by Charles Cowman, who took the title from Isaiah 35:3-7: "*Strengthen the weak hands . . . make firm the feeble knees. Say to those who are fearful-hearted, 'Be strong, do not fear! Behold, your God will come with vengeance. . . . He will come and save you.' . . . The eyes of the blind shall be opened, and the ears of the deaf shall be unstopped. Then the lame shall leap like a deer, and the tongue of the dumb sing. For waters shall burst forth in the wilderness, and streams in the desert. The parched ground shall become a pool, and the thirsty land springs of water. . . .*"

Perhaps this is your prayer today: "Lord, I'm in a dry place, and I either do or don't know why or what brought me here, but I do know this: I'm ready to be delivered." Never forget that God calms the storm, or He may calm the one in the storm, allowing the storm to rage. Sometimes He delivers from the wilderness, and other times he provides streams in the desert until He delivers. Sometimes our dryness comes from unrepentant sin, which grieves the Holy Spirit. If that's the case, the burden is on your own shoulders. Repent and be set free (Acts 3:19)! The Lord will refresh you. And if you're living, loving, and serving the Lord but suddenly find yourself in a spiritual wilderness, this psalm will be your guide to finding streams in the desert.

Divine Refreshing

¹O God, You are my God; early will I seek You; my soul thirsts for You; my flesh longs for You in a dry and thirsty land where there is no water. ²So I have looked for You in the sanctuary, to see Your power and Your glory. ³Because Your lovingkindness is better than life, my lips shall praise You. —Psalm 63:1-3

THE OPENING VERSES of this psalm are replete with wisdom regarding locating streams in the desert. The first tip is in verse one. David recognizes that his physical situation has created his spiritual dryness, and thus he declares that God is the God of dry places as well as of palaces. He shares a nugget of wisdom when he says, "*Early* will I seek you." Maybe this dry time came out of nowhere, but meanwhile, what do you do?

Perhaps your dryness is due to your circumstances. Maybe it was a personal loss or an extended trial. It might be an unfair situation that doesn't make any sense. But whether the cause is known or not, our marching orders are reflected by "Early will I seek You!" Seek God! He hasn't forsaken you. "*For I know the thoughts that I think toward you, says the Lord, thoughts of peace and not of evil, to give you a future and a hope. . . . Call upon Me, and go and pray to Me, and I will listen to you. And you will seek Me and find Me, when you search for Me with all your heart*" (Jer 29:10-13).

David knew that he was in a place of physical dryness and thirst, which also contributes to the cause of spiritual dryness and thirst, so he began to look for God first in the sanctuary. He longs to see God's power and glory. Too often, we tend to look for the exit from our situation, not for the streams that run through it. "Sanctuary" means a sacred place or thing, something consecrated, dedicated, hallowed, holy. David was looking for a way to make this dry place a sacred place. Can we do the same?

Consider Jacob's experience. On the run from his brother, Esau, having been sent by his father to find a bride among his own people, he falls asleep in the desert and dreams of a ladder with angels going up and down on it. In the dream, the Lord promises that He will be with him, and there, with a rock for a pillow, he arises in the morning saying, "God is with me in this place" (Gen 28:16-19). Are you in a "desert" right now? God's *perfect will* for your life may include wilderness experiences in dry and thirsty lands! He allows and even causes these times in our lives to create trust and endurance and to show us that He alone is our sanctuary. The heart of God and His desire for us is this: "*Seek first the kingdom of God and His righteousness, and all these things shall be added unto you.*

Therefore, do not worry about tomorrow, for tomorrow will worry about its own things. Sufficient for the day is its own trouble" (Mat 6:33-34).

Whether you know the cause of your dry season or not, you must search for those streams in the desert and not merely for the way of escape. Divine refreshing doesn't require a change in circumstances. Through David, God says, "Seek me early and look for Me, for I am the stream in the desert of life that will refresh you until things change." Are you able to see Him in this way, not only as your Deliverer but also as your Provider and Sustainer even in the midst of your difficult situation? The Lord says through David, "Seek Me early. Look for me. For I am the stream in the desert of life that will refresh you until things do change." God has not forsaken you. Go to the stream and wait for Him there.

April 29

An Attitude of Gratitude

⁴Thus I will bless You while I live; I will lift up my hands in Your name. ⁵My soul shall be satisfied as with marrow and fatness, and my mouth shall praise You with joyful lips. ⁶When I remember You on my bed, I meditate on You in the night watches. ⁷Because You have been my help, therefore in the shadow of Your wings I will rejoice. —*Psalm 63:4-7*

DAVID MAKES the point once again of the importance of praising God during times of trial, *even when* words seem empty and the night hours are spent in sleeplessness, and the desert experience continues on into the day without relief.

He writes: "I will bless You . . . I will lift up my hands in Your name. . . . My mouth will praise you with *joyful* lips." In the middle of this dry place, he mentions being satisfied as with marrow and fatness, figurative terms for feasting or bounty. He finds reason to rejoice in the knowledge that God is still caring for him and seeing him through this trial. Remember, David is in the wilderness of Judah. It's hot. He's thirsty in body and soul, but he doesn't first go looking for water for his flesh but for that which will water his soul. And this is why he can lift up his hands in praise.

We may well wonder where he finds the desire and ability to do this under his present circumstances. He meditates, remembering that God has *always* been his help. Now, in the shadows of the night that bring relief from the scorching sun, he meditates on God's love and goodness as he rests in the shadow of His wings.

Sometimes during those night watches we may think about things that frighten us and cause us to question God. Those things are certainly out there, but David tells us that when we're in the wilderness, the best action we can take is to look to the God of Judah, the Lion of the tribe of Judah, and allow our souls to follow closely after Him.

When you find yourself in one of these desert experiences, remember this: Some things can be learned only during those dry seasons. Have you ever toured a cave or a mine that was well lit, and then, while you're deep in its recesses, the guide turns out the lights, and it becomes so dark that you literally can't see your hand in front of your face? Then he lights a match, and the entire cave is illuminated by that one tiny light!

The same is true for our lives when it comes to God's manifested power, whether it's the power to deliver or to comfort or anything else. We find that power highlighted during the difficult and dry seasons in which we find ourselves. How many testimonies have you heard of God pouring out His love and care and protection during a time when someone felt like they were passing through the floodwaters but knew that He was holding them closely to Himself *through* it all?

Some things can be learned only through the dry times of life. God loves you, no matter how you feel. He knows everything about you (see Ps 139:6-12). John wrote, "God is light and in Him is no darkness at all" (1 John 1:5). Sometimes, He allows situations to come into our lives that create a thirst for Him because He wants to lead us to those streams in the desert where we will find Him and find refreshment for our souls. Although we must search for those streams, they aren't hard to find. Look for the Lord! Praise Him, and you'll find His hand ready to help in whatever way you need it. He'll guide you and satisfy your thirsty soul in the drought. You will be like a watered garden, a spring whose waters do not fail. Wait for the Lord, and while you're waiting, remember to look for those waters and serve Him, even in the desert places.

April 30

The Things Not Seen

8My soul follows close behind You; Your right hand upholds me. 9But those who seek my life, to destroy it, shall go into the lower parts of the earth. 10They shall fall by the sword; they shall be a portion for jackals. 11But the king shall rejoice in God; everyone who swears by Him shall glory; but the mouth of those who speak lies shall be stopped. —Psalm 63:8-11

AS WE CLOSE out our time in this psalm today, David is still on the run in a hot, dry, and thirsty place, both in his flesh and in his spirit. He states that even while his soul follows closely behind the Lord, his enemies are closing in on him with the intent of killing him. But David has confidence that those who pursue him will meet their end, and he himself will be saved.

It's often the things not seen that are the most important to reflect upon. The apostle Paul wrote to the Corinthians: *"For our light affliction, which is but for a moment, is working for us a far more exceeding and eternal weight of glory, while we do not look at the things which are seen, but at the things which are not seen. For the things which are seen are temporary, but the things which are not seen are eternal"* (2 Cor 4:17-18).

Always remember this (especially during the dry times of life): Every difficulty in life is only temporary. Heaven lies before the believer no matter what hell one may have to endure in this life. I talk about heaven a lot, but can you think of a better subject? It's a place where we'll live forever, a place where there will be no death, sorrow, sickness, or crying, and where nothing that causes those things can enter. We must also remember that all those who have not repented of their sins will one day stand before God and give an account of their lives to the One who created them.

David maintains that although he is in a very dry place, the Lord will be his stream in the desert. His situation is tough right now, but it's only temporary. Those who seek to destroy him and are telling lies about him may have impacted him for the moment, but not for long. When our own dry times come, look to the Lord alone as your sanctuary! A change in circumstances doesn't necessarily assure times of refreshing, even though they may feel a little more comfortable. The best time to view God's glory is during those seasons when situations in our lives seem the worst. Stay close to the Lord, and remember that whatever you're going through, it's only temporary!

In the Gospel of Mark, chapter 45, verses 35-41 Jesus told the apostles one evening, "Let us cross over to the other side" of the lake. As they began to cross, a great windstorm arose, "and the waves beat into the boat, so that it was already filling." And where was Jesus? "He was in the stern, asleep on a pillow." Alarmed, the apostles woke him up, saying, "Teacher, do you not care that we are perishing?" We are told that Jesus arose, rebuked the wind, and said to the sea, "Peace, be still!" The wind immediately ceased and everything grew calm. The disciples then said to one another, "Who can this be, that even the wind and the sea obey Him!" Who, indeed?

This is the same Jesus who tells us to "get into the boat. We're going over to the other side. Whatever we go through on this journey, remember that it's only temporary, and I am with you." There are streams in the desert, and if you know where and how to find them, the desert experiences of life won't be absent of divine light. In fact, the light will be more vivid then than at any other time! Enduring until the end isn't easy, but enduring is best done by remembering that this situation will have an end. The Lord is with us.

MAY

How Great Is Our God

1 [To the chief Musician. A Song. A Psalm] Make a joyful shout to God, all the earth! *2* Sing out the honor of His name; make His praise glorious. *3* Say to God, "How awesome are Your works! Through the greatness of Your power Your enemies shall submit themselves to You. *4* All the earth shall worship You, and sing praises to You; they shall sing praises to Your name." Selah —*Psalm 66:1-4*

WE AREN'T GIVEN much information about the backdrop of this psalm, although there's a hint of internal evidence that it may be attributed to David.

Our title, "How Great Is Our God," although an exclamation, could also be a rhetorical question, since no one can really give an answer that would satisfy. Anything we might say would fall far short of His greatness and leave much about Him unsaid. We will, however, attempt to scratch the surface in describing God as we go through our psalm and as we find five reminders of His greatness in our text.

Of course, this won't be a Top 5 list, because God's attributes are unparalleled in scope and majesty. For example, He's the King of kings, and Lord of lords; He's the Maker of heaven and earth; He rides the clouds; He is love; He is the Authority over all creation; He is our Savior, our Redeemer, our Deliverer, and our Provider. There is so much more that could be said!

The greatness of our God is placed in full view for us in these verses as we're told that all the earth shall worship Him. We're reminded that every knee will bow and every tongue will confess that Jesus Christ is Lord. Even His enemies will submit themselves to Him! This will be an unwilling submission and admission, however, as they are forced to confess that He is who He said He is and has been since time began. This submission will be the opposite of the joyful shout to the God of all the earth and the singing out in honor of His name. Nonetheless, *everyone* will bow before Him one day, in the literal sense—some with joyful shouts of praise and adoration, and others with forced submission and disdain.

As we begin to answer the question, "How great is our God?" let's begin with just one point: *All of creation is subject to Him*. This may seem overly simplistic, but let me explain. There seems to be a mindset today that if you don't believe God or believe in God, He'll just go away and leave you alone, letting you go your own merry way. Not so! Our God is so great that all creation will be subject to Him, not only those who want to be. Everyone and everything will worship Him, some sincerely and joyfully, and others out of forced obeisance.

Worship means to prostrate oneself in *submission*. Belief is irrelevant when it comes to the greatness of our God. He is so great that *all creation* is subject to Him and all will bow before Him one day. One group will do so with exceeding joy; the other in disgust. But they will bow, nonetheless. Personally, I've chosen to be on the winning side and to submit to Him willingly and joyfully, in the light of all that He has delivered me from and for which He has forgiven me. It's good to reflect on these things and realize where we do indeed stand. Remember to pray for those around you who still may not understand the seriousness of this "choosing of sides."

May 2

Together Forever!

> [5]Come and see the works of God: He is awesome in His doing toward the sons of men. [6]He turned the sea into dry land; they went through the river on foot: there we will rejoice in Him. [7]He rules by His power forever; His eyes observe the nations; do not let the rebellious exall themselves. Selah. —*Psalm 66:5-7*

THE AUTHOR of these words makes an important point that is often overlooked as he reminds the reader of the awesome works of God toward the sons of men. He uses the partings of the Red Sea and the Jordan River as evidence of the lengths to which our God will go for the sake of His people. When the verse reads "sons of men" here, in the Hebrew "men" means "Adam." It's significant that the Holy Spirit chose to use this word instead of "Israel," which would limit the scope of the text. By using "Adam," He invites all of us to recall the incredible doings of God toward *all* the descendants of Adam.

Our psalms over the past few weeks have been very practical, teaching us how to wait on the Lord with a proper heart and attitude and also what we should do when those dry seasons encroach upon our lives. We must admit our own tendency to overlook the acts of God on our behalf in the past while waiting for Him to act in the present. It might be that you need a "Red Sea" experience this morning, or you're waiting for the swollen waters of the Jordan River to stand up in a heap so that you may cross over on dry ground to safety. Our great God can and does do such things, but never forget that He does them for people and not as a performance.

If you're waiting for a miracle, please remember this truth: God loves us enough to prove His love for us. In what way, you ask? In that He has already swallowed up our great enemy, Death, and has made a way for us to cross over into the Promised Land.

Romans 5:8-9 tells us, "*But God demonstrates His own love toward us, in that while we were still sinners, Christ died for us. Much more then, having now been justified by His blood, we shall be saved from wrath through Him.*" Just as the rebellious Egyptian army was not allowed to exalt themselves above the will of God as they pursued His people through the parted sea, neither will your enemies' plans prevail over you. You are the Lord's, and nothing can separate you from the love of God or snatch you from the Father's hand.

"*When you pass through the waters* [which you may have to do], *I will be with you; and through the rivers, they shall not overflow you. When you walk through the fire, you shall not be burned, nor shall the flame scorch you. For I am the Lord your God, the Holy One of Israel, your Savior . . .*" (Isaiah 43:2-3a).

Hold on to these precious words, which could be companions to these in the New Testament as well: "*I am persuaded that neither death nor life, nor angels nor principalities nor powers, nor things present nor things to come, nor height nor depth, nor any other created thing, shall be able to separate us from the love of God which is in Christ Jesus our Lord*" (Romans 8:38-39).

Let's begin our day with praise to our great God who loved us so much that He sent His precious Son to die in our place that we might live with Him forever!

What Wondrous Love Is This?

8Oh, bless our God, you peoples! And make the voice of His praise to be heard, 9Who keeps our soul among the living, and does not allow our feet to be moved. 10For You, O God, have tested us; You have refined us as silver is refined. 11You brought us into the net; You laid affliction on our backs. 12You have caused men to ride over our heads; we went through fire and through water; but You brought us out to rich fulfill-ment. —Psalm 66:8-12

IN OUR TIMES, it seems as though love, even God's love, is defined as one that accepts everything that one does or sees as right in their own eyes. It's necessary for us to be reminded that within the scope of ultimate, demonstrated love, there must also be testing and loving discipline. Some people seem to be under the impression that if God loves us, He should let us do whatever we want and not "force" any moral code upon us. If one believes this, they hold a dangerously low view of God.

Real love has a refining element within it. We all make adaptations within our personal relationships in the way we show our love, particularly with our children. Why, then, should we have a hard time accepting that there must be corrective behavioral adaptations between oneself and God? Sometimes true love involves discipline, and the same is true when it comes to God's loving discipline of His children. *"My son, do not despise the chastening of the Lord, nor be discouraged when you are rebuked by Him, for whom the Lord loves He chastens, and scourges every son whom He receives. . . . But if you are without chastening . . . then you are illegitimate and not sons . . ."* (Hebrews 12:5-11).

In fact, the discipline of God toward His children is *proof* of His great love for us. His discipline is one means of not only preventing us from sinning again in that way, but it is also often a means of saving our lives as well! God's love for us is so great that He wants to see us grow in our faith and love and trust for Him as He tests and refines us through the trials of this life. There will be times of affliction and persecution, perhaps even through fire and water, that through all of these we may be brought into the glorious ultimate fulfillment of His plan for our lives.

Please keep in mind that God gains nothing by saving us. It doesn't improve Him, because He is already perfect. He isn't fulfilled by it, because He is the source of all fulfillment. The hard things that He allows to come into our lives are *for our betterment, not for His!* We may wonder why He needs to refine and test us at all once we belong to Him. Listen, we must never begin to believe that here on this earth we are perfect. Perfection would need to be conformed into the image of

Christ. But God can work all things together for His glory and for our benefit. Yes, we have an obligation to Him to grow and become conformed into His image, but we must not despise His discipline in our lives as He works to bring about that same truth.

Folks, we're told to resist the devil, not to resist the Lord. God *will* test you and refine you if you belong to Him. He doesn't do it for fun or just because He can. He does it because He loves you beyond anything you could ever imagine, and He wants to bring you out into rich fulfillment in Christ. What wondrous love is this!

May 4

"Working Out" Our Salvation

¹³I will go into Your house with burnt offerings; I will pay You my vows, ¹⁴which my lips have uttered and my mouth has spoken when I was in trouble. ¹⁵I will offer You burnt sacrifices of fat animals, with the sweet aroma of rams; I will offer bulls with goats. Selah *—Psalm 66:13-15*

WE CONTINUE with this psalm by an unidentified author about whom we know little. One thing we do know is that it was written by a Jew who lives under the ceremonial Law of Moses. And here's where I personally find evidence indicating that perhaps David is the author, due to the repeated phrase, "pay my vows." This expression is common in his writings and usually points to commitments that he made to the Lord when he was on the run or when he feigned madness in the city of Gath.

We do know that David wrote Psalm 51, in which he said, "*Deliver me from the guilt of bloodshed, O . . . God of my salvation, and my tongue shall sing aloud of Your righteousness. . . . You O God, do not desire sacrifice, or else I would give it. . . . The sacrifices of God are a broken spirit, a broken and a contrite heart—these, O God, You will not despise*" (vv. 14-19).

In those verses, David has confessed his sin against the Lord with Bathsheba, revealing that he well understood that God wasn't looking for some religious activity from him but rather brokenness over his sin. Even so, he didn't forsake his vows and sacrificial offerings, although they weren't the Lord's primary concern. And the same is true for us! Yes, we should go to church, but that won't save us. Yes, we should give to the Lord, but that won't get us into heaven. Yes, we should serve the Lord, but works won't gain salvation for anyone. So what's the point of works at all? We serve Him because we love Him! Philippians 2:12 tells us to "*work out your own salvation with fear and trembling.*" Paul wasn't telling us that we can work for our salvation, but we are to work before the Lord to do the things that He has asked us to do, based on the generosity of His great salvation, which He has provided, and to show our love for Him!

Keep in mind that no one will *ever* regret having served God. In fact, I think that one day we will all regret not having served Him more. When we look back at how much the Lord has brought us through, in spite of all the "inconveniences" and personal sacrifices of serving Him and the ridicule and persecution we may have to endure, I seriously doubt that any of us will regret it. Paul wrote, "*For we must all appear before the judgment seat of Christ, that each one may receive the things done in the body, according to what he has done, whether good or bad*" (2 Cor 5:10). I'm pretty sure that no one standing before the Lord is going to be wishing that they had taken more vacations or that they hadn't spent so much time serving the Lord because they had "missed so much." In fact, this psalmist reminds us that even the *rituals of service* from a heart that is right in the eyes of God are a sweet-smelling aroma to Him.

Why do some balk at the idea of obeying God? This is easily remedied by looking back on His proven love to mankind through His sacrifice on the cross and His displays of miraculous power. God saves us by the blood of His own Son, He gives us the Holy Spirit to empower us to serve Him, He gives us the ability to obey His commands by that power, and He stirs our hearts for love and good works that we might serve Him by serving others. And then He rewards us for what He did through us! And that is how, as His children, we work out what He has worked in us already. Hallelujah!

May 5

Unanswered Prayer?

*16*Come and hear, all you who fear God, and I will declare what He has done for my soul. *17*I cried to Him with my mouth, and He was extolled with my tongue. *18*If I regard iniquity in my heart, the Lord will not hear. *19*But certainly God has heard me; He has attended to the voice of my prayer. *20*Blessed be God, who has not turned away my prayer, nor His mercy from me! —*Psalm 66:16-20*

DO YOU EVER stop to think of all that the Lord has done for your soul? The state of our soul is of the utmost importance to our God, and so it should be of concern to us. It's a sad truth that many today have lost sight of the fact that God is more interested in our holiness than in our happiness. Happiness is an emotion that's based primarily upon our circumstances. It is fickle and fleeting and subject to change when our situation changes. "Cheer today, gone tomorrow," we might say.

God's work on us goes far deeper than the fleshly realm of happiness and materialism that we "feel." This psalmist tells us that it is this *deep* work of God that he will declare to those who fear the Lord. He describes the heartfelt passion with which he cried out to the Lord, whom he extolled with his mouth. Verse 18 is pivotal to this passage because it warns us that God may disregard our prayers! This refutes the mindset of today that "the Man upstairs" is sitting there in heaven waiting for instructions from earth on how to bless and perform for his children.

In Psalm 119:156-60, King David praises God's tender mercies, His truthfulness, His lovingkindness, and he views the acts of many who disparage and diminish the Word of God as a treacherous and disgusting practice. How sad that many in the so-called church of today are doing that very thing! This is the tactic of Satan, and it has been so since the Garden of Eden, causing people to question the inspiration and infallibility of the Word of God.

In our Psalm 66 today, the writer says, "*If I regard iniquity in my heart, the Lord will not hear me.*" What he is saying is "If I disregard the Bible's definition of morality and spirituality, my prayers won't be heard." His conscience is clear in this regard, as he continues with "But certainly God has heard me. . . ." God has not hidden His will from us, folks. Many today try to make God out to be unfair in His dealings with us, but the exact opposite is true. God knows that it would be unfair to hide His will from us and leave us guessing as to what He wants from us, and we wouldn't even know He was displeased until we stood before Him. Romans 1:16-17 tells us that Paul is "*not ashamed of the gospel of Christ, for it is the power of God to salvation for everyone who believes. . . . [A]s it is written, 'The just shall live by faith.'*" Faith is not a power in and of itself, but it must be attached to an objective reality, and in this case that is the Word of God.

How great is our God! He hasn't hidden His will from us. He's told us up front that He desires to save us, and through His Word we read why we need saving in the first place and how we can become His child! "Blessed be God!" cries the Psalmist, "who has not turned away [our] prayers nor His mercy from [us]." God loves us enough to warn us of the consequences of turning to the world, choosing darkness instead of His marvelous light where we will be guided and protected by His Word. And when we are obedient to do those things that please Him, He will hear and answer our prayers.

Reasons to Sing

Introduction to Psalm 67

To the Chief Musician. On stringed instruments. A Psalm. A Song.

WE'RE TAKING a look at another anonymously written psalm today, and although we know that the Holy Spirit is the inspiration behind the writing of all Scripture, the human author is useful in providing an understanding of the history behind the psalm, book, or epistle. In this case, the authorship is particularly significant because the content isn't directed or limited to one person, nor is there any one historical or prophetic setting where it might be more relevant.

Psalm 19:1-4 states, "*The heavens declare the glory of God; and the firmament shows His handiwork. Day unto day utters speech, and night unto night reveals knowledge. There is no speech or language where their voice is not heard. Their line has gone out through all the earth, and their words to the end of the world.*" Just as the heavens give evidence of the creative majesty of God, declaring His existence to the world in *all seasons* of history, so, too, our psalm today is generic in that it is always applicable no matter our circumstances or season of history, including the times in which we now live.

But even when our nation is falling apart, and good is called "evil" and evil "good," when the world is spiraling toward the Tribulation at breakneck speed, when culture has become so corrupt that it has no moral compass, or it has become so delusional that evil is practiced and protected by the majority—*even then*, we still have and always will have *reasons to sing*.

Do you remember in the book of Acts, when Paul and Silas were arrested for delivering the demon-possessed slave girl of an evil spirit? They were beaten with "many stripes," thrown into prison, locked up, and their feet were fastened in the stocks. Such a shameful, painful situation they were in! So did they protest that they were innocent? Did they curse the ones who had beaten them and locked them up? The Bible says that "*at midnight Paul and Silas were praying and singing hymns to God, and the prisoners were listening to them*" (Acts 16:25).

In our flesh, it would seem as if they had every right to complain and groan against their captivity. Locked up in the stocks, one would understand if they were weeping and moaning in pain. They had reason to cry to God that they were being unfairly treated in *His name*! But what did they do?" They maintained their focus on their *reason* to sing, and then, "*There was a great earthquake, so that the foundations of the prison were opened and everyone's chains were loosed*" (v. 26)

Do any of you need an earthshaking deliverance, doors to open, chains to be loosed? Our God is able, and He can do those things today! One day, He will do them for all and forever, but until then we still have reasons to sing.

Not all of the psalms are actually songs, but this one is identified as such and is addressed to the Chief Temple Musician to incorporate into the Temple worship. Let's be looking for our own reasons to sing, both in this psalm and also in our lives as we go through these verses the next few days as living temples of the Holy Spirit.

May 7

In the World but Not of It

¹God be merciful to us and bless us, and cause His face to shine upon us, Selah ²that Your way may be known on earth, Your salvation among all nations. —Psalm 67:1-2

WHAT WAS TRUE in 1000 BC is still true today: the Word of God itself is an unequaled source of inspired lyrics for hymns and songs. The writer of this psalm looks back on Israel's recorded history, drawing from the book of Numbers for his opening stanza: "*The Lord bless you and keep you; the Lord make His face to shine upon you . . . and give you peace*" (Numbers 6:22-27).

The Lord is our Provider, our Strength, our Healer, Deliverer, Protector, Redeemer, Defender, and Savior, who crowns us with tender mercies (Psalm 103:1-5). Why does He do all of these things? So "*that His ways may be known in all the earth and His salvation to all nations,*" according to our Scripture for today.

As we look at the first verse of this psalm above, we see that it begins with a petition for mercy. This is inspiration for singing, because we know that we can always count on the tender mercies of God in our lives. Hallelujah! Jeremiah wrote: "*This I recall to mind, therefore I have hope. Through the Lord's mercies we are not consumed, because His compassions fail not. They are new every morning; great is Your faithfulness. 'The Lord is my portion,' says my soul, 'therefore I hope in Him!' The Lord is good to those who wait for Him, to the soul who seeks Him*" (Lam 3:21-24).

Did you notice that it says it is "through the Lord's mercies that we are not consumed"? Think about that, especially those of us who may tend to have a "soft, squishy" idea of the character of God. Is our God a "consuming fire"? Hebrews 12:29 tells us that He is! Have you ever done rotten things? Maybe even since you've come to know the Lord? And yet, we're not consumed. Why not? Because— precious truth—"His mercies are new every morning." God is faithful in His mercy, and His compassion is unfailing.

The psalmist is saying that the life experience of the believer is a means through which the world sees and learns of the way to the salvation of God. The church seems to have moved away from the thinking that we are in the world but not of it. The message the world is getting from the church is often that we're *of the world*, but we're saved. "We're just like you," we try to placate people, "only we know Jesus." Does this attitude please God? Actually, the teaching of universalism proceeds from that school of thought, leading to the belief that a "loving God couldn't create a place like hell," let alone send anyone there!

The truth is that as Christians we're not to try to blend into the world so that we're indistinguishable from those who are in it. No! We are to be distinguished from the world and its ways because only God's way leads to salvation. The world should see the distinction between themselves and those who are of the Lord, and it should lead some to Christ. Do we always excel at presenting our lives this way? Do we ever even succeed when we try? Maybe not, but one thing you can count on is that the mercy of God is new every morning. The fact that we weren't consumed yesterday proves it, and that, my friend, is reason to sing!

May 8

"That's Not Fair!" Really? (part 1)

> ³Let the peoples praise You, O God; let all the peoples praise You. ⁴Oh, let the nations be glad and sing for joy! For You shall judge the people righteously, and govern the nations on earth. Selah —*Psalm 67:3-4*

AS BELIEVERS in God, we must settle it in our hearts that *God is sovereign*. He doesn't become sovereign because we believe in Him. He isn't the judge only of those who believe, nor does He govern only the nations who acknowledge His existence. He is Lord of all creation, and He is actively engaged in governing the affairs of men, whether or not they know Him or believe in Him or even hate Him. God has clearly told man in His Word what is acceptable and unacceptable to Him, and rulers will rise and fall within those parameters. We read in the book of Daniel, "*Blessed be the name of God forever and ever, for wisdom and might are His. And He changes the times and the seasons; He removes kings and raises up kings; He gives wisdom to the wise and knowledge to those who have understanding. He reveals deep and secret things; He knows what is in the darkness, and light dwells with Him*" (Daniel 2:20-22).

This is a difficult concept for some to grasp. Nebuchadnezzar had carried Judah away captive, yet He was still under the control of the Almighty God. Why did God permit him to do this to His children? In fact, Nebuchadnezzar was being *used by*

God as an instrument of judgment on them! He ultimately became filled with pride at his own greatness, and then God held him accountable for the knowledge He had given him, which he had abused. The Lord humbled him for seven years until he recognized God as the only sovereign God who is the true King over all (Daniel 3-4).

The psalmist tells us that God will judge righteously as He governs the nations on the earth, and in the future Millennium He will rule and reign. This will be a wonderful time for all. Because He is wholly righteous, we can trust that He will never do anything that is unfair.

Most of us have had experiences when we felt we were being unfairly treated. It's true that God permits some hard things to come into each of our lives at some point. But even though these times may have been difficult—possibly even brutal—to endure, God is never unfair when He renders His judgments. And also note that sometimes these difficult life situations aren't judgment at all but merely life experiences that God is permitting for His own good and pure reasons. Read Ezekiel 18:25-31, which begins, "*Yet you say, 'The way of the Lord is not fair.' Hear now, O house of Israel, is it not My way which is fair, and your ways which are not fair?*" The Lord then proceeds to defend His righteous judgments on those who complain that they're not getting a fair deal. The passage ends, "'*I have no pleasure in the death of one who dies,' says the Lord God. 'Therefore turn and live!'*" Isn't that wonderful? God wants no one to die, and the provision is given: "Turn to Me and live forever!" (continued)

"That's Not Fair!" Really? (part 2)

> [3] Let the peoples praise You, O God; let all the peoples praise You. [4] Oh, let the nations be glad and sing for joy! For You shall judge the people righteously, and govern the nations on earth. Selah —*Psalm 67:3-4*

WE ALL HAVE our own way of reasoning through things, and the truth is that most of the outcomes that we devise arise from our own selfish hearts. We want our lives to be happy, fruitful, and productive. Is that wrong? Of course not, but God has never promised that everything will go the way we think it should. You've heard it said, "Bad things *do* happen to good people." The Bible says, "*For He makes His sun rise on the evil and on the good, and sends rain on the just and on the unjust*" (Mat 5:45).

Please understand this: God isn't judging us for asking from Him the things we want when we believe them to be good things. But many today who accuse God of being unfair think that because He is good, our lives should contain *only* good things—blessings, and not hardship or trials or evil. We must always keep in mind that God is *perfectly* fair. He will never allow people who reject Him to enter into heaven, nor will He ever keep anyone out who has accepted Him. In fact, the Bible tells us that "it is by His mercies that we are not consumed" (Lamentatons 3:22)!

Listen, it's not difficult to grasp. The Lord God has said to the world, "Surrender your life to Me, accept My Son as Your Savior, and you'll live forever and ever in heaven. Reject My Son and do your own thing, and you'll live forever and ever in hell." What's not to understand? And yet, people revolt at the idea of having to obey God. They want to do what they want to do, and they don't want anyone to challenge them. Would it be right that these should be allowed into heaven? That wouldn't be fair, and furthermore, they would be miserable in the presence of the Savior of the world whom they rejected in order to follow their own desires.

The reverse is also true, and it's good news! With Christ as your Savior, who has completely satisfied your sin debt with His own blood, you can trust that He will not reject you when you stand before Him. There's no hidden clause or fine print in the gospel. Everyone in Christ is a *new creation* and old things have all passed away.

God is completely fair, but life is not. Our loving Father permits trials and testing to come into our lives not to punish us or to make us miserable but to try us. He wants to test us to prove (not to Himself but to us) that He is faithful to see us through hard times and sorrows and pain. He wants the world to see how we're able to endure struggles and hardships gracefully, guided and held by His loving hands. He wants to draw people to Himself as they see strength and joy in us even in the midst of suffering. We can have full assurance that the Lord is with us at every moment of our lives, through the joys and through the sorrows. Whether we are the pictures of health or wasting away in pain, He is there. "It is well with my soul!"

No one comforts like our God. No one loves us like our Father. May the Lord allow us this day and every day, no matter what our circumstance are, to praise His name with all our hearts as we consider the many thousands of reasons that we have to sing to our God! Praise Him!

Fear the Lord (Part 1)

⁵Let the people praise thee, O God; let all the people praise thee. ⁶Then shall the earth yield her increase; and God, even our own God, shall bless us. ⁷God shall bless us; and all the ends of the earth shall fear him. —Psalm 67:5-6

THE PSALMIST seems to be looking ahead to a time when the Jews would be longing for the Messiah to come and rule the world, thus lifting the curse, and the earth would return to an Eden-like state. I love the expectancy and the blessing the psalmist realizes, as the people are exhorted in this song to praise the Lord, followed by a reason to sing: God! Their own God will bless them, and all the ends of the world shall fear Him!

That concept, the fear of the Lord, is one that many shy away from today, but can you imagine what a different world it would be if everyone feared the Lord? It would be a huge understatement to say that the world would be a far better place.

But also within these verses we find the reminder that this world is not our home. We should recall those verses that speak of our time in heaven and focus less on the ones that speak of our time upon the earth. Even so, this psalm is still meant to be sung today. It was intended to be a reminder for our times even though it speaks of the future.

So, continuing with our theme in this series, we must remember that we have a reason to sing, and it is this: God will always honor His Word. Jeremiah wrote of this very thing: "*He who scattered Israel will gather him, and keep him as a shepherd does his flock. . . . I will turn their mourning to joy, I will comfort them, and make them rejoice rather than sorrow . . .*" (Jer. 31:10-14). Although Jeremiah wrote this several hundred years later, we can see that he had the same expectation as the psalmist. And although we are reading their words a few *thousand* years later, we, too, can have the same expectation: *the Lord will keep His Word*!

Jesus said that He will come for His bride, and He will! He said that He will rule and reign on the earth for a thousand years—and He will. He said there will be a new heavens and a new earth, in which righteousness dwells, and there will be. He said that we will live there forever, and, praise the Lord—we will! He said there will one day be no more sickness nor death, and the streets are paved with gold, and . . . are you getting the picture?

In Revelation 22, Jesus said, "*Behold, I am coming quickly, and My reward is with Me, to give to every one according to his work. I am the Alpha and the Omega, the Beginning and the End, the First and the Last.*" He continues, "*I, Jesus, have sent My angel to testify to you of these things in the churches. I am the Root and the Offspring of David, the Bright and Morning Star.*" The verse ends with "*And the Spirit and the bride say, 'Come!' And let him who hears say, 'Come!' And let him who thirsts come. Whoever desires, let him take of the water of life freely*"(vv. 12-17).

We should be looking and longing for that day, and we should be living our lives according to the hope that lies within these promises. Maranatha!

May 11

Fear the Lord (Part 2)

⁷God shall bless us; and all the ends of the earth shall fear him. —Psalm 67:5-7

IN OUR READING yesterday, we saw that Jesus said He is "coming quickly," which means suddenly, and He is. He said that some will be banned from heaven forever, and they will be. We can count on His tender mercies every day, and even though life is hard, He is never unfair. He acts righteously in the lives of both those who are His and those who are not. We have much cause to sing His praises because He will always honor His Word.

Maybe for some who are reading this, the idea that the Lord always keeps His Word is a *negative* thought. Perhaps you don't yet truly know the great God of heaven. His promises are exclusive to *His people*, and they cannot be enjoyed apart from knowing and loving Him. Jesus said that you must be born again, and you must be. He said that apart from being born again, you can't go to heaven, and that's true, too. It's in God's Word, and He cannot deny His Word. Is there any help for you then? Absolutely!

First of all, you must examine your own heart. The Bible says, "*Examine yourselves as to whether you are in the faith. Test yourselves. Do you not know yourselves, that Jesus Christ is in you? —unless indeed you are disqualified. But I trust that you will know that we are not disqualified*" (2 Corinthians 13:5-6).

How do you know if you're in the faith and not disqualified? "*Now by this we know that we know Him, if we keep His commandments. He who says, 'I know Him,' and does not keep His commandments, is a liar, and the truth is not in him. But whoever keeps His word, truly the love of God is perfected in him. By this we know that we are in Him. He who says he abides in Him ought himself also to walk just as He walked*" (John 2:3-6).

Examine yourselves honestly. Test yourselves. Walk as He walked. Listen, friend, if you don't have reasons to sing today about the joy that lies before us who love Him, you can have those reasons right now! Come to Jesus. Surrender your life to Him. Live by His ways, which are always better and more satisfying, and He'll give you reasons to sing every day, even when the tough things in life come your way. He is coming soon on a day that no one will suspect. We need to be ready to meet our King and our God and be waiting for Him in joyful anticipation.

Look up!

The Champion of the Chosen

Introduction to Psalm 68

To the chief Musician, A Psalm or Song of David.

THE PSALM that we're about to study is authored by King David. Much like the song of Deborah in Judges 5, which extols the majesty and power of the God of Israel, it's a song of victory. How wonderful that we have two leaders of Israel, Deborah and David, both singing to the same God because the same God was the reason the two leaders had to sing!

Our psalm for the next few days is considered a royal psalm. We'll find the character names of God throughout these verses by the Hebrew titles "Elohim," "Jehovah," "Jah (the abbreviated form)," "Adonai," and "Shaddai."

The apostle Paul quoted verse 18 from this psalm in Ephesians 4:8, writing, *"When He ascended on high, He led captivity captive, and gave gifts to men."* This Messianic assignment to the words of King David not only incorporates a Trinitarian application to the royal song, but it also reminds us that one of the more poetic titles of Jesus concerning the nation of Israel is expressed in these verses: *"When you pass through the waters, I will be with you; and through the rivers, they shall not overflow you. When you walk through the fire, you shall not be burned, nor shall the flame scorch you. For I am the Lord your God, The Holy One of Israel, your Savior"* (Isaiah 43:2-3a).

The Holy One of Israel is Israel's Savior, and He is ours as well! All of these elements take us to our title by looking back to Deborah in the time of the Judges of Israel and forward to the Church Age. Then, combined with the words of David in Psalm 68, the only rightful conclusion we can draw about our God and His people is that He is the Champion of the Chosen!

He stood behind Abraham, Moses, Joshua, Rahab, Deborah, David, Mary, James, John, Paul, Spurgeon, Moody, Graham, and He stands also behind you and me. Elohim, Jehovah, Yah, Adonai, Shaddai is the champion of the chosen, whether the chosen be the Jews, whom He chose to set His love upon and through whom He would bring His Messiah into the world, or those who become the chosen by faith and trust in the Holy One of Israel as their Savior.

We will find within this psalm some very needful and timely reminders of what knowing God means to our everyday lives as His chosen people on this earth, awaiting our transport home to heaven. Are you ready? Let's go out today with this thought in our hearts and minds: God loves us, and He has a plan for us, as He did with David and Deborah, that includes bigger things than we can even imagine!

The Mighty God

*1*Let God arise, let His enemies be scattered; let them also who hate Him flee before Him. *2*As smoke is driven away, so drive them away; as wax melts before the fire, so let the wicked perish at the presence of God. *3*But let the righteous be glad; let them rejoice before God; yes, let them rejoice exceedingly. *4*Sing to God, sing praises to His name; extol Him who rides on the clouds, by His name Yah, and rejoice before Him. *5*A father of the fatherless, a defender of widows, is God in His holy habitation. *6*God sets the solitary in families; He brings out those who are bound into prosperity; but the rebellious dwell in a dry land.
—Psalm 68:1-6

DAVID USES a series of contrasts, which he often did, as he petitions God to arise and then follows up with a series of comparisons between feeble man, false gods, and JAH (or YAH), the true and living God. David says that when God chooses to move, His enemies will be scattered. They'll be like smoke driven by the wind or like wax before the flame, completely incapable of resisting the greater force, and they will perish in their efforts to oppose God.

On the other hand, the righteous will have an experience of gladness, exceeding joy, and reasons to sing, all because the Champion of the chosen rides the clouds. He is a Father to the fatherless, the Defender of the widows; He sets lonely people into God's family, and He brings those who are bound in the horror of sinfulness into the bountiful blessings of the wonderful newness of life in Christ.

Sadly, rebellious people live in a contrasting state of constant drought, and David tells us in verse 6 that this is a long-established pattern among the rebellious, using the Exodus from Egypt as an example (Exodus 3:19-22).

In those verses, God tells Moses that Pharaoh won't let them go, even by a mighty hand (i.e., military might), so He himself will stretch out His hand. This tells us that God's hand is mightier than any human *army*! David presents the Lord in the poetic terms as "a rider of the clouds." This phrase is commonly associated with the Canaanite deity Baal, and David follows this statement with a qualifier, lest any mistake his statement, *"His name is Yah"* (which is a contraction of YHWH, meaning "the Existing One").

Notice the Holy Spirit's choice of title for the Lord here, which contains a bit of sarcasm that the God of Israel actually exists, unlike Baal. So how does all of this play out for you and me—all of these comparisons between feeble man, false gods, and Yah, the Existing One? The Bible tells us that the Existing One is *the Champion of the chosen*. Remember this: Our enemies will *never* have the advantage over us. No matter how many there are, or who they are, or what they have, say, or do, or even the size of their army—when God arises, they are like smoke in the wind and wax before the flame. They don't stand a chance!

Some of you may be thinking, "What can man do to me?" Well, sadly, the answer is "plenty!" But the truth is that man can do nothing of *eternal* consequences. Even in this life when God allows things we may not like or understand, no one who belongs to Him is ever snatched out of the Father's hand or separated from His love. He is a Champion of the chosen, and so we can know that our enemies will never have the advantage over us. Go out in confidence today!

May 14

"You Will Go out with Joy and Be Led Forth with Peace"

[7]O God, when You went out before Your people, when You marched through the wilderness, Selah [8]the earth shook; the heavens also dropped rain at the presence of God; Sinai itself was moved at the presence of God, the God of Israel. [9]You, O God, sent a plentiful rain, whereby You confirmed Your inheritance, when it was weary. [10]Your congregation dwelt in it; You, O God, provided from Your goodness for the poor. [11]The Lord gave the word; great was the company of those who proclaimed it: [12]"Kings of armies flee, they flee, and she who remains at home divides the spoil. [13]Though you lie down among the sheepfolds, You will be like the wings of a dove covered with silver, and her feathers with yellow gold." [14]When the Almighty scattered kings in it, it was white as snow in Zalmon. [15]A mountain of God is the mountain of Bashan; a mountain of many peaks is the mountain of Bashan. [16]Why do you fume with envy, you mountains of many peaks? This is the mountain which God desires to dwell in; yes, the Lord will dwell in it forever. [17]The chariots of God are twenty thousand, even thousands of thousands; the Lord is among them as in Sinai, in the Holy Place. [18]You have ascended on high, You have led captivity captive; You have received gifts among

men, Even from the rebellious, That the Lord God might dwell there. ¹⁹Blessed be the Lord, who daily loads us with benefits, the God of our salvation! Selah —*Psalm 68:7-19*

THESE BEAUTIFUL WORDS are the way David describes God's absolute faithfulness to Israel in the past, continuing His tribute to the Lord, the Champion of the chosen. He begins with God's faithfulness during the wilderness wanderings, and then leads us to God's majesty when Mount Sinai quaked in His presence at the giving of the Law. He references Deuteronomy 11:11, in which God is presented as always faithful to water the earth the way a man would water his garden. He reflects upon the crossing of the Jordan River into the Promised Land, and he describes how the Lord drove out the enemies of Israel before them. He refers to the rich bounties of the land itself, the vineyards, and the houses that they were given to occupy, which they hadn't even had to build.

He waxes poetic in verse 13, where he compares the life of God's chosen ones to the beauty of a silver-winged dove with feathers of gold! Describing the mountain peaks in Israel from Samaria to North of the Galilee, Zalmon, and Bashan respectively, he asks why the other mountain peaks (which can also be a metaphor referring to people or nations) are envious, the answer being because God has *chosen* to dwell on Mt. Zion *forever*. He continues, describing the thousands and thousand chariots of *El Shaddai*, as compared to the contrast between the greatest human armies of earth.

Pointing back once more to the deliverance of Israel from bondage under the Egyptians, he mentions the many gifts that they had been blessed with upon their exodus from Egypt, which were later used to build the tabernacle in which God would dwell.

When we belong to the Lord and seek to live for Him, we'll see that our own provision isn't limited to earthly means. Who, reading this, has ever faced an impossible situation and could see no solution, when suddenly, the problem was solved in ways that couldn't have been imagined? It was God doing that, not just a wild coincidence! Who but God could take His people from under the whip of the taskmaster and, on the way out of town, see that they were given the taskmaster's treasures to take with them?

Do you question the love of God? Even though we may face impossible situations, God isn't bound by natural ways of providing for us! He is Jehovah Jireh, "The Lord Will Provide," and He will do so in ways that will astound us. He is the *Champion of the chosen.* Let's go out today in faith, realizing that He knows our trials and our needs, and He is always faithful in His time.

Don't Be a "Hairy Scalp"!

²⁰Our God is the God of salvation; and to God the Lord belong escapes from death. ²¹But God will wound the head of His enemies, the hairy scalp of the one who still goes on in his trespasses. —*Psalm 68:20-21*

AS WE READ through these verses, we are comforted knowing that we belong to the God of power and might. David's description of the "procession" (reading ahead in verse 24) may refer to God leading His people through the wilderness with the cloud by day and the pillar of fire by night, as they carried the ark of God from place to place. It could also refer to the conquests of the Canaanites, who were certainly a people mightier and greater than little Israel. Whatever is being described here, it unquestionably refers to *anything that God does*, for He is the mighty, unstoppable King, our Champion.

Verse 21 mentions God wounding the head of his enemies, and it refers to the "hairy scalp of the one who still goes on in his trespasses." The Hebrew word for "head" can mean "captain" or "chief." God easily defeated the greatest military leaders in the world, including Gog. The word can also mean "pride," and the mention of the hairy scalp in verse 21 could mean "youth." Isn't it often true that the young see themselves as invincible, believing they have no need for God?

In John 8, the Scribes and Pharisees sought to get Jesus to violate the law by bringing to Him a woman who had been caught in adultery. They quoted from the Law of Moses to Him that the penalty was stoning. Trying to entrap Him, they asked Him what they should do. He ignored them, bending down and writing in the dirt. They persisted asking Him until He stood and said, "He who is without sin among you, let him throw a stone at her first." One by one, "being convicted in their conscience," they walked away. Jesus asked the woman, "Has no one condemned you?" She replied, "No one." Jesus told her, "Neither do I condemn you; go and sin no more."

What He wasn't saying here was that since we're all sinners, we have no right or responsibility to recognize someone's sin. What He was saying to these prideful, arrogant Christ rejecters, who had sought to set a trap for Him according to the Law, and who believed they alone knew the Law, was that they were *all* violating the Law, because the Law required both the guilty man and woman to be present (Lev 20:10), and that only the witnesses who had actually caught the sinning pair in the act could convict them. None of them met these qualifications, including Jesus himself. They got the message, from the oldest to the youngest, i.e., the hairy scalps.

How loving is our God! He alone can see into the hearts of everyone and knows exactly how to convict us of our sin and lead us to repentance, rather than leaving us to mourn in our misery. How much better to be like the bald-headed Elisha, who operated in the wisdom of the Lord, than to be like the "hairy scalps" who continue on in their trespasses!

May 16

It's Supernatural!

²²The Lord said, "I will bring back from Bashan, I will bring them back from the depths of the sea, ²³that your foot may crush them in blood, and the tongues of your dogs may have their portion from your enemies." ²⁴They have seen Your procession, O God, the procession of my God, my King, into the sanctuary. ²⁵The singers went before, the players on instruments followed after; among them were the maidens playing timbrels. ²⁶Bless God in the congregations, the Lord, from the fountain of Israel. —*Psalm 68:22-26*

IN THE GOSPEL of Matthew, we learn that even though Jesus was sought after in other places for His miracles, He was scoffed at in His own hometown. The people asked, "*Where did this Man get this wisdom and these mighty works? Is this not the carpenter's son? Is not His mother called Mary? And His brothers James, Joses, Simon, and Judas? And His sisters, are they not all with us? Where then did this Man get all these things?*" And it says that they were offended by Him. And Jesus said, "*A prophet is not without honor except in his own country and in his own house.*" Sadly, because of their unbelief, the Bible tells us that He didn't do many miracles there.

How does this relate to our verses today? Could Jesus not do many mighty works in His hometown because the people didn't believe in miracles? No! His power is not hindered by unbelief. He didn't do many miracles there because they were offended by His claims that He was the prophet of God and even the Son of God.

David tells a different story in our verses today. He writes of miraculous escapes from death for His chosen people, of God bringing them through the Red Sea, of conquering enemy after enemy, even though they were greatly outnumbered. These victories caused the singers, musicians, and maidens to play their instruments and dance before God in the midst of the congregation.

Because God is the Champion of His people, our lives will be filled with supernatural events. Saints, God is doing more for us that we *don't* know about than things that we do know of. We have no idea of all the times and ways He has delivered us from death. We don't know of all the ways He has brought us through "Red Sea" experiences. We don't know of all the thwarted attacks by the enemy.

"I look up to the mountains—does my help come from there? My help comes from the Lord, who made heaven and earth! He will not let you stumble; the one who watches over you will not slumber. Indeed, he who watches over Israel never slumbers nor sleeps. The Lord himself watches over you! The Lord stands beside you as your protective shade. The sun will not harm you by day, nor the moon at night. The Lord keeps you from all harm and watches over your life. The Lord keeps watch over you as you come and go, both now and forever" (Psalm 121:1-8).

We are God's chosen people in the form of the church. Who else would there be who would watch over us besides the One who watches over Israel? The Lord is your protective shade, who keeps you from all harm and watches over your life, both now and forever. And He, our Champion, never sleeps, and because He doesn't, we can! Our lives as His children are a series of supernatural events, known and unknown, because we love and serve the One who cares for us as no other could.

May 17

The God of the Feeble

[27]There is little Benjamin, their leader, the princes of Judah and their company, the princes of Zebulun and the princes of Naphtali. [28]Your God has commanded your strength; strengthen, O God, what You have done for us. [29] . . . Kings will bring presents to You. [30]Rebuke the beasts . . . , the herd of bulls . . . till everyone submits himself with pieces of silver. Scatter the peoples who delight in war. [31]Envoys will come out of Egypt; Ethiopia will quickly stretch out her hands to God. [32]Sing to God . . . [33]to Him who rides on the heaven of heavens . . . ! [34]Ascribe strength to God; His excellence is over Israel. . . . You are more awesome than Your holy places. The God of Israel . . . gives strength and power to His people. Blessed be God! —*Psalm 68:27-35*

IN THIS SONG, David refers to tiny Benjamin and their leader, King Saul, in contrast to the great tribes of Judah, Zebulun, and Naphtali. There is another member of that little tribe through whom God worked mighty works. Indeed, it was through the apostle Paul, who wrote, *"For we are the circumcision, who worship God in the Spirit, rejoice in Christ Jesus, and have no confidence in the flesh. . . . If anyone else thinks he may have confidence in the flesh, I more so: circumcised the eighth day, of the stock of Israel, of the tribe of Benjamin, a Hebrew of the Hebrews; concerning the law, a Pharisee; concerning zeal, persecuting the church; concerning the righteousness which is in the law, blameless. But what things were gain to me, these I have counted loss for Christ"* (Philippians 3:3-8).

Paul is saying what David pointed out in his psalm above, which is that compared to God, there are *no great men*. It is God who does great things through small and *feeble men*. He gives strength those who do His will. David looks forward to the day when kings will present gifts to the Holy One of Israel as He sits in the Temple, having scattered all who delight in war. The earth will sing praises and ascribe strength to the Lord as His mighty voice goes out to all the earth, and He gives strength and power to His people.

"In that day, there will be an altar to the Lord in . . . Egypt, and a pillar to the Lord at its border. . . . It will be for a . . . witness to the Lord of hosts . . . ; for they will cry to the Lord because of the oppressors, and He will send them a Savior and a Mighty One, and He will deliver them. . . . Israel will be one of three with Egypt and Assyria—a blessing . . . whom the Lord of hosts shall bless, saying, 'Blessed is Egypt My people, and Assyria the work of My hands, and Israel My inheritance'" (Is 19:19-25). Egypt and Assyria will bow before and worship the Creator one day, but through Christ, we are the chosen, and earthly rulers and systems don't determine or control our destiny!

Friend, the Lord is our Provider, and the Bible says that the wealth of the wicked is stored up for the righteous. Just as God plundered the Egyptians to give wealth to Israel, He can do the same kind of move now to provide for His people. Sadly, many miss God's miracles because they don't believe that He will provide for them. We must remember always that earthly rulers and systems do not determine our destiny, either eternally or temporally. God is in control, and He is the only One to whom we must look.

"Trust in the Lord with all your heart, and lean not on your own understanding; in all your ways acknowledge Him, and He shall direct your paths. Do not be wise in your own eyes; fear the Lord and depart from evil. It will be health to your flesh, and strength to your bones. Honor the Lord with your possessions and the first fruits of all your increase; so your barns will be filled with plenty, and your vats will overflow with new wine" (Proverbs 3:5-10). Why settle for the help of natural man when a supernatural God has made a way for you, no matter how feeble you may think you are!

Go Where You're Watching!

Introduction to Psalm 73

A Psalm of Asaph.

PSALM 73 is a favorite psalm for many. It's one with which most of us can relate, being a very honest portrayal of what happens to us when we set our eyes on others and what they are doing and not on ourselves, minding our own business. It's one of those "Been there, done that" kind of psalms by one of David's chief musicians, Asaph.

In the previous psalm, David's son King Solomon had written about all of the mighty works of God and His saving hand on His people. It's a wonderful tribute that glorifies our mighty God. But sometimes we look at things with different eyes. We observe that the people of God may suffer lack and pain and may face one difficulty after another while God's enemies seem to flourish despite their rejection of Him. *Why is this so?*, we wonder.

To paraphrase Asaph, "This reality almost tripped me up and caused a crisis of faith when I saw how the wicked *do* prosper." We might all feel this way at times, and our study of this psalm will help us to learn to deal with our minds and emotions when they begin to wander down such paths.

Have you ever run into something because you weren't watching where you were going? Have you ever had your mind and emotions run away with you and take you places (mentally or physically) where you didn't want to go, or cause you to run into situations that you didn't expect or want?

Both scenarios may turn out the same way if you don't watch where you're going. Eventually, you'll run into some thing or some situation that you didn't anticipate. We need to stay focused on the things that are true and right, or we will *go where we're watching* instead!

"Go where you're watching" is a play on words and is mostly a warning that when we face such things as Asaph describes, we must be wary, or his experience in his mind and emotions will become ours.

Proverbs 4:25-26 tells us, "*Let your eyes look straight ahead, and your eyelids look right before you. Ponder the path of your feet, and let all your ways be established.*" Sound advice!

Asaph will warn us, as we dive into his psalm, that we will indeed go where we are watching if we don't heed his advice as he relates his personal experience of having a very close call that led to a slippery slope when his thoughts almost took him away from the truth.

Let's pray before we dive into these verses with Asaph that the Lord will remind us to keep our eyes looking straight ahead, and that we may continue to be aware of the importance of keeping our minds on things above, not on things that are on the earth (Colossians 3:2).

God Is Good . . . to the Wicked?

¹Truly God is good to Israel, to such as are pure in heart. ²But as for me, my feet had almost stumbled; my steps had nearly slipped. ³For I was envious of the boastful, when I saw the prosperity of the wicked. ⁴For there are no pangs in their death, but their strength is firm. ⁵They are not in trouble as other men, nor are they plagued like other men. ⁶Therefore pride serves as their necklace; violence covers them like a garment. Their eyes bulge with abundance; they have more than heart could wish." —*Psalm 73:1-8*

THIS PSALM is about trusting God. With Asaph, we see that it has become of a struggle for him to trust Him. Why is this? In his opening verse, Asaph describes what he knows to be true. This truth has been the one constancy of his life regarding the consistency of God. *God is good to such as are pure in heart*—always. And yet . . .

What Asaph was struggling with was the real definition of "good." As he looked around him, he saw the prosperity of those who were filled with pride. They were arrogant and boastful. They were blasphemers, who scoffed at God and spoke wickedly and brazenly against heaven itself. Yet their lives appeared to be blessed and easy. The more they had, the more they increased! Something seemed so wrong with this picture!

Poor Asaph! He said that as he considered all of this, his own path went from stable to slippery, and he says that he *almost* fell into a full-blown crisis of faith.

Jesus, in the Gospel of Luke, said: *"If you love those who love you, what credit is that to you? For even sinners love those who love them. And if you do good to those who do good to you, what credit is that to you? For even sinners do the same. And if you lend to those from whom you hope to receive back, what credit is that to you? For even sinners lend to sinners to receive as much back. But love your enemies, do good, and lend, hoping for nothing in return; and your reward will be great, and you will be sons of the Most High. **For He is kind to the unthankful and evil**. Therefore be merciful, just as your Father is also merciful"* (Luke 6:32-36).

And there's the key that opens the door to the first part of the solution to Asaph's misery! It's true: God is good, even to the unthankful and the evil. Jesus says that loving those who are like us is easy. But loving those who hate us is necessary, because God does it, and He tells us to do the same! And it's not easy, but then Asaph points us to something else that relates to what the Lord has said, and that is that when we're dealing with our enemies, we mustn't look at what they have. Look at who they are. And remember that they are perishing.

The key for us to keep in mind is this: Be careful what you look for, because you will always find it. Asaph said, "Truly God is good to Israel." And he should have stopped looking further right there! But he didn't. Then he saw the prosperity of the wicked and the good things that seemed to always happen to them even as they continued in their evil—and it almost caused his foot to slip.

Life is hard. It has its ups and downs, but our eyes must always be fixed on what is immovable and unchanging, and that is our God and His love for us! This is the only way for us to avoid the slippery slope to envy and anger instead of peace.

May 20

"Keep Your Mind on Your Drivin' "

⁹They set their mouth against the heavens, and their tongue walks through the earth. ¹⁰Therefore his people return here, And waters of a full cup are drained by them. ¹¹And they say, "How does God know? And is there knowledge in the Most High?" ¹²Behold, these are the ungodly, who are always at ease; they increase riches. —*Psalm 73:9-12*

WE CONTINUE with Asaph and his dilemma today as we study his psalm, and hopefully, as we go, we'll learn some things that will prevent our falling into the same trap. (Isn't it wonderful that God has left us so many examples in the Scriptures of people who were weak and even sinful, yet He loved them and us enough to not only see them through their troubles but also to leave a record for us to give us hope? God is so good!)

Isaiah wrote God's words, "*Fear not, for I am with you; be not dismayed, for I am your God. I will strengthen you, yes, I will help you, I will uphold you with My righteous right hand*" (Isaiah 41:10). Wonderful words! Are they still true today? Very much so! But if we turn our minds and eyes away from that and begin to think, "Look at those people over there. They don't love God, and they're not struggling to make ends meet!" Or "I know that my neighbors are having an immoral relationship, but they drive brand new cars, while I can barely keep mine running."

If you look for reasons to complain, you'll find them and complain. If you look for things to envy, it'll be right there in front of you. And conversely, if you look for reasons to rejoice, you'll find those also! Why? Because *we will always go where we are looking*.

Consider these wonderful words by the author of Hebrews: *"Seeing then that we have a great High Priest who has passed through the heavens, Jesus the Son of God, let us hold fast our confession. For we do not have a High Priest who cannot sympathize with our weaknesses, but was in all points tempted as we are, yet without sin. Let us therefore come boldly to the throne of grace, that we may obtain mercy and find grace to help in time of need"* (Hebrews 4:14-16). Wow! Could it get any better? God not only knows our ugly thoughts, but He has compassion on us for having them! Jesus Christ himself was tempted in all things also, so He understands our hearts. But He never sinned, so that's where we should run when our mind starts going where our eyes have taken us. If we keep our eyes on the road before us, we won't drive off into a ditch!

Let's balance this out in light of what Asaph is telling us. He had the wrong definition of "blessing." He thought, as many of us do, that blessings are things you can put in the bank. But God's blessings come in the form of "mercy and grace to help in time of need." Jesus said that it's hard for the rich to enter the kingdom of heaven. Their minds are often on their riches. God desires that those who are pure in heart will experience His mercy and grace and help in every situation we may encounter. And material wealth by no means always indicates His blessing. In fact, nobody wishes for more money when they're going through a tragedy, such as having a child who is sick and near death. What they want is God's mercy and grace! And on one's deathbed, no one is thinking about how to get richer. They, too, need God's mercy and grace, "a very present help in time of need" (Psalm 46:1).

Asaph issues a warning for us to heed. When he took his eyes off of the true goodness of our heavenly Father, he went straight to where he was watching, and his feet almost slipped because of what he saw.

God truly is good to us, as Asaph began his psalm. If you keep your eyes on that, you *will* go where you are watching, and it will be exactly where God wants you to be.

Feelings Can't Be Trusted

*13*Surely I have cleansed my heart in vain, and washed my hands in inno-cence. *14*For all day long I have been plagued, and chastened every morning. *15*If I had said, "I will speak thus," behold, I would have been untrue to the generation of Your children. *16*When I thought how to under-stand this, it was too painful for me—*17*until I went into the sanctuary of God; then I understood their end. *18*Surely You set them in slippery places; You cast them down to destruction. *19*Oh, how they are brought to des-olation, as in a moment! They are utterly consumed with terrors. *20*As a dream when one awakes, so, Lord, when You awake, You shall despise their image. *—Psalm 73:13-20*

POOR ASAPH! He continues struggling in his mind and heart over what he has seen. He's having a terrible time getting those images out of his head. Remember, now, that Asaph was in ministry, and when he went into the Sanctuary of God, he was doing so as King David's worship leader. This tells us that if Asaph could be tempted to get his eyes off the Lord even as he is serving Him, we're all in danger of doing the very same thing.

Every Christian is tempted at times to turn his or her eyes from the truth, whether they're mature believers or babes in Christ, so it's very important that we follow the progression in this psalm as a warning and also as a guide to the way of escape.

Asaph confesses his sin, revealing that he was in a hypocritical place and he knew it. And yet, he really struggled with getting his feet back onto solid ground and into a right relationship with the Lord. To paraphrase verse 13, he says "What good does it do to believe? I've kept the law for no good reason, apparently. It's the wicked who have it easy. But I'm being plagued and chastened every morning!"

What was Asaph doing? He was expressing what he *felt*, not what was true. And what happened? His mind and emotions went straight to where he was watch-ing, not to the Lord. As an honorable man, he even confessed that if he had said to others what he was thinking, he knew that he'd be lying to God's children about Him, but he still couldn't shake those horrible thoughts and feelings that churned inside of him—until he went into the sanctuary.

Have you ever been in a place where you couldn't help but wonder why God did or didn't do something, and you even began to feel frustrated about it? Asaph gives us the cure. Go into the sanctuary, which for us can simply mean to go to the Lord himself, who is our sanctuary, our refuge (Isaiah 8:14; Ezekiel 11:16). This was where Asaph finally found peace. He began to understand the other side of the picture as he looked at the wicked through God's eyes. And he also began to realize the ultimate difference between the wicked and the saved, and this brought comfort.

It may seem too simple, but it's true: When life seems like a living hell, remember that you're not going there. Asaph realized that the wicked are the ones on the slippery slope that leads to destruction. Their lives may appear trouble-free on this side of eternity, but keep in mind that this life is but a vapor, and then comes an eternity of destruction and desolation and being consumed by terrors for the ungodly. To put it another way, Christians: "Your worst day in life is better than any day in hell."

Thus, no matter what we may be facing or going through at the moment, God is with us and we can run to Him in the sanctuary of His arms, where we will find peace and rest and hope for today in the midst of the worst of storms. Let us praise His holy name!

May 22

"On the Road Again"

[21]Thus my heart was grieved, and I was vexed in my mind. [22]I was so foolish and ignorant; I was like a beast before You. [23]Nevertheless I am continually with You; You hold me by my right hand. [24]You will guide me with Your counsel, and afterward receive me to glory. [25]Whom have I in heaven but You? And there is none upon earth that I desire besides You. [26]My flesh and my heart fail; but God is the strength of my heart and my portion forever. [27]For indeed, those who are far from You shall perish; You have destroyed all those who desert You for harlotry. [28]But it is good for me to draw near to God; I have put my trust in the Lord God, that I may declare all Your works. —*Psalm 73:21-28*

AT LAST Asaph is on the road to recovery. In essence, what he is saying is "I can't believe I let my mind and emotions get the best of me! I was so foolish and ignorant that I acted like an animal before you." And then we have those blessed words "Nevertheless." I'm so glad that God allows us those "nevertheless" moments of clarity in our lives without getting angry at us. His will and plan for us is always the best. Nevertheless . . . we don't always follow it, yet He waits patiently for us to find our way.

Asaph gives us some important insight into going where you're watching in verse 24, where he mentions the guidance of God's counsel. Where may we find God's counsel? We find it in His Word. Everything we need to know is in the Word of God.

In John 17, Jesus prayed to His Father, "*Those whom You gave to Me, I have kept; and none of them is lost except the son of perdition, that the Scriptures might be fulfilled. . . . I have given them Your word; and the world has hated them because they are not of the world, just as I am not of the world. I do not pray that You should take them out of the world, but that you should keep them from the evil one. They are not of the world, just as I am not of the world. Sanctify them by Your truth. Your word is truth. As You sent Me into the world, I also have sent them into the world*" (vv.12-18).

Jesus prayed over all believers because they have His Word. He doesn't say their lives will be problem-free. In fact, because they have the Word, the world will hate them!

In verse 25, Asaph hints that he felt alone. He wrote, "Whom have I in heaven but You, and there is none on earth like You." Then he confesses that his heart and flesh fail, and he even "goes where he is watching," except for God! God is the strength of his heart and his portion forever! How beautiful are those words! Without God, we have nothing! There are certainly people and things in our lives that make us richer and better, but none compares to God. Jeremiah wrote, "*Ah, Lord God, You have made the heavens and the earth by Your great power and outstretched arm. There is nothing too hard for You*" (Jeremiah 32:17).

God, who has made heaven and earth, has also made a way for us to get from earth to heaven. Nothing is too hard for Him! God is our strength and our portion forever!

As for Asaph, he took his eyes from the Lord, looked at the wicked, and became double-minded. But then, he humbled himself before God. His heart was purified, and the Lord lifted him up from the slippery slope of envy, doubt, and despair. And the same can be done for us today. If you find that you have been going where you are watching, submit to God, resist the devil, and watch him go on the run! Draw near to God, and He will draw near to you. Remember: if you don't watch where you're going, you'll soon go where you're watching, and if it's the way of the wicked that you're watching you'll end up in envy and despair. But if you're watching the Word of God, you'll see that God is good to the pure in heart and you'll be lifted up. Do you want to get on the right road again? Open your eyes to see His road before you and follow God in all of His ways. There's nothing better than that!

Battlefield Supremacy

Introduction

A Contemplation of Asaph [Psalm 74]

THE AUTHOR of our psalm is named Asaph, although no one knows if he is the same as the Asaph of Psalm 73. It's written in a different time period, in which it sounds as if the Temple has been under attack. We know that there wasn't yet a Temple during the time when King David reigned and had "Asaph," with whom we've become familiar over the past few days, as his worship leader. But is it possible that this could be David's Asaph, writing prophetically? Perhaps. Or is it David's Asaph writing figuratively with more of a spiritual connotation than physical? Or is it someone else entirely? The Scriptures don't tell us.

Regardless of who the man is, there is definitely a relevant message for us in our day, and that is this: There are those who seek to destroy the House of God, the church, the Temple, God's people—and some of them have infiltrated the church even now.

Like Israel, the church is a single entity comprising individuals, and both are under attack. The enemy is trying to silence the collective church and nullify the only hope the world has with its life-changing message, and he is also trying to kill individual believers as he has since the birth of the church. What is the hope for us today as the battle rages more and more furiously?

The apostle Paul wrote: *"Finally, my brethren, be strong in the Lord and in the power of His might. Put on the whole armor of God, that you may be able to stand against the wiles of the devil. For we do not wrestle against flesh and blood, but against principalities, against powers, against rulers of the darkness of this age, against spiritual hosts of wickedness in the heavenly places. Therefore take up the whole armor of God, that you may be able to withstand in the evil day, and having done all, to stand"* (Ephesians 6:10-13).

Paul isn't denying the fact that we have flesh-and-blood enemies as well as spiritual ones, but he's pointing out that behind our flesh-and-blood enemies are principalities and powers and rulers of the darkness of this age. We're fighting an enemy that we can't see.

We are at war, Church, and we have always been. The only change we see in our portion of history is that the persecution of the church has come closer to home than ever before. We cannot let down our guard.

In Asaph's song of lament, he gives us a great reminder that no matter what the enemy does or tries to do against the church, and no matter what group he uses to confront us, we, as the church, have battlefield supremacy.

Psalm 124 gives us assurance: " '*If it had not been the Lord who was on our side,*' *let Israel now say—'If it had not been the Lord who was on our side, when men rose up against us, then they would have swallowed us alive, when their wrath was kindled against us; then the waters would have overwhelmed us, the stream would have gone over our soul; then the swollen waters would have gone over our soul'. . . . Our hope is in the name of the Lord, who made heaven and earth.*" As with Israel, so with us. Our hope is in the same Lord-over-all-creation. Let us praise Him today, who is worthy of all praise, and keep one eye on the battle before us and the other looking upward. Come quickly, Lord Jesus!

May 24

No End in Sight

¹O God, why have You cast us off forever? Why does Your anger smoke against the sheep of Your pasture? ²Remember Your congregation, which You have purchased of old, the tribe of Your inheritance, which You have redeemed—this Mount Zion where You have dwelt. ³Lift up Your feet to the perpetual desolations. The enemy has damaged everything in the sanctuary. ⁴Your enemies roar in the midst of Your meeting place; they set up their banners for signs. ⁵They seem like men who lift up axes among thick trees. ⁶And now they break down its carved work, all at once, with axes and hammers. ⁷They have set fire to Your sanctuary; they have defiled the dwelling place of Your name to the ground. ⁸They have said in their hearts, "Let us destroy them altogether." They have burned up all the meeting places of God in the land. ⁹We do not see our signs; there is no longer any prophet; nor is there any among us who knows how long. ¹⁰O God, how long will the adversary reproach? Will the enemy blaspheme Your name forever? *—Psalm 74:1-10*

IF YOU LOOK CLOSELY at this passage, which may sound like Asaph is complaining and lacking in faith, you'll see something much deeper. Asaph is *agonizing in prayer* to the only One who can possibly help them, asking God to do what God does, which is to defend His Word and His people.

As the church, collectively, we may feel like Asaph did, wondering, "How long is the enemy going to prevail, Lord? They're burning churches and killing Christians all over the world. They're destroying Christian businesses and threatening the church in the United States with prosecution for believing Your Word. Lord, aren't we the sheep of Your pasture and Your congregation, Your purchased possession? Then why has the enemy damaged everything in Your sanctuary and infiltrated Your meeting place? They have raised their own banners over Your house, and ours have been torn down."

No matter what the history of this psalm is, Asaph is setting the example of what we ourselves should be doing as we see the persecution of the church growing: he knew that God truly hears and answers our prayers, and he is going to the One who alone can help. And this is why we can say that we have "Battlefield Supremacy." There is one God, one Lord, one Ruler over all. Baal never existed. There is no Allah. They are nonexistent. And although "Allah" is the name of "a god," the true God never inspired the Qu'ran, because it conflicts with the Word that God had given to His prophets centuries before the Qu'ran even came to be. And we can trust God's Word and know that He hears our prayers for help. I can't tell you why God doesn't send fire from heaven to consume the murderous cults in the world today, other than the fact that He is not willing that any should perish, and perhaps some of them will be saved.

Even though Asaph was in an extreme situation of distress and trouble, He did the right thing by turning to the Lord with his fears, and so must we. God hears our prayers even when we're in dire straits and feel like we're all alone. Unlike the false gods of other religions, our God is real. He is loving and kind and caring, and he elevates women instead of denigrating them, as is the norm in places like Saudi Arabia. He loves the little children, and woe to those who would do them any harm! He is the one true and living God, and those who hate Him and hate us will not prevail in end. No matter how long we may have to endure our trials, God is with us, and our God is an awesome God! He is the one true and living God and our enemies will not prevail in the world. Take heart. The end *is* in sight.

The Battle Belongs to the Lord

*[11]*Why do You withdraw Your hand, even Your right hand? Take it out of Your bosom and destroy them. *[12]*For God is my King from old, working salvation in the midst of the earth. *[13]*You divided the sea by Your strength; You broke the heads of the sea serpents in the waters. *[14]*You broke the heads of Leviathan in pieces, and gave him as food to the people inhabiting the wilderness. *[15]*You broke open the fountain and the flood; You dried up mighty rivers. *[16]*The day is Yours, the night also is Yours; You have prepared the light and then sun. *[17]*You have set all the borders of the earth; You have made summer and winter. —Psalm 74:11-17

HAVE YOU ever felt this way? "Lord! Take Your hand out of Your bosom and destroy those guys!" When I read of horrendous events like the gang rapes of nine- and ten-year-old girls by Isis and other atrocities, my thoughts are the same as Asaph's. I mourn, "How long will the cries of Allahu Akbar be allowed to continue without a divine response?"

In verse 12, Asaph does what we should do when confronted by horrifying situations: he calls to mind the myriad of divine interventions by the Lord, beginning with the deliverance of the Israelites from Egypt to the miraculous parting of the Red Sea to the breaking of the heads of the sea serpents and Leviathan, giving them as food to the people in the wilderness. ("Leviathan" represents evil and even Satan, the great dragon.) We, too, must keep in mind that God is the God of the night and of the daytime; He has set the boundaries of the earth and is the One who made the seasons. He is the God of all creation! What Asaph is doing is good and healthy for us to do in times of difficulty and persecution, and that is to run down the list of God's credentials and attributes (see Job 26:7-14, for example). Not only will it fill your mind with the wonders of our great God, but it will also bring peace to your heart. No one is higher or greater than He!

Our minds are often incapable of understanding the immensity of great evil that seems so inconsistent with God's promise of divine protection. But remember this: Only God can determine the outcome of any battle. We, as children and soldiers of the Lord have battlefield supremacy in every situation, even though, like Asaph, we may be presently baffled by the situation before us. When you are doubting or fearful, ask yourself, "Did God make the heavens and the earth and all that is within them? Can any difficulty or situation prove that He did not create all things?" You see, no matter who or what enemy we face, no matter how fierce his advances and persecutions, that enemy is still under the sovereign Lord of all creation! God said: "Behold the day of the Lord is coming, and . . . I will gather all nations to battle against Jerusalem.... But the remnant of the people shall not be cut off from the city. Then the Lord will go forth and fight against those nations . . ." (Zec 14:1-4).

No matter what enemy we face, always remember that God is in control. We tend to believe that the enemy is getting away with murder, forgetting that the real battle is over souls, not flesh and blood. When the enemies of God gather against Jerusalem, when they gather to condemn and silence the church, there is no battle over which God is not in ultimate control. Every enemy of this world or the next are creations of God and subject to Him and His will, even if it appears to us that they are getting away with their crimes. God is ready for every enemy advance always. The battle is His. Victory is His. There are no surprise attacks or battlefield maneuvers of which He is unaware. And it is He who will determine the outcome every single time. Our job is to wait patiently, even as the souls under the altar in Revelation 6, "who had been slain for the word of God and for the testimony which they held," who were told to rest a little while longer. Everything is under God's control, and no matter what we face, or how dire it appears, the battle belongs to the Lord!

May 26

No Greater Love

[18]Remember this, that the enemy has reproached, O Lord, and that a foolish people has blasphemed Your name. [19]Oh, do not deliver the life of Your turtledove to the wild beast! Do not forget the life of Your poor forever. [20]Have respect to the covenant; for the dark places of the earth are full of the haunts of cruelty. [21]Oh, do not let the oppressed return ashamed! Let the poor and needy praise Your name. [22]Arise, O God, plead Your own cause; remember how the foolish man reproaches You daily. [23]Do not forget the voice of Your enemies; the tumult of those who rise up against You increases continually. —*Psalm 74:18-23*

THIS MORNING, we will come to the real heart of the matter, and this is that fools are blaspheming God by oppressing and attacking His own people. Asaph calls Israel the Lord's turtledove, asking God to deliver this poor little nation from the wicked ones. He reminds God that they are poor, oppressed, and needy, and asks God to give them something to praise Him for by their deliverance from those who reproach Him daily.

As it was with Israel during the time of this psalm being written, so it is with us today. The tumult of those who are against the Lord is increasing today, as Asaph wrote. Is it right for us to cry out to God, asking that He defend His great name? Yes, it is, and we honor Him by doing so! God's people never have to fight in their own strength, and they shouldn't even try.

There are two things that we must keep in mind. In John 10, Jesus said, *"Therefore My Father loves Me, because I lay down My life that I may take it again. No one takes it from Me, but I lay it down of Myself. I have power to lay it down, and I have power to take it again. This command I have received of My Father"* (vv. 17-18). And, in Acts 22, Paul wrote, *"Now it happened, as I journeyed and came near Damascus at about noon, suddenly a great light from heaven shone around me. And I fell to the ground and heard a voice saying to me, 'Saul, Saul, why are you persecuting Me?' So I answered, 'Who are You, Lord?' And He said to me, 'I am Jesus of Nazareth, whom you are persecuting'"* (vv. 6-8).

No one was in control of Jesus' life but Jesus. No one took it. He gave it of Himself. And no one is control of our lives but God. He does allow us to lay down our lives at times, but, as Paul learned, those who persecute God's people are persecuting Jesus! Just as Asaph reviewed in his mind the history of Israel's victories through God in the past, even back to the days of Noah, so let us keep in mind that Moses didn't part the Red Sea. God did! Joshua didn't bring down the walls of Jericho. God did. The Medo-Persians didn't defeat Babylon. God did. Our God cooled the flame for Shadrach, Meschech, and Abed-nego; He shut the lions' mouths for Daniel; He opened the prison doors for Peter, and He caused the chains to fall off the hands of Paul and Silas. No Christian will ever fight or face the enemy of death in their own strength. This gives us battlefield supremacy over every enemy and takes out the sting of even death for our faith. Be bold, and stand firm in the face of attack. Our King is coming, and no one will be able to stand against Him. Meanwhile, He has given us the *power* to stand until He comes and meets us in the air! That might even be today!

May 27

The Waiting List

[1]To the Chief Musician. Set to "Do Not Destroy." A Psalm of Asaph. A Song. We give thanks to You, O God, we give thanks! For Your wondrous works declare that Your name is near. [2]"When I choose the proper time, I will judge uprightly. The earth and all its inhabitants are dissolved; I set up its pillars firmly. Selah —*Psalm 75:1-3*

WHETHER this Asaph is the author of Psalm 73 or 74, or of both, or of neither, we see a real interaction between the human and the Divine. As Asaph prays, God answers. If we reflect back on the impassioned writing of Psalm 74, we might conclude that this psalm, which we're just beginning, records God's response, with the situation still unchanged.

It's likely that some of you reading these words today are in a situation in which you're having to wait on the Lord for something. Your prayers, pleas, and petitions have been passionate and heartfelt, and yet, at this point, nothing has changed, even though you know that God has heard your prayers. As we begin this chapter, you'll easily be able to understand what Asaph and others, including ourselves, have had to experience in one way or another, and that is being put on "The Waiting List." What we want to do is to compile a list of things we can do while we wait for the Lord, and we'll see how Asaph continues to engage in conversation with God even though nothing appears to have changed. He is still waiting.

In verses 1-3 we see an exchange between the two. Remember in Psalm 74, Asaph wrote, "*Arise, O God, plead Your own cause; remember how the foolish man reproaches You daily. Do not forget the voice of Your enemies; the tumult of those who rise up against You increases continually*" (vv. 22-23).

The Lord's response in verse 2 of our psalm today is this: "*When I choose the proper time, I will judge uprightly.*" This is followed by a prophetic reminder of the ultimate judgment that awaits the earth and all of its inhabitants: they will be dissolved, and the Lord will then set up its pillars firmly. The "setting up of pillars" reminds us: "*The works of His hands are verity and justice; all His precepts are sure. They stand fast forever and ever, and are done in truth and righteousness*" (Psalm 117:7-8). God's moral and ethical code is unchanging, which is essential to His upright judging of the world and all who have ever lived on it. If what was right and true for one generation wasn't so in another, then one could cry "foul" against God on Judgment Day.

The first thing we want to add to our waiting list is exactly what Asaph exhibits in verse 1. Remember, Asaph doesn't have any evidence that his situation has been remedied, and God's response in verses 2 and 3 seems to indicate that it was yet future. So what's the first item on the list? *Begin to thank and praise God for what He is going to do*. We must recognize that whatever God does and whenever He does it will be perfect. We praise Him when He answers our prayers, but we should also praise Him *whether we see the answers or not*. We can always know that His answer will be best for all concerned, including the one praying, and it can't be anything less than perfect, because He is a perfect God!

Asaph thanks God, acknowledging that His "name is near" ("name" means "honor," "authority," "character") and Asaph performs the first thing on our waiting list. He begins to praise God for who He is, not just for what He does. He seeks God's face, not just His hand.

That's for us, Saints! It's at the top of the list. Begin to thank and praise God *for what He is going to do*. Do it not because of how you feel. Do it in spite of how you feel. And in doing that, you will be giving honor and glory to our Lord and will be blessed in one way or another (whether it's what you expected or not) because He loves you.

"I Brought You into This World, and I Can Take You Out"

⁴"I said to the boastful, 'Do not deal boastfully,' and to the wicked, 'Do not lift up the horn. ⁵Do not lift up your horn on high; do not speak with a stiff neck.'" ⁶For exaltation comes neither from the east nor from the west nor from the south. ⁷But God is the Judge: He puts down one and exalts another. —*Psalm 75:4-7*

WHAT GOD SAYS in these verses today is true for every person in every age and refers to the abuse of power by those in high places and the boasting that often accompanies it. When God says, "Do not lift up your horn" in verse 5, He is referring to the horn as a symbol of power. He is accusing those who speak with the stiff neck of rebellion and stubbornness. We see the same today among some who are powerful and/or famous.

In Acts 7, Philip accused the religious leaders, "*You stiff-necked and uncircumcised in heart and ears! You always resist the Holy Spirit; as your fathers did, so do you. Which of the prophets did your fathers not persecute? And they killed those who foretold the coming of the Just One, of whom you now have become the betrayers and murderers, who have received the law by the direction of angels and have not kept it*" (vv. 51-53). He was stoned to death for this bold speech, but he saw Jesus standing next to His Father in heaven as he died!

God is sovereign when it comes to the affairs of men. The Bible says that He puts down one and exalts another. He has brought everyone into this world, and He can take them out if and when He wants to. This by no means indicates that God is the cause and initiator of every action of every person, good or evil. He knows the future, and everything is working out according to His plan. He "takes no pleasure in the death of the wicked" (Eze 33:11). His desire is that *all* would be saved, but in our verses today, He's dealing with the arrogant blasphemers who think they can overturn His will and persecute His people.

Some of us may be waiting for deliverance from a situation—maybe reconciliation with an estranged family member or friend. Or perhaps you're experiencing the ceaseless attacks of an enemy in school or in your workplace. It could be that you've been betrayed by a spouse and find yourself on the losing side of a monetary or custody battle. Maybe you're being persecuted for the sake of righteousness, and you're praying for it to stop.

Well, add this to your "While You're Waiting" List: "God never leaves matters unresolved concerning His children." He will deal with the proud and boastful. It's true that some are exalted and others are put down, as our verse today states, but God will leave no matter concerning you or me unaddressed. Psalm 138:6-8 (precious words!) state: *"Though the Lord is on high, yet He regards the lowly; but the proud He knows from afar. Though I walk in the midst of trouble, You will revive me; You will stretch out Your hand against the wrath of my enemies, and Your right hand will save me. The Lord will perfect that which concerns me; Your mercy, O Lord, endures forever; do not forsake the work of Your hands."*

Keep your eyes off others and don't fall into the pity trap, thinking, "They don't have to go through these things. They have plenty of money. Their family relationships have been healed. God punishes their enemies. . . ." The Lord says, *"Let your conduct be without covetousness; be content with such things as you have. For He Himself has said, 'I will never leave you nor forsake you"* (Hebrews 13:5).

Do you believe this today? Then there should be corresponding actions and attitudes to accompany that belief, such as praise and thanksgiving while waiting. Jesus said, *"Come to Me, all you who labor and are heavy laden, and I will give you rest. Take My yoke upon you and learn from Me, for I am gentle and lowly in heart, and you will find rest for your souls. For My yoke is easy and My burden is light"* (Matthew 11:28-30). Rest on this today!

May 29

Don't Refuse the Cup of Blessing

> [8]For in the hand of the Lord there is a cup, and the wine is red; it is fully mixed, and He pours it out; surely its dregs shall all the wicked of the earth drain and drink down. [9]But I will declare forever, I will sing praises to the God of Jacob. [10]"All the horns of the wicked I will also cut off, But the horns of the righteous shall be exalted." —*Psalm 75:8-10*

OUR FRIEND Asaph now shows us the contrasting life and eternal experiences between the righteous and the wicked. At the Last Supper, we saw that the third of the four cups poured out represented the New Covenant in Christ's blood. The cup of blessing is also the cup of wrath, for it was the *blood* of the Lamb slain that provided forgiveness of sins to the whole word. Those who refuse to partake of the cup of blessing have no alternative but to experience the cup of God's undiluted wrath.

Look at the opening words of verse 8 above: "*In the hand of the Lord there is a cup, and the wine is red and fully mixed, and He pours it out. . . .*" God knows everything. He is perfectly just. So the completion to our Waiting List is: "Know that every injustice will be repaid."

Let's reflect for a moment on the contrasting destinies of the righteous and the wicked. The apostle John wrote: "*The Father loves the Son, and has given all things into His hand. He who believes in the Son has everlasting life; and he who does not believe the Son shall not see life, but the wrath of God abides in Him*" (John 3:35-26). In other words, all those who reject Christ as Savior and Redeemer will experience the wrath of God, and all who *have* accepted Christ will have had the wrath of God that was intended for them *laid upon Jesus.* (Note: this in no way endorses the teaching of Limited Atonement. According to 1 John 2:2, Christ died for the sins of the whole world. "Whole world" does not mean "the elect." It means the *whole world.*)

God will never permit injustice to reign forever. So what is His plan for us? What is the best thing that could happen to your enemy or persecutor? That they die? No! It is that they *get saved*! This is very important, because there are so many who feel as Asaph did in Psalm 74, that the enemy was having his way unchecked. It seemed as though God were doing nothing to stop him, and things would never be made right again.

Why does God permit the wicked to live? Why doesn't He just take him out? Listen, God does not rejoice in the death of the wicked (Ezekiel 33:11), and neither should we. We must not allow our thoughts and emotions to reign as we see the way the wicked live. Remember that every injustice will be repaid. There is no escaping God. "I will repay," said the Lord, in many verses of the Bible. He will repay, either through the blood of Jesus and the cup of blessing—or by Christ and the cup of His wrath and indignation. The point is this: God has not been unfair to you, and He will never be so. If it seems as if He has treated others better, He may simply be giving your enemies or oppressors time to repent! Jesus is coming back soon, but it feels like He should have come back yesterday, or *right this very minute*! Meanwhile, we need a waiting list, and here it is: 1) Thank and praise God for what He is going to do. 2) Remember that God never leaves matters concerning His children unresolved. 3) Know that every injustice will be recompensed. That's a great start. Are you ready to go out and face the day, equipped with the knowledge that God loves you and will protect you from the snares of the evil one?

As Good As It Gets

Introduction

To the Chief Musician. On an instrument of Gath.
A Psalm of Asaph. [Psalm 81]

TODAY WE'LL BEGIN to look at this psalm of lament, which is, again, by Asaph. In an earlier lament, he wrote: "*And I said, 'This is my anguish; but I will remember the years of the right hand of the Most High.' I will remember the works of the Lord; surely I will remember Your wonders of old. I will also meditate on all Your work, and talk of Your deeds. Your way, O God, is in the sanctuary; who is so great a God as our God? You are the God who does wonders; You have declared Your strength among the peoples*" (Psalm 77:10-14).

Asaph had anguish. Do you ever feel anguished? There are two cures for it: if it's self-inflicted (i.e., caused by your own sin), then repent; if the cause of anguish is outside of your control, then *remember God's faithfulness.*

This psalm is of dual character—it's a psalm of praise and also an admonition to the hearers to listen to the Lord. Here, similar to what we saw in Psalms 74 and 75, a petition is made in one song, and the divine response is in the next. Look back in your Bible to Psalm 80, where the psalmist wrote, "*Restore us, O God; cause Your face to shine, and we shall be saved! O Lord God of hosts, how long will You be angry against the prayer of the people? You have fed them with the bread of tears, and given them tears to drink in great measure. You have made us a strife to our neighbors, and our enemies laugh among themselves. Restore us, O God of hosts; cause Your face to shine, and we shall be saved!*" (vv. 3-7).

Psalm 81 is a *prescriptive* psalm. In other words, "If such-and-such happens, here's what you need to do," says the Lord. Although God through Asaph is address-ing the nation of Israel, our own country would do well to heed these words. Sadly, our nation also comprises many individuals who have rejected the Lord, or have a false idea of who He is. For example, there's a popular mindset among some, especially in the United States, that God just wants everybody to be happy, healthy, and wealthy. There's even a book about that, familiar to most: *Your Best Life Now.* The fact is, we *don't* have full control over the circumstances in our lives. We can't "attract" wealth; we can't repel sickness and disease by merely "having enough faith." There are poor and sick godly Christians of great faith all over the world!

Saints, we live in a fallen world, where sickness, death, disease, and poverty impact people of faith every day. What we need and want to do is to learn how to arrive at a place in life, even in this world such as it is, that we can describe as "As good as it gets."

Israel's sin was the cause of Asaph's plea, and God graciously responds with the cure. This also comes down to a personal level in the way of the need in this land for national repentance, but that's probably not going to happen. So the point is, how can this life be "as good as it gets" and remain content with that until we arrive at our "best life" in the next life? Listen, no matter what comes our way, no matter how far our country slides or how hard life becomes, God has a plan, and He will show us how to live our lives under any circumstances with the attitude that this is as good as it gets here, and He will be with us through it all. There's a lot that is praiseworthy in that thought. May we lift our praise to Him for seeing us through this day, giving us hearts and voices that can still sing of the wonders of His love—in the good, the bad, the mundane, the ugly, the scary, and the sad. "Weeping may endure for a night, but joy comes in the morning." God is with us, and nothing gets any "gooder" than that.

May 31

When Life Gives You Lemons . . .
Give Thanks for God's Gifts

¹Sing aloud to God our strength; make a joyful shout to the God of Jacob. ²Raise a song and strike the timbrel, the pleasant harp with the lute. ³Blow the trumpet at the time of the New Moon, at the full moon, on our solemn feast day. ⁴For this is a statute for Israel, a law of the God of Jacob. ⁵This He established in Joseph as a testimony, when He went throughout the land of Egypt, where I heard a language I did not understand. ⁶"I removed his shoulder from the burden; His hands were freed from the baskets. ⁷You called in trouble, and I delivered you; I answered you in the secret place of thunder; I tested you at the waters of Meribah. Selah —*Psalm 81:1-7*

IN THE PSALMS problems and praise are often paired together. Yesterday we saw Asaph expressing the need for restoration, and now he calls on the nation to sing aloud to God, who is our strength! He encourages the people to make a joyful shout to Him raise up a song, and strike up the band unto the Lord. Then he goes on to mention the feasts of the new and full moon, as was commanded by the Lord in Numbers 29:1-6: "*In the seventh month, on the first day of the month, you shall have a holy convocation. You shall do no customary work. For you it is a day of blowing the trumpets. You shall offer a burnt offering as a sweet aroma to the Lord . . . [with a] grain offering . . . [and] also one kid of the goats as a sin offering, to make atonement for you . . . as a sweet aroma, an offering made by fire to the Lord."* And also: *"On the fifteenth day of the seventh month you shall have a holy convocation. You shall do no customary work, and you shall keep a feast to the Lord seven days"* (Num 29:12).

Israel operated on a lunar calendar, and the feast on the day of the *new* moon was Rosh Hashanah, or the Feast of Trumpets; the feast on the day of the *full* moon was the Feast of Tabernacles, or Sukkoth. Asaph reminds the nation that this is part of the Law as a reminder of the exodus from Egypt and God's provision and protection as they wandered all those years through strange lands in the wilderness.

Asaph also mentions the rock at Meribah that gushed forth water when Moses struck it with his rod. This was a test, and God does test His people. But He also lifted their heavy burden of brick making, removing from them the responsibility of gathering straw to make those bricks. The Lord answered their prayers, delivering them in a thunderous way!

How does this relate to us? All the feasts of Israel caused the people to look back in remembrance of what God had done, but each feast also pointed to what lay ahead: the coming of the Messiah! And He would show us how our lives can be "as good as it gets."

If you want your life to be lived with shouts of joy to the Lord, proclaiming His glory, you must do this: *Always remember your forgiveness and deliverance!* Asaph points Israel back to God's faithful deliverance of them from Egypt and the miracles He did during the Exodus, but we also see those who had become spiritual brats: *"We remember the fish which we ate freely in Egypt, the cucumbers, the melons, the leeks, the onions, and the garlic; but now . . . there is nothing at all except this manna . . . !"* (Num 11:5-6). Seriously? That's the only thing they remembered from those horrible years in Egypt as slaves of Pharaoh?

Any of this "ringin' a bell" in *your* conscience? Remember: even if the bills are piling up, at least you're no longer headed for hell. The car won't run? You've been forgiven all your sins and reconciled to God! If you're weary from things not going your way, remember that the Holy Spirit lives in you, and the devil can't have his way in your life. You belong to God, and the one whom the Son sets free is free indeed! Looking back on our own forgiveness and deliverance will remind us that this may be as good as it gets now, but the best is yet to come—and it lasts forever. Count your many blessings! Hallelujah!

JUNE

Don't Live a Life of "If Only . . . "

8"Hear, O My people, and I will admonish you! O Israel, if you will listen to Me. *9*There shall be no foreign god among you; nor shall you worship any foreign god. *10*I am the Lord who brought you out of the land of Egypt; open your mouth wide, and I will fill it. *11*But My people would not heed My voice, and Israel would have none of Me. *12*So I gave them over to their own stubborn heart, to walk in their own counsels. —*Psalm 81:8-12*

THIS SECTION begins with an admonishment and a plea for them to listen. God himself has joined the dialog! Are they listening? The Lord is telling Israel, "Listen to Me! I want to restore you. I want to relieve and lift you up." Why did He need to admonish them? Because they weren't listening! Idol worship was rampant all around them, and God was warning them of the dangers therein. He reminds them "*I am* the Lord your God." He encourages them, jogging their memories regarding the miraculous delivery of them by His hand from the land of Egypt. He makes this gracious offer: "Just open your mouth wide. I want to fill it!" But we see that this is conditional. The end of verse 8 says, " . . . *if you will listen to Me.*"

There is a tremendous life application in these verses for us, as well as for the Israelites. If we tune out the Word and the will of God in our lives, we can't expect a positive outcome—ever—and there's no way we can expect life to be lived "as good as it gets."

God turns next from admonishment to indictment when He says in verse 11, "*But My people would not heed My voice, and Israel would have none of Me. So I gave them over to their own stubborn heart, to walk in their own counsels.*" In other words, God was saying, "You wanted to do your own thing without Me, so go ahead."

To whom was He speaking? To His people! What can we ourselves glean from this passage? *God wants us to do and believe what He says and not what we feel or think*. It really isn't complicated. But sometimes we need to be awakened to the fact that we aren't here to live the lifestyles of the rich and famous. In fact, we're to be at war with the principalities and powers of this fallen world!

This means that, yes, we will have sickness and sorrow, pain and trials, but we can at least eliminate our self-inflicted wounds that result in God's disciplinary action in our lives by simply doing what the Word says we're to do. And what is that? In Joshua, we read what God spoke to him: "*This Book of the Law shall not depart from your mouth, but you shall meditate in it day and night, that you may observe to do according to all that is written in it. For then you will make your way prosperous, and then you will have good success. Have I not commanded you? Be strong and of good courage; do not be afraid, nor be dismayed, for the Lord your God is with you wherever you go*" (Joshua 1:8-9).

Was the Lord speaking of Scripture memorization? Or did He mean for us to literally observe the Word in our own lives? Obviously, it was the latter. The Lord himself says to Joshua that the key to living a prosperous and successful life is to know and live by the Word of God. Listen, friends, God will let you do things your way, and He will allow you to think or feel whatever you want. But do you know what? When you choose to go that way, it won't be long before you will moan, "If only I had listened. . . ." God says, "I asked you to hear My words, but you refused, so I gave you over to your stubborn hearts and desires."

If your desire is for your life not to be a long list of regrets and "if onlys," then do exactly what God says, not what you feel. He is your Father, who formed your inward parts, and covered you in your mother's womb (Psalm 139:13). Surely He knows what's best for you in this life! Trust Him right now to show you what is *His* best for you. You won't ever regret it.

Some People's Kids . . .

> [13]"Oh, that My people would listen to Me, that Israel would walk in My ways! [14]I would soon subdue their enemies and turn My hand against their adversaries. [15]The haters of the Lord would pretend submission to Him, but their fate would endure forever. [16]He would have fed them also with the finest of wheat; and with honey from the rock I would have satisfied you." —*Psalm 81:13-16*

IT'S EXTREMELY important to listen to the Lord and do whatever He tells us. Have you ever been appalled as you've observed the behavior of a child who's old enough to know better but is acting rebelliously and disobediently to his parents in public despite their weak attempts to discipline him? Most of us feel disgusted at both the parents and the child.

We must never forget that what God said to Israel in this psalm is also meant for us in our day. Sadly, we tend to forget that the way we respond to God is a reflection on Him, for good or for bad. When nonbelievers observe Christians acting in ways that mock or take away from God's perfect image, their hatred of God only grows more intense, and they also despise the hypocrites who are flaunting their "freedom" to act as they want. God's warnings and promises in these verses are not exclusive to national Israel. We, too, are God's chosen by second birth even as the Jews are by first birth. If deliverance and protection are promised to the chosen people who walk in His ways, then it's certainly appropriate to embrace this conditional covenant as individual saints.

What does our loving God promise to His children who are obedient to Him, reflecting His character? "*If you diligently obey the voice of the Lord your God, to observe carefully all His commandments . . . the Lord your God will set you high above all nations of the earth. And all these blessings shall come upon you and overtake you, because you obey the voice of the Lord your God*" (Deut 28:1-2). It continues with the blessings that His children would enjoy in all aspects even in this fallen world.

Then we read: "*But it shall come to pass, if you do not obey the voice of the Lord your God, to observe carefully all His commandment and His statutes . . . that all these curses will come upon you and overtake you*" (Deut 28:15). From here proceeds a list of "cursings" in those lives, where blessings would have been possible, if only. . . .

The same is true for us as the saints of God, but many, like spoiled children, expect the blessings of obedience even as they live in disobedience. They're like those bratty kids that moral people don't even enjoy being around. How must our perfect heavenly Father view them, when He's given them so many blessings?

Actions have consequences. Yes, we are saved by grace through faith, but saving faith will always manifest itself through our actions that reflect obedience to God, which glorifies Him, so that others will know that we serve a loving God for whom we would do anything. We want to be the "King's kids," and act like it, not like "some people's kids."

Never minimize or deny the relationship between personal obedience and divine blessings. In 1 Peter 2:11-12, the apostle urges us to "*abstain from fleshly lusts which war against the soul, having your conduct honorable among the Gentiles, that when they speak against you as evildoers, they may, by your good works which they observe, glorify God. . . .*" Obedience matters to God. Life is hard, but we can experience it "as good as it gets" if we never forget God's forgiveness and our deliverance, doing what He says, not what we feel or think. Jesus and the Father are one, and they both have the same set of commandments. We can be seen as "the King's kids," honoring our Father, or we can be like "some people's kids," disgracing the parents who are raising them. It's something to think about.

One Nation

Introduction

A Song. A Psalm of Asaph. [Psalm 83]

Our psalm for the next few days is again by Asaph and is a lament that includes an imprecatory prayer. He prays against the nations that are conspiring against Israel and petitions God to act on Israel's behalf and make their enemies as chaff in the wind.

THERE ARE a broad range of interpretations for these verses, due to the fact that the "confederacy of nations" mentioned and the implied battle that some see here has never taken place, which would make this psalm prophetic regarding a future war. Some commentators believe this psalm is predictive of the Ezekiel 38-39 battle (unlikely, since Ezekiel names a different set of nations as aggressors against Israel). Others see it as prophetic of a battle yet to take place, viewing this war as a precursor to, or even the cause of, the battle of Ezekiel 38-39, placing it early in or just before the Great Tribulation.

One of these interpretations may be right, or all of them could be wrong. There could even have been a battle then, which appears to be implied, but there's a core issue we don't want to overlook and one that is critical to the understanding of the entire narrative. In Genesis 9, God said, "*I set My rainbow in the cloud, and it shall be for a sign of the covenant between Me and the earth. It shall be, when I bring a cloud over the earth, that the rainbow shall be seen in the cloud; and I will remember My covenant which is between Me and you and every living creature of all flesh; the waters shall never again become a flood to destroy all flesh. The rainbow shall be in the cloud, and I will look on it to remember the everlasting covenant between God and every living creature of all flesh that is on the earth*" (vv. 13-16).

Some seek to "hijack" the rainbow for their own purposes, but there's a true spiritual reason for this sign: God established an everlasting covenant with all on earth that He will never again judge the world by a global flood. Therefore, if the earth *does* experience another one, either God doesn't keep His word, "everlasting" doesn't mean forever, or God has been overthrown by a greater being. None of these is possible, so we know that when we see a rainbow and He calls it His everlasting covenant, then it's everlasting!

God made a covenant with Abraham that he would birth from his loins many nations, and to them He would give the land of Canaan as an everlasting possession (Gen 17:5-8). In an age where Replacement Theology is the predominant belief, there's a great need to understand the central theme of this psalm: *God has made an everlasting covenant with one nation—Israel*. Israel is the only nation that God has chosen for His many purposes and whom He opted to set His love upon, to whom He gave a geographical everlasting inheritance, through whom the Messiah would be given, and who will stand alone against the world in the last days. (See also Deut 4:7-8.) To the replacement theologians who believe that Israel's rejection of Jesus as the Messiah and that the church has replaced Israel in the covenantal scheme of things, I'll say this: If Replacement Theology is right, then God is wrong, which is a dangerous concept, at least. Israel is the one nation in the Old Testament that has been scattered throughout the world and is now regathered into the land by God himself! The church can no more replace Israel than a man can become a woman. DNA and biology say so. You can't change Israel into the church because Israel is the only nation with whom God himself has made an everlasting covenant! Let's pray that the Lord will open our hearts and minds to understand His plan for the world and His love for His chosen people, Israel—not because of anything that they have done, but because it was God's plan from eternity past that He would use this tiny nation in this unbelievable way!

A Little History Lesson Is in Order

> [1]Do not keep silent, O God! Do not hold Your peace. And do not be still, O God! [2]For behold, Your enemies make a tumult; and those who hate You have lifted up their head. [3]They have taken crafty counsel against Your people, and consulted together against Your sheltered ones. [4]They have said, "Come, and let us cut them off from being a nation, that the name of Israel may be remembered no more." —*Psalm 83:1-4*

ASAPH OPENS this psalm crying out for the Lord to take action against their enemy. He gives a detailed description of some of the enemy's own actions that would seem to require God's intervention. Their plots against the tiny nation are vengeful and hate-filled.

Zechariah foretold such times for Israel: *"Thus says the Lord . . . 'Behold, I will make Jerusalem a cup of drunkenness to all the surrounding peoples, when they lay siege against Judah and Jerusalem. And it shall happen in that day that I will make*

Jerusalem a very heavy stone for all peoples; all who would heave it away will surely be cut in pieces, though all nations of the earth are gathered against it'" (Zech 12:1-3). Sixteen times in chapters 12-14 we find the phrase "in that day." The "day" refers to the Day of Jacob's Trouble, the Great and Terrible Day of the Lord, the Seventieth Week of Daniel, or the Great Tribulation, as we call it. But in Zechariah 3, it says that *"all nations of the earth are gathered against"* Israel.

It sounds like a confederacy, or a global coalition. Confederacies against Israel are not new. There was a coalition against Israel in Joshua's day, and in Nehemiah we saw a growing coalition regarding the rebuilding of the Wall of Jerusalem. In 1948, when Israel was "born in a day," the very next day they were attacked by Egypt, Syria, Jordan, Lebanon, and Iraq. Border incidents between Israel and Syria, Egypt, and Jordan increased during the early 1960s until June 5, 1967, when Israel launched a massive air assault that led to the Six-day War and the capture of the Old City and the Golan Heights, all territories given to them by God in the everlasting covenant, and, with His help, they drove out the occupiers.

October 6, 1973, on Yom Kippur, Egyptian forces struck eastward across the Suez Canal and pushed the Israelis back while the Syrians advanced from the North. Iraqi forces joined the war and, in addition, Syria received support from Jordan, Libya, and the smaller Arab states. All had the same desire as the Iranians: to cut Israel off from being a nation.

Why is Israel important to the church? Why is it critical that we reject Replacement Theology, or any "ism" that minimizes Israel's right to exist or to dwell in the land covenanted to them by God? Because Israel is essential to understanding God's faithfulness. Zechariah 7:14: *"But I scattered them with a whirlwind among all the nations which they had not known."* And in Zechariah 8:7-8: *"Behold, I will save My people from the land of the east and from the land of the west; I will bring them back. And they shall dwell in the midst of Jerusalem. They shall be My people, and I will be their God, in truth and righteousness."*

How many nations have had land eternally covenanted to them directly by God, had coalitions of nations seeking their destruction for millennia, been scattered among the nations for nearly 2,000 years by the disciplinary hand of God, been regathered without losing their national identity into the exact land areas given them by God 3,500 years prior? *One nation.* Israel! Israel is crucial to understanding God's faithfulness. The confederacy against which Asaph prayed was not the first nor the last. But of the many, none prevailed, and Israel is *in the land promised to them by God* himself and will never be uprooted (Amos 9:15). This is not only food for thought, but a reason to be praying for Israel, as Scripture tells us (Ps 122:6).

The Righteousness of God

⁵For they have consulted together with one consent; they formed a confederacy against You: ⁶The tents of Edom and the Ishmaelites; Moab and the Hagrites; ⁷Gebak, Ammon, and Amalek; Philistia with the inhabitants of Tyre; ⁸Assyria also has joined with them; they have helped the children of Lot. Selah ⁹Deal with them as with Midian, as with Sisera, as with Jabin in the Brook Kishon, ¹⁰who perished at En Dor, who became as refuse on the earth. ¹¹Make their nobles like Oreb and like Zeeb, yes, all their princes like Zebah and Zalmunna, ¹²who said, "Let us take for ourselves the pastures of God for a possession." —Psalm 83:5-12

WHO ARE these nations, and why were they consulting together against Israel? Let's look at what we can know. These nations are all contiguous, i.e., touching, or very near, the nation of Israel. Historically, we have no record of their ever forming a coalition and attacking Israel. Nor are any of them named in the Ezekiel 38-39 scenario.

Seeing this as a future battle has two major weak spots, and the first is with the people group Edom. The Edomites were the descendants of Esau and the nearest of kin, yet enemies of Israel. According to the historian Josephus in his work, *Antiquities*, the Edomites were eliminated as a people by the Romans after the time of the Maccabees, thus making future involvement of Edom in a war with Israel impossible.

Some believe that the Edomites, Philistines, and Tyrinans represent the Palestinians, Hamas, and Hezbollah of today, which is speculation. Then we have the Hagrites. Those who draw the conclusion that this is a yet future battle believe that the Hagrites were the Egyptians, with Hagar as their matriarch. Hagar was Sarai's handmaid from Egypt. Egypt was well-established before Hagar and was ruled by Pharaohs. Egyptians are always referred to as Egyptians in Scripture, never Hagrites. They appear to be an offshoot of the Ishmaelites, making them Arabs. (The Egyptians are not Arabs.)

One more point about this psalm: nowhere does our text indicate that there is a battle, but only plotting. Isaiah wrote of Israel: *"'No weapon formed against you shall prosper, and every tongue which rises against you in judgment You shall condemn. This is the heritage of the servants of the Lord, and their righteousness is from Me,' says the Lord"* (Isaiah 54:17). Asaph prays, calling to the Lord's mind the victories of Gideon over the Midianites and the slaying of their princes, Oreb and Zeeb, and Zebah and Zalmuna, kings of Midian, and also Deborah and Barak and their victories over Sisera and Jabin, King of Canaan. In verse 12, he says, in essence, "They're coming after your land, Lord!"

Although there are facts and speculations concerning our text, there is something that can apply to only one nation, and that is this: *Israel is essential to understanding God's righteousness.* One nation alone has taught the world that God is righteous in that He does not allow sin to go unpunished, even in the life of those upon whom He has set His love. Even in the wilderness, God didn't reward rebellion and hardness of heart. He disciplined and scourged Israel for their sin, yet He never ceased loving them! When they rebelled, He sent them into captivity. When they rejected their Messiah, He scattered them among the nations and let the land lie desolate, and then He brought them back because of the everlasting covenant that He had made with them. God doesn't let those who hate Him and who attack His people go unpunished, and history has proven time and time again that to attack Israel is to provoke God.

One nation is essential to understanding God's faithfulness and righteousness. Apart from Israel's existence today, these things could not be fully understood. May we meditate on this in our hearts and grow even closer to our wonderful God!

June 6

Judgment Begins in the House of God

[13]O my God, make them like the whirling dust, like the chaff before the wind! [14]As the fire burns the woods, and as the flame sets the mountains on fire, [15]so pursue them with Your tempest, and frighten then with Your storm. [16]Fill their faces with shame, that they may seek Your name, O Lord. [17]Let them be confounded and dismayed forever; yes, let them be put to shame and perish, [18]that they may know that You, whose name alone is the Lord, are the Most High over all the earth. —*Psalm 83:13-18*

ASAPH REFERENCES the whirling dust on the edges of the millstone and the threshing floors located on the hills where the wind consistently separated the wheat from the chaff. He asks God to deal with the enemies like a great fire in the forest and to pursue them like an approaching tempest and raging storm, filling their faces with shame. He prays for this judgment with righteous anger against those come against God's people, and he makes a statement that should ring in our hearts today in the face of all the weak, watered-down teaching in most churches: *The judgment of God will cause people to know that He is the Lord, and it will even cause some to seek after Him.*

Peter wrote, "*For the time has come for judgment to begin at the house of God; and if it begins with us first, what will be the end of those who do not obey the gospel of God? Now 'If the righteous one is scarcely saved, where will the ungodly and the sinner appear?'"* (1 Peter 4:17-18). Notice where judgment begins? At the house of God. Why is that? Because God is righteous and all His judgments are right and true.

This isn't a judgment regarding our salvation. That judgment was already paid in full by Christ on the cross, and all who receive His payment for their sin are saved. This judgment is one of purification and sanctification that reveals God's righteousness to the world. Looking through Asaph's eyes, a battle is looming, and he turns to the righteousness of God throughout Israel's past, asking that it might be repeated in the present.

Today the entire world is gathered against Israel in spite of the fact that history reveals God's faithfulness, righteousness, and judgment regarding His chosen ones. What many don't seem to understand is that *Israel is essential in understanding God's prophetic timeline.* The prophet Ezekiel wrote: *"Thus says the Lord God: 'Now I will bring back the captives of Jacob, and have mercy on the whole house of Israel; and I will be jealous for My holy name—after they have borne their shame, and all their unfaithfulness . . . to me. . . . And they shall know that I am the Lord their God, who sent them into captivity . . . but also brought them back to their land. . . . And I will not hide My face from them anymore; for I shall have poured out My Spirit on the house of Israel,' says the Lord God"* (Ezekiel 39:25-29). The Lord will pour out His Spirit on Israel during the Tribulation when He fulfills the last and final seven-year period (See Daniel 9:24).

How many nations hold the key to identifying the nearness of that time period? One nation: Israel. Have you noticed a theme through our look at this psalm over the past few days? It is Israel. Israel cannot be cast aside or replaced if you hope to understand the sovereignty and providence and progressive revelation of God. And we know from Scripture that no matter how many rise up against her and plot for her demise, Israel will win. Israel is essential to the plan of God, because it is through this nation that all the nations of the earth are blessed (through the birth of Jesus our Savior), and because of this, all the nations who fight against them will be judged.

O Lord, the time of the end is surely drawing near. Hold our hearts in Your hand and keep us steadfast as we move forward in these exciting times.

The Hunger Gains

Introduction

To the Chief Musician. On an instrument of Gath. A Psalm of the sons of Korah. —*Psalm 84*

OUR SUBJECT this morning and over the next few days as we study this psalm of Zion is best introduced through the Sermon on the Mount and the words of Jesus in the Beatitudes: "*Blessed are those who hunger and thirst for righteousness, for they shall be filled*" (Matthew 5:6).

Now, let's go back to this psalm of the sons of Korah. It's one of my favorites because of the way it reflects the character of God. These verses remind us that the past cannot control the present nor can it determine our spiritual future, which is one of the reasons why this psalm is often referred to as the "pearl of the Psalms."

The sons of Korah were the descendants of a man by that name who, 500 years earlier, had erred exceedingly and played the fool. In short, he went to Moses, God's appointed and anointed leader of Israel, and challenged him, in essence saying: "Who do you think you are? We're all God's chosen people and just as capable of leading them as you are. We want to have a say in what goes on around here!"

Moses said to Korah and his partners, "We'll let the Lord decide this matter. Come back tomorrow and we'll see what He has to say." The next day, the Bible says that "*The glory of the Lord appeared to all the congregation. And the Lord spoke to Moses and Aaron, saying, 'Separate yourselves from among this congregation, that I may consume them in a moment.'*" At that point, Moses and Aaron fell on their faces, pleading that God would not destroy the entire congregation for the sins of a few. God responded, "*Speak to the congregation, saying, 'Get away from the tents of Korah, Dathan, and Abiram.'*" And then what followed was shocking. "*The ground split apart under them, and the earth opened its mouth and swallowed them up, with their households and all the men with Korah, and all their goods. So they and all those with them went down alive into the pit; the earth closed over them, and they perished from among the assembly*" (Numbers 16:28-33).

The point of this lengthy introduction is to say this: from the illustration of God's dealings here, we can understand that there is *no such thing as generational curses*. One person does not have to bear the penalty of another person's sins. Although sin may impact the generations that follow, God does *not* punish you for what your ancestors did. Even though you or your family has a terrible past, God has a wonderful plan for you in the present, and eternal glory awaits you in the future in heaven—*if you know Christ as Savior and Lord.*

The ones writing this song are the descendants of the wicked Korah, and yet here they are, leading worship and honoring the Lord in the Temple of God! God did not hold them accountable for the sins of their fathers in the past, nor does He do so with us today. Do you want to be filled with the blessings that result from hungering and thirsting after righteousness? There is a key, and it's written in Jesus' words in the verse from the Beatitudes with which we opened this devotional. We will learn what some of those blessings are and be reminded that the past is behind us, and in Christ we are dead to the sins of our ancestors. We'll take a closer look at the joys God has for us when we hunger and thirst for His righteousness. Are you ready? Begin by thanking Him today for His wonderful provision of salvation and His awesome love in not holding us responsible for another's sins. Hallelujah!

June 8

Where Two or Three Are Gathered

¹How lovely is Your tabernacle, O Lord of hosts! ²My soul longs, yes, even faints for the courts of the Lord; my heart and my flesh cry out for the living God. ³Even the sparrow has found a home, and the swallow a nest for herself, where she may lay her young—even Your altars, O Lord of hosts, my King and my God. ⁴Blessed are those who dwell in Your house; they will still be praising You. Selah —Psalm 84:1-4

TODAY, WE'LL BEGIN to look at the first of three things that we gain when we hunger for the Lord. The psalmist speaks of the tabernacle, the courts, and the house of God. These are poetic terms that refer to Solomon's Temple in Jerusalem. The words express a longing for the collective gathering of God's people and the wonder and beauty of *corporate* praise and worship. Keep in mind that even though the Temple and, specifically, the Holy of Holies, were places where the Lord was present, the Jews didn't believe that His presence was *limited* to the Temple grounds. "*Our God is greater than all gods. But who is able to build Him a temple, since heaven and the heaven of heavens cannot contain Him?*" said Solomon (2 Chronicles 2:5-6). In other words, the Temple wasn't a place for God to be kept but a place for God to be *met*; it was a place to come and meet together as His people, bringing a sacrifice of praise and worship with us.

There's a growing movement today that denies the necessity of attending church or being part of a corporate gathering of believers, citing that "we are the temples of the Holy Spirit," and spouting the popular saying, "You don't have to go to church to be a Christian." It's true that we *are* the temple of the Holy Spirit, but as Christians, we should, like the sons of Korah, *long* to be in the house of the

Lord. *"And let us consider one another in order to stir up love and good works, not forsaking the assembling of ourselves together, as is the manner of some, but exhorting one another, and so much the more as you see the Day approaching"* (Hebrews 10:24-25).

The sons of Korah remind us that there is something significant about the corporate gathering of God's people, and that our hearts and flesh should cry out for the living God. These worshipers speak to God personally, saying, "Blessed are those who dwell in Your house"! They mention the altars, and we are reminded that this is the house of prayer and not because it was the only place God could be found. They could worship Him anywhere, even all by themselves. But what a hunger and thirst for God with other believers will do is to give us unparalleled opportunities to experience God as we join with them. And although I hesitate to use such verbiage because of the rampant experientialism today, I'm not willing to allow abusers to diminish or rob us of the truth.

Here's what I mean: You can't glean from a concert, observing others perform, what you can experience during praise and worship in which you're a participant. You can't get from a speech what you learn from an anointed biblical message. You can't get from attending a seminar what you gain from gathering with the saints to hear the Word of God. A hunger for the house of the Lord grants you unparalleled opportunities to experience God. The world has nothing even remotely close to it, by comparison.

The apostle Paul would not agree, nor would the Holy Spirit, that we don't need a church or a pastor in order to learn about or worship God. The sons of Korah are reminding us of the "hunger gains," or what our hunger for the Lord yields for us, as we gather together to worship the living God. Things happen in God's house when we are gathered together with one another that don't happen anywhere else, and we should long for those moments.

June 9

Hungering and Thirsting for Righteousness

⁵Blessed is the man whose strength is in You, whose heart is set on pilgrimage. ⁶As they pass through the Valley of Baca, they make it a spring; the rain also covers it with pools. ⁷They go from strength to strength; each one appears before God in Zion. ⁸O Lord God of hosts, hear my prayer; give ear, O God of Jacob! Selah —*Psalm 84:5-8*

TODAY WE AGAIN encounter blessings being offered to those whose hearts are set on pilgrimage. What does this mean? To some, it's viewed as the annual feast associated with trips to Jerusalem. Personally, I believe the context isn't about the journey but the destination: Zion, the house of God. For us, that would be the church.

The Valley of Baca is mentioned as a place through which one must pass. It literally means, "The Valley of Weeping." It's figurative for a place of difficulty or sorrow, much like David's mention in Psalm 23:4: *"Yea, though I walk through the valley of the shadow of death, I will fear no evil; for You are with me; Your rod and Your staff, they comfort me."* The psalmist goes on to say that the Valley of Baca becomes a spring covered with pools. The people go from strength to strength, and each one appears before God in Zion. The last phrase means that the weak and weary have access to God at all times, as do we all!

The next thing we gain from hungering for God is the *strength and hope that are exclusive to those who know God.* Have you noticed that our world is growing more and more evil, with crimes becoming more frequent, senseless, and sociopathic? The reason for this is the denial of God as Creator. When you deny that man is created in God's image and likeness, you have taken any value away from human life and made life into a meaningless and purposeless existence, which means that life has no value, so you can slaughter people both in or outside the womb, and it doesn't matter.

People are hopeless today, and it stems primarily because of the teaching of evolution, which robs mankind of value and steals from man's ability to reason. But don't you lose hope! There is a group of people today who know very well that the world is spiraling out of control; they know that judgment is coming, and they see that the end of all things is at hand, yet at the same time, they are the most hopeful and joyful people in all the earth. Believers in Christ know and understand the evidence that is all around them that *in the beginning, God created....* They know this Creator God personally! And in times of difficulty and darkness, they find strength and hope that is exclusive to them because they know Him. Peter tells us, *"Beloved, do not think it strange concerning the fiery trial which is to try you, as though some strange thing happened to you; but rejoice to the extent that you partake of Christ's sufferings, that when His glory is revealed, you may also be glad with exceeding joy. ... [If] anyone suffers as a Christian, let him not be ashamed, but let him glorify God in this matter"* (1 Peter 4:12-16).

Saints, are you hungering and thirsting for righteousness? I hope so, because there are hunger gains available to you and me, and they can be found by remembering first of all that this world is not our home.

These Are the Good Ol' Days

⁹O God, behold our shield, and look upon the face of Your anointed. ¹⁰For a day in Your courts is better than a thousand. I would rather be a doorkeeper in the house of my God than to dwell in the tents of wickedness. ¹¹For the Lord God is a sun and shield; the Lord will give grace and glory; no good thing will He withhold from those who walk uprightly. ¹²O Lord of hosts, blessed is the man who trusts in You! —*Psalm 84:9-12*

—

"I WOULD RATHER *be a doorkeeper in the house of my God than to dwell in the tents of wickedness*," write the sons of Korah. Matthew 11:11 states, "*Among them that are born of women there hath not risen a greater than John the Baptist: notwithstanding he that is least in the kingdom of heaven is greater than he*," meaning that the one of lowest stature who is in heaven is far greater than the greatest person alive on earth! The closer we remain to the Lord in our spirit now, the better our lives will be, no matter what adversities and trials we face, even unto death. And of course, "absent from the body [is to be] present with the Lord" (2 Corinthians 5:8). It's a win-win situation!

The "tents of wickedness" are clearly a reference to Korah, and the descendants of Korah are saying that they want no part of such rebellion. Some scholars see the "work of service" assigned to the Korahites as janitorial in nature, there's also the possibility that they were the temple guards. The word "keepers" means to guard or protect. Regardless, they were content to do whatever they did, compared to the wickedness of their ancestors.

They refer to the Lord as a *sun*, meaning that He is the source of light—not just a ray of light, as from the physical sun, but the source from which light emanates! The mention of the Lord being a *shield* implies God's defense and protection. So regardless of whether they were mere doorkeepers or the guardians of the Temple didn't matter. They would rather be "least" in the Temple than to dwell in the tents of the wicked.

We see that the Lord *will* give grace and glory, a tremendous relief to these men whose ancestors had sinned so grievously again the God whom they honored. We hear stories of the relatives of those who have committed heinous crimes going into hiding out of shame. But in God's family, those whose ancestors have sinned greatly can become the guards of the Temple (v. 11)! Verse 12 tells us why they walk uprightly: they trust in God.

Right here we come to another one of the things we gain by hungering and thirsting after the Lord and after righteousness: We can *expect* to see great and mighty things! Are you still waiting for the Lord to "do something" about a situation in your life? Remember, God isn't doing only "one thing," so make sure that you look around for other great and mighty things that He is doing meanwhile. And while you wait, take heart! Psalm 27 states, "*I would have lost heart, unless I had believed that I would see the goodness of the Lord in the land of the living. Wait on the Lord; be of good courage, and He shall strengthen your heart; wait, I say, on the Lord!*" (vv.13-14).

Never forget that every day of being a Christian is better than any day before you came to Christ. Your unsaved past is not "the good ol' days." Yes, things are hard, but you have Jesus. Yes, you will be attacked for your faith, but you have Jesus. Yes, you've made mistakes in the past, but you have Jesus, and "*No good thing will He uphold from those who walk uprightly.*" So let's go back to where we began: "*Blessed are those who hunger and thirst for righteousness, for they shall be filled*" (Mat 5:6). Let's move forward, walking in a way where great and mighty things are possible through God. Call upon the name of the Lord!

June 11

The Closer You Get

Introduction

He who dwells in the secret place of the Most High. —*Psalm 91*

SOME SCHOLARS believe the author of this psalm is Moses. Whether or not this is so, the Holy Spirit is the true inspiration for this and every chapter of the Bible, and He has a word for us today through these verses. It's a very timely word in this world of terror, corruption, and evil leadership—a world where political correctness stifles truth, and evil is called good and good is called evil.

There is a "woe" pronounced against these things. Isaiah 5:9 states, "Woe to those who call evil good, and good evil," but we still must live in this fallen world. That's why we need a message that we can trust in our day. It's important that we remember what to do when times are terrible and even frightening.

But take heart! There's a key word in our text that's a bit of hinge upon which all that we're going to study hangs upon, and that word is "dwell." In Hebrew, the word means "remain, sit, abide, to have one's abode, endure, and establish." Another way to understand it would be to take a fixed position or to be steadfast. The author of Hebrews wrote, "*Let us hold fast the confession of our hope without wavering, for He who promised is faithful*" (v. 10:23). This gives us an idea of what is meant when the Scripture speaks of dwelling "in the secret place of the Most High." But there's also an antithesis of "dwelling in" that we must recognize, because it leads to the opposite of the results, benefits, and blessings that are recorded in our verse.

In Mark, we read, *"They led Jesus away to the high priest; . . . But Peter followed Him at a distance, right into the courtyard of the high priest. And he sat with the servants and warmed himself at the fire"* (Mark 14:53-54). Although the idea of Peter "warming" himself may have been more of a practical gesture than spiritual, much like Peter's following Jesus at a distance, the facts are irrefutable: *Peter's decision to enter into that courtyard tragically led to his denials of knowing Jesus Christ.*

Here's the lesson for us: to follow God at a distance is never a good idea. The use of the word "dwell" in the opening phrase of this psalm of trust, and the blessings in that, is a lesson all by itself. To dwell in the secret place of the Most High is what allows the rest of the verses of this psalm to be appropriated. In a world where many believe that the blessings of God belong to us no matter how we act or behave, there's a valuable lesson before us that will remind us of the dangers of warming ourselves at the fires of complacency, and this is why the title of the message for this psalm is "The Closer You Get." Implied in that phrase is the idea of getting closer to God, of course. There aren't only blessings that we will receive from that closeness, but there are other benefits, too—among them, protection!

We'll walk through all of this for a few days, so that the difference between "following at a distance" and "walking beside" becomes clearer, and the choices that we should make will become evident as well. Even though it messes up the rhythm a little bit, we may find ourselves singing, "I have decided to follow [close to] Jesus, no turning back, no turning back."

June 12

Tearing Down the "Blessing Blockers"

> [1]He who dwells in the secret place of the Most High shall abide under the shadow of the Almighty. [2]I will say of the Lord, "He is my refuge and my fortress; My God, in Him I will trust." [3]Surely He shall deliver you from the snare of the fowler, and from the perilous pestilence. [4]He shall cover you with His feathers, and under His wings you shall take refuge; His truth shall be your shield and buckler. —*Psalm 91:1-4*

IN THESE beautiful verses, the psalmist establishes a pinnacle of truth for us as he proclaims the marvelous greatness of God's character and capabilities. He acknowledges God as El Elyon, God Most High, and then as El Shaddai, God Almighty. He personalizes these names, saying *"My* God" (my Elohiym). After establishing God's credentials, he moves on to His attributes and capabilities: He is my refuge, my fortress, my Deliverer, my covering, my shield, and my Protector. But notice that all of these are based upon the author's proximity to the Lord, which is the safest and best of all places: in the secret place of the Most High, under His shadow, with

God's truth as his shield and buckler. (The meaning of "buckler" in this passage is a bit different from usage in some other places, in that here it means a large shield that protects the entire body.) This is obviously the safest of all places to be!

James, whom many scholars agree was likely the half-brother of Jesus, concurred. He wrote: "*Submit to God. Resist the devil and he will flee from you. Draw near to God and He will draw near to you. Cleanse your hands, you sinners; purify your hearts, you double-minded. . . . Humble yourselves in the sight of the Lord, and He will lift you up*" (James 4:7-10). What is he saying? He's implying that dirty hands, impure hearts, and double-mindedness (being two-spirited or vacillating) all put a distance between a person and God, and thus the admonition to "draw near," as opposed to following at a distance and warming one's hands at the fires of complacency. Another beautiful phrase used is "under His wings," clearly an allusion to the Mercy Seat of God (See also Ex 25:17-22). Of God's mercies, Jeremiah wrote: "*This I recall to mind, therefore I have hope. Through the Lord's mercies we are not consumed, because His compassions fail not. They are new every morning; great is Your faithfulness. 'The Lord is my portion,' says my soul, 'Therefore I hope in Him!' The Lord is good to those who wait for Him, to the soul that seeks Him. It is good that one should hope and wait quietly for the salvation of the LORD*" (Lam 3:21-26). In those closing lines, the word "salvation" means "deliverance." This implies that when we were saved, we were delivered from something, namely hell! God saves us from hell and delivers us from the practices that send people there.

Remember this, as you focus on following the Lord closely: ***The closer you get to God, the less likely you are to encounter moral or spiritual failure.*** Although we won't become perfect and sinless in this life (but we will when we see Jesus and are like Him [1 John 3:2]), we can always take shelter under the shadow of His wings at the Mercy Seat.

Are you guilty of putting up blessing blockers in your life, following the Lord at a distance, or, worse, treating Christianity like a salad bar, from which you can pick and choose the things you like and disregard the rest, exalting your feelings over God's truth? That's about as helpful as shooting yourself in the foot. We live in a world in which man has exalted himself above God. We know the cure: Draw near to God, and He will draw near to you. Then there won't be any more blessings being blocked and no distance between you and your Savior and the precious Mercy Seat under His wings.

June 13

Reflecting God's Light

⁵You shall not be afraid of the terror by night, nor of the arrow that flies by day, ⁶nor of the destruction that lays waste at noonday. ⁷A thousand may fall at your side, and ten thousand at your right hand; but it shall not come near you. ⁸Only with your eyes shall you look, and see the reward of the wicked. ⁹Because you have made the Lord, who is my refuge, even the Most High, your dwelling place, 10no evil shall befall you, nor shall any plague come near your dwelling. . . . —*Psalm 91:5-10*

WE NOW FIND that the message of Psalm 91 moves from spiritual purity to personal protection (which, obviously, can be spiritual in nature, too). It's not hard to agree with the scholars that Moses is the likely author of this psalm, because the background could be understood as the death of the firstborn in Egypt for all who didn't apply the blood of an unblemished lamb to the doorposts at the Passover. The people would also be reminded of the thousands of Egyptian soldiers lying dead on the shores of the Red Sea during the Exodus. In both instances, Israel saw the awful reward of the wicked, unlike that of those who had obeyed the Lord and were covered by the blood, making God their refuge and dwelling place.

Our Lord's protection is still active today, although many who don't "follow closely" to Him may doubt this when they look around. Charles Spurgeon tells of a time when London was experiencing a great cholera outbreak. He described his experiences of walking from one funeral to another of friends and loved ones, and in between, his time was spent visiting the sick and the dying. Fear for his own health and that of his family was becoming an overwhelming burden to him. One day, between two funerals, as he walked down a road in Dover, he saw a sign in a cobbler's shop that read, "*Because you have made the Lord, who is my refuge, even the Most High, your dwelling place, no evil shall befall you, nor shall any plague come near your dwelling*" (our verses 9-10 above). From that moment on, Spurgeon said that he ministered without fear, knowing that his life was in the *Lord's hands*. How could he do so? Because he had made the Lord Most High his own dwelling place! And just like the tenth plague in Egypt, the evil did not come near him.

In days such as the ones in which we live, the plagues of ISIS and immorality are all around us. This should only serve as further cause to draw nearer to God, for the truth is: ***The closer we get to Him, the more obvious He becomes to others.*** Think about it. When the death angel passed over the house of all who had applied the blood to the doorposts, what happened? Pharaoh let the people go. Why? Was it the Israelites whom he feared? No, it was the Lord God Almighty! When the army of the Egyptians lay dead on the banks of the Red Sea, who was exalted? The Lord of heaven and earth! When Spurgeon ministered fearlessly in the midst of the cholera plague, was he the reason for being spared? Of course not! God gets the glory when He does what He does, and shame on us if we try to steal any of it for ourselves.

We need to draw ever nearer to Him and ask Him to help us to truly shine *His* light into this decaying, dark world. And one glorious day, we will be *so close* to Him that we will no longer "see in mirror, dimly, but then face to face . . . then [we] shall know [Him] just as [we] are also known." Let us reflect His light in this old world.

June 14

Is Jesus Obviously in Your Life?

> [11]For He shall give His angels charge over you, to keep you in all your ways. [12]In their hands they shall bear you up, lest you dash your foot against a stone. —*Psalm 91:11-12*

OUR MINDS, I'm sure, latched onto these two verses and classified them as messianic, but we must also remember who quoted them to the Lord: "*Then the devil took Him up into the holy city, set Him on the pinnacle of the temple, and said to Him, 'If you are the Son of God, throw Yourself down. For it is written: "He shall give His angles charge over you," and "In their hands they shall bear you up, lest you dash your foot against a stone." Jesus said to him, 'It is written again, "You shall not tempt the Lord your God"'*" (Matthew 4:3-10).

Satan's quoting of these passages is a misappropriation of their meaning, and Jesus points it out as such by quoting Deuteronomy 6:16: "*You shall not put the Lord Your God to the test, as you tested him at Massah (Meribah)*." Satan was using his old ploy of twisting Scripture in an effort to get Jesus to violate the Scripture. Does that still happen today? Saints, the "you" in these verses includes you and me. We must always be on our guard. When we listen to Satan, we draw away from the Lord and run the risk of making terrible mistakes that could ruin our lives.

God deals with sin, no matter where it originates or in what form it comes. Ezekiel wrote: "*The word of the Lord came to me, saying, 'Son of man, when the house of Israel dwelt in their own land, they defiled it by their own ways and deeds. . . . Therefore I poured out my fury on them for the blood they had shed on the land, and for their idols. . . . I scattered them among the nations . . . I judged them according to their ways and their deeds. . . . Wherever they went, they profaned My holy name— when they said of them, "These are the people of the Lord, and yet they have gone out of His land." But I had concern for My holy name, which the house of Israel had profaned among the nations . . .*'" (Ezekiel 36:16-21).

God wanted to bless Israel, but they refused to draw near to Him and kept Him at a distance, so they were scattered among the nations. Every moment they were outside of the Land of Promise was, in essence, profaning His name because they weren't near to Him.

We're not helping the world to see the Lord by trying to convince them that we're just like them only with Jesus. We should be distinct! Is God distinct from all others? Does He live in us? Then the more *different* we are from the world around us, the more obvious He becomes, but every moment that we are *outside* of His promises, we cause His name to be profaned. When we draw near to Him, and He draws near to us, we reflect His love to a dying world.

The carnality in the church today is of Satan. He puts up a blockade against the church being blessed, and every moment that the church doesn't remain under the protective shield and buckler of truth, the name of the Lord is profaned. How grievous! What does He desire for and from us? Exodus 19:5-6 says, "*Now, therefore, if ye will obey my voice indeed, and keep my covenant, then ye shall be a peculiar treasure unto me above all people: for all the earth is mine: And ye shall be unto me a kingdom of priests, and an holy nation*" (KJV). And 1 Peter 2:9 says, "*But ye are a chosen generation, a royal priesthood, an holy nation, a peculiar people; that ye should shew forth the praises of him who hath called you out of darkness into his marvelous light*" (KJV).

God wants His people to be different from other people. It's hard to convince someone of the need for God in their life when they don't see any difference in ours. The key is in this: **the closer you get to God, the more obvious He becomes to others.** Do you want to make a difference in this world? Draw near to the Lord in your own life first.

June 15

What's Your "God Proximity"?

[13]You shall tread upon the lion and the cobra, the young lion and the serpent you shall trample underfoot. [14]"Because he has set his love upon Me, therefore I will deliver him; I will set him on high, because he has known My name. [15]He shall call upon Me, and I will answer him; I will be with him in trouble; I will deliver and honor him. [16]With long life I will satisfy him, and show him My salvation." —*Psalm 91:13-16*

THE OPENING WORDS set the context: the treading upon of the lion and the cobra. A lion and a cobra—to whom do you suppose the psalmist refers? Peter wrote: "*Be sober, vigilant; because your adversary the devil walks about like a roaring lion, seeking whom he may devour*" (1 Peter 5:8). And in Revelation we read, "*So the great dragon was cast out, that serpent of old, called the Devil and Satan, who deceives the whole world; he was cast to the earth, and his angels were cast out with him" (vv. 12:9).

The young lion and the serpent would refer to the devil's spiritual offspring, the false prophets and teachers, cult leaders, and deceivers. To tread on them (v. 13 in our psalm) figuratively means to be in authority over them. Mark wrote: "*These signs will follow those who believe: in My name they will cast out demons . . . speak with new tongues; . . . take up serpents; and if they drink anything deadly, it will by no means hurt them; . . . lay hands on the sick, and they will recover*" (Mark 16:17-18). And in 1 John we read, "*You are of God, little children, and have overcome them, because He who is in you is greater than he who is in the world*" (v. 4:4).

Do you ever wonder why the church today doesn't look like this? Here's why: proximity to God. The cure for it? Get closer to Him! Don't be like Peter and follow along at a distance. We need to draw near to our Redeemer.

Note that the subject of our power and authority over demons is introduced with a qualifier: "because." *Because He has set His love upon me*, the One in whose power we live and move and have our being (Acts 17:28), He will deliver us! The one who sets his love on the Lord will be set on high. God knows his name, his nature, and his character.

What about long life (v. 16)? That would be identified with the phrase "show him my salvation (eternal life)." There are temporal blessings in these verses, and here is the last of the three: The closer you get to God, the greater His power is manifested in you. We need only mention two names here: David and Saul. "*The Philistine said, 'I defy the armies of Israel this day; give me a man, that we may fight together.' When Saul and all Israel heard these words of the Philistine, they were dismayed and greatly afraid*" (1 Samuel 17:10-11 –emphasis added). Had Saul moved away from his closeness to God? Yes! David, on the other hand, was a man after God's own heart. Did one walk in *fear* for his life and the other in the power of the Lord? We can answer that by looking at the encounter that David had with Goliath: "*David spoke, 'Who is this uncircumcised Philistine, that he should defy the armies of the living God?'*" (1 Samuel 17:26).

Are there giants in your life? Are you dwelling under the shadow of God's wings, so that His truth can be your shield and buckler? Or are you justifying your weakness because of the size of the giants or legitimizing carnality because of our culture? Listen, if you are weak and overcome by sin and the love of this world, change your nearness to God, and things will change for you! "*Greater is He that is in me than He that is in the world*" (1 John 4:4).

Yesterday, Today, and Forever

Introduction

A Psalm. A Song for the Sabbath day. —*Psalm 92*

THE AUTHOR of this psalm is unknown, but most identify him as Moses. The character of this psalm is a *hallel*, or a psalm of praise, and is easily paired with Psalm 91. Remembering our look at Psalm 91 over the past few days, we recall that the author wrote, "*He who dwells in the secret place of the Most High shall abide under the shadow of the Almighty. I will say of the Lord, 'He is my refuge and my fortress; my God, in Him I will trust'*" (Psalm 91:1-2). That psalm was filled with phrases like "perilous pestilence," "arrows by day," "terror by night," "plagues," "lions," and "serpents"! All of these were met with the promised protection and deliverance by the Most High God as they put their trust in Him.

We also saw, as we keep these verses in context, that some really difficult things do come near to the chosen people of God, including Christians. Although the first three plagues when they were still slaves in Egypt did come near to the people, the last seven did not. Only the Egyptians suffered. We can take heart that when God plagues the world with wrath, it will not come near to us, His children.

There's a truth contained in this psalm that will open the door of our hearts and minds to something that we may not always recognize but that will help us from being merely religious or mechanical in our praise and thanksgiving. Just as Psalm 91 was a song of trust, Psalm 92 is a song of praise. This is in the correct order, because learning to trust is essential to truly being able to praise. Praise absent of trust is merely insincere lip service and even hypocrisy. Job wrote, "*Though He slay me, yet will I trust Him. Even so, I will defend my own ways before Him. He also shall be my salvation, for a hypocrite could not come before Him*" (Job 13:15-16).

Remember, praise isn't an expression of happiness but one of faith, *no matter what may come*. It can feel mechanical yet not be mechanical. How is that possible? It means that we can trust God when our hearts are broken and life is brutal and mean. It's not that we must "feel good," or get the warm fuzzies when we praise Him. Job declared that he would trust and defend his own ways before the Lord, meaning that he would justify his circumstances based on his pain and sorrow, and yet, out of heartbroken or even fearful sincerity, he would express his hope and trust in God and His Word, *no matter what*. Our psalm over the next few days will help us in this by reminding us of three things that are true yesterday, today, and forever.

This psalm is titled "A Psalm for the Sabbath." The word Sabbath means "rest," and resting in the Lord is an idiom for trusting in Him. For many, our psalm will take you to a place of trust and sincere praise, even if current or recent circumstances may leave you feeling as though He has slain you. Three things that were true yesterday are true today and will be true forever. They don't change because the Lord never changes. He is the same—always. *"For who is God, except the Lord? And who is a rock, except our God?"* (2 Samuel 22:32). We can trust in the Rock of our salvation no matter what may lie before us. He sees down the road ahead of us, and if we trust Him, will bring us exactly to where He wants us to be.

June 17

Rest for the Weary

[1]It is good to give thanks to the Lord, and to sing praises to Your name, O Most High; [2]to declare Your lovingkindness in the morning, and Your faithfulness every night, [3]on an instrument of ten strings, on the lute, and on the harp. . . . [4]For You, Lord, have made me glad through Your work; I will triumph in the works of Your hands. —*Psalm 92: 1-4*

I LOVE THE WAY this psalm opens, as we're given the instruments that played harmoniously accompanying this "Song for the Sabbath" bookended by reasons for trust-based praise: God's lovingkindness and His faithfulness. These verses also provide us the frequency with which we are to engage in this praise: morning and night (v. 2). This would certainly imply "at all times"!

Notice the benefits of praise in these verses, beginning with the opening stanza, which reads, "It is good to give thanks to the Lord and to sing His praises." The work of the Lord's hand made Moses glad and gave him a sense of triumph through them. That's what praise will do for us! Looking back at Psalm 91, we see the necessity of trust in the establishing of true praise when perils, plagues, and arrows are coming at you from all sides. Isaiah wrote, *"You will keep him in perfect peace, whose mind is stayed on You, because he trusts in You"* (Isaiah 26:3). But there's a condition on our part that must be met in order to obtain a peace that only God can give us. What is it? Simply this: trust. And this is true, yesterday, today, and forever.

Moses says, "It is good to give thanks. . . ." Good for whom? God is pleased with our thanks and blessed by our praise, but He isn't changed by it, nor is He made better from it. Yet He commands it. Why is that? Because He knows that yesterday, today, and forever, praise is an ointment for our soul. *Our soul?* I think of the words of C. S. Lewis, who wrote, "You don't have a soul; you *are* a soul. You *have* a body." Much of modern "praise" today focuses on the body and not on ministering to the soul. Many praise songs now are about *us* and not about or to *Him*. Although there are some wonderful, powerful praise songs written today, there are many others that aren't about who God is at all but rather about what He can do *for us* to enhance our life circumstances!

The mention of morning and evening in this psalm pictures for us good times and dark times and the necessity of praise in both of them. In Psalm 91, we saw the proximity of plagues, pestilence, arrows, and terrors in our lives. At times like those, the soul needs much more than flesh-gratifying songs about ourselves. True praise is an outward expression of trust, and we see the connection between trust and personal blessing, including comfort for the hurts that wound the soul. Peter wrote: "*In this you greatly rejoice, though now for a little while . . . you have been grieved by various trials, that the genuineness of your faith, being much more precious than gold . . . though it is tested by fire, may be found to praise, honor, and glory at the revelation of Jesus Christ, whom having not seen you love . . . believing, you rejoice with joy inexpressible and full of glory, receiving the end of your faith—the salvation of your souls*" (1 Pet. 1: 6-9).

Trials that grieve us, but that we meet with genuine faith and trust, can praise, honor, and glorify Jesus Christ, resulting in joy inexpressible and full of glory, knowing that there is an end result of our faith in Him: the salvation of our souls. Meanwhile, our souls are grieved, and we have sorrow at times, but trust-based praise is a soothing ointment to them. *Lord, help us to praise You, day and night and in between. Let our praise be a glory to You and a soothing ointment to our hurting hearts.*

June 18

Why, God?

> ⁵O Lord, how great are Your works! Your thoughts are very deep. ⁶A senseless man does not know, nor does a fool understand this. ⁷When the wicked spring up like grass, and when all the workers of iniquity flourish, it is that they may be destroyed forever. ⁸But You, Lord, are on high forevermore. —*Psalm 92: 5-8*

WHEN YOU ATTEMPT to deal with things foreign to your thinking, remember the likely author and setting for this Sabbath song. After the Jews had spent more than 400 years in captivity, and following a harrowing exodus from Egypt after the death of all the firstborn in the households of those who didn't know the Lord, Moses looks back, rejoicing that the people at last have rest. Israel's enemies, who were also God's enemies, had been dealt with by the Lord himself at the waters of the Red Sea.

For us today, instead of the Egyptians insert the names ISIS, Boko Haram, the Muslim Brotherhood—and, Christians, and you'll get a better idea of the context for this psalm and how it relates to us. Verse 5 helps us to understand the reverence and respect this author had for the Lord. No matter what things may look like from our standpoint, God is good. Always. His ways are not our ways nor His thoughts our thoughts. We must trust that the deep thoughts of the Lord are justice and righteousness, and we can always lean on Him. "His word endures forever," Peter wrote in 1 Peter 1:22-25. And although we may not always understand Him, we can understand this: God always deals righteously. Even when it seems that the wicked are rising up all around us (something we can really relate to in our times), the wicked will be destroyed, and the righteous will be with the Lord forever. Hold onto this idea, even in the darkest of situations: Truth and justice will ultimately prevail.

Isaiah understood the plight that we're in, although he never saw our day. And he held onto his faith throughout whatever trials he was made to endure, writing, *"The Lord of hosts has sworn, saying, 'Surely, as I have thought, so it shall come to pass, and as I have purposed, so it shall stand'* (14:24). Did you read that? The same concept is true yesterday, today, and forever that whatever God thinks and purposes will ultimately come to pass. Those today who are slaughtering Christians around the world, inflicting torturous and barbaric acts upon women and children, will answer before a pure and righteous God regarding every evil deed they have done to Him and to His people. Unless they repent and turn to Jesus, there will be no paradise awaiting them but only the place of fire that burns with brimstone.

We may find ourselves wondering why God doesn't just wipe these evildoers off the face of the earth with a single word. Why does He allow terrorists to stab and wound and kill Jews every day in Israel? Why does He allow the innocent to perish and the drunk driver to live through the accident they caused? Friends, I don't know, but this I do know: every one of them will give an account to a holy God someday, and although it always has and always will be that in this life God allows the wicked to flourish for a time, their roots are as shallow as grass.

Just as Moses did, we can and must praise God that His enemies do not now and never will triumph over Him. Their temporary victories in life mean nothing in God's great scheme of things because ultimately truth and justice will prevail. This is true of yesterday, today, and forever!

"If the Lord Is on Our Side . . . "

⁹For behold, Your enemies, O Lord, for behold, Your enemies shall perish; all the workers of iniquity shall be scattered. ¹⁰But My horn You have exalted like a wild ox; I have been anointed with fresh oil. ¹¹My eye also has seen my desire on my enemies; my ears hear my desire on the wicked who rise up against me. ¹²The righteous shall flourish like a palm tree, he shall grow like a cedar in Lebanon. —Psalm 92: 9-12

AS MOSES LOOKS back to God's victories on behalf of the nation of Israel, he also remembers the personal victories of God for him personally. He exalts over the Lord's lifting him up and anointing him with fresh oil. Again and again, God proved Himself strong to Moses, working great miracles through him, protecting him and the nation of Israel as He brought them into their promised land. And although Moses still had enemies, he knew that the Lord was with him, and Moses exclaims that he has both heard and seen God's hand against those came against him.

It's likely that those who rose up against him in verse 11 refers to the sons of Korah and the event we read about in our devotional time earlier. The "horn," which he refers to in verse 10, is symbolic of power and the anointing of oil. The power and anointing of Moses by God were confirmed when Korah and company rose up against him, and we know what happened to them!

It would be appropriate to summarize verses 10-11 by another thing that is true in keeping with our theme of "Yesterday, Today, and Forever," and that is: "'*No weapon formed against you shall prosper, and every tongue which rises up against you in judgment you shall condemn. This is the heritage of the servants of the Lord, and their righteousness is from Me,' says the Lord*" (Isaiah 54:17).

Earlier in Isaiah 54, the Lord clearly told Israel that He is their Redeemer. Is God also the Redeemer of the body of Christ today? Then the Lord also says to the true church that weapons formed against you will not prosper.

God's power in us, and His anointing on us, is far greater than any weapon in the enemy's arsenal. Then why do we see such a marked power shortage in much of the church today? Ephesians 6:14-17 provides much of the answer: "*Stand therefore, having girded your waist with truth, having put on the breastplate of righteousness, and having shod your feet with the preparation of the gospel of peace; above all, taking the shield of faith with which you will be able to quench all the fiery darts of the wicked one. And take the helmet of salvation, and the sword of the Spirit, which is the word of God*" (Ephesians 6:14-17).

It's true that when one ignores and then completely abandons truth, that person eliminates the ability to stand in power. True power is divine power, and divine power is truth-based. When you abandon truth, you've abandoned God's power.

Yes, the wicked will spring up like grass, but the righteous will stand tall like a cedar of Lebanon. The wicked may flourish for the moment, but they will be destroyed forever. The righteous may see the wicked rising up against them temporarily, but those who dwell in the house of the Lord will flourish forever. Take heart! Forever may be coming very soon. Are you ready?

June 20

"To Obey Is Better Than Sacrifice"

¹³Those who are planted in the house of the Lord shall flourish in the courts of our God. ¹⁴They shall still bear fruit in old age; they shall be fresh and flourishing, ¹⁵to declare that the Lord is upright; He is my rock, and there is no unrighteousness in Him. —*Psalm 92: 13-15*

DID YOU KNOW that if you are planted in God's house now, you will flourish in His courts one day? It's so easy to get our eyes off of that idea and onto the wickedness that surrounds us. But in these verses we're reminded that although the wicked spring up like grass (and they do seem to!), the righteous stand tall like the cedars of Lebanon. The wicked will indeed flourish, but it will only be for "a moment," and then they will be destroyed forever, while those who dwell in the house of the Lord will *flourish* forever.

When I read verse 14, I think of Caleb. In Numbers 32:11-12, the Lord speaks: "*Surely none of the men who came up from Egypt, from twenty years old and above, shall see the land of which I swore to Abraham, Isaac, and Jacob, because they have not wholly followed Me, except Caleb . . . and Joshua . . . for they have wholly followed the Lord.*"

Caleb appears before Joshua, saying, "*The Lord has kept me alive . . . these forty-five years, ever since the Lord spoke this word to Moses while Israel wandered in the wilderness; and now, here I am this day, eighty-five years old. As yet I am as strong this day as on the day that Moses sent me; just as my strength was then, so now is my strength for war. . . . Now therefore, give me this mountain of which the Lord spoke in that day; for you heard in that day how the Anakim were there. . . . It may be that the Lord will be with me, and I shall be able to drive them out as the Lord said*" (Josh14:10-12).

Biblical righteousness is twofold. There is positional, or imputed, righteousness, which is directly from the Lord. And there is practical righteousness, or obedience, which is what is in view here. Obedience to the Lord will always be met with divine power and opportunity. There may not be many 85-year-olds like Caleb, who can say, "I am as physically strong as I was when I was 40," but our spirits never age. We can still bear fruit and bring God glory even in our old age. In fact, we ought to be stronger in trust and praise than ever before, the older we get, because God's faithfulness has been evidenced in our lives so many times in the past.

And this, too, is reason to trust and praise the Lord yesterday, today, and forever. God blesses our obedience with divine power and opportunities to bear fruit, independent of age: "*I have been young, and now I am old; yet I have not seen the righteous forsaken, nor his descendants begging bread*" (Ps 37:25). We should be fresh and even flourishing in these last days, friends. Our purpose, as God's chosen people, is the same: "*To declare* [publicly proclaim] *that the Lord is upright and is our Rock, and there is no unrighteousness in Him.*" Although the words of a known compromiser are seldom believed and have no power, the words of those who are obedient to God will bear fruit all the days of their lives as they glorify the upright and righteous God whom they serve.

True praise is an expression of thankfulness for all that God has done, is doing, and will do. The will of God cannot change, for He changes not. So praise Him in the morning for His lovingkindness, and praise Him for His faithfulness at night, when those plagues of life keep you awake. Praise is an ointment to your soul. In a world of lies and injustice, remember this: in the end, truth and justice will prevail. Finally, obey God, and you'll be blessed with power and opportunities to bear fruit all the days of your life. Obedience brings what is better than anything the enemy or the world has to offer every time. And this is true, yesterday, today, and forever.

June 21

The King Is Coming

Introduction

O sing to the Lord . . . [Psalm 96]

—

AS WE'VE CONTINUED our journey through the psalms, we have seen the pattern of contrasting both the life experience and the eternal destinies of the righteous and the wicked. The contrast is great, to say the least! In these verses, we'll see the bar raised exponentially as the contrast is set for us, and it's not between the wicked and the righteous but between the King of kings (the Lord of lords) and the false Gods and idols of the nations.

This psalm is presented also in 1 Chronicles 16, which helps us to establish it in context as the contrast between the false gods of the Canaanites and the true and living God of Israel. The Canaanites had many gods, who seemingly had domains of their own. Yamm was the god of the sea; Mot was the god of death; Lotan was a sea-monster god; and the chief god of the Canaanites was El, the "King of the Gods." According to Canaanite mythology, El was attacked by Baal, the god of storms and fertility, and was overthrown. In the battle against Yamm, Mot, and Lotan, Baal was mortally wounded and resuscitated by his wife-sister, Anat. His victories and resuscitation made Baal, in the minds of the Canaanites, king of the gods. Yet the questions remained for them: Who could overthrow Baal? For how long would he reign?

It's against this backdrop of historical and cultural thinking that the contrast between El, Baal, Mot, Yamm, and Lotan (and any other false god) can be seen in contrast to the true and living God. Keep this in mind as we visit the powerful words of this royal psalm in contrast to the many false gods worshiped around the world today.

There are prophetic elements to this psalm that point to a time when the King of kings and Lord of lords rules and reigns on the earth. Our psalm will remind us majestically that our God, the true and living God, is nothing like the false gods of the nations. He is the King of kings and Lord of lords, who was and is and is to come! Let us begin now to prepare our hearts to meet the Lord Jesus Christ, soon, and very soon. . . .

June 22

"Soon and Very Soon, We Are Going to See the King"

¹Oh, sing to the Lord a new song! Sing to the Lord all the earth. ²Sing to the Lord, bless His name; proclaim the good news of His salvation from day to day. ³Declare His glory among the nations, His wonders among all peoples. ⁴For the Lord is great and greatly to be praised; He is to be feared above all the gods. ⁵For all the gods of the peoples are idols, but the Lord made the heavens. ⁶Honor and majesty are before Him; strength and beauty are in His sanctuary. —Psalm 96:1-6

WE LIVE in interesting times. Our previous government mandated that prayer be replaced by government action as it pertains to the growing terrorism in our country. Our psalm says that they're wrong, and although prayer isn't directly stated here, the One to whom we pray is clearly in view. When the world is increasingly influenced by false gods and religions, God's command to David is clear: *Sing to the*

Lord expressions of praise! Proclaim His gospel every day, and declare His glory to all the nations!

Psalm 95 has a wonderful exhortation that has been put to melody and is helpful in arriving at our first observation. "*Oh come, let us worship and bow down; let us kneel before the Lord our Maker. For He is our God, and we are the people of His pasture, and the sheep of His hand. Today, if you will hear His voice: 'Do not harden your hearts, as in the day of rebellion, as in the day of trial in the wilderness, when your fathers tested Me; they tried Me, though they saw my work . . .'*" (Psalm 95:6-9).

Let me ask you a question: is there any hope for our nation and our world apart from God? We can look at these verses as an Old Testament "Great Commission" to sing, proclaim, and declare the greatness and glory of our God to all nations. And this leads us to the first of our exhortations in this psalm, which is this: **The King is coming!** This is *not* the time to go soft on who God is. The reality is that when God's people fail to sing, proclaim, and declare the greatness of our God, it becomes impossible for the nations to hear of the His greatness and to understand what it is to fear of the Lord.

The Bible tells us that all the "gods" of the nations are idols, which means that they're the results of human imagination. But God made the heavens! Honor and majesty are rightfully His. Strength and beauty are in His sanctuary. This portion of the song of Moses expresses it well: "*Who is like You, O Lord, among the gods? Who is like You, glorious in holiness, fearful in praises, doing wonders? You stretched out Your right hand; the earth swallowed them. You in Your mercy have led forth the people whom You have redeemed; You have guided them in Your strength to Your holy habitation. . . . Fear and dread will fall on them; by the greatness of Your arm they will be as still as stone . . . O Lord, till the people pass over whom You have purchased*" (Exodus 15:11-16).

This is what it looks like to sing, to proclaim, and to declare, the greatness of God! The end result? It should produce the fear of the Lord among the nations. Why don't we see this happening today? Are we doing what Moses did? Our message is still one of good news, even though we also live in a time much as Moses did, where judgment is at hand. And yet, King David, under the inspiration of the Holy Spirit, tells us to sing, sing, sing, and proclaim and declare the very things that the world hates us for and for which it is attacking us today!

The God of Israel is the God of the church, and He doesn't change. The enemies of the church will meet the same fate as did Israel's enemies unless they repent. This isn't a time for us to "take a stand." It's a time for us to remain standing. God is the only God. He is the King. And He is coming back soon!

"To the Glory of God"

⁷Give to the Lord, O families of the peoples, give to the Lord glory and strength. ⁸Give to the Lord the glory due His name; bring an offering, and come into His courts. ⁹Oh worship the Lord in the beauty of His holiness! Tremble before Him, all the earth. —Psalm 96:7-9

DO YOU STILL have the same excitement and enthusiasm for the things of God that you had as a new believer? Is it a joy for you to praise and sing "unto the Lord"? It's likely that many of us find our relationship with Him waxing and waning, depending upon our circumstances. These verses don't appear to leave much room for our "feelings."

This psalm is a call to action. Let's jump in and allow ourselves to be brought back to where we really need to be in our lives. There are some wonderful exhortations in these verses that serve as a constant reminder of where our hearts and actions should be focused. First, we're told to *sing, sing, sing, proclaim and declare* in verses 1-3, and to *give, give, give, bring, worship, and tremble* in our verses today. The first section indicates what our actions should be in the eyes of the world, and the second reflects how they are in the eyes of God.

In Genesis 12:1-3, God said to Abraham (then Abram): "*Get out of your country . . . to a land that I will show you. I will make you a great nation; I will bless you and make your name great; and you shall be a blessing. I will bless those who bless you, and I will curse him who curses you; and in you all the families of the earth shall be blessed.*" This Abrahamic covenant hangs as a banner over this psalm, establishing God as the source of blessing for *all people*. The exhortation to "all the earth" in verse nine that we are to "tremble" before the Lord literally means "to twist and swirl." Figuratively, it means either to dance or to writhe in pain! Thus it reflects the eternal experiences of everyone, depending on what they did with the Gospel, resulting either in eternal joy or eternal pain.

What we take away from these verses is that we are to *give to the Lord glory and strength and bring offerings to His courts* (His house). Also we are to *worship in the beauty of holiness*. We often sing these words as a song, and somehow the pronoun "His" has wrongly made its way into our lyrics before "holiness." It actually isn't God's holiness in view here, but our own. This tells us that *our holiness is an act of worship, and it is beautiful to the Lord*!

The apostle Paul warned us, "Do not be unequally yoked together with unbelievers. . . . 'Come out from among them and be separate,' says the Lord. . . . And I will receive you'" (see 2 Cor 6:14-18 for the full context). God's people are to sing, proclaim, and declare the glory of God! He is greatly to be praised before all the nations of the earth. They are to worship God by being separated from worldliness and carnality as they give the Lord His due.

So since we have already understood from the past two days' reading that the King is coming, what should be our response? We are to **live and do all for His glory and Kingdom!** Paul warned us to come out and be separated from the world, and Peter wrote, "*As He who called you is holy, you also be holy in all your conduct, because it is written, 'Be holy, for I am holy*" (1 Peter 1:13-16).

I think a question is in order here, and the likelihood of its being convicting is high, but it begs to be asked, and that is, have you surrendered to the Lord all you are and have—or just the parts you can live without? Are you giving God your spare time and your spare change? Is His glory and kingdom your top priority? The King is coming, saints. We need to be all in. Has the Lord laid something on your heart to do for Him? Has He called you to repent of some habit or attitude in life? The King is coming! Pull out all the stops. Sing, sing, sing. Proclaim and declare. Give, give, give. Bring, worship, and tremble. And do it all to the glory of God.

June 24

He Is Coming . . . Soon!

[10]Say among the nations, "The Lord reigns; the world also is firmly established, it shall not be moved; He shall judge the peoples righteously. [11]Let the heavens rejoice, and let the earth be glad; Let the sea roar, and all its fullness; [12]Let the field be joyful, and all that is in it. Then all the trees of the woods will rejoice before the Lord. *—Psalm 96:10-12*

"LET THE SEA ROAR. . . ." The Holy Spirit is speaking here, saying, "Let the sea roar and all its fullness . . . let the earth be glad and the heavens rejoice . . . let the field be joyful, and all that is in it, and the let the trees of the woods rejoice, for . . . " the King is coming to judge the earth! Our God is not limited in scope or in power. He isn't the "god" of this or of that, but He is the Lord of all Creation, the mighty King! He isn't worried about being challenged. He isn't worried that He will be overthrown. He isn't concerned about Allah ruling the world, nor is He fearful of any of the millions of Hindu gods. The New Age movement doesn't frighten Him, nor does Buddhism or Scientology restrain Him or threaten Him with overtaking His kingdom. He is the King! He is coming to judge the world with His truth.

God's truth is the only absolute, moral truth. His truth, His Word, stands fast in the heavens. It is the measure by which all men will be judged. His truth is the very definition of righteousness. Psalm 33 states: "*For the word of the Lord is right, and all His work is done in truth. He loves righteousness and justice. . . . By the word of the*

Lord the heavens were made, and all the host of them by the breath of His mouth. . . . Let all the earth fear the Lord; let all the inhabitants of the world stand in awe of Him. For He spoke, and it was done; He commanded, and it stood fast. The Lord brings the counsel of the nations to nothing; He makes the plans of the peoples of no effect. The counsel of the Lord stands forever. . . . Blessed is the nation whose God is the Lord, the people He has chosen as His own inheritance" (Psalm 33:4-12).

Anyone who thinks they are going to stand before God and say, "But, Lord, I practiced tolerance and was politically correct all my life. I never offended anyone," has their concept of access to heaven sorely mistaken.

God wants His Good News proclaimed, and He wants His children to be fully committed to doing so with all they have and with all they are, because His truth is the earth's most precious commodity and only His truth can save the human soul from eternal death! In this world, which is growing increasingly more fragile, and where tensions around us are mounting to what seems like an unbearable degree at times, remember that God has a plan, and part of that plan includes our witness of Him to a dying world. Let's ask Him to show us someone today with whom we might be able to share the wonderful news of His love even in the midst of the horror stories we see and hear all around us.

June 25

Here Comes the Judge

> [13] For He is coming to judge the earth. He shall judge the world with righteousness, and the people with His truth. —*Psalm 96:13*

JUST LOOK around you. You can see that the King is coming soon. Why do I say that? Because *man is only getting worse and worse, and things can't be turned around.* What would bring peace? Gun control, border patrol, political party change, religious coexistence, tolerance of all sexual lifestyles, a two-state solution in Israel—none of these things will bring about world peace.

World peace can be brought about only by the Prince of peace, the King who is coming to judge the world, so there is much that must happen before we truly see peace. The Bible tells us that after the saints who have died and the believers on earth have all been taken up in the Rapture (See 1 Corinthians 15:51-54), *"Then they will deliver you to tribulation and kill you, and you will be hated by all nations for My name's sake. And then many will be offended, will betray one another, and will hate one another. Then many false prophets will rise up and will deceive many. And because lawlessness will abound, the love of many will grow cold. But he who endures to the end shall be saved. And this gospel of the kingdom will be preached in all the world as a witness to all the nations, and then the end will come"* (Matthew 24:9-14).

It certainly sounds as if it's going to get worse before it gets better. Hatred of Jews and Christians will be rampant in the Last Days, and the only way there will ever be peace on earth is when the King of kings returns to bring it at the end of the Tribulation.

Imagine this: during the Millennium, when Christ rules with a rod of iron from the city of Jerusalem, there will be no Islam, Buddhism, Hinduism, Sikhism, Mormonism, or any other false religion. The prophet Zechariah wrote: *"It shall come to pass that everyone who is left of all the nations which came against Jerusalem shall go up from year to year to worship the King, the Lord of hosts, and to keep the Feast of Tabernacles. And it shall be that whichever of the families of the earth do not come up to Jerusalem to worship the King, the Lord of hosts, on them there will be no rain. . . . They shall receive the plague with which the Lord strikes the nations who do not come up to keep the Feast of Tabernacles. . . . In that day 'HOLINESS TO THE LORD' shall be engraved on the bells of the horses. The pots in the Lord's house shall be like the bowls before the altar. Yes, every pot in Jerusalem and Judah shall be holiness to the Lord of hosts. Everyone who sacrifices shall come and take them and cook in them. In that day there shall no longer be a Canaanite in the house of the Lord of hosts"* (Zech 14:16-21).

"Canaanite," in this context, represents false beliefs, cults, and godless enemies of the Lord. In the Millennium, there will be no false religion and there will be world peace! It won't be anything like what we see today. Justice will be meted out swiftly and fairly from the Righteous One, the King of Glory, who will sit on David's throne, ruling the nations.

"Who is this King of glory? The Lord strong and mighty, The Lord mighty in battle. Lift up your heads, O you gates! Lift up, you everlasting doors! And the King of glory shall come in. Who is this King of glory? The Lord of hosts, He is the King of glory" (Ps 24:8-10).

We don't need to explain Him, just proclaim Him! We must not hold anything back from Him but give our all to Him and live fully for Him. He is coming back because man is on a downward spiral that only the Lord can stop by His return. The King is coming, perhaps today! *Lord Jesus, we long for Your return. Come quickly!*

Good Housekeeping

Introduction

A Psalm of David (Psalm 101)

THE PSALM that we're beginning today is a royal psalm, written before David had ascended to the throne as king of Israel. It's considered a *hallel*, or a praise psalm. The historical backdrop highlights the content for us very clearly. Israel was divided at this time. Saul, Israel's first king, had recently been killed, and loyalties were divided.

Let's take a brief look at the history of Saul's coming to the throne in the first place: "*Now it came to pass when Samuel [Israel's judge] was old that he made his sons judges over Israel. . . . But his sons did not walk in his ways; they turned aside after dishonest gain, took bribes, and perverted justice. Then all the elders of Israel gathered together and came to Samuel at Ramah, and said to him, 'Look, you are old, and your sons do not walk in your ways. Now make us a king to judge us like all the nations.' But the thing displeased Samuel. . . . So Samuel prayed to the Lord. And the Lord said to Samuel, 'Heed the voice of the people in all that they say to you; for they have not rejected you, but they have rejected Me, that I should not reign over them. . . . However, you shall solemnly warn them, and show them the behavior of the king who will reign over them*'" (1 Samuel 8:1-9).

Then Samuel proceeded to tell the people that the king they want will take their land, send their sons to war, take their daughters to be cooks, perfumers, and bakers, take a tenth of their herds, flocks, and servants, and cause the people to cry out against him. The response of the people when they heard these words? Essentially, they said, "Great! We'll take it."

As this psalm opens, King Saul, the people's choice, who had done all of the things that Samuel had warned them he would do, is dead, along with his son, Jonathan, who was David's beloved friend and kindred spirit. Loyalties among the people were divided, and it is into this atmosphere that David, as *God's* choice for the position, now steps into his role as king of Israel, a position that he will hold for 40 years.

As we make our way through this psalm over the next few days, we'll see that it isn't only a psalm of praise but also one of determination. David isn't offering a synopsis in these verses of how he'll rule as the new king but rather how he is going to live *as a man*. He is concerned about how he'll conduct himself even in the privacy of his own home. The truth is, the way he acts at home will determine how he rules as king. David is basically saying that he intends to practice *good housekeeping*.

Warren Wiersbe, writing on this psalm, said, "What is the most important part of a house? At first you might say the foundation, the heating system, or the plumbing. But the most important part of a house is the home. And the most important part of that home is the hearts of the people who live there. That's what David said when he was dedicating his house to the Lord. 'I will behave wisely in a perfect way. Oh, when will You come to me? I will walk within my house with a perfect heart' (v.2). If you want to wreck your house, start wrecking your home. And if you want to wreck your home, start wrecking your heart. But if you want your house and home to be all that God wants them to be, then make your heart perfect. What is a perfect heart? It's one that has integrity, wholeness, and oneness—a heart that is not divided. Nobody can serve two masters."

Do you want your house to enjoy the blessings and benefits of God? Then let's begin to learn how to practice good housekeeping!

June 27

"Come, Let Us Worship and Bow Down"

1I will sing of mercy and justice; to You, O Lord, I will sing praises. 2I will behave wisely in a perfect way. Oh, when will You come to me? I will walk within my house with a perfect heart. 3I will set nothing wicked before my eyes; I hate the work of those who fall away; it shall not cling to me. —Psalm 101:1-3

THERE ARE ACTUALLY eight uses of "I will" in this psalm in which David determines that he will do or not do certain things. He wasn't always successful at this. In fact, at times he failed miserably, but his failures didn't alter God's divine standards. The target never moved for David, even when he fell. And the same is true for us. When we fail, we must pull ourselves back to our feet and position ourselves to try once again.

The first goal that David sets is in our verses for today. He begins by determining that his house is going to be a house of praise (v. 1), followed by his determination to practice the same things as the One he praises: to be merciful and just.

Mercy and justice, grace and truth—they remind us of keeping the fullness of God always in view in our homes. Too many homes today teach *grace* but not *truth*, giving an unbalanced and unscriptural view of God. David declares that he will behave wisely and walk perfectly in his house, and then he petitions the Lord for help in this. He commits to keeping his focus on things that are pure and lovely. The things that draw him away from the Lord he will not allow to cling to him.

In a similar way, the apostle Paul commended and encouraged the believers in Rome by saying, *"For your obedience has become known to all. Therefore I am glad on your behalf; but I want you to be wise in what is good, and simple concerning evil. And the God of peace will crush Satan under your feet shortly. The grace of our Lord Jesus Christ be with you. Amen"* (Romans 16:19-20).

Paul's use of the word "simple" here means "unmixed." What David is determining, and what Paul is communicating, is that it is wise not to get mixed up with evil things. Spurgeon put it like this: "Piety must begin at home. Our first duties are those within our own abode. We must have a perfect heart at home, or we cannot keep a perfect way abroad. Notice that these words are part of a song, and that there is no music like the harmony of a gracious life, no psalm so sweet as the daily practice of holiness. Reader, how fares it with your family? Do you sing in the choir and sin in the chamber? Are you a saint abroad and a devil at home? For shame! What we are at home, that we are indeed. He cannot be a good king whose palace is the haunt of vice, nor he a true saint whose habitation is a scene of strife, nor he a faithful minister whose household dreads his appearance at the fireside."

To summarize David, Paul, and Spurgeon: If you want your home to be blessed, anointed, and powerful, then the first determination in good housekeeping is to **treat your home like a house of worship**. David said, "To the Lord I will sing praises and prostrate and submit to him in all my ways." Your house is a house of worship. Someone is being prostrated before and submitted to. The question is, who is it? Is it the God who made heaven and earth? Or is it the god of wickedness and the world? Good housekeeping begins with declaring your home to be a house of worship of the Lord and not just a place where praise songs are played. Set nothing wicked before your eyes, hate what God hates, and love what He loves, and don't follow those who lead people astray from a proper perspective of God. Begin to treat your home like a house of worship, and you've taken a major step toward good housekeeping.

June 28

The Dark Side

⁴A perverse heart shall depart from me; I will not know wickedness. ⁵Whoever secretly slanders his neighbor, him I will destroy; the one who has a haughty look and a proud heart, him I will not endure.
—Psalm 101:4-5

DAVID MOVES ON to an area of good housekeeping that few enjoy: cleaning out closets and those unseen places where "stuff" is stored and seldom seen. Most houses have a "junk drawer," or a side of the house or closet that becomes a catchall for things you want hidden from view but don't really want to throw away. Spiritually speaking, junk drawers and hidden sides of our minds or catchall closets, whether physical or mental, are dangerous. The perverse heart is one that is "divided," or even "crooked." David says that he will not "know," meaning to learn or practice, wicked things. Luke 16:13 says, "*No servant can serve two masters; for either he will hate the one and love the other, or else he will be loyal to the one and despise the other. You cannot serve God and mammon.*" Notice that it doesn't say, "should not." You *cannot* serve two masters, i.e., God and treasure, regardless of its form.

Along with the idea of secretly loving our treasure (whether monetary or other things that can stir up evil desires, etc.), David includes his interpersonal relationships in his housekeeping activities. Listen to Spurgeon again: "We cannot turn out of our family all whose hearts are evil, but we can keep them out of our confidence, and let them see that we do not approve of their ways. I will not know a wicked person. He shall not be my intimate, my bosom friend. I must know him as a man or I could not discern his character, but if I know him to be wicked, I will not know him any further, and with his evil I will have no communion. 'To know' in Scripture means more than mere perception; it includes fellowship, and in that sense it is here used. Princes must disown those who disown righteousness; if they know the wicked they will soon be known as wicked themselves."

David is saying that he will surround himself with people going the same direction that he is. He's not going to have as his closest companions people who can merely benefit him, or who are "fun," or because they just "click" with him. He is going to surround himself with people who aren't going to drag him down and increase the possibility of the king himself being associated with evil.

This brings us to the second determination of good housekeeping in your heart, which is: ***Don't be two-faced about your faith, or, Don't be a radical at church and take a sabbatical when you're not.*** We see that David was serious about this part of his life. In verse 5, he even uses the word "destroy" regarding those who are morally displeasing to God. The word "destroy" here means to cut off, i.e., to not endure or morally enable. To put it simply, David would not be a companion of those who displease God morally.

How do we balance this with the command to love sinners and to be kind to everyone? Think about Jesus when He walked on this earth, and follow His example. We *are* to be friends of sinners, but we're not to be friends of sin! We must not simply ignore things that damage our witness. When we're with sinners, we should be in ministry. When we're with the saints, we're in fellowship. It can't be any other way.

Has God been showing you that there are people or things in your life that need to be cut off as part of your housekeeping chore, because they cause you wander to the dark side of your mind, depositing wicked thoughts and dirty ideas? Cut them off! Do not endure them. Don't try to be one thing with some people and another thing with others. Be radical *all the time*. Be pure *all the time*. Be holy *all the time*. Come out of the dark side and into the light. And then stay there. Your Spirit-filled heart will know the difference and will rejoice.

June 29

Into the Light

⁶My eyes shall be on the faithful of the land, that they may dwell with me; he who walks in a perfect way, he shall serve me. ⁷He who works deceit shall not dwell within my house; he who tells lies shall not continue in my presence. —*Psalm 101:6-7*

DAVID TAKES a strong stand in these verses, vowing that rather than setting his eyes on wicked things and establishing relationships that compromise his own integrity, he will put his eyes on the faithful of the land. David is perfectly in tune with the Lord on this, being called in the Bible in a few places "a man after God's own heart." We see the Lord's heart echoed in 2 Chronicles 16, which says, "*For the eyes of the Lord run to and fro throughout the whole earth, to show Himself strong on behalf of those whose heart is loyal to him*" (v. 9a).

David continues with his commitment to "good housekeeping," reiterating his declaration to distance himself from lies and deceit in any form and to limit his inner circle of friends to those who walk in the same perfect way. "Perfect" means "without blemish," which is consistent with the New Testament admonition to remain unspotted from the world. Centuries later, James would write, "*Pure and undefiled religion before God and the Father is this: to visit orphans and widows in their trouble, and to keep oneself unspotted from the world*" (James 1:27).

Here we see a masterful pairing of faith and works, a topic that James handled well. Works would be actions such as visiting orphans and widows who were facing difficult times, and faith would be the act of keeping oneself unspotted from the world. *How is that faith?* you ask. Track with this concept for a moment: keeping oneself unspotted, or without blemish, is admonished in God's Word. It means to be without glaring defect. It can even mean something as simple as one's having overcome basic sins. I say "simple," and really, it is. There are two things necessary for overcoming basic sins: sin must be defined, and that definition must be believed. There is only one source where sin is defined, and that is in the Bible, the Word of

God. The Bible also tells us that faith comes by hearing, and hearing, by . . . what? By the Word of God!

Putting this whole concept together, James states that faith by itself (in other words, faith that is unaccompanied by good works) is dead. He explains that without our faith being evidenced by our good works, who would know that we had faith at all? If we have true faith in God and recognize everything that He has done for us, shouldn't our lives and works also reflect that faith and love by our putting "feet" to our words as we love and care for others? In James 2, he wrote: *"But someone will say, 'You have faith, and I have works.' Show me your faith without your works, and I will show you my faith by my works. The Lord Jesus said, 'A new commandment I give to you, that you should love one another; as I have loved you, that you also love one another. By this all will know that you are My disciples, if you have love for one another'"* (John 12:34-35).

How will the world know Christ's love? By the Word of God, but also as we display that love through our works of love and kindness. As we obey Christ's command to love one another, just as the "good Samaritan" did, we will be demonstrating that love by our good deeds to those in need.

June 30

When Silence Is Not Golden

⁸Early I will destroy all the wicked of the land, that I may cut off all the evildoers from the city of the Lord. —Psalm 101:8

AS WE FINISH this psalm and the examination of our own "spiritual housekeeping," we find David adding another determination to his goal of cleaning things up to which we would do well to pay attention: *Do not be silent or indifferent on matters of sin.* Keep in mind that David is speaking here as God's appointed king, who was responsible for the protection and spiritual health of the nation. He states, "Early [meaning immediately] I will deal with wickedness in the land that I may keep the city of the Lord pure and, therefore, secure."

Folks, the same thing is necessary for the security of our homes. (See also 1 Peter 2:9-10.) Through our own adoption by the King of kings and Lord of lords into the royal family of God, as believers we now have the responsibility of being the world's only source of spiritual salt and light. Remember what Jesus told those whom He had commanded to tarry in Jerusalem? *"You shall receive power when the Holy Spirit has come upon you; and you shall be witnesses to Me in Jerusalem, and in all Judea and Samaria, and to the end of the earth"* (Acts 1:8).

Consider this: We're told to be witnesses to the grace and mercy and holiness of God. How can we do that if we're not walking with Him? If our hearts are messed up, our homes will be messed up. And if those are messed up, our witness is messed up. If we've lost our witness, we've lost the most important thing on earth: the ability to be a purifying and preserving influence in this world by reflecting the Lord Jesus through our lives.

Listen, there is no command in the Bible that says, "Don't offend anyone." Nor does it tell us, "Just go with the flow of the culture, and you might win some over to the Lord's side." In fact, it clearly states the opposite: "*You are the salt of the earth; but if the salt loses its flavor, how shall it be seasoned? It is then good for nothing but to be thrown out and trampled underfoot by men. You are the light of the world. . . . Let your light so shine before men, that they may see your good works and glorify your Father in heaven*" (Matthew 5:13-16).

If there's no light at home, there'll be no light in the world. It may be that some of us need to do some thorough housekeeping so we can again be salt and light to the world. Perhaps that means to stop setting wicked things before our eyes, or to cut off relationships that influence us badly, or transitioning from fellowship with darkness to a ministry of light. Church, we need to be bold for Jesus in front of those who drag us down. Speak up! Worship like you're in church when those people are around, and you won't have to cut them off! They'll either get saved or get lost.

This is not the time to go soft on who God is, nor is it the time to go soft on what sin really is, especially in our own home, and even more so regarding our own sin. This is war! It's a war for souls. Your own battle is already won if you've been born again. But the bigger battle is this: "*Deliver those who are drawn toward death, and hold back those stumbling to the slaughter. If you say, 'Surely we did not know this,' does not He who weighs the hearts consider it? He who keeps your soul, does He not know it? And will He not render to each man according to his deeds?*" (Proverbs 24:11-12).

Are you ready to begin practicing good housekeeping so that you can effectively rescue those drawn toward death? Clean out that junk drawer, that secret closet, and that side of the house with the closed doors. God will be pleased and your home will be blessed, anointed, and empowered because of it. Fling open those doors and be free!

JULY

Smart Praise

Introduction

A Psalm of David. [Psalm 103]

AS WE READ through this psalm in our Bibles before we even begin our study, we want to note that this psalm, as are some others, is both a *wisdom* psalm and a *praise* psalm. It is personal, written by David, and corporate, in other words, intended for worship among the people. No explanation or title is given in the opening. It's merely referred to as "A Psalm of David." David opens the psalm by speaking for himself, blessing the Lord, in verses one and two, and then he includes his readers from that point.

I love the way that David speaks of the Lord, blessing Him as he writes. It's similar to Psalm 16:7-9: "*I will bless the Lord who has given me counsel; my heart also instructs me in the night seasons. I have set the Lord always before me; because He is at my right hand, I shall not be moved. Therefore my heart is glad, and my glory rejoices; my flesh also will rest in hope.*" Note David's statement: I WILL BLESS THE LORD. And as we think on that, our response might well be, "Am *I* a blessing to the Lord?"

The word "bless" in Hebrew literally means to kneel (implying submission) in adoration. But it can also mean "to curse," and "treason"! It may also mean "to blaspheme," or it can mean "to praise." Obviously, David is speaking of adoration here, but isn't it interesting that the word can mean things that are polar opposites?

In the book of James, we find that this is indeed possible, "*For every kind of beast and bird, or reptile and creature of the sea, is tamed and has been tamed by mankind. But no man can tame the tongue. It is an unruly evil, full of deadly poison. With it we bless our God and Father, and with it we curse men, who have been made in the similitude of God. Out of the same mouth proceed blessing and cursing. My brethren, these things ought not to be so. Does a spring send forth fresh water and bitter from the same opening? Can a fig tree, my brethren, bear olives, or a grapevine figs? Thus no spring yields both salt water and fresh*" (James 3:7-12).

Have you ever heard the old adage warning of the danger in being quick to speak because you often say things you haven't thought of yet? Have you ever said something you hadn't thought through before saying it out loud, but then, there it hung in the air, never to be reeled back in? Do you ever regret those words that somehow escaped your lips and hurt someone whom you love?

We can see that the concept of the same thing being the source of good or evil is not that abstract. David had done wrong in his own life, and he was not always a "blessing" to the Lord, even though the Lord remained faithful to David even in his faithlessness.

Most scholars believe that David was an old man when he wrote this psalm and is looking back over his life, remembering those times when he didn't "bless the Lord with all that is within" him. Those are hard things for all of us to look back upon, wishing that we could take those times back and have a "do over." But that isn't to be. What we *can* do is to remember that God is always worthy of our highest praise, and we are to bless Him with *all* that is within us, *no matter what our circumstances are*. And David, who knew what it was like to truly bless the Lord and also what it was like to enter into serious, deadly sin, will help us to understand applying wisdom in our praises to the Lord. Smart praise will be thought out and purposeful, not mindless repetitions or vague, dreamy descriptions. Are you ready to find out more about how to do that? David, the man after God's own heart, but also the man who knew what it was like to be overcome by his own evil heart, is going to teach us.

"Thou Art Worthy"

Bless the Lord, O my soul; and all that is within me, bless His holy name!
—*Psalm 103:1*

AS WE BEGIN our look at verse one of this psalm of praise, let's jump to the last verse: "*Bless the Lord, all His works, in all places of His dominion. Bless the Lord, O my soul!*" (v. 22). In that closing line, we find summed up the idea that our soul is the source of true praise. We are to praise the Lord at all times, in any circumstance, and in any situation, whether we're happy or sad or angry or tired. God is always good and deserving of our praise. He knows all things, and He sees beyond our circumstances to the future. He knows our thoughts—the good, the bad, and the ugly, and He is always deserving of our praise.

Is there anyplace in the universe where the Lord does not have dominion or where His works do not prevail? Doesn't this lead us to the conclusion that the Lord is *worthy* of our praise? There's no one and nothing greater than, or who even comes close to, our God. His name is "Wonderful, Counselor, Mighty God, Everlasting Father, Prince of Peace" (Isaiah 9:6). Our praise for the Lord must be genuine, and as we make our way through the rest of this psalm of praise, I hope that our hearts will be enlarged more and more to understand not only the beauty of our Lord and His worthiness to be praised but also the fact that when we praise Him in sincerity, we are lifted above our circumstances. Yes, our praise may be insincere at times. Perhaps we're caught up in the moment rather than in the glory of the Lord. It may be that we're moved by the music or by the crowd around us. And sometimes we may feel that it's impossible to praise the Lord at all in our present circumstances, because our hearts are downcast, or because we feel ugly and mean inside. Here is the key that we need to remember: ***Praise from the soul is not governed by circumstance.***

If we're told to praise the Lord in all His works and in all of His dominion, then we're to praise Him everywhere all the time. There may or may not be music associated with our praise. Praising wisely doesn't require music or a particular time or setting, because there's a communion of our eternal soul with the eternal God whenever we praise Him!

It isn't always possible to praise the Lord *for* everything that happens, but we're to praise Him *through* everything. Look at Job. From the very depths of despair, in his confusion and anguish over his devastating circumstances, Job was able to lift himself momentarily from his misery and cry out, "*For I know that my Redeemer lives, and He shall stand at last on the earth; and after my skin is destroyed, this I know, that in my flesh I shall see God*" (Job 19:25-26). That is praise, exhibiting hope and faith in His Lord, regardless of his anguish.

You may even now be undergoing circumstances for which you simply *cannot* be thankful. You can still bless God from the soul and with all that is within you because, whether you see it or not, the Lord has dominion over the place and season where you are even now. We can still praise God *for who He is*, not just what He does. Praise is to come from the soul, because it is the soul that He has saved! We need to remember that praise is not for us! It is for Him, and He is always worthy, regardless of how we *feel*. And sometimes, when our faith seems weak, as the man who brought his possessed son to Jesus for deliverance, we may cry, "*Lord, I believe; help me with my unbelief!*" (Mark 9:24), and even then our Lord is gracious and will give us the faith we need to support our praise to Him. What a loving

God we serve! He understands our weaknesses and He loves us anyway. Let's give praise to Him this day: "Thou art worthy, Thou art worthy, Thou art worthy, O Lord, to receive glory, glory and honor, glory and honor and power!"

July 3

"The Lord God Almighty Reigns" (part 1)

²Bless the Lord, O my soul; and forget not all His benefits: ³Who forgives all your iniquities, who heals all your diseases . . . —Psalm 103:2-3

THESE VERSES are instrumental as we consider the wisdom of praise, and they bring us face to face with our first truth found here, which is that **praise from the soul is not governed by circumstance.** We see David moving from his personal commitment to praise the Lord to his all-inclusive statements of everyone's reasons for praise. We can examine these as we consider a series of questions:

1) Does God forgive everyone? 2) Does God heal everyone? 3) Has God made a way for everyone to be forgiven? 4) Is God able to heal everyone?

Crucial to understanding the text of our verses today is realizing that what's in view here are God's *attributes*, not His *actions*. Yes, when God responds positively to our prayers, it's certainly an occasion for praise, but it isn't the *reason* for our praise. David is saying that yes, God is capable of healing any disease and forgiving all iniquities, but what he wants to highlight is God's power.

In Nehemiah we read, "*Now on the twenty-fourth day of this month the children of Israel were assembled with fasting, in sackcloth, and with dust on their heads. Then those of the Israelite lineage separated themselves from all foreigners; and they stood and confessed their sins and the iniquities of their fathers. And they stood up in their place and read from the Book of the Law of the Lord their God for one-fourth of the day; and for another fourth they confessed and worshiped the Lord their God. . . . And the Levites . . . said: 'Stand up and bless the Lord your God forever and ever! "Blessed be Your glorious name, which is exalted above all blessing and praise! You alone are the Lord; You have made heaven, the heaven of heavens, with all their host, the earth and everything on it, the seas and all that is in them, and You preserve them all. The host of heaven worships You"'*" (Nehemiah 9:1-6).

Altogether in this great prayer of Nehemiah in chapter nine, the personal pronouns for God—"You" and "Your"—were used 67 times. That is the wisdom of praise. Yes, Nehemiah mentioned some glorious events of Israel's past, and, yes, the faithfulness of God to a rebellious people was recalled, but it was the *object* of these things, God himself, to whom the praise and prayer were directed. This brings us to the next element of the wisdom of praise: ***Praise is the acknowledgment of God's sovereignty and power.***

The most tragic thing that has happened in recent world history is not ISIS or cataclysmic world events and natural disasters, as grave and concerning as those things are. The greatest catastrophe the world has experienced in recent years is the diminishing and demeaning of God himself. And, tragically, it often comes from the people who stand behind the pulpits. Nehemiah 9 contains a truth that we need to heed today: when the people heard the uncompromised and undiluted Word of God, then began the confession of sin and repentance followed by praise and worship! God was seen in His sovereignty and power. His works of old were recalled, and His majestic name and character were revered. This is so unlike the "good buddy God" of today, who is treated as someone who puts up with anything and everything, as long as it makes you happy. I'll leave you with a question: How can we justify such a "god" in light of the beauty of the verses from Nehemiah that showed repentance being brought forth from the sincere offering of praise and worship to the Lord?

July 4

"The Lord God Almighty Reigns" (part 2)

²Bless the Lord, O my soul; and forget not all His benefits: ³Who forgives all your iniquities, who heals all your diseases . . . —*Psalm 103:2-3*

IT'S INTERESTING to note that, as with Nehemiah in chapter 9, which we looked at yesterday, David never asked the Lord for anything in this psalm. He merely declares the sovereignty and power of God. Let's look at another psalm like this, only because we see and hear so little of this kind of praise from men's lips today: "*I will extol You, my God, O King; and I will bless Your name forever and ever. Every day I will bless You, and I will praise Your name forever and ever. Great is the Lord, and greatly to be praised; and His greatness is unsearchable. One generation shall praise Your works to another, and shall declare Your mighty acts. I will meditate on the glorious splendor of Your majesty, and on Your wondrous works. Men shall speak of the might of Your awesome acts, and I will declare Your greatness. They shall utter the memory of Your great goodness, and shall sing of Your righteousness*" (Psalm 145:1-6).

Many of those standing in pulpits today are preaching a "god" that man will accept instead of preaching how man needs to and can become acceptable to God. This is catastrophic, and we see it reflected in the hardening of hearts all around us. Yes, God could heal everyone, and He is capable of doing so. That's the power of

God. But He doesn't, even though He could. That's His sovereignty. I can't justify His actions to you or to anyone else. I'm simply stating the truth.

Peter wrote: "*The Lord is not slack concerning His promise, as some count slackness, but is longsuffering toward us, not willing that any should perish but that all should come to repentance*" (2 Peter 3:9). God isn't willing that any should perish.... That's where the story ends for many today. They never get around to preaching how *not to perish*. They preach the grace of God without mentioning our need for repentance. The truth is that it's God's grace that He forgives the one who is repentant. He doesn't *owe* them salvation because they repent. He *chooses* to do so in His sovereign power and His love for all.

The fear of the Lord has taken a back seat to the "glory of mankind," which the world, and even the church, has fallen into the trap of believing. But the writer of Hebrews wrote: "*Therefore, since we are receiving a kingdom which cannot be shaken, let us have grace, by which we may serve God acceptably with reverence and godly fear. For our God is a consuming fire*" (Hebrews 12:28-29). "Fire" speaks of purity and refining, but it also speaks of judgment. The purity of God refines by fire those who believe, and the very same fire consumes those who do not. You cannot bargain with God.

It's funny (tragic, really) how people today are afraid of offending *everyone* except God. We would do well to remember that the wisdom of praise includes acknowledging the sovereignty and power of the true and living God! Let us praise him in truth and with respect and reverence for who He is and the fact that He has forgiven our sins based on His Son's own sacrifice, and not on anything that we are or have done or could do. How great is our God!

July 5

"Money Can't Buy [God's] Love" (part 1)

⁴Who redeems your life from destruction, who crowns you with lovingkindness and tender mercies, ⁵who satisfies your mouth with good things, so that your youth is renewed like the eagle's. —*Psalm 103:4-5*

WHAT ARE SOME of the benefits that we enjoy, both temporally and eternally, when we know the living God? Well, for starters, we're delivered from permanent destruction to experiencing God's everlasting loving-kindness and mercy; we go from having emptiness in our hearts to deep satisfaction with the good things that He gives to us; we go from being weary and heavy laden to being renewed as youths in our spirits. There are many who are hurting from personal loss or illness who can still experience the joy of knowing the Lord and having His grace and mercy and love shine into their hearts despite their suffering. The ungodly don't enjoy this comfort.

Money can bring temporary happiness and a sense of pleasure, and although we may find ourselves envying those who never have to worry about expenses, believing that somehow they must be "happier" than we are, there are multitudes of things that we enjoy that they can never purchase or experience apart from a relationship with God. Because of Jesus, I never have to worry about what happens when I die. I know where I'm going. Jesus said, *"Let not your heart be troubled; you believe in God, believe also in Me. In My Father's house are many mansions; if it were not so, I would have told you. I go to prepare a place for you. And if I go and prepare a place for you, I will come again and receive you to Myself; that where I am, there you may be also"* (John 14:1-3).

Money and "things" can't calm a troubled heart or redeem a life from perdition. Our lives aren't always easy, but we are always redeemed from destruction. We may not have all the pleasures and treasures of this world, but what awaits us is far better than anything that can be bought or experienced in this life. Psalm 16:11 says, *"You will show me the path of life; in Your presence is fullness of joy; at Your right hand are pleasures forevermore."*

When you were redeemed by the blood of Jesus upon being born again, you began a journey on the path of life that is showered with the loving-kindness and tender mercies of God. When you stop to think about it, aren't you glad that God doesn't give us everything we ask for? Aren't you glad that God doesn't give us what we deserve? Aren't you glad that through Jesus we are richer than Bill Gates, Warren Buffet, and even the Walmart heirs and heiresses, whose combined net worth tops $140 billion?

Sometimes we tend to think things like, "Well, if I just had their money, my life would be better." Not necessarily. There is no better life than living for and with Jesus. Don't miss the connection between "satisfying our mouths with good things," and having "renewed youth [meaning strength] like an eagle." What does Philippians 4:19 say? *"And my God shall supply all your need according to His riches in glory by Christ Jesus."* And that's a promise that we take to the "bank," so to speak. Let us praise Him today!

"Money Can't Buy [God's] Love" (part 2)

⁴Who redeems your life from destruction, who crowns you with lovingkindness and tender mercies, ⁵who satisfies your mouth with good things, so that your youth is renewed like the eagle's. —*Psalm 103:4-5*

PUTTING ALL of the thoughts of the previous few days together, we can understand better why we can say that praise is recognition of God's mercy and grace. We live in an age where most people's sense of entitlement is robbing society of its sense of good and evil. I read an article about how a man had been shot while robbing a Family Dollar Store and survived. His family was considering bringing a lawsuit against the concealed-carry-permit holder who had defended the shoppers and store clerks from potential harm and even death. The family of the criminal claimed that the man should have minded his own business and just walked out of the store when he saw the robbery in progress!

Many people view God the same way, thinking that because He's good, He should give them whatever they want and then just look the other way when they do wrong. We'll see in the days ahead that the Lord is slow to anger, but this doesn't mean He isn't angry over the sinfulness of mankind. The prophet Jeremiah lived and wrote during a time and in a nation much like ours in the United States, with no fear of the Lord, even though they once had had that fear. He wrote: "*This I recall to my mind, therefore I have hope. Through the Lord's mercies we are not consumed, because His compassions fail not. They are new every morning; great is Your faithfulness. 'The Lord is my portion,' says my soul, 'Therefore I hope in Him!' The Lord is good to those who wait for Him, to the soul who seeks Him. It is good that one should hope and wait quietly for the salvation of the Lord*" (Lam 3:20-26).

If we are going to bless the Lord—as Jeremiah did, and as David himself did in the opening of this psalm—"with all that is within" us—then we need to be certain that we understand what praise truly is. Praise isn't just a response to good things happening in our lives or in the lives of others, although it's appropriate that we praise Him when they do. It's also an *offering* to God no matter how things are going. We shouldn't praise the Lord only when He blesses us with good things and then remain silent when we're hurting or going through hard times. Praise acknowledges that God is omnipotent and sovereign over all creation *all the time*, and in love and respect, we bow down to Him in that.

"*Blessed be the Lord, who daily loads us with benefits, the God of our salvation!*" (Psalm 68:29). To praise God means that we also recognize that the Almighty and Sovereign Lord hasn't dealt with us as we deserve, but in fact He has done the exact opposite. He has loaded us with benefits! This is the wisdom of praise—praise from the very depths of our souls, with all that is within us, to the powerful and sovereign God of the universe who hasn't give us what we do deserve and who has loaded our lives with good things that we don't deserve. We must remember this and move past our petty whining that God gives His good things to others—to the rich, the well-known, the successful—and leaves the scraps for us. God is no respecter of persons. Money means nothing to Him. We can't buy His help, nor can we shame Him into helping us. We must seek to praise Him *through all things.*

Friends, there's a fine line between true and false praise, and true praise is much deeper than emotion-based experientialism. No matter what life may bring our way, God is always God and worthy of our praise. This is the wisdom of praise, and we would do well to learn its ways.

Smart Praise Too!

> ⁶The Lord executes righteousness and justice for all who are oppressed. ⁷He made known His ways to Moses, His acts to the children of Israel. ⁸The Lord is merciful and gracious, slow to anger, and abounding in mercy. ⁹He will not always strive with us, nor will He keep His anger forever. *—Psalm 103:6-9*

WE CONTINUE today with our look at praising the Lord from Psalm 103 and how we can praise Him with our minds and our spirits. We'll begin with a look a favorite verse, Psalm 97:6-10: *"The heavens declare His righteousness, and all the peoples see His glory. Let all be put to shame who serve carved images, who boast of idols. Worship Him, all you gods. Zion hears and is glad, and the daughters of Judah rejoice because of Your judgments, O Lord. For You, Lord, are most high above all the earth; You are exalted far above all gods. You who love the Lord, hate evil! He pre-serves the souls of His saints; He delivers them out of the hand of the wicked."*

We see in these verses the contrasting life experiences of the righteous and the wicked and how the righteous will always ultimately prevail. The contrast we'll look at will be between the majestic, all-powerful God and fallen, feeble man. Another thing we'll see is that the majestic, all-powerful God has bridged the dis-tance between Himself and man with a supernatural love that knows our frame and remembers that we are but dust.

David remembers back to the oppressed Israelites living under tremendous bondage in Egypt as he makes his first point about the nature and character of God. He notes that God revealed His ways through His giving of the Law to Moses and also through His actions on behalf of the Israelites and against the Egyptians.

He then reminds us of the abounding mercy and manifested grace of God in being slow to anger. In verse nine, David gives us a beautiful truth that can bring us comfort today also: "*He will not always strive with us, nor will He keep His anger forever.*"

We know that God puts up with a lot from us. How many times have we doubted Him, questioned His timing, been ungrateful for His provision because it wasn't what we had hoped for? We're reminded in Proverbs 3:11-12, "*My son, do not despise the Lord's discipline or be weary of his reproof, for the Lord reproves him whom he loves, as a father the son in whom he delights*" [ESV]. The parent-child illustration is one of the most outstanding examples of our relationship with God in all of Scripture.

We'll see more of that later, but first let's consider this: Most people understand that raising kids is hard. It's both wonderful and worrisome. It's a blessing and trial at times. It's a season of holding them close and then a season of letting them go as they grow up and sometimes seeing them making wrong choices.

Verse nine of our psalm tells us that someday things are going to change. There won't always be the need for loving discipline. Someday, God will never again have to watch us do things the wrong way or make the same poor choices. He'll end the misery by perfecting us and making us like Jesus! His anger won't continue into eternity, and His righteous judgment will be seen for the oppressed, and the righteous and the wicked will be forever separated. God is good, and greatly to be praised. Let's continue to give our "smart praise" to Him, the kind of praise that He himself has shown to us, and not something that we ourselves consider to be praise.

July 8

According To . . .

¹⁰He has not dealt with us according to our sins, nor punished us according to our iniquities. —*Psalm 103:10*

THE PHRASE "according to" occurs hundreds of times in the Bible. Many times the words are applied to the Lord himself, as in "*according to* His will" or "*according to* the grace of God." Other times they relate to the Word of God, as in "*according to* the Scriptures." The meaning can be a warning, as in judgment, with each person receiving rewards, good or bad, "*according to* what he has done."

In our verse from Psalm 103 today, the word is used to remind us that God never gives us everything we deserve. Some of you may be thinking, *That's right. I've asked God for things and I never got them.* I'm pretty sure that we could all say that we've had God answer *no* to some of our petitions for things, but remember, if He said *yes*, it wouldn't be because you deserved it. He never gives us everything we deserve, and I praise Him for that, because none of what we actually *deserve* is good!

Jeremiah wrote, "*The heart is deceitful above all things, and desperately wicked; who can know it? I, the Lord, search the heart, I test the mind, Even to give every man according to his ways, according to the fruit of his doings*" (Jeremiah 17:9-10).

I know that I've had to bear "the fruit of my doings" at times, and I'm pretty sure you've had to as well. But, on the other hand, none of us have ever had to suffer the full extent for the things we've done that were born out of a deceitful heart.

Something that I love about some of the "heroes of the faith" is that they never seemed to get too far away from their initial forgiveness. Isaiah wrote: "*Woe is me, for I am undone! Because I am a man of unclean lips, and I dwell in the midst of a people of unclean lips; for my eyes have seen the King, The Lord of Hosts*" (Isaiah 6:5). And the apostle Paul wrote, "*O wretched man that I am! Who will deliver me from this body of death? I thank God—through Jesus Christ our Lord!*" (Romans 7:24-25).

And yet, Isaiah never said, "Whoa! Look at me! I've seen the Lord of Hosts!" Nor did Paul say, "Hey, check me out! I'm delivered from the body of this death!"

I believe that all of us would do well to remember that God hasn't dealt with us *according to our sins and iniquities*. Sins are violations of God's law, and iniquities are moral perversities. And we wish that God would give us "what we deserve"? We should be in a constant state of thankfulness—not a mentality of personal deservedness! None of us has ever gotten everything we deserve for our violations of God's law and our perversities. That isn't to say that there haven't been consequences, but even those will one day come to an end.

No one now alive has ever received from God what they actually deserved. Someone else, however, did receive what we deserved, and we'll get to that a little later.

But for now, let's bless the Lord with all that is within us because He hasn't dealt with us *according to* our sins, nor has He punished us *according to* our iniquities. I can't tell you how grateful I am for that truth!

Gone with the Wind

[11] For as the heavens are high above the earth, so great is His mercy toward those who fear Him; [12] as far as the east is from the west, so far has He removed our transgressions from us. [13] As a father pities His children, so the Lord pities those who fear Him. [14] For He knows our frame; He remembers that we are dust. [15] As for man, his days are like grass; as a flower of the field, so he flourishes. [16] For the wind passes over it, and it is gone, and in its place remembers it no more. —Psalm 103:11-16

God, who is as high as the heavens are above the earth, looks down on man, who is like a blade of grass or a flower of the field—here today, gone tomorrow, framed out of dust, and, eventually just dust in the wind. Verse 13 is a pinnacle of Scripture in the father/child illustration that draws us into a deeper understanding of God's love for us. We know that as parents we sometimes strive, but eventually we must simply let go and trust that training them up in the way they should go will be the way that they will finally keep going.

God is watching over our lives. Psalm 144:3-4 says, "*Lord, what is man, that You take knowledge of him? Or the son of man, that You are mindful of him?*" Yet it is to this feeble man, who is like grass and the flower, that God has shown mercy when that man is one who fears God in measure as high as the heaven is above the earth and from whom God has removed his transgressions, sins, and iniquities as far as the east is from the west.

Why is this? Because our God, like the good and loving Father that He is, pities His children! The parents of a seriously injured or very ill child would readily say, "I would do anything to take away my child's pain. I wish it were me and not him (or her). I would do anything to take his place." Friends, this is exactly what God has done! He looked down upon the earth, saw our frame, and knew that we were but dust—desperate and sick, seriously wounded by sin, suffering with the disease of death, and completely incapable of saving ourselves—and He traded places with us! (See Isaiah 53:4-11 for a beautiful description of what He did for us.)

Man was suffering under the plague of sin, along with every human, headed for hell, and no one could do anything about it. No one was righteous. Not one among them was perfect. Not one among them could live up to the righteous requirements of the Law. In fact, the Law exposed them all as sinners.

God looked down at man as a father would his sick child and became sin for us, dying the death that we deserved! God endured for us what we could not. We're but dust and fading flowers, yet the mercy of God is from everlasting to everlasting, as we shall see.

The apostle Peter wrote, " . . . *because Christ also suffered for us, leaving us an example, that you should follow in His steps: . . . who, when He was reviled, did not revile in return; when He suffered, He did not threaten, but committed Himself to Him who judges righteously; who Himself bore our sins in His own body on the tree . . .* " (1 Peter 2:21-25).

Peter understood that the grave had every right to us. As the One who bore our sins on a tree and by whose stripes we were healed, Jesus endured what we could not. No one is good enough to go to heaven. You can't give enough or do enough good deeds to outweigh your sins. The only thing that will save us is God's mercy, which is as high as the heavens, and His forgiveness, which stretches the same distance. The Bible tells us that flesh and blood cannot inherit the kingdom of God (1 Cor 15:50-56), and that is what we are. Christ endured *in our place* what we deserved. Death would have been the victor were it not for the mercy of our God and His pity for His children. Smart praise is to praise God for enduring what we could not. Let's begin to thank Him for that now.

July 10

Is Heaven Your Future Home? Praise the Lord!

[17]But the mercy of the Lord is from everlasting to everlasting on those who fear Him, and His righteousness to children's children, [18]to such as keep His covenant, and to those who remember His commandments to do them. [19]The Lord has established His throne in heaven, and His kingdom rules over all. [20]Bless the Lord, you His angels, who excel in strength, who do His word, heeding the voice of His word. [21]Bless the Lord, all you His hosts, you ministers of His, who do His pleasure. [22]Bless the Lord, all His works, in all places of His dominion. Bless the Lord, O my soul! *—Psalm 103:17-22*

AS WE NEAR the end of this psalm, remember that it begins and ends with the same phrase, telling us that praise is to be offered to God. This means in all places of His dominion and including everyone everywhere and under every circumstance. What we haven't noted yet is that "everyone everywhere" includes the unseen realm of the Spirit as well as the angels and the hosts of heaven who do God's pleasure as His ministers (v. 21). In Hebrews 2 we learn that originally, man's position was higher than the angels, and that someday we will judge angels (1 Corinthians 6:3) when we're restored to God's original intent and position for us.

David recognizes the angels as ministering spirits, proclaiming to them, *"Bless the Lord, you His angels, who excel in strength and who do His word."* Then David extends the same directive to "all the hosts," meaning armies. It pleases God that

His army of angels ministers to those who are inheriting salvation. David also says, "*Bless the Lord, you ministering spirits*," and we are to bless Him also. But who are the recipients of God's everlasting mercy from verse 17? It's those who belong to Him, proving their salvation by their fear of Him and keeping His covenant by doing His commandments. How can we do that, frail as we are in our faith sometimes?

God knows our weakness, and He has provided all that we need. The apostle John, quoting Jesus, wrote, "*If you love Me, keep My commandments. And I will pray the Father, and **He will give you another Helper**, that He may abide with you for-ever—the Spirit of truth, whom the world cannot receive, because it neither sees Him nor knows Him; but you know Him, for He dwells with you and will be in you. I will not leave you orphans; I will come to you*" (John 14:15-18). So God himself provides the help we need to worship Him in spirit and in truth!

Although many minds struggle with it in this politically correct era, the truth is that heaven is not the future home of everyone whom God loves. It's the future home of everyone *who loves God* and who keeps His commandments and in whom the power of the Spirit abides forever. It's important to examine ourselves from time to time, even as we know where we're headed eternally, to see if we can truly call ourselves lovers of God, filled with the Holy Spirit, and eager to see the Lord in our future heavenly home. It's time to offer to Him our thoughtful, heart-felt praise for His generous love and provision for our future no matter what we may be experiencing right now.

July 11

Are You Smart, or Are You Foolish?

Bless the Lord, O my soul! —*Psalm 103*

I WANT TO LEAVE you with some food for thought. John 3:16 says, "God so loved the world. . . ." Some still don't understand: If God loves everyone in the world, shouldn't everyone go to heaven? Jesus said that the world (in general terms) can-not receive the Spirit of truth because it neither sees nor knows Him (nor wants Him). It's a sad truth that people don't want God involved in their lives. Yet, amaz-ingly, they still expect to go to heaven when they die! Yes, God's loving-kindness is available to all who . . . do what? . . . *Keep His covenant and obey His commandments*. But those actions are merely identifiers. *No one* deserves or earns heaven by doing those things, but those who love Him *will* do them.

What may we glean from all of this? One thing is that God is greater and more powerful than the human mind can ever fathom. The more we truly understand this, the more readily we'll surrender to His will and praise Him from our hearts.

Who else could offer us mercy as high as the heavens are above the earth? Who else could endure the suffering that you and I could not? Who else never gives you "everything you deserve?" When someone has sinned, people might say, "You made your bed; now lie in it." Or, "I hope they get what's coming to them!" But God said, "Look at pitiful humanity. If I don't do something to save them, none of them will make it here, and they would have to suffer all that they deserve. I will endure for them what they never could."

There is really one sin that is at the core of them all. It was the sin of Satan himself that caused his fall and caused a third of the angels to fall with him. It is the sin of pride, and man falls victim to it all the time, resulting in the inability to admit that *God is greater than us and has every right to do as He pleases*. Once you accept that, the rest is easy.

Have you done so? If not, you should. If you don't, you'll never bless the Lord, and He'll never bless you—certainly not with heaven. "I thought that God loves everyone!" you say. He does. But the question is: Do you love Him? The answer isn't just to say the word "yes," but to live a *life* that says "yes" by keeping His covenant and doing His commandments, believing in the huge sacrifice that He paid to cover your sins—suffering and dying in your place—and then proving His infinite life and love by rising from the dead, showing Himself to many after His resurrection as proof that the grave couldn't hold Him, and ascending into heaven before the eyes of many, promising that He will come again to take us to our home to be with Him in heaven forever!

How smart are you? In Matthew 7, Jesus said, "'*Whoever hears these sayings of Mine, and does them, I will liken him to a wise man who built his house on the rock: and the rain descended, the floods came, and the winds blew and beat on that house; and it did not fall, for it was founded on the rock. But everyone who hears these sayings of Mine, and does not do them, will be like a foolish man who built his house on the sand: and the rain descended, the floods came, and the winds blew and beat on that house; and it fell. And great was its fall.' And so it was, when Jesus had ended these sayings, that the people were astonished at His teaching, for He taught them as one having authority, and not as the scribes*" (Matthew 7:24-28).

Jesus taught as one who has authority because He does have it—over all creation! And knowing Him is the only way we'll be able to endure the storms of life with our praise intact. And if you're smart, you'll praise Him, too! *Lord, we thank You for your love and Your great salvation that cost You so much and yet is so easy for us to obtain. We praise You with our lips and our hearts and our minds as we go out into the world today, because You alone are worthy.*

Putting God Before Us

Introduction

O give thanks unto the Lord . . . —Psalm 105

AS WE BEGIN our devotional look at Psalm 105, we would do well to examine another psalm that extols some of the same praiseworthy attributes of our Lord. Our psalm today, to begin with, addresses the faithfulness of God's people—both the presence of that faithfulness and the lack thereof. Psalm 66:1-5 gives us many reasons and ways that we should be praising God: "*Make a joyful shout to God, all the earth! Sing out the honor of His name; make His praise glorious. Say to God, 'How awesome are Your works! Through the greatness of Your power Your enemies shall submit themselves to You. All the earth shall worship You and sing praises to You; they shall sing praises to Your name.' Come and see the works of God; He is awesome in His doing toward the sons of men.*"

And this is what is in view here: the *awesome* works of God toward the sons of men. *Is* God always faithful? Can we access the blessings of His faithfulness? The answer to both questions is *yes*! Here's how we can we gain His blessings: "*Seek ye first the kingdom of God and His righteousness, and all these things shall be added to you*" (Matthew 6:33). That, very simply, is how we may appropriate the promises and faithfulness of God in our own lives.

Romans 8:31 asks the question: "If God is on our side, who can come against us?" Well, we need to ask ourselves, "Is God on our side?" And taking that up a notch, do we really believe this and act as if it is true? Do we really seek first the kingdom of God and His righteousness? What would life be like if we lived according to God's definitions of righteousness, obedience, and service, and made those our top priorities? What might we begin to see manifested in this life while we wait for the next? What might be "added" to us if we were to seek God first?

And why would we not want to seek Him? The Bible tells us of the faithfulness of God: "*If we are faithless, He remains faithful; He cannot deny Himself*" (2 Timothy 2:13). So His faithfulness is never in question! It's a part of His nature, and since He never changes, the ways in which God has always been faithful to Israel are the same ways that He will always be faithful to us. He cannot do otherwise, because "*He cannot deny Himself.*"

So, as Romans 8:31 says, "*If God is for us, who can be against us?*"; and the promise that we see in 2 Chronicles 7:14 holds true: "*If My people who are called by My name will humble themselves, and pray and seek My face, and turn from their wicked ways, then I will hear from heaven, and will forgive their sin and heal their* land," and the similar admonition in the New Testament: *"If you know these things, blessed are you if you do them*," then we can expect to see God's faithfulness manifested in countless areas of our lives, and this is what we will be looking at over the next few days.

Are you ready to learn what it really means to say, "If God be for us, who can be against us?"

July 13

Keeping God Before Us

¹Oh, give thanks to the Lord! Call upon His name; make known His deeds among the peoples! ²Sing to Him, sing psalms to Him; talk of all His wondrous works! ³Glory in His holy name; let the hearts of those rejoice who seek the Lord. ⁴Seek the Lord and His strength; seek His face evermore! ⁵Remember His marvelous works which He has done, His wonders, and the judgments of His mouth. —*Psalm 105:1-5*

WE LIVE in interesting times. The normal attacks and trials of keeping a "God before us" life seem to have stepped up. Lately I've found myself doing what the psalmist does here—recounting the faithfulness of God and reminding myself of the times when I couldn't see how things could work out, but they did! I've remembered when my eyes were blind to the "all things working together for good" aspect of keeping God *before* me, yet in 20/20 hindsight, recognizing that they did work out!

There isn't one time in my life where God has ever failed me. The blood of Jesus is far greater than my sin. And though I don't live in the past, it's good sometimes to recall the depth of His forgiveness in my life, making even more real the knowledge that my sin is "as far as the east is from the west" removed because God's mercies are as high as the heavens are above the earth. Think about that!

What the psalmist is doing on a national level in these verses is to consider God's faithful track record over the course of Israel's history of both faithfulness *and* faithlessness, yet never once did God abandon who He was or His promises to them because of their actions. God will never deny Himself. As we look through that lens, so to speak, let's see what He is saying: "Give thanks. Call upon; make known, sing, talk, glory, rejoice!" What is all of this? The writer of Hebrews knew: *"Therefore by Him let us continually offer the sacrifice of praise to God, that is, the fruit of our lips, giving thanks to His name"* (13:15).

The psalmist is calling on the people to offer the fruit of their lips through the sacrifice of praise, which is described for us here as all of those commands listed above. This translates into the first magnificently simplistic but ever-so-important truth: ***If we put God first, there will always be something good to talk about.***

Think about it. If we're continually giving thanks, calling upon Him, singing, talking about Him, etc., we'll never have to say, "Remember that time when God let me down? When He didn't keep His word?"

If we put *ourselves* before God, then we won't be praising the Lord but reviewing our list of failures and miseries. Is that what you want the fruit of your lips to be? There's a time to share our concerns with someone and ask for prayer, but I think you get the point. We can't say that there's nothing good to talk about, because we can always talk about God! Look at the similarity between the verses of this Old Testament psalm and Paul's words in Philippians 4:8-9: *"Finally, brethren, whatever things are true . . . noble . . . just . . . pure . . . lovely, whatever things are of good report, if there is any virtue and if there is anything praiseworthy—meditate on these things. . . . [A]nd the God of peace will be with you."*

There is never a time when we can't seek the Lord, His strength, His face, remember His marvelous works, wonders, and judgments. The result? Thanksgiving, singing, rejoicing, and all of the other reactions that we should have when we consider our Lord! All the good things that God has done in our lives can never be numbered because they're infinite. That's what the "God before us" life should be like—an endless string of good things to talk about because *God is good when nothing else is.* If we keep "God before us" as our outlook, we will never run out of good things to say!

July 14

God's Faithfulness to Israel

[6]O seed of Abraham His servant, you children of Jacob, His chosen ones! [7]He is the Lord our God; His judgments are in all the earth. [8]He remembers His covenant forever, the word which He commanded, for a thousand generations, [9]the covenant which He made with Abraham, and His oath to Isaac, [10]and confirmed it to Jacob for a statute, to Israel as an everlasting covenant, [11]saying, "To you I will give the land of Canaan as the allotment of your inheritance," [12]when they were few in number, indeed, very few, and strangers in it. —Psalm 105:6-12

THERE ARE THOSE who deny that anything in the Old Testament has application to the church or to Christians. The truth is that when discussing or examining matters concerning the nature and character of God, those things will always be true—regarding the Law, to the Jews, and regarding faith, to the Church. Let's look at Romans 4:12-16: *"For the promise that he would be the heir of the world was not to Abraham or to his seed through the law, but through the righteousness of faith. For if those who are of the law are heirs, faith is made void and the promise made of no effect, because the law brings about wrath; for where there is no law, there is no transgression. Therefore it is of faith that it might be according to grace, so that the promise might be sure to all the seed, not only to those who are of the law, but also to those who are of the faith of Abraham, who is the father of us all."*

So you can see that we're not infringing on the context by making personal application of things pertaining to national Israel, because it's actually God who's in view here and not the Jews. God did the choosing. He is the Lord; they are His judgments and it is He who remembers His covenants forever.

In Deuteronomy, the Lord said, *"Therefore know that the Lord your God, He is God, the faithful God who keeps covenant and mercy for a thousand generations with those who love Him and keep His commandments . . ."* (Deuteronomy 7:9). You can see that this unconditional and everlasting covenant wasn't without condition for those experiencing the blessings of it, but God's *faithfulness* to His covenant is absolutely unconditional and everlasting.

Verse 9 of our text today begins a walk through the history of the Israelites as the writer moves from Abraham to Isaac to Jacob and then to Israel as a nation, mentioning that the land in this covenant was given to them as the "allotment of their inheritance," meaning in the future, forever!

Today, there's much debate over the land that is blasphemously referred to by some as "Palestine." Saints, we are talking about the land of *Israel*, and it doesn't matter who else has lived there—God has given it specifically to Israel *forever*. He is true to His promises both to Israel and the New Testament church. And although we live in troubled and uncertain times, one thing is always sure: God is faithful. Numbers 23:19 says, *"Has He said, and will He not do? Or has He spoken, and will He not make it good?"* We can rely on His faithfulness no matter what man may do.

July 15

Are You Being Directed by the Faithful Promises of God?

[13]When they went from one nation to another, from one kingdom to another people, [14]He permitted no one to do them wrong; yes, He rebuked kings for their sakes, [15]saying, "Do not touch My anointed ones, and do My prophets no harm. *—Psalm 105:13-15*

IN THESE VERSES, the writer continues to march through time. He mentions these people who had been few in number but had grown into a great multitude during their time in Egypt. He traces their move to the Promised Land, where God protected them as they took possession of their inheritance one city at a time. Even though we can see some lapses in the covenant due to periods of persecution and captivity, God remained faithful to His judgments and promises in all the earth, and Israel is still a nation to this day because of His faithfulness to His covenant! It's a mistake to say that it was the resilience of the Jews that allowed them to remain a people today. They exist only because God is faithful to His promises, and He can never lie. He is faithful to bless and He is faithful to discipline, all according to His covenant.

What does this mean for us today? If we allow God to go before us, then **our lives will be directed by covenant promises!** This doesn't mean that we don't have free will, or that every step we take or don't take is being directed by Him, or that we won't sometimes need to be redirected. But God is faithful to His covenant and to His promises. When He brought Israel back to the land that He had given them after they were scattered among the nations, they returned under the same name and covenant that He had made with Abram.

What's the takeaway here? *"Thus says the Lord: 'Stand in the ways and see, and ask for the old paths, where the good way is, and walk in it; then you will find rest for your souls.' But they said, 'We will not walk in it'"* (Jer 6:16). Here we see illustrated that it's impossible for someone to stand in the ways of God and ask for the old paths and walk in them, and not be able to find rest for their souls. It's equally impossible for someone to find true rest for their souls by *not* standing in the way and asking for the old paths. When we live a life of asking God to always go before us, then His Word *will* be our guide, and His covenant promises will direct and lead us into the blessings associated with obedience to Him!

Many in this entitled era expect the blessings without the obedience. What does the New Testament say? *"All the promises of God in Him are Yes, and in Him Amen, to the glory of God through us. Now He who establishes us with you in Christ and has anointed us is God, who also has sealed us and given us the Spirit in our hearts as a guarantee"* (2 Cor 1:20-22).

Back the 1950s, A. W. Tozer said, "A whole new generation of Christians has come up believing that it is possible to accept Christ without forsaking the world." How accurate! The term "postmodern" has become a description of the age of history in which we live. The meaning of it is that we have moved past the thinking of the so-called modern era, which was "industrial age thinking." This notion has also taken hold in the church itself, and many have moved on to a different way of thinking, saying, "Different doesn't necessarily mean wrong. It's just different!" But when it comes to the Word of God "different" can be very wrong and often is. Sadly, the postmodern church in many ways is actually "post mortem."

We can't look at the Scriptures as if the interpretations are unlimited. We don't have "my" interpretation vs. "your" interpretation. The Word of God is not subjective! It is absolute and unchanging. So is God, and we would do well, as did the writer of this psalm, to revisit the past and ask for the "old paths" because that is the only good way, and to walk in that way means your life will be directed by the promises of God going before you.

July 16

God's Faithfulness to Israel through Joseph

16Moreover He called for a famine in the land; He destroyed all the provision of bread. 17He sent a man before them—Joseph—who was sold as a slave. 18They hurt his feet with fetters, he was laid in irons. 19Until the time that his word came to pass, the word of the Lord tested him. 20 The king sent and released him, the ruler of the people let him go free. 21He made him lord of his house, and ruler of all his possessions, 22to bind his princes at his pleasure, and teach his elders wisdom. —Psalm 105:16-22

NOW THE PSALMIST moves on to the more personal application of the faithfulness of God as he introduces Joseph in this march through the history of God's faithfulness to His people. If we were ever looking for a life that could illustrate the verse, *"All things work together for good to those who love God, to those who are the called according to His purpose"* (Romans 8:28), it could be epitomized through Joseph! Sold into slavery by his jealous brothers, falsely accused and jailed for a crime he did not commit, forgotten by those whom he had helped while in prison, and then finally, after two years in the prison cell, he was remembered only because Pharaoh had a dream that none of his magicians could interpret, and his former cell mate let it be known that Joseph was able to interpret dreams accurately.

He was called before the Pharaoh, and the Lord gave him the correct interpretation regarding a coming famine, thus impressing Pharaoh, who set Joseph over all the land, second only to himself. When the earlier prophesied years of plenty in the dream had ended and the famine had begun, the brothers who had sold Joseph into slavery years before had to stand before him (whom they didn't recognize), begging him to sell them grain. A series of events ensued that finally led to Joseph's revelation of his identity to his brothers: *"Then his brothers also went and fell down before his face, and they said, 'Behold, we are your servants.' Joseph said to them, 'Do not be afraid, for am I in the place of God? But as for you, you meant evil against me; but God meant it for good, in order to bring it about as it is this day, to save many people alive . . .'"* (Gen 50:18-21).

There are times when we see general truths that apply to the church as a body, but somehow we skip over them. Just as there were covenantal promises made to national Israel, even so, both Israel and the church are made up of individuals, and we can learn from these covenantal truths. Even though Joseph had had to endure so many wrongs against him, having been betrayed by his own brothers, imprisoned in fetters of iron, tested by the Word of God (which proved faithful), he was later made a teacher of the elders of Egypt who saved many people, including his brothers, through whose loins, one, Judah, would come both David and the Messiah! What had been intended as evil against Joseph by his brothers was turned into the wonderful story of God's salvation available to all who will receive it! And it can be traced back to Joseph's living his life with God before him. What a marvelous thing to ponder. As we quoted earlier in this study, "*If God is for us, who can be against us?*" (Romans 8:31). Let's continue to ask the Lord to go before us every day and do our best to follow His lead.

July 17

Divine Opportunities through Difficulties

²¹He made him lord of his house, and ruler of all his possessions, ²²to bind his princes at his pleasure, and teach his elders wisdom. —Psalm 105:21-22

JUST TO SUM UP what we covered yesterday, after all that Joseph, a just man, had to endure, God used it all in a beautiful way to ultimately bring Jesus Christ into this world to save us all from our sin and bring us to the home in heaven created for all who will believe in Him. What we can learn and hold onto as a promise is this: **We can expect divine opportunities even in difficulties.**

Do you ever think about those who face many of the same trials and traumas that we do as Christians but who don't know the Lord and have no hope whatsoever of ever seeing any good from their difficulties? We know that for those who live their lives asking God to go always before them, the outlook is much different.

One of the oft-overlooked elements of the wonderful promise of Romans 8:28 is that God has a purpose for us, and we can therefore expect divine opportunities even in the midst of life's difficulties. In fact, sometimes it will be from those very difficulties that He will create the opportunities! God wastes nothing. Although we all experience the normal course of life's events, including painful ones, there is always something good to talk about when your subject matter is God, His will, and His purposes. There are always divine opportunities because when we keep God ever before us, our lives will be directed by His promises into the things that bring Him glory and bless His children.

The Israelites were instructed to "*Remember the days of old, consider the years of many generations. Ask your father, and he will show you; your elders, and they will tell you: when the Most High divided their inheritance to the nations when He sepa-rated the sons of Adam, He set the boundaries of the peoples according to the number of the children of Israel. For the Lord's portion is His people; Jacob is the place of His inheritance. 'He found him in a desert land and in the wasteland, a howling wilder-ness; He encircled him, He instructed him, He kept him as the apple of His eye. As an eagle stirs up its nest, hovers over its young, spreading out its wings, taking them up, carrying them on its wings, so the Lord alone led him, and there was no foreign god with him'"* (Deut 32:7-12).

The point of our study of this portion of Scripture isn't to remember what God did for Israel through Joseph. The point is to remember God through His marvelous works, wonders, and judgments, and if our priorities are to seek first the kingdom of God (i.e., if God comes before us), then good words will come frequently from our lips and our lives will be a series of steps ordered by the Lord. If those steps should lead through difficult places, even there His hand will guide us into divine opportunities.

I simply can't see a downside to putting God first every day of my life, and in the end, hearing Him say those precious words, "Well done." Can you?

July 18

How Can You Question the Faithfulness of the Lord?

[23]Israel also came into Egypt; and Jacob sojourned in the land of Ham. [24]He increased His people greatly, and made them stronger than their enemies. —*Psalm 105:23-24*

SINCE THE BEGINNING of creation and until the heavens and the earth pass away and on into eternity, the Lord is faithful and true to His word. These verses continue to prove this to us today. That means that to question the inspiration and inerrancy of God's Word is to question His faithfulness. God promised this land to Israel, and He has continued to oversee His promise. Even with all the evil that Israel committed through the centuries, God has remained faithful, for He cannot deny Himself. This is also true in our own lives as they relate to Him.

To emphasize this point, look at Revelation 19:11, which says, *"Now I saw the heaven opened, and behold, a white horse. And He who sat on him was called Faithful and True, and in righteousness He judges and makes war."* Since the beginning of creation and until the heavens and the earth pass away, and even on into eternity, the Lord is faithful and true to His Word. Thus, to question the inspiration and inerrancy of God's Word is to question His faithfulness.

Isaiah wrote: "*For thus says the Lord, Who created the heavens, Who is God, Who formed the earth and made it, Who has established it, Who did not create it in vain, Who formed it to be inhabited: 'I am the Lord, and there is no other. I have not spoken in secret, in a dark place of the earth; I did not say to the seed of Jacob, "Seek Me in vain"'; I, the Lord, speak righteousness, I declare things that are right'*" (Isaiah 45:18-19).

As we look at the nature, character, and faithfulness of God, we can also apply some of these promises to ourselves. God was faithful to those who believed before there was ever an Israel, and His faithfulness then is the same faithfulness that we enjoy now as a church. Remember Jesus' command in Matthew 6:33? "*But seek first the kingdom of God and His righteousness, and all these things shall be added to you.*" The Lord didn't say to Jacob, "Seek Me," in vain, nor has He ever said such to the church. In fact, our seeking will add to us "all these things." What things? If God is truly put before us as we go through our lives, we can expect that:

1. There will always be something good to talk about.

2. Our lives will be directed by God's covenant promises.

3. We can find divine opportunities even in our difficulties.

Let's press on in faith as we keep God before us in all that we do, looking *toward the goal for the prize of the upward call of God in Christ Jesus*!

We Are the Champions . . . Through Christ

> [25]He turned their heart to hate His people, to deal craftily with his servants. [26]He sent Moses His servant, and Aaron whom He had chosen. [27]They performed His signs among them, and wonders in the land of Ham. *—Psalm 105:25-27*

SOME COMMENTATORS believe this psalm was authored after the Babylonian captivity, serving as a reminder to the Jews returning to Jerusalem of God's faithfulness to Israel during and after the exodus from Egypt. The post-captivity Jews could expect God to be just as faithful as He was to those in Moses's day. We have the same expectation today because God is for us! We continue to see the personal pronouns "He" and "His" in reference to God.

And what do we learn? *God is for His people!* Look at the first two verses of this psalm that recall the families of Jacob making their trek to Egypt where Joseph was in a position of great power as a part of God's plan to save many alive. One family entered Egypt. A nation exited. God increased His people and made them stronger than their captors. Just as "Israel" is the new name given to Jacob, we are the "chosen people" when we come to Christ.

Israel still had a lot of Jacob in them, just as Peter had a lot of Simon left in him in the New Testament. And yet, God was faithful when Israel acted like Jacob, the supplanter, and when Peter acted like Simon. God is faithful to us even when we have lapses. There's no better illustration of this than the words of King David, who knew a bit about personal failure and God's faithfulness (to say the least!): *"Where can I go from Your Spirit? Or where can I flee from Your presence? If I ascend into heaven, You are there; if I make my bed in hell, behold, You are there. If I take the wings of the morning, and dwell in the uttermost parts of the sea, even there Your hand shall lead me, and Your right hand shall hold me. If I say, 'Surely the darkness shall fall on me,' even there Your hand shall lead me, and Your right hand shall hold me. If I say, 'Surely the darkness shall fall on me,' even the night shall be light about me"* (Psalm 139:7-11).

God blessed Israel even when they were under the heavy hands of the taskmasters, which caused the Egyptians to hate them and deal with them dishonestly. The Lord sent Moses and Aaron, who performed miracles, thus validating Israel as His chosen people who exalted their God above the many "gods" of the Egyptians. All of this brings us to this truth: **"If God be for us . . . we are ensured a life of victory and not defeat!"** Even if we are hated by the world and oppressed by the government, we still have a *real* understanding of the truth, which is that the government may try to thwart God's will just as Pharaoh did in slaying the infant boys of the Israelites. We may be silenced by their threats at times, but the "gates of hell will not prevail" against God's church.

If the great enemy of the second death has been defeated, and we are victorious over it through Christ, then what can feeble man do to come against us? If he takes our lives, we have a glorious home awaiting us in heaven with our Savior! We've already won the battle! Therefore, we must be steadfast, immovable, abounding in the work of the Lord while we are still here, for our labor for His name's sake is never in vain. We are the champions—we're not *"going* to be," or *"hope* to be." We are already numbered among those who, when evil was meant against them, God used it for good.

Remember this, saints: A Christian is so mighty in God that not even death can harm one: " . . . *whatever is born of God overcomes the world. And this is the victory that has overcome the world—our faith. Who is he who overcomes the world, but he who believes that Jesus is the Son of God?"* We have millennia to look back upon to see that if God be for us, we can walk in victory and not defeat. Walk on!

No Weapon Formed
against You Shall Prosper

²⁸He sent darkness, and made it dark; and they did not rebel against His word. ²⁹He turned their waters into blood, and killed their fish. ³⁰Their land abounded with frogs, even in the chambers of their kings. ³¹He spoke, and there came swarms of flies, and lice in all their territory. ³¹He spoke, and there came swarms of flies, and lice in all their territory. ³²He gave them hail for rain, and flaming fire in their land. ³³He struck their vines also, and their fig trees, and splintered the trees of their territory. ³⁴He spoke, and locusts came, young locusts without number, ³⁵and ate up all the vegetation in their land, and devoured the fruit of their ground. ³⁶He also destroyed all the firstborn in their land, the first of all their strength. —*Psalm 105:28-36*

WHAT WAS GOD'S response to the treatment of His chosen people by the Egyptians? His love was demonstrated in our verses today as eight of the ten plagues are recorded here, beginning with the plague of darkness (which was actually the ninth). The seven that follow are mentioned in closer-to-chronological order, skipping the fifth and sixth plagues (of diseased livestock and boils). Let's take a look at what the Bible tells us.

"*Then the Lord said to Moses, 'Stretch out your hand toward heaven, that there may be darkness . . . which may even be felt.' So Moses stretched out his hand toward heaven, and there was thick darkness in all the land of Egypt three days. They did not see one another; . . . But all the children of Israel had light in their dwellings*" (Exodus 10:21-23). The Egyptians were sun worshipers. So God sent them three days of darkness so intense they could *feel* it, but the Israelites had light in their dwellings! That must have shown Pharaoh something.

Why was God plaguing the Egyptians? Because they were preventing the Israelites from being free to worship Him, the one true God. The plagues of frogs, lice, hail, and locusts all led to the final plague of the death of the firstborn in every household that didn't strike the doorposts and lintels of their homes with the blood of a spotless and innocent lamb, and finally caused Pharaoh and the Egyptians to let God's people go.

What do we learn from this for today? If God is for us, we are under the protection of a supernatural defense system, so to speak. In other words, you're not dying 'til God says you're dying! One of my favorite verses that highlights God's omnipotence is regarding His defense of Israel during the Tribulation: "*Then the Lord will go forth and fight against those nations, as He fights in the day of battle*" (Zechariah

14:3). And how did we see the Lord fight against the nation of Egypt? With bloody water, bugs, boils, hail, disease, darkness, and death! These are comparable to many of the plagues we see in the book of Revelation during the Tribulation period.

We could certainly say that God defends His children in ways that may seem unconventional and are definitely supernatural! Even though at times we feel that we're being oppressed and attacked, we need to remember that not only *will* God defend us; He already has. If you're a born-again Christian, your soul is completely protected from going to hell. It won't happen. It can't happen. You are supernaturally defended from those of Satan who only want to steal, kill, and destroy right to the end. Yes, Christians today are being abused and executed around the world, but their persecutors are not the victors. The Christians are the victors! And unless the oppressors repent, they, as did the Egyptians, will become the victims of the wrath of the Almighty God!

"In God I have put my trust; I will not be afraid. What can man do to me?" (Psalm 56:11). Saint, you're not going anywhere until God says it's time. Satan cannot choose the hour of your death. As we've seen, God is in control of that, and nothing the devil tries can change that, because God is for us (Romans 8:31)!

July 21

With God, We Can Believe What We Hear

> [37]He also brought them out with silver and gold, and there was none feeble. . . . [38]Egypt was glad when they departed, for the fear of them had fallen upon them. [39]He spread a cloud for a covering, and fire to give light in the night. [40]The people asked, and He brought quail, and satisfied then with the bread of heaven. [41]He opened the rock, and water gushed out; it ran in the dry places like a river. [42]For He remembered His holy promise, and Abraham His servant. [43]He brought out His people with joy . . . with gladness. [44]He gave them the lands of the Gentiles . . . [45]that they might observe His statutes and keep His laws. Praise the Lord! *—Psalm 105:37-45*

THINK ABOUT what's being said in these verses. Pharaoh held tightly to the Israelites through nine horrible plagues, refusing, out of sheer stubbornness and pride, to let them go to worship their God. And then, after the tenth plague, the Egyptians *paid* them to leave!

What finally forced Pharaoh to acknowledge his impotence before the mighty God of the Israelites? God told Moses: *"So I will stretch out My hand and strike Egypt with all My wonders which I will do in its midst; and after that he will let you go. And I will give this people favor in the sight of the Egyptians; and it shall be . . . that you shall not go empty-handed. But every woman shall ask of her neighbor . . . articles of silver . . . of gold, and clothing. . . . So you shall plunder the Egyptians"* (Exodus 3:20-22).

God spoke these words to Moses long before any of it happened. This is a good reminder to us that God's promises are true *when He says them*, not when they're seen. Has God made promises to us that are yet unrealized? Is there more to His plan for us when we leave "Egypt," i.e., the world? Won't that be when things will be at their best—forever?

Look at how all of this came about: their oppressors, who had refused to let them go, were suddenly glad to see them leave. God protected His children after they left, covering them with a cloud by day and a pillar of fire by night. He fed them every day with bread from heaven. They asked for meat, and he sent quail into their midst. He brought forth water from a rock that renewed life and defeated death. Why did He do all of this? Because He was faithful to the covenant that He had made, long before, with Abraham.

Things didn't always go so well for the Israelites during their long trek in the wilderness. At one point they began to murmur and complain, scorning the manna from heaven that God had sent to them: *"Why have you brought us up out of Egypt to die in the wilderness? . . . Our soul loathes this worthless bread."* God's response? He sent fiery serpents who bit the people and many of them died! Then God told Moses to make a "fiery serpent and set it on a pole." Whoever looked at it after being bitten would live (Numbers 21:4-9).

Just a day into their journey the people were complaining about being thirsty. God gave them water, fed them with manna from heaven, which they called "worthless bread." Some of them even longed to go back to Egypt, apparently forgetting the sting of the taskmaster's whip. We live in a day where many hate the bread of life and want to fulfill the longings of their flesh. People speak against the Lord and complain about His ways. There is a time of judgment coming on the world for doing so.

And yet, God saved those who found the joy of the Lord to be their strength and brought them into a land flowing with milk and honey, with houses and vineyards planted by others—a place where they might observe His statutes and keep His law. Hold onto this thought very tightly: *If God be for us, everything we need is already ours.* Strength when we're weak, mourning turned to dancing, a blessed hope of His glorious appearing, a promise of His faithfulness, a satisfied sin debt— and the list goes on. In closing, remember this: God *is* for you! Go and live like it from here on!

Our PTA Meeting Is Called to Order

Introduction to Psalm 108

A Song or a Psalm of David [Psalm 108]

THIS PSALM is actually a mash-up of two of David's previous psalms, Psalm 57:7-11 and Psalm 60-5-12. Another intriguing thing to notice is that the opening verses of this psalm are the closing verses of Psalm 57.

The background of that psalm, as you may recall, was that David was hiding from King Saul in a cave at En Gedi. He begins this psalm where he left off in Psalm 57, and it appears that experience has become David's teacher. He begins with praise first and moves into another difficult season .

He sets a good example in doing that. If you recall, in Exodus, after being miraculously delivered from Pharaoh and the Egyptians, Moses and the Israelites sang this song: *"I will sing to the Lord, for He has triumphed gloriously! The horse and its rider He has thrown into the sea! The Lord is my strength and song, and He has become my salvation; He is my God, and I will praise Him; my father's God, and I will exalt Him. The Lord is a man of war; The Lord is His name"* (Exodus 15:1-3). In truth, Moses and the children of Israel could have sung this song on either side of the Red Sea. It was as true of the Lord before the sea parted as it was afterward. And this is what David seems to have learned and perhaps why he chose to open with the words of praise from a previous psalm: God is worthy of praise *before deliverance comes*. He is worthy of praise *before the battle is won*. He is worthy of praise before provision is given. What David seems to fully understand now is that God is worthy of praise *because of who He is*, not just because of what He does.

As we make our way through this psalm, we'll discover the same thing for our own lives. Let's look at what Isaiah wrote: " . . . *Behold, God is my salvation, I will trust and not be afraid; 'For Yah, the Lord, is my strength and my song; He also has become my salvation.' . . . 'Praise the Lord, call upon His name; declare His deeds among the peoples, make mention that His name is exalted. Sing to the Lord, for He has done excellent things. . . .*" This is similar to what David has said in these verses, even though Isaiah wrote 300 years later. And you and I can say these exact same things as well, even though we are reading it 3,000 years later! *Truth is unchanging.* Our God is the way, the truth, and the life. What we read today is ours to appropriate and carry with us always, as these truths about who God is never change.

We need to have a meeting as believers about how to live our lives with the mindset and manner that has been described here. "What kind of meeting?" you ask. Well, let's call it a P.T.A. meeting! Why would we call it that? We're going to be learning through the words of David how to have a vibrant Christian life. People often talk about being "on fire" for the Lord, and our P.T.A. meeting is going to show us what that looks like. The "on-fire" Christian life is one that is filled with Praise, Trust, and Action (P.T.A.), even in perilous times and in the face of adversity. There is much to be learned from David here, so let's call this meeting to order and dig in!

PTA (Praise, Trust, Action)

¹O God, my heart is steadfast; I will sing and give praise, even with my glory. ²Awake lute and harp! I myself will awake the dawn. ³I will praise You, O Lord, among the peoples, and I will sing praises to You among the nations. ⁴For Your mercy is great above the heavens, and Your truth reaches to the clouds. —*Psalm 108:1-4*

AS WE OPEN our "PTA meeting" today to learn how to implement God's work and will in our own lives, let's look at the opening of Psalm 108. The verses above show us the "*Praise*" element of the on-fire Christian life as we also look back at Psalm 57. Whereas David opened that psalm with a cry for God's mercy, he opens this psalm with praise to the Lord. In Psalm 57, David began by describing the troubles that surrounded him with phrases such as: "*My soul is among the lions; I lie among the sons of men who are set on fire, whose teeth are spears and arrows, and their tongue a sharp sword. They have prepared a net for my steps; my soul I bowed down; they have dug a pit before me . . .*" (Psalm 57:3-6).

As he opens this psalm, David displays a faith-filled attitude. Not until he has listed several ways that he will praise the Lord, proclaiming God's greatness, does he finally begin to describe the difficult situation in which he finds himself. But, to repeat, notice that he now *opens* with his proclamations of faith and trust! What this tells us about how to live as an on-fire Christian, and as related to the "P" in our PTA meeting, is this (and this is important!): **Praise is a conscious decision, not an uncontrollable emotion.** That's not to say that our praise should be an unemotional recitation, but it does mean that the realities of David's being surrounded by his present calamities were every bit as hard for him as they had been back in Psalm 57. But this time, he said *first*, "God, my heart is steadfast." In other words, what David said is, "Oh, God, I am *determined* to sing and give praise!" When he says "even with my glory" in verse one, he is saying, "Even as King, I will sing praise to You, and although it's still a dark time in my life, I will praise You among your people and among the nations, because Your mercy is great, and Your truth reaches to the clouds."

In the New Testament, the apostle Peter wrote, "*In this you greatly rejoice, though now for a little while . . . you have been grieved by various trials, that the genuineness of your faith, being much more precious than gold that perishes, though it is tested by fire, may be found to praise, honor, and glory at the revelation of Jesus Christ, whom having not seen you love. . . . [Y]et believing, you rejoice with joy inexpressible and full of glory, receiving the end of your faith—the salvation of your souls*" (1 Peter 1:6-9). This is much like what David and Isaiah both wrote, meaning that true, faith-based praise can't be quenched—not by fiery trials nor by anything else!

Sometimes we have to make a conscious decision to praise the Lord. It may not even feel natural, but we must do it no matter what our emotions are saying. Why? For one thing, there are benefits when we make that decision. The King James Bible tells us in Psalm 22:1-3 that the Lord "inhabits the praises of Israel" (or, "His people"). When you and I make a decision to lift ourselves above our situation, and we sing and praise the Lord with all that is within us, no matter what we're going through, God will inhabit those praises. That alone may touch your perceptions and emotions, and your praise time will honor God and be a blessing to you, too! This is why David now puts his praise *before* his calamities: the conscious decision to praise God helps us to control our emotions as we face up to our pending battles. May the Lord continue to teach how to praise Him in ways that honor and bless Him!

July 24

"I Will Trust and Not Be Afraid"

> [5]Be exalted, O God, above the heavens, and Your glory above all the earth; [6]that Your beloved may be delivered, save with Your right hand, and hear me. [7]God has spoken in His holiness: "I will rejoice; I will divide Shechem and measure out the Valley of Shechem and measure out the Valley of Succoth. [8]Gilead is Mine; Manasseh is Mine; Ephraim also is the helmet for My head; Judah is My lawgiver. [9]Moab is My washpot; over Edom I will cast My shoe; over Philistia I will triumph." —*Psalm 108:5-9*

PSALM 57 had to do with David's personal problems, but in Psalm 108, he begins by exalting the Lord, praising Him and His glory above all the earth, and he distinguishes the Word of God itself as holy! The Lord speaks in this psalm, describing how He will divide and measure the lands of Israel, demonstrating His sovereignty over them. Meanwhile, David looks back at how the tribe of Ephraim had stood by him through his difficulties, as had Manasseh, and they had supplied him with "mighty men of valor" assigned to take David back and make him King over Israel.

The Lord states that Judah is His also. But remember: the sovereignty of God isn't limited by geography or loyalty! God also states that Moab, who detested Israel, was to Him as the dirty water of a washpot meant for the dusty feet of travelers in those days. He described Edom as a dirty shoe that had been cast upon the floor.

In 1 Chronicles 29, we read, "*Therefore, David blessed the Lord before all the assembly; . . . 'Blessed are You, Lord God of Israel, our Father, forever and ever. Yours, O Lord, is the greatness, the power and the glory, the victory and the majesty; for all that is in heaven and in the earth is Yours; Yours is the kingdom, O Lord, and you are exalted as head over all. Both riches and honor come from You, and You reign over all. In Your hand is power and might; in Your hand it is to make great and to give strength to all*" (vv. 11-13).

This is what David wrote after hearing that he wouldn't be the one to build the house of the Lord because he had been a man of war, and that, instead, his son Solomon would build God's house. Even after hearing those words, David remained on fire for the Lord, advising the people that God had chosen his son Solomon to accomplish the work of building the Temple of the Lord.

God is sovereign over both His people and His enemies. All that we are and have are His, and He is faithful to His own. So our PTA meeting today will call our attention to the second word in the title of our PTA association: "Trust." Trust is truth, based upon expectation that God will be faithful to His Word.

So we see David go from apparently thinking, "I'm hiding in a cave from King Saul" to remembering, "Nevertheless, I'm going to praise the Lord"; and "God is sovereign over all men. I can praise the Lord no matter what's going on around me, because national or international circumstances cannot hinder or hamper the Word of God from prevailing." *Trust* is based on truth. It's based on the expectation that God will be faithful to His Word, and, no matter what anyone in any position of power says, God's Word will prevail. His Word is truth, and, therefore, *trusting* in God's unchanging truth is part of on-fire Christian living. God's Word will prevail, friends, and we should expect it to. That's what trust actually is: truth-based expectation. Are you in a place where you can really appreciate this? May the Lord give you the grace to grasp and to keep this trust today.

"I Did It My Way" . . . to My Dismay

[10]Who will bring me into the strong city? Who will lead me to Edom? [11]Is it not You, O God, who cast us off? And You, O God, who did not go out with our armies? [12]Give us help from trouble, for the help of man is useless. [13]Through God we will do valiantly, for it is He who shall tread down our enemies. —Psalm 108:10-13

AS WE CLOSE out our PTA "meeting" with this psalm today, we find David taking a slightly different tone. He seems to be asking who will give him power over his enemies. But notice that he isn't doubting God here, and he actually answers his own question, saying that ultimately it will be God, who, even in wrath, remembers mercy. David knows that God had cast them off before for their disobedience and had left them to their own devices. David now appears to be looking at his situation from God's perspective, admitting that when he did things *his* way, instead of God's way, it was disastrous, resulting in defeat.

Now he's eager to resume his praise, showing his confidence in God, through whom, he declares, *"we will do valiantly, for it is He who shall tread down our enemies."*

What can we learn from this? Praise and trust will always be visible in our *actions*. And there's the "A" of our PTA meeting. It's a sad truth in our day that Christianity for many means going to church. That's not wrong, but it certainly isn't the whole of the Christian experience nor the definition of on-fire Christian living!

The apostle Matthew wrote: *"When the Son of Man comes in His glory. . . . All the nations will be gathered before Him . . . and He will set the sheep on His right hand, but the goats on the left. Then the King will say to those on His right hand, 'Come, you blessed of My Father, inherit the kingdom prepared for you . . . : for I was hungry and you gave Me food; I was thirsty and you gave Me drink; I was a stranger and you took Me in; I was naked and you clothed Me; I was sick and you visited Me; I was in prison and you came to me"* (Matthew 25:31-36).

Some see this as the Great White Throne Judgment and others see it as the dividing of the survivors of the Tribulation according to their faith and deeds. Either way, the principle remains the same, and we can examine ourselves by it. Those who praise and trust the Lord will have actions as manifestations of that praise and trust.

Can we Christians really have the single most important piece of information in the universe and keep it to ourselves? Shouldn't it impact our decisions about what we do and how we structure our lives? Shouldn't we want to feed the hungry in the hope of being able to tell them about the love of Jesus? Shouldn't we give to the thirsty water in the hope of telling them of salvation through faith in Christ and the *living water* that He offers to all who come to Him? Shouldn't it make us hospitable, having a love for strangers, taking them into our lives in the hope of telling them about Jesus? Shouldn't we clothe the naked for God's glory? Shouldn't we visit the sick and imprisoned so we might tell them of a God who heals and sets free human souls? As people who PRAISE God and TRUST in His Word, would not these be the identifying features through our ACTIONS?

Our "meeting" is about to adjourn, but we want to remember that God has called us to action, and a big part of the on-fire Christian life is "doing"—not for salvation, but for evidence of lives that are given to our Savior. Merely going to church is not serving God. Praising God and preaching of Him is the way that God has given us to share the Lord with the world, and as we exhibit our trust in Him through our actions, may we draw many to Him.

Our meeting is now adjourned, but our journey continues. And remember, even in these perilous times, the Lord our God is with us!

July 26

Yes, The King Is Coming!

Introduction

A Psalm of David [Psalm 110]

IN THIS FASCINATING psalm of David, he presents the coming Messiah as priest, ruler, and conqueror. He is King of kings and Lord of lords. This is the most-quoted psalm in the New Testament. In fact, verse one, "The Lord said to my Lord, 'Sit at My right hand, till I make Your enemies Your footstool,'" is quoted or alluded to 25 times! Verse 4 is quoted five times, and there are ten references to Psalm 110 in the book of Hebrews alone (remember that the people of Hebrew nationality in those days needed this instruction about Christ and how the prophecies related to Jesus of Nazareth, who had been rejected at His first coming).

The subject of the coming Messiah is further complicated because although this psalm portrays the coming King as conqueror and ruler, other Messianic verses present a different picture: *"To whom has the arm of the Lord been revealed? For He shall grow up before Him as a tender plant, and as a root out of dry ground. He has no form or comeliness; and when we see Him, there is no beauty that we should desire Him. He is despised and rejected by men, a Man of sorrows and acquainted with grief. And we hid, as it were, our faces from Him; He was despised, and we did not esteem Him. Surely He has borne our griefs and carried our sorrows; yet we esteemed Him stricken, smitten by God, and afflicted. But He was wounded for our transgressions,*

He was bruised for our iniquities; the chastisement for our peace was upon Him, and by His stripes we are healed" (Isaiah 53:1-5). Here we see not a conquering but a suffering Messiah.

Add to that verses such as: *"The Lord has said to Me, 'You are My Son, today I have begotten You. Ask of Me, and I will give You the nations for Your inheritance, and the ends of the earth for Your possession. You shall break them with a rod of iron; You shall dash them to pieces like a potter's vessel'"* (Psalm 2:7-9). To complicate things even further, Daniel wrote: *"And after sixty-two weeks Messiah shall be cut off, but not for Himself; and the people of the prince who is to come shall destroy the city and the sanctuary. The end of it shall be with a flood, and till the end of the war desolations are determined"* (Daniel 9:26).

Putting this all together, what you see is that Psalms 2 and 10 present a conquering King, Priest, and Lord in the person of the Messiah. Daniel and Isaiah present a suffering and murdered King, Priest, and Lord as the Messiah. What do the rabbis conclude? There must be two Messiahs! Jesus addressed this very question: *"While the Pharisees were gathered together, Jesus asked them, saying, 'What do you think about the Christ? Whose Son is He?' they said to Him, 'The Son of David.' He said to them, 'How then does David in the Spirit call Him "Lord," saying: "The Lord said to my Lord, 'Sit at My right hand, till I make Your enemies Your footstool'"? 'If David then calls Him "Lord," how is He his Son?' And no one was able to answer Him a word, nor from that day on did anyone dare question Him anymore"* (Matthew 22:41-46). He's making the point that this psalm is about Him! He is the one for whom His Father is going to make His enemies His footstool (i.e., utterly humiliate them).

When Jesus walked on earth, did this happen? No, but He is right now sitting at the right hand of the Father awaiting that very day and hour. Since Christ refers to Psalm 110 as applying to Himself as the conquering King, Priest, and Lord, that means there are not two Messiahs. There is one Messiah, who comes twice! Once to suffer, and the second time to conquer. Are you ready? The King is coming!

July 27

Life as It Was Meant to Be

[1]The Lord said unto my Lord, Sit thou at my right hand, until I make thine enemies thy footstool. [2]The Lord shall send the rod of thy strength out of Zion: rule thou in the midst of thine enemies. —*Psalm 110:1-2*

KING DAVID seems to see beyond the first coming of the Messiah and His ascension. In Luke 1, we read, *"Then the angel said to her, 'Do not be afraid, Mary, for you have found favor with God. And behold, you will conceive in your womb and bring forth a Son, and shall call His name Jesus. He will be great, and will be called the Son of the Highest; and the Lord God will give Him the throne of His father David. And He will reign over the house of Jacob forever, and of His kingdom there will be no end"* (vv. 30-33). "Son of David," which is implied in these verses, refers to the human family through which the Son of the Highest would be born as the God Man. David was born of the lineage of Judah, the tribe of kings, and Jesus rightfully entered the world as prophesied. Interestingly, this "Son of David" is also David's Lord, as the king prophesies here of seeing beyond the first coming of Jesus and into the heavenly arena, which is the present day "reality" concerning the whereabouts of the Son of the Highest— "at the right hand of the throne of the Majesty in the heavens" (Hebrews 8:1).

David sees beyond the first coming of Jesus, past His ascension, and now he says that Jesus's presence in heaven at the right hand of the Father is a time of waiting. We're in that process now, waiting until the Lord makes His enemies His footstool. The Lord, Jehovah, will send the rod of His strength out of Jerusalem! What will He do? He will rule right in the midst of, and even surrounded by, His enemies. Obviously, this isn't a description of Christ's first appearance on earth, when He was falsely accused, arrested, tried in a mock trial, found guilty, and ultimately executed for things He didn't do . . . but we did. And that's why He came. Thus we see that this psalm is yet unfulfilled and still requires the return of the Messiah. But for the present time, He is seated at the right hand of the Father. When that day and hour arrive, the King will return to the earth. And then what?

First, He will bring righteousness and justice to an unrighteous and unjust world. The Bible teaches the physical return of Christ to the earth when He comes to rule on earth for the thousand years of the Millennium. Here is how the Bible describes that time: *"Out of His mouth goes a sharp sword, that with it He should strike the nations. And He himself will rule them with a rod of iron. He himself treads the winepress of the fierceness and wrath of Almighty God"* (Revelation 19:15). We want to remember that the "nations being ruled with a rod of iron" means that there will be sin even in the Millennium with Christ on the throne! Otherwise, what would be the purpose of a rod of iron? The standard by which all nations are judged will be the Word of God, the sharp sword coming from the mouth of the Lord. When Jesus returns and rules on the earth, there will no longer be people who "get away with murder." There won't be any more "loopholes" or technicalities that let criminals off the hook. No one will lie to the judge in an attempt to fool him, because the Judge of all the earth is omniscient. He knows all, and therefore no one will be convicted of a crime they didn't commit, nor will anyone be able to lie themselves out of a just penalty. Abortion won't be allowed. False worship and cults won't be permitted either, and disobedience to the King will be met with swift consequences (Zechariah 14:17-19). The King is coming! When He arrives on the earth, things will return to the way they should have been run all along. No more injustice, no more promoted and protected unrighteousness. What a day that will be. Are you ready for Him if He should make His appearance today?

July 28

"When the Saints Go Marching In"—Part 1

³ Your people shall be volunteers in the day of Your power; in the beauties of holiness, from the womb of the morning, You have the dew of Your youth. —Psalm 110:3

WE CONTINUE this look at life in the Millennial Kingdom through these verses, written many, many years prior to the still-future event. David's "people," who are identified as the Lord's people, are "volunteers" who, in the day of the Lord's power, are clothed in the beauty of His holiness and the brightness of a new day, and who have the dew, vigor, and vitality of youth about them. Who are they? Jude writes: "*Now Enoch, the seventh from Adam, prophesied about these men also, saying, 'Behold, the Lord comes with ten thousands of His saints, to execute judgment on all, to convict all who are ungodly among them of all their ungodly deeds which they have committed in an ungodly way, and of all the harsh things which ungodly sinners have spoken against Him'*" (vv. 14-15).

Who are the ungodly ones prophesied by Enoch? They are the apostates, the false teachers. But what's important to our time (as we look ahead) is that the Lord is coming with ten thousands of His *saints*! This will be the Lord's 100-percent volunteer army. They won't be drafted; they'll enlist of their own free will. Yes, the Father draws them, but people resist His drawing all the time. These will not— they'll choose to follow the Lord, recognizing that God's offer of mercy and grace is the best offer they'll ever get, and they'll accept gladly His terms and conditions.

Revelation describes this event: "*I saw heaven opened, and behold, a white horse. And He who sat on him was called Faithful and True, and in righteousness He judges and makes war. His eyes were like a flame of fire, and on His head were many crowns. He had a name written that no one knew except Himself. He was clothed with a robe dipped in blood, and His name is called the Word of God. And the armies in heaven, clothed in fine linen, white and clean, followed Him on white horses*" (Revelation 19:11-14).

Picture that! The King is coming, with multitudes of saints who have surrendered to His will. Remember this: saying you're a Christian doesn't make you one. Being extremely "religious" doesn't make you one either. The only way to become a Christian is to be born again—born spiritually, by the regeneration of the Holy Spirit. Being a Christian isn't a claim you make or a box you check on a form as your "religious affiliation." Being a Christian is the result of having been born of *the Spirit of God*.

The apostle John explains a bit more about what takes place when we surrender our lives to Christ: "*Behold what manner of love the Father has bestowed on us, that we should be called children of God! Therefore the world does not know us, because it did not know Him. Beloved, now we are children of God; and it has not yet been revealed what we shall be, but we know that when He is revealed, we shall be like Him, for we shall see Him as He is. And everyone who has this hope in Him purifies himself, just as He is pure*" (1 John 3:1-3).

As then, as the pure saints of God, we will gladly join Jesus Christ in His triumphant return to rule the world.

July 29
"When the Saints Go Marching In"—Part 2

> [3]Your people shall be volunteers in the day of Your power; in the beauties of holiness, from the womb of the morning, You have the dew of Your youth. —*Psalm 110:3 cont'd*

AS WE LOOK again at this beautiful verse above, we see that these saints who appear with the Lord will be holy, as He is holy, strong, as He is strong, and vigorous as youths in their new glorified bodies (1 John 3:2). We see it again in Isaiah: "*Those who wait on the Lord shall renew their strength; they shall mount up with wings like eagles, they shall run and not be weary, they shall walk and not faint*" (Isaiah 40:31).

What is meant in this verse by the word "wait" as in "waiting on the Lord"? It can literally mean to "wait," as in to look forward to expectantly, or it can be translated as "bind together to." In other words, those who bind their hope to the Lord will have renewed strength that is similar to that of an eagle soaring through the sky or a tireless runner who's able to keep going without fainting or giving up. Isn't that a wonderful thought?

There's one more thing we must look at before we move on in this psalm, and that is this: In order for the volunteer army of the Lord, who are now like Him, to be in this place of returning to the earth with Him, *something had to happen beforehand to make them like Him and be taken with Him to where He is*. What might that have been? We know that every born-again Christian has been forgiven of all sin, but we still sin. We're not yet perfect. We're certainly not "complete," like Jesus, even though we are "in" Him as new creations. First Corinthians 15 describes an amazing event that leads up to this triumphant re-entry to our planet: "*Now this I say, brethren, that flesh and blood cannot inherit the kingdom of God; nor does corruption inherit incorruption. Behold, I tell you a mystery: we shall not all sleep, but we shall all be changed—in a moment, in the twinkling of an eye, at the last trumpet. For the trumpet will sound, and the dead will be raised incorruptible, and we shall all be changed. For this corruptible must put on incorruption, and this mortal must put on immortality*" (vv. 50-53).

Think about that! In a single moment, in the twinkling of an eye, all who are alive and in Christ Jesus at the time of the Rapture will be made instantly and eternally immortal! Then, seven years later, we will come back with Jesus when He returns—because during this life we willingly surrendered to His will.

Are you looking forward with anticipation to that day? Or is there something in your life that needs to happen first? Don't wait another moment. You can ask the Father to receive you as His child, in humility and faith, in Jesus' name, and He will do it. Then you need not fear the days ahead! Your sins will all be washed away. The apostle Paul wrote: "*For [God] says: 'In an acceptable time I have heard you, and in the day of salvation I have helped you.' Behold, now is the accepted time; behold now is the day of salvation*" (2 Corinthians 6:2). You can make today the day of your salvation and know with certainty that you will forever be with the Lord, returning with Him in victory along with all the saints!

July 30

"I'm in the Lord's Army"

⁴The Lord has sworn and will not relent, "You are a priest forever according-ing to the order of Melchizedek." ⁵The Lord is at Your right hand; He shall execute kings in the day of His wrath. ⁶He shall judge among the nations, He shall fill the places with dead bodies, He shall execute the heads of many countries. ⁷He shall drink of the brook by the wayside; therefore He shall lift up the head. —Psalm 110:4-7

FOR SOME, these verses present a problem. For the Jew, the problem would be the son of David being a priest. The priestly tribe was Levi, not Judah, and the Messiah was clearly to come through the tribe of Judah and, specifically, through the lineage of King David. The problem for the Jew is handled easily by the introduction of a priestly order that is neither of the Jews or even of the Levites. In the book of Hebrews, we read: "*For this Melchizedek, king of Salem, priest of the Most High God, who met Abraham returning from the slaughter of the kings and blessed him, to whom also Abraham gave a tenth part of all, first being translated 'King of righteousness,' and then also King of Salem, meaning 'King of peace,' without father, without mother, without genealogy, having neither beginning of days nor end of life, but made like the Son of God, remains a priest continually"* (Hebrews 5:6-10).

Melchizedek was a "priest of God" before there were ever any Jews and certainly before the Levitical line of earthly priests. Melchizedek is a type of Christ in that Christ is not limited to human ordinance or life span. He is a priest forever, and it was not through birth that he received his priesthood like the Levites do. The more contemporary problem arises when we look at verses 5-7, where the Lord is presented as judge of the nations, who executes the heads of countries and kings in His wrath. People don't like to hear that. They only want a God who meets their definitions and even their code of behavior.

Some believe that the Lord lets them define their own moral code, and no one can tell them that they're wrong and that they won't be going to heaven. They'd never accept that. This type of thinking is called "universalism," promoted by many preachers today who seek to build their own kingdoms instead of contributing to growing God's kingdom.

Christ came once to suffer for our sins, but He is coming back to conquer His enemies. Why should He let into heaven people who hate Him and don't want to go there? The blatant truth is this: The King is coming, and He will destroy all His enemies. Some of you may not like that, but I'm not trying to make you happy. I'm here to tell you that you *must* be holy. And you can't be made holy apart from Christ. And if you're not made holy, then what are you? You're God's enemy. In a not-too-distant future, a soon-to-come generation will experience the fullness of God's wrath if they enter into the coming Tribulation continuing to reject the Lord's offer of forgiveness.

True love means not letting one do what he or she wants without consequence. Luke wrote: [Jesus said] *"If anyone desires to come after Me, let him deny himself, and take up his cross daily, and follow Me. For whoever desires to save his life will lose it, but whoever loses his life for My sake will save it"* (Luke 9:23-26). Jesus makes the same offer to us today. If you want to come after Him, you have to stop putting yourself first and stop living by what you think is right and follow Him and His ways. As for me, I know that God sent His Son to die for my sins, proving beyond question that He loves me—and He loves you too!

The King is coming, first for His church to meet them in the air, and then seven years later *with* His church, to rule the nations with a rod of iron. Have you volunteered for the Lord's army? You can join of your own free will by being born again.

The Time Has Come

Introduction

Praise ye the Lord! [Psalm 111]

A FEW INTERESTING notes about our psalm today and also Psalm 112, which we'll be looking at in a few days, is that both are considered to be "wisdom" psalms, and both are acrostics, meaning that each line begins with the successive letters of the Hebrew alphabet (which was likely an aid in remembering or memorizing the content). In addition, neither psalm gives us any indication of the historical setting at the time of writing.

One thing we can be thankful for is that the Author of the Scriptures, the Holy Spirit, never makes mistakes or accidentally omits vital information. Psalm 119:160 confirms this: *"The entirety of Your word is truth, and every one of Your righteous judgments endures forever."*

It's highly possible that the historical context of this pair of wisdom psalms is unmentioned so that later readers wouldn't be restricted by the times and would thus be free to appropriate the majestic content during any point in history, including now! What we read in these verses we can "take to the bank," speaking figuratively. We can depend on them, we can act on them, we can rest in them—because the wisdom contained within these psalms is still true and apropos for today.

Taking a quick peek at the first line of the upcoming Psalm 112, we read: *"Praise the Lord! Blessed is the man who fears the Lord, who delights greatly in His commandments."* So we see that both of these psalms open with the phrase *"Halalyah,"* with "Yah" being the contracted form of Jehovah. The words contained in these verses are a vow to praise Jehovah no matter what. Praise Him when things are good, praise Him when they are not. We don't praise the Lord because our *circumstances* are good. We praise Him because *He* is good, regardless of our circumstances.

I'm calling this series of devotionals over the next several days, "The Time Has Come." We'll be reading about how wisdom comes from fearing the Lord, and receiving blessings from fearing Him is predicated on doing things, not just knowing them. Proverbs 11 tells us: *"The fruit of the righteous is a tree of life, and he who wins souls is wise"* (v. 30). For us to be aware that souls around us are perishing is knowledge. Leading them to Jesus is *wisdom*. So wisdom, then, is applied knowledge. What we know is irrelevant if we fail to act on it.

Some of us will be convicted as we make our way through these verses, but that's a good thing, isn't it? If we're not convicted, we'll never be convinced that something needs to change and thus begin to improve that situation. Could we do better at serving God? We know that we need to, and now is the time, because there isn't much time left!

Today, let's prepare our hearts to begin this study, asking the Lord to teach us, convict us, soften us, and help us, that we might be about our Father's business of saving souls.

AUGUST

Is God's Kingdom Your Top Priority?

¹Praise the Lord! I will praise the Lord with my whole heart, in the assembly of the upright and in the congregation. ²The works of the Lord are great, studied by all who have pleasure in them. ³His work is honorable and glorious, and His righteousness endures forever ⁴He has made His wonderful works to be remembered; The Lord is gracious and full of compassion. —Psalm 111:1-4

THIS PSALM opens with the admonition to praise the Lord, and then the author describes how and where he will praise Him, along with many reasons why God is worthy of our praise. In the first verse, he declares that he will praise the Lord in the assembly of the upright—in other words, when he's in the midst of friends and others in the congregational gathering. In Revelation 19 we're given a beautiful picture of that taking place: *"And the twenty-four elders and the four living creatures fell down and worshipped God who sat on the throne, saying, 'Amen! Alleluia!' Then a voice came from the throne, saying, 'Praise our God, all you His servants and those who fear Him, both small and great!'"* (vv. 4-5). This psalm opens with praise being issued as a command for all, because God is worthy of all praise.

In verse two, the author says that the great works of God are "studied" by all who desire to know them. Is that you? Do you desire to know more about the works of God? Are you willing to put time and effort into doing that? Do you often find that other things get in the way of your seeking to know the wonderful works of God? Track with me for a minute. Many Christians today complain about the sex and violence we see portrayed on television, in the movies, and even in commercials. There are also many wonderful Christians whose children are involved in sports on teams that have games on Sunday. They naturally worry that their children will soon begin to think that sports are more important than church.

But listen: there are more professing Christians in our country than any other special interest group, and if *just the Christians* would stop watching inappropriate movies, Hollywood would stop making them, because they're all about the money. The same goes for sports. As a kid, I was involved in three sports: track, baseball, and football. *Not once was there ever a sports event on Sunday.* If earlier on, Christians of today had spoken up the first time a Sunday sport event was proposed, saying: "We won't be there. Sunday is the day we meet to praise the Lord and study His Word," Christian parents wouldn't be facing this situation today.

Saints, the time has come *for Christians to make God's kingdom their top priority*! Our gracious and compassionate God made His wonderful works to be remembered. He even instituted the corporate gathering of His people for the purpose of doing just that. We don't *have* to go to church to worship God, of course, although that's a wonderful place to gather with others to do so. But God recorded in His Word that the corporate gathering together of believers is something that He *wants* us to do (Hebrews 10:25). God has given to His people the responsibility of being salt and light to the world, and that requires that we put His kingdom first, leaving everything else to Him. Matthew wrote: "*Seek first the kingdom of God and His righteousness, and all these things shall be added to you*" (6:33).

Consider this: Is our nation getting better and better or worse and worse? You know the answer. And I can assure you that the reason is because man's desires are being sought after and satisfied far more than remembering the works of the Lord. The time has come to make God and His kingdom our top priority, and let's not just give it lip service. Let's prove it by our actions, because God is an awesome God, and He deserves it!

Our God Is a Consuming Fire

> ⁵He has given food to those who fear Him; He will ever be mindful of His covenant. ⁶He has declared to His people the power of His works, in giving them the inheritance of the nations. ⁷The works of His hands are verity and justice; all His precepts are sure. ⁸They stand fast forever and ever, and are done in truth and uprightness. —*Psalm 111:5-8*

IN THESE VERSES, the author reminds the people of the wanderings of the Israelites and God's miraculous provision of manna from heaven. He refreshes their memories about God's faithfulness to His covenant, bringing them back to the power He displayed in places like Jericho, and when He made the sun stand still over Gibeon so that Joshua's army could conquer the five kings of the Amorites, leaving a heritage to His chosen people. The writer declares that all the works of God's hands are absolutely certain and unchangeable.

Acts 19: "*Some of the itinerate Jewish exorcists [called upon] the name of the Lord Jesus over those who had evil spirits, saying, 'We exorcise you by the Jesus whom Paul preaches.' Also there were seven sons of Sceva . . . who did so. And the evil spirit answered . . . , 'Jesus I know, and Paul I know; but who are you?' Then the man in whom the evil spirit was leaped on them . . . and prevailed against them, so that they fled . . . naked and wounded. This became known . . . in Ephesus; and fear fell on them all, and the name of the Lord Jesus was magnified. And many . . . came confessing . . . their deeds. Also, many . . . who had practiced magic brought their books . . . and burned them. . . . So the word of the Lord grew mightily and prevailed*" (19:13-20).

Unlike the seven sons of Sceva, we know the Lord, and the Bible says, "*Greater is He who is in us than he who is in the world,*" so the demon world has no power over us. In fact, we have power over the demons! But any power we have is directly related to our living by the truth, and the time has come for the church to tell the world the *whole truth* about God.

Notice that fear fell upon those present, and the name of the Lord was magnified. The sorcerers of the land were so convicted when they saw the power and heard the name of the Lord being magnified in connection to the event, that they brought their books of magic to be burned, and God's Word grew mightily.

Whose kingdom is growing by leaps and bounds today? Are we seeing mass burnings of pornography, drugs, and drug paraphernalia, along with repentance from the distributors of such things? Sadly, no, because today God's Word is watered down, compromised, and cut and pasted into a powerless blob of silliness that is powerless. Where is the church? Too many preachers have removed any mention of hell, repentance, and the fear of the Lord from their sermons. We need to remember what Spurgeon said: "The church's job is to feed the sheep, not to entertain the goats."

So what does a loving person tell their unsaved friends? They should be telling them to fear God, who has the power to kill and to cast into hell! When hell isn't preached, no one fears God. The truth of God's Word is the only thing that can set people free and save their souls from hell. Friends, it's time for the church to get angry at what the devil is doing. We need to get out there and tell the world the truth about God. Yes, He is love; no, He did not send His Son into the world to condemn the world but to save it, because it was already condemned. He *showed* His love by sending His Son to die in our place. There's no middle ground. God is love and has prepared a wonderful place for those who love Him. But those who refuse His love will find out at the end of their life on this earth that He is a consuming fire! Is there someone you know who needs to hear this? Let's begin by praying for them today and seeking for opportunities to speak the truth without being hindered by fear.

Are You In?

9He has sent redemption to His people; He has commanded His covenant forever: Holy and awesome is His name. 10The fear of the Lord is the beginning of wisdom; a good understanding have all those who do His commandments. His praise endures forever. —Psalm 111:9-10

WE MIGHT SUMMARIZE this beautiful psalm like this: "Wisdom is accessed by fearing the Lord." James wrote: "*Who is wise and understanding among you? Let him show by good conduct that his works are done in the meekness of wisdom. But it you have bitter envy and self-seeking in your hearts, do not boast and lie against the truth. This . . . is earthly, sensual, demonic. For where envy and self-seeking exist, confusion and every evil thing are there. But the wisdom that is from above is first pure, then peaceable, gentle, willing to yield, full of mercy and good fruits, without partiality and without hypocrisy*" (James 3:13-17).

As you look at the world around you, what do you see? Do you see most people exhibiting good conduct? Or do you see envy and self-seeking? Why? What is missing? It's the *fear of the Lord*. The fear of the Lord brings understanding to those who obey God, and "do His commandments" (Psalm 111:10). But accessing this pure wisdom that James writes of is only possible because of verse 9: God sent redemption to His people, and His commanded covenant is forever, because His name is holy and awesome.

People try to find "religion" in every way but through the Word of God, which is so easily found within the Bible. Some think redemption can be found through certain "religions" or schools of thought. So they seek, hoping to find Nirvana, a higher state of consciousness. Some believe the paths to enlightenment and spiritual healing are through meditation and the Eastern religions. Some within the "church" claim to be healers anointed by God. But take a close look at verse 9 again. It says that "He," i.e., Jehovah, *sent redemption to His people*. What is significant about that? Redemption represents the *finished work*! Unlike other belief systems and practices, God sent a Redeemer in person, who actually redeemed us! He sent us a Healer who actually healed us; a Deliverer who actually delivered us; a Provider who provided for us, and a Savior who saved us.

It's time for us as the people of God to walk in the fullness of our calling. Stop reading this right now, and turn to Romans 6:16-23 in your Bible. Read it carefully, and then come back to this page. Based on those words, here's what we find: God said that it's a sin to be drunk, so upon your salvation, He gave you the power to be sober. He said it's a sin to commit adultery or to fornicate, so He gave you the power to be pure. He said that sin shall not have dominion over you, so He gave you the spirit of self-control. Fiery darts thrown at you can now be quenched by faith; the Holy Spirit who indwells you is greater than the spirit of darkness who is after you; when the enemy forms weapons against you, they will not succeed; when people speak evil of you, you shall condemn them, because your righteousness is from the Lord.

There will be no more getting pushed around by Satan or failing to take the provided escape from every temptation; no more fearing man to the point of being silent about the fear of the Lord. God has given you all you need, and you can do all things through Christ who strengthens you! The time has come for us as the church to rise up and rescue those who are drawn toward death and those stumbling toward slaughter, and we have already been redeemed, empowered, and commissioned to do so. We know it, and the time has come to turn it into the wisdom of doing it! Are you ready to stand for Jesus, for righteousness, for His Word, and in His power? Who's in?

August 4

Time Will Tell

Introduction

Praise the Lord! [Psalm 112]

THE PAST FEW DAYS, we've been looking at Psalm 111, which is a companion to our current psalm. Neither gives us any idea of the historical setting in which they were written, nor are we told the author's name. In a way, this is a good thing, because it releases those verses from being restricted to the moment or situation. We talked about how Psalm 111 dealt with such words as "delight," "righteousness," "grace," "compassion," and "justice" as they apply to God, and in Psalm 112, we'll see how those same ideas impact man.

Remember when we looked at Psalm 1:1-3? *"Blessed is the man who walks not in the counsel of the ungodly, nor stands in the path of sinners, nor sits in the seat of the scornful; but his delight is in the law of the Lord, and in His law he meditates day and night. He shall be like a tree planted by the rivers of water, that brings forth its fruit in its season, whose leaf also shall not wither; and whatever he does shall prosper."* This holds true just as much today as it did when it was written, and we can apply the words "man," "his," and "he," to ourselves, whether male or female. The progression and the reward is the same for all of us.

In today's psalm, the author opens with praise to God. There's never a time when we shouldn't praise our Lord. Back in Psalm 111, we clearly saw that the time has come for Christians to make God's kingdom their top priority. Now is the time for the church to be telling the world the whole truth about God. It's time for God's people to walk in the fullness of their calling. And as we do these things, we should expect the benefits of our decisions to manifest themselves in our lives.

We live in "interesting" times, to say the least. Look back to the early days of the Christian church, which was just in its beginning phases in the book of Acts: "*Then the churches throughout all Judea, Galilee, and Samaria had peace and were edified. And walking in the fear of the Lord and in the comfort of the Holy Spirit, they were multiplied*" (Acts 9:31). Why don't we see much of this today? There are churches that have spent millions of dollars on church-growth programs, when all they had to do was to fear the Lord, and He would have multiplied their churches and comforted them with the Holy Spirit! The time has come for the *true* church to take a stand in the fear of the Lord.

Remember as we closed out Psalm 111, the last words had to do with the fear of the Lord being the beginning of wisdom. Wisdom is applied knowledge, and doing God's commandments is far different from just knowing them. Let's read on to find out how we can begin to really understand the fear of the Lord, and how we can gain and apply the wisdom that we are promised by the Lord as we study and learn from His Word.

August 5

The Faithfulness of the Lord

[1]Praise the Lord! Blessed is the man who fears the Lord, who delights greatly in His commandments. [2]His descendants will be mighty on the earth; the generation of the upright will be blessed. [3]Wealth and riches will be in his house, and his righteousness endures forever. —*Psalm 112:1-3*

"FOR THIS IS THE LOVE OF GOD, that we keep His commandments. And His commandments are not burdensome" (1 John 5:3). God didn't *burden* us with commandments. He *blessed* us with commandments, and those blessings are illustrated throughout the verses of this psalm. The person who fears the Lord, delighting to do God's will and obeying His commands will realize blessings in their lives and in the lives of their children as well. " . . . *No good thing will He uphold from those who walk uprightly. O Lord of hosts, blessed is the man who trusts in You*" (Ps 84:11).

And it's not about money. When Jesus walked on earth, there were many Jews who believed that wealth was a sign of personal righteousness. The disciples were shocked when they heard Jesus say, "'*Assuredly, I say to you that it is hard for a rich man to enter the kingdom of heaven. . . . [It] is easier for a camel to go through the eye of a needle than for a rich man to enter the kingdom of God.' When His disciples heard it, they were greatly astonished, saying, 'Who then can be saved?'*" (Matthew 19:23-25).

What can we learn from this? Those who fear the Lord and "delight greatly" in obeying Him will have descendants who are strong and brave, and whose homes will be filled with good things that make one's life rich. Does this mean only material wealth? Listen to Timothy: "*Now godliness with contentment is great gain. For we brought nothing into this world, and . . . we can carry nothing out. . . . Having food and clothing, with these we shall be content. But those who desire to be rich fall into temptation and a snare, and . . . harmful lusts which drown men in destruction and perdition. For the love of money is a root of all kinds of evil, for which some have strayed from the faith in their greediness . . . [piercing] themselves through with many sorrows*" (I Timothy 6:6-10).

So we see that the actions of those who fear the Lord will have an impact further down the road in that their righteousness will pass down to their descendants who fear the Lord. The legacy of living a godly lifestyle penetrates far deeper than we often see on the surface.

Are Christians held in high esteem? Not in most cases. But, here's the truth as we await the coming of the Lord: Time will tell that the plan and people of God will always prevail. "*You will be hated by all for My name's sake. But he who endures to the end shall be saved*" (Mark 13:13).

Jesus said this, so we know it's true. Sadly, many today have adopted political correctness and seeker-sensitivity in an effort to make people love us at the expense of truth. We need to live for the future *now*. We don't have the "upper hand" now, but as believers we will have it forever one day! Socialism and Marxism will never prevail, although many believe they will. There will a one-world ruler, and I don't mean the Antichrist. It will be the true Christ, and those who delighted in doing His commandments in this life will rule and reign with Him in glory in the next. How do we know that the Antichrist won't win and end up ruling the world forever? Because his power is limited to that of Satan. God is Almighty and nothing and no one can ever be greater than He is! We live in times when God is still allowing the enemy to advance. Countries will have to reap what they've sown, as will those who have claimed to follow the Lord but have not. But in the end, the plan and the people of God will always prevail.

Saints, do you want your homes to be blessed and your children valiant? Then teach them the fear of the Lord through your own great desire to obey God's commandments. We may not see instant results, but time will tell that the plan and people of God will always prevail.

"Father Knows Best"

⁴Unto the upright there arises light in darkness; he is gracious, and full of compassion, and righteous. ⁵A good man deals graciously and lends; he will guide his affairs with discretion. ⁶Surely he will never be shaken; the righteous will be in everlasting remembrance. —Psalm 112:4-6

AREN'T GOD'S PROMISES wonderful? He asks us to be faithful to His commands, gives us explicit examples so that we'll understand, and then He pours out His blessings upon us for doing as He asked!

Yesterday we looked at life in the home of the believer. Now we move out into public life, looking at the impact of fearing the Lord and delighting in His commandments as we interact with the world. He tells us that the upright person will be a light in dark places, exhibiting graciousness and compassion to others. Verse 5 tells us that the good man is kind and generous, holding loosely to material things and "guiding his affairs with discretion." There's a lot being said there!

Proverbs 19:17 states, "*He who has pity on the poor lends to the Lord, and He will pay back what he has given.*" Have you ever considered that? It tells us that whatever we do unto others we're doing unto the Lord. When Jesus was teaching the disciples about helping others, He spoke of the rewards that would be given to those who took care of people in need, stating, "*Assuredly, I say to you, inasmuch as you did it to one of the least of My brethren, you did it to Me*" (Matthew 25). God's people are to be a generous people, meeting the needs of those around them, thoughtfully, and with discernment, letting the Holy Spirit direct us.

Verse six is comforting as well, assuring us that if we're among the upright and doing the things that God wants us to do, we'll never be shaken, in a spiritual sense. God will give us discernment as we do His will, and we won't be pushed around by false emotions or teachings.

The apostle Paul wrote: "*You know, from the first day that I came to Asia, in what manner I always lived among you, serving the Lord with all humility, with many tears and trials which happened to me. . . . Now I go bound in the spirit to Jerusalem, not knowing the things that will happen to me there, except that the Holy Spirit testifies in every city, saying that chains and tribulations await me. But none of these things* move me; nor do I count my life dear to myself, so that I may finish my race with joy, and the ministry which I received from the Lord Jesus, to testify to the gospel of the grace of God" (Acts 20:17-24).

This is what we see in Psalm 112: Hold back nothing, and with that attitude, you'll be unmoved by the experiences of life! God knows what's best for us and for our children. If we put His things first in our own lives and demonstrate this before them, they'll learn to put God first in their lives also. Then we will reap the blessings and benefits of having done so. It's no guarantee that they won't wander off or question things, but with the truth in their hearts, they'll have the opportunity to prevail over the challenges around them.

This is important, because in the world today, it seems that anything the Bible says, people want to do the opposite. God says, "Humble yourself, and you'll be exalted." Man says, "Exalt yourself by humbling others." God says, "Deny yourself, and take up your cross and follow Me." Man says, "The cross is for the weak. Don't deny yourself anything." Who is right? *Time will tell* and one day it will be proven forever that God's ways are right! For now, however, God's ways have been forsaken. As Christians, we need to stand on His Word and trust Him no matter what the world says or does. We may face rejection, we may experience persecution and mockery, but time will tell that God was right, and we were right to believe Him. Our Father truly knows what's best for His children, and we can trust in His promises.

August 7

Prepare to Meet Your God

> [7]He will not be afraid of evil tidings; his heart is steadfast, trusting in the Lord. [8]His heart is established; he will not be afraid, until he sees his desire upon his enemies. [9]He has dispersed abroad, he has given to the poor; his righteousness endures forever; his horn will be exalted with honor. [10]The wicked will see it and be grieved; he will gnash his teeth and melt away; the desire of the wicked shall perish. —*Psalm 112:7-10*

WE'VE ALL SEEN the cartoons that show an old bearded man walking around with a cardboard sign that says, "The End Is Near." In truth, many people prefer to deny what the Bible clearly teaches: there will be an end to everything as it now exists, and the Bible doesn't shy away from that subject. Peter wrote: "*The end of all things is at hand; therefore be serious and watchful in your prayers. Above all things have fervent love for one another, for 'love will cover a multitude of sins.' Be hospitable to one another without grumbling. As each one has received a gift, minister it to one another, as good stewards of the manifold grace of God*" (1 Pt 4:7-10).

Peter says it, and Paul tells us through his letters to Timothy that the last days are not only coming but they will be perilous. Men will be lovers of themselves and haters of God. They won't endure sound teaching but will flock to those who will tell them what they want to hear. They'll try to sell the idea that you can walk in darkness and still be in the light.

The truth is that those who delight in God's commandments won't be afraid of evil tidings but will trust the Lord with a steadfast heart that is established on the *truth*. The man referred to in the psalm above has maintained the gracious and compassionate spirit even in the face of evil times, and God says that that man will be exalted with honor.

We also read that the righteous will see his desire on his enemies. God's plan will always prevail, and His ways will be proven right far above the ways of man. Time will tell us that the Word of God cannot return empty. Every word in the Bible will be fulfilled; every prophecy will come to pass, every foretold judgment will happen exactly as stated. The Word of God will never be revised to accommodate anybody. In verse nine it says that the wicked will look upon the reward of the righteous and be grieved. Then he'll go away to a place of gnashing of teeth, where all of his desires will perish.

The time has come, saints, as we've been seeing over the past few days, for Christians to make God's Kingdom our top priority. Jesus Himself mandated that we seek first His Kingdom and leave everything else up to Him. Even though we may not see any rewards in this lifetime, God's promise of blessing will not return void. By the same token, you can't live a life denying Christ, degrading the Bible, and still hope to reap good things in the end.

This isn't new. In Malachi 1:6-11, we read that a son honors his father, a servant honors his master, but God the Father isn't honored or revered. And then the Lord says, "*I have no pleasure in you . . . nor will I accept an offering from your hands. For from the rising of the sun, even to its going down, My name shall be great among the Gentiles; in every place incense shall be offered to My name, and a pure offering; for My name shall be great among the nations, says the Lord of hosts.*" God is telling them that they despise His name, giving Him their leftovers and discards and then expecting Him to be pleased and reward them! God says, "I'll take My blessings elsewhere and give them to those who put Me first and make My name great."

God's Word *will not* return void. If you put Him first, your life experience and eternity will come together exactly as the Word of God promises. The wicked will reap everything they've sown. The Bible says so, thus rendering all other outcomes void. The plan and people of God will always prevail. Time will prove it, and that time is even at the door.

What's the Point?

Introduction

A Hallel Psalm [Psalm 115]

THE HISTORICAL SETTING for this psalm isn't really known, although many believe there's evidence that it was written after the seventy-year Babylonian captivity by one of the Jews who had returned to Jerusalem. Some scholars point to the strong stance against idolatry in this psalm that is similar to that of the prophetic books of the Old Testament. What was the predominant sin of the nation of Israel? Just a quick look at Israel's history will reveal that idolatry was rampant in the land.

God's word on that subject was made very clear early on: "*Do not turn to idols, nor make for yourselves molded gods: I am the Lord your God*" (Leviticus 19:4). Yet despite that strong warning, Israel turned to idols time and again, and they were chastened time and again, until finally their city was destroyed by the Babylonians along with their temple. It's very telling that after the harsh discipline they endured during those long years in captivity, Israel never again turned to idol worship. So it's possible—and perhaps even likely—that Psalm 115 was written as a corporate psalm of praise by the returning Babylonian captives to their homeland.

The theme of this psalm is "pointless worship." Jeremiah, quoting the Lord, wrote, "*Because My people have forgotten Me, they have burned incense to worthless idols. And they have caused themselves to stumble in their ways, from the ancient paths, to walk in pathways and not on a highway, to make their land desolate and a perpetual hissing; everyone who passes by it will be astonished and shake his head. I will scatter them as with an east wind before the enemy; I will show them the back and not the face in the day of their calamity*" (Jeremiah 18:15-18).

In the New Testament, Mark recorded Jesus's words: "*This people honors Me with their lips, but their heart is far from Me*" (Mark 7:6).

So just as in both the Old and New Testaments, idolatry is alive and well today, and just as it was to Israel, it is to the church—spiritual adultery. The title for this psalm, which we'll be looking at over the next few days, is "What's the Point?" This psalm continues the wonderful progression we began several days ago as we studied the pair of Hallels in Psalms 111 and 12. Putting those two psalms together with our title for Psalm 115, shows us that "The Time Has Come" and "Time Will Tell" that worshiping idols is pointless as well as dangerous and even debilitating. This psalm presents a timely word for a nation such as ours today that is steeped in idols and idolatrous behavior: What's the point . . . of pointless worship?

My Way, or God's Way?

¹Not unto us, O Lord . . . but to Your name give glory, because of Your mercy, because of your truth. ²Why should the Gentiles say, "So where is their God?" ³But our God is in heaven; He does whatever He pleases. ⁴Their idols are silver and gold, the work of men's hands. ⁵They have mouths, but they do not speak; eyes they have, but they do not see; ⁶they have ears, but they do not hear; noses they have, but they do not smell; ⁷they have hands, but they do not handle; feet they have, but they do not walk; . . . ⁸Those who make them are like them; so is every-one who trusts in them. —*Psalm 115:1-8*

If this psalm had been written by someone who had been close to Nehemiah for the past seventy years, it would be an understandable backdrop for the satirical verses we read today as the Lord of glory is compared to the idols of the nations. Imagine yourself, for a moment, after seeing the futility of idol worship for seventy years from the seat of pagan idolatry, Babylon, the golden city, home of the great King Nebuchadnezzar, who was the ruler of the world! Picture living in the most powerful nation on earth and being surrounded by silver and gold and people who sell their very souls to idols who can neither see nor speak nor hear.

It seems fitting that the returning captives, having been exposed to the point-less worship of pagan idols and their emptiness, say, "Not unto us, O Lord, not unto us, but to Your name give glory!" We can see why Israel, who continually wandered away from the Lord, now says, " . . . because of your mercy and truth. Why should the Gentiles say, 'Where is their God?'" That taunting question was likely what they heard, day after day, while they were in Babylon. The Jews would be hearing, "Why isn't their God helping them? Why doesn't He show His great power?" Isaiah spoke similarly in Isaiah 44:14-20, speaking of the heathen: "*He cuts down cedars for him-self, and takes the cypress and the oak; he secures it . . . among the trees of the forest. He plants a pine. . . . Then it shall be for a man to burn, for he will take some of it and warm himself; . . . indeed he makes a god and worships it; . . . He burns half of it in the fire; . . . he eats meat; he roasts a roast, and is satisfied. . . . And the rest of it he makes into a god. . . . He falls down before it and . . . prays to it and says, 'Deliver me, for you are my god!' [For] He has shut their eyes so that they cannot see, and their hearts, so that they cannot understand. And no one considers his heart, nor is there knowledge nor understanding to say, 'I have burned half of it in the fire, yes I have also baked bread on its coals; I have roasted meat and eaten it; and shall I make the rest of it an abomination? Shall I fall down before a block of wood? a deceived heart has turned him aside; and he cannot deliver his soul, nor say, 'Is there not a lie in my right hand?'"*

We read this and think, *How foolish!* And yet that happens every day in our own country and even in our own lives. People ask, "Why is your God so special? Where is He? What gives you the right to say that your God is the true God and the gods of other religions are wrong?"

God does whatever He pleases. He is the maker of *all things*! He doesn't jump through hoops to please foolish humans. He is the true and living God, who has made a way for everyone who believes in Him to have an eternal home in heaven, where they will be separated from all the things that hurt and cause pain and sorrow. What's the point of worshiping what cannot save or help you? Worship means to submit to something or someone. The Bible is not anti-money, anti-pleasure, anti-happiness. The God of the Bible is anti-idolatry in any form. What's the point of surrendering your life to the pursuit of something that can't help you eternally? If you want your life to be rich and filled with purpose, meaning, and value, worship the Lord! Nothing compares to the Christian life, because only the Christian life offers eternal rewards and peace in our hearts on earth, no matter what circumstances we may be in. What's the point of worshiping something that can't help or save you? Go with God's way. It's the only way!

August 10

The God Who Cannot Lie

⁹O Israel, trust in the Lord; He is their help and their shield. ¹⁰O house of Aaron, trust in the Lord; He is their help and their shield. ¹¹You who fear the Lord, trust in the Lord; He is their hell and their shield. ¹²The Lord has been mindful of us; He will bless us; He will bless the house of Israel; He will bless the house of Aaron, ¹³He will bless those who fear the Lord.
—Psalm 115:9-13

Are you beginning to see a pattern? The author calls upon the nation to trust in the Lord, for He is their help and shield; he calls on their spiritual leaders to trust Him, for He is their help and shield; he calls on the individual Jew to trust in the Lord, for He is their help and shield.

The writer declares that the Lord "has been mindful of us." This may be a hint that this is a post-exilic psalm. Jeremiah wrote: *"For thus says the Lord: after seventy years are completed at Babylon, I will visit you . . . and cause you to return to this place. For I know the thoughts that I think toward you, says the Lord, thoughts of peace and not of evil, to give you a future and a hope"* (Jeremiah 29:10-11). The Lord had told Israel that because they had forsaken the Sabbath year for 490 years, not allowing the land to rest, as He had told them to do, that He would remove them from the land for one year of every year that they had disobeyed Him in that command. But He also said that while they were in Babylon, they were to remember that His thoughts toward then were of peace and not of evil, to give them a future and a hope. This psalm reminds them that the Lord is still thinking of them and blessing them. We see repeated: "Trust in the Lord; trust in the Lord; trust in the Lord."

Has someone you trusted ever lied about you? Did it damage your friendship with them, and maybe even destroy it because you couldn't trust them anymore? God isn't like that! Paul wrote: "*[I] Paul, a bondservant of God and an apostle of Jesus Christ, according to the faith of God's elect and the acknowledgment of the truth which accords with godliness in hope of eternal life which God, who cannot lie, promised before time began . . .*" (Titus 1:1-2).

Listen, God cannot lie, and therefore, He can always be trusted, He will never be responsible for damaging a relationship, and He said He is never out to hurt you. So trust Him! He is your help and your shield.

What's the point of listening to things that aren't true? Sadly, in our own nation, lies about people in positions of authority have become the new normal. They lie about one another and they lie about themselves. In all honesty, it doesn't matter *who* sits in the Oval Office, because America's problem isn't political; it's spiritual. America has a heart problem, and this is true for every other nation and for people the world over. If our nation is ever to be made great, it must start by acknowledging God as creator and endow-er of anything good. This applies to all nations, America, Israel, Iran, et al., that if they will trust in the true and living God, He will be their help and their shield. And yet, people seem to prefer to listen to lies. College professors are turning their backs on what they learned as children and are perverting truth on college campuses. Many now reject God's offer of salvation because someone with a PhD lied to them, telling them that evolution *proves* there is no God. "Intellectuals" write books filled with hatred and fallacy, and gullible people flock to them to hear their lies.

As it was in the days of our psalm above, so it is today. We're told that "God doesn't want you to feel guilty! You don't have to lower yourself by repenting. God loves you just the way you are." If you believe those things, then you're believing in something that isn't true. Our Father, who cannot lie, says, "Trust Me. I am your Help and Shield, your Provider and Protector." We must trust and believe in Him, or, like Humpty Dumpty, we'll have a great fall, and unless we repent of having believed lies against our God, we can't be put back together again.

Who Do You Love?

¹⁴May the Lord give you increase you more and more, you and your children. ¹⁵May you be blessed by the Lord who made heaven and earth. ¹⁶The heaven, even the heavens, are the Lord's; but the earth He has given to the children of men. ¹⁷The dead do not praise the Lord, nor do any who go down into silence. ¹⁸But we will bless the Lord from this time forth and forevermore. Praise the Lord! —Psalm 115:14-18

These last verses in our portion of this psalm today sounds like a benedictory blessing that might be spoken over a meal. "May the Lord who made heaven and earth give you and your children increase and blessing" followed by the acknowledgment that the heaven and the heavens are the Lord's. But the earth He has given to man. Reminding them that the dead don't pray to God, the psalmist is saying that now is the time to praise and bless Him, while we have breath. Look at Psalm 103: *"Bless the Lord, O my soul; and all that is within me, bless His holy name! Bless the Lord, O my soul, and forget not all His benefits: Who forgives all your iniquities, Who heals all your diseases, Who redeems your life from destruction, Who crowns you with lovingkindness and tender mercies, Who satisfies your mouth with good things, so that your youth is renewed like the eagle's"* (Psalm 103:1-5).

That carries the same thoughts as our verses today. God is the source of all blessing, so praise Him and bless His name! He is the God of heaven and the heavens, the realm of the stars—and He is worthy to be praised, from this time forth and forevermore. Psalm 27:12-14 gives us a little more to consider: *"Do not deliver me to the will of my adversaries; for false witnesses have risen against me, and such as breathe out violence. I would have lost heart, unless I had believed that I would see the goodness of the Lord in the land of the living. Wait on the Lord; be of good courage, and he shall strengthen your heart; wait, I say, on the Lord!"*

We know that our lives will be filled with trials and tribulations, but we will see the goodness of the Lord in the land of the living, which leads us to our third, and very probing question: **What's the point of living for self and not for God?** I believe that most of you feel the same as I do when I say that I want my life to count for God's Kingdom. I want to make a difference. I *long* to hear those words, "Well, done, good and faithful servant."

Can you see the progression in these verses, where trusting the Lord as our help and shield leads to the blessings of more and more increase from the Lord? I don't want to waste my life on meaningless things. I don't merely want the temporal blessings of God, especially where there is a danger of making those *things* my god and the object of my worship. We can even do this when it comes to reading the Bible itself. I was thinking about the book of Acts the other day, and the Lord pricked my heart that we often look at the book of Acts in awe of the God of that first century church. He is the exact same great God that we worship and serve today!

We should always want to put Him in first place, and our works should be seen as being done for the glory of the Lord. What's the point of being a church that's known for the fancy building that it's in, or by the size of its congregation, or by the name of its pastor? We should want our churches to known because of the name of our God, who lives and dwells among us, and is known by His works through us! Otherwise—*what's the point*?

Friends, it's time to storm the gates of hell. Jesus is coming soon!

The End Result

Introduction

I love the Lord [Psalm 116]

—
THIS PSALM is a Passover psalm, which was read by Jews during the Passover meal each year as one of the Hallel psalms, 113-118. The Passover was a time when the Jews remembered the grace of God as they were about to exit Egypt (See Exodus 12:12-14). It is a psalm of thanksgiving, recalling the original Passover, when the blood of an innocent lamb, spread upon the lintels and doorposts of their houses, allowed Death to pass over their homes. And we know today that without the shed blood of a spotless lamb, with Christ Himself as the final sacrifice, the remission of sin is impossible. It is also wonderfully true that Christ, as the perfect sacrifice, didn't remain in the tomb but arose from the grave, thus making Him, as Paul points out in 1 Corinthians, " . . . *the firstfruits of those who have fallen asleep [died]. For since by man [Adam] came death, by Man also came the resurrection of the dead. For as in Adam all die, even so in Christ all shall be made alive*" (vv. 20-22).

Christ's resurrection is what allows others to be made alive. People are now able to live for Him, being conformed into His image. Breaking this very deep subject down to its simplest from, and through the lens of this psalm over the next few days, we're going to look at the benefits of being a Christian—benefits that are exclusive only to those who belong to Him.

In Ephesians, Paul wrote, "*But God, who is rich in mercy, because of His great love with which He loved us, even when we were dead in trespasses, made us alive together with Christ (by grace you have been saved), and raised us up together, and made us sit together in the heavenly places in Christ Jesus, that in the ages to come He might show the exceeding riches of His grace in His kindness toward us in Christ Jesus"* (Ephesians 2:4-7). This Passover psalm is going to remind us not only of the end result of applying blood to the doorposts and lintels of the enslaved Israelites, but we are also going to see how Christ's death, resurrection, and ascension changed everything about everyday life for those who have been made alive in Him! We're going to take a close look at how the Resurrection impacts us today. And we must always remember those wonderful words of the "two men" who stood at the tomb in shining garments, who said to the women who had come to the tomb and found the stone rolled away, *"Why do you seek the living among the dead? He is not here, but is risen!"* (Luke 24:1-6a).

We'll begin our journey by examining this Passover psalm, which was read by Jesus in the upper room with His disciples the night before three days that would change the world would begin, and we'll discover the end result of all that He endured for you and for me.

Life Is But a Dream

¹I love the Lord, because He has heard my voice and my supplications. ²Because He has inclined His ear to me, therefore I will call upon Him as long as I live. ³The pains of death surrounded me, and the pangs of Sheol laid hold of me; I found trouble and sorrow. ⁴Then I called upon the name of the Lord: "O Lord, I implore You, deliver my soul!"
—Psalm 116:1-4

WE DON'T KNOW who the author of this psalm is, but a traditional association with the Passover has been made over the years. It's good for us to remember that connection, because it reminds us that deliverance isn't limited by our circumstances. In fact, God is able not only to deliver individuals but entire nations from the grip of death. So what we really have here is a personal testimony that is shared on a night where a national deliverance was celebrated!

Notice that the author of these verses implores the Lord to deliver *his soul*. The Exodus, as incredible as that deliverance was, removed the people from their physical suffering in Egypt, but this psalmist seeks help for his soul. He declares his love for the Lord, thankful that God hears his voice and supplications. In verse two, because of his confidence that God hears him and cares for him, he says that he will call upon Him as long as he lives.

Although we don't know what the pains were that surrounded him, we know that they were serious by the way he refers to them as the "pangs of Sheol." Thus he called upon the Lord to deliver his soul from death.

For believers today, because of the cross of Christ and His resurrection, we know that He has put our sins behind us, we have been made alive in Him, and thus we should praise Him all the days of our lives. It's because of what Christ did that our souls have been delivered, and that also means that we can call upon Him as long as we live.

To bring this home, we can say that *the end result* of the life, death, and resurrection of Jesus includes this wonderful assurance: **We have lifetime access to supernatural help.** The book of Hebrews tells us that we can " . . . *come boldly to the throne of grace, that we may obtain mercy and find grace to help in time of need*" (Hebrews 4:16).

What it all comes down to is this: In order for man to approach God, a change in his state needed to take place. Man had to be made holy. He needed to have a right standing before God. It was necessary for his sinful state, which would result in eternal death, to be changed. Because of what Christ did on the cross, and His resurrection from the dead, we now have lifetime access to supernatural help. God is a very present help in all times and for every need. In comparison with eternity, we are all living on the brink of death in this life that the Bible describes as but a vapor. The end result of the cross and resurrection was our being made alive, and we now have access to God through Christ and can call on Him, knowing that He will incline His ear to us all the days of our lives.

August 14

Blessed Assurance

> [5]Gracious is the Lord, and righteous; yes, our God is merciful. [6]The Lord preserves the simple; I was brought low, and He saved me. [7]Return to your rest, O my soul, for the Lord has dealt bountifully with you. [8]For You have delivered my soul from death, my eyes from tears, and my feet from falling. —*Psalm 116:5-8*

SWEET WORDS: "The Lord preserves the simple." God's grace and mercy are on full display here. God has long been using the foolish things of the world to confound the wise. In the case of the psalmist here, he was "brought low, and [God] saved me." James wrote: "*Humble yourselves in the sight of the Lord, and He will lift you up*" (James 4:10). This is exactly what the psalmist experienced. When he was in terrible distress, he was lifted above death and his soul was at rest. He says that his soul was delivered and his eyes were relieved of their tears. We don't know the cause of his sorrow, but it's highly likely that in this case the Holy Spirit was using him to write something far greater—something that would, in fact, be read by Jesus on the very eve of the day that He would deliver all souls who believe from the death grip of the grave.

And what a day we have to look forward to! Look at what John wrote in Revelation 21: "*Now I saw a new heaven and a new earth, for the first heaven and the first earth had passed away. Also there was no more sea. Then I, John, saw the holy city, New Jerusalem, coming down out of heaven from God, prepared as a bride adorned for her husband. And I heard a loud voice from heaven saying, "Behold, the tabernacle of God is with men, and He will dwell with them, and they shall be His people. God himself will be with them and be their God. And God will wipe every tear from their eyes; there shall be no more death, nor sorrow, nor crying. There shall be no more pain, for the former things have passed away*" (vv. 1-4).

Of course, to live in a place where "the former things have passed away," and where tears will cease from flowing forever, is only possible through faith in the life, death, resurrection, and ascension of Jesus Christ as God's provision for salvation. *The end result* of the cross and resurrection is that we will have complete assurance in this life about the next. The apostle Paul encouraged his readers with these words: "*If in this life only we have hope in Christ, we are of all men the most pitiable*" (1 Corinthians 15:19). In other words, there is more than this life! The end result of the spotless Lamb of God, slain for our sins in the person of Jesus Christ, is complete assurance right now about living in eternal glory in the next.

During some very hard times for the young Christian church, the apostle Peter wrote to them, saying, "*Beloved, do no think it strange concerning the fiery trial which is to try you, as though some strange thing happened to you; but rejoice to the extent that you partake of Christ's sufferings, that when His glory is revealed, you may also be glad with exceeding joy. If you are reproached for the name of Christ, blessed are you, for the Spirit of glory and of God rests upon you. . . . If anyone suffers as a Christian, let him not be ashamed, but let him glorify God in this matter*" (1 Peter 4:12-16). It would be hard to take comfort if this life was all there is. Could you honestly rejoice that you had suffered for Christ knowing you would soon die and fade into oblivion? There isn't much to rejoice in there! Instead, we're told not to consider it strange that we suffer, because Christ suffered. Rejoice if you're reproached for the name of Christ. It means that someone can see the difference in you as you reflect the glory of the Lord. Suffering for being a Christian will end one day when He himself returns in glory. Knowing about the next life helps to make this one bearable. And there will be rest for our souls one day, the result of Christ's death and resurrection for you and for me.

When Life Gets Hard

⁹I will walk before the Lord in the land of the living. 10I believed, therefore I spoke, "I am greatly afflicted." ¹¹I said in my haste, "All men are liars." ¹²What shall I render to the Lord for all His benefits toward me? ¹³I will take up the cup of salvation, and call upon the name of the Lord. ¹⁴I will pay my vows to the Lord now in the presence of all His people. ¹⁵Precious in the sight of the Lord is the death of His saints. —*Psalm 116:9-15*

AT THE PASSOVER meal, the listener would be reminded that the exodus was also meant to be an entrance. It was essentially an exit from slavery and an entrance into the Promised Land. The writer expresses his desire to walk before the Lord while he is living and promises to pay his vows to the Lord in front of everyone. After the reading of this psalm, the cup of salvation would be shared at the meal, thus making the connection between this psalm and the Passover vital, because it brings us face-to-face with what Jesus did on the very night these words were read. John writes: "*So when He had washed their feet, taken His garments, and sat down again, He said to them, 'Do you know what I have done to you? You call me Teacher and Lord, and you say well, for so I am. If I then, your Lord and Teacher, have washed your feet, you also ought to wash one another's feet. For I have given you an example, that you should do as I have done to you. Most assuredly, I say to you, a servant is not greater than his master; nor is he who sent greater than he who sent him. If you know these things, blessed are you if you do them*" (John 13:12-17).

There is a beautiful thread that is woven within this history. Just as Israel was brought out of Egypt and eventually into the Promised Land, we, by the cross of Christ, are called out of our former lives to a life of joyfully serving Him. As the Israelites were delivered from the bondage of slavery into a land of freedom, we were delivered from the bondage of sin and into a life of serving the Lord *freely* with all of our hearts.

It wasn't all sunlight and roses for the children of Israel upon their departure from Egypt. Exodus describes the situation: "*And when Pharaoh drew near, the children of Israel lifted their eyes, and behold, the Egyptians marched after them. So they were very afraid, and the children of Israel cried out to the Lord. Then they said to Moses, 'Because there were no graves in Egypt, have you taken us away to die in the wilderness? Why have you so dealt with us, to bring us up out of Egypt? Is this not the word that we told you in Egypt, saying, "Let us alone that we may serve the Egyptians"? For it would have been better for us to die in the wilderness.' And Moses said to the people, 'Do not be afraid. Stand still, and see the salvation of the Lord, which He will accomplish for you today. For the Egyptians whom you see today, you shall see no more forever. The Lord will fight for you, and you shall hold your peace'* (Exodus 14:10-14).

The people were afraid, but God had the situation well in hand. As for us, because Jesus went to the cross, conquered death, delivered us from darkness, and conveyed us into the kingdom of the Son of His love, we know that the Lord will fight for us, even when we go through dark times. We can rest assured that the end result of the death and resurrection of Jesus included the promise that we live every day under God's divine providence. When you "take up the cup of salvation" [get saved], having called upon the name of the Lord, your life is under His divine protection and providence. You've come out of Egypt and are headed for the Promised Land, and in your journey, as you live for the Lord, you have these assurances: *"The steps of a good man are ordered by the Lord, and He delights in his way. Though he fall, he shall not be utterly cast down; for the Lord upholds him with His hand"* (Ps 37:23-24). And *"But even if you should suffer for righteousness' sake, you are blessed"* (1 Pet 3:13-17).

August 16

Free at Last!

¹⁶O Lord, truly I am Your servant; I am Your servant, the son of Your maid-servant; You have loosed my bonds. ¹⁷I will offer to You the sacrifice of thanksgiving, and will call upon the name of the Lord. ¹⁸I will pay my vows to the Lord now in the presence of all His people, ¹⁹In the courts of the Lord's house, in the midst of you, O Jerusalem. Praise the Lord! —*Psalm 116:16-19*

IT'S ENCOURAGING to read about someone who keeps his promises, but we don't hear of it very often. The author of our verses today is making a public statement before the people and the Lord that he will stand by his commitment. Verse 16 tells us that the Lord has loosed his bonds. Through Isaiah, God said to the people, *"Is this not the fast that I have chosen: to loose the bonds of wickedness, to undo the heavy burdens, to let the oppressed go free, and that you break every yoke? Is it not to share your bread with the hungry . . . bring to your house the poor who are cast out; when you see the naked that you cover him, and not hide yourself from your own flesh. Then your light shall spring forth like the morning, your healing shall spring forth speedily, and your righteousness shall go before you; the glory of the Lord shall be your rear guard. Then you shall call, and the Lord will answer; you shall cry, and He will say, 'Here I am . . .'"* (Isaiah 58:6-11).

We know that Jesus is same yesterday, today, and forever (Heb 13:8). God doesn't change (Mal 3:6). Through Isaiah, the Lord spoke of loosing the bonds of wickedness, breaking bondage of every kind. And Jesus died for our sins, our wickedness, the things that held us in bondage—not so that we could live for ourselves but so that we could live for Him! He released us from our heavy burden of sin so that we could do the same for others. He shared with us the bread of life so that we could offer it to others. He clothed us in His righteousness so that we could bring others under His covering. He healed us by His stripes so that others could hear and see for themselves His healing power.

The Passover Lamb that allowed the Death Angel to pass over the house of those who had applied the blood was pointing to the ultimate sacrificial lamb who would die to take away the sins of the world. And it wasn't just any lamb, but it was the Lamb of God in the person of the Son of God! One of the marvelous end results of the cross of Christ and the second death having passed over us is that now we're able to live with power over the things that used to have power over us!

People today talk a lot about not being able to help their sinfulness because they were "born that way," and they "can't help it." I agree—to a point. They *were* born sinners, and there's nothing they can do to change that. It doesn't matter what the manifestation of the sin in their lives is. All sin requires someone greater than us to effect change in our lives and obtain freedom from bondage—*all* bondage.

The cross of Christ says that you don't have to remain in your sin. Some people speak of wanting to break free of their bondage, but they don't go to the source of Power to do that. By His death and resurrection, Jesus Christ makes that power accessible to you! And unless you come to Him, the only One who can set you free, you'll remain in your sin. What kind of sins are we talking about? How about adultery, fornication, impurity, lewdness, idolatry, sorcery, hatred, contentions, jealousies, outbursts of wrath, selfish ambitions, dissensions, heresies, envy, murders, drunkenness, revelries—these are all things that people naturally do because they are born with a nature bent toward sin.

Only God, through Christ, is able to effect the kind of change we need, and it's only because it cost so much for Christ to go to that cross in our place so that we can be truly free,if we'll only avail ourselves of that provision. Choose this day if you will grasp the end result of the death and resurrection of Christ, which is the saving of our soul, and you can be free at last!

Fierce Faith

Introduction

Give thanks to the Lord . . . [Psalm 118]

WE'RE NOW COMING to the last of the Passover Hallels. This psalm is placed between the shortest psalm in the Bible (117) and the longest psalm (119). And a fun fact to note is that the middle verse of the entire Bible is contained within this psalm. But the best thing to observe is the way that Christ (who hadn't yet been born) is presented in each one of these psalms.

Let's review: Psalm 113 presents God as being willing to humble Himself to lift man up, which Christ did when He came in the flesh. Psalm 114 presents the Lord in power and authority over creation, which Jesus displayed when He walked on the earth. Psalm 115 reveals the faithfulness of God in contrast to the futility of idols, which Jesus proved when He fulfilled the Scriptures through what He said and did. Psalm 116 is a psalm of thanksgiving for deliverance from the death of our souls, which Jesus accomplished when He lived, died, and rose from the dead, to live eternally. Psalm 117 is a call to the Gentiles to trust in the Lord, which is exactly what happened after national Israel rejected their Messiah. Psalm 118, the last Passover Hallel, praises God for His mercy, which endures forever, as we will see repeated five times in our psalm, and, like the other five Passover Hallels, is filled with Messianic references.

We followed the progression of these five psalms all the way to their fulfillment, moving from the humility of God the Son, who came in the likeness of sinful flesh, to the displays of divine power manifested during His time on Earth. We saw His death and resurrection and His calling of the Gentiles to trust in Him, and the everlasting mercy of God, which spans all generations and is manifested specifically in the lives of those who believe. Looking at this from beginning to end, what we have is a description of what life can be for us because of the resurrection and ascension of Christ! *"For I have been crucified with Christ; it is no longer I who live, but Christ lives in me; and the life which I now live in the flesh I live by faith in the Son of God, who loved me and gave Himself for me"* (Galatians 2:20).

As we seek to understand the idea of an "I am crucified with Christ" life, we see a hint of defiance in the tone of this psalm, which is where we derive our title, "Fierce Faith." The word "fierce" means something different from what it used to mean. Today, if you look it up in the Urban Dictionary, it means "something of exceptional quality." But the older definition of the word "fierce" was "ferocious," or "fearless," so keep that in mind over the next few days.

There are many examples of those who exhibited fierce faith named in the Bible, and some of them are not identified, although they are still remembered and respected. "*The time would fail me to tell of Gideon and Barak and Samson and Jephthah, also of David and Samuel and the prophets: who through faith subdued kingdoms, worked righteousness, obtained promises, stopped the mouths of lions, quenched the violence of fire, escaped the edge of the sword, out of weakness were made strong, became valiant in battle, turned to flight the armies of aliens. Women received their dead to life again*" (Hebrews 11:32-35). It's that kingdom-subduing, righteousness-working, lions'-mouths-shutting, fire-quenching, sword-escaping, strength-receiving, valiant-in-battle, dead-raising kind of fierce faith that we're talking about! Some might say, jokingly, "This ain't your grandma's faith," but in truth, our Bible-believing grandmas probably had a lot better understanding of this kind of faith than most people today. And the culmination of all of this is that because Christ is risen, death has been conquered, friends! And we can live in full defiance of our defeated enemy, the devil, because of it. Let's go forward the next several days with anticipation of learning how to live with fierce faith ourselves!

August 18

His Mercies Never Come to an End

¹Oh, give thanks to the Lord, for He is good! For his mercy endures forever. ²Let Israel now say, "His mercy endures forever." ³Let the house of Aaron now say, "His mercy endures forever." ⁴Let those who fear the Lord now say, "His mercy endures forever." ⁵I called on the Lord in distress; the Lord answered me and set me in a broad place. ⁶The Lord is on my side; I will not fear. What can man do to me? ⁷The Lord is for me among those who help me; therefore I shall see my desire on those who hate me. ⁸It is better to trust in the Lord than to put confidence in man. ⁹It is better to trust in the Lord than to put confidence in princes.
—*Psalm 118:1-9*

HOW CAN FIERCE faith manifest itself in our lives? Are you ready to get fierce?

The psalmist begins by calling on the nation to give thanks for the Lord's goodness, which is evidenced by His mercy. The Hebrew word for "mercy" simply means kindness. God never has a bad day. He is ever and always *kind*. Lamentations tells us: "*Through the Lord's mercies we are not consumed, because His compassions fail not. They are new every morning; great is Your faithfulness*" (Lam 3:22-23). And Luke writes, "*Love your enemies, do good, and lend, hoping for nothing in return; and your reward will be great, and you will be sons of the Most High. For He is kind to the unthankful and evil. Therefore be merciful, just as your Father is also merciful*" (Luke

6:35-36). Although technically we aren't reading about being kind to our enemies here, we do see the consistent kindness of the unchanging and all-merciful God. It's because He is kind that we aren't consumed! We should thus understand that we are also to be kind!

The psalmist speaks of being in distress and seeing God reach down to set him "in a broad place." That would indicate into a place of freedom from captivity. Have you ever felt frozen, unable to make a decision because you were being held captive by a terrible situation? We're going to see that the author refers to being set free from such fears, reminding us that God will often use other people to bring relief to our suffering, and He himself will fight against the ones who are causing it. Just remembering that He is on our side should bring some relief.

Our author arrives at the conclusion that it's better to trust in God than in man or in the government—always! Why? Because honestly, there are few in this earthly realm that can really be trusted. God is *always* trustworthy. Putting this all together, we see that God's mercy is eternal and never fails. He is *there* when we're surrounded by our enemies, showing us His kindness! He's on our side, so why do we fear? Why aren't we looking up and looking out for the evidence of His tender mercies even during the hard times?

Understanding what it means to live with fierce faith, we must remember that no weapon or personal attack can deactivate God's mercy. He is merciful and kind to the thankful *and* to the unthankful. Habakkuk prayed that God, in His wrath, would remember His mercy (Hab 3:2). And we read in the book of Hebrews: "*My son, do not despise the chastening of the Lord, nor be discouraged when you are rebuked by Him; for whom the Lord loves He chastens, and scourges every son whom He receives*" (Heb 12:3-6). Yes, God chastens us, and sometimes He even scourges us, but has He ever given us what we deserve? No, in fact, that's what He laid upon Jesus, because only He could bear that torture, and He did it out of love for those who would believe in His Son as their Savior. God shows His mercy to all sinners, but it will endure forever for those who are on His side. God's chastening of His children, like that of a good parent, is for the purpose of correcting our direction and restoring our fellowship with Him.

We can have fierce faith because God is merciful to us *always*, even when we, as His children, do evil, because His mercies are as infinite as He himself is, and although Satan hates this, there's nothing he can do to change it.

Greater Is He That Is in You

*10*All nations surrounded me, but in the name of the Lord I will destroy them. *11* They surrounded me, yes, they surrounded me; but in the name of the Lord I will destroy them. *12* They surrounded me like bees; they were quenched like a fire of thorns; for in the name of the Lord will I destroy them. *13* You pushed me violently, that I might fall, but the Lord helped me. *14* The Lord is my strength and song, and He has become my salvation. *15* The voice of rejoicing and salvation is in the tents of the righteous; the right hand of the Lord does valiantly. *16* The right hand of the Lord is exalted; the right hand of the Lord does valiantly. *17* I shall not die, but live, and declare the works of the Lord. *18* The Lord has chastened me severely, but He has not given me over to death.
—Psalm 118:10-18

IF THESE WORDS in verse 14 sound somewhat familiar, it's because they're a direct quote from the song of Moses in Exodus 15:2-7, and "the right hand of the Lord" mentioned above in verses 15 and 16 seem to proceed from that song as well.

Today our psalmist mentions that all the nations around him have surrounded him like bees and have pushed him, hoping to bring about his downfall. These verses are prophetic in the sense that Israel will be (and we already see this in our times) a "burdensome stone" for all nations (Zech 12:3). In addition, the severe chastening that we see in verse 18, combined with the reference to the gates in tomorrow's verses 19 and 20, has led some to see the returning Jews after their seventy-year captivity as they begin to rebuild Jerusalem.

Have you wondered why the author referred three times to the "right hand of the Lord"? It's to bring to the mind of the reader or hearer the reminder that the right hand was representative of a position of power, or even of a person's best attribute or greatest strength. In Hebrews 8, the writer stated, *"We have such a High Priest, who is seated at the right hand of the throne of the Majesty in the heavens, a Minister of the sanctuary and of the true tabernacle which the Lord erected, and not man"* (vv. 1-2). "The right hand of the Lord" here is clearly a Messianic reference. We also see a hint of defiance in this chapter when the writer says, "I am surrounded by all nations, yet in the Lord's name, I will destroy them" (v.11). They came at him like a swarm of bees, but they were quenched in their efforts. They were like a dried thorn bush thrown into the fire, and in the name of the Lord he vowed to destroy them. He complains that they pushed him violently, but God was there to help him. Thus he could sing, even in the face of all of this trouble, that the Lord was his deliverer, his salvation, and the source of his rejoicing. We see God responding with valiant actions on the writer's behalf. And, ultimately, he would live, and not die, even though having to endure severe chastening by the God himself.

Thus we see again today a cause for us to have a fierce faith, and it is this: *No power around us is greater than the power within us*. Yes, our faith can be fierce. It can even be ferocious. Satan, who prowls about as a roaring lion, is no match for the ferocity of a faith in the true and living God and His ability to deliver. Yes, Christians are being killed for their faith, but Satan still loses, because all he accomplished was to bring another believer from earth to heaven, where his evil can never touch them again. If the Spirit of Him who raised Jesus from the dead dwells in you, He who raised Christ from the dead will also give life to your mortal bodies through His Spirit who dwells in you (See Romans 8:9-11).

There is no power greater than the power that is within you. It is Resurrection power. It is Divine power that is greater than that of any person or spirit. There may be much that is against us on this earth, but through the Lord we will prevail. In the end, they, not we, will fall.

August 20

In Christ, We Cannot Lose

19 Open to me the gates of righteousness; I will go through them, and I will praise the Lord. *20* This is the gate of the Lord, through which the righteous shall enter. *21* I will praise You, for You have answered me, and have become my salvation. *22* The stone which the builders rejected has become the chief cornerstone. *23* This was the Lord's doing; it is marvelous in our eyes. *24* This is the day the Lord has made; we will rejoice and be glad in it. *25* Save now, I pray, O Lord; O Lord, I pray, send now prosperity. *26* Blessed is he who comes in the name of the Lord! We have blessed you from the house of the Lord. *27* God is the Lord, and He has given us light; bind the sacrifice with cords to the horns of the altar. *28* You are my God, and I will praise You; You are my God, I will exalt You. *29* Oh, give thanks to the Lord, for He is good! For His mercy endures forever . —*Psalm 118:19-29*

THE MESSIANIC references in this psalm are very clear, e.g., the stone that the builders rejected (Mt 21:42, Mk 12:10, Lk 20:17, 1 Pt 2:7); *"Blessed is he who comes in the name of the Lord"* (Mt 21:9, 23:39; Mk 11:9; Lk 13:35; Jn 12:13); and the Light (Mt 4:16; Lk 1:78-79; Jn 1:4-5; 8:12 9:5, etc.). Jesus also presented Himself as "the door" (or "the gate") to the sheepfold. He was greeted as the blessed One who came in the name of the Lord at His triumphal entry, yet the builders of the earthly temple rejected Him as the "foundation stone" of the temple.

You may notice that the psalmist personalized these truths (and so can we). He says that he enters through the "gates of righteousness." He will praise the Lord, for He has answered his prayers. He says that "we," including himself, rejoice in the day that the Lord has made and are glad in it. He prays, "Save now" (translated as "Hosanna") and "send prosperity," which in Hebrew means "to break out mightily." Are you praying this way? Are you praying for the Lord to break out mightily in your life? In verse 27, "light" is used as an idiom for "truth." The Lord sent us the Light of the world, because He is the way, the truth, and the life.

Then the psalmist arrives at the peak of personalized truth: "The Lord is *my God*, and I will praise Him. The Lord is *my God*, and I will exalt Him." He ends where he began, with the enduring mercy and kindness of our God. Is Jesus the blessed one who came in the name of the Lord? Is He able to save? Did He break forth mightily, although rejected by many? Did He heal the sick and deliver the demon possessed? Is He our light and our truth? Is He the sacrifice for our sins? We can answer yes to all of these, so we can give thanks, for *He is good*, and His mercy endures forever! Why should we have fierce faith? Friends, we have the advantage in every battle we face. Our government tries to silence the voice of the church. It can't, for Christ is our Head. The world tries to push us into falling apart by their violence and rejection of Christ, but they won't succeed, for God is our Deliverer! "*For you once were darkness, but now you are light in the Lord. Walk as children of light . . . finding out what is acceptable to the Lord. And have no fellowship with the unfruitful works of darkness, but rather expose them. . . . See then that you walk circumspectly, not as fools but wise, redeeming the time, because the days are evil*" (Eph 5:8-15).

It takes a fierce faith to redeem the time in evil days, but with Christ as the object of our faith, we can do it! It means that we have the power to walk in the light and truth as children of the light in an world of increasing darkness. We can walk with fierce faith, remembering that no weapons formed against us will prosper; the gates of Hades will not prevail against us; no one can separate us from the love of God, nor can we be snatched from the Father's hand. We have every advantage in every battle, because the Lord is on our side. Our bodies may face death, but our souls never will! The enemy may try to make us fall, but we will not. God is with us. There is no power greater than the power that is within us through Christ, and remember: If we ever start truly believing this and acting on it, the devil's kingdom is in big trouble!

The One Book

Introduction

Aleph [Psalm 119]

TO say that the journey before us is epic, monumental, or any other appropriate cliché would be to grossly understate what we're about to encounter. Psalm 119 is the most exhaustive and comprehensive declaration and validation of the inspired Word of God in the entire Bible. It contains 176 verses dedicated to elevating God's Word to its rightful place in our hearts and minds. All but seven of the verses directly mention the words "Word of God" using eight different descriptive terms: Law (Torah), Testimony, Precept, Statute, Commandment, Judgment, Word, and Promise. Five of these same terms are used in Psalm 19, which has led some to believe that King David is the author of this otherwise anonymous psalm.

Take a look at those verses: "*The law of the Lord is perfect, converting the soul; the testimony of the Lord is sure, making wise the simple; the statutes of the Lord are right, rejoicing the heart; the commandment of the Lord is pure, enlightening the eyes; the fear of the Lord is clean, enduring forever; the judgments of the Lord are true and righteous altogether*" (Psalm 19:7-11).

Besides the similarity of this and other psalms written by David, this psalm is a literary masterpiece. King David used the acrostic as a poetic device in other psalms, meaning that each line of the psalm or section begins with the sequential letters of the Hebrew alphabet. More impressive, though, is that this psalm is an *octadinal* acrostic, which means there are eight lines for each Hebrew letter. In other words, there are eight lines that start with the letter *Aleph*, then eight lines beginning with *Beth*, followed by eight lines beginning with *Gimel*, and so forth.

We know that many psalms were intended to be sung during temple worship. The eight lines of each letter that begin the verses of this psalm, and the fact that there are eight notes that make up an octave, gives us a hint, perhaps, that Psalm 119 also was intended to be sung.

This psalm is considered to be one of the "wisdom" psalms, and there's certainly much wisdom within these verses that may be gleaned from a careful study. This psalm is a chapter unlike any other and is contained within a book unlike any other. Hebrews 4:12 tells us that "*The word of God is living and powerful, and sharper than any two-edged sword, piercing even to the division of soul and spirit, and of joints and marrow, and is a discerner of the thoughts and intents of the heart.*"

I've read many books in my lifetime, but there is only one that can be defined by those verses, and that is the Word of God. It is unique in many ways, but one way in particular is that it can be read over and over and over, for years on end, and the depths of it will never be completely mined. It contains a narrative of the past, profitable directives for the present, and reliable revelations of the future. You may ask how we can know that the future revelations are reliable. In one word: *history*. This is the one and only book of progressive revelation whose prophecies were written long before they began to be fulfilled in all truth, one by one, and are still being fulfilled to this day. Not one of them thus far has failed to come to pass. Thus we can know with certainty that the ones remaining will surely be proven true as well.

God's Word is alive, and that's why parts of it will truly come alive to us—even individually at times—as we seek to plumb the depths of His wisdom and help. This is going to be a wonderful adventure! Are you ready to be blessed and inspired? Let's go!

August 22

Step by Step

¹Blessed are the undefiled in the way, who walk in the law of the Lord! ²Blessed are those who keep His testimonies, who seek Him with the whole heart! ³They also do no iniquity; they walk in His ways. —*Psalm 119:1-3*

AS WE BEGIN our journey through this beautiful psalm, we notice that the author opens with the same principle that we saw many months ago when we looked at Psalm 1, which is that there are blessings associated with seeking God with our whole hearts and walking according to the Law, i.e., the Word, of the Lord.

"Blessed is the man who walks not in the counsel of the ungodly, nor stands in the path of sinners, nor sits in the seat of the scornful; but his delight is in the law of the Lord, and in His law he meditates day and night. He shall be like a tree planted by the rivers of water, that brings forth its fruit in its season, whose leaf also shall not wither; and whatever he does shall prosper" (Psalm 1:1-3).

That section of Psalm 1, which we looked at months ago, presents the same truth as Psalm 119 but in both the positive and negative way. Notice that Psalm 1 states that blessings are to be found by *walking not* in ungodly counsel, etc., and by delighting in God's Law.

In the New Testament, we find that Jesus began His public teaching ministry in much the same way. Encouraging the common and hurting people of the land (and offending the self-righteous), He instructed them thus: *"Blessed are the poor in spirit, for theirs is the kingdom of heaven. Blessed are those who mourn, for they shall be comforted. Blessed are the meek, for they shall inherit the earth. Blessed are those who hunger and thirst for righteousness, for they shall be filled"* (Matthew

5:3-6). Paraphrasing this, we might say: "Whether you're poor, hurting, or humble, you can lead a full life if you hunger and thirst after righteousness."

Verse 1 of Psalm 119 defines being "undefiled" as walking in the Law of the Lord. "Law" means the Word, and verse 2 says that there are blessings for those who keep His testimonies (we might phrase it "who keeps His witness). Verse 3 summarizes such a life as one that isn't conducted by taking part in wickedness in any form, because that is how we are to live if we live according to God's Word.

Although the psalmist has presented this solely from the perspective of what we have to gain by walking in the Law of the Lord, it's also clear that this book is the *one* book that has a guaranteed avoidance plan for all our wounds, even they that are self-inflicted! We all know folks who aren't Christians, and we might look at their lives and, just from a material perspective, conclude that they live a blessed life. They have nice things, extra money, and take great vacations. They live in big, beautiful homes. But remember this: the same things that destroy the lives, marriages, and families of the less "fortunate" are no strangers to their homes, either. We are all people, we all have feelings, and we all need the Lord in our lives.

There are countless self-help books, and books about how to get rich, but none of them tells you how to keep from ruining your lives. There's only one incredible book that describes and defines how to live a blessed life and avoid the sins that bring such pain and destruction into our lives, and that is the Book of the Word of God.

Learn from Solomon, who wrote: "*The highway of the upright is to depart from evil; he who keeps his way preserves his soul. Pride goes before destruction, and a haughty spirit before a fall. Better to be of a humble spirit with the lowly, than to divide the spoil with the proud. He who heeds the word wisely will find good, and whoever trusts in the Lord, happy is he*" (Proverbs 16:17-20).

August 23

When Bad News
Becomes Good News

⁴You have commanded us to keep Your precepts diligently. ⁵Oh, that my ways were directed to keep Your statutes! ⁶Then I would not be ashamed, when I look into all Your commandments. ⁷I will praise You with uprightness of heart, when I learn Your righteous judgments. ⁸I will you're your statutes; oh, do not forsake me utterly! —Psalm 119:4-8

IT SEEMS TO be built into human nature to resist a command given by someone else. And when the phrase "righteous judgment" is used in reference to God's prerogative, many are even offended. This indicates a low view of God. The truth is that if you can accept and believe in Genesis 1:1: "*In the beginning God created the heavens and the earth,*" the rest is easy. Think about it. If God is the Creator of this earth and of the entire universe, including the angels and all people—who are we to question His right to command and righteously judge His own creation?

I'm no different from anyone else. I don't like to be told what to do. *I* want to be the captain of my ship. Unfortunately, I tried that and wound up with a life that was a shipwreck. But the Lord rescued me and turned everything around. I still don't always understand the things that He wants me to do, or why He allows some things in my life, but I know and believe that He's God—and I'm not. He knows what's best for me, and the same goes for you!

The Bible says some things that are offensive. It talks about hell and judgment and God's hatred of sin. Who wants to hear that? "Tell me the good stuff. I don't like all that bad news about eternal punishment and all. I like to hear good news. And besides, who made God the judge?" It's like the foolish little kid who, on being told to pick up his toys, turns to the babysitter, hired by the parents, and says, "You're not the boss of me!"

Suppose you go to the beach with a friend, and as soon as you get there he drops everything and sprints off into the water and swims out toward the waves. Suddenly you notice a dorsal fin sticking up from the water. A great white shark is approaching your friend. That's bad news! So do you run toward the water yelling, "Hey, man, you're a great swimmer!" Would they feel good if you said that? Sure! But would it help them in their present situation, or is it the bad news that's what they *must* hear? The same is true with the Word of God. It doesn't try to make people feel better about themselves. It tells the truth that they need to hear, and even though it may sound like bad news: "*You have sinned against the Lord, and be sure your sin will find you out*" (Num 32:23) and "The soul who sins shall die" (Eze 18:20), it really can be good news if it alerts you to your future, unless you change the direction you're headed. We need One greater than ourselves to direct our path—one who can the see the "Great Whites" ahead of us and direct our steps instead to a life of health in our bodies and strength to our bones and assure us of a glorious destiny instead of the "something terrible" that otherwise awaits us.

If you haven't understood yet or seen your need for the Lord, listen: God loves us enough to tell us the bad news and not only how to avoid the pains of self-inflicted wounds on this earth but also the eternal consequences of ignoring His commands and rejecting His love and forgiveness. We have the One Book that will show us ours sins and our need for a Savior. If you read the Bible sincerely, wanting to know the truth, I promise that you will be convicted by its words and understand the help that is *promised* if you receive Christ into your life. The Bible is clear:

all have sinned and come short of the glory of God. "All" means *all*. You, me, the best person you can think of, the nicest person, the smartest person—all. There is *no one* who can escape eternal death apart from knowing Jesus Christ as your Savior, which was God's plan all along. Once we're safe in His arms as believers in Him, no matter what lies before us, we can praise and thank Him, knowing that it's all being allowed for our benefit, and that a glorious future lies before us in the end. Do you want to be safe at last? Seek Him.

Prone to Wander

⁹ Beth How can a young man cleanse his way? By taking heed according to Your word. ¹⁰ With my whole heart I have sought You; Oh, let me not wander from Your commandments! ¹¹ Your word I have hidden in my heart, that I might not sin against You. ¹² Blessed are You, O Lord! Teach me Your statutes. ¹³ With my lips I have declared all the judgments of Your mouth. *—Psalm 119:9-13*

WE SEE TWO important things in verse one today. The first is that a person's way, or manner of living, needs to be cleansed. The second is that the Bible is the only source from which we can obtain that cleansing, or moral purity, in our lives. Paul said the same thing: "*For what I am doing, I do not understand. For what I will to do, that I do not practice; but what I hate, that I do*" (Rom 7:15). Have you ever sworn that you'd never do something again and then found yourself doing that very thing? That's what both Paul and our psalmist are saying. Even though our hearts are fully committed to the Lord, we still live in *bodies of flesh* that are committed to ourselves, much like the hymn writer who wrote, "Prone to wander, Lord, I feel it; prone to leave the Lord I love. Here's my heart, oh, take and seal it, seal it for Thy courts above."

We need to hide God's Word in our hearts—not just practicing religion, or "doing" good works, following rituals, or even attending church. What God wants is for His Word to penetrate our hearts and govern our lives so that *everything* we do is committed to Him first and done simply because we love Him. We need to make certain that His will and purposes direct us, letting His Word alone define for us what is pure and right. In Ephesians, Paul writes, "*You once were darkness, but now you are light in the Lord. Walk as children of light . . . , finding out what is acceptable to the Lord. And have no fellowship with the unfruitful works of darkness, but rather expose them*" (vv. 5:8-11). "Darkness" and "light" are synonyms for evil and good, so walking as "children of light" requires finding out what is truly acceptable to the Lord.

Is there a place where we can learn how to walk in and live by what pleases God? As believers, we ourselves are already acceptable to God because of the finished work of Christ on the cross. But how do we make our lives pleasing to God on a day-to-day basis as His children? It would require that we understand what such a lifestyle would entail. Today many truly believe that we're morally accountable to ourselves alone, with each person determining what's right and what's wrong *for himself.* But the psalmist makes a point here when He says that He hides God's Word in his heart that he might not sin against Him. This tells us that *the One Book contains a single moral standard for all cultures and generations*, which is of critical importance, undoing all subjectivism and universal moral absolutes.

All sin is against God. Sins aren't measured differently from one culture to another, or in one generation compared to the next. "*For I am the Lord, I do not change; therefore you are not consumed, O sons of Jacob*" (Mal 3:6). People hate the idea of a single set of moral absolutes that pertain to everyone for all time, but it's not only necessary, it's the best thing! Imagine if, under a system where everyone lived by his or her own moral code, one person believed in monogamy and the other spouse didn't. Who's right? Does one person's moral code give them the right to break the heart of their mate through infidelity because they believe it's okay?

Under a single moral code, right is right and wrong is wrong. There's only one place where we find the standard set and meant to be lived by, and that's in the Bible. When all is said and done, this is God's planet. We're His creation, and He knows what's best. He designed a single moral code to cover every situation, and it's our responsibility to live by it and not wander around in our self-made cocoons doing whatever we "feel" is right. Prone to wander? Prone to leave the Lord you love? You, too, can ask Him to "take your heart and seal it," and then let Him do it!

August 25

Where Are You Going?

[14] I have rejoiced in the way of Your testimonies, as much as in all riches. [15] I will meditate on Your precepts, and contemplate Your ways. [16] I will delight myself in Your statutes; I will not forget Your word. —*Psalm 119:14-16*

THERE'S A BEAUTIFUL truth concerning this section of Psalm 119, and it's unlike any other. First, we see that the testimonies within God's Word are the source of true riches, and His statutes are a source of true delight. And, for those very reasons, His Word won't be forgotten. In the verse above, "precepts" are mandates, and "statutes" are customs and ordinances, i.e., things prescribed. So the rituals, feast days, and other Jewish traditions were a blessing to the psalmist. It's much like when we do some things that won't save us but they're simply things that saved people do, like going to church, helping the poor, visiting the sick—these would be viewed as blessings, not burdens, by one who understands that these are the Lord's ways.

Another element to this is what's written in the book of Hebrews: "*By faith Moses, when he became of age, refused to be called the son of Pharaoh's daughter, choosing rather to suffer affliction with the people of God than to enjoy the passing pleasures of sin, esteeming the reproach of Christ greater riches than the treasures in Egypt; for he looked to the reward*" (11:12). Moses chose the latter and better way. For us, the One Book offers us everything that money can't buy. There's only one Book that promises health in a future home, where sickness, death, pain, and sorrow are banned forever. Moses looked forward to this reward, but we don't have to wait for the next life to enjoy the things that money can't buy. We can have them now: peace that passes understanding and the ability to face life's sorrows with hope, joy, and expectation.

In Second Corinthians, regarding that very thing, Paul wrote: "*We have this treasure in earthen vessels, that the excellence of the power may be of God and not of us. We are hard-pressed on every side, yet not crushed; we are perplexed, but not in despair; persecuted, but not forsaken; struck down, but not destroyed . . .*" (4:7-8). Yes, life is hard and painful, but we don't need to face those times alone as we await the end and our safe arrival in heaven. The things that money can't buy are exclusive to those who don't follow a book but who know the God of whom the Book speaks. It's only then that the things in the Book become our own personal reality. In Ecclesiastes, we read, "*I made my works great, I built myself houses . . . planted vineyards. I made myself gardens and orchards . . . I planted all kinds of fruit trees. . . . I made myself water pools from which to water the growing trees of the grove. I acquired . . . servants, and . . . had greater possessions of herds and flocks than all who were in Jerusalem before me. . . . So I became great and excelled. . . . Whatever my heart desired I did not keep from them. I did not withhold my heart from any pleasure, for my heart rejoiced in all my labor. . . . Then I looked on all the works that my hands had done and on the labor in which I had toiled; and indeed all was vanity and grasping for the wind. There was no profit under the sun*" (Eph 2:4-11).

Jesus said something similar: "*What profit is it to a man if he gains the whole world, and loses his own soul? Or what will a man give in exchange for his soul?*" (Mt 16:26). Having the things that money can buy will do nothing for you in the end. The Bible is the only book that will tell us how to be reconciled to God after having been separated from Him by sin. Only by having our sin debt paid in full by Jesus can we access now what money can't buy, understand the single moral standard that defines sin for all people, grasp our need for a Savior, and avoid our self-inflicted wounds. There's only one way to heaven, your future home, where you'll have all your sins forgiven, and that's through God's one Son, who died on the cross for all of your sins. He is the one way, and eternal life come only through Him! Are you going to be there?

The One Book—Part II

Introduction

Gimel [Psalm 119:17-32]

THERE ARE MANY self-help books in the world that can give you some information in our present day about how to do many things. But there's only one Book that can actually *do* something to you—and for you—just by your reading it. I'm talking about things like "how to cleanse your way," and "how to not sin against the Lord." And it's this Book that will continue to be the source of our study over the next several weeks.

We mentioned that this is a wisdom psalm, which means that it has the capability to make one wise. In fact, because this is the one Book that has proven itself true and has provided for us all things pertaining to life and godliness, it's pretty much a given that if we study with our whole heart and mind, we stand to gain a *lot* of wisdom!

For example, here are some marching orders from the apostle Paul: "*I charge you therefore before God and the Lord Jesus Christ, who will judge the living and the dead at His appearing and His kingdom: Preach the word! Be ready in season and out of season. Convince, rebuke, exhort, with all longsuffering and teaching. For the time will come when they will not endure sound doctrine, but according to their own desires, because they have itching ears, they will heap up for themselves teachers; and they will turn their ears away from the truth, and be turned aside to fables. But you be watchful in all things, endure afflictions, do the work of an evangelist, fulfill your ministry*" (2 Timothy 4:1-5).

Our world and nation are in a terrible mess, and there's only one Book that can turn things around. It's the one Book that tells of God's only Messiah and the means of our salvation, Jesus Christ, the Son of the true and living God. There are many people out there who absolutely despise God's Word. They attack it, disparage it, and even deny it. But none of them can stop the Word today. In the book of Acts we read, "So the word of the Lord grew mightily and prevailed" (Acts 19:20). If this was true in idolatrous Ephesus, it can be true for idolatrous America. The Bible is the one Book that contains the one hope for our country and our world. Psalm 119 will continue to remind us of the wonderful life-changing truths in the Book that is truly the Word of the Almighty God himself.

You've got your marching orders. Are you going to be ready in season and out of season, to convince, rebuke, and exhort others, no matter how you are received? Remember that the results aren't your responsibility. Our job is simply to get the Word out about the blessings and freedom contained in the one Book that has all the answers we need to live our lives in a way that blesses the Lord. Let's go!

August 27

The Lord of the Word

17 Deal bountifully with Your servant, that I may live and keep Your word. *18* Open my eyes, that I may see wondrous things from Your law. *19* I am a stranger in the earth; do not hide Your commandments from me. *20* My soul breaks with longing for Your judgments at all times. —*Psalm 119:17-20*

IT'S HELPFUL sometimes to take a close look at the individual words in the Bible and see how perfectly they come together to yield deep truths. You may have noticed that these verses focus on the words "word," "law," "commandments," and "judgments" and are paired with "live," "see," and "longing," revealing the faith and passion that we, too, should have for the Word of God. There's another interesting element of this psalm that we may not quite understand but possibly lends itself to the musicality of the poetic aspect of this acrostic poem. You'll recall the structure: eight lines that begin with the same letter, followed by eight lines beginning with the next letter, and so on. The third line of the second letter "Beth" says, *"Your word I have hidden in my heart, that I might not sin against You" (v. 11).* And the third line of the third letter, "Gimel," says, *"I am a stranger in the earth; do not hide Your commandments from me"* (v. 19). So together we have "I have hidden the Word in my heart that I might not sin. Do not hide Your commandments from me," which brings up the possibility that this may have been a responsive song in the same pattern that we see elsewhere in Psalm 119. Either way, the psalm calls us to revere the Word of God and reminds us that it has the power to change us.

To Joshua, the Lord said, *"This Book of the Law shall not depart from your mouth, but you shall meditate in it day and night, that you may observe to do according to all that is written in it. For then you will make your way prosperous, and then you will have good success. Have I not commanded you? Be strong and of good courage; do not be afraid, nor dismayed, for the Lord your God is with you wherever you go"* (Joshua 1:8-9).

There are many, many books that tell you what you should do, but there's only one Book that tells you what it will do for you! In fact, there's a qualifying feature of the Bible concerning its capabilities, and it is this: Only the Bible has a *100 percent* success rate for its claims. This is highlighted in God's promise to Joshua that his way would be prosperous, fruitful, and successful because the *Lord* of the Word was with him wherever he goes.

John 1:1 tells us that "In the beginning was the Word, and the Word was with God, and the *Word was God*" (Jn 1:1—emphasis added). What was true for Joshua is true for us. When the Word of the Lord is hidden in you, the Lord of the Word is with you wherever you go. The success rate for the Word is 100 percent. God deals bountifully with all who keep His Word, and they'll see wondrous things in His law, but they'll also live as strangers on the earth, looking to the Lord and longing for His righteous judgments. The Bible also tells us that all who call upon the Lord will be saved. All who are saved are filled with the Holy Spirit. All who are filled with the Holy Spirit are taught by God; all who are taught by God desire to please Him. All who desire to please Him will experience tribulation. But all who experience tribulation will be with Him in glory. That's just a handful of the truthful claims that we can read in the Bible—and there's never been one instance when they haven't proven themselves to be true. We can call upon the Lord and trust that He hears our cries and is already preparing us for whatever comes next. God is good and He loves His people. We can trust that everything He does or allows in our lives is what is the very best for us.

August 28

Everything Is Beautiful— Really?

[21] You rebuke the proud—the cursed, who stray from your commandments. [22] Remove from me reproach and contempt, for I have kept Your testimonies. [23] Princes also sit and speak against me, but Your servant meditates on Your statutes. [24] Your testimonies also are my delight and my counselors. —*Psalm 119:21-24*

THE APOSTLE Paul wrote, "*All Scripture is given by inspiration of God, and is profitable for doctrine, for reproof, for correction, for instruction in righteousness*" (2 Tm 3:16). The Bible is the only Book that can cut through everything and get right to the heart. The wicked are identified as those who stray from the Commandments, disgracing and disrespecting God's Word. God calls them the proud and the cursed! But the psalmist humbly pleads with God, acknowledging that it's only God's Word that will keep him from falling himself.

Habakkuk wrote: "*Behold the proud, his soul is not upright in him; but the just shall live by his faith*" (Hab 2:4). Remember, in and of itself, faith has no power. It must have an object. The object of our faith is God and His Word. Those who disgrace and disrespect God's Word don't have an upright soul and will be rebuked by God unless they repent.

But there's something else about the Word that we need to understand, and it's that no other book deals more accurately with the human condition than the Bible. The world tries to sell us on the idea that all behaviors are normal, and that everyone is basically good. The Bible, written by the Creator of this same world and of everyone and everything in it says, "There are none good!" All are sinners; all need a savior. The good news is that God has provided just that through a Savior who can save all. Sadly, as we see in the Scriptures, many won't seek Him or respond to Him when they're presented with the truth of the Gospel. This isn't a new thing. In Matthew, we see Jesus's sad account of the wedding invitation to the marriage of the king's son. His servants went out to call all who were invited to this joyful celebration, but they weren't willing to come (Matt 22:1-3). And in the next chapter of Matthew we see Jesus crying out, "*O Jerusalem, Jerusalem, the one who kills the prophets and stones those who are sent to her! How often I wanted to gather your children together, as a hen gathers her chicks under her wings, but you were not willing!*" (23:37).

Today there are books that tell you how to "unlock your power potential" and how to realize your dreams and achieve greatness. They make it sound as if anyone can have anything they want if they just know the secret. Everyone's a winner. Anything is permissible, if it helps you to reach your goals. There isn't really any "bad" anymore, just "alternative ways of looking at things." Everything has its own beauty. We mustn't judge. We can create our own reality—be whatever we want to be—and no one can judge us!

There's one Book, however, that is more honest and insightful than anything ever written, and because its Author is Lord of the Universe, it's the only book that can set a standardized moral code for all of mankind, and by that code it assesses the human condition in a way that is applicable to all seasons of history, all cultures, and all countries. And it's the best book for all, because God loves everyone, and He is all good. He tells us how He wants us to live! As we saw above, the Lord longs to gather *everyone* to Himself and to pour out His love on them. But the sad truth is that the human heart is ugly, deceitful, and desperately wicked (Jer 17:9). Most people would rather believe the lie that everything is good if it's good in their own eyes. Beauty is in the eye of the (sinful) beholder.

There Is Nothing Greater

DALETH— [25]My soul clings to the dust; revive me according to your word. [26]I have declared my ways, and You have answered me; teach me Your statutes. [27]Make me understand the way of Your precepts; so shall I meditate on Your wonderful works. [28]My soul melts from heaviness; strengthen me according to Your word. —*Psalm 119:25-28*

THIS SECTION begins with the Hebrew consonant DALETH, which tells us that the Word, when meditated on, will give one an understanding of its statutes and precepts. The author speaks of "clinging to the dust," which is another way of saying that he's on the brink of death. Whether it was emotional or literal death, we don't know, but it highlights for us another capability of God's Word. The Word has the potential to revive one even from the brink of death.

It's possible, and even likely, that the reason the psalmist's soul was clinging to the dust was from betrayal or maybe the constant attacks of an enemy. But the Word of God is able to deliver one from unreasonable and wicked men: *The Lord is faithful, who will establish and guard you from the evil one"*—2 Thess 3:1-5.

Another blessing of the Bible is that it also directs our hearts into the love of God and the patience of Christ. When our soul is overwhelmed with sorrow or heaviness, His Word will strengthen us. And we must always remember (especially in times of trouble): *There is no greater help in life than God's Word.* Let's take a quick look at what the apostle John wrote in the New Testament. This scene took place when Jesus had "detoured" into Samaria. While He stood by a well, a woman came near to draw water, and He asked her to draw a drink for Him. During the course of their conversation, He revealed to her things about her life that no stranger should have known. She ended up bringing the men of the city to meet this One, claiming that He had to be the Christ. Meanwhile the disciples were urging Him to eat, knowing that He hadn't had sustenance in a long time. His reply was *"I have food to eat of which you do not know. . . . My work is to do the will of Him who sent Me, and to finish His work"* (John 4:27-39). The story continues: *"And many of the Samaritans of that city believed in Him, because of the word of the woman who testified, "He told me all that I ever did. . . . And many more believed because of His own word."*

Although Jesus spoke figuratively about the food, He was illustrating a literal point. God's Word does feed our spiritual life, bringing fruitfulness and success as we meditate on it day and night. Based on what we see in the church today, I wouldn't hesitate to say that there are many Christians whose souls are clinging to the dust because they're starving themselves to death by not being in the Word daily. The matter is complicated further because they attend churches that aren't really feeding them the Word. There's no greater or more sufficient proven help for you than the Word of God. It will strengthen you, instill immovable hope, enable you to quench the fiery darts thrown by the enemy, transform and renew your mind, give you power to control your lusts, and implant in you a soul-saving assurance that will endure until the end. Is that something you want to ignore? This Book needs to be read and meditated on every single day! Only the Bible, God's Word, can revive and strengthen us. We are not alone in our walk through this life, but God has given us His Word to guide, teach, and strengthen us, and His Holy Spirit to help us to discern. There's nothing greater in this life than that!

August 30

Prognosis: An Enlarged Heart

> 29Remove from me the way of lying, and grant me Your law graciously. 30I have chosen the way of truth: Your judgments I have laid before me. 31I cling to Your testimonies; O Lord, do not put me to shame! 32I will run the course of Your commandments, for You shall enlarge my heart.
> —Psalm 119:29-32

TODAY WE'RE reminded of the capabilities of the Word of God, but also there's a descriptive element included here that highlights the majesty of the one Book that is truly authored by God found in verse 30: *the way of truth*. The psalmist calls upon the Lord to use His Word to free and cleanse him of the most common sin of all mankind: lying. What an open and honest admission and request! He states that He has thoroughly examined the judgments and commandments of God, and that he'll cling to His testimonies. "Running the course of God's commandments" reminds us that these are directives, not suggestions. Our steps will be ordered on the path God wants us to take.

Psalm 37 says, *"The steps of a good man are ordered by the Lord, and He delights in his way. Though he fall, he shall not be utterly cast down; for the Lord upholds him with His hand. . . . He is ever merciful and lends; and his descendants are blessed. Depart from evil, and do good; and dwell forevermore"* (vv. 23-27). The fruitfulness of following the ordered steps of the Lord according to His Word will have a trickle-down effect that will impact even our descendants! The end result? *"You will enlarge my heart."* This may not be a good thing medically, but it's a wonderful thing metaphorically! "Enlarge" means "to broaden or make room for." God sees our hearts. He knows what's in them. Jeremiah wrote, *"The heart is deceitful above all things, and desperately wicked; who can know it? I, the Lord, search the heart, I test the mind, even to give to every man according to his ways, according to the fruit of his doings*" (Jeremiah 17:9-10). The capabilities of the one Book that is truly a holy Book is this: Only the Word of God has the capacity to change a person's heart so that it might make room for His Word and, through that, change a person's ways.

The subject is the Word, which is described as the Way of Truth. Shouldn't we realize that the way to a changed heart is through the One who is the Way, the Truth, and the Life, and who is the Word? Jesus speaks to us through the Gospel of John: "*Let not your heart be troubled; you believe in God, believe also in Me. . . . I go to prepare a place for you. And . . . I will come again and receive you to Myself; that where I am, there you may be also. . . . 'I am the way, the truth, and the life. No one comes to the Father except through Me'*" (John 14:1-6).

The only way to having an enlarged heart that can receive the Word and be strengthened and revived is through Jesus. There's no other way to the Father but by Him, and no other book gives us the truth about Him. Jesus is the One the Father sent, the One the Holy Spirit followed after, who hung on the cross paying the penalty for our sins, who gives us access to the Father and grants us the indwelling Spirit, who revives and strengthens us by enlarging our hearts to receive the implanted Word. Ask yourself honestly: Are you doers of the Word or hearers only? Have you truly asked Jesus to be *your* Savior? If you haven't yet been revived and strengthened to run the course of the commandments but you're willing to have that new life, you can! You just learned from the one Book that is able to change your heart and turn your life in the right direction. Don't wait. Go humbly before Him, confessing that you're a sinner in need of a Savior, and ask Him to enlarge your heart that you might receive His life into yours. You'll never be the same again. An enlarged heart is the best prognosis you'll ever get.

SEPTEMBER

From Here to Eternity

Introduction

He [Psalm 119:33-48]

—

AS YOU'VE NOTICED, certain phrases of Psalm 119 are repetitive. In fact, eight descriptive terms are used 184 times. Why? It would seem that the purpose is to keep our attention on the inspiration and infallibility of the Word of God, and the lessons within these verses are many and varied. Deuteronomy 30 tells us that God's commandments are for our good, and He wants to make them real and doable for us. He doesn't make them difficult to find or hard to understand. In fact, He promises that "*The word is very near you, in your mouth and in your heart, that you may do it*" (Deuteronomy 30:11-14).

This is what Psalm 119 does. It makes the commands, testimonies, precepts, and statutes of God available to us and not difficult to understand. As we read through them and think on them, we're reminded that we are to be "doers of the Word and not hearers only," a fact that James also understood when he wrote his epistle.

We've been seeing that when we study the Word it will bring about change in our lives if we're seeking to not only *know* what it says but to *do* the things that we're reading about.

You may also have observed that some of the commands of God are strictly for the advancement of His kingdom and to give Him glory; others command us to do things that will benefit others besides us. And the psalmist repeatedly reminds us that blessings will ultimately be ours as we live according the Word of God.

As we've gone through the early verses in the lengthy psalm, we've been looking at the theme of the entire chapter, which is the elevation of the Word of God in the hearts and minds of His people. There is nothing more important for us in

319

our lives than to know, understand, and live by His Word! The writer of Hebrews reminds us, *"The Word of God is living and powerful, and sharper than any two-edged sword . . . "* (Hebrews 4:12). If we don't fully grasp that truth and begin to see it as divinely inspired, we probably won't live by it, doing the things that God asks of us.

Doing what God says is going to lead to blessings, as promised and proven in His Word. And we can be assured that the blessings of God will last from now throughout eternity! Of course, assuming that you've already made the wise decision to "follow Jesus" throughout your life, let's continue to explore what our lives should and will look like until we see Him face to face.

"Bless the Lord, O my soul; and all that is within me, bless His holy name! Bless the Lord, O my soul, and forget not all His benefits: Who forgives all your iniquities, who heals all your diseases, who redeems your life from destruction, who crowns you with lovingkindness and tender mercies, who satisfies your mouth with good things, so that your youth is renewed like the eagle's" (Psalm 103:5). What's not to love in that?

As we press on, we'll be taken deeper into the realm of "doing" God's Word, thus benefiting from living it according to His instructions. We can have all our iniquities forgiven, be healed of our diseases, and have our lives redeemed from destruction, both temporally and eternally, through Christ. He will crown us with His tender mercies and satisfy us with good things and renewed youth like an eagle's.

Are you ready to go deeper? Let's dig in!

September 2

Don't Ever Change . . .

[33]Teach me, O Lord, the way of Your statutes, and I shall keep it to the end. [34]Give me understanding, and I shall keep Your law; indeed, I shall observe it with my whole heart. [35]Make me walk in the paths of Your commandments, for I delight in it. —*Psalm 119:33-35*

YESTERDAY WE SPOKE of how we're to live our lives until we go into eternity. We've established the necessity of God's truth being unchanging—something that can always be depended upon. Looking further into this idea, we must understand that truth, if it really is *truth*, can't change from one generation to the next, or it's not truth. There can't be more than one truth. In other words, would it be truth if a person in one generation were condemned for all eternity while one who lived the same way was allowed to live in heaven forever? We can see why a single absolute moral code is necessary if there's to be any sense of justice both here and forever. If truth never changes, then there's a way that we're to live that *never changes* when our desire is to live for God.

Jeremiah wrote, "*Thus says the Lord: 'Stand in the ways and see, and ask for the old paths, where the good way is, and walk in it; then you will find rest for your souls.' But they said, 'We will not walk in it'*" (Jeremiah 6:6). These words are true for us today. God still says, "My Word shows you the good path. It's an old path, and you should walk in it." Yet some are still saying, "We will not."

Our psalmist prays that the Lord would teach him the way of His statutes, His unchanging truths, and help him to understand them and delight in them as he lives his life according to them. Watch the progression in the verses above: Teach—understand—keep—walk—delight. That is to be our life experience as well! We're to be taught by the Word of God, striving to understand and keep it (which means that we're not at liberty to change or amend it). We're to live by it, and if we do, our lives will be filled with delight. Look at Psalm 40: "*I delight to do Your will, O my God, and Your law is within my heart*" (v. 8).

This leads us to what is true from here to eternity when it comes to living for God: **We obey God to express our love for Him, not to avoid His discipline.**

This is why the Bible is constantly showing us the idea of family rather than the slave/master or owner/employee relationship. Yes, God is our Master, and we are His possession, and we do work for Him. But it comes down to this: we serve Him because we love Him. Jesus said, "*If you love Me, keep My commandments*" (John 14:15). And again: "This is the love of God, that we keep His commandments. And His commandments are not burdensome" (1 John 5:3). And our keeping His commands shows our love for Him!

Of course I want to avoid God's discipline, and yes, we all should. But it shouldn't be like what we see so often in this life, where people put on a good front when they think God's watching, but the rest of the time, they live as they please. It's like someone driving down the freeway, seeing a cop on the side of the road, and slamming on the brakes. Did they do that because they love the speed limit? No, they did it to avoid getting a ticket. But we should obey God because His commandments are a *blessing*, not a burden, and we love Him and delight to do His will. He has forgiven all of our sins, He will (ultimately) heal all our diseases, He has redeemed our lives from destruction, and He has crowned us with His lovingkindness and tender mercies that are new every morning and never run out.

God has fed me good things. Sometimes I still get taken to the woodshed, but even then, it's not out of fear of punishment that I obey Him but out of adoration. And this will be true from here to eternity.

You Are What You Eat

*36*Incline my heart to Your testimonies, and not to covetousness. *37*Turn away my eyes from looking at worthless things, and revive me in Your way. *38*Establish Your word to Your servant, who is devoted to fearing You. *39*Turn away my reproach which I dread, for Your judgments are good. *40*Behold, I long for Your precepts; revive me in Your righteousness. —*Psalm 119:36-40*

ONLY ONE BOOK has the capacity to change the human heart. The verses that you are reading are in that Book. Our first verse says, "Incline my heart." "Incline" means to bend toward something. The word "bent" can mean a tendency or inclination. For example, "He had a bent for getting into trouble." The psalmist prays, "Lord, make *Your testimonies* my inclinations and not the things my flesh desires."

Next he asks the Lord to turn his eyes away from worthless things. That warning would refer to things that are vain, evil, or idolatrous. In Genesis, we find Adam and Eve in the Garden of Eden, pure and innocent. The Bible says that they were "naked . . . and were not ashamed" (Genesis 3:1-7). Then along came Satan in the form of a serpent and seductively engaged Eve in a conversation in which she should never have been involved. He planted doubts in her mind about God's goodness and honesty, and she fell for it. You know the rest of the story. We've heard that the eyes are the windows to the soul, and in this case, Eve saw that the tree was good for food and pleasant to look at. What she saw made its way into her soul. The tree was desirable and could make her wise! She wanted that. And suddenly all that God had given her and had done for them went by the wayside. So she took, and she ate, and from that point her life took a terrible turn. Remember, the devil doesn't wrap temptation in ugly packaging. He never tempts anyone with how amazing it would be to become a junkie or a Skid Row drunk. He lies and hides in places where drugs and drunkenness will lead. Otherwise, no one would be tempted. He hides the broken homes, the lost jobs, the ruined health, and the destroyed lives as he seeks to secure one's soul.

Our psalmist prays, "Lord, revive in me Your way by establishing Your Word, for I am devoted to fearing You. Turn me away from things of disgrace (reproach) for Your judgments have no hidden surprises, and they lead only to good." What we face is a simple matter of "What you see is what you'll get," or, even more serious to consider, "What we feed on is what we will become." If we feed our lusts with material things, we'll live a materialistic life. If we feed on the good things of God in His Word, we'll live a spiritual life. The story of Abram in the Bible is instructive. God had shown him the land that He had set apart for him. When Abram and his nephew Lot came to a certain place, some issues arose between Abram's shepherds and Lot's shepherds. Abram offered Lot whatever land he wanted, and Abram took the "leftovers." That turned out to be a real blessing however. Lot *saw* the land of Sodom, he wanted it; he moved there, and, ultimately, he barely escaped with his life. Sodom grew to be so wicked that it had to be permanently destroyed. Even now, the very name is an idiom for carnality and debauchery! Abram, on the other hand, didn't look toward what *his* eye desired but rather what the Lord desired, and we know what God did in that situation: Abram was given a land where God later said that His name would dwell perpetually.

The same is true today. Instead of submitting to the God of heaven, worthy of all respect and honor, people do what they want, chasing after what they desire, and often end up in places like Sodom, surrounded by evil. Don't follow your eyes. Feed on the good things of the Lord, and your life will be far better as you become what He desires.

September 4

Tell It Like It Is

> [41]WAW—Let Your mercies come also to me, O Lord—Your salvation according to Your word. [42]So shall I have an answer for him who reproaches me, for I trust in Your word. [43]And take not the word of truth utterly out of my mouth, for I have hoped in Your ordinances. [44]So shall I keep Your law continually, forever and ever. —*Psalm 119:41-44*

THE PSALMS are filled with real-life scenarios to which we can all relate. Have you ever felt reproached by someone? It's an awful feeling, especially if the accusations against you are false. What should your response be?

Back in verse 23, we saw that *"Princes also sit and speak against me, but Your servant meditates on Your statutes." And in 1 Peter we read: "If you are reproached for the name of Christ, blessed are you, for the Spirit of glory and of God rests upon you. On their part He is blasphemed, but on your part He is glorified"* (1 Pt 4:14). Our psalmist prays against the opposition when he asks the Lord to "take not the word of truth utterly out of my mouth." Twice in this section he speaks of "Your word" and defines it as the "word of truth." It seems that he's making a declaration that no matter what attacks he faces, he'll remain focused on the Word of God. There's much comfort in doing that, especially considering Peter's words above: you are *blessed* when reproached for the name of Christ, because God's Spirit rests on you! Try to keep that in mind when you're struggling against the mental slings and arrows of the enemy. Be bold, and continue to tell it like it is. The fact is, God has equipped us to be able to live surrounded by adversity! We need to learn how to handle it, not how to avoid it, as so many do today who preach a weak message, removing any offensive statements that are in the Bible so that people will like them. You'd have a pretty hard time selling that idea to the Old Testament prophets or the apostles—or to today's martyrs.

If you think about the lives of those whom we admire in Scripture, who comes to mind? Abram had to fight to rescue Lot; Jacob and Esau wrestled in the womb; Moses had to confront Pharaoh; Joshua fought for the Promised Land; Nehemiah faced constant and growing opposition; the prophets were stoned and lived in caves, Jeremiah was imprisoned and spent his whole life being hated because of the "bad news" that God had sent him to share; Paul and Peter and John were all imprisoned; Stephen was stoned to death, and on it goes. But there was one more who was constantly surrounded by adversity—Jesus.

God, in His sovereign will, has chosen to place His people in precarious and difficult settings in order to rescue those being drawn toward death. Many of them hate Him, and they also hate us. Jesus comforts us with these words: "*These things I have spoken to you, that in Me you may have peace. In the world you will have tribulation; but be of good cheer, I have overcome the world*" (Jn 16:33).

That should give us much comfort. Are we under fire from our government? So was Jesus. Are we being oppressed and under pressure to deny what we believe? So was Paul. We're told that our claims of Jesus being the only pathway to heaven is offensive and they try to silence us. So they did to Peter, who even wrote: "*Beloved, do not think it strange concerning the fiery trial which is to try you, as though some strange thing happened to you; but rejoice to the extent that you partake of Christ's sufferings, that when His glory is revealed, you may also be glad with exceeding joy*" (1 Pt 4:12-13). We've been called and equipped by God for such a time as this (See Est 4:14). Pray for strength and help from the Lord, who is with you and in you that you may be strong and of good courage in proclaiming the Good News about our Good Savior who has gone before us to prepare a Good Place for us forever.

September 5

Broken Bonds

> 45And I will walk at liberty, for I seek Your precepts. 46I will speak
> of Your testimonies also before kings, and will not be ashamed.
> —Psalm 119:45-46

TODAY, the psalmist reminds us that living for God is to truly walk in liberty! It's interesting that many people see it as walking in bondage. But James wrote: "*He who looks into the perfect law of liberty and continues in it, and is not a forgetful hearer but a doer of the work, this one will be blessed in what he does"* (Jas 1:23-25).

This brings us back to the commandments of God not being burdensome. The psalmist said that he loves and delights in them; he wouldn't be ashamed of them, ever! Not even before kings or political rulers. He states that he will meditate on them always. It's interesting that the world today sees Christians as the ones who are in subjugation and not themselves. They believe that we aren't free to do what we want. Yes, we are! And what I want to do is to please my Father! Listen to Peter: *"For we have spent enough of our past lifetime in doing the will of the Gentiles—when we walked in lewdness, lusts, drunkenness, revelries, drinking parties, abominable idolatries. In regard to these, they think it strange that you do not run with them in the same flood of dissipation, speaking evil of you. They will give an account to Him who is ready to judge the living and the dead"* (1 Pt 4:3-5).

Some see us and think that we're living under burdensome restrictions. But in truth, we're under the law of liberty and are truly free! "You don't drink!" I don't want to. "You don't party!" Yes, I do. But not with drugs or alcohol or immoral behavior.

I'm free! I'm free from accidental drug overdose. I'm free from getting a DUI. I'm free from ruining my marriage through infidelity. I'm no longer bound by the fear of death. I'm free from worrying about where I'm going when I die. I'm not in bondage to materialism. I'm free to live every day for Jesus because every word of God is true, and I trust in, rely on, and cling to them all.

There's an old song whose lyrics express the joy of this freedom well:

> *Once like a bird in prison I dwelt;*
> *No freedom from my sorrow I felt.*
> *But Jesus came and listened to me,*
> *And, glory to God, He set me free.*

> *Now I am climbing higher each day;*
> *Darkness of mine has drifted away.*
> *My feet are planted on higher ground,*
> *And, glory to God, I'm homeward bound.*

> *Goodbye to sin and things that confound;*
> *Not all the world can turn me around.*
> *Daily I'm working; I'm praying, too,*
> *And glory to God I'm going through.*

He set me free, yes, He set me free,
And He broke the bonds of prison for me;
I'm glory bound, my Jesus to see,
For, glory to God, He set me free!

—*Alfred Edward Brumley*

The real truth is that being born again is the only way to be truly free!

No Shame

⁴⁷And I will walk at liberty, for I seek Your precepts. ⁴⁸I will speak of
Your testimonies also before kings, and will not be ashamed.
—*Psalm 119:47-48*

IN THE BOOK OF ROMANS, the apostle Paul wrote: "*There is therefore now no condemnation to those who are in Christ Jesus, who do not walk according to the flesh, but according to the Spirit. For the law of the Spirit of life in Christ Jesus has made me free from the law of sin and death. For what the law could not do in that it was weak through the flesh, God did by sending His own Son in the likeness of sinful flesh, on account of sin: He condemned sin in the flesh, that the righteous requirement of the law might be fulfilled in us who do not walk according to the flesh but according to the Spirit. For those who live according to the flesh set their minds on things of the flesh, but those who live according to the Spirit, the things of the Spirit. For to be carnally minded is death, but to be spiritually minded is life and peace. Because the carnal mind is enmity against God; for it is not subject to the law of God, nor indeed can be. So then, those who are in the flesh cannot please God*" (Romans 8:1-8).

In those verses, the law of sin and death is referring to the "second death," which is eternal separation from God in hell. This condemnation isn't intended for those who are in Christ Jesus, because they don't walk (i.e., live) according to the flesh but according to the Spirit. The Law of Moses couldn't save them, because no one could keep it perfectly, but Christ could, and He did. Those who have been made alive in Christ set their minds on things above. Those who have not been set free are still carnal, which means fleshly, or immoral, in their thinking—as were most of us before we came to know Jesus!

Paul also wrote, "*Do you not know that to whom you present yourselves slaves to obey, you are that one's slaves whom you obey, whether of sin leading to death, or of obedience leading to righteousness? But God be thanked that though you were slaves of sin, yet you obeyed from the heart that form of doctrine to which you were delivered. And having been set free from sin, you became slaves of righteousness. I speak in human terms because of the weakness of your flesh. For just as you presented your members as slaves of uncleanness, and of lawlessness, leading to more lawlessness, so now present your members as slaves of righteousness for holiness"* (Romans 6:16-19).

What Paul is saying, in modern language, is "Hey, guys, I'm using an illustration here so that you can understand. Sin is your master if you don't know Jesus, and the only way to be free from sin is to be delivered from it by Jesus, so that you can live in holiness."

As we've already seen, God has equipped us to live at such a time as this, just as He has all who have gone before. Our message is the same, whether before kings or commoners, and we're not to be ashamed of it! You must come to fully understand that we alone are the truth bearers in this world, and no one and nothing else has the capacity to make men free besides those who proclaim the Word of the Lord.

We all live lives that are filled with desires. If our desires are for the things of the Lord, then our life will reflect that and will have no shame. The reason we obey God is because we trust Him and believe that He's right and knows what's best for us. He's done more for us than we could ever hope to deserve, and every day from here to eternity should be lived in loving gratitude that we express by being obedient to His Word for all that He has done. This was true of the saints of old, it's true for us today, and it will be true from here . . . to eternity!

The Father Hood

Introduction

TETH—Psalm 119:65-72

AS WE APPROACH the midpoint of this majestic wisdom psalm, we're going to continue on our usual course of examining the text for nuggets of truth that we can apply to our lives. We're going to specifically focus on one particular subgroup of the greater body of Christ, and that is the fathers.

When many men think of whom they would consider role models, they might think of great athletes, financial giants, rock stars, or self-help gurus. If any of those are the kind of man that we admire and attempt to emulate, guys, our aim is set far too low. Those kinds of talents may be impressive, but they all pale when compared to this: *"He stretches out the north over empty space; He hangs the earth on nothing. He binds up the water in His thick clouds, yet the clouds are not broken under it. He covers the face of His throne, and spreads His cloud over it. He drew a circular horizon on the face of the waters, at the boundary of light and darkness. The pillars of heaven tremble, and are astonished at His rebuke. He stirs up the sea with His power, and by His understanding He breaks up the storm. By His Spirit He adorned the heavens; His hand pierced the fleeing serpent. Indeed these are the mere edges of His ways, and how small a whisper we hear of Him! But the thunder of His power who can understand?"* (Job 26:7-14).

That, of course, is our Father, and He is the perfect example and role model of the high calling of being a father. The apostle Paul wrote: *"And because you are sons, God has sent forth the Spirit of His Son into your hearts, crying out, 'Abba, Father!' Therefore, you are no longer a slave but a son, and if a son, then an heir of God through Christ"* (Galatians 5:6-7).

Christian men and dads, you are sons of God, heirs of the One who hangs the earth on nothing and created the expanding heavens. Your Father is so powerful that the heavens tremble and are astonished at His rebuke. He can stir up or calm the seas of the entire world. His Spirit adorns the heavens. Yet these are only a fraction of the marvels of His ways!

Why settle for such small and powerless human figures for our "heroes" on earth? You are sons of the Most High God! Throughout the Scriptures we find many references to our heavenly Father, such as in Psalm 68:5, which calls Him a father of the fatherless, a defender of widows, who dwells in His holy habitation. What a role model!

Ecclesiastes 5:2 reminds us that God is in heaven and we're on earth, so our dwelling place is a bit different from His. He resides in glorious perfection; we live in a sinful and fallen world. Nevertheless, we're called to make our homes holy habitations. And our Father will lead and guide us in that as we seek His wisdom (See Ephesians 6:4).

Over the next few days, we'll be looking at some ways that we can do just that as we follow along with Psalm 119 and take a deeper look into the subject of The Father Hood, which will be explained a little more tomorrow.

Women will appreciate this study as well, so let's pray today that God will open all of our hearts and minds to learn from Him what His plan is for all of His children, as the good, good Father that He is.

The word "hood," an abbreviated form of "neighborhood," is slang for "where you live. We're going to take a look a this portion of this great psalm through the lens of how men can live like sons of the King of kings and Lord of lords as fathers, seeking to make our homes holy habitations in an unholy world. We'll be looking at three things over the next few days that will help us to be and do that for which our Father made us through the blood of His own Son, Jesus Christ.

A Holy Habitation

TETH—[65]You have dealt well with Your servant, O Lord, according to Your word. [66]Teach me good judgment and knowledge, for I believe Your commandments. [67]Before I was afflicted I went astray, but now I keep Your word. —*Psalm 119:65-67*

IN OUR READING yesterday, we began looking at fathers and their importance in the home. Their responsibility isn't only to provide for their family but also to set a good example and be leaders in things like prayer, standards, etc. Mothers are to set good examples in these areas as well, of course, but I especially want to encourage men, because sometimes in this world in which we live, many of them didn't have godly examples in their own childhood, or I might say, in their "child hood."

"Hood" is a slang word, an abbreviation of "neighborhood." A hood would be the place where you grew up and is now where you reside. We're going to take a look at this portion of the our great psalm through the lens of how men can live like sons of the King of kings and Lord of lords as fathers in their own right, seeking to make their homes holy habitations in an unholy world. We'll be looking at three things over the next few days that will help us to be and do that for which our Father made us through the blood of His own Son, Jesus Christ.

Now I know that these verses don't directly address fathers, but neither do they exclude them, so although I'm going to present this case to dads, its also applicable for all, as you'll see in the verses of the psalm itself. God, in His Word, has made men to be the heads the of their households (Eph 5:22, 24; Col 3:18; Titus 24-5; 1 Pet 3:1, 5), so the man must embrace the Word of God as his primary information source for the high calling of headship and fatherhood that has been placed upon him.

In our verses today, the psalmist recalls the goodness of God and states that good judgment and knowledge come only through His Word. Then he asks the Lord to help Him to do what it is that he already believes. In verse 67, he makes an honest admission, which far too many would never acknowledge. He confesses that when he strayed from the Word of God, he suffered afflictions. The word "afflicted" in our text means to "deal hardly with," to "depress, as in, to press down," or "to humble." Our psalmist says, in essence, "Before Your Word pressed me down and humbled me, I went astray, but now that I have been transformed, I keep Your Word."

This is the first key to making our own "father hood" a holy place: Our households are called to live by higher standards than the world's standards. And yes, this applies to moms and kids and everyone else. But let me put some skin on it for dads out there.

Men, it really doesn't matter what the world thinks or how they define success. Your fatherhood is under a different standard, and your calling is higher even than the unsaved dads. It doesn't matter what other parents allow their kids to wear, watch, or do. Your home is to be a holy habitation that doesn't submit to the world, but to the Word. *"I press toward the goal for the prize of the upward call of God in Christ Jesus."* (Phil 3:14-16).

Yours, Dads, is an upward call, not a downward or lateral call. You are called to advance the cause of Christ in your homes. You set the standards for TV viewing by your example and words. The standards for communication in general within your home is established by you also. You're the thermostat for the spiritual temperature in your homes. Is your territory, your "father hood" moving upward toward the goal of a higher standard than the world's? (Phil 3:13-14).

September 9

When Lies Are Forged against You

[68] You are good, and do good; teach me Your statutes [69] The proud have formed a lie against me, but I will keep Your precepts with my whole heart. —*Psalm 119:68-69*

WE ENDED our study yesterday with the admission by the psalmist that when he went astray he suffered affliction. Today he affirms that even with all of that, *God is good*! And He is good, always! In 1 John 1:5 we read, *"This is the message which we have heard from Him and declare to you, that God is light and in Him is no darkness at all."* "Darkness" and "light" symbolize good and evil. Since God always does good, then for Him to teach us hard lessons is also good. Keeping His statutes is of value when one is being lied about by the proud. But the Bible says, "[although] *a righteous man may fall seven times and rise again, but the wicked shall fall by calamity. Do not rejoice when your enemy falls, and do not let your heart be glad when he stumbles; lest the Lord see it and it displease Him, and He turn away His wrath from him. Do not fret because of evil doers, nor be envious of the wicked; for there will be no prospect for the evil man; the lamp of the wicked will be put out. My son, fear the Lord and the king; do not associate with those given to change; for their calamity will rise suddenly"* (Proverbs 24:16-22). And in Romans, we read, *"Repay no one evil for evil. Have regard for good things in the sight of all men. If it is possible, as much as depends on you, live peaceably with all men. Beloved, do not avenge yourselves, but rather give place to wrath; for it is written, 'Vengeance is Mine, I will repay,' says the Lord. Therefore, 'If your enemy is hungry feed him; if he is thirsty, give him a drink;*

for in so doing you will heap coals of fire on his head.' Do not be overcome by evil, but overcome evil with good" (Rom 12:17-21).

People often idolize those who are "winners," even if they're utter failures in other ways. But not only are we called to a higher standard as sons of God, but His people define success differently from the world's idea of success. Early role models in the lives of many Christians are men like Chuck Smith, Billy Graham, D. L. Moody, or Charles Spurgeon—fallible men, to be sure, but dedicated men because of the cross of Christ. Therefore, they're associated with "success" in the Christian realm. Whose name comes up in your family when talking with your kids about "heroes"? A moral failure who can put a ball in a hoop or run across a goal line? Or someone who's seeking to bring glory to God?

Let's go back to the *Shema* in the Old Testament." Take a look at the "Father Hood" from that perspective: *"Hear, O Israel: The Lord our God, the Lord is one! You shall love the Lord your God with all your heart, with all your soul, and with all your strength." And these words which I command you today shall be in your heart. You shall teach them diligently to your children, and shall talk of then when you sit in your house, when you walk by the way, when you lie down, and when you rise up. You shall bind them as a sign on your hand, and they shall be as frontlets between your eyes. You shall write them on the doorposts of your house and on your gates"* (Deut 6:4-9).

Men, if you're teaching the Word to your children through words and actions, God sees you as a success, and you'll be prosperous and successful, according to His definition. My hope is to sharpen the ax for all of us that we might succeed as God's children and that every home here today would be a holy habitation. If you're a success in the things of God, you'll be rewarded greatly in heaven. Success in God's eyes means living by His Word—even when you're lied about—and returning good for evil, doing good to those who hate you.

September 10

Coals of Fire

[68] You are good, and do good; teach me Your statutes [69] The proud have formed a lie against me, but I will keep Your precepts with my whole heart. *—Psalm 119:68-69*

AS WE CONTINUE to look at these two verses, I want to ask the dads a question: Do your children hear you talk about how you'd like to get even with someone? Or do they hear you mourn over your burden for the lost soul who forged a lie against you in order to hurt you?

As parents, we have to remember that our children hear and see everything we do. They often take on characteristics of ours that cause us to cringe. We ought to be especially careful of what we say or how we act when they are nearby, especially as we're instructing them in the ways of the Lord.

I'm afraid that many of us men today have lost our edge to some degree because we've moved away from what *God* defines as success, which includes keeping His precepts even when lies are told about us and remembering to return such actions with good.

I'm sure that some might be asking, "What are you *saying*? You want me to just roll over and let people walk over me, hurting me and my family?"

The prophet Isaiah wrote: "*Therefore please hear this, you afflicted, and drunk but not with wine. Thus says your Lord, the Lord and your God, who pleads the cause of His people: 'See, I have taken out of your hand the cup of trembling, the dregs of the cup of My fury; you shall no longer drink it. But I will put it into the hand of those who afflict you, who have said to you, "Lie down, that we may walk over you."'*"

God is telling the people that He sees everything that is being done against them, and that He will place His anger onto those who have afflicted them.

Remember what we saw that the Lord said in our reading a couple of days ago? "*If your enemy is hungry, feed him; if he is thirsty, give him a drink; for in so doing you will heap coals of fire on his head*" (Romans 12:20). That sounds a bit vengeful, doesn't it? Our first reaction might be, "Yeah, that's exactly what I want to do—heap coals of fire on their heads!" The term actually means "to bring to shame and repentance," which would be a wonderful result if it came to pass. You do your part, and let the Lord take care of the rest.

That's what would be a successful "father hood" in God's eyes and is simply basic God-pleasing Christian living for all of us. Our homes should be places where the Word of God is often spoken of, applied, and lived by, and then your time of fatherhood will be a success in the eyes of God. And truthfully, He is the only one whose opinion matters.

Play It Again, Psalm

70 Their heart is as fat as grease, but I delight in Your law. 71 It is good for me that I have been afflicted, that I may learn Your statutes. 72 The law of Your mouth is better to me than thousands of coins of gold and silver.
—Psalm 119:70-72

THE LAST VERSES of this section are basically a replay of and a conclusion to what we've been reading of our heavenly Father in correcting us in His love, even when it amounts to real hardships. The psalmist elevates the Word to its rightful place, which is far higher than the position that the world gives to it: *"The law of the Lord is perfect, converting the soul; the testimony of the Lord is sure, making wise the simple; the statutes of the Lord are right, rejoicing the heart; the commandment of the Lord is pure, enlightening the eyes; the fear of the Lord is clean, enduring forever; the judgments of the Lord are true and righteous altogether. More to be desired are they than gold, yea, than much fine gold; sweeter also than honey and the honey-comb. Moreover by them Your servant is warned, and in keeping them there is great reward"* (Ps 19:7-11). We continue to be reminded that God's Law is perfect, sure, right, pure, clean, enduring and righteous. The judgments of the Lord are eternal, of more value than gold, and sweeter than honey, which refers to the material things in life. Proverbs 10:22 states that *"The blessing of the Lord makes one rich, and He adds no sorrow to it,"* while Paul reminds us that *"the love of money is a root of all kinds of evil, for which some have strayed from the faith in their greediness, and pierce themselves through with many sorrows"* (1 Tim 6:10). God gives us the power to get wealth, but wealth isn't the definition of success. It just means that God has blessed us, and we should express our gratitude to Him (Deut 8:18). God's Word is worth far more than any amount of silver or gold.

How do we relate the subject of gold and silver to the way our "father hood" can be a holy habitation? *Always maintain an eternal perspective.* Another expression for the same thing is called future-first thinking, which means that part of having a father hood that's also a holy habitation is to continually check oneself. What do I mean?

Let me ask you this, dads: Is this world your home? I hope not. Everything we encounter in life—the forged lies, the afflictions at the hand of our adversaries, and even our own disobedience—are to be filtered through this one truth: **This world is not our home.** Remember this verse? *"Let not your heart be troubled; you believe in God, believe also in Me. In My Father's house are many mansions; if it were not so, I would have told you. I go to prepare a place for you. And if I go and prepare a place* *for you, I will come again and receive you to Myself; that where I am, there you may be also*" (John 14:1-3).

I recently had something on my mind that was troubling me. Then the Lord reminded me that He's never failed me yet, and He brought to my mind a series of eleventh-hour miracles that He had worked in my life. He may not have been as early as I liked, but He was never late! He won't let you down, so continue to trust in Him, and let your father hood be one that can be described as a holy habitation like your heavenly Father's house.

If you're having trouble when you see the prosperity of the wicked or the lies against you and the advancement of evil, remember: This is not all there is! Your future will be nothing like your present (See Phil 2:12-16). Your father hood is to be a temporary situation but a very important one. Let's not run in vain, that we may rejoice in the Day of Christ, when we are where He is forever. And if this seems to be a repeated theme throughout this psalm, God meant that for a reason. And thus we can gladly say, "Play it again, Psalm!" We can never hear it enough.

September 12

Sheep Wars

Introduction

YOD —*Psalm 119:73-80*

THERE ARE any number of self-help books that can tell you how to do almost anything, but there's only one Book that can actually *do* something to and for you just by your reading of it. What kinds of things? How about cleansing your way and helping you not to sin against the Lord, just for starters?

We're going to begin this segment of Psalm 119 by addressing the issue of conflict resolution between believers. In James, we read: "*So then, my beloved brethren, let every man be swift to hear, slow to speak, slow to wrath; for the wrath of man does not produce the righteousness of God*" (James 1:19-20). It seems incredible that the Holy Spirit-inspired words seem to have little or no effect on many believers today, which is very sad. Check out social media between Christians, and you'll also see little evidence of many being "slow to speak and slow to wrath."

James wrote more about the dilemma we face: "*Out of the same mouth proceed blessing and cursing. My brethren, these things ought not to be so. Does a spring send forth fresh water and bitter from the same opening? Can a fig tree, my brethren, bear olives, or a grapevine bear figs? Thus no spring yields both salt water and fresh*" (James 3:10-12).

Good words, but have they been overlooked in the conflict-resolution practices we see taking place between believers today? It seems so, as we're far more likely to see this: *"For all the law is fulfilled in one word, even in this: 'You shall love your neighbor as yourself.' But if you bite and devour one another, beware lest you be consumed by one another!"* (Galatians 5:14-15).

David often spoke of harassment from his enemies and how he cried out to the Lord for deliverance from them, but this is different. Why? In Psalm 119:85 the psalmist writes, *"The proud have dug pits for me, which is not according to Your law."* In this, we see that there is obviously no expectation of adherence to the Law from those who aren't under it. So the author is saying that those who were digging the pits and causing him grief and sorrow by their attacks were "under the law," i.e., fellow Jews.

What do we see today? Christians biting and devouring one another, with few even attempting to practice biblical conflict resolution. This is a heavy topic, and one that is needful of explanation. Why did I call this segment "Sheep Wars"? You'll soon see.

One must be careful these days. With the plethora of communication devices that we all seem to live with, it can happen that if you say the wrong thing about politics or a certain ministry, person, or doctrine, in an instant you'll see sheep attacking other sheep instead of fending off the wolves, taking refuge in our Shepherd, and resisting the devil. Every church family will have disputes among themselves, and Christians, as a body, aren't always going to agree on everything. But within our fellowships, we need to find better means of conflict resolution and bring an end to the sheep wars of our day.

We'll be considering all of these things over the next few days, but in the meantime, may we honestly search our own hearts and make sure that we aren't sheep that are contributing to the problem.

September 13

"They Will Know
We Are Christians by Our Love"

[73] Your hands have made me and fashioned me; give me understanding, that I may learn your commandments. [74] Those who fear You will be glad when they see me, because I have hoped in Your word. *—Psalm 119:73-74*

WE'RE GIVEN a clue in the first few verses of this section of Psalm 119 that the source of the division among the people was close to home, because "those who fear the Lord" are mentioned. This seems to imply that there were some who didn't, and we're reminded that these people were living among pagans.

We also recall that we've been fashioned by God and supernaturally assisted to understand His commandments and to place all of our hope in His Word. Never forget: God made us; He gave us His commandments; He is the source of our hope, and if He made us, then there's a plan and purpose for us.

What might that plan be? We don't really know, except that we're to follow where He leads us, with prayer and study of the Word. Psalm 100 tells us, "*Know that the Lord, He is God; it is He who has made us, and not we ourselves; we are His people and the sheep of His pasture. Enter into His gates with thanksgiving, and into His courts with praise. Be thankful to Him, and bless His name. For the Lord is good; His mercy is everlasting, and His truth endures to all generations*" (Psalm 100:1-5).

In our verses today, we're given a wonderful reminder about conflict resolution, as God's sheep seem committed to butting heads, and it is this: **Life is far better spent seeking whom you can bless than whom you can blame.**

What does the Bible say? Galatians tells us, "*Therefore, as we have opportunity, let us do good to all, especially to those who are of the household of faith*" (6:10). Paul is saying that we should be focusing on doing good to other believers, and sheep wars are definitely *not* good!

Look at verse 74 above again. That's a pretty bold statement! Is it true of us? Are we known for always being a blessing, or are we the ones who are always blaming? Are we continually finding fault in others instead of seeing the best in them as people who were fashioned by God, just like us?

Colossians contains a wonderful admonition to us: "*Let the peace of Christ rule in your hearts . . . and be thankful. Let the word of Christ dwell in you richly in all wisdom, teaching and admonishing one another in psalms and hymns and spiritual songs, singing with grace in your hearts to the Lord*" (Colossians 3:15-16).

Search your heart: When others see you coming, do they think, *this will be a blessing,* or, *Oh, no, I wonder what their problem is this time?* We really need to work harder at being one body. The apostle John, quoting Jesus, wrote: "*By this all will know that you are My disciples, if you have love for one another*" (Jn 13:35). Does this speak of you? Does the world know that you're His disciple by the loving way you deal with others, or are you known more for fighting sheep wars? The world shouldn't have a hard time distinguishing us from them! Our lives are meant to be spent blessing, not blaming. People should be glad to see us coming—not running inside and locking the door. Pray for wisdom in all of these things.

Do Trials Make You Bitter or Better?

[75]I know, O Lord, that Your judgments are right, and that in faithfulness You have afflicted me. [76]Let, I pray, Your merciful kindness be for my comfort, according to Your word to Your servant. [77]Let Your tender mercies come to me, that I may live; for Your law is my delight. *—Psalm 119:75-77*

IN THIS SECTION of the psalm, we've established our goal to bless one another, giving testimony that we're the disciples of the Lord. Through this, we hope to bring some reality and balance into our sheep wars. It may seem strange to realize that there are divisions among Christians, but it's not something common only to our generation. Look at what Paul wrote to the church at Corinth: "*Now . . . I do not praise you, . . . For first of all, when you come together as a church . . . there are divisions among you, and in part I believe it*" (1 Corinthians 11:17-19). Our psalmist recognizes that the afflictions he has incurred were God allowed. This implied that he was at fault, yet still he prayed for God's mercy. Paul said to Corinth, "*I hear that there are divisions in the church, and I believe it. There are factions* (Greek for "heresies"), *for these heresies expose those who are approved to the Lord.*" Likewise, King David says that the Lord allowed his afflictions, and Paul says there were divisions and factions in his day. So not every conflict is avoidable, but they can all be learned from.

Years ago, my wife and I realized that the barrage of attacks would continue as long as we were in ministry, so instead of getting mad every time something happened, we decided to scan every accusation for shreds of truth. Was there anything in this that we could learn and grow from? Could we have done something differently when a conflict arose or an attack came our way? As we proceeded this way, we prayed for God's merciful kindness, seeking His comfort according to His Word, and remembering the adage: *Trials can make you either bitter or better*. We chose the latter, hard as it was sometimes.

There will always be disagreements between Christians and among families. All have the potential to create a more Christ-like you, even when they hurt. Luke wrote: "*Woe to you when all men speak well of you, for so did their fathers to the false prophets*" (Luke 6:26).

Paul and Barnabas had a great relationship in ministry. But what happened? "*Paul said to Barnabas, 'Let us now go back and visit our brethren in every city where we have preached the word of the Lord, and see how they are doing.' Now Barnabas was determined to take with them John called Mark. But Paul insisted that they should not take with them the one who had departed from them in Pamphylia, and had not gone with them to the work. Then the contention became so sharp that they parted from one another. And so Barnabas took Mark and sailed to Cyprus; but Paul chose Silas and departed, being commended by the brethren to the grace of God."* (Acts 15:36-41). That's sad, right? But later, we hear again from Paul: *"Get Mark and bring him with you, for he is useful to me for ministry"* (2 Timothy 4:9-11).

A sheep war had developed between Paul and Barnabas that led to their separation. History would seem to say that Paul was right. Barnabas took Mark and sailed to Cyprus and right on out of the pages of the Bible, never to be heard of again. Paul, however, wrote numerous epistles, planted churches, and was extremely fruitful in ministry. Yet later Paul sent for Mark. He had bailed out on Paul and Barnabas in the past but somehow, later on, Mark had learned from experience and had become useful for the ministry.

When there's a dispute between believers, search it out for yourself that you might learn from it. Not every conflict can be avoided, and some God uses to help us grow. We can certainly learn something from every conflict when we seek the Lord, trying to see things through His eyes. Do you have your discernment and mercy glasses handy?

September 15

You Can Fool Some of the People Some of the Time . . .

78Let the proud be ashamed, for they treated me wrongfully with falsehood; but I will meditate on Your precepts. —Psalm 119:78

THE NEXT TRUTH we're going to examine is a zinger and a profundity combined. The psalmist says, essentially, that those who afflicted him should be ashamed of themselves for what they've said about him. It wasn't true, and he was treated wrongly, but . . . "I will meditate on Your precepts." Is that you? Is that your response when you're wrongfully attacked? It should be! We need to remain focused on the precepts of the Word when we're dealing with "the proud" antagonists that we seem to encounter in this life.

Proverbs 26:12 says, *"Do you see a man wise in his own eyes? There is more hope for a fool than for him."* To bring this wise saying home, every war between sheep is foolish. Think about it. We love the same God, and He has given us directives and precepts on how to deal with each other, including during disputes.

What I'm about to say next is true. We all know it's true, and yet we often act like it isn't when it comes down to conflict resolution. Are you ready? Prepare yourself! **If you think you're always right, you couldn't be more wrong.** The only one who is always right every time is God, and you're not Him. Proverbs 27:17 tells us, *"As iron sharpens iron, so a man sharpens the countenance of his friend."* Have you ever met one of those saints who seems to always see themselves as the sharpener and never the sharpen-ee? Are you glad to see them coming? Then don't be one of "those people." A wise individual once said, "The true test of a servant is how he responds when he is treated like one." If we have to be right, or if we actually do believe that we are right all the time, it flies under the banner of the word "Pride." What do the Scriptures say? *"Bless those who persecute you; bless and do not curse. Rejoice with those who rejoice, and weep with those who weep. Be of the same mind toward one another. Do not set your mind on high things, but associate with the humble. Do not be wise in your own opinion"* (Romans 12:14-16).

Here's a thought: You may have been right; and you may have been wronged. But the question is did you handle it with humility? Or did you take your toys and go home? Were you only fooling people with your "spirituality," or do you remember that the servant of the Lord is to be humble, able to take abuse? No one is right all the time, and when the proud treat you wrongly by telling lies about you, or when another sheep treats you as if you were nothing, ask yourself, is there any truth in it? And the first rule in divine conflict is to stay humble. People see through façades. A true Christian is humble; he doesn't fake humility. James wrote: *"Humble yourselves in the sight of the Lord, and He will lift you up. Do not speak evil of one another, brethren. He who speaks evil of a brother and judges his brother, speaks evil of the law and judges the law. But if you judge the law, you are not a doer of the law but a judge. There is one Lawgiver, who is able to save and to destroy. Who are you to judge another?"* (James 4:10-12). There's a high probability that someone out there may owe someone an apology. Consider this: the question isn't "Was I right?" or "Was I wronged?" but "Was I humble in how I handled this?" That's what matters most to God. The truth is, we're to be "strong, and of good courage," no matter what opposition we may have to endure. It doesn't matter what man says about us. We know that ultimately mercy and comfort from the Lord will be ours through the Word of God, so we meditate on His precepts, not lick our wounds. The sheep aren't fooled by someone who comes across with all the answers and who is "never wrong." Take the high road of humility in those situations, or you may end up being someone no one likes to see coming.

How to Deal with Frenemies

[79]Let those who fear You turn to me, those who know Your testimonies. [80]Let my heart be blameless regarding Your statutes, that I may not be ashamed. —*Psalm 119:79-80*

FRIENDSHIP is a rather tenuous thing. We all have friends and family members who are steadfast believers, and we have others who aren't interested in the things of the Lord at all. Then there are all the rest who fall somewhere in between. We're going to take a look at how we're to live in the midst of all of these relationships in this thing called "life." We've talked before about how "agreeing to disagree" sometimes has its place, but it also has its limitations. Psalm 133 reads, "*Behold, how good and how pleasant it is for brethren to dwell together in unity!*" Unity is important, of course, for getting things done in any situation. But one thing to remember is that we can't simply unite for the sake of uniting. The Lord has laid out standards when it comes to how and when and why we are to unite.

The apostle Paul wrote, "*I beseech you to walk worthy of the calling . . . with all lowliness and gentleness . . . longsuffering, bearing with one another in love, endeavoring to keep the unity of the Spirit in the bond of peace.*" (Eph 4:1-6). Unity of the Spirit is our objective, not the spirit of unity. Many Christians treat each other more like enemies than family. Yes, false doctrine is worth dividing over. We can't unite in any "religious" sense with those who try to change what the Bible says to fit their own desires. But for other things, division may not be not the solution. The psalmist wrote: "*Let those who fear You turn to me,*" meaning that he's asking God to bring support for him from those who also love God and are likeminded. What's the unifying feature here? Belief and adherence to the statutes of God.

Turning again to Ephesians, we read, "*For you were once darkness, but now you are light in the Lord. Walk as children of light . . . finding out what is acceptable to the Lord. Have no fellowship with the unfruitful works of darkness, bur rather expose them*" (5:8-13).

There's a limit to unity: exposing evil. We're called to do that, and it may cause division. But most sheep battles center on politics, personalities, and opinions. Stop! Jesus is coming soon! Some of you may be realizing that you need to humble yourself, pick up the phone or walk across the room, taking the high road of humility, letting go of pride, and mending that relationship. *But they were wrong*, you may be thinking. It's possible. But were you honestly humble? Did you seek to bless them or blame them? Have you done as much as depends on you to be at peace, or have you left it all up to them (See Romans 12:18)?

One caveat: we are talking about sheep fighting sheep here. We're not suggesting that you should "make things right" with physical or sexual abusers. Some need to be forgiven from a distance and perhaps only in our hearts, with no restoration of the relationship. But when our hurt feelings get in the way of a humble reply and opinion acts like biblical doctrine, or conflicting personalities rub one another the wrong way, a sheep war is in the making. "*Where there is no wood, the fire goes out; and where there is no talebearer, strife ceases.*" (Prov 26:20-22). It's time to start talking to someone instead of about them. The gates of hell can't prevail against the church, but a gossiping church is going nowhere fast. Our psalmist says, "*Let my heart be blameless regarding Your statutes, that I might not be ashamed.*" Ongoing hard feelings among the sheep are a shame to any fellowship. So where do we draw the line? At false doctrine. Everything else is pretty much just politics, personalities, and opinions. We're to walk in grace and humility, remembering Proverbs 26:12: "*Do you see a man wise in his own eyes? There is more hope for a fool than for him.*" Seek to turn your "frenemies" back into friends by humbling yourself and letting go of your anger. You'll sleep better, pray better, and your conscience will thank you.

The Word for Today

Introduction

[81]KAPH—Psalm 119:81-104

THE FOCUS NOW is going to be on the majesty, sufficiency, and supremacy of the Word of God over all life and literature and also on the benefits and blessings of living according to God's statutes, precepts, and commandments. Psalm 119, the longest chapter in the Bible, establishes the reason that the Bible stands alone among all books written throughout history: It's because of its Author. In John 17, one of the most beautiful passages in the Bible, we see the heart of our Lord Jesus as He spoke to His Father in front of the disciples saying, "*I have given them Your word; and the world has hated them because they are not of the world, just as I am not of the world. I do not pray that You should take them out of the world, but that You should keep them from the evil one. They are not of the world, just as I am not of the world. Sanctify them by Your truth. Your word is truth. As You sent me into the world, I also have sent them into the world. And for their sakes I sanctify Myself, that they also may be sanctified by the truth*" (vv. 14-19).

Jesus, who is the Word made flesh, says that God's Word is what separates His people from the world. No wonder Satan has been trying to get the church to set the

Word aside and teach ear-tickling fables instead of life-changing truth. The word *sanctify* means to make holy, to separate from profane things, or to consecrate to God. As we consider great men of the Lord throughout the ages who stood behind pulpits around the world, sanctified by the Word, yet having different personalities and dispositions, but who were all separated from the world in this: they knew and lived by the Word of God. We read of Polycarp, Luther, Wycliffe, Edwards, Wesley, Spurgeon, Moody, Mueller, et al., who all shared a love for God's Word that set them apart for a holy work.

In recent times, some who have recently gone to be with the Lord, and who had the same mind as the above, were ones such as Chuck Smith, William MacDonald, Dr. Henry Morris, and many others, who wouldn't compromise in their stand for the Lord. Their entire lives were dedicated to carrying on the tradition of proving that God's Word truly is *the* Word for today! And there are still faithful servants of the Lord working quietly and diligently to get the Gospel message into the hands and minds and hearts of all who have an ear to hear, as they strive to save souls and teach people how to be set apart from the world.

Listen to what Moses instructed the people to do: *"Now, O Israel, listen to the statutes and the judgments which I teach you to observe, that you may live. . . . You shall not add to the word which I command you, nor take from it, that you may keep the commandments of the Lord your God which I command you . . . "* (Deut 4:1-4). There were blessings for the people of Israel that were associated with keeping God's Word, and there were consequences for ignoring it, adding to it, or taking away from it. The same goes for us today. The Word for today is the same Word of God that has changed lives for centuries and is still in the business of curing society's ailments. But many choose to ignore it. Others add their own ideas to it, and still others water it down, removing the warnings and judgments. The Bible tells us they'll reap what they've sown.

The pastor's job is to *equip the church for the work of ministry*. It's not to tickle the ears of the saints by removing sound doctrine and adding fables in place of the truth of Scripture. Let's strive to look to the Word, learn from the Word, and live by the Word.

"How Dry I Am!"

[81]Kaph My soul faints for Your salvation, but I hope in Your word. [82]My eyes fail from searching Your word, saying "When will You comfort me?" [83]For I have become like a wineskin in smoke, yet I do not forget Your statutes. [84]How many are the days of Your servant? When will You execute judgment on those who persecute me? [85]The proud have dug pits for me, which is not according to Your law. [86]All Your commandments are faithful; they persecute me wrongfully; Help me! [87]They almost made an end of me on earth, but I did not forsake Your precepts. [88]Revive me according to Your lovingkindness, so that I may keep the testimony of Your mouth. —*Psalm 119:81-88*

I DON'T UNDERSTAND "dry" times. We can go from feeling spiritually supercharged one day, and then feel as dry as a bone the next. Our psalmist is experiencing just such a time, so we know we're in good company and that God, who knows and understands everything, must be allowing these times in our lives.

The author describes feeling "like a wineskin in smoke." In modern vernacular, it would probably be similar to feeling "shriveled up like a prune." Used wineskins used to be hung inside the tent, where there was a fire burning during the cold months, which would cause the wineskin to become dry and shriveled—and basically useless. He moves on, expressing his feelings and asking the Lord how long this must last. We learn that he's experiencing persecution from the proud, who have ignored God's Word and seek to destroy him. He even says that they almost succeeded! But there's a beautiful hopeful note attached to this situation when he states that even in all that he was going through, *he hadn't forsaken God's precepts.* So although he was emotionally spent, mentally and physically weary, feeling like this situation would never end, and even despairing of his life, what did he do? He looked to the Word for hope, comfort, help, and revival. God is the only who can truly help in situations like this, and He can lead us to conclusions that could come only from Him.

"*No one puts ... new wine in old wineskins, or else the wineskins break, the wine is spilled, and the wineskins are ruined. But they put new wine into new wineskins, and both are preserved*" (Mat 9:16-17). Just as the psalmist did here, Jesus used a commonly known fact to illustrate a point. Dried-up wineskins can't hold new wine. As the new wine expands during fermentation, the old skins will burst, having lost their elasticity. And sometimes we feel like that. We're so dried up spiritually that we feel as dead and dried up as on old wineskin.

What do we do? Well, we can't put new wine into old wineskins. But God can! He can take someone who feels fed up, dried up, and used up, and He can revive them and give them new hope and life. God can take someone who feels as if life is just one long trial and comfort and help them. He can take someone who's been persecuted and help them to stay faithful to His Word even though they continue to be wronged. He even packaged a plan on how He would do this in a Book, and we must go to that Book ourselves when we're "grieved by various trials" (1 Pet 1:6). That Book *is* the Word for today! And what does it tell us? "*God, who is rich in mercy, because of His great love with which He loved us, even when we were dead in trespasses, made us alive together with Christ . . . and raised us up together . . . in the heavenly places in Christ Jesus that . . . He might show the exceeding riches of His grace in His kindness toward us in Christ Jesus*" (Eph 2:4-7).

The best way to deal with circumstances you're weary of is to focus your attention instead on searching His Word. Psalm 60:11 says, very succinctly, "*Give us help from trouble, for the help of man is useless,*" but God's Word is and has always been our Word for today.

September 19

God's Lesson Plan

> [89]LAMED—Forever, O Lord, Your word is settled in heaven. [90]Your faithfulness endures to all generations; You established the earth, and it abides. [91]They continue this say according to Your ordinances. [92]Unless Your law had been my delight, I would then have perished in my affliction. [93]I will never forget Your precepts, for by them You have given me life. [94]I am Yours, save me. . . . [95]The wicked wait for me to destroy me. . . . [96]I have seen the consummation of all perfection, but Your commandment is exceedingly broad. —*Psalm 119:89-96*

WE NOW understand that we must look to the Word as our source of help and hope above all else. We are reminded that it isn't enough to just know the content of the Word—we must apply what we know to our own lives. Jeremiah wrote: "*O Lord . . . ; remember me and visit me, and take vengeance for me on my persecutors. In Your enduring patience, do not take me away. Know that for Your sake I have suffered rebuke. Your words were found, and I ate them. And Your word was to me the joy and rejoicing of my heart; for I am called by Your name, O Lord God of hosts*" (Jeremiah 15:15-16).

Jeremiah was a man who knew a little bit about betrayal, having had pits dug for him to fall into by his fellow Jews. He makes the point that hope in the Word goes beyond a mere *awareness of its content*, and he illustrates acting upon the Word through the phrase, "Your words were found and I ate them."

Our psalmist declares why His source of hope is our source of hope, and why it remains the Word for today. God's Word is settled in the heavens, which means that it stands upright. Heaven has established God's Word, which will be faithful to all generations.

Next, he illustrates his point through creation when he says that the Lord established the earth, and the heavens and the earth continue according to what God has already determined. By contemplating the power of creation through God, the psalmist realizes that there is so much for us to learn (See Hebrews 11:3)!

The Holy Spirit inspired Jeremiah to look at the ordinances of the universe that God had established by His Word and to look at the written Word with the very same expectation of constancy. Jeremiah also wrote, "*Thus says the Lord, who gives the sun for a light by day, and the ordinances of the moon and the stars for a light by night, who disturbs the sea. . . . 'If those ordinances depart from before Me, says the Lord, then the seed of Israel shall also cease from being a nation before Me forever'*" (Jeremiah 31:35-37). Did the sun rise this morning? Did the moon maintain its orbit last night? Then God has not cast off Israel. Why did the sun come up this morning and the moon maintain its assigned orbit? Because God declared it to be so!

The psalmist appears to have found that remembering and applying God's precepts is what has saved him in the past, even while his enemies were waiting for the opportunity to destroy him. God's Word will teach us how to *avoid* learning things the hard way. It's like this with our own children. We hope they'll learn by listening instead of through experience, but look at what we find in the Bible: a loving Father trying to teach His children how to avoid the heartache and pains of self-inflicted pitfalls in life, including the lapses of faith when the unavoidable happens and the pains of life come our way, but with loving forgiveness whenever we're willing to admit our failure.

God's Word is settled in heaven even now. As we learn from it, we can understand how we're to live on this earth. Thus we can avoid having to learn things the hard way. God's precepts and statutes will sustain us throughout our lives. Look for His Word today. Learn from it. As we live by it, we'll know that there is nothing more important!

Got Questions? He's Got Answers!

*[97]*MEM—Oh, how I love Your law! It is my meditation all the day. *[98]*You, through Your commandments, make me wiser than my enemies; for they are ever with me. *[99]*I have more understanding than all my teachers, for Your testimonies are my meditation. *[100]*I understand more than the ancients, because I keep Your precepts. *[101]*I have restrained my feet from every evil way, that I may keep Your word. *[102]*I have not departed from Your judgments, for You Yourself have taught me. *[103]*How sweet are Your words to my taste, sweeter than honey to my mouth! *[104]*Through Your precepts I get understanding; therefore I hate every false way. —*Psalm 119:97-104*

I ONCE SAW a poster that I thought was rather ironic. It read: "Those of you who think you know everything are very annoying to those of us who do." That's human nature! But have you ever considered the fact that you really do know someone who knows it all? His counsel gives more understanding than any teacher; He has more understanding than anyone in history. Why would we not look to the Book by the perfect Author every time we need perfect answers to life's questions?

Here is wisdom: *"Who is wise and understanding among you? Let him show by good conduct that his works are done in the meekness of wisdom. But if you have bitter envy and self-seeking in your hearts, do not boast and lie against the truth. This wisdom does not descend from above, but is earthly, sensual, demonic. For where envy and self-seeking exist, confusion and every evil thing are there. But the wisdom that is from above is first pure, then peaceable, gentle, willing to yield, full of mercy and good fruits, without partiality and without hypocrisy"* (James 3:13-18). Pure wisdom as opposed to earthly, sensual, and demonic "wisdom"—which one should we choose? Where can we find this wisdom from above? Some people think that when thoughts or ideas come into their minds, they must be from God. That's not biblical, and it's also very risky. We all know people who do terrible things, claiming that God told them to do it!

What is the wisdom that the psalmist loves so much that he wants to meditate on it all day? It's the wisdom that truly comes from God. What's the fruit of meditating on God's Word? It is better decision-making skills than that of those who come against us, more understanding than any earthly teacher, and the ability to be restrained from evil. Look at what he says in verse 103: God's words are sweeter than honey! And yet some people view the Bible as they would swallowing bitter medicine instead of as the sweet honey that it is. The Word of God is authored by the only One in the universe who created everything, and whose commandments, if obeyed, will make you wiser than your enemies and more understanding than the ancients.

The author ends this section with the conclusion that he hates every evil way. In Colossians we read, *"Beware lest anyone cheat you through philosophy and empty deceit, according to the tradition of men, according to the basic principles of the world, and not according to Christ"* (Colossians 2:8). We live in such times when worldly philosophies have crept in, and they won't produce godly people. Saints, listen: there's no better way to live than according to God's Word. Period.

Do you believe that? Would others see it? Or are we listening to the world, whose wisdom is earthly, sensual, and demonic? I want to make wise decisions. I want to live a blessed life, and I can do that only by living according to God's Word. The Word for today is perfect, and it has all of the answers to all of the questions.

September 21

Watch Your Step!

Introduction

NUN —Psalm 119:105-136

KEEP IN MIND as we progress through this masterpiece psalm that the focus throughout is on the exaltation of the Word of God. We see it described for us repeatedly as the Law (Torah), Testimony, Precept(s), Statute(s), Commandment(s), Judgments, Word, and Promise. There's another component to this psalm that we've touched on a bit throughout our studies but haven't yet identified, and that is the psalmist's *response* to the Law, Testimony, Precept(s), Statute(s), Commandments(s), Judgments, Word, and Promises of God. Also, intermingled with these descriptive terms for "The Word of God" we find words like "walk," "keep," "look," "learn," "heed," "meditate," and "live." We're reminded in this that the Word of God is of little value or benefit at all if it's merely ignored, and we don't do our part to walk according to it, keep it in our hearts, look to it always as our source of hope and truth, learn from it and obey it, meditate on it, and live by it.

Remember the admonition in Psalm 1? *"Blessed is the man who walks not in the counsel of the ungodly, nor stands in the path of sinners, nor sits in the seat of the of the scornful; but his delight is in the law of the Lord, and in His law he meditates day and night. He shall be like a tree planted by rivers of water, that brings forth its fruit in its season, whose leaf also shall not wither; and whatever he does shall prosper. The ungodly are not so. . . . The Lord knows the way of the righteous, but the way of the ungodly shall perish"* (Psalm 1). The contrasting life experiences, the eternal destinies revealed all through the Scriptures, and the defining factor in how our lives are experienced and how our eternal destinies are determined is the way we respond to the Word of God. The blessed man doesn't walk in ungodly counsel or hang around with sinners or join forces with scorners. Instead he delights in and meditates on God's Word, experiencing the blessings, both temporal and eternal, as a result. The implied negative for the unrighteous is that they will have the exact opposite experience, both here on earth and in eternity.

How can this have been laid out so long ago and yet we are to live by it today? It's because the Word of God itself is unchanging and is authored by the eternal God, who does not change! Although the world is rejecting the Word, and though many in the church are diluting and even changing the Word, we want to offer a warning. Actually, it's both a warning and encouragement: Watch your step! Those who dismiss and disparage the Word of God had better watch their step. And conversely, those who live by the Word of God will be shown how to watch their step.

Psalm 37:23-24 says, "*The steps of a good man are ordered by the Lord, and He delights in his way. Though he fall, he shall not be utterly cast down; for the Lord upholds him with His hand.*" Saints, God has ordered the steps for each of our lives. Morally, they will lead us all in the same direction. Practically, they are individually designed for our own lives, and our paths may be different from someone else's. But ultimately, He will guide us in all of these things, and they will turn out to be the most effective for His name and beneficial to us and our loved ones. Since God has ordered our steps, we need to make certain as we make our way through life that we're walking in the ones that He has ordered! Let's move forward with hope and confidence that our Lord is leading us to where He wants us to go, and all we need to do is to pay attention and follow closely. The result can only be good!

"The Light Shines in the Darkness, and the Darkness Did Not Comprehend It"

[105]NUN—Your word is a lamp to my feet and a light unto my path. [106]I have sworn and confirmed, that I will keep Your righteous judgments. [107]I am afflicted very much; revive me O Lord, according to Your word. [108]Accept, I pray, the freewill offerings of my mouth, O Lord, and teach me Your judgments. [109]My life is continually in my hand, yet I do not forget your law. [110]The wicked have laid a snare for me, yet I have not strayed from Your precepts. [111]Your testimonies I have taken as a heritage forever, for they are the rejoicing of my heart. [112]I have inclined my heart to perform your statutes forever, to the very end. —*Psalm 119:105-112*

A LAMP to the feet and a lighted path imply surrounding darkness. Think about it: is a flashlight more effective at midnight or at noon? As the days darken, the light of the Word becomes increasingly necessary if we're to navigate our way safely through life. "*You are all sons of light and sons of the day. We are not of the night or of darkness*" (1 Thess 5:5).

"Light" and "dark" here are used metaphorically for multiple things in Scripture: good and evil, spiritual enlightenment, and spiritual depravity, and, in a sense, they even represent life and death. We know that the source of light for our planet is the sun, and without the sun's light, life would be impossible here on earth. We need to see and treat the Word of God the same way, because the Christian life is impossible without it.

Friends, the Bible is a necessity, not a luxury. It isn't something that you read when you "have the time," or that you pull off the shelf when you're in trouble and need comfort. J. Vernon McGee said, "It is always more important for the Shepherd to talk to you than it is for you to talk to Him." John wrote: "*This is the message which we have heard from Him and declare to you, that God is light and in Him is no darkness at all*" (1 Jn 1:5). And writing of the New Jerusalem, he also wrote, "*I saw no temple in it for the Lord God Almighty and the Lamb are its temple. The city had no need of the sun or of the moon to shine in it, for the glory of God illuminated it. The Lamb is its light*" (Rev 21:22-23). In "light" of this (pun intended), how can you love God, who is light, and not love His Word, which is His light to our paths? How can you say you love His Word but disagree with parts that don't fit your beliefs? The fact is, in this world of darkness in which we live as children of the light, we need to watch our step and not plow ahead in the darkness without it!

In verse 106, we see the depth of the commitment to keep the Word even in the midst of trials and afflictions (v. 107). The psalmist wasn't going to silence his praises as He called to the Lord to revive him. "*My life is continually in my hand,*" he wrote in verse 109, meaning that his life was continually in danger, yet he didn't forget the Word of God even during the worst of times. When his enemies were trying to entrap him, the testimonies of the Lord were his heritage, and his heart was filled with joy! Thus, he determined within himself that he would perform God's statutes, live by the Word forever, to the very end, even if hell or high water should come against him.

What this means to us is this: there is a right way for us to walk in every situation. Sometimes, the best thing for us to do is to walk *away* from something. The Lord will direct us in and out of those situations. But there are also times when we must endure the afflictions, waiting and trusting on the Lord to deliver us out them all. He may tell us to move, or He may tell us to stand still. But how will you know if you're never in His Word, the primary means by which He communicates to us?

September 23

The Fear of the Lord
Is the Beginning of Wisdom

[113]SAMEK—I hate the double-minded, but I love Your law. [114]You are my hiding place and my shield; I hope in Your word. [115]Depart from me, you evildoers, for I will keep the commandments of my God! [116]Uphold me according to Your word, that I may live; and do not let me be ashamed of my hope. [117]Hold me up, and I shall be safe, and I shall observe Your statutes continually. [118]You reject all those who stray from Your statutes, for their deceit is falsehood. [119]You put away all the wicked of the earth like dross; therefore I love your testimonies. [120]My flesh trembles for fear of You, and I am afraid of Your judgments. —*Psalm 119:113-120*

WHAT DOES IT MEAN to be double minded? In our verses today, it indicates skepticism or half-heartedness. James uses the word in his epistle: "*If any of you lacks wisdom, let him ask of God, who gives to all liberally and without reproach, and it will be given to him. But let him ask in faith, with no doubting, for he who doubts is like a wave of the sea driven and tossed by the wind. For let not that man suppose that he will receive anything from the Lord; he is a double-minded man, unstable in all his ways*" (Jas 1:5-8). It makes for unstable thinking.

Proverbs 23:7 warns: "*As a man thinks in his heart so he is.*" Our psalmist hates the instability that doubt can bring into life, so to keep himself on the right path, he focuses on loving the law, or the Word. The Word hides and shields him, giving him hope, he keeps God's commandments, and he is upheld and lives unashamed of his hope.

Have you ever felt confused or disappointed by the direction in which you felt that God was leading you? During those times, it's imperative that we hold onto the Word, because the Word will hold you up even as God is rejecting those who stray from His statutes. When that happens, by their own doing, they are left facing the enemy alone.

Since God removes the wicked from the earth like dross, according to our verses above, even as the psalmist trembles in fear of God's righteous judgments, he continues to love the Lord's testimonies. We read in the Book of Acts, "*The fear of the Lord is the beginning of wisdom*" (Acts 9:31). Yes, today we should fear the righteous judgment of God. We should fear going to hell, and we should long for God to deliver us by the shed blood of Jesus upon the cross, which He has already done for those who have put their faith and trust in Him. And He also admonishes us again to watch our steps in this way: the Word exposes all of the enemy's tactics and pitfalls. It's much like a map through the minefield of life.

In John we read, "*The thief does not come except to steal, and to kill, and to destroy. I have come that they may have life, and that they may have it more abundantly*" (John 10:10). That's all that Satan wants to do: he wants to steal the Word from our hearts, kill our hope by leading us into minimization of God's statutes, and steal our stability by means of planting doubt and encouraging divided thinking.

God tells us what Satan is up to and how to fight it. We read, "*Stand therefore, having girded your waist with truth, having put on the breastplate of righteousness, and having shod your feet with the preparation of the gospel of peace; above all, taking the shield of faith with which you will be able to quench all the fiery darts of the wicked one*" (Eph 6:14-16).

Satan hates it when we fear the Lord. He never feared God, and it cost him everything. He thought that he could replace God. He'll end up eternally in the Lake of Fire—and his plan is to take as many of us as he possibly can with him. God's plan is different. He warns us to walk carefully, to love His testimonies, and to reject the wicked. Why? Because His plan leads right on into eternity. The choice is not difficult.

Don't Blame God!

[121]AYIN—I have done justice and righteousness; do not leave me to my oppressors. [122]Be surety for Your servant for good; do not let the proud oppress me. [123]My eyes fail from seeking Your salvation and Your righteous word. [124]Deal with Your servant according to Your mercy. And teach me Your statutes. [125]I am Your servant; give me understanding, that I may know Your testimonies. [126]It is time for You to act, O Lord, for they have regarded Your law as void. [127]Therefore I love Your commandments more than gold, yes, than fine gold! [128]Therefore all Your precepts concerning all things I consider to be right; I hate every false way. *—Psalm 119:121-128*

TODAY WE FIND our psalmist petitioning the Lord for deliverance from his oppressors, and he repeats what he said in verse 82 about his eyes growing weary from searching God's righteous Word. Pleading for mercy, he states that he understands that he is the servant of the Lord, not the other way around. He prays for God to help him to better understand the testimonies of the Lord. What a wonderful, honest prayer!

He makes a statement that we might just as easily make as we look around at conditions on this earth, saying, "It's time for You to act, O Lord!" Let's look at Psalm 127:1, where we read, *"Unless the Lord builds the house, they labor in vain who build it; unless the Lord guards the city, the watchman stays awake in vain."* Our psalmist in today's reading isn't saying, "Come on, Lord! It's time for you to do something. This has gone on long enough!" Instead, he's saying, "Lord, you're the only one who can help us now, or this will never end." That's also true of our nation. Only God can turn things around. He's the only one who can reach into the human soul and reveal to us what He wants us to hear. Only He has the power to right the thinking of our immoral nation. Our own efforts to effect change are in vain.

God's Word is worth far more than gold, and His precepts teach us all things that are right. If God isn't right about *everything*, He can't be God, and if He's not God, then He can't forgive and save us, and we're lost in our sins. When you begin to think deeply about your life and your trials and frustrations and begin to charge God with not acting on your behalf, remember this: *God's plans and will are not subject to human approval.* Whether people believe His Word or not has absolutely no effect on God or His plans. He will always prevail.

No matter how hard atheists may try, God cannot be legislated off of His throne. He may allow politicians to have their moment, but they'll be judged by His righteous Word in the end. Paul wrote to Timothy: *"Know this, that in the last days perilous times will come: for men will be lovers of themselves . . . of money, boasters, proud, blasphemers, disobedient to parents, unthankful, unholy, unloving, unforgiving, slanderers, without self-control, brutal, despisers of good, traitors, headstrong, haughty, lovers of pleasure rather than lovers of God"* (2 Timothy 3:1-4). That's a pretty fitting description of our culture. We feel in our hearts that it's time for God to act. And He will! He doesn't just fade into the background because people don't believe in Him. He doesn't change His plans or His will because people disagree with Him or dislike what He is doing. Our culture is the way it is today because of one thing,: people regard God's Word as void, irrelevant, and out of step with our modern culture.

Some may be surprised to learn that God doesn't arrive at His statutes and precepts by popular vote. He does what is right, and He'll never be wrong. If you hold a particular opinion on a moral or ethical matter that's different from what the Bible says about it, you're the one who's wrong, not God. God is eternal and omniscient. He's never out of step or out of touch. He's so far ahead of us in every way that we should humbly bow before Him, repenting of our arrogance and disdain for His Word. In truth, our God is the only hope not only for America but for any country and for any individual.

September 25

Do You Truly "Heart" the Lord and His Word?

[129]PE—Your testimonies are wonderful; therefore my soul keeps them. [130]The entrance of Your words gives light; it gives understanding to the simple. [131]I opened my mouth and panted, for I longed for Your commandments. [132]Look upon me and be merciful to me, as Your custom is toward those who love Your name. [133]Direct my steps by Your word, and let no iniquity have dominion over me. [134]Redeem me from the oppression of man, that I may keep Your precepts. [135]Make Your face shine upon Your servant, and teach me Your statutes. [136]Rivers of water run down from my eyes, because men do not keep Your law. —*Psalm 119:129-136*

WE HAVE IN THESE VERSES today a beautiful word picture painted for us of receiving the Word of God into our hearts. Back in verse 11 we read, *"Your word I have hidden in my heart, that I might not sin against You."* That's how it *should* be. Our first two verses today remind us that there's a difference between religious observance and personal transformation. If you're trying to do things by the power of your mind and the power of the converted soul, then you'll never be successful at walking as the Lord directs. To "deny self" as some kind of ethereal decision serves only to satisfy one's love of religion, rather than love of God.

The psalmist speaks of keeping the testimonies of God in his soul. This means that the Word has entered into his *heart* and has shed light on the truth, giving him understanding. This totally destroys any of our sense of obligatory discipline or legalism, and puts us in the correct place of having right desires and being obedient to the Lord. James wrote: *"Therefore lay aside all filthiness and overflow of wickedness, and receive with meekness the implanted word, which is able to save your souls"* (James 1:21). God tells us in our hearts those things that He doesn't want us to do. It's our choice to obey or to disobey, but we do have to live with the consequences, whether of the joy of freedom or the pain of having been disobedient. When the Lord directs our steps, we walk in divine authority, which is a great place to walk. Then our enemies won't have dominion over us, because God has saved us from their efforts to do so. When we walk in the steps ordered by Him, we're in a good place, because He is always right, and His plans will never be defeated. The phrase above, *"Make Your face shine on Your servant,"* is a poetic way of saying that to live in divine favor, your steps must be directed by the Word of God.

It comes down to this: Do you believe that hell is real or not? Do you realize that unbelievers will all be consigned to an eternity in hell? Should we not be weeping and grieving over those who are destined to that awful future? In fact, some today even act as if the church were subject to their approval in the decisions that it makes. We should be grieved over this! The Word of God tells us that the Lord is grieved, and the entrance of God's Word, which will shed light, will also break our hearts and grieve our spirits.

Do you truly love the Lord? Do you "heart" Him by welcoming Him into your heart? Or is your love really for yourself and how you might stand to gain by applying some of God's principles to your life? May the Lord give us hearts that long to be like Him and with Him as we watch our steps in these final days.

September 26

The Day That Changed the World

Introduction

137—Psalm 119:137-160

I'M FAIRLY CERTAIN that on September 11 each year there are many who still are reminded of what happened in our nation on that day in 2001. They may be asking in their minds, "God, where were you?" Many, many people lost loved ones, and some still haven't found the answer to their question. Let's look at this in light of history and God's dealings with His children.

The basic theme of the Psalm 119 is the exaltation of the Word of God as the only completely divinely inspired book ever written. It was authored by God the Holy Spirit, and we'll be reminded today that this means not only that all of it is true but that it is *truth itself.* Psalm 138:2 tells us that God has magnified His word above His name, meaning that even though we can be saved only through the name of the Lord, His word is esteemed above even that name! We can understand the converse of that in this way: If someone's word is no good, neither is their name.

Our writer was having a difficult time, as we see in these verses, because four times he pleaded with the Lord to revive him. He was besieged by attacks from the enemy. A cataclysmic event had shaken him to his core. In verse 153, we'll read his prayer, *"Consider my affliction and deliver me."* If, as many believe, David was the author of this psalm, we can conclude that his nation, Israel, was under attack from without and within. David was also under attack as a "man after God's own heart." As the nation's leader, he looked to the King of kings and Lord of lords for direction and deliverance.

The United States has been attacked from without, but it's also under even worse attack from within. As Christians, we are the only salt and light this country has, and it's only to the true church that access to God's has been granted. As we think about the horror of the 9/11 attack, we're comforted through Psalm 34:17-22: *"The righteous cries out, and the Lord hears, and delivers them out of all their troubles. The Lord is near to those who have a broken heart, and saves such as have a contrite spirit. Many are the afflictions of the righteous, but the Lord delivers him out of them all. . . ."* Ultimately, wickedness will not prevail, and righteousness will reign.

Our world is a mess, and we have every reason to be concerned. Immorality and lawlessness abound, the natural affection of a mother for her child has been lost in many cases, the thoughts and intents of men's hearts is only evil continually. Good is called evil, and evil is called good (which was foretold in the Bible way back in the days of Isaiah—see Isaiah 5:20). When we think about a "day that changed the world," many events in history could claim that title, including what happened on September 11, 2001.

Personally, I would love to think that the very day on which you are reading this page could be called "the day that changed the world." *In what way?* you ask. Perhaps if the church started *being the church* instead of a self-help group focused on materialism, our entire country would change. Or some may have their own life-changing day by asking the Lord earnestly, "Revive me!" No matter what we're experiencing, the Lord can change things in a moment, even in the twinkling of an eye! Let's keep our hearts on Him and a watchful eye on ourselves as we seek

God's will no matter what is going on outside and all around us. The Lord looks on the heart. And if our hearts belong to Him, then we have no need to fear anything or anyone.

Never Forget

> [137] TSADDE—Righteous are You, O Lord, and upright are Your judgments. [138]Your testimonies, which You have commanded, are righteous and very faithful. [139]My zeal has consumed me, because my enemies have forgotten Your words. [140]Your word is very pure; therefore Your servant loves it. [141]I am small and despised, yet I do not forget Your precepts —*Psalm 119:137-141*

NOTICE HOW our psalmist opens this portion of his writing: he declares the righteousness of the Lord, followed by acknowledging the purity of His Word, identifying God's Word as truth and His testimonies as everlasting. We're reminded of many out there, even among "ministers," who believe that the Bible "contains" the words of God but is not entirely divinely inspired. Well, there's a problem there. Who gets to decide which portions are inspired and which parts are human insertions? Surely many, even among themselves, would have strong disagreements, no matter how many degrees they have or how spiritually they may speak. Should we each try to decide for ourselves as we read the Bible?

Spurgeon wrote: "As God is love, so His law is truth, the very essence of truth . . . applied to ethics . . . in action . . . upon the judgment seat. We hear great disputes about, 'What is truth?' The Holy Scriptures are the only answer. . . . Note, that they are not only true but the truth itself. We may not say of them that they contain the truth, but that they are the truth: 'thy law is the truth. . . .' Those who act contrary thereto are walking in a vain show."

Our psalmist also reminds us that God's enemies (our enemies are God's enemies) *forget* His Word. To forget means to mislay, to misapply, to be oblivious to, or to ignore. Is our country paying the penalty today for having forgotten or ignored God's Word? How important is His Word? The psalmist wrote, "*Your word is lamp to my feet and a light to my path*" (v. 105). You'll recall that "lamps" and "light" are used metaphorically for truth, and "darkness" represents wrong or evil. So if God's Word is ignored or misapplied, then one can't walk in truth or on the lighted path but can only walk in darkness, i.e., evil.

We also read today that God's testimonies (commandments) are ignored by His enemies. There's a heavy price to pay for despising His Word: "*He who is often rebuked and hardens his neck, will suddenly be destroyed, and that without remedy.*

When the righteous are in authority, the people rejoice; but when a wicked man rules, the people groan" (Prv 29:1-2).

We need "a day that changed the world," but we must face the reality that the cause of our affliction is that we as a people don't revere the Word of God. When His Word is revered, people and nations are awakened and revived. No one will experience revival if they despise the truth that the Bible is God's inspired Word and *is* truth. We need two things more than anything else: we need a great awakening and revival. Paul wrote: *"You he made alive, who were dead in trespasses and sins, in which you once walked according to . . . this world, according to the prince of the power of the air, the spirit who now works in the sons of disobedience, among whom also we all once conducted ourselves in the lusts of our flesh, fulfilling the desires of the flesh and of the mind, and were by nature children of wrath, just as the others. But God, who is rich in mercy, because of His great love with which He loved us, even when we were dead in trespasses, made us alive together with Christ (by grace you have been saved)"* (Eph 2:1-5). *That* is a great awakening: dead sinners being made alive in Christ through the mercy and great love of God, even when we were still dead in our trespasses! And that is something we must *never* allow ourselves to forget.

September 28

Do You Truly Believe in the Power of the Word?

[142]Your righteousness is an everlasting righteousness, and Your law is truth. [143]Trouble and anguish have overtaken me, yet Your law is truth. [144]The righteousness of Your testimonies is everlasting; give me understanding, and I shall live. —*Psalm 119:142-144*

THE APOSTLE PAUL, writing to believers, said, *"For you once were darkness, but now you are light in the Lord. Walk as children of light (for the fruit of the Spirit is in all goodness, righteousness, and truth), finding out what is acceptable to the Lord. And have no fellowship with the unfruitful works of darkness, but rather expose them. For it is shameful even to speak of those things which are done by them in secret. But all things that are exposed are made manifest by the light, for whatever makes manifest is light. Therefore He says, 'Awake, you who sleep, arise from the dead, and Christ will give you light"* (Ephesians 5:8-14).

That is what revival looks like—the church awakening to her calling and true purpose of being salt and light to a lost and dying world. But it won't happen, because it can't happen, apart from recognizing that the Word of God is just that: *the Word of God.*

Examine your hearts to see what you really believe. Do you believe that God's Word truly has the power to change lives for all eternity? Do you believe that the Word of God has the power to save individuals and shape the future of the nations? Yes? Then we must preach the Word as truth!

Who originally came up with the idea that only parts of the Bible are divinely inspired? It was Satan himself, and those who believe his lies are his followers, no matter how "wise" or sophisticated they may consider themselves to be. It's the devil who is glorified when people who claim to be Christians sneer at the Bible as being outdated and out of touch with society. It's the devil who promotes the idea that man can pick and choose his approach to the Bible as though it were some kind of smorgasbord and still believe that he's going to heaven.

Satan is the great deceiver of all times, and he is the very father of lies. But keep this in mind: "*Beloved, do not believe every spirit, but test the spirits, whether they are of God; because many false prophets have gone out into the world. By this you know the Spirit of God: Every spirit that confesses that Jesus Christ has come in the flesh is of God, and every spirit that does not confess that Jesus Christ has come in the flesh is not of God. And this is the spirit of the Antichrist, which you have heard was coming, and is now already in the world. You are of God, little children, and have overcome them, because He who is in you is greater than he who is in the world. They are of the world. Therefore they speak as of the world, and the world hears them. We are of God. He who knows God hears us; he who is not of God does not hear us. By this we know the spirit of truth and the spirit of error*" (1 John 4:1-6).

If we want to see our nation turned around and blessed by the Lord, there is no one alive who is capable or qualified to do so. It's only when the Word of God is revered that nations awaken and the church is revived. Only when God's testimonies are viewed as commands to be obeyed and the pure truth of His Word is preached unashamedly and without compromise will we see "a day that changed the world," and that, friends, will only happen when the Word of God is treasured. We must search our own hearts to make sure that we are innocent in that regard, and then we ought to go out and share the Good News with others. There is true power in the Word of God that's unlike any power anywhere else. Shouldn't we avail ourselves of that precious gift from God that will help us to preach the truth unafraid and unashamed?

How Do We Change the World?

[145]QOPH—I cry out with my whole heart; hear me, O Lord! I will keep Your statutes. [146]I cry out to You: save me, and I will keep Your testimonies. [147]I rise before the dawning of the morning, and cry for help; I hope in Your word. [148]My eyes are awake through the night watches, that I may meditate on Your word. [149]Hear my voice according to Your lovingkindness; O Lord, revive me according to Your justice. [150]They draw near who follow after wickedness; they are far from Your law. [151]You are near, O Lord, and all Your commandments are truth. [152]Concerning Your testimonies, I have known of old that You have founded them forever.
—Psalm 119:145-152

THE PSALMIST declares that he'll keep God's commands, committing to rising early to meditate on the Word day and night, acknowledging God's loving kindness and His willingness to hear our cries. He pleads for justice, which will bring revival. He knows many who follow after wickedness because they're far from God's law.

"Those who live according to the flesh set their minds on the things of the flesh, but those who live according to the Spirit, the things of the Spirit. For to be carnally minded is death, but to be spiritually minded is life and peace. Because the carnal mind is enmity against God; for it is not subject to the law of God, nor indeed can be. So then, those who are in the flesh cannot please God. But you are not in the flesh but in the Spirit, if indeed the Spirit of God dwells in you. Now if anyone does not have the Spirit of Christ, he is not His" (Romans 8:5-9).

The psalmist affirms that God is near and that all of His commandments are truth, having existed from the beginning. The wicked are far from His law. Paul said the same in Romans above. Those who are in the flesh can never please God and are at enmity with Him.

A few days ago we read that those who were afflicting the writer regarded God's law as void. We're surrounded by the same situations in our lives as the psalmist was in his day. In fact, there's much deception even among those who consider themselves Christians as there was among the Jews back in the psalmist's day. It's important to understand this in light of recent attempts to promote sin within the church under the banner of "grace" in an effort to reach the world. God says that He sent His Son to destroy the works of the devil. He didn't do it so that the church could practice the sins that He sent His Son to overcome.

The psalmist says he will focus on the commandments of the Lord because by them, he is saved. If we did the same, we, too, could expect to be revived even in the midst of our troubles, because all of God's commandments are truth and justice. Changing the world won't take place by changing the church, however. The postmodern church movement isn't merely moving away from the old methods of "doing church." It's moving away from the timeless message that comes directly from God himself. What a travesty!

The Bible tells us that we're to be bound by *unity of the Spirit*. The Spirit teaches us all things that are within the Word of God. We don't join arms with cults and false teachers for the sake of unity. The church appears to say, "Live by your own moral code, because we're all saved by grace." That's not from the Bible but from the pit of hell. All of God's commandments are truth. If there's ever going to come a "day that changed the world," it won't come from changing the church to suit the desires of the world, nor will it be from watering down the message. Without the truth of God, people will never be made free. Jesus is coming soon, and we'll meet Him in the air in the twinkling of any eye. I fear that many who attend church will miss the Rapture, because in their "churches" they don't learn the Word, and without the Word they will never be delivered from their sins.

September 30

What Did You Expect?

[153]RESH—Consider my affliction and deliver me, for I do not forget Your law. [154]Plead my cause and redeem me; revive me according to Your word. [155]Salvation is far from the wicked, for they do not seek Your statutes. [156]Great are Your tender mercies, O Lord; revive me according to Your judgments. [157]Many are my persecutors and my enemies, yet I do not turn from Your testimonies. [158]I see the treacherous, and am disgusted, because they do not teach Your word. [159]Consider how I love Your precepts; revive me, O Lord, according to Your lovingkindness. [160]The entirety of Your word is truth, and every one of Your righteous judgments endures forever. —*Psalm 119:153-160*

THE PSALMIST seems to understand better than many that there are temporal benefits to living according to God's will and Word. He reiterates the fact that he doesn't forget God's testimonies as others do and asks the Lord to deliver and revive him. He states that because of the way they treat the Word of God, the wicked shouldn't expect salvation, He prays for the Lord to revive him according to His judgments. What might that mean?

In 2 Thessalonians, we read: *"We are bound to thank God always for you, brethren . . . because your faith grows exceedingly, and the love of every one of you all abounds toward each other, so that we ourselves boast of you among the churches of God for your patience and faith in all your persecutions and tribulations . . . which is manifest evidence of the righteous judgment of God . . . and to give you who are troubled rest with us when the Lord Jesus is revealed from heaven . . . in flaming fire taking vengeance on those who do not know God, and on those who do not obey the gospel of our Lord Jesus Christ"* (2 Thessalonians 1:3-8).

God will repay with tribulation those who trouble us, and we'll have our rest when He comes to take vengeance on the earth! We can expect His tender mercies as we await His coming to us—or our going to Him. Those who don't keep God's word are deceitful and can only expect judgment (v. 158). He implies that, unlike them, he continues to seek God's loving kindness, displayed by revival in his own life (v. 159). The theme is that God's Word is truth: immutable, unchanging. If we keep His Word, we'll be rewarded with tender mercies, but salvation is far from those who don't obey Him. God, through His Word, instructs us to choose between mercy and judgment. The choice should be simple. We can only experience His mercy as it relates to His truth. This doesn't mean that if we fail we can't expect mercy, because that would deny the meaning of the Word. But the *eternal* mercies that accompany salvation are exclusive to those who see God's Word as pure truth and who love His precepts.

Can one love God and deny or reject His Word? How so, when God is inseparable from His Word? If you say you love Him but reject His Word, you're in darkness. If you say you love Him and believe that the Bible *contains* words from God but isn't all *the* Word of God, you're in darkness. If you say you love God but reject His moral code, you're in darkness. In other words, you'll need a day that changes your world. God gives us a choice: choose mercy or choose judgment. Mercy is for those who accept His Word. Judgment is reserved for those who reject it. We must be willing to tell the truth to those who are heading for judgment. They need to hear that they're perishing but that God's mercy is available through Jesus, the very Word of God. Only when His Word is revered will people and nations be awakened and revived.

Our world changed a little after 9/11, but then it changed back. What is desperately needed is a change that lasts, which will only come from and through the Word of God. And then the day that changed the world could be today!

OCTOBER

More or Less

Introduction

Shin—Psalm 119:161-176

TODAY, we'll begin drawing near to the peak of the biblical "Mount Everest" as we approach the last few sections at the end of the longest chapter in the Bible, Psalm 119. Looking back over this monumental work, a quick review highlights where we've been. First we focused on the exclusivity of God's Word among a sea of religious writings and the ponderings of men. We learned that the Bible is the One Book that stands alone in its majesty and authority, and we've been mining nuggets of personal application as we've ascended. We learned that the Bible has a guaranteed avoidance plan for all of our self-inflicted wounds, i.e., avoiding sinful situations. The amazing Bible exposes every person's need for a Savior. It contains a single moral standard for all cultures and generations and offers to us everything that money can't buy.

We found some pinnacle truths about hiding God's Word in our hearts that we might not sin against Him (v. 11), and we learned that *all* of His words are truth. His righteous judgments are not affected by time or culture, and His judgments endure forever (v. 160). We gleaned insights from the Word, realized its impact, and recognized its integrity. It isn't a "container" of truth but is truth itself. We read of the benefits and blessings of knowing the Word of God and hiding it in our hearts, meditating on it day and night. We saw that because they never change, His Words still hold true for us today. According to Revelation 3:7-10, those who keep God's Word will be kept from the hour of trial that's going to come upon the entire world.

Our title for this last series relates to some of the implied negatives in these verses and also to the wonderful and positive truths of Scripture. We're told to hide the Word in our hearts that we might not sin against the Lord. If we don't take that to heart, we *will* end up sinning against Him.

As we begin this final series in Psalm 119, we're going to look at a choice we must all make and the corresponding life experiences that will result from that choice. What is the choice? It's what we do with God's Word on a personal and daily level. For example, Paul said to Timothy, "*Be diligent to present yourself approved to God, a worker who does not need to be ashamed, rightly dividing the word of truth*" (2 Timothy 2:15). There's a blessing to be had in being diligent when it comes to studying the things of God in that we're less likely to end up being ashamed. Each day we have a choice to make between focusing on God's law, His precepts, statutes, commandments, judgments, words, and promises—or not. Either way, our lives will reflect our choices.

I don't know about you, but I want *more* of the Word to be manifested in and through me, not less. I want to know the Lord more, not less. I want Him to be more involved in my life, not less. Yes, I realize that He's already in me and in all believers by means of the Holy Spirit, so how is it possible to have "more" of Him in our lives? It's really the result of the choices we make between having more of God's blessings, insights, impact, and the integrity of the Word of God acting in our lives—or having less.

Let's make the decision to choose "more" as we finish our climb to the summit of this Mount Everest-like chapter.

October 2

Better and Better

161SHIN—Princes persecute me without a cause, but my heart stands in awe of Your word. 162I rejoice at Your word as one who finds great treasure. 163I hate and abhor lying, but I love your law. 164Seven times a day I praise You, because of Your righteous judgments. 165Great peace have those who love Your law, and nothing causes them to stumble. —Psalm 119:161-165

WE RELATE to our psalmist's plight of being persecuted by the government without cause, but how does he deal with it? "*My heart stands in awe of Your Word.*" God's Word brought much rejoicing to him, as if he had found something very valuable. And indeed he had! The Hebrew word for "treasure" means "spoil," implying the expectation of a victorious reward. He says that he hates lies, but he loves God's law, and proves it by praising the Lord as His righteous Judge. Look, friends, no matter what our personal difficulties may be, we can handle them the same way: by looking to, leaning on, and treasuring God's Word.

Back in Ecclesiastes, Solomon wrote: "*Here is what I have seen: It is good and fitting for one to eat and drink, and to enjoy the good of all his labor in which he toils under the sun all the days of his life which God gives him; for it is his heritage. As for every man to whom God has given riches and wealth, and given him power to eat of it, to receive his heritage and rejoice in his labor—this is the gift of God. For he will not dwell unduly on the days of his life, because God keeps him busy with the joy of his heart*" (Eccl 5:18-20).

My, how things have changed! God said through King Solomon that there's joy in our labors and toils, but today *not* laboring, letting the government take care of you, seems to be the goal for many. The Bible says the opposite is the right way. If our heritage is to be *busy* all the days of our lives for the glory of God, then we can certainly understand this: The more we live by the Word, the less the enemy can steal our joy!

Do you ever wish you had more money? Or dreamed of taking the vacation of a lifetime or fulfilling something high on your "bucket list"? Did you know that you can be perfectly content if you *never* have more money, take that trip, or have that experience? How often does the devil come along and rob people of the joy of their salvation because of what they don't have or get to do! Our psalmist declares that seven times a day he will praise the Lord! Even though he's being persecuted by people in power, he knows a better Power and will continue to rejoice in Him all day long. Psalm 19 tells us that God's law is *perfect*, able to convert our souls; His commandments are pure, and the fear of Him is clean and eternal; His judgments are true and righteous and desirable. There are warnings contained within those words, which, if we keep them will yield a great reward.

Have you ever done something that you regretted? Something that hurt yourself or grieved God's Spirit, and you experienced a loss of a sense of peace? Obedience and adherence to the Word will take care of that! But even more than that, do we see and live as if God's Word is more to be desired than gold and sweeter than honey? Listen to me: part of the heritage of knowing the Lord is joy of heart, even when we're being persecuted without cause, overlooked, belittled for belief, and even when you can't ever seem to get ahead and trials seem to be without end. What's our heritage? It's a heart that rejoices all day because of the righteous judgments of God!

One day, you'll walk on streets of gold. One day, you'll never be sick again or be treated unfairly. It only gets better! Knowing what's coming will affect how we handle what is now. The more we live by the Word, the more time we'll spend rejoicing, because, friends, there is great peace in not stumbling.

Standing on the Promises of God

[166]Lord, I have hoped for Your salvation, and I do Your commandments. [167]My soul keeps Your testimonies, and I live them exceedingly. [168]I keep Your precepts and Your testimonies, for all my ways are before You. —*Psalm 119:166-168*

WE CONTINUE to see the depth of the commitment and devotion of this psalmist to God's Word. I'm reminded again of his words back in verse 97: *"Oh, how I love Your law! It is my meditation all the day";* and verse 113: *"I hate the double-minded, but I love Your law";* and verse 163: *"I hate and abhor lying, but I love Your law."* Here, he states that his hope is in salvation, understanding, and deliverance, and since all of these are taught throughout God's Word, it certainly isn't a vain hope but an absolute confidence!

Notice how he connects "doing God's commandments" with the hope of salvation. In truth, salvation comes before keeping the commandments because the commandments can't save, and no one can ever keep them perfectly in and of themselves. He loves God's testimonies, i.e., the witness of the Lord, and keeps them *exceedingly*, along with all of God's precepts (His statutes or commands). The Hebrew word for salvation as used in the first verse above is Yešû'â, and the Greek translation of the Old Testament uses the word σωτηρία, *soteria*, which describes the present condition of Christians as being saved from hell.

Putting all of this together, we have a man who hopes in Yešû'â and obeys God's commandments because he loves them, and he proves his love by living them out before the Lord. Even so, his personal current experience still leads him to cry out to God for deliverance from this persecution that he is being forced to endure, which seems to have no cause. What does the Bible say about these kinds of situations? *"These things I have spoken to you, that in Me you may have peace. In the world you will have tribulation; but be of good cheer, I have overcome the world"* (John 16:33).

Have you noticed in recent years that the more perverse a practice is, the more the world tries to protect it and demean those who stand against it? Have you noticed that the tolerance crowd only tolerates those who agree with them, thus proving that they have no tolerance at all? Have you noticed how often what we know is evil is approved of as "good," and what is really good is called "evil"? What does the Bible say? *"Know this, that in the last days perilous times will come: for men will be lovers of themselves . . . of money, boasters, proud, blasphemers, disobedient . . . unthankful, unholy, unloving, unforgiving, slanderers, without self-control, brutal, despisers of good, traitors, headstrong, haughty, lovers of pleasure rather than lovers of God, having a form of godliness but denying its power. And from such people turn* away!" (2 Tim 3:1-5); and also *"Scoffers will come in the last days, walking accord-ing to their own lusts . . ."* (2 Pet 3:3). Loving God's commandments, keeping His testimonies and precepts, will lead to persecution without cause. It happened to Jesus, it will happen to us.

But Jesus reminds us, *"Blessed are you when they revile and persecute you, and say all kinds of evil against you falsely for My sake. Rejoice and be exceedingly glad, for great is your reward in heaven, for so they persecuted the prophets who were before you"* (Matt 5:11-12). This means that we have a choice to make: Who are you going to serve? Be forewarned: The more we live by the Word, the less we'll be tolerated by the world. Our natural choice would not be to choose persecution but that's what we've chosen when we decide to take up our cross and follow Jesus. Are you ready to make that choice?

October 4

Choose Ye This Day . . .

[169]TAU—Let my cry come before You, O Lord; give me understanding according to Your word. [170]Let my supplication come before you; deliver me according to Your word. —*Psalm 119:169-170*

I WAS SPEAKING at a conference recently, and someone had mentioned that they couldn't believe that I was so bold as to have DVDs and CDs on our product table covering the topic of homosexuality. That's the kind of world we live in now, where what once was normal now requires a new boldness to speak about it, and we can either change our message to accommodate the world, or we can preach God's message and be hated by the world. What did Jesus say? *"When you lift up the Son of Man, then you will know that I am He, and that I do nothing of Myself; but as my Father taught Me, I speak these things. And He who sent Me is with Me. The Father has not left Me alone, for I always do those things that please Him"* (John 8:28-29).

Saints, the more we live by the Word, the less we will be tolerated by the world. So do we do more to please the Father in such a time, or less? Jesus *always* did what pleased the Father, even when it led Him to the cross. Will you stand for God in times where the cost is getting higher and higher for doing so? Will you stand on His Word even when doing so stirs accusations of bigotry and hatred from the world?

What is it worth to you? Have you been blessed with covered sin and had your transgressions forgiven, no matter how heinous? Would you keep silent about that? When we confess our sins and transgressions, God is our hiding place and our preservation in times of trouble. He will deliver us, the psalmist says, "according to His Word."

I will *not* keep silent about Jesus being the only way to heaven. I will *not* remain silent about all people being sinners in need of a Savior. I will *not* stay silent about false Christs and religions that rob men of their souls. The psalmist, when speaking of holding it inside regarding his sin, said, "*When I kept silent, my bones grew old through my groaning all the day long. For day and night Your hand was heavy upon me . . .*" (Psalm 32:1-7). If Jesus hung naked on a cross made from a tree that He had created, then I am going to stand for Him even though the more I live by the Word, the less tolerated I will be by the world.

But the world can't save me! The world can't forgive me. The world can't conquer the second death for me. The world can't get me into heaven. The world can't offer me immortal incorruptibility and a peace that passes understanding and a heart of rejoicing.

This day, I choose to have more of Jesus and less of the world, even though they'll hate me for it. How much love do you have, both for Jesus and for others?

October 5

Don't Be Ruled by Your Failures

> [171] My lips shall utter praise, for You teach me Your statutes. [172] My tongue shall speak of Your word, for all Your commandments are righteousness. [173] Let Your hand become my help, for I have chosen Your precepts. [174] I long for Your salvation, O Lord, and Your law is my delight. [175] Let my soul live, and it shall praise You; and let Your judgments help me. [176] I have gone astray like a lost sheep; seek Your servant, for I do not forget Your commandments. —*Psalm 119:171-176*

THESE ARE FITTING words to conclude this long chapter about the incredible value of the Word of God. The psalmist's mouth is dedicated to praising the Lord and preaching the Word, because all of God's commandments are righteous. Think about it: how much more could we be like Christ and less like the world if we saw as our purpose in life (and even the reason for our existence as born-again believers) to praise God and to preach His Word? Paul wrote: "*How then shall they call on Him in whom they have not believed? And how shall they believe in Him of whom they have not heard? And how shall they hear without a preacher? And how shall they preach unless they are sent? . . . So then faith comes by hearing, and hearing by the word of God*" (Rom 10:14-17).

Although choosing to dedicate our lives to the admonitions in the Word may mean that we have fewer of the "things" of the world, what a treasure we have in store for us in heaven! When we choose God's way, He will be our help. The more we understand His righteousness and realize that His commandments are good and perfect, the more we will delight in Him and praise Him with our very lives.

In the end, the writer confesses that he has not forgotten the commandments of the Lord but admits that he hasn't always kept them. He asks God to come looking for him when he strays. Will God do that? Jesus said, *"What do you think? If a man has a hundred sheep, and one of them goes astray, does he not leave the ninety-nine and go to the mountains to seek the one that is straying? And if he should find it, assuredly, I say to you, he rejoices more over that sheep than over the ninety-nine that did not go astray. Even so it is not the will of your Father who is in heaven that one of these little ones should perish"* (Matt 18:12-14).

Aren't you thankful that the Lord seeks His servants? He doesn't just let us wander off, but with His rod and staff He corrects and redirects us. We know we're to love one another, but we sometimes stray from that as well. Even so, God's hand and judgments are there to help us! The more we live by the Word, the less we'll be ruled by our failures. Proverbs 24:16 says, *"For a righteous man may fall seven times and rise again, but the wicked shall fall by calamity."* If you find yourself "prone to wander," as the hymn writer mourned, remember that when we fall we can always come home to the Father and be welcomed with open arms. Thus, we can also forgive one another! *"The end of all things is at hand; therefore be serious and watchful in your prayers. And above all things have fervent love for one another, for 'love will cover a multitude of sins'"* (1 Pet 4:7-10). The word "cover" here means to set aside. What if the church stopped sniffing for sins and started covering sin with love and prayer? I'm not talking about heresy or unrepentant immorality. But what about the mistakes, the unkind words, the insults spoken in the heat of the moment? What if we let love cover those times when a Christian behaves rudely or is puffed up and boastful, or is slow to listen and quick to speak (See 1 Cor 13)?

Dear sinning saint, the Word of God says that you can rise up and come home, where you will find God's judgments to be loving and where you may receive a helping hand. Don't wait another moment. Your failures don't have to rule you. Come home, and be free!

Up, Up, and Away!

Introduction

A Song of degrees—Psalm 121

OVER THE PAST months, we've encountered various types of psalms. We've seen that some psalms share more than one characteristic, mixing wisdom and praise, petition and praise, lament and praise, gratitude and praise! Now we come to a different category of psalm. These are called the Psalms of Ascent, also referred to as the Gradual Psalms, Psalms of Degrees, Pilgrim Psalms, or the Psalms of Steps. That last title has led some to believe that these fifteen psalms were sung by the Levite singers as they ascended the fifteen steps of the temple in Jerusalem, where they performed their ministry. Four of them are written by King David, one by King Solomon, and the other ten are anonymous.

Many believe that these psalms were originally sung when the pilgrims made their way each year to the Holy City. All able-bodied males were required to attend three of the seven feast days celebrated by Israel: Passover, Pentecost, and the Feast of Tabernacles in the City of Jerusalem. Let's think about that for a moment in our time: Passover was fulfilled by Jesus on the Cross, Pentecost was fulfilled when the Holy Spirit was poured out on the church, and the Feast of Tabernacles will be fulfilled when Christ rules and reigns from Jerusalem for one thousand years!

The apostle Paul wrote, "*For He Himself is our peace, who has made both one, and has broken down the middle wall of separation, having abolished in His flesh the enmity, that is, the law of commandments contained in ordinances, so as to create in Himself one new man from the two, thus making peace, and that He might reconcile them both to God in one body through the cross, thereby putting to death the enmity. And He came and preached peace to you who were afar off and to those who were near. For through Him we both have access by one Spirit to the Father*" (Ephesians 2:14-18).

The fulfilling of Passover on the cross made God accessible not through Judaism but through Jesus! The wall that separated Jew and Gentile was brought down when the veil that separated the sanctuary from the Most Holy Place was torn in two from top to bottom. God symbolically opened the door for Jew and Gentile, rich and poor, slave and free, to be made one in Christ! Those Jews who believed in Him then experienced the outpouring of God's Spirit at Pentecost, and the Gospel was sent to the Gentile world. Ultimately, the "one new man made from the two," meaning all believers in Christ as Savior, will rule and reign with Him during the Millennium.

Back in the time when this psalm was written, most would travel on foot to the Holy City, which could have been a very long journey. They incorporated celebration and joy along the way, as many would soon be seeing some of their friends whom they seldom saw. As they went along, they sang these Psalms of Ascent. We don't know the exact order in which the psalms were sung, but there is a tradition about Psalm 121, which was to be sung on the last night's journey as the hills of the Holy City of Jerusalem came into view. It was an encouragement and reminder that God is their help and their watchman along the road of life. This psalm deals with the character and nature of God and is therefore still applicable to us today. God *is* our help. He watches over and protects us along our paths in life, and, saints, I believe we are almost at our journey's end. We can know that the Lord will help us up, keep us up, and someday will take us up! Are you ready to begin this journey as we go . . . up, up, and away?!

October 7

Where Are Your Eyes Looking?

¹I will lift up my eyes to the hills—from whence comes my help? ²My help comes from the Lord , who made heaven and earth. —Psalm 121:1-2

WE'VE BEEN READING about the pilgrims approaching Jerusalem, and no matter which direction they may have been coming from, they'd have been able to see the hills of Jerusalem in the distance. Our psalmist reminds them to keep their eyes lifted to the hills. This is the same exhortation that we've seen over and over on our journey through the psalms: Keep our eyes on the end of the road and lift them above life's circumstances. This isn't to say that we go into a mindless state of oblivion, nor are we being told to just "believe" and "have faith" and we won't get hurt or discouraged ever again.

The mention of lifting one's eyes implies that sometimes we encounter seasons and events on the road where we need God to help us, because our eyes, our focus, and our attention are set on things lower than what He wants us to see. "*It came to pass, when Joshua was by Jericho, that he lifted his eyes and looked, and behold, a Man stood opposite him with His sword drawn in His hand. And Joshua went to Him and said to Him, 'Are You for us or for our adversaries?' So he said, 'No, but as Commander of the army of the Lord I have now come.' And Joshua fell on his face to the earth and worshiped, and said to Him, 'What does my Lord say to His servant?' Then the Commander of the Lord's army said to Joshua, 'Take your sandal off your foot, for the place where you stand is holy.' And Joshua did so*" (Josh 5:13-15).

There's a lesson in that for us. We, too, need to stop at times, lift our eyes from the moment and circumstance, and remember the holiness of the Lord. The fact that He is the Captain of our salvation means that He is in command and control of our lives. The psalmist lifts his eyes to the hills of Jerusalem, the city in which the Lord said His name will be perpetually (2 Chr 7:16), and remembers that his help comes from the Lord. Then he elevates his thoughts to contemplation of God's omnipotence and adds that He is the Maker of heaven and earth.

Likewise, we, as people of faith in the true and living God, are pilgrims and strangers, heading for a city prepared for us by God himself. Like those in Hebrews 11, we will encounter hardship, trauma, and trial in our lives, so we need to heed the exhortation to lift our eyes to the Lord, the Maker of heaven and earth, who is our help! We were all born defective, you know. We all came into this world with a sin nature, which is what separated us from God and destined us for a life of sin, leading to hell. Powerless to revert to what we had lost in the Garden of Eden, we, in our flesh, could never live a life that would grant us access to heaven, because the standard, sinless perfection, was too high. But God handled that obstacle through His Son on the Cross.

The Bible never says the Christian life is easy. It does say that it's the difficult way. It's goes against our culture, it brings tribulation and even persecution for righteousness' sake, but look at Galatians 1: *"Grace to you and peace from God the Father and our Lord Jesus Christ, who gave Himself for our sins, that He might deliver us from this present evil age, according to the will of our God and Father, to whom be glory forever and ever. Amen"* (vv. 3-5).

Remember that God's specialty is handling difficulty, and the fact that He has already handled your biggest problem tells us that all the others are miniscule by comparison. Sometimes it seems like He's moving too slowly or doing things differently from what we think He should, but He's better than we are, so, stop, lift your eyes, and remember: even though we may not be in the city whose Maker is God yet, we will be soon.

Now I Lay Me Down to Sleep

[3]He will not allow your foot to be moved; He who keeps you will not slumber. [4]Behold, He who keeps Israel shall neither slumber nor sleep. [5]The Lord is your keeper; the Lord is your right hand. [6]The sun shall not strike you by day, nor the moon by night. —Psalm 121:3-6

READ THROUGH the verses above a second time. Think about what the psalmist is saying! We learned yesterday that the Lord will help us up, and today we see that He will keep holding us up, even as we sleep, because He himself never sleeps nor slumbers. Night or day, He is keeping us. The Lord told Moses that they were to bless the children of Israel by saying, "*The Lord bless you and keep you; the Lord make His face to shine upon you, and be gracious to you; the Lord lift up His countenance upon you, and give you peace.*" And then He said, "*So they shall put My name on the children of Israel, and I will bless them*" (Num 6:22-27).

As Christians, we, too, bear the name of the Lord. We're saved by the same name that was put on the children of Israel. The God of Israel is the God of the church. In Revelation, speaking of those who overcome evil, the Lord said He would make them pillars in the temple and write on them His name and the name of the City of the Lord, the New Jerusalem.

Regarding that Name, the Jews refer to Him as *Hashem*, meaning "the Name." Of course, the name they will not say is the name of the Lord, *Yeshua*, that name by which we are saved, by which we are kept, and that is above every other name. It's the name at which one day every knee will bow and every tongue confess what we knew all along: that Jesus Christ is the Lord!

To you pilgrims who are on a long, difficult journey but trying to keep your eyes lifted even as the enemy tries to pull them down to looking at your circumstances, remember this: not only is handling difficulty God's specialty, but He never slumbers nor sleeps! His eye is ever upon you, even in the midst of trials. I can't explain why He allows some situations and averts others, but I know this: as His children, He helps us up and keeps us up. To believe the devil's lies that He has forsaken or forgotten you is from the pit.

We don't have to *like* a painful situation, but just because you feel alone doesn't mean you *are*! God didn't nod off, and something bad happened to you while He was sleeping. He hasn't forgotten you or your circumstances. He's right there with you! You can rest and sleep sweetly, knowing that He who never sleeps will always take care of you.

This psalm tells us that the Lord is our *keeper*, meaning one who hedges in or guards someone or something—in this case, us! But we need to be on guard ourselves. Paul wrote: "*Stand therefore, having girded your waist with truth, having put on the breastplate of righteousness, and having shod your feet with the preparation of the gospel of peace; above all taking the shield of faith with which you will be able to quench all the fiery darts of the wicked one*" (Eph 6:14-16). Notice that God didn't promise that the fiery darts would stop coming during our lifetime, but He said that *faith in Him* can quench them all as *you* use the shield of faith! Faith in what? Faith in Jesus, who helps us up and keeps us up!

If this is where you find yourself, lift your eyes up to where your help comes from. You haven't been left to your own devices! That would be contrary to the nature and character of our loving Father! Friends, the Lord is your keeper. Say it to yourself often, "The Lord is my keeper, all night and all day long, every day." Then you can lie down and sleep in peace in spite of the battle that rages all around you.

The Keeper of Our Souls

> [7]The Lord shall preserve you from all evil; He shall preserve your soul.
> [8]The Lord shall preserve your going out and your coming in from this time forth. —*Psalm 121:7-8*

GOD WILL KEEP us from evil. It's clear, however, that we're not in for an easy ride, because we will encounter evil. What does this evil force want? It seeks after our *souls*. In Psalm 119:167 we read, "*My soul keeps Your testimonies. . . .*" That's an action on our part. But in Proverbs we read, "*If you faint in the day of adversity, your strength is small. . . . He who keeps your soul [emphasis added], does He not know it? And will He not render to each man according to his deeds?*" (Proverbs 24:10-12). We've already observed that we're not promised a pain- and problem-free life as we journey toward our final home. That sweet rest won't begin until we're there. Here, we must experience trials and troubles, but God will help us up and keep us up along the way. The battle is far more than just a fleshly one. "*Beloved, I beg you, . . . abstain from fleshly lusts which war against the soul, having your conduct honorable among the Gentiles, that [they] may, by [observing] your good works . . . glorify God in the day of visitation*" (1 Peter 2:11-12).

The war that's raging for souls today is fierce, and it comes back to bite us because its weapons and tactics are the lusts of the flesh. Paul wrote: "*The carnal mind is enmity against God; for it is not subject to the law of God, nor indeed can be. . . . [I]f anyone does not have the Spirit of Christ, he is not His*" (Romans 8:6-9). Those in the flesh can't please God. Their soul is in peril, thus Jesus's statement that "you must be born again." Verse 8 refers to our day-to-day experiences, victories, and defeats—doing God's will, and failing to do so. Yet He preserves our soul. The enemy can't win! The war that rages against us engages principalities and powers and is aimed at the Lord and His host of angels. What is the enemy after? Our souls. But fear not! You can't lose what God preserves. Your soul is eternal. Where will that soul spend eternity? Jesus said that He came to offer eternal life (implying the saving of the soul) to all who would come to Him and believe. Once the soul is saved, God helps us up when we fall, keeps us up, and seals our souls to Himself forevermore.

We still have a battle to be won, and we are often our own worst enemy. The apostle Paul understood this well, and he wrote: "*We know that the law is spiritual, but I am carnal, sold under sin. . . . What I am doing, I do not understand. For what I will to do . . . I do not practice; but what I hate, that I do. . . . (In my flesh) nothing good dwells; for to will is present with me, but how to perform what is good I do not find. . . . I find then a law, that evil is present in me, the one who wills to do good*" (Romans 7:14-21).

So what of those who claim to be Christians but their actions contradict what they say? Paul says that he *wills* to do good but sometimes doesn't. It isn't sin from the soul but sin from the flesh. That means that his perfected soul still lives on in an imperfect body. Romans tells us that we cannot continue in sin counting on grace to cover our shame (Romans 6:1-4). Even so, those who are truly saved "will" to do good, but sometimes they don't. Must we, then, fear losing our soul to the darkness after this life? You can't lose what God preserves. All born-again believers share the same moral convictions. Some are better at working them out than others, but no one can defend his sin or say that God is wrong. The Holy Spirit, residing within, leads us to grieve over our sin, and we seek repentance and forgiveness from our Lord. Remember this: if you *could* lose your salvation, you already would have. But *God* has preserved your soul from this time forth and forevermore! God has helped you up, kept you up, and one day will take you up, that where He is, you may be also. Even so, come quickly, Lord Jesus!

October 10

"There's No Place Like Home"

Introduction

A Song of Ascents. Of David—Psalm 122

PSALM 121, which we just finished, was to be sung the evening before the final day's journey into Jerusalem. The pilgrims would make camp for the night with the hills of Jerusalem in view and sing about how their help doesn't come from the hills of their beloved Jerusalem but from the One who made those hills! The tradition behind Psalm 122, which we'll be looking at over the next few days, was that it was intended to be sung or recited responsively the day after the pilgrims had arrived within the city and were about to go up to the House of the Lord to give thanks, bringing their offerings and sacrifices before Him.

In our last psalm, we learned that all able-bodied males were required to attend three of the seven feast days celebrated by Israel: Passover, Pentecost, and the Feast of Tabernacles. Today, as Christians, we realize that we're not under the Law of Moses, nor are we required to make the pilgrimage or even to observe the feast days. But one thing we do want to acknowledge regarding the beauty of these passages is this: The things that were "written before" (see Romans 15:4) are the Old Testament Scriptures, which were written for our *learning*. This means that there are things that are spoken of within this pilgrimage journey to Jerusalem from which we can learn.

We speak of "going to church," yet we know that as Christians we *are* the church. Hebrews 10:24-25 tells us that as the church, we're to *go* to church for the purpose of assembling ourselves together and being exhorted and built up.

What we see in the words of King David in this beautiful psalm is the importance of making our way to God's house (even in our hearts) as pilgrims and sojourners on earth, and what David will be reminding us of is that when it comes to going to God's house of worship and prayer, *there's no place like home*.

These "Psalms of Ascent" have established for us that it is the Maker of heaven and earth who is the object of our worship, and the pilgrimage and the feasts were merely to highlight His glory and majesty. Today we are the temple of the Holy Spirit, yet we meet in a place that we rightfully refer to as God's House. We're His sons and daughters, and there's truly no place like home. What was written in these verses that we can learn from is the significance of the church and its importance in the life of every believer and to the world.

We already understand that this world is not our home, and we're going to begin to take a closer look at our true "home" and what that really means. Ask the Lord to give you wisdom as we go down that road to our real home.

Home, Sweet Home

¹I was glad when they said to me, "Let us go into the house of the Lord."
²Our feet have been standing within your gates, O Jerusalem!" —*Psalm 122:1-2*

NOTICE WHAT David says when they said, "Let us go into the house of the Lord." He was glad. The time had arrived for them to go inside! Are you glad when Sunday comes or when it's time for your Bible study group to meet?

It was always the pattern and practice in Scripture for God to meet with His people when they gathered to seek Him. And it's the same for us! Jesus said, "*Where two or three are gathered together in My name, I am there in the midst of them*" (Matt 18:20). And Paul wrote in his first letter to the Corinthians: "*In the name of our Lord Jesus Christ, when you are gathered together, along with my spirit, with the power of our Lord Jesus Christ . . .*" (1 Cor 5:3-8). Jesus promises to be present when we gather in His name! Paul wrote that, assuming that the people accepted this as a matter of fact regarding their walk with the Lord.

People like to argue that you don't have to go to a church to be a Christian. It's true that attending church doesn't *make* you a Christian, but the Bible actually does say that all believers should go to church. In Hebrews we're told not to forsake the "*assembling of ourselves together . . .*" (Heb 10:25), meaning that we're to gather together with other believers regularly for the purposes of praying for one another, encouraging and challenging one another, and it says that this grows ever more important as we move along in the Last Days.

Another objection put up by those who don't agree with the idea of meeting with our believing church body regularly is that "there are hypocrites present." That's probably true. In most assemblies, there are what the Bible refers to as "tares" among the "wheat," meaning that there are people who may appear to be saved, but in truth they're not. One thing to note is that the stronger and more biblical the teaching, the less likely there are be "tares" in the fellowship, because the message definitely won't titillate or flatter the "itching ears" crowd.

Saints, remember this as you ponder these thoughts: the most important entity in the world is a Bible-teaching church. Even the tiniest among them is more vital to the world than the greatest of royal palaces on earth! This is because there's nothing the world needs more than to hear the Word of God. They need this more than money and more than any other kind of "news," and for one simple reason: the Word will stand forever (Isaiah 40:8)!

Just how important should attending our local fellowship be to us? In fact, our lives should be *planned* around going to the house of the Lord—and not going to the house of the Lord only when it fits into our plans. Hebrews 12 says, "*But you have come to Mount Zion and to the City of the living God, the heavenly Jerusalem, to an innumerable company of angels, to the general assembly and the church of the firstborn who are registered in heaven, to God the Judge of all, to the spirits of just men made perfect, to Jesus the Mediator of the new covenant, and to the blood of sprinkling that speaks better things than that of Abel"* (Heb 12:22-24).

So although we are citizens of the heavenly Jerusalem, we're also the general assembly and the church of the firstborn. There's nothing that will help you throughout your life, comfort you in your afflictions, or teach you how to handle your enemies better than hearing the Word of God faithfully taught. There is no single entity, enterprise, group, or organization on the earth that can contribute more to the betterment of society and the world than a Bible-teaching church, and we ought to be glad when it's time to go into the house of the Lord, because there's no place like home! 'Nuff said!

October 12

Doing Our "Homework"

³Jerusalem is built as a city that is compact together, ⁴where the tribes go up, the tribes of the Lord, to the Testimony of Israel, to give thanks to the name of the Lord. . . . *—Psalm 122:3-4*

THE WORD "COMPACT" in verse three can mean simply to join. But it can also mean to fascinate or charm, or it can mean to fellowship! The overall context is that there is a fascination about the city of Jerusalem that supersedes its buildings and infrastructure. Jerusalem was a city that worshiped the true and living God. It was a destination for the tribes of Israel to ascend, on the annual feast days, to the "Testimony of Israel," which is likely a reference to the Ark of the Covenant during a time when the entire city would be joined in fellowship to worship the Lord, in obedience to His ordinances.

Psalm 133 states, *"Behold, how good and pleasant it is for brethren to dwell together in unity! It is like the precious oil upon the head, running down on the beard . . . of Aaron, . . . down the edge of his garment. It is like the dew of Hermon, descending upon the mountains of Zion; for there the Lord commanded the blessing—life forevermore"* (vv. 1-3).

The "good and pleasant" blessings of dwelling in the city in unity are pictured as oil running down onto Aaron's beard and garments, representing God's blessings on His people when they gather together for worship. It also symbolized the agreement among the people as their praises were accompanied by offerings of animals, grain, wine, and oil. There would come a day under the reign of David's son Solomon where the unity of the people in God's house would bring about what we all long for and what can only happen among God's people (see 2 Chronicles 5:11-6:1a). The essence of what happened on that day under Solomon, was this: As the band and singers were united for the purpose of praising God and singing and playing solely for Him, the Lord *inhabited* the praises of His people and moved among them, manifesting His glory to them! This was their *true* home!

"And it came to pass when the priests came out of the Most Holy Place . . . and the Levites who were the singers . . . with their sons and their brethren, stood at the east end of the altar, clothed in white linen, having cymbals, stringed instruments and harps, and with them one hundred and twenty priests sounding with trumpets— . . . when the trumpeters and singers were as one, to make one sound to be heard in praising and thanking the Lord, and when they lifted up their voice with the trumpets and cymbals and instruments of music, and praised the Lord, saying: 'For He is good, for His mercy endures forever,' that . . . the house of the Lord was filled with a cloud, so that the priests could not continue ministering because of the cloud; for the glory of the Lord filled the house of God" (2 Chronicles 5:11-6:1a).

This is an excellent text for worship leaders to ponder, recognizing the importance of what they do and how crucial unity (with the Lord and with one another) really is. It's not meant to be a display or a "show" or a talent contest. The sole purpose is to draw and unite all the people to corporately *worship* our heavenly Father. When we enter the church, our purpose is to praise God through verbal thanksgiving and sacrificial offerings of praise, but it's also to be equipped in this house for the work of ministry.

Saints, when we enter this place of worship, our purpose is twofold, according to Scripture. It's so that we can praise God through our verbal thanksgiving and sacrificial offerings and also that we might be equipped for the purpose of ministering to one another. It's pretty exciting when we think of it this way, and we should all consider this as we prepare to "go to church" on Sunday. God has something there for you to do, and you are to "do it with your might." Have you been doing *your* "home" work?

October 13

The Heart of the Home

> [5]Thrones are set there for judgment, the thrones of the house of the Lord. —Psalm 122:5

EVEN THIS BEAUTIFUL setting of gathering together with believers to worship the Lord as one, there is an enemy of which we must beware and that the

Lord hates. God hates? Yes! Proverbs 6 tells us, *"There are six things the Lord hates, yes, seven are an abomination to Him: a proud look, a lying tongue, hands that shed innocent blood, a heart that devises wicked plans, feet that are swift in running to evil, a false witness who speaks lies, and one who sows discord among brethren"* (vv. 16-19). "Discord" means strife or contentions. As the pilgrims in this psalm were one in purpose and praise while they made their way into Jerusalem, so, too, ought we to be each week as we enter God's house. Wherever there are people gathered, there will be personality clashes, but we must strive to be singular in purpose. Keep this in mind: the unity we share in Christ has no earthly equal! There is nothing else quite like it among any other gathering, because this is of the Holy Spirit, not just the human bonds that bring some together.

We know, of course, who is behind sowing discord, and he is our worst enemy, Satan. God is our righteous Judge, who sits upon His throne, observing all things. He watches over His children, protecting them, but also stretching them, testing them to see not only how they do but also to help them to learn to work and to love as He himself does.

Christianity comprises an interesting bunch. Some of us are a little rough around the edges. We many not always say or do the right thing; some may not always keep their word or follow through on things well. Some are quiet and retiring, others are loud and bristly. Some are happy-go-lucky and some are grumpy-go-lucky! But whether snippy and snarky or passive and patient, *we are still one in Christ!* And God hates it when there is division among His children. Paul wrote to the church at Ephesus: *"I, therefore, the prisoner of the Lord, beseech you to walk worthy of the calling with which you were called, with all lowliness and gentleness, with longsuffering, bearing with one another in love, endeavoring to keep the unity of the Spirit in the bond of peace. There is one body and one Spirit, just as you were called in one hope of your calling; one Lord, one faith, one baptism; one God and Father of us all, who is above all, and through all, and in you all"* (Ephesians 4:1-6).

J. Vernon McGee used to say, "The church is not for you. You are for the church." We come to church not to *do* something, or to *get* something, although we may be blessed by both doing and getting as we give our hearts wholly to worshiping the Lord. We come to be united in spirit, praising God with one accord. Singing worship is neither about nor for you. It's about and for God. As God's children, we have what the world does not: unity of the Spirit and the bond of peace. Satan loves to throw a wrench into the works, disrupting and causing discord among the saints, thus rendering them no different from the world and even irrelevant and unnecessary rather than as lights on a hill.

The bond we share in Christ is why Christians from anywhere in the world can meet by chance and recognize a connection among themselves—a sense of unity, of family. Other close-knit groups may share a common love or recreation, but only the church is actually one *body*, of which Christ is the head. Our endeavor is to keep the unity of the Spirit in the bond of peace as we make our pilgrimage here each week. And it's then that we realize that here is the heart and that there truly is no place like home!

October 14

Seek the Good of God's House

⁶Pray for the peace of Jerusalem: may they prosper who love you. ⁷Peace be within your walls, prosperity within your palaces." ⁸For the sake of my brethren and companions, I will now say, "Peace be with you." ⁹Because of the house of the Lord our God I will seek your good.
—Psalm 122:6-9

KING DAVID calls for the people to pray for the beloved city of Jerusalem and for peace within its walls and prosperity in its palaces. He points to the tabernacle of the Lord, the focal point of the city. In Jerusalem, the pilgrims were told to seek the peace of the city. David, too, declares that because Jerusalem is the center for worship as established by God, he will strive for what is good for the house of the Lord, and in turn, for the city. We see that seeking the good of God's house will bless our own! The most important entity in the world is a Bible-teaching church. A godly, prosperous church will be a blessing to the city in which it exists and a blessing to the believers.

Part of the worship during the feast days was to bring an offering as an expression of thanksgiving to the Lord. In a farm community such as Israel, animal, grain, wine, and oil would be offered and were the equivalent of the giving of our money today. A lot of people disdain the idea of giving money to a church, and no wonder. There are many charlatans out there who are fleecing the "flock." But we can't allow liars and thieves to rob us of the blessing of being obedient to the Lord in this. The prophet Malachi, in the Old Testament, wrote: *"Will a man rob God? Yet you have robbed Me! But you say, 'In what way have we robbed You?' In tithes and offerings. You are cursed with a curse, for you have robbed Me. . . . Bring all the tithes into the storehouse, that there may be food in My house, and try Me now in this,' says the Lord of hosts. . . ."* (3:8-12).

Many debate over whether tithing is a New Testament principle. In Second Corinthians we read, *"He who sows sparingly will also reap sparingly, and he who sows bountifully will also reap bountifully. . . . God loves a cheerful giver"* (9:6-7). Isn't this the principle in Malachi? God blesses the houses of those who strive to bless

His. *"The word of the Lord came by Haggai the prophet, saying, 'Now, therefore . . . consider your ways! You have sown, and bring little; you eat, but do not have enough; you drink, but you are not filled with drink; you clothe yourselves, but no one is warm; and he who earns wages, earns wages to put into a bag with holes.' Thus says the Lord of hosts: Consider your ways! . . . You looked for much, but indeed it came to little; and when you brought it home, I blew it away. Why?' says the Lord of hosts. 'Because of My house that is in ruins, while ever one of you runs to his own house'"* (Hag 1:3-9).

We see here that giving is a principle, not an amount. Does God deserve top priority when it comes to our finances? He does! Since a Bible-teaching church is an asset in the community, and since there is a unity within the body that passes understanding and guards the hearts and minds through Jesus Christ, isn't that something worth striving for—to seek the good for the benefit of the community? And we will be blessed by God for doing so!

There's no place like home. Nothing compares to God's house and His people. He has spoken, and He does not change. We *are* the church. We're called to go to church and also to support the church, because there is no place like our (church) home. May we seek to bless our churches, our fellowships, and in so doing may we recognize the blessing of the Lord in our lives, because nobody can out-bless God, and one day we'll all be with Him forever in our permanent homes that He has been preparing for us since Jesus ascended into heaven!

October 15

Immovable

Introduction

A Song of Degrees—Psalm 125

PILGRIMS MAKING their way to Jerusalem for one of the Feasts encountered many hardships along the way. The road grew narrow and steep as they neared the City of Jerusalem. The possibility of being accosted by thieves was always a concern. Families traveling with children would have to be especially watchful.

In the same way, we Christians are pilgrims and strangers on this earth, headed for the New Jerusalem! The path of life is narrow, steep, and treacherous, and we must always be on guard for the thief, who comes to steal, kill, and destroy (Jn 10:10). The closer we get to heaven, the more difficulties we'll encounter in our spiritual journey. Jesus warned that the time of "the last days" will be as it was in the days of Noah, when man's heart was evil and violence filled the earth.

Paul prophesied that the last days would be perilous because of man's love of himself and his hatred of God. Sound doctrine won't be endured, but people will seek smooth-talking, ear-tickling teachers to make them feel better about themselves, and the mood of many will be more like, "Don't worry. Be happy." Paul, who understood what was to come, wrote: "*Therefore . . . be steadfast, immovable . . . abounding in the work of the Lord, knowing that your labor is not in vain . . .* " (1 Corinthians 15:58).

Our context is the trek to Jerusalem. The application is that the pilgrims should trust in the Lord while on the way. The takeaway is like a banner that we can hang over our own lives. It's our testimony, but it must become our belief. It's a word that defines how we're to live on this journey. We must be "Immovable." I don't mean that in the sense of being stubborn but of being steadfast, trusting in the One "*who keeps our soul among the living, and does not allow our feet to be moved*" (Psalm 66:9). When the Lord orders our steps, our feet can't be wrongly moved.

In Psalm 73, Asaph wrote: "*Truly God is good to Israel, to such as are pure in heart. But as for me, my feet had almost stumbled; my steps had nearly slipped. For I was envious of the boastful, when I saw the prosperity of the wicked*" (vv. 1-3). Asaph continues with his complaint that the wicked don't seem to experience the struggles that he had even though they were violent mockers of God. They have everything and they get away with everything. They scoff at God, yet their lives are easy. And here's poor Asaph, "always" being chastened, struggling to live a pure life, but in vain!

But, oh, look at what happens: "*It was too painful for me until I went into the sanctuary of God; then I understood their end. . . . You set them in slippery places; you cast them down to destruction. . . . [T]hey are brought to desolation, as in a moment! . . . Thus my heart was grieved, and I was vexed in my mind. I was so foolish and ignorant . . . like a beast before You. Nevertheless, I am continually with You; You hold me by the right hand, . . . guide me with Your counsel, and afterward receive me to glory. Whom have I in heaven but You? . . . there is none upon earth that I desire besides You. My flesh and my heart fail; but God is the strength of my heart and my portion forever*" (Psalm 73:16-26).

This world is not our home! We can't allow our eyes and minds and hearts to rest upon this place, but we must put our trust and faith in the Lord and remember that in Him we can have peace and be *immovable* regardless of our situation. God holds us, guides us, and will receive us into glory. He promises to be our strength and portion forever, even when we fail and our feet almost slip. Our position in Christ never changes, and as we keep our eyes upon Him, we'll find that our status in life will remain immovable.

October 16

"None of These Things Move Me . . . "

[1]Those who trust in the Lord are like Mount Zion, which cannot be moved, but abides forever. [2]As the mountains surround Jerusalem, so the Lord surrounds His people from this time forth and forever. —*Psalm 125:1-2*

THIS PSALM is a psalm of trust, as we see in the first verse. Those who trust in the Lord will be like Mount Zion, which not only can't be moved but will abide forever. The Holy City that is surrounded by the mountains illustrates the safety that we have when we trust the Lord. What does this mean? Well, Psalm 32:10 tells us that *mercy* surrounds those who trust God. Psalm 34:8 says that the man who trusts in the Lord is *blessed*. The author of Proverbs 16 says that *happy* is the man who trusts in the Lord (v. 20). Proverbs 28 says that he who trusts in the Lord will *prosper . . .* will be *delivered* (vv. 25-26). And Proverbs 29 says that whoever trusts the Lord will be *safe* (v. 25). What is the mechanism that makes this blessedness, happiness, prosperity, and safety a reality? *Trusting in the Lord!*

So, in this season of rampant corruption where good is called evil and evil good, where murdering a child days before its due date is applauded as a good political stance, how do we get to that place of blessedness and the rest? How can we trust when we see that the things that God has forbidden are the very things that qualify one to be nominated to the Supreme Court? Where do we find trust when Christians are martyred daily by murderers who are financed and protected by their own government? How can we live an immovable life in such a time as we live now? Remember this: no spiritual or earthly powers are greater than our God!

If we trust in this truth alone, we can live as if we are surrounded by mountains of safety, in a city of mercy, blessedness, happiness, and prosperity. But what about the innocent people who are being killed all around us? Remember this: "*For to me, to live is Christ, to die is gain. But if I live on in this flesh, this will mean fruit from my labor; yet what I shall choose I cannot tell. For I am hard-pressed between the two, having a desire to depart and be with Christ, which is far better. Nevertheless to remain in the flesh is more needful for you*" (Philippians 1:21-24). Paul, when faced with arrest, chains, and tribulations, wrote, "*But none of these things move me; nor do I count my life dear to myself, so that I may finish my race with joy . . .* " (Acts 20:24).

According to the historian Eusebius, Paul was about to be beheaded by Caesar Nero, and yet Paul considered that being with the Lord was far better, although to remain was more necessary for the people. Christian martyrs today are now in a far better place, safe with Christ, and God only permitted their deaths for that very reason. Heaven is a far better place than earth. "To live is Christ, to die is gain," said Paul. Although we know that heaven is better, we'll be here on earth as long as God determines—no more and no less. Everyone who is in heaven now got there through death except for Enoch and Elijah, who were supernaturally translated into heaven. And we can even dare to hope for the same!

While we wait to go there, we must remain here and *not be moved*, no matter how much wickedness surrounds us. Through the Lord we can be immovable. Nothing is greater or stronger than our God. He will win the battle, and He is coming to fight very soon!

October 17

We Shall Overcome

³For the scepter of wickedness shall not rest on the land allotted to the righteous, lest the righteous reach out their hands to iniquity. —*Psalm 125:1-2*

A SCEPTER is a symbol of rulership. The Holy Spirit gives us a reminder that has prophetic implications along with the personal application. He says that the scepter of wickedness will never rest in the land that has been allotted to the righteous. The word "rest" in this case means to dwell or to stay. The prophetic implication is greater:

"Now I saw a new heaven and a new earth, for the first heaven and the first earth had passed away. Also there was no more sea. Then I, John, saw the holy city, New Jerusalem, coming down out of heaven from God, prepared as a bride adorned for her husband. And I heard a loud voice from heaven saying, 'Behold, the tabernacle of God is with men, and He will dwell with them, and they shall be His people. God Himself will be with them and be their God. And God will wipe away every tear from their eyes; there shall be no more death nor sorrow, nor crying. There shall be no more pain, for the former things have passed away.'

Then He who sat on the throne said, 'Behold, I make all things new.' And He said to me, 'Write, for these words are true and faithful.' And he said to me, 'It is done! I am the Alpha and the Omega, the Beginning and the End. I will give of the fountain of the water of life freely to him who thirsts. He who overcomes shall inherit all things, and I will be his God and he shall be My son. But the cowardly, unbelieving, abominable, murderers, sexually immoral, sorcerers, idolaters, and all liars shall have their part in the lake which burns with fire and brimstone, which is the second death' " (Rv 21:1-8).

What are we reading about here? This is the future Promised Land allotted to the righteous, where no wickedness will be allowed. Yet, the earthly, or "in this life," context reminds us that this is also true in our own lives. There will always be evil present in the world, but it will never *prevail or prosper* over God's people. It may impact us, but it will not influence us. Remember how Asaph said that the prosperity of the wicked "almost" caused his foot to stumble? But what he heard in the sanctuary stabilized his feet, his walk.

Verse 3 of our psalm today hints at immorality and idolatry, because "reaching out the hand to iniquity" implies participation or getting caught up in sin. So although a day is coming where the scepter of wickedness will not be permitted in the land of the righteous, we see that in our day, its presence is very real. Remember that it is neither permanent nor prevailing. First Corinthians 10 says, "*Let him who thinks he stands take heed lest he fall. No temptation has overtaken you except such as is common to man; but God is faithful, who will not allow you to be tempted beyond what you are able, but with the temptation will also make the way of escape, that you may be able to bear it*" (vv. 12-13). We will overcome!

Temptations that can cause our feet to slip have ways of escape, or else God wouldn't allow them to happen. He won't permit wickedness to rule to the degree that the righteous reach out their hand to it. God promises that although He allows temptations, He will never allow them to be more than we can bear. Evil has its limits. They are governed by God. Those who trust in the Lord will be like Zion. Keep this in mind as we head into darker days: *darkness cannot prevail over us, because we are surrounded by our God*! There will always be evil, but it won't prevail over God's people. But be forewarned, "*your adversary the devil walks about like a roaring lion, seeking whom he may devour*" (1 Pt 5:8-11).

We may suffer as brothers and sisters in Christ, but suffering doesn't diminish the eternal glory that awaits us. And meanwhile we want to hold fast to our goal of remaining immovable before the Lord.

October 18

Well Done . . . ?

> ⁴Do good, O Lord, to those who are good, and to those who are upright in their hearts. ⁵As for such as turn aside to their crooked ways, the Lord shall lead them away with the workers of iniquity. Peace be upon Israel!
> —Psalm 125:4-5

THESE VERSES raise some hard questions. What about someone who was walking with the Lord and then walked away? Were they saved but lost their salvation? Or were they never saved? God knows. Our psalmist says, "Lord, do good to those who are . . . upright in heart." He tells us that those who turn aside to crooked ways will be led away with the workers of iniquity. Who are they? They are the ones who habitually run after unrighteousness. In Matthew, Jesus warned, "*Not everyone who says to Me, 'Lord, Lord,' shall enter the kingdom of heaven, but he who does the will of My Father in heaven. Many will say . . . in that day, 'Lord, Lord, have we not prophesied in Your name, cast out demons in Your name, and done many wonders in Your name?' And then I will declare to them, 'I never knew you; depart from Me, you who practice lawlessness!'*" (Matthew 7:21-23). To practice lawlessness is the equivalent of being workers of iniquity.

What's the future for those who love and follow the Lord? They will get to hear, "*Well done, good and faithful servant; you have been faithful over a few things, I will make you ruler over many things. Enter into the joy of the Lord*" (Matthew 25:23). Many seem to have a very casual idea of what it means to be a servant of the Lord. They think that grace gives one a free pass regarding sin. They "identify" as Christians but are easily turned aside to the crooked ways of the workers of iniquity. Who will hear the words "Well done, good and faithful servant?" That is reserved for those for all who actually enter heaven!

Listen, we all mess up. We sin. I'm not talking about a "works-righteousness" attempt here but a truly righteous *life*, filled with good works that glorify the Lord through the Holy Spirit. The psalmist prays, "*Do good, O Lord, to those who are good and to those who are upright in heart.*" The Bible speaks of uprightness of heart. (See Psalm 36:10-12 and Psalm 64:9-10 as examples.) But see the balance: Jeremiah wrote: "*The heart is deceitful above all things, and desperately wicked; who can know it?*" (17:9-10); and "*I will put My law in their minds, and write it on their hearts; and I will be their God, and they shall be My people*" (31:33).

Making a deceitful heart upright is God's work, and this work is written in the minds and hearts of His people. What our hearts and minds are filled with will be what our lives are filled with. So if someone claims to be a Christian but follows sinful ways, then the Lord will allow them their desires as they head into the eternal destiny of the unrighteous. Yes, Christians also sin and fail, but they don't seek to redefine sin and habitually follow crooked paths under the banner of grace. Living for God is never a waste of time. But—not living for Him always is. Time is a precious commodity. We don't have forever. Are we wasting precious time that could be spent blessing our Lord? (See 1 Peter 4:1-3). I personally wasted ten years of my life doing my own will, but now my desire is to live for God's will. If you've been thinking, "I'm going to get right with God after I finish college, or after I get married, or after I've 'lived' a little"—we're not guaranteed tomorrow. You could die tonight and face your Lord. How do you want to appear before Him? I want to hear, "Well done, good and faithful servant." Serving Him is the desire of my heart, which is now made flesh with God's law written on my mind. I am immovable. God is the one who set me free. He changed my heart and mind, does good things to and for me. He is immovable, and I am in Him. Are you?

Home Security System

Introduction

A Psalm of Ascents. Of Solomon. —Psalm 127

TODAY WE'RE GOING to begin to study one of the fifteen Psalms of Ascent said to be written by, about, or for King Solomon, the son of David and Bathsheba. You'll recall Solomon's visit from the Lord one night:

"God appeared to Solomon, and said to him, 'Ask! What shall I give you?' And Solomon said to God: 'You have shown great mercy to David my father, and have made me king in his place. Now, O Lord God, let Your promise to David my father be established, for You have made me king over a people like the dust of the earth in multitude. Now give me wisdom and knowledge . . . for who can judge this great people of Yours?' Then God said . . . : 'Because . . . you have not asked riches or wealth or honor or the life of your enemies, nor . . . long life—but have asked wisdom and knowledge for yourself, that you may judge My people over whom I have made you king—wisdom and knowledge are granted to you; and . . . riches and wealth and honor, such as none of the kings have had who were before you, nor shall any after you . . . '" (2 Chronicles 1:7-12).

And later, sadly: *"But King Solomon loved many foreign women . . . : of the Moabites, Ammonites, Edomites, Sidonians, and Hittites— . . . of whom the Lord had said to . . . Israel, 'You surely shall not intermarry with them, nor they with you. Surely they will turn away your hearts after their gods.' Solomon clung to these in love. And he had seven hundred wives, princesses, and three hundred concubines; and his wives turned away his heart. For . . . when Solomon was old . . . his wives turned his heart after other gods; and his heart was not loyal to the Lord his God, as was the heart of his father David"* (1 Kings 11:1-4).

Have you ever heard someone say, "Do as I say, not as I do"? Perhaps you've even offered advice to someone although you had failed to follow the same wisdom in a similar situation? Have you reminded others that "all things work together for good," and then needed to be reminded of it yourself? Solomon, blessed by God with incredible wisdom, is a case in point, because he didn't heed the counsel in the Psalm of Ascent above. We might say that he didn't implement his "home security system." The idea of a "system" is a set of connected things forming a complex whole, and in these verses the home is represented. Solomon failed to follow his own reliance of that "home security system." Our individual homes may share many things in common yet may be very distinct from one another. We have in common the same basic needs but to different degrees and in varying tastes. One thing that we all want within our homes is a sense of security—safety and peace.

Solomon also wrote, "*The perverse person is an abomination to the Lord, but His secret counsel is with the upright. The curse of the Lord is on the wicked, but He blesses the home of the just. Surely He scorns the scornful, but He gives grace to the humble. The wise shall inherit glory, but shame shall be a legacy of fools*" (Proverbs 3:32-35).

The three main features of our "home security system" in the psalm of Solomon concern protection, provision, and preparation, which all relate to the counsel of the Lord, His blessings, and His grace. The home security system that we'll be featuring through this psalm is the best on the "market." It has only two manufacturers, and we'll do some "product" comparison as we go along. Our model has some wonderful features, but keep this in mind as you examine the system offered by our competitor: "*He who troubles his own house will inherit the wind, and the fool will be servant to the wise of heart*" (Proverbs 11:29).

The system offered by the world can't protect, provide, or prepare our homes. It can only bring trouble into our house in all three of these areas. Let's not be like Solomon and fail to install the very home security system that we have recommended to others!

October 20

Under Warranty

[1]Unless the Lord builds the house, they labor in vain who build it; unless the Lord guards the city, they watchman stays awake in vain. —Psalm 127:1

NOTICE THE FIGURATIVE language in this verse. It is rich with meaning and promises of protection. The word "build" here means "establish" or "cause to continue," implying that the means through which our homes are established and protected is because the Lord is watching over them. As we continue with our illustration of the Home Security System, which we all need if we're to keep our homes safe in Christ, let's see what God has to say about our dwelling places: "*Therefore whoever hears these sayings of Mine, and does them, I will liken him to a wise man who built his house on the rock: and the rain descended, the floods came, and the winds blew and beat on that house; and it did not fall, for it was founded on the rock. 'But everyone who hears these sayings of Mine, and does not do them, will be like a foolish man who built his house on the sand: and the rain descended, the floods came, and the winds blew and beat on the that house; and it fell. And great was its fall.' And so it was, when Jesus had ended these sayings, that the people were astonished at His teaching, for He taught as one having authority, and not as the scribes"* (Matthew 7:24-29).

What is said in this psalm is that unless the Lord establishes and causes our homes to continue, our labors to build and watch over them are in vain. The only way to protect our homes (and I'm not just talking about the structure) is this: The most effective home security system is a home that honors the Word of God. Nothing can offer more protection from the storms and temptations of life than building your house (your life) on the Rock of His Word.

"As it was in the days of Noah, so it will be also in the days of the Son of Man: They ate, they drank, they married wives, they were given in marriage, until the day that Noah entered the ark, and the flood came and destroyed them all. Likewise, as it was in the days of Lot: they ate, they drank, they bought, they sold, they planted, they built; but on the day that Lot went out of Sodom it rained fire and brimstone from heaven and destroyed them all. Even so will it be in the day when the Son of Man is revealed" (Luke 17:26-30).

My illustration may seem a bit esoteric, but I hope you're getting the point. Far too many "homes" (think "lives") are built of inferior materials and protected by a "security system" installed by one who has a terrible reputation in the industry, although he promises great things. The system that you're depending on to keep you safe and happy offers freedom but delivers only bondage. In fact, those who have believed the promises of this competitor may discover from the Manufacturer of the true system that they've been victimized by a thief: *"The thief does not come except to steal, and to kill, and to destroy. [On the contrary] I have come that they may have life, and that they may have it more abundantly"* (John 10:10). Too many don't bother to read the fine print of the lying competitor's contract (which is also revealed as lies in the Bible) and thus they are unprotected from the liar's invasion into their homes, bringing emptiness, broken hearts, and lying, worthless, morally destructive conduct.

There's only one home security system that has never been breached or had a systems failure or overload, and that is the Word of God. It comes with an unbreakable warranty! Build your home on the Word by reading it regularly and speaking it often in your home. Let your prayers go before the Good Manufacturer, and your home will be protected from empty speech, vain lies, and moral destruction, and will instead operate in peace, love, and contentment, no matter what the "weather" out there in the world is like.

Free to You,
But Provided at Great Cost

²It is vain for you to rise up early, to sit up late, to eat the bread of sorrows; for so He gives His beloved sleep. —*Psalm 127:2*

FOR THE WORRIERS out there, notice above that God's "home security system" continues to function even as we sleep. It's so effective that you can sleep peacefully, knowing that your home is fully protected. Nor do we have to wonder how much it's going to cost us. The psalmist makes the point that to get up early and stay up late worrying about how to pay for equipment that can't guard your home, heart, and mind, means that you've chosen an idolatrous and useless system, while God gives to His beloved the gift of rest from our labors.

Proverbs 23:4-5 says, "*Do not overwork to be rich . . . , cease! Will you set your eyes on that which is not? For riches certainly make themselves wings; they fly away like an eagle toward heaven.*" The competition may offer luxurious vacations, fancy cars, success in the world—but when the storms come (and they will) their idolatrous false system is useless.

Take a look at a product review from the "Spiritual Consumer Reports" and compare the two security systems: "*Do not love the world or the things of the world. If anyone loves the world, the love of the Father is not in him. For all that is in the world—the lust of the flesh, the lust of the eyes, and the pride of life—is not of the Father but is of the world. And the world is passing away, and the lust of it; but he who does the will of God abides forever*" (1 John 2:15-17).

The world system is passing away, but God's system is secure forever. Which is the better product? Which provides better protection for your home? Which will let you sleep? The "lust of the flesh, lust of the eyes, pride of life," or doing the will of God? May I submit that rather than striving to pay for a security system that offers no security at all because it is passing away, you might consider this: God's system comes with free installation and no hidden fees. Now, understand that the system itself is not free, although it is free to you. It was bought at great cost: "*May the God of peace who brought up our Lord Jesus from the dead . . . through the blood of the everlasting covenant, make you complete in every good work to do His will . . . through Jesus Christ, to whom be glory forever and ever. Amen*" (Hebrews 13:20-21).

God's security system was paid for by the blood of His only Son, thus establishing an everlasting contract (covenant) with those who sign up for His plan. The competition may promise you the world, but the installation costs and hidden fees are astronomical. "*Jesus said to His disciples, 'If anyone desires to come after Me, let him deny himself, and take up his cross, and follow Me. For whoever desires to save his life will lose it, but whoever loses his life for My sake will find it. For what profit is it to a man if he gains the whole world, and loses his own soul? Or what will a man give in exchange for his soul? . . .'"* (Matthew 16:24-27).

The competition's plan may promise the world—and it might even come through on that—but the fine print asks for your soul. What are the conditions of the contract with God? *"The law of the Lord is perfect, converting the soul; the testimony of the Lord is sure, making wise the simple; the statutes of the Lord are right, rejoicing the heart; the commandment of the Lord is pure, enlightening the eyes; the fear of the Lord is clean, enduring forever; the judgments of the Lord are true and righteous altogether. . . . Moreover by them Your servant is warned, and in keeping them there is great reward"* (Psalm 19:7-11).

Warned, did that last verse say? In other words, through the Word of God and by the enlightenment of the Holy Spirit, we are warned of dangers that lie ahead if we go in a certain direction. The competition offers no such protection. Why invest in a system that can cost you a fortune, even your very life, when God will install one for free that comes with a lifetime guarantee and eternal rewards? The answer should be abundantly clear by now.

October 22

Satisfaction Guaranteed

³Behold, children are a heritage from the Lord , the fruit of the womb is a reward. ⁴Like arrows in the hand of a warrior, so are the children of one's youth. ⁵Happy is the man who has a quiver full of them; they shall not be ashamed, but shall speak with their enemies in the gate. —Psalm 127:3-5

IT'S A SHAME that many today view what God has deemed a heritage and a reward as a consequence and inconvenience, even denying the very right to life by aborting the fruit of the womb. That's one of the hidden costs associated with going against God and teaming up with the competition. In our verses today, the author likens the children of the household that has God's home security system in place to arrows in the hand of a warrior whose home that is filled with children is like a quiver filled with arrows, and he will not be ashamed (or afraid).

Asaph, regarding the importance of the preparation-for-the-future feature of God's system, wrote: *"Give ear, O people, to my law; . . . I will open my mouth in a parable . . . which we have heard and known, and our fathers have told us. We will not hide them from their children, telling to the generation to come the praises of the Lord, and His strength and His wonderful works that He has done. For He established a testimony in Jacob, and appointed a law in . . . that they should make them known to their children; that the generation to come might know them . . . that they may arise and declare them to their children, that they may set their hope in God, and not forget the works of God, but keep His commandments . . .* (Psalm 78:1-8).

Asaph says the system can't be inherited but must be installed in our children through product awareness. We need to tell them what God has done and will do, so that future generations are prepared to reach their peers through product knowledge and customer satisfaction testimonials about the supremacy of God's security system! It's a system that has never been marketed by Wall Street but has been offered for generations one at a time by satisfied customers who assure its continuance by transferring it on.

There are only two manufacturers of the types of home security systems of which we speak. One has a 100-percent success rate, and the other has a 100-percent failure rate. Sadly, the majority of consumers in the world choose the failed system, even some within the church. Children will often choose the system that was in their parent's home. Are our children being prepared to be arrows in the hand of warrior or defeated by an enemy at the gate? Nothing prepares your children for life better than teaching them the Word and the ways of God. They can face their enemies; they are like arrows in the hands of a warrior, and God rewards a home when children are taught about Him. What does the competition offer? *"Your adversary the devil walks about like a roaring lion, seeking whom he may devour"* (1 Peter 5:8).

I'll include here the old adage, "When you find a Bible that's falling apart, it's owned by a Christian who isn't." Homes are falling apart today because they've installed a worldly home security system. They have pursued things that money *can* buy, often at the expense of things that money cannot. Just because the other system is offered with promises of pleasure and success, remember that its manufacturer is an experienced con man who has been wrecking homes for a long time, leading people to believing that they are safe. He does it by false advertising (see Genesis 3:1-7). He destroyed the very first home on earth with the same false advertising he uses today: "Did God *really* say . . . ?"

Don't buy the lie! God's home security system is the only one that protects, provides, and prepares your home—satisfaction guaranteed!

Courageous Fear

Introduction

A Song of Degrees—Psalm 128

WE CONTINUE our journey with the pilgrims who are ascending to Jerusalem, and we cannot miss the connection between our own lives in Christ as we ourselves continue on our trek toward the New Jerusalem! This is identified as a Psalm of Zion, and the main subject of it is the fear of the Lord. *"The fear of the Lord is the beginning of wisdom; a good understanding have all those who do His commandments. His praise endures forever"* (Psalm 111:10). Proverbs 9 reads, *"The fear of the Lord is the beginning of wisdom, and the knowledge of the Holy One is understanding"* (Proverbs 9:10).

The character of this psalm is one of wisdom and of Zion, but the subject of the benefits and blessings on the family who fears the Lord along with the promise to them of reaching their destination is for all of us.

First Corinthians 3:18 tells us, *"Let no one deceive himself. If anyone among you seems to be wise in this age, let him become a fool that he may become wise."* In other words, life in the Lord may be defined as living the exact opposite of the way the world tells us we should live. We may well become fools in the eyes of the world but wise in the ways of the Lord. The paradoxes continue: We must humble ourselves if we're to be exalted. We give that we might receive. We must die in order to live. Thus our title, "Courageous Fear."

When Christians mention the "fear of the Lord," many perceive this in a negative way. In fact, the postmodern "seeker" today isn't searching for a God who is a fearful being in the case that they should "fall into His hands." Many are looking for a God who just grants their wishes—a genie instead of Jehovah, or maybe a God who is indifferent regarding evil, who cares nothing about how we act, and who is happy to let everyone into heaven.

Even within the church, Christians become uncomfortable when thinking about *fearing* God. They prefer to picture Him as a gentle, permissive Father, and Jesus as our understanding "buddy."

Let's examine this honestly for a moment. *Is* the "fear of the Lord" a part of the Christian life? Should we teach it in our homes? Is it part of the New Testament teaching? One thing we do know: it takes courage today to live in a world where we're looked down upon for recognizing that we are to fear the Lord, but in the end, God's rewards will make it all worthwhile. We may be mocked, ridiculed, and challenged, but the Bible assures us of this: *"Be strong and of good courage; do not be afraid, nor be dismayed, for the Lord your God is with you wherever you go"* (Joshua 1:8-9).

As we continue our journey with these pilgrims, we will find the blessings in fearing the Lord in our labors and in our lives, and we will begin to understand the impact of our legacy as we make our way to Zion to be forever with the Lord!

"Heigh-Ho, Heigh-Ho, It's off to Work We Go"

[1]Blessed is every one who fears the Lord, who walks in His ways. [2]When you eat the labor of your hands, you shall be happy, and it shall be well with you. —Psalm 128:1-2

THESE FIRST VERSES speak of fear of the Lord and joyful labor. "Fear" means "to be afraid" or to have "moral reverence." If we fear the Lord, we should also fear becoming irreverent in our jobs and in our lives, realizing the poor legacy we would leave. Our founding fathers described the United States as a people endowed by our Creator with certain unalienable rights, including life, liberty, and the pursuit of happiness; but a quick glance at the news reveals that few Americans have been successful in that.

This would have to mean that people aren't really following God's instructions for happiness. What does He tell us should be our attitude? *"Whatever you do, do it heartily, as to the Lord and not to men, knowing that from the Lord you will receive the reward of the inheritance; for you serve the Lord Christ"* (Col 3:23-24). But it appears that many have decided that "what we do," and not *"how we do* it," is the key to happiness. God tells us that as believers who serve the Lord first of all, *whatever we do* we are to do it heartily as unto Him.

Obedience will always be blessed, and blessings begin with fearing the Lord, which will show itself by our walking in His ways. This will resulting in contentment when we eat the labor of our hands.

Here's something to consider: *Work is meant to feed you, not fulfill you.* I'm not saying that we shouldn't have a sense of fulfillment in our labors, but I am talking about a point of identity—what satisfies our life and our heart's desires? Listen, God isn't anti-education, anti-success, or anti-wealth. But He is anti-"finding your identity" through any of those things! In fact, fearing the Lord and walking in His ways makes the fruit of your labors, no matter what those labors may be, a source of happiness and success—or, as our psalmist writes, that "it shall be well with you."

The fact is, far too many people are looking for a sense of "wholeness," a sense of fulfillment, from their labors, when those things are only truly found in serving the Lord. "*Do not overwork to be rich; . . . cease! . . . For riches certainly make themselves wings; they fly away like an eagle toward heaven*" (23:4-5). Paul wrote: "*Godliness with contentment is great gain. . . . [H]aving food and clothing, with these we shall be content. Those who desire to get rich fall into a temptation and a snare, and into many foolish and harmful lusts which drown men in destruction and perdition. For the love of money is a root of all kinds of evil . . .*" (1 Tim 6:6-10).

The word "contentment" means "A perfect condition of life in which no aid or support is needed; sufficiency of the necessities of life, and a mind contented with its lot." We need to ask ourselves some serious questions at this point. Do we truly believe that we have all we need if we have Christ in our lives? Is His grace sufficient for us? Is our mind content with the things we have? Or are we "chasing the dream," thinking that at the end of the pursuit lies something that we've been thus far able to attain: true happiness?

Do you realize that work is a source of provision and not your true identity? Do you understand that no matter what we do, if we do it as *unto the Lord*, we will always find blessings in our lives? Your job title may be "Dr." It may be District Attorney or Professor or something else. But your true calling as a disciple of Christ is to preach the gospel to every creature, and your identity is in Him, not in your career! Your *true* calling is as a servant of God. It's a good idea to stop and search our hearts in these matters from time to time, and if we gain a godly perspective on working for a living and working for the Lord, we can truly head off for both jobs singing in our hearts!

October 25

A Haven from the Storm

> ³Your wife shall be like a fruitful vine in the very heart of your house, your children like olive plants all around your table. ⁴Behold, thus shall the man be blessed who fears the Lord. —*Psalm 128:3-4*

WE COULD PARAPHRASE these verses like this: "Walk in the ways of the Lord, and the fruit of your labors will be a happy home." In these verses, we see that when the people in the house fear the Lord, the wife, who is the heart of the home, will be fruitful in the things that make the home a refuge. If children are present, they will be reflections of their parents, much like sprouts from a mature olive tree.

We also see that the blessing of the home ultimately depends upon the man who fears the Lord. Proverbs 18:22 reads, *"He who finds a wife finds a good thing, and obtains favor from the Lord."* Men, did you ever stop to consider that when your wife feels like you see her as an expression of God's favor upon you, the heart of your home will bear fruit all around your table? I've sometimes heard people say that in a marriage God takes two people's decisions to marry and makes it work. I don't believe that, although I believe that God is involved in every Christian marriage. I believe that He gave me *my* wife—not just *a* wife but the wife that He had for me. She is strong where I am weak, compassionate where I am stern. I didn't marry from happenstance or coincidence, but I obtained favor from the Lord when my wife, Teri, and I said, "I do!"

Peter wrote, *"Husbands . . . dwell with them with understanding, giving honor to the wife, as to the weaker vessel, and as being heirs together of the grace of life, that your prayers may not be hindered"* (1 Pet 3:7). Husbands, do you practice courageous fear at home? Your home will be blessed if you do. Your wife will blossom as the heart of the home, and your children will be like olive plants around your table. In fact, a home that fears the Lord will be a safe haven in an evil world.

Let me ask some direct questions here: What's more important for you to teach your children: how to win souls or how to play soccer? (You know the answer, but is that really what receives the most attention?) If your child were asked, how would he or she answer that question?

Remember the Bible illustration of Jesus washing the disciples' feet? He wasn't instituting foot washing. He was offering an example of how to take the position of the lowest of household slaves, washing the dirty feet of the guests, saying to the disciples, "You'll be blessed if you follow My example."

Husbands, love your wives like Christ does the church, giving Himself for her. Wives, respect your husband as head of the home. Let your God-fearing home become a safe haven from the storms of life in this wicked world. Our homes need to be places where there's no fear that the children will be exposed to pornography, where wives feel safe, and where husbands can enjoy seeing the fruit of courageous fear around the table. This can be true as well for the single home! Our home should be a haven where, in a world that dishonors God, God is honored by all that takes place there. It should be a place where the Lord is sought first, and the other necessary things of life are added unto us by Him. There's no greater benefit to your home than the *fear of the Lord*. (See Psalm 25:14.)

Your home can become a haven that is blessed by the counsel of the Lord and a place of intimate relationship with Him. Creating a haven from the storm begins with courageous fear and will yield a safe place for all who enter it in the midst of an evil world.

The Agony of Disobedience

5The Lord bless you out of Zion, and may you see the good of Jerusalem all the days of your life. —*Psalm 128:5*

WE'VE BEEN LOOKING at the blessings of courageous fear in our labors and in our home life, and now we see the potential legacy that is created when we live in the fear of the Lord. These pilgrims were promised that they would see the good of Jerusalem and be blessed all the days of their lives.

In Proverbs we read some sound advice: *"My son, do not forget my law, but let your heart keep my commands; for length of days and long life and peace they will add to you. Let not mercy and truth forsake you; bind them around your neck, write on them on the tablet of your heart, and so find favor and high esteem in the sight of God and man. Trust in the Lord with all your heart, and lean not on your own understanding; in all your ways acknowledge Him, and He shall direct your paths. Do not be wise in your own eyes; fear the Lord and depart from evil. It will be health to your flesh, and strength to your bones. Honor the Lord with your possessions, and with the firstfruits of all your increase; so your barns will be filled with plenty, and your vats will overflow with new wine"* (3:10).

I don't know about you, but one thing I can say for certain as I look back beyond the last 35 years or so of my life is that disobedience to the will of God is hard on your health! And these verses are saying the same thing. There are great blessings to be had in living a life pleasing to the Lord. A life that is lived for God is free from the consequences of disobedience, the shame and fear of being caught and exposed, and a weakened immune system from the anxiety and stress of hiding your shame.

I heard a story once about a country sheriff who had an uncanny ability to discern whether a person was innocent or guilty. He said, "It's simple! I watch them sleep. The innocent person tosses and turns all night, distraught over being falsely accused. The guilty person sleeps like a rock because endless nights and days with the fear of being captured have now come to an end."

Make no mistake, friends. God sees our hearts. All the time. And He has provided relief for us from the guilt and shame and stress of hiding our sin! David, who understood possibly better than most what it's like to live in despair caused by his own sin and attempting to keep that sin hidden, also understands the *blessed* relief of finally having it exposed! *"Blessed is he whose transgression is forgiven, whose sin is covered. Blessed is the man to whom the Lord does not impute iniquity, and in whose spirit there is no deceit. When I kept silent, my bones grew old through my groaning all the day long. For day and night Your hand was heavy upon me; my vitality was turned into the drought of summer"* (Psalm 32:1-4). David, who had lived through this shame, says, in essence, "When I lived in unconfessed sin, it was horrible, and I felt like an old man, groaning all day long."

That's no way to live! God wants better things for us! Being blessed "out of Zion" (v. 5, at top) refers to heaven's blessings on us—spiritual blessings in heavenly places. "Seeing the good of Jerusalem" refers to the good things of God in this life, as in the prosperity and success that we read about in Joshua. This is what our Father desires for us to experience. What is missing today, as we've talked about, is the *fear* of the Lord. Our lives are truly in His hands. His desires for us are that we would turn to Him with everything, good, bad, and ugly, and let Him wash us, purify us, and strengthen us to follow His lead as we head toward the future that He has in store for those who love Him!

October 27

Do You Have the Courage to Fear the Lord?

⁶Yes, may you see your children's children. —Psalm 128:6

THE PRONOUNCED blessing at the end of this chapter regarding peace upon Israel, seeing the good of Jerusalem all the days of your life, and seeing your grandchildren, speaks to us of a legacy that is exclusive to the Christian and gives us our final truth in this psalm: no one will impact the world more for good than a person with the courage to fear the Lord.

A lot of people in our times claim that some athlete or actor has impacted their life in a major or positive way. That's nice. But can you name one *first-century* athlete or actor? Yet everyone has heard of Noah and Moses, mighty men of God who feared the Lord.

Some may admire philosophers like Socrates and Confucius, but most people can't tell you one thing they said. Conversely, nearly everyone knows the Golden Rule from the Sermon on the Mount. In fact, most people, including atheists and agnostics, know the story of Daniel in the lions' den, or David's defeat of Goliath, or have heard of John the Baptist and the apostles Peter and Paul.

Why might this be? Because all of them lived with the courage to fear the Lord! In the Book of Acts, we read that many of the Jews who did not believe that Christ was the Messiah became jealous of the attention the disciples were getting, so they gathered a mob, set the city in an uproar, and *"attacked the house of Jason, and sought to bring [the disciples] out to the people. But when they did not find them, they dragged Jason and some brethren to the rulers of the city. . . ."* What were the charges against them? *"These who have turned the world upside down have come here, too"* (Acts 17:5-6).

I love that! What a legacy! What Christian doesn't long to have that as the description of his or her life: someone who had turned the world upside down? In truth, folks, we can and we should, if we only have the courage to fear the Lord when others call it foolishness.

It's imperative that we train up our children in the ways of the Lord and not of the world if we hope to leave a legacy of good behind us. We must strive to make our homes safe havens in the midst of great evil that is growing ever greater; our homes should be places of purity, where righteousness and holiness are the governing influences over all that happens within those walls.

Then we can have an impact on those who have ears to hear and eyes to see and who are willing to be influenced for good, hopefully carrying the banner to those who come after them. *"Therefore be very courageous to keep and to do all that is written in the Book of the Law of Moses, lest you turn aside from it to the right hand or to the left. . . . One man of you shall chase a thousand, for the Lord your God is He who fights for you, as He promised you. Therefore, take careful heed to yourselves that you love the Lord your God"* (Josh 23:6-11).

I want to be used of the Lord for good, for His kingdom, and for His glory. I want my name to be associated with those who "turn the world upside down," who withstand evil, and, having done all, to continue to stand in dark days to come (see Eph 6:13). If we're to do that, we must be very careful that we love the Lord our God above all else. How do we do that? Jesus said, *"He who has My commandments and keeps them, it is he who loves Me. And he who loves Me will be loved by My Father, and I will love him and manifest Myself to him. . . . If anyone loves Me, he will keep My word; and My Father will love him, and We will come to him and make Our home with him"* (Jn 14:21-23).

We must have the courage to fear God if we want to have an impactful life. There's no other way. Some may choose to go after the things of the world, but "as for me and my house, we will serve the Lord."

October 28

Wait Watchers

Introduction

A Song of Degrees—Psalm 130

MOST OF US HATE to wait, but we've learned over the past months that God hears and answers every prayer in one of three ways: He may say, "yes"; He may say, "no"; or He may say, "wait." As we go through this psalm we'll be reminded of various times and seasons of life when we can do nothing but wait. The author of Psalm 69:3 wrote, "*I am weary with my crying; my throat is dry; my eyes fail while I wait for my God.*"

We all have times when we find ourselves waiting on the Lord to answer our personal prayers. We may be praying about things that are causing pain and sorrow in our lives, or times where we cry out to God, feeling like we desperately need help from a situation where someone is causing us harm, only to realize that He is telling us to wait. Proverbs 20:22 reads, "*Do not say, 'I will recompense evil'; wait for the Lord, and He will save you.*"

Wait. It sounds easy, but it isn't. How many times do we finding ourselves looking around at the world and say, "Lord! Things can't possibly get any worse! They are calling good 'evil,' and evil 'good.' Please, come and get us out of here!" And He tells us in our hearts, "I will, but you must wait."

As our pilgrims in these verses made their journey to Jerusalem, quoting the Psalms of Ascent along the way, we know that they must have encountered difficulties, had family squabbles, and found the path difficult, narrow, and steep. There would have been dangerous encounters as they traveled, and the journey may have seemed like it was taking far too long. In another of the Psalms of Ascent we read that even though Jerusalem was in view, the people had to wait before entering the city. In another we read that the people had arrived in the city but were made to wait before they could make their way to the Temple Mount.

We frequently find ourselves in situations similar to those, and our manner in response to this could probably use a lot of improvement. Therefore, I've decided to sign us all up for a "group plan" to help us while we are waiting. The name of the plan, as you may read at the top of today's message, is "Wait Watchers." If truth be told, we're all pretty good at grumbling while we wait. Sometimes we experience doubt and discouragement as time passes by without an answer or a release from the waiting time. Sometimes, we've even pouted a bit, while we wait, and that's why I've titled this section "Wait Watchers."

Over the next few days I'll be giving you four things to consider as we make our way through the last couple of months of this year and will likely encounter times of waiting—two of them are things to watch *out* for and two are things to watch *for* when the answer to your prayers is "Wait." As we proceed, do cling to this verse, especially when you begin to feel discouraged: "*We know that all things work together for good to those who love God, to those who are the called according to His purpose*" (Romans 8:28).

I'm pretty sure we all know that between "all things" and "work together for good" usually comes a period of having to wait, and it may seem to be far longer than we would like. Consider the fact that we live in an age of instant gratification. We have express lines at the grocery store, we microwave some of our dinners, cutting the wait time from an hour to five minutes. Theme parks now have "fast passes" so their patrons don't have to . . . well . . . wait! Our attitude is often like the old cartoon character who said, "I want instant gratification, and I want it *now*!"

Rather than being "wait grumblers, doubters, or pouters," let's join Wait Watchers and renew our strength during those times of waiting on the Lord!

October 29

Just You Wait!

Out of the depths have I cried unto thee, O Lord. ²Lord, hear my voice: let thine ears be attentive to the voice of my supplications. —Psalm 130:1-2

WHAT SHOULD our response be when we're put in the position of waiting on the Lord? In verse one, the author is crying out from *the depths*. That implies sinking. Sinking takes time. And time means waiting. To paraphrase the psalmist, "I have sunk to the depths, Lord, and I have cried out to You all the way down! Hear my voice and answer my earnest prayers."

Look at Christ in the Garden of Gethsemane: " . . . *He knelt down and prayed, saying, 'Father, if it is Your will, take this cup way from Me; nevertheless not My will, but Yours, be done.' Then an angel appeared to Him . . . strengthening Him. And being in agony, He prayed more earnestly. Then His sweat became like great drops of blood falling down to the ground*" (Luke 22:41-44). Truly, no one can ever say that they've suffered during a period of waiting in the way that Jesus did. He knew what lay before Him, and even though He was the second Person of the Godhead, He had to endure in real time and with real emotions the horror that lay before Him. So He continued to "pray more earnestly." And He certainly wasn't praying a "Now I lay me down to sleep" kind of prayer, or any other memorized lines. This was an earnest, "great drops of blood" kind of prayer that came from the depths of His soul.

And the writer of our psalm today has also been waiting on God's answer to his prayer, and though still in the depths, he cries out to the Lord, the only One who can deliver him. This brings us to one of those points we mentioned yesterday that we should watch *for* while waiting, and that is this: *Do not allow waiting to cause you to grow weary in prayer.* Some may ask, "What's the use of praying, since God is sovereign, and provision, deliverance, or healing will come in His time, not ours, and according to His will? What's the point?"

The answer is simple. First of all, God *tells* us to pray. Look at these examples: "*Hear, O Lord, when I cry with my voice! Have mercy also upon me and answer me.*

When You said, 'Seek My face,' my heart said to You, 'Your face, Lord, I will seek" (Ps 27:7-8). And, Jesus speaking: *"Ask, and it will be given to you; seek, and you will find; knock, and it will be opened to you. For everyone who asks receives, and he who seeks finds, and to him who knocks it will be opened"* (Mat 7:7-8). And again, *"Rejoice always, pray without ceasing, in everything give thanks; for this is the will of God in Christ Jesus for you"* (1 Thes 5:16-18). So we see that we're to pray because God tells us to, and He tells us not to stop even when we feel like we are sinking to the depths.

Another thing that we wait watchers need to consider is this: For some of us, sadly, if we didn't have problems and never had to wait, we might not even have a prayer life. Friends, we need to pray without ceasing. In other words, we're to be people of prayer at all times. During times of waiting, when we feel like we're sinking, or we feel like God is taking too long in delivering us, or providing for us, or healing us, even then we must never allow ourselves to stop crying out to the Lord.

We must guard our hearts from growing weary of praying during those times of silence. It is crucial both to our own wellbeing and to our relationship with our heavenly Father that we continue to cry out to Him even during the darkest of nights. He *does* hear our cries, and He *does* know our hearts. We're promised that He will not allow us to be tried or tempted beyond what we're able, but that He himself will provide the deliverance (1 Cor 10:13). But deliverance will come in His time and not ours. Can you trust Him enough to wait? He will rescue you, but many times we must discipline ourselves to *wait for it*, trusting that He knows what is best.

October 30

While You're Waiting (Part 1)

³If You, Lord, should mark iniquities, O Lord, who could stand? ⁴But there is forgiveness with You, that You may be feared. —Psalm 130:3-4

—

TODAY'S VERSES give us something to "watch for" while we are waiting, and it's something that we should always keep in mind. As we wait on the Lord for His answer to our prayers, often we will be led to examine our lives a little more deeply.

"If I regard iniquity in my heart, the Lord will not heart" (Psalm 66:18). Hold up! Can it be that sometimes we're the cause of being in this position of having to wait? What is the Lord trying to tell us? It's natural and good for our minds to go here when the answer to our prayers doesn't appear to be forthcoming. *Have I done something wrong? Have I displeased God in some way?* The Hebrew word translated "regard" in Psalm 66 means to approve, to enjoy, or to look upon with favor. If

you've been looking on sin of any kind with favor, enjoying it, or even approving of it, in your life or in the lives of others, the Lord will not hear your prayer, and you need to repent. That may seem obvious, but it needs to be considered.

In most cases, however, God isn't making us wait due to some sin in our lives but more often it has to do with helping us to grow in our trust and faith in Him. Remember this example? *"Now when evening came, His disciples went down to the sea toward Capernaum. And it was already day, and Jesus had not come to them. Then the sea arose because a great wind was blowing. So when they had rowed about three or four miles, they saw Jesus walking on the sea and drawing near the boat; and they were afraid. But He said to them, 'It is I; do not be afraid.' Then they willingly received Him into the boat, and immediately the boat was at the land where they were going"* (John 6:16-21).

In chapter six of Mark's gospel, we learn a little more of the story. Jesus came to them walking on the water during the fourth watch of the night *just before dawn*. He also mentions that when Jesus got into the boat, the sea was instantly calmed. Putting these two versions of that night together, we want to consider a few things. It was *evening* when they set out, and the Bible tells us that while Jesus was still on the shore, He saw them straining at the oars (Mark 6:48). And yet He didn't go to them immediately but waited until it was almost daylight!

Although we can't try to read their thoughts, I know what I would probably be thinking: *Why did Jesus send us into this?* And after arriving safely on shore after He had come walking on the water, I would likely be wondering, *Why did He wait until the last minute and let us row against the wind all night for miles?*

But stop right there! We need to combat that kind of thinking, fellow wait watchers, and we must watch for and remember that when the end of waiting comes, also comes the end of struggle and fear. Always, always remember: your greatest need has already been met. Our psalm today states, "If You, Lord, should mark (meaning *preserve* or *keep* or *heed*), iniquities, O Lord, who could stand? But there is forgiveness with You." Hallelujah!

To paraphrase, if human imperfections and failures would keep us from God, no one would have the right to stand before Him, but He's not like that. He forgives us, and he doesn't hold onto our sins. Saints this is something that we can hold onto, especially during those times when we find ourselves falling apart at the seams and help appears to be far away. We have to guard against our tendency to "unravel" when waiting seems especially wearisome. The psalmist checks his own heart here, saying, in essence, "Lord, even if I messed up and my circumstances are my fault, there is forgiveness in You, and I can still come before You!" What a blessing to know that we can always call upon Him, cling to Him, and trust Him, even while we're still waiting for the light at the end of the tunnel.

October 31

While You're Waiting (Part 2)

*[3]If You, Lord, should mark iniquities, O Lord, who
could stand? [4]But there is forgiveness with You,
that You may be feared.* —Psalm 130:3-4

FOR YOU AND ME, these verses serve to keep our countenances in check as we remember that what we need more than anything else in life—more than the answer to any prayer or cry from the depths—is God's forgiveness.

Remember, God has already said "yes" to your greatest need—the forgiveness of your sins. He didn't say, "Sorry, your sins are too great." He didn't say, "Nope, you have to wait. You haven't earned it yet." When you were truly convicted of your own sinfulness and cried from the depths of your heart, "Forgive me, Lord, for I am a sinner," He said, "Done!"

Look at the mercy of our Lord: "*You gave them bread from heaven for their hunger, and brought them water out of the rock for their thirst, and told them to go in to possess the land which You had sworn to give them. But they and our fathers acted proudly, hardened their necks, and did not heed Your commandments. They refused to obey, and they were not mindful of Your wonders that You did among them. But they hardened their necks, and in their rebellion they appointed a leader to return to their bondage. But You are God, ready to pardon, gracious and merciful, slow to anger, abundant in kindness, and did not forsake them*" (Nehemiah 9:15-17).

And now, when your cries are that you thirst or are hungry or in need of help of any kind, remember this: when God's answer is "Wait," don't allow your thoughts to run away with you and your emotions to rule your mind and fill you with doubt, despair, or feelings of being abandoned by Him. Never forget that *your greatest need has already been met!*

If you said yes to Jesus, He said yes to you. You're *forgiven!* This means that you are His forever and ever. That should create in us the moral reverence that we read about earlier and that we see here in verse four above. When doubts begin to creep in that maybe He doesn't really love you or He doesn't care or hear; when you feel like maybe you've messed up too badly and He doesn't want you anymore; when you begin to wonder if maybe you're even saved at all—then you need to surrender once again to His loving arms.

If you've truly received the Lord Jesus Christ as your Savior, then let these words assure you of His great love for you: "*For I am persuaded that neither death nor life, nor angels nor principalities nor powers, nor things present nor things to come, nor height nor depth, nor any other created thing, shall be able to separate us from the love of God which is in Christ Jesus our Lord"* (Romans 8:38-39).

What wonderful news! So despite your present struggles, the ultimate battle has already been fought and won, and now, while you're still waiting for your present situation to be settled, solved, or removed, rest in His love and know that you are safe in His arms, no matter what is going on in your life.

NOVEMBER

Whistle While You Wait . . .
or Work, or Praise

> [5]I wait for the Lord, my soul waits, and in His word I do hope. [6]My soul waits for the Lord more than those who watch for the morning—yes, more than those who watch for the morning. —*Psalm 130:5-6*

WELL, FELLOW Wait Watchers, in these verses today we're given some pretty powerful reminders of what else to "watch out for" as we wait. Remember when we recently read Isaiah 40:31? *"But those who wait on the Lord shall renew their strength; they shall mount up with wings like eagles, they shall run and not be weary, they shall walk and not faint."* This verse alone establishes for us that waiting doesn't need to be a negative experience. It can actually turn out to be a productive time in our lives, bearing the fruit of renewed strength, mounting up with wings, running without wearying, and walking without fainting.

We've all experienced the unpleasantness of pushing ourselves past what we're usually able to do and reaching the point where we felt like we were going to pass out. Sometimes waiting on God can feel like this. To wait just one more minute seems impossible.

The word "wait," as it's used in Isaiah 40 above, can mean "active hope," which fits nicely with the idea of mounting up, running, and walking without fainting or growing weary. But the word "wait" as it's used in our text (though the same word in Hebrew) fits best with the primary definition of it, which means to bind together. The psalmist is saying, "I am waiting for the Lord from the depths of my soul and binding myself together with His Word."

The verse about the watchman waiting for the morning takes our minds back to what we saw when Jesus waited to come to the frantic disciples in the boat until the fourth watch of the night, between three o'clock AM and six o'clock AM, a time

associated with sayings like, "It's always darkest before dawn." So our psalm is saying, "It's been a long night, getting longer, and a dark season of difficulty. Like the
watchman awaiting the morning sun, I look to Your word for my hope."

So the next thing for us to be aware of while waiting for God's response to our
prayer is to keep this in mind: Waiting is the worst time for spiritual inactivity or
apathy. Did you catch that? If we combine the meanings of the word "wait" that
we read just above, we see that active hope is found by binding ourselves to the
Word—not just reading it, or even heeding it, but doing it. "*Therefore, since we are
receiving a kingdom which cannot be shaken, let us have grace, by which we may
serve God acceptably with reverence and godly fear*" (Hebrews 12:28). We need to
guard fiercely against pouting and whining and telling God that we're not going to
do another thing until we get an answer from Him or at least an explanation of why
this is happening. Note that the verse in Hebrews tells us that we're to continue to
serve Him acceptably with reverence and godly fear while we're waiting.

Satan will try to exploit our emotions and inflame our doubts. He wants to
isolate us and keep us from doing anything productive, telling us not to read the
Word (which is the primary place where hope can be found), and convincing us
to stop serving God until provision arrives. But listen, wait watchers, waiting on
the Lord and serving the Lord are not mutually exclusive. We can, and should, do
both! Think about it: under normal circumstances when you're waiting for something to happen—maybe just the end of the workday—what makes the day go by
faster? Doing nothing or keeping busy? The same applies as you wait for the Lord.
Maintain an active hope by binding yourself to His Word. So while you're waiting,
continue to seek His face, pray, concentrate on the beautiful attributes of God and
the things for you are thankful. Beware of spiritual inactivity—continue to pray,
read, gather together with other believers and avoid apathy. It's all part of the Wait
Watchers plan!

November 2

When the Wait Is Over

> [7]Let Israel hope in the Lord: for with the Lord there is mercy, and with
> him is plenteous redemption. [8]And he shall redeem Israel from all his
> iniquities. —*Psalm 130:7-8*

THE ORIGINAL context of this psalm isn't known, but the tradition of reading
these verses as the pilgrims headed to Jerusalem is. As we've followed the cries of
the psalmist, we know that an enemy threat was the likely cause of their prayers.
And even though we don't know the source of concern, the psalmist prays for Israel

to hope in the Lord, whose mercy and redemption is promised to all who trust in Him, including deliverance from iniquities!

The apostle Paul wrote: "*At my first defense no one stood with me, but all forsook me. May it not be charged against them. But the Lord stood with me and strengthened me, so that the message might be preached fully through me, and that all the Gentiles might hear. Also I was delivered out of the mouth of the lion. And the Lord will deliver me from every evil work and preserve me for His heavenly kingdom . . .*" (2 Timothy 4:16-18). By Paul's comment, "At my first defense," we know that there was some waiting involved on his part. Whether the "mouth of the lion" was literal or not is irrelevant in light of the fact that God is able to deliver us from every evil and preserve us for His kingdom.

We've now arrived at the concluding truth for our Wait Watchers meetings: *Every time of waiting should be approached with a spirit of expectancy.* Most of us have been through seasons of waiting, feeling like nothing would ever change. Nothing would get better. The wrong against us would never be made right, and God would never change the answer from "wait" to a solution. Can you justify those "feelings" from Scripture? How did Paul view such times? "*Finally, there is laid up for me the crown of righteousness, which the Lord, the righteous Judge, will give to me on that Day, and not to me only but also to all who have loved His appearing*" (2 Tim 4:8). And, "*The grace of God that brings salvation has appeared to all men, teaching us that, denying ungodliness and worldly lusts, we should live soberly, righteously, and godly in the present age, looking for the blessed hope and glorious appearing of our great God and Savior Jesus Christ, who gave Himself for us, that He might redeem us from every lawless deed and purify for Himself His own special people, zealous for good works*" (Titus 2:11-14).

How will we rise up to meet Jesus in the air? Are the wrongs done against us going to matter? Are those times of waiting going to be on our minds as we look at the face of our Savior? One day, at the glorious appearing of our Lord Jesus Christ, everything else will fade away: the check in the mail that never came, the apology from one who betrayed you, the injustice that was never settled. Meanwhile, we should face every period of waiting with the expectant hope of mercy and ultimate redemption. That should give us the impetus needed to do as Jesus instructed us in Luke 12:35-38: "*Let your waist be girded and your lamps burning; and . . . be like men who wait for their master . . . that when he comes and knocks, they may open to him immediately. Blessed are those servants whom the master will find watching. . . . I say to you that he will gird himself and have them sit down to eat, and will come and serve them. And if he should . . . find them so, blessed are those servants.*"

Friends, Jesus is coming! The fact that we think He should have come before we rowed most of the night through the storms of life won't even be a fleeting memory at that time. He's coming to get us! Until then, watch how you wait, not as "wait grumblers," "wait doubters," or "wait pouters." He is going to answer our prayers, whether by "yes," "no," or "wait." And one glorious day, all of our waiting will be over. In that day, we'll no longer be wait watchers but will find ourselves rejoicing in the presence of the Lord Jesus as we sit with Him at the Marriage Supper of the Lamb!

November 3

The Jews, Jerusalem, and Jesus

Introduction

A Psalm of Degrees—Psalm 132

CHRISTIANS are pretty much in agreement that we're living in the last of the last days. For any who don't understand that statement, see how Paul described what would take place as we near the time of the end: *"In the last days perilous times will come: for men will be lovers of themselves . . . of money, boasters, proud, blasphemers, disobedient . . . unthankful, unholy, unloving, unforgiving, slanderers, without self-control, brutal, despisers of good, traitors, headstrong, haughty, lovers of pleasure . . . having a form of godliness but denying its power"* (2 Tim 3:1-5). A careful reading of those verses makes it clear that the character defects of the last days are clearly seen today! We read, *"God, who . . . spoke in time past to the fathers by the prophets, has in these last days spoken to us by His Son, . . . appointed heir of all things . . ."* (Heb 1:1-2). The last days characterized here and foretold by God are approaching a climax.

God's own words about these times are recorded: *"I will make Jerusalem a cup of drunkenness to all the surrounding peoples, when they lay siege against Judah and Jerusalem. . . . I will make Jerusalem a very heavy stone for all peoples; all who would heave it away will surely be cut in pieces, though all nations of the earth are gathered against it"* (Zec 12:1-3).

We also know that we're in the last days because, along with the multitude of signs that reveal this, we also see the world gathered together against Jerusalem, seeking to divide the city and the nation of God's chosen people, the Jews. In January 2017, seventy nations gathered in Paris for the purpose of determining the future of Israel and Palestine. UNESCO, the United Nations Educational and Scientific and Cultural Organization said that it strongly condemns "Israeli aggressions and illegal measures against the freedom of worship and Muslims' access to their holy site, Al Aqsa Mosque" and "firmly deplores the continuous storming" of the mosque compound by "Israeli right-wing extremists and uniformed forces." Pope Francis recently welcomed Mahmoud Abbas to the Vatican, celebrating the Embassy for the

Palestinian State. Israel, and Jerusalem specifically, has taken center stage of world events in recent years, a good sign that our redemption is nigh. Many in the church itself are either unclear concerning the nation of Israel or actively oppose them.

The content of our psalm seems to be that the pilgrims are now inside the City of Jerusalem. The subject, as you see in the title above, is the Jews, Jerusalem, and Jesus. One note: although we don't find the name "Yeshua" (Jesus) in these verses, nor the name Jerusalem, nor "Jews," we do find the name Anointed, or Messiah, and Zion, a city chosen by God for His dwelling place, and we see the promise from God made to the Jews implied in verse one as a plea offered to the Lord by the words, "Remember David." This triad of "J"s is pivotal if we're to understand how close to then end of time we really are. The author of the book of Daniel was a Jew. The Holy City is Jerusalem, and the anointed Most Holy One is Jesus.

Please read Daniel 9:24 for a better understanding of the incredible biblical timeframe in which we now live. How many seven-year periods were determined for the Jews? The Bible itself tells us this: On March 14, 445 BC, a command was given to Nehemiah to rebuild the torn-down wall around Jerusalem. Sixty-nine seven-year periods later, 173,880 days total, Jesus rode into Jerusalem as Messiah, and a week later he was killed, exactly as foretold. If the first 69 "weeks" are for God's people, His city, and Messiah, can the seventieth week be nullified or forfeited? Are the Jewish people excluded from the seventieth week? No! We will be learning about three particular "J"s: the Jews, Jerusalem, and Jesus, and all have unfinished business to take care of that will last for one seven-day week of years!

November 4

Jerusalem Forever

¹Lord, remember David and all his afflictions; ²how he . . . vowed to the Mighty One of Jacob: ³". . . I will not go into the chamber of my house . . . ⁴I will not give slumber or sleep to my eyelids, ⁵until I find . . . a dwelling place for the Mighty One of Jacob." . . . We heard of it in Ephrathah. . . . ⁷Let us go into His tabernacle; let us worship at His footstool. ⁸Arise, O Lord, to Your resting place, You and the ark of Your strength. ⁹Let Your priests be clothed with righteousness, and let Your saints shout for joy. —Psalm 132: 1-9

IN THESE opening verses, the writer appeals to the Lord to "remember David." This refers to God's promises to His people and to David. In 2 Samuel, we read of David's heart's desire to build a resting place for the Ark of the Covenant. The Lord spoke to Nathan the prophet, and told him to speak this promise to David: "*When your days are fulfilled and you rest with your fathers, I will set up your seed after you, who will come from your body, and I will establish his kingdom. He shall build a house for My name, and I will establish the throne of his kingdom forever. I will be his Father, and he shall be My son. If he commits iniquity, I will chasten him. . . . But My mercy shall not depart from him, as I took it from Saul, whom I removed from before you. And your house and your kingdom shall be established forever before you. Your throne shall be established forever"* (2 Samuel 7:12-16).

The author of our psalm today is reminding the Lord of that response to David's zeal, and he asks God to remember His promise regarding Jerusalem and the One whose throne would be established forever. We can see the connection between the physical temple at the time of the psalms and the future Temple with Jesus reigning eternally!

To try to separate Israel's role in the past from their purpose in the present damages the integrity of Scripture. Denying that the Jews of modern Israel are biblical Israel takes some serious interpretive gymnastics and requires a cut-and-paste approach to the Bible. In addition to this, remember that genetics link modern Israelites to the ancient Israelites and also that the Jews have lived in the same region of the world with the same capital city that they had 2,000 years ago! It's imperative that we understand the seventy weeks of Daniel, the *fact* of the Holy City of Jerusalem, and the coming of the Most Holy One, Jesus. If the first coming of the Most Holy One involved the Jews and Jerusalem, then the return of the Most Holy One must also involve the Jews and Jerusalem!

Let's take a quick look at what two Old Testament prophets wrote under the inspiration of the Holy Spirit. *"The day of the Lord is near in the valley of decision. The sun and moon will grow dark, and the stars will diminish their brightness. The Lord also will roar from Zion, and utter His voice from Jerusalem; but the Lord will be a shelter for His people, and the strength of the children of Israel. 'So you shall know that I am the Lord your God, dwelling in Zion My holy mountain. Then Jerusalem shall be holy, and no aliens shall ever pass through her again"* (3:14-17). And Zechariah wrote: *"I will gather all the nations to battle against Jerusalem. . . . Half of the city shall go into captivity, but the remnant . . . shall not be cut off. . . . Then the Lord will go forth and fight against those nations. . . . His feet will stand on the Mount of Olives, which faces Jerusalem on the east. And the Mount of Olives shall be split in two, from east to west, making a very large valley . . . "* (Zechariah 14:2-4).

These events are still in the future, and they share the same three elements that we've been looking at: the Jews, Jerusalem, and Jesus. The seventieth week of Daniel can't be nullified without denying the very purpose for God's people and city. He will reign in Jerusalem, which will again be known not as the capital of Palestine but as the capital of Israel!

God Says What He Means
and Means What He Says (part 1)

*¹⁰*For Your servant David's sake, do not turn away the face of Your Anointed. *¹¹*The Lord has sworn in truth to David; He will not turn from it: "I will set upon your throne the fruit of your body. *¹²*If your sons will keep My covenant and my testimony which I shall teach them, their sons also shall sit upon your throne forevermore." *¹³*For the Lord has chosen Zion; He has desired it for His dwelling place: *¹⁴*This is My resting place forever; here I will dwell, for I have desired it. *¹⁵*I will abundantly bless her provision; I will satisfy her poor with bread. *¹⁶*I will also clothe her priests with salvation, and her saints shall shout aloud for joy. *—Psalm 132:10-16*

THERE'S A LOT to unpack in these incredible verses. First of all, although there have been exceptions in history, it's the norm for the throne of a monarch to be set in the nation's primary city or capital. In today's verses we read of the promise made to David concerning his descendants ("the fruit of [his] body") and their sons as well. It is very clear: the Lord has chosen Zion and desires it to be His dwelling place and His resting place forever!

Look at what Zechariah wrote: "*The word of the Lord of hosts came, saying, 'Thus says the Lord of hosts: 'I am zealous for Zion with great zeal; with great fervor I am zealous for her.' Thus says the Lord: 'I will return to Zion, and dwell in the midst of Jerusalem. Jerusalem shall be called the City of Truth, the Mountain of the Lord of hosts, the Holy Mountain.' Thus says the Lord of hosts: 'Old men and old women shall again sit in the streets of Jerusalem, each one with his staff in his hand because of great age. The streets of the city shall be full of boys and girls playing in its streets. . . . If it is marvelous in the eyes of the remnant of the people in these days, will it also be marvelous in My eyes? . . . Behold, I will save My people from the land of the east and from the land of the west; I will bring them back, and they shall dwell in the midst of Jerusalem. They shall be My people and I will be their God I truth and righteousness'*" (Zechariah 8:1-8).

Listen, if the Lord says that He will *return* to Zion in the verses above, doesn't it mean that He must have been there before? If He says that He will bring His people *back*, doesn't that meant that he people must have been out of the land?

Zechariah, who wrote these verses, was a contemporary of Haggai, and both men were post-exilic prophets, so we know that he can't be referring to Jerusalem's return after the Babylonian captivity, because that had already happened. It *must* mean refer to the 2,000-year-long Diaspora that ended May 14, 1948! He also mentions the old men and women sitting in the streets of Jerusalem watching the children playing happily and safely in the streets. Isn't that a comforting picture? But it hasn't happened yet. To what could the Lord have referred as He spoke to the prophet Zechariah? It is the peace that will reign when the Prince of Peace rules on the earth for a thousand years. And from what city will He reign? That's right! Jerusalem.

Jerusalem is the only city in the entire world with the right to claim divine association. It was a city that was ordered by the Lord from the very beginning as the place from which He would, one day, rule and reign, and nothing could ever stop that from happening.

There are many temples around the world that lay claim to being "holy places" where deity dwells or is worshiped, such as Mecca and Medina, whose inhabitants both claim divine associations.

But there is only one city that can truly make the claim of being the site of the throne from which the Lord would reign because there is only one God, and, by His own words, He has chosen the dwelling place that is to be His resting place forever. *O Jerusalem!*

God Says What He Means
and Means What He Says (part 2)

¹⁰For Your servant David's sake, do not turn away the face of Your Anointed. ¹¹The Lord has sworn in truth to David; He will not turn from it: "I will set upon your throne the fruit of your body. ¹²If your sons will keep My covenant and my testimony which I shall teach them, their sons also shall sit upon your throne forevermore." ¹³For the Lord has chosen Zion; He has desired it for His dwelling place: ¹⁴This is My resting place forever; here I will dwell, for I have desired it. ¹⁵I will abundantly bless her provision; I will satisfy her poor with bread. ¹⁶I will also clothe her priests with salvation, and her saints shall shout aloud for joy. —Psalm 132:10-16

TO CONTINUE with our thoughts from yesterday: If Jerusalem is no longer the chosen city of God and the Jews no longer His chosen people, then we're going to have to redefine both "forever" and "perpetually." God's statement in verse 12 concerning the sons of David refers to David's throne—not to the status of national Israel in the eyes of God.

One of the main arguments of the replacement theologians relates to Israel's sin and the rejection of their Messiah. But this ignores the terms and conditions of the *one-sided* covenant that God made, which was dependent solely upon Him and not on Israel. Were there serious consequences for Israel's rejection of the

Messiah? Yes, indeed! But when Christians mess up in life and miss an opportunity, do we lose our salvation? Upon what is the assurance of our salvation based? Is it on our performance or on God's faithfulness?

Read these comforting words from the Lord spoken through the prophet Jeremiah: "*The days are coming . . . when I will make a new covenant with . . . Israel and with . . . Judah—not according to the covenant that I made with their fathers . . . which they broke. . . . But this is the covenant that I will make with . . . Israel after those days . . . : I will put My law in their minds, and write it on their hearts; and I will be their God, and they shall be My people*" (Jer 31:31-33).

The very mention of Egypt solidifies the fact that we're not talking about national Israel, who broke the covenant, but instead it is a *law* written on the minds and hearts of the national Israel yet to come. It won't happen until they realize that Jesus, whom they despised when He walked on earth, is their Messiah. This will be during the Tribulation. So we see that the same national people group who exited Egypt are going to exist in the last days, and despite the fact that they broke God's covenant, He will never break His. Were there consequences to their rebellion? Did they forfeit blessings? Absolutely!

Look at what the Lord spoke through the prophet Ezekiel: "*When the house of Israel dwelt in their own land, they defiled it . . . ; their way was like the uncleanness of a woman in her customary impurity. I poured out My fury on them for the blood they had shed . . . and for their idols with which they had defiled it. So I scattered them among the nations, . . . I judged them according to their ways and their deeds. . . . Wherever they went, they profaned My holy name. . . . But I had concern for My holy name, which the house of Israel profaned . . . wherever they went*" (Eze 36:16-21).

God had made a covenant with the Jews and Jerusalem. Their disobedience robbed them of the blessings of a national homeland and, even worse, cost them the negative consequences of profaning the name of the Lord. Jerusalem is the only city in the world that God has chosen for His name and that was created for only one people, the Jews. He promises that they will once again inhabit the land, and it will be a rich and beautiful place. God promised to bring His people back to the land, and they will build houses and plant gardens, and God will rule and reign over them all (Amos 9:14-15). One fine day, the poor will be satisfied with bread, the Jewish priests will be clothed at last with salvation, and the saint will be shouting for joy! The Lord said it, and He means what He says!

"His Mercies Never Come to an End"

[17]There I will make the horn of David grow; I will prepare a lamp for My Anointed. [18]His enemies I will clothe with shame, but upon Himself His crown shall flourish. —*Psalm 132:17-18*

IN VERSE TWELVE of our psalm we read God's promise to David that his sons' sons would sit on his throne forever. Sons, of course, in this case means descendants. Our verse today mentions the horn of David. This refers to his kingdom and power. So from David's kingdom would come one who will sit on David's throne forever, whose reign (crown) shall flourish!

This was also foretold in the New Testament. In the gospel of Luke, we find the account of the angel Gabriel coming to Mary at God's command. He spoke to this young virgin: *"Rejoice, highly favored one, the Lord is with you; blessed are you among women" (1:26-28).* Mary was troubled by what he said, but the angel comforted her: *"Do not be afraid, Mary, for you have found favor with God. . . . Behold you will conceive in your womb and bring forth a Son, and shall call His name Jesus. He will be great, and will be called the Son of the Highest; and the Lord God will give Him the throne of His father David. And He will reign over the house of Jacob forever, and of His kingdom there will be no end" (vv. 30-33).*

Who was this Child who would be born to Mary? His name was Jesus, and He will be the one King of the Jews yet to rule from Jerusalem! How does He qualify for this, aside from being God's only begotten Son? David himself was his ancestral father. To what national people group did David belong? The nation of Israel. Where will His throne be? In Jerusalem!

Through all of this we need to understand that if, as some claim, God has cast Israel off forever because of their disobedience, then Jesus would have forfeited the right to sit on David's throne, and biblical prophecy would be a lie. Saints, God's Word doesn't lie, and it doesn't change. There can be no other culmination of the history of mankind than what is foretold will happen as we approach the last of the last days.

The lamp spoken of in verse 17 speaks of enlightenment. We see it is prophesied that from the lineage of David will come the Light of the world, whose enemies will be clothed with shame. *"Since we are surrounded by so great a cloud of witnesses, let us lay aside every weight, and . . . sin . . . and let us run with endurance the race that is set before us, looking unto Jesus, the author and finisher of our faith, who for the joy that was set before Him endured the cross, despising the shame, and has sat down at the right hand of the throne of God" (Heb 12:1).*

Jesus came as the Lamb of God to take away the sins of the world. He bore the shame of the cross to accomplish that. Did we then see the shame with which His enemies were to have been clothed (see v. 18 above)? *"My anger is kindled against the shepherds [the religious leaders]. . . . For the Lord of hosts will visit His flock, the house of Judah, and will make them as His royal horse in the battle. . . . They will be like mighty men, who tread down their enemies in the mire of the streets in the battle. They shall fight because the Lord is with them, and the riders on the horses shall be put to shame. I will strengthen the house of Judah, and I will save the house of Joseph. I will bring them back, because I have mercy on them. They shall be as though I had not cast them aside; for I am the Lord their God, and I will hear them"* (Zec 10:3-6).

Even now we see God protecting Israel and strengthening Judah because of His mercy. Nationally, even now He has not totally cast them aside. But there remains one unfinished piece of business regarding the Jews, Jerusalem, and Jesus. Jesus must return to the earth, this time as King, the descendant of David, who was divinely ordained to rule from Jerusalem, but who has yet to ascend to the throne. *He is coming again soon!* The veracity of the Scriptures regarding these events is essential when it comes to biblical integrity and infallibility, which are inseparable prophetic companions. Even so, come quickly, Lord Jesus!

November 8

El Shaddai

Introduction

Praise Ye the Lord. —*Psalm 135*

WITH THE PILGRIMS now safely in Jerusalem, this closing psalm of ascent would be on their lips, and their hearts and minds would be focused on the purpose of their journey to the one city that rightfully claims a divine association. The pilgrimage wasn't merely an opportunity to visit the sacred city as a tourist, but the people came in obedience to the commandment (Law) that they were to celebrate and commemorate the faithfulness of God to His chosen people and to bless His name!

The Law stated that every year all able-bodied males were required to attend three of the seven feast days: Passover, Pentecost, and the Feast of Tabernacles, which were all held in the holy city of Jerusalem. As the pilgrims traveled along the way, these psalms of ascent were recited or sung, and concluded with Psalm 134: *"Behold, bless the Lord, all you servants of the Lord, who by night stand in the house of the Lord! Lift up your hands in the sanctuary, and bless the Lord. The Lord who made heaven and earth bless you from Zion!"*

Our psalm today opens with the closing words of the Psalms of Ascent. The date of authorship is irrelevant to the context. We know that whoever compiled the quotes of the various psalms in our text did so under the inspiration of the Holy Spirit for a specific purpose, and that purpose will guide our approach to this psalm.

Let's take a side trip for a moment to the story of Nebuchadnezzar in the book of Daniel. The King had been warned that his pride would be his downfall, and he was continually reminded that God was the one who had given him such a great kingdom. One day, the king was walking about the royal palace and said, "Is not this great Babylon, that I have built for a royal dwelling by my mighty power and for the honor of my majesty?" Daniel tells us that while the words were "still in his mouth," a voice from heaven came down and said, "The kingdom has departed from you." Nebuchadnezzar became a madman, driven from men, eating grass like oxen. He was wet with the dew until his hair had grown like eagles' feathers and his nails like birds' claws. After seven years the Lord restored his mind and kingdom.

Listen to what he said, "*At the end of the time, I, Nebuchadnezzar, lifted my eyes to heaven, and my understanding returned to me; and I blessed the Most High and praised and honored Him who lives forever: For His dominion is an everlasting dominion, and His kingdom is from generation to generation. All the inhabitants of the earth are reputed as nothing; He does according to His will in the army of heaven and among the inhabitants of the earth. No one can restrain His hand or say to Him, 'What have you done?' At the same time my reason returned to me, and for the glory of my kingdom, my nobles resorted to me, I was restored to my kingdom, and excellent majesty was added to me. Now I, Nebuchadnezzar, praise and extol and honor the King of heaven, all of whose works are truth, and His ways justice. And those who walk in pride He is able to put down*" (Daniel 4:34-37).

The purpose of Psalm 135 is to extol and honor the King of Heaven. Our world has gone mad. Pride has reached a level in the hearts of so many and leads them to march in celebration of the greatest evil the world has ever seen: abortion. Yet God is willing to restore the sanity and the sanctity of life. The truth is that America will only become great again when her people come to the place that Nebuchadnezzar did, recognizing God for who He is! Who is He? Our God is El Shaddai, the Lord God Almighty!

The God of
People-changing Power

*1*Praise ye the Lord! Praise the name of the Lord; praise Him, O ye servants of the Lord! *2*You who stand in the house of the Lord, in the courts of the house of our God, *3*Praise the Lord, for the Lord is good; sing praises to His name, for it is pleasant. *4*For the Lord has chosen Jacob for Himself, Israel for His special treasure. *—Psalm 135:1-4*

THE APOSTLE JOHN repeatedly referred to himself as "the disciple whom Jesus loved." Paul personalized the redemptive act of Christ on the cross as being for himself: "*I have been crucified with Christ; it is no longer I who live, but Christ lives in me; and the life which I now live in the flesh I live by faith in the Son of God, who loved me and gave Himself for me*" (Galatians 2:20). What we want to remember is that El Shaddai, our God, loves us and gave Himself for us, and we, too, are called His beloved.

What's the first thing this psalm reminds us? We are to praise the Lord. And the Lord has a name! "God" is a title that means Supreme Being. God's name is a tetragrammato, YHWH, or "God is salvation." In the first verse from Psalm 135, the first word for "Lord" is *Jah* and the second "Lord" in verse one is *YHWH*. God is a *personal* God, and He has a name that is to be praised. Those who served in the Lord's temple were to sing praises to the Lord, for "His name is pleasant."

Verse four gives us the first reason why we are to extol El Shaddai: "He has chosen Jacob for Himself, and Israel for His special treasure." In other words, God took a heel catcher (supplanter) and made him into a prince (Israel means Prince of God). So why are *we* to praise Him? Because our God alone has "people changing" power! This is why we can have hope today. Millions of Americans call evil good and good evil. They hate anything that is sacred and holy. They hate the church and Christians and everything they stand for.

But what does God do? He take supplanters, schemers, and those who take what belongs to others by force or deception, and He makes them into princes and princesses in His kingdom! But doesn't the Bible tell us that the unrighteous will not inherit the kingdom of God (1 Corinthians 6:9-11)? Yes, but the verse continues, "*But you were washed, but you were sanctified, but you were justified in the name of the Lord Jesus and by the Spirit of our God.*"

Praise the Lord! Praise the Lord alone who has people-changing power to turn us from darkness to light, who makes friends of former enemies, transforms the mind, and restores understanding. He alone washes, sanctifies, and justifies those who once practiced things that were contrary to His holy moral code. How does He do it? He is El Shaddai, God, the Almighty! Nothing is impossible with Him!

Who Is Like Our God?

⁵For I know that the Lord is great, and our Lord is above all gods. ⁶Whatvever the Lord pleases, He does, in heaven and in earth; He makes lightning for the rain; He brings the wind out of His treasuries. ⁷He causes the vapors to ascend from the ends of the earth; He makes lightning for the rain; He brings the wind out of His treasuries. —*Psalm 135:5-7*

WHO IS EL SHADDAI? Just when we think we know Him, we find out even greater things than we could have imagined. God speaks in the book of Job, asking some unanswerable questions that prove our limited capacity to understand just how great He is: "*Have you entered the treasury of snow, or . . . seen the treasury of hail, which I have reserved . . . for the day of battle and war? By what way is light diffused, or the east wind scattered over the earth? Who has divided a channel for the overflowing water, or a path for the thunderbolt, to cause it to rain on a land where there is no one . . . to satisfy the desolate waste, and cause to spring forth the . . . tender grass?*" (Job 38:22-27). In Isaiah we read, "*He . . . sits above the circle of the earth . . . stretches out the heavens like a curtain, and spreads them out like a tent to dwell in. He . . . makes the judges of the earth useless*" (Isa 40:22-23). That's our God, El Shaddai!

We see here that God does as He pleases. He is above *all* gods, exercising authority over the heavens and earth and all that is within them. His power is greater than the combined forces of the universe! What do we actually know about the universe? With high-powered telescopes traveling through space, astronomers and astrophysicists are telling us of the great power of black holes and supernovas. But isn't the Creator of all these greater than what He created? Wouldn't the One who created the hydrologic cycle, causes lightning, and commands the wind be greater in power than the created forces? He who names and numbers the stars and sets them in their places must be more powerful than they!

How can people today push the idea of the universe's ability to *create itself* (think about that for a moment!) given enough time? They dream up scenarios, denying God in the creation of the human race. The more advanced we become in the realm of astrophysics and the subatomic sciences, the more questions arise about the "self-creating universe" theory.

Complicating matters even more, a concept called the "multiverse theory" has become popular. It reasons that since scientists can't be sure what shape the space-time continuum takes, then it is most likely flat (as opposed to spherical or even donut shaped), stretching out *infinitely*. But if space-time goes on forever, it must begin to repeat itself at some point. Because there's a finite number of ways that particles can be arranged in space and time, they reason that there must be multiple universes, with ours being simply a product of the replication process. *But they still can't explain where the first universe came from.*

There's the theory of "eternal inflations," suggesting that some pockets in space stop inflating while other regions continue to inflate, giving rise to the concept of many isolated "bubble universes." Another theory suggests parallel universes that hover just out of reach of our own. Quantum mechanics describes the world in terms of probabilities, rather than definite outcomes, suggesting that all possible outcomes of a situation occur in their own separate universes, and we just happen to be in one of those. None of this is provable, nor is it even remotely possible. We do have the answer to all of this, of course: "*In the beginning God created the heavens and the earth*" (Genesis 1:1). No matter how many universes there may be, God is more powerful than all of them, and He is their Creator. He sits over the circle of the earth, riding the clouds, and He is El Shaddai!

November 11

"There Is None Like Thee"

[8]He destroyed the firstborn of Egypt, both of man and beast. [9]He sent signs and wonders into the midst of you, O Egypt, upon Pharaoh and all his servants. [10]He defeated many nations and slew mighty kings. [11]Sihon king of the Amorites, Og king of Bashan, and all the kingdoms of Canaan—[12]and gave their land as a heritage, a heritage to Israel His people. —*Psalm 135:8-12*

—

MOST PEOPLE are familiar with the Exodus of the Israelites from Egypt and the series of supernatural plagues that were initiated by God because of Pharaoh's refusal to let His people go that they might worship the Lord. But the *reason* why God used the plagues and subsequent exodus needs to be remembered also. "*The Lord said to Moses, 'Rise early in the morning and stand before Pharaoh, and say to him, "Thus says the Lord God of the Hebrews: 'Let My people go, that they may serve Me, for at this time I will send all My plagues to your very heart, and on your servants and on your people, that you many know that there is none like Me in all the earth'"'*" (Exodus 9:13-14).

El Shaddai does things that set Him apart from the rest of creation that it might be known that there is none like Him in all the earth. The kingdoms of Sihon and Og are not familiar to most people, but they were the first to oppose Israel's progress to the Promised Land and were the mightiest of all the kingdoms who would ever oppose the Jews. When Israel requested passage through the land of the Amorites, Sihon, whose name means "warrior," refused to let them enter. In fact, they came out to fight against Israel, but Israel defeated them and took possession of their land.

Next they went up the road to Bashan, where King Og came out against them. God told His people not to be afraid, and then He delivered Og, one of the last representatives of the giants, and the people over to Israel, who slew them and took all of their cities.

What did Israel learn from this, and what do we learn? Our God is greater than any giant or warrior that the enemy throws at us! In fact, God is the world's *only rightful authority*. He is the authority over all human power, no matter how high, by right as Creator, and He can give the land to whomever He chooses, no matter who was there before them.

Our God also has the right to define morals and determine truth. This is His planet, and He does what pleases Him, including defending His people against warriors and giants.

Truly, there is none like our God!

November 12

Our God Actually Is God!

13 Your name, O Lord, endures forever, Your fame, O Lord, throughout all generations. 14 For the Lord will judge His people, and He will have compassion on His servants. 15 The idols of the nations are silver and gold, the work of men's hands. 16 They have mouths, but they do not speak; eyes they have, but they do not see; 17 They have ears, but they do not hear; nor is there any breath in their mouths. 18 Those who make them are like them; so is everyone who trusts in them. —*Psalm 135:13-18*

ALTHOUGH moral relativism and political correctness are popular today, they haven't gained any traction in heaven. God hates them both, and He is the one true authority over the world. He is against "equalization," as well, when it comes to religious beliefs. He disagrees with such statements as "We are *all* God's children" or "We all worship the same God."

God doesn't go by many names. His name is Yahweh (YHWH). That is the only name that endures forever. His fame is to be declared in successive generations, and He will judge His people and have compassion on those who serve Him.

The prophet Isaiah painted a great picture of how foolish it is to follow a man-made religion, no matter how sincere are its adherents: "*[A man] cuts down cedars for himself, and takes the cypress and the oak; he secures it for himself among the trees of the forest. He plants a pine, and the rain nourishes it. Then it shall be for a man to burn, for he will take some of it and warm himself; yes, he kindles it and bakes bread; indeed he makes a god and worships it; he make it a carved image, and falls down to it. He burns half of it in the fire; with this half he eats meat; he roasts a roast, and is satisfied. He even warms himself and says, 'Ah, I am warm, I have seen the fire.' And the rest of it he makes into a god, his carved image. He falls down before it and worships it, prays to it, and says, 'Deliver me, for you are my god!'*" (Isaiah 44:14-17).

Today, whether the central figure of a religion is crafted or molded by men's hands or fashioned and fabricated in their minds, they all result in the same thing as cutting down a tree, carving an image, and then bowing down to it, while using other parts of the same wood to warm himself and cook his food. God says that those who make them are like them.

But here's the truth about El Shaddai: Our God actually *is* God! Remember, the title "God" means Supreme Being. If there is more than one "Supreme Being," then none are "supreme," and the title means nothing.

What about the "COEXIST" movement? In Zephaniah 2:9-11 we read: "*Therefore, as I live, says the Lord of hosts, the God of Israel, 'Surely Moab shall be like Sodom, and the people of Ammon like Gomorrah—overrun with weeds and saltpits, and a perpetual desolation. The residue of My people shall possess them.' This they shall have for their pride, because they have reproached and made arrogant threats against the people of the Lord of hosts. The Lord will be awesome to them, for He will reduce to nothing all the gods of the earth; people shall worship him, each one from his place, indeed all the shores of our nations.*"

He isn't the product of human hands or imaginations that can neither hear nor speak. Our God hears our prayers. He answers them! And someday He is going to answer our cry for His kingdom to come and His will to be done, on earth as it is in heaven.

Make no mistake about it. El Shaddai actually is God, and He is the *only* God!

His Name Is YHWH

19Bless the Lord, O house of Israel! Bless the Lord, O house of Aaron! 20Bless the Lord, O house of Levi! You who fear the Lord, bless the Lord! 21Blessed be the Lord out of Zion, who dwells in Jerusalem! Praise the Lord! —Psalm 135:19-21

THIS PSALM ends along the very same lines as it began, calling upon the people to praise the Lord, including the priests and everyone who fears God. Psalm 150:6 reminds us, "*Let everything that has breath praise the Lord. Praise the Lord!*"

The City of Jerusalem, along with Mount Zion, located just outside the walls of the old city, was to be a place where blessing the Lord continued perpetually. If we combine both fear of the Lord and blessing the Lord, as in the previous verses, we gain further insight, and the door opens upon our last takeaway from this psalm. The idol makers (vv. 15-18) make idols that are like themselves, deaf and dumb.

In contrast, the fear of the Lord imparts to man the very wisdom of God! The fear of the Lord initiates *true* religion as opposed to the *appearance* of religion (Colossians 2:23). The fear of the Lord inspires praise. The fear of the Lord makes our praises acceptable. Peter is quoted in the Book of Acts stating, " . . . *God shows no partiality. But in every nation whoever fears Him and works righteousness is accepted by Him.*"

We'll close this mini-series with a final observation regarding this call to praise: Our God is the source of all blessing and alone is worthy of the highest praise. Remember what we learned in Psalm 128 in our message on courageous fear? We saw that a home that fears the Lord will be a safe haven in an evil world. Isn't that a wonderful blessing from God? Shouldn't we always praise God for His blessings?

Who is this God whom we love and fear? He is El Shaddai, God Almighty, and His name is YHWH. God alone has people-changing power, a power that is greater than the combined forces of the universe(s), and that makes Him the only rightful authority over all, including our own little lives and homes. He is very source of *all* blessing, and He alone is worthy of our highest praise. So what is the only way we can respond to all of this? *Praise the Lord!*

Living in the Last Days

Introduction

A Psalm of David—Psalm 138

THERE ARE beliefs that all Christians hold in common, but not all share the same life experiences. To be a Christian in Syria is exactly what it is in America, but the actual way we live out our Christianity might be vastly different from one another. The same idea is true when it comes to seasons of history. In the book with his name, Daniel was visited by a "certain man" (whose description is nearly identical to the description of Christ in His glorified body in Revelation 1:13-16), who spoke to Daniel, saying, "*Daniel, shut up the words, and seal the book until the time of the end; many shall run to and fro, and knowledge shall increase*" (Dan 12:4). And later, Jesus spoke to the disciples of things to come: "*There will be signs in the sun . . . moon, and . . . stars; and on earth distress of nations . . . , the sea and the waves roaring; men's hearts failing them from fear . . . of those things which are coming on the earth, for the powers of the heavens will be shaken. . . . They will see the Son of Man coming in a cloud with power and great glory. . . . When these things begin to happen . . . lift up your heads, because your redemption draws near*" (Lk 21:25-28).

Through Daniel, the Lord was saying that there will be a season in human history called "the time of the end," when knowledge of Daniel's prophecy will increase, setting those times apart from all others. God also said in Luke that there will be signs in the heavens, indicating that we should lift our heads and look up, because our redemption is near, and the Son of Man will soon appear in a cloud, with power and great glory!

We are now living in a season unlike any other, and experiences among Christians during this time will be distinct from those of times past, even though our beliefs will be just the same. What are we to watch for? How can we know that the times of the end are drawing near? In Matthew we read, "*The Pharisees and Sadducees came, and testing Him asked that He would show them a sign from heaven. He answered and said to them, "When it is evening you say, 'It will be fair weather, for the sky is red'; and in the morning, 'It will be foul weather today, for the sky is red and threatening.' Hypocrites! You know how to discern the face of the sky, but you cannot discern the signs of the times*" (Mat 16:1-3). And again in Matthew, Jesus spoke: "*Of that day and hour no one knows, not even the angels of heaven, but My Father only. But as the days of Noah were, so also will the coming of the Son of Man be. For as in the days before the flood, they were eating and drinking, marrying and giving in marriage, until the day that Noah entered the ark, and did not know until the flood came and took them all away, so also will the coming of the Son of Man be"* (24:36-27).

Jesus rebuked the religious leaders for not discerning what the signs of His first coming had been, and then He told Peter, Andrew, James, and John that the same thing will again occur prior to His Second Coming. Again, people will ignore or deny the signs.

Even though we don't have much information on this Psalm of David, the content tells us that what was going on in David's time is the same as what we're experiencing in our own times. Thus, it's crucial that we read and understand what is being said. Over the next few days, we'll learn that during David's time, idolatry was rampant, and society was corrupt and prideful. They hated God's children, yet the Lord was faithful to His Word, even in the midst of all their troubles. What can we glean from David's own experience about how to actually *live* during these last days? Let's press on joyfully and see!

"In the Beginning Was the Word"

¹I will praise You with my whole heart; before the gods I will sing praises to You. ²I will worship toward Your holy temple, and praise Your name for Your lovingkindness and Your truth; for You have magnified Your word above all Your name. *—Psalm 138:1-2*

ARE THERE things that we see creeping into our lives and churches that was also seen in Old Testament times? Verse one implies the influence of pagan deities way back then, and in the New Testament, in Matthew, regarding the last days, we read: *"Then many false prophets will rise up and deceive many. And because lawlessness will abound, the love of many will grow cold. But he who endures to the end shall be saved. And this gospel of the kingdom will be preached in all the world as a witness to all nations, and then the end will come"* (Matthew 24:11-14).

Are false witnesses rising up today? Is lawlessness abounding even now? Is the natural love of many growing into selfish, cold indifference to others? Are those who endure to the end, no matter what conditions they go through, still going to be saved?

The information within the Bible is amazing! No other work comes even close to the living Word of God laid out within its pages. What was prophesied so long ago regarding God's plan for this world has been taking place exactly as He warned and promised.

As we move forward through this psalm, let's allow the words of David in these verses to guide us and give us our marching orders for living in these last days. What do we know about those prophesied "end times"? We were warned that false men would rise up, but David says that, no matter what, *he* will praise the Lord with his whole heart right in front of the pagan deities! That gives us a clue as to what we should do as we encounter false prophets on the rise. What is it? Praise the Lord with our whole heart! And David would continue to do that right in front of the false teachers and pagan religions with boldness, publicly!

There's a beautiful truth in verse two that we need to remember: "*You have magnified Your word above all Your name*" (v. 2b). It's important to recall that a person's name is directly associated with their word. If one doesn't keep one's word, or if his words aren't true, his name and reputation is tarnished. What does the name of the Lord reflect? Let's take a look at some of the most beautiful verses in the Bible: "*In the beginning was the Word, and the Word was with God, and the Word was God. He was in the beginning with God. All things were made through Him, and without Him nothing was made that was made. In Him was life, and the life was the light of men. And the light shines in the darkness, and the darkness did not comprehend it*" (John 1:1-4).

There is so much contained within those verses! To begin with, Jesus is the Word, and He is God. Why is this especially important in these days in which we live? Because there is a growing movement that teaches and believes that as long as you "accept Jesus as Savior," you can pick and choose what other parts of the Bible you want to believe or adhere to, implying that everything else is subjective. Some reject the importance of prophecy in the Scriptures, and some deny any need for a "changed life" after being saved, in essence saying that the Bible's moral commands are subservient to cultural thinking and beliefs. Doesn't this take away from the verses we just read about the Word (Jesus) being God himself, and *with* God, revealing the truth of the Trinity: Father, Son, Holy Spirit—three in one? We must reject any teaching that denies the inspiration and authority of all of God's Word! He is all God and the only God. Be careful what you read and hear! There is only one truth, and the enemy hates it.

"Life in the Fast Lane?"

³In the day when I cried out, You answered me, and made me bold with strength in my soul. —Psalm 138:3

WHO IS the One who really knows us? Who knows our thoughts, our hearts, our feelings? Of course it is the Lord God Almighty. The *Lord God Almighty*? And He cares about us? There are some who hear this and step right over it as if were nothing, but it's something that should be the heartbeat and foundation of every single thing we do or say—ever. Listen friends, as we speed down the fast lane toward the very last days, wondering how we can keep up with everything going on around us, let's un-complicate things a bit. The first thing we want to remember as we hold the truths of the Bible in our hearts and minds is that we must *reject any teaching that denies the inspiration and authority of all of God's Word*. And we must also reject the teacher who is belittling the Word of God, as we saw yesterday.

So if someone says, "Ignore Bible prophecy," run! If someone says the Bible doesn't define absolute truth, run. If someone says anything that denies the inspiration, infallibility, and absolute authority of *all* of the Word of God? You guessed it: run!

Verse two of our psalm spoke of worshiping the Lord and praising His name. In the New Testament we read, "*Therefore lay aside all filthiness and overflow of wickedness, and receive with meekness the implanted word, which is able to save your souls*" (Jas 1:21). And look at this one, where Jesus himself is speaking to one of the churches in the last days: "*These things says He who has the sharp two-edged sword: 'I know your works, and where you dwell, where Satan's throne is. And you hold fast to My name, and did not deny My faith even in the days in which Antipas was my faithful martyr, who was killed among you, where Satan dwells. But I have a few things against you, because you have those who hold to the doctrine of Balaam, who taught Balak to put a stumbling block before the children of Israel, to eat things sacrificed to idols, and to commit sexual immorality. Thus you also have those who hold the doctrine of the Nicolaitans, which thing I hate. Repent, or else I will come to you quickly and will fight against them with the sword of My mouth*'" (Rev 2:12-16).

So the Word and the Lord Jesus cannot be separated from one another. The implanted Word is able to save souls! Holding fast to His name is an expression of "saving faith." Conversely, to deny the Word and its inspired, infallible authority is to deny Jesus, the only *Name* that can save. David had learned that when life got tough, when he found himself in the fast lane and realized that he didn't belong there because things were getting out of control, he turned to *praise the Lord*! When false gods were all around him, he praised and worshiped the true God, as

Psalm 119:60 says, "*The entirety of God's Word is truth.*" Saints, we need to be bold with the strength in our souls that comes by honoring the Word and rejecting all other teaching or teacher who denies the inspiration and infallibility of any portion of Scripture.

Get out of the fast lane when you feel like you're being pushed in directions that you don't want to go. You may not appear to be the "coolest" Christian, and you may lose a few friends, but as you cling to the truth of the Word and let the Lord guide your steps, what peace can fill your soul! The devil is watching you. Why not let him see you running with the Lord—not in the fast lane, but in the good path, led of God: "*Teach me Your way, O Lord, and lead me in a smooth path because of my enemies*" (Ps 27:11). God's Word is a lamp to your path and a light to your feet. It magnifies God's name and is the *only* name on the *only* path that can save!

November 17

"Humble Yourself in the Sight of the Lord" (part 1)

4All the kings of the earth shall praise You, O Lord, when they hear the words of Your mouth. 5Yes, they shall sing of the ways of the Lord, for great is the glory of the Lord. 6Though the Lord is on high, yet He regards the lowly; but the proud He knows from afar. —Psalm 138:4-6

DAVID HOPED that by maintaining his praise and proclamation of God's loving kindness and truth it would lead to the salvation of other rulers who heard the Word, causing them to praise the Lord and sing of His ways. He states that the kings of the earth will praise the Lord, but although God desires that, He's interested in the poor, the lowly, and the humble. Those who are too proud to acknowledge him, sadly, "He knows from afar" (v. 6).

The apostle Peter wrote: "*Likewise, you younger people, submit yourselves to your elders. Yes, all of you be submissive to one another, and be clothed with humility, for God resists the proud, but gives grace to the humble.' Therefore humble yourselves under the mighty hand of God, that He may exalt you in due time, casting all your care upon Him, for He cares for you*" (1 Pet 5:5-7). Humility isn't a popular idea for most people, but it's only those who humble themselves before the mighty hand of God through the blood of Jesus Christ who can be exalted to the status of "child of God."

In verse four, David speaks of the importance of hearing the words of *God.* Unfortunately, many who bear the title "pastor" or "elder" or "Christian leader" are not bringing the Word of God that gives life to the ears of their listeners. They substitute marketing tactics in place of teaching truth from the Bible. In the seventies and early eighties the late singer/songwriter Keith Green wrote about this travesty in his song, "How Can They Live without Jesus?" Referencing the religious leaders, he said: "He's [God's] not just a religion, with steeples and bells, or a salesman who will sell you the things you just want to hear; for His love was such that He suffered so much to cause some of us just to follow...."

Salvation cannot be marketed. Phony teachers will yield phony "Christians." When churches resort to tactics that eliminate or diminish the clear teaching of Scripture, which alone is able to save men's souls, what they are saying is that the Word of God isn't enough to reach and save our culture today. But David says that the loving kindness and truth of God's Word is able to save *anyone* whether king, pauper, or anyone in between. But where will they hear this truth?

In the book of Romans we read: "*How then shall they call on Him in whom they have not believed? And how shall they believe in Him of whom they have not heard? And how shall they hear without a preacher? And how shall they preach unless they are sent? As it is written: 'How beautiful are the feet of those who preach the gospel of peace, who bring glad tidings of good things!' But they have not all obeyed the gospel. For Isaiah says, 'Lord, who has believed our report?' So then faith comes by hearing, and hearing by the word of God*" (10:14-17).

Some churches, in an effort to create a level of comfort and familiarity for the nonbelievers who may be attending their church, play popular secular music. But in truth, I have never heard of a church that uses that tactic and also boldly preaches the uncompromised Word of God afterward. I've heard it said, sarcastically but truthfully, that the fact that there is a "stairway to heaven" and "highway to hell" (to quote some secular songs) gives a pretty good indication about the level of traffic in each direction.

Being proud of a church because it's "cool" enough to not "force" people to listen to "corny" religious music shows a tragic lack of understanding of what the gospel message even is and reveals a very confused concept of what it means to know the Lord. May the Lord give us wisdom in all these things.

"Humble Yourself in the Sight of the Lord" (part 2)

4All the kings of the earth shall praise You, O Lord, when they hear the words of Your mouth. 5Yes, they shall sing of the ways of the Lord, for great is the glory of the Lord. 6Though the Lord is on high, yet He regards the lowly; but the proud He knows from afar. —Psalm 138:4-6

AS WE SEEK to humble ourselves before the Lord, blessing Him and bringing Him honor, we need to ask ourselves a few important questions. Of course our hearts yearn to draw others to Christ, and it's great to invite them to come to church with us. But at some point, we need to realize that what happens while they're there is a matter between them and the Lord. Are we bringing them, hoping that they'll have a good time? That they'll feel comfortable? Or are we bringing them, knowing that the Lord *will* be working on their hearts while they're there, and it might not be very comfortable at all! We bring them, praying that they will hear the Word of God, authored by the Holy Spirit, and be convicted of their sin, which definitely *won't* be a comfortable time, but it may prove to be the very best day of their entire life! Of course, we want them to feel welcomed and loved, but we should also pray that God will be touching their heart in a way that it has never been touched before.

The problem with making sinners feel "comfortable" in church means that the Holy Spirit is stifled, and the Word spoken from the pulpit may well go right over their head. We should pray that salvation would be preached from the pulpit, and if it isn't, we must be prepared to fill in the gaps, perhaps after the service is over. Some may come and leave unchanged. Others may be stirred and be filled with questions and a desire to know more. Still others will have their hearts broken as they are convicted of their sins and their need of a Savior. You must be ready to hold their hand and encourage them further, as the Holy Spirit leads. It goes deep. This is the most important decision that one can make in life, and we want to be ready for the Lord to fill us and use us in ministering to these new baby Christians, or perhaps friends who have now become true seekers.

Remember that it is the truth that sets us free. Nothing else will do it. Pray that the Lord will fill your mouth with the right words, boldly yet humbly speaking of what it means to receive salvation and letting them know that their lives will never be the same again, because now they have the Lord himself to walk beside and guide them for the rest of their lives! The follow-up isn't in your hands alone. There are many Christians whom the Lord will touch who will come alongside these new babes.

Are you ready to be there to help them along the way? If they have been broken at the recognition of what they are apart from Christ, you must be ready to encourage, comfort, and even lead them for a little bit as they begin taking those baby steps. Paul wrote to Timothy: *"I charge you therefore before God and the Lord Jesus Christ, who will judge the living and the dead at His appearing and His kingdom: Preach the word! Be ready in season and out of season. Convince, rebuke, exhort, with all longsuffering and teaching. For the time will come when they will not endure down doctrine, but according to their own desires, because they have itching ears, they will heap up for themselves teachers; and they will turn their ears away from the truth, and be turned aside to fables. But you be watchful in all things, endure afflictions, do the work of an evangelist, fulfill your ministry"* (2 Timothy 4:1-5).

Paul warns that the time will come when people won't put up with sound doctrine. What do we do then? Preach the Word to them anyway! Fulfill your ministry even when others are forsaking theirs and turning from the truth to "feel-good" fables. Remember, our job isn't to attract people to the *church* but to attract them to the Lord himself. In fact, when tactics meant to draw crowds replace the clear teaching of the truth, no one can be made free.

November 19

Preach the Word . . .

⁷Though I walk in the midst of trouble, You will revive me; You will stretch out Your hand against the wrath of my enemies, and Your right hand will save me. ⁸The Lord will perfect that which concerns me; Your mercy, O Lord, endures forever; and Your right hand will save me. —*Psalm 138:7-8*

WE, LIKE DAVID, walk in the midst of trouble, and so we, too, can expect the Lord to revive us. Notice that while David, as King, could expect God's help in defeating their enemies, stretching out His hand against their wrath, we also know that there's a future that is coming by the hand of God against the enemies of His chosen people, the Jews and the Church.

Paul wrote, *"We . . . thank God always for you . . . because your faith grows exceedingly, and the love of every one of you all abounds toward each other, so that we . . . boast of you among the churches of God for your patience and faith in all your persecutions and tribulations that you endure, which is manifest evidence of the righteous judgment to God, . . . "* (2 Thes 1:3-10).

We live in the midst of trouble today, but we know that the right hand of God will save us and perfect that which concerns us because His mercy endures forever. He will never forsake the work of His hands. Our faith can and should grow exceedingly, and our love should abound. We need patience and faith while we endure persecutions. God will repay with tribulation those who trouble us when the Lord Jesus appears with His mighty angels from heaven taking vengeance on those who do not know God. He's coming again to the earth with His saints. In the midst of trouble and perilous times, there's an important truth regarding living in the last days: The mission of the church has always been to seek and to save our enemies! *"You will be hated by all for My name's sake. But he who endures to the end will be saved"* (Matthew 10:22; see also Matthew 10:34-39).

Before you were saved, you were God's enemy. How did *you* get saved? Most likely, it was because one of God's former enemies, who is now His friend, proclaimed to you the Word of God, or even brought you to church, and you heard, heeded, and were saved. We live in the midst of trouble, but that's nothing new. David did, too, 3,000 years ago, and so has every one of God's chosen people since. Although some seasons of history have been more "Christian-friendly" than others, the last season to come will be the worst of all, and yet, our primary mission remains unchanged. We are still to preach to the homosexuals and the transvestites; preach to the cult member and the heretic the Word of God. Preach to the adulterer and the fornicator, the protestor and the rioter. Preach to the evolutionist, the atheist, the agnostic, the spiritualist, the liar, the thief, the Republican, and the Democrat— the Word of God. Our mission is to preach whether our message is popular or not, and it has always been our mission to save our enemies. That's how you got saved, as did I! We're living in the last days, friends. Reject any and all efforts to diminish the authority of the Word of God. Remain truthful. Don't become tactical, trying to formulate a message and method that people will embrace. Remember: *every person ever saved was once an enemy of God and filled with wickedness*. We're living in such times as in Noah's day, but the mercy of the Lord endures forever, and that means that He is still unwilling that any should perish but that all should come to repentance!

November 20

God Knows

Introduction

To the Chief Musician, a Psalm of David—Psalm 139

A. W. TOZER wrote, "The essence of idolatry is the entertainment of thoughts about God that are unworthy of Him." This psalm by King David is addressed to the chief musician. It was used in temple worship. Although there are more than fifty psalms that begin with the same introductory words, this psalm is distinct from the others for one reason. In the twenty-four verses that this psalm comprises, there are close to fifty personal pronouns used, each one connecting *us* with *God*. They are paired throughout this psalm in this way: I-You, You-my, You-me, Your-my, over and over. We see that King David is connecting our minds to the intimacy of our relationship and also interaction with our Lord.

What Tozer wrote above is fitting in that we have all had thoughts at times that were less than worthy of God. Perhaps we've felt like God has forsaken or forgotten us, or maybe He didn't handle something the way we think He should have. Did He allow something that hurt you? Did He let someone get away with something that you think He should have, could have, stopped? But look at what the author of Hebrews tells us: "*Let your conduct be without covetousness; be content with such things as you have. For He Himself has said, 'I will never leave you nor forsake you.' So we may boldly say: 'The Lord is my helper; I will not fear. What can man do to me?'*" (Hebrews 13:5-6).

The contents of this psalm is nothing short of glorious, as we will find within these twenty-four verses the omniscience, omnipresence, and omnipotence of God and the way that all of these attributes are directly connected to His relationship with us. In fact, God's omniscience reminds us that He knows *all*, His omnipresence means that He is *everywhere* at all times, and His omnipotence tells us that He is *all-powerful*. Nothing compares to our God! Thus the little title of this little series: "God Knows."

Now, when we think about that idea, it can either be comforting or frightening, depending on where we stand with Him. Remember that Jesus on earth was God, and His all-knowing nature was just one of His incredible ways of interacting with the apostles and disciples. Remember this? "*All the multitudes were amazed and said, 'Could this be the Son of David?' Now when the Pharisees heard it they said, 'This fellow does not cast out demons except by Beelzebub, the ruler of the demons.' But Jesus knew their thoughts, and said to them: 'Every kingdom divided against itself will not stand. If Satan casts out Satan, he is divided against himself. How then will his kingdom stand?'*" (Matthew 12:23-25).

Jesus knew their thoughts! Think about that. I wonder how the disciples felt when they realized this about Him. He heard inside of their heads when they thought such things as "How long are we going to keep walking?" or "Why doesn't He tell Peter to shut up?" or maybe "Why would He choose a tax collector?" or any other random thoughts that might enter into the minds of a group of competitive men. Do you suppose that His knowing their thoughts made them think about what they were allowing into their minds? I'm sure it was cause for concern, but it wasn't the main point of their knowing about His knowing. God knows all about us, but He knows us in an understanding, loving, and compassionate way.

"*He remembers our frame; He knows that we are but dust*" (Psalm 103:14), lest we start thinking too highly of ourselves! He said, "*You will seek Me and find Me, when you search for Me with all your heart*" (Jeremiah 29:11-13). Are you seeking Him today, with all of your heart?

He Sees You
When You're Sleeping

¹O Lord, You have searched me and known me. ²You know my sitting down and my rising up; You understand my thought afar off. ³You comprehend my path and my lying down, and are acquainted with all my ways. ⁴For there is not a word on my tongue, but behold, O Lord, You know it altogether. ⁵You have hedged me behind and before, and laid Your hand upon me. ⁶Such knowledge is too wonderful for me; it is high, I cannot attain it. —*Psalm 139:1-6*

"O LORD, You. . . ." This simple introduction flips the title of this series, "God Knows" from being an ominous negative: "God knows what you're doing, so you'd better watch out," to "God is watching over you. He sees everything that's going on with you right now." John, one of the Lord's disciples, recorded the Jesus' words: "*You did not choose Me, but I chose you and appointed you that you should go and bear fruit, and that your fruit should remain, that whatsoever you ask the Father in My name, He may give you*" (John 15:16); and "*We love Him because He first loved us*" (1 John 4:19).

This "choosing" in John 15 isn't for salvation, but, as disciples, we *choose* to love God as a response to His first loving us. David says, "O Lord, You have known all my ups and downs and are acquainted with all my ways, and there is not a word that I am about to speak that you don't know." Who initiates this intimate relationship and knowledge of us? God does! He knows everything—when we get up, when we lie down, when we're happy or sad, when our thoughts wander and our feet do, too—He knows it all. David continues: "And, Lord, knowing me the way You do, you've protected me and hedged me in, in a safe place."

God knows our failures and struggles, and He's always there to help us through them. Remember what Jeremiah said? "*For thus says the Lord of hosts, the God of Israel: Do not let your prophets and your diviners who are in your midst deceive you, nor listen to the dreams. . . . For they prophesy falsely to you in My name; I have not sent them, says the Lord. For thus says the Lord: After seventy years are completed at Babylon, I will visit you and perform My good work toward you, and cause you to return to this place*" (Jer 29:8-10).

Here, God told Judah that even though their seventy-year captivity was deserved and self-inflicted, He would still hedge them in, behind and before, and they were to remember that His thoughts toward them, especially as they headed into hard times, were thoughts of peace and not of evil. We're all sinners. Look at David, God's anointed, who made serious errors, entertaining thoughts that he shouldn't have that led him into grievous sin. The Lord knew, and watched, as David followed his feet to his neighbor's house and his neighbor's wife. He knew what David would later say to the husband of Bathsheba, the woman with whom he had physical relations while Uriah was away, fighting for David's kingdom. God knew the lies David would tell as he tried to hide Bathsheba's pregnancy, and worst of all, He knew of the subsequent murder of a good man in David's attempt to cover up his sin. And yet—God's love was so great for David, his *repentant* servant, that He hedged him in, before and behind.

Likewise, God knows *your* failures, struggles and doubts, and yet He actively makes Himself available as a "very present help in time of need," not because we deserve it or have earned it, but because of the great love He has for us. He understands our weaknesses and our faults, and what He wants from us are repentant hearts and sorrow over our sinfulness. That He loves us still is too wonderful to comprehend, and yet it's absolutely true. And He promises that He will never leave us nor forsake us as we seek to walk on His path, letting Him guide us as we go through this life. Precious words again from Psalm 127:2 "He gives His beloved sleep." Rest in the Lord.

November 22

No Place to Hide

> [7]Where can I go from Your Spirit? Or where can I flee from Your presence? [8]If I ascend to heaven, You are there; if I make my bed in hell, behold, You are there. [9]If I take the wings of the morning, and dwell in the uttermost parts of the sea, [10]even there Your hand shall lead me, and Your right hand shall hold me. —*Psalm 139:7-10*

HAVE YOU ever tried to hide from God? Perhaps you've said or done something that you're ashamed of, but instead of running to Him, asking for His forgiveness, you try to ignore what your heart is telling you and keep on running away from Him. How'd that work out for you? Very likely you learned that it's impossible to run or hide from God if you're truly His child. David understood this well. What he's saying, in essence, is that as a prodigal, he had made his bed in "hell"—not literal hell, but he had become comfortable with the things that would send him there. But even then he found that the Lord was there to convict him and eventually lead him back to His Father's house, where life is far better than the hell that he had made for himself.

There's a wonderful literal application for us in these verses that goes beyond David's figurative descriptions: "*Do you not know that you are the temple of God and that the Spirit of God dwells in you?*" (1 Cor 3:16). In Old Testament times, the Holy Spirit spoke through the prophets to direct God's chosen people. Today His chosen ones are *indwelt* by the Holy Spirit, who teaches them all things and is always with them because He is in them! Think about that. It means that whether you soar to the heights of heaven in your thoughts and actions or delve into the depths of hell by the same means, *the presence of the Lord never leaves you*! That should be a very sobering thought. Even if we try to run from God, as did Jonah, or Adam and Eve, taking the "wings of the morning" to the "uttermost parts of the sea," even there the Spirit is within His children, leading us, and God's right hand holds us. Consider the gentleness and kindness of our Father!

There's no getting around it: God knows that we can do nothing without Him, so He's arranged it that we never *are* without Him. Having an imputed righteousness through the blood of Jesus Christ, we can rise from any fall by the presence of the Holy Spirit, and since He is in us and always with us, no failure or fall can hold us down. Paul wrote, "*I know how to be abased, and I know how to abound. Everywhere and in all things I have learned both to be full and to be hungry, both to abound and to suffer need. I can do all things through Christ who strengthens me*" (Phil 4:12-13). Think about that! It means that there is nothing that we will face that we won't have the strength for, because Jesus Christ is with us through it all.

Consider Peter in Luke 22. He was ready to go to death himself with the Lord, and yet Jesus warned him that he would deny Him three times before the rooster crowed. You know what happened. After the third denial, when the rooster crowed, Peter realized the awfulness of what he had done, even though the Lord had warned him of this. He went out and wept bitterly, we are told. But Christ had also said that Peter would return to Him and be used to strengthen his brethren, and that's exactly what happened. Even at Peter's lowest point, as he wept bitter tears, God was there!

Friends, God is there to lift us when we make our bed in hell, and He is there to temper us when things are going well. John warned us "*Do not love the things of the world. . . . [All] that is in the world . . . is not of the Father but is of the world. And the world is passing away . . . but he who does the will of God abides forever*" (1 John 2:15-17). God knows that we can't handle either adversity *or* prosperity without

Him, so He promises that we are never without Him. There's no place to hide. And isn't that wonderful?

The Battle for the Mind

[11]If I say, "Surely the darkness shall fall on me," even the night shall be light about me; [12]Indeed, the darkness shall not hide from Your but the night shines as the day; the darkness and the light are both alike to You.
—*Psalm 139:11-12*

WE'RE NOW brought back to the source of so many of our struggles—our thought life, our mind. Sometimes it seems as though our mind has become a battlefield, and our thoughts turn into words that indicate our hopelessness and despair. How well David understood these things! Psalm 31: *"Have mercy on me, O Lord, for I am in trouble; My eye wastes away with grief, yes, by soul and my body! For my life is spent with grief, and my years with sighing; my strength fails because of my iniquity, and my bones waste away"* (vv. 9-10). And again, *"My soul melts from heaviness; strengthen me according to Your word"* (Psalm 119:28).

What was the source of David's grief in Psalm 31? It was due to his iniquity, his moral perversity. And although the source isn't mentioned in Psalm 119, the cure is given, as it is in our verses today. When David begins verse 11 with "If I say . . . " and then expresses his fear, he also reminds himself of the wonderful truth that God's light will be with him even then. Darkness and night often have the connotation of evil and deception. So David is saying that even if he reaches the point in his own mind that this wickedness will never end, he also acknowledges the comforting thought that because the Lord is with him, the darkness shall be as light, and the night will shine like the day. (Keep in mind that "light" and "day" are metaphors for truth and goodness.) In other words, God is not influenced or altered in His actions by either one.

The author of Psalm 43 wrote, *"Vindicate me, O God, and plead my cause. . . . Deliver me from the deceitful and unjust man! For You are the God of my strength; why do You cast me off? Why do I go mourning because of the oppression of the enemy? Oh, send out Your light and Your truth! Let them lead me; let them bring me to Your holy hill and to Your tabernacle"* (vv. 1-3). And we also read, *"Your word is a lamp to my feet and a light to my path"* (Psalm 119:105).

The Bible continually reminds us that God is the One who orders our steps and directs our paths, making a way for us that leads us right back to remembering

His Word! He knows that we will go through difficulties in life, and He gave us His Word to light our path through those times.

As we close out our reading this morning, let's look at some of the words of wisdom that He has given to us through the Scriptures: *"There is therefore now no condemnation to those who are in Christ Jesus, who do not walk according to the flesh, but according to the Spirit"* (Romans 8:1); *"I say then: Walk in the Spirit, and you shall not fulfill the lust of the flesh"* (Galatians 5:16); and *"If we live in the Spirit, let us also walk in the Spirit"* (Galatians 5:25).

So whether we walk in the darkness or in the light, He promises to be with us. He will guard our minds and our hearts as we commit them to Him, and no battle will be so great that we cannot over it. So what should we do then? Walk on!

November 24

The Living Word of God

Summary conclusions—Psalm 139:1-12

THERE IS so much to consider in this psalm that I want to take us through a few more thoughts. We've seen that we're to walk in the Spirit being directed by the Word of God. Why am I bringing this up again? Because there's a trend in the church today regarding so-called "extra-biblical revelation," meaning that God tells people things beyond what is in His Word, and many proponents are elevating these statements to the status of Scripture.

Never, ever forget that the Spirit will never contradict the Word, nor is the prophetic revelation of God incomplete. God's desire regarding what He wants us to know, from the beginning of time on this earth to the very end, is all contained within the Bible. We have everything we need to arrive in heaven and to make our way through this life both now and when our "redemption draws near." We can rest in His promise that *"He who has begun a good work in you will complete it until the day of Jesus Christ"* (Phil 1:6).

Peter wrote: *"Grace and peace be multiplied to you in the knowledge of God and of Jesus our Lord, as His divine power has given to us all things that pertain to life and godliness, through the knowledge of Him who called us by glory and virtue, by which have been given to us exceedingly great and precious promises, that by these you may be partakers of the divine nature, having escaped the corruption that is in the world through lust"* (2 Peter 1:2-4).

This isn't to deny that God gives special words of knowledge, grants discernment, and offers wisdom through the gifts of the Holy Spirit. The Word says that in fact He does. But remember that it is the written Word of God that has guided the church and Christians through difficult times for centuries, and it is still sufficient and capable of doing so today.

Yes, the Holy Spirit still speaks to us. And yes, we are to walk in the Spirit. But we must not add to or ignore His Word in order to do so. Why else would God warn us that we are to *"test the spirits, whether they are of God,"* and *"do not believe every spirit . . . because many false prophets have gone out in the world"* (1 John 4:1)?

Have you ever had a sensing or an impulse and wondered if it was the Lord telling you to do or not to do something? Have you ever come to a crossroads in your life and needed the direction of the Lord but weren't sure if what you thought or felt was actually from Him? Don't you realize that we need an unchanging and constant infallible filter for our thoughts and inspirations? In addition to all of these, isn't it usually in the middle of difficulties that our thoughts and emotions run away with us, causing us to do things that we later regret? God knows all about this! And He has given us the stability of His written Word as a light to our path and lamp to our feet.

How can we balance both walking in the Spirit and being directed through His Word? *"He [Jesus] said to them, 'Go into all the world and preach the gospel to every creature'"* (Mark 16:15). So the Word of God sends us out to all the world to preach the gospel. But it is the Spirit who will guide us to *where* and to *whom.* "Preach the gospel" is a concrete instruction for all of us. The specifics of where we will go or to whom we will preach is not. Not everyone is called to be a foreign missionary, though we all share that commission. Not everyone is called to be a street evangelist, but all are called to evangelize. The Holy Spirit will direct us in those callings. We're to trust the Lord and lean not on our own understanding, and we're especially not to read into the Word of God things that aren't there. God often shows us through His Word to "wait." If we wait upon the Lord, He *will* direct our steps, and we will know that we're walking on the path that He has set out for us.

November 25

Where You Lead, I Will Follow

Final Thoughts—Psalm 139:1-12

WALKING IN the Word and by the Spirit are not mutually exclusive, but the Holy Spirit is the one who will empower us to walk in the Word. And then when difficulties arise, as the Spirit leads us to the Word, the Word will tell us such things as: "*He who dwells in the secret place of the Most High shall abide under the shadow of the Almighty. I will say of the Lord, 'He is my refuge and my fortress; my God, in Him I will trust.' Surely He shall deliver you from the snare of the fowler and from the perilous pestilence. He shall cover you with His feathers, and under His wings you shall take refuge; His truth shall be your shield and buckler. You shall not be afraid of the terror by night, nor of the arrow that flies by day, nor of the pestilence that walks in darkness, nor of the destruction that lays waste at noonday. A thousand may fall at your side, and ten thousand at your right hand; but it shall not come near you. Only with your eye shall you look, and see the reward of the wicked. Because you have made the Lord, who is my refuge, even the Most High, your dwelling place, no evil shall befall you, nor shall any plague come near your dwelling . . ."* (Psalm 91: 1-10).

Truthfully, I can't imagine anything else that we might need to know during seasons of trial and difficulty besides these words from our Father. He knows what we need—His Word, to guide us, and His Spirit to empower and direct us. He freely gives us both! A good verse to memorize—or at least to copy and keep close at hand—is 2 Timothy 3:16-17: *"All Scripture is given by inspiration of God, and is profitable for doctrine, for reproof, for correction, for instruction in righteousness, that the man of God may be complete, thoroughly equipped for every good work."*

We've noted before that God knows our hearts, that we're prone to wander and to wonder, so He has given us His Word as a light in times of darkness and to thoroughly equip us for every good work. Those works will require the Holy Spirit's power, which also enables us to deny the lusts of the flesh. In fact, our God is so good that He knows and has supplied *all* we need to get through our secret failures and struggles, and we need never face them by ourselves in our own strength. When we feel like the darkness is winning, He holds our hand and reminds us that will never happen. The gates of Hades will never prevail against God's church. And as a loving Father, He knows that we need to continually be reminded of these things during such times as those in which we now live.

November 26

The Sovereignty of God (Part 1)

Introduction—Psalm 139:13-18

WE'VE BEEN seeing that God is the One who initiates an intimate relationship with His children, and we learned that we could be assured of three things: (1) God knows our secret failures and struggles and He is always there to help us through them. (2) God knows that we can do nothing without Him, so we are never left without Him. (3) God knows that we will go through difficulties in life, and He has given us His Word to light our way.

We saw David's observation about God's omnipresence: *"Where can I go from Your Spirit? Or where can I flee from Your presence?"* (Psalm 139:7-8). God is with us when we soar the heavens and when we plunge the depths and through all the highs and lows of our lives. We're going to take a closer look at the omnipotence of God.

The main lesson of the whole of Psalm 139 is that you can't fool God, you can't flee from God, and you can't fight God, so we should just follow God! There are some pretty deep theological concepts in this psalm, but we want to try to break it down the best we can to gain an understanding of this One who loves us so much that He sent His Son to die for our sins so that we might spend the rest of eternity with Him!

In Matthew 5, Jesus said, *"You have heard that it was said, 'You shall love your neighbor and hate your enemy.' But I say to you, love your enemies, bless those who curse you, do good to those who hate you, and pray for those who spitefully use you and persecute you, that you may be sons of your Father in heaven; for He makes His sun rise on the evil and on the good, and sends rain on the just and the unjust"* (vv. 43-45).

Many people have a hard time with the idea of God having enemies whom He will ultimately have to judge. It's important that we look at the Lord's heart when it comes to those enemies who have made a choice to continue in their wickedness even though salvation is right in front of them. Never forget that God is good. He causes His rain to fall on the wicked and the just, and He makes His sun to rise on the evil and the good. How can we explain our God?

Over the next few days in this psalm, we're going to take another look at that wonderful attribute of His: Sovereignty. The word itself means "Supreme Ruler," even as "God" means "Supreme Being." In order to be the Supreme Ruler, one must be omniscient, omnipresent, and omnipotent, and there is no one besides our God who fits that description. Therefore, as Supreme Ruler, both evil and good are under His providential control. Because of this, some ask, "Why does He even allow evil at all?" and "Why do the evil experience the goodness of God when they hate Him?" and "Why doesn't He just make everyone behave and do His will?" The answer is that if He did that, there would be no such thing in this world as love, including love for God, because *love requires a choice*, and submission without love is called "servitude," which is the exact opposite of the relationship that God longs to have with His people. In fact, He desires a more familial relationship.

We are going to be looking at some observational reminders of the truths that expose the real consequences of those who have thoughts about God that are unworthy of Him, even though He is sovereign over all creation. These are the ones who hate and reject Him. May the Lord use these next few days to impress on our hearts just how wonderful, kind, and majestic is our Lord. And may we be led to pray for those who do not understand the beauty of His holiness and grace and His desire for all to be saved.

Bless the Lord, O My Soul!

¹³For You formed my inward parts; You covered me in my mother's womb.
¹⁴I will praise You, for I am fearfully and wonderfully made, marvelous are Your world, and that my soul knows very well. —Psalm 139:13-14

AS WE CONSIDER these next verses, we see the beautiful imagery of the Lord creating life within the womb of the mother. David understood that God was involved in the creation of his own body and states that this is something that his "soul knows very well." The word for "formed" implies divine involvement in the constructing of humans within the womb. The word "covered," in verse 13, means to protect. What a precious picture! C. S. Lewis stated, "We don't *have* a soul; we *are* a soul. We *have* a body." In other words, where there is a living human body there is a soul. In Exodus 21:22-23, we read that if an altercation of some sort injures a pregnant woman and the baby is born prematurely but healthy, then the father of the child shall determine the punishment of the perpetrator. But if the child is stillborn due to the altercation, the Lord calls for the death of the one who caused the child's death. A life for a life.

God declares that the child being formed inside the womb is a precious, living human being, whose right to life is equal to that of those outside the womb. Both are human lives, and thus the child in the womb also must have a soul. Tragically, our present culture protests that the growing child within the womb is mere tissue and not something to be treasured and protected. They ignore the miracle of conception and the divine involvement in the creation, protection, and formation of children within the womb. This denial of the humanity of unborn children seems to be reserved for the depravity of the time of the end, which we are surely in today.

Jeremiah wrote: "*The word of the Lord came to me, saying, 'Before I formed you in the womb I knew you; before you were born I sanctified you; I ordained you a prophet to the nations'*" (Jer 1:4-5). Thus both David and Jeremiah understood that God created, protected, and wonderfully made them. Does this mean that God's hand is active in the physical creation of all life within the womb? If we follow this train of thought to the end, it would mean that God also is hands-on in the creation the mentally and physically impaired as well as the miscarried and stillborn children. This is a difficult concept. What we do know is this: God is sovereign, and

He is omniscient—all knowing. One consideration is that God at one point set in motion the process for the conception and development of every child within the womb, but as Adam and Eve had sinned against God, there were natural consequences that followed, including, over time, the introduction of faulty genes that have grown more mutated with each generation as part of the fact of sin on this earth. It has nothing to do with God's love for each child in the womb. It's that after the fall of man, in many ways He removed His protection from the human race as a result of sin and evil. God loves these children as much as any others. In fact, often they are the greatest blessings to their parents and to others as God's love shines through their innocent lives.

Remember David's sin with Bathsheba that resulted in the birth of a child whom the Lord took shortly after his birth? David knew that the child was innocent, and that he would see him in heaven when he himself died. We can't state for certain why God allows some things to happen in the womb, but we do know that God loves those babies and will attend wonderfully to their lives on earth and in heaven. But people today have a different view, which has been tarnished by their lack of belief and appreciation for the Lord himself, and a diminished view of God leads to a disregard for *all* life.

"You Can't Make Me!"

15 My frame was not hidden from You, when I was made in secret, and skillfully wrought in the lowest parts of the earth. 16 Your eyes saw my substance, being yet unformed. And in Your book they all were written, the days fashioned for me, when as yet there were none of them. —Psalm 139:15-16

DAVID DESCRIBES his own formation as a baby in the womb of his mother. "Frame" simply means "substance" and speaks of the combined elements of which we are all formed. He writes of being "skillfully wrought in the lowest parts of the earth [a poetic reference to the womb]." For millennia, what happens in the womb, although secret and hidden from view, was always known to be the creation of a living, growing child. Incredibly, now that man can actually look inside the womb and observe the wonderful process of the development of the child, it is now referred to as "fetal tissue." That "tissue," not long after conception, has fingers, toes, eyes, ears, and pulmonary, respiratory, and nerve systems just like we who live outside the womb, yet it's not considered a child the right to life!

David goes so far as to say that before even one day of his life had begun, God had a purpose for him, fashioning, as it were, the course upon which He would later direct him. And here's a fascinating concept: God's purpose for our lives is written when we are yet unformed, so we must ask, "Does God's sovereignty over-rule man's free will during the course of his life?" *Must* we do all that God has ordained, or do we have the freedom to do our will, ignoring His plan? All we need to do is to look at the history of the Jews and Israel.

In Deuteronomy, we read, *"You are a holy people to the Lord . . . [who] has cho-sen you . . . for Himself, a special treasure above all the peoples on the face of the earth. The Lord did not . . . love . . . nor choose you because you were more in number than any other people, for you were the least of all peoples; but because the Lord loves you, and keep[s] the oath which He swore to your fathers, . . . [He] brought you out with a mighty hand, and has redeemed you from . . . bondage, from the hand of Pharaoh. . . . 'Therefore know that the Lord your God, He is God, the faithful God who keeps covenant and mercy for a thousand generations with those who love Him and keep His commandments; and He repays those who hate Him to their face, to destroy them. . . . Therefore you shall keep the commandment, the statutes, and the judgments which I command you today, to observe them'"* (7:6-11). And in Luke, *"O Jerusalem, Jerusalem, the one who kills the prophets and stones those who are sent to her! How often I wanted to gather your children together, as a hen gathers her brood under her wings, but you were not willing!"* (Lk 13:34).

God is the initiator of the intimate relationship that He desires to have with His people. If His sovereignty means that everything that happens is because it's His will, then a willing heart to observe His commands, statutes, and judgments becomes moot. In fact, man's free will doesn't impose upon the sovereignty of God, because in that sovereignty, He has given man the freedom to choose to obey or to disobey Him. In Luke we saw that Jesus longed to gather the Jews to Himself but they weren't willing! Can God *make* people do whatever He wants them to do? He's the Creator of the universe! He can do all things. But *does* He force men to do His will? No, because that would make us like robots, unable to choose for ourselves how we act. The real question, though, is this: Is it *best* for us to always obey the will of God? The answer, of course, is a resounding yes! Don't be like the stubborn child who, even knowing what is best for him, still digs in his heels, crying, "Don't tell me what to do! You can't make me!" In fact, God *has* made us, from the begin-ning of our lives, and He has every right to ask of us whatever He wants and that He knows is the absolute best for us.

What's It Worth to You?

¹⁵My frame was not hidden from You, when I was made in secret, and skillfully wrought in the lowest parts of the earth. ¹⁶Your eyes saw my substance, being yet unformed. And in Your book they all were written, the days fashioned for me, when as yet there were none of them.
—Psalm 139:15-16

CONTINUING our thoughts from yesterday, we can truly say that life is best when we follow God's plan, not when we ask Him to bless ours. His will and purpose for us was written in His book before we even existed. As we live according to His plan for us. God will direct our steps. He will light our path, and He will lead us in the way everlasting. Are we intelligent enough to understand what a blessing this is and yield our lives to Him?

In 1 Corinthians, Paul wrote, *"We are God's fellow workers; you are God's field, you are God's building. According to the grace of God which was given to me, as a wise master builder I have laid the foundation, and another builds on it. But let each one take heed how he builds on it. For no other foundation can anyone lay than that which is laid, which is Jesus Christ. Now if anyone builds on this foundation with gold, silver, precious stones, wood, hay, stray, each one's work will become clear; for the Day will declare it, because it will be revealed by fire; and the fire will test each one's work, of what sort it is. If anyone's work which he has built on it endures, he will receive a reward. If anyone's work is burned, he will suffer loss; but he himself will be saved, yet so as through fire"* (1 Cor 3:9-15).

A good line to remember, which has been quoted by many, says, "Only one life, 'twill soon be past; only what's done for Christ will last." "We're saved by grace," Ephesians tells us, "through faith for good works, and we should walk in them." Those works will be tested by fire, and only the gold, silver and precious stones, representing the works we did in *God's* will and for *His* glory will remain. But the things that we did for our own glory, even if done in the name of the Lord, will prove to be but wood, hay, and stubble.

Look at it this way: the best life is one that impacts the next life. To arrive in heaven saved, yet "so as through fire" (we could say, "by the skin of our teeth") and suffering the loss of any rewards, isn't the description I want hung on my eternal existence. We need to quit wasting time on things that have no eternal value! They may not even necessarily be bad things or things that are wrong, but if they rob us of fulfilling God's will and purpose for our lives, then we're settling for second-best in this life, and sowing nothing into the next. Is that worth it?

Do you believe in eternal rewards, which are promised in God's Word? Do you seek to earn them by asking God to bless your plans, or do you seek to live according to *His?* Matthew makes it pretty clear what we're to do: "*Seek first the kingdom of God and His righteousness, and all these things shall be added to you*" (Matthew 6:33). The word "seek," as used here, means to strive after. Ask yourself, are you striving first for the kingdom of God and His righteousness? Or are you striving first for your own kingdom, asking God's blessings on it?

I believe, more so today than I did yesterday, that Jesus is coming soon. I believe that this life is a short opportunity to sow into eternity. I believe that God has works for all of us to do, and we should walk in them. I also believe that other interests may keep many from doing so, and it could mean for those having a saved soul but a wasted life. I want to live for God and strive first for His kingdom. I want to see the "things added to me," because He is pleased with me. After all, He's the one who formed and fashioned my days while I was still in the womb! How precious a reminder is that! How much is that worth to you?

November 30

What Can I Do?

17 How precious also are your thoughts to me, O God! How great is the sum of them! *18* If I should count them, they would be more in number than the sand; when I awake, I am still with You. —*Psalm 139:17-18*

DAVID DRAWS our minds back to earlier verses and how we are constantly on God's mind. He describes the thoughts of God as precious, saying that these prized and valuable thoughts, if it were even possible to count them, would be more numerous than the grains of sand on the earth. Then he adds, "When I awake, I am still with you." Psalm 121:4 tells us, "*Behold, He who keeps Israel shall neither slumber nor sleep.*" On a personal side, having had a little one in the house last week as our daughter and youngest granddaughter visited, I was reminded of an interesting contrast. When you have a toddler, they take a nap, and then it's time to get other things done (or take a nap yourself!) before the miniature whirlwind wakes up. But David says, "When I awake, you have continued here with me." God never says, "Oh, good, they're finally asleep. I can get some other things done." He watches over us and continues with us throughout the night, no matter how long that night may last.

Looking at the New Testament, we read, "*With many other words [John the Baptist] testified and exhorted them, saying, 'Be saved from the perverse generation.' Then those who gladly received his word were baptized; and that day about three thousand souls were added to them. And they continued steadfastly in the apostles' doctrine and fellowship, in the breaking of bread, and in prayers. Then fear came upon every soul, and many wonders and signs were done through the apostles. Now all who believed were together, and had all things in common, and sold their possessions and goods, and divided them among all, as anyone had need. So continuing daily with one accord in the temple, and breaking bread from house to house, they ate their food with gladness and simplicity of heart, praising God and having favor with all the people. And the Lord added to the church daily those who were being saved"* (Acts 2:40-47).

Personally, I wish that some Christians would read Peter's sermon in Acts 2 today, and see where he used prophecy, history, theology, miracles, conviction, warnings, and a call to repentance to preach a message that resulted in 3,000 souls being added to the church! And they and the rest of the church continued steadfastly in that practice and teaching, resulting in the Lord's adding to the church daily those being saved!

Friends, no matter what you're going through, hold onto this thought: There is never a day that God doesn't have plans for you. When you awake, He continues to be with you, and in that continuance, He has works every day for you to walk in. God is still adding to the church daily those who are being saved. He has continued to do this every day since the church was born. In every case, He has used someone to either plant, water, or harvest those seeds. Even in the Middle East, where the gospel is forbidden, we hear of reports of those to whom Jesus has appeared in visions and dreams, and they knew who He was because they had heard from someone else of this One in whom the Christians believe.

We are nearing the times of the end. Some Christians today may not exactly be doing the will of the Gentiles, but they are spending their time pursuing their own will, while God's will daily takes a back seat. May we all, from this day forward, begin our days with the question that Paul asked when accosted by Jesus on the road to Damascus: "Lord, what would You have me to do?" And then add the word, "today." Pray this today. Pray this tomorrow—and the next day, and every day, until the trumpet sounds. The dead in Christ shall rise, and we will meet Him in the air!

DECEMBER

The Sovereignty of God (Part 2)

Introduction

Search me, O God . . . —Psalm 139:19-24

WE'VE BEEN looking at some of the most personal and thought-provoking words ever written, and we've seen beyond doubt that our God isn't the god of the Deists—a distant, impersonal being; nor is He the "god" of the pantheists—a force within everything, whether inanimate, animal, and human. He isn't in the rocks or the trees, nor is he inside all of us. Nature is not God. Nor is God a "genie" (which is essentially what the word-faith crowd likes to believe), obligated to say "yes" to our every demand if we just have enough "faith."

In review, Psalm 139 is a masterpiece, using forty-eight pairings of personal pronouns, with one representing God, and the other, man. God is sovereign *over* all creation, not merely present among us, and He is deeply involved in the world He has created. He knows *everything* about *everything*. We've seen that: 1) God knows our failures and struggles, and He will always help us. 2) He knows we can do nothing without Him, so He never leaves us. 3) He knows that our paths will be difficult, but His Word lights our way.

In verses 13-18, we noted that not only does God know all, but also, He is present and active everywhere, including during our formation in the womb (see Ps 139:13-14 and Jeremiah 1:4-5). We addressed some difficult questions about why some children are handicapped or deformed, or even stillborn. We saw that God sees the child in the womb as a real human being, who is alive, has a heart-beat, experiences sensations while still inside the mother, and even cries. (Read Ex 21:22-23 to see God's love for those little ones.)

We also saw through King David's own experience of losing a child that he firmly believed he would see his child again, which indicates through God's Word that babies in the womb and young children who die *do* go to heaven.

In all of the instances that are touched on throughout this psalm, one glorious truth shines through, and it is this: *God knows all and is actively engaged in His creation.* He alone is sovereign over everything and everyone. Over the next few days, we'll examine some difficult issues that arise in life that cause people to draw wrong conclusions about the Lord. Some examples people give are that it seems there are two Gods in the Bible: the angry God of the Old Testament (the Father) and the "meek and mild" Jesus of the New Testament (the Son). Some use these faulty impressions to reject the Lord God altogether.

What do we know about our God? We see that within His sovereignty over all is also His absolute *justness*, which, whether some like it or not, includes rendering justice to his enemies, a fact that some find unacceptable. They argue that since God is portrayed as being loving and inclusive of all, retributive justice is inconsistent with the idea of Him. Psalm 7 reminded us that God is just and *righteous*. He tests hearts and minds. He saves those who are upright in heart, but as a just judge, He is angry with the wicked every day.

Wrong thoughts of God come from books and movies and minds that dwell on what they don't understand and then form their own conclusions. But let's go deeper and learn about the Almighty God from His *autobiography*, in which we see that He truly knows *all*, He is sovereign over *all*, and His love is for *all*, including those who hate Him. This explains why His justice won't allow those who willfully misunderstand Him to have a place in His eternal heaven. Imagine how miserable they would be if forced to go there! These are difficult concepts, but we'll continue to work our way through them, looking to the Author of the Book and the Creator of the Universe himself to help us find the way.

December 2

When Loving Is Hard

[19]Oh, that You would slay the wicked, O God! Depart from me, therefore, you bloodthirsty men. [20]For they speak against You wickedly; Your enemies take Your name in vain. —*Psalm 139:19-20*

DAVID IS ASKING God to *slay those who slander the Lord and take His name in vain.* The third commandment states, "*Thou shalt not take the name of the Lord thy God in vain.*" David is crying out to the Lord that his enemies are doing exactly that.

Are we likewise guilty? Do we use God's name as a curse word or claim that we know Him but live like we don't?

Now, we need to do some heavy thinking here. In Matthew 5, Jesus references the Old Testament, saying, "*You have heard that it was said, 'You shall love your neighbor and hate your enemy.' But I say to you, love your enemies, bless those who curse, you, do good to those who hate you, and pray for those who spitefully use you and persecute you, that you may be sons of your Father in heaven; . . . For if you love those who love you, what reward have you?. . . . And if you greet your brethren only, what do you do more than others? . . . Therefore you shall be perfect just as your Father in heaven in perfect*" (Matthew 5:43-48).

There's something we need to consider in order to correct the concept of the "God of the Old Testament vs. the God of the New Testament," or the "angry God" vs. "gentle Jesus." In Matthew's words above, was Jesus introducing a new way of thinking? On the contrary! He was actually correcting a wrong way of thinking. "Love your neighbor" was part of the Law! Leviticus 19:18 states: "*You shall not take vengeance, nor bear any grudge against the children of your people, but you shall love your neighbor as yourself: I am the LORD.*"

"Hate your enemy" wasn't a part of the Law, and in fact Jesus himself was teaching the Jews from the original Old Law, because the New Covenant age couldn't begin until the final Passover Lamb was offered as the perfect sacrifice, fulfilling the righteous requirements of the Law. Nor had Jesus yet risen from the dead, conquering the second death for us.

In the book of Leviticus we read, "*You shall not take vengeance, nor bear any grudge against the children of your people, but you shall love your neighbor as yourself: I am the Lord*" (19:18). Of course, some might wonder, "If the law said to love your neighbor, then why would God command His people to go out and destroy the nations and occupy their land?" For one thing, Leviticus and the Sermon on the Mount are addressing *interpersonal* relationships, not national or international ones. In many places in the Old Testament, God instructed the Israelites to drive out or destroy the people of the land lest the Jews might be tempted to worship their pagan gods. God even called for the complete destruction of those who killed infants as sacrifices and employed other abominable practices.

For those who say, "Well, Jesus would *never* do that," may I suggest that you read the end of the Book? Jesus does exactly that when He returns in glory! In Matthew, He dealt with the way people are to treat one another as individuals. Vengeance was reserved for the *Lord* both in the Old *and* in the New Covenants. (See Romans 12:19 and Hebrews 10:30.) Loving one's neighbor was nothing new, nor was loving one's enemy, in the realm of interpersonal relationships. So what was David saying in verses 19 and 20 under the inspiration of the Holy Spirit?

David was defending God, not himself. He said, "They speak wickedly against You and take Your name in vain." As we begin to fit all of these pieces together, here is what we see: Righteous indignation is not only our right; it's our responsibility. David took a courageous stand in speaking out against these people. Do we ever waffle in similar situations, asking, "Is it safe?" or "What will people think?" If so, we've moved away from what the Bible really says. We'll look at this a little more deeply tomorrow. Meanwhile, take a few minutes to examine your own heart along these lines.

December 3

Holy Anger

[19] Oh, that You would slay the wicked, O God! Depart from me, therefore, you bloodthirsty men. *[20]* For they speak against You wickedly; Your enemies take Your name in vain. (Cont'd) —*Psalm 139:19-20*

TODAY WE WANT to make David's statements a little more understandable, so let's look at them through the eyes of modern situations. Might we cry out, "Oh, Lord, that you would slay the Nazis who slaughter Your chosen people, the Jews;" or, "Oh, Lord, that you would slay the members of ISIS who are killing your chosen people, the Church, and others!" or "Oh, Lord, that you would slay the members of Boko Haram, who are kidnapping and using little girls as sex slaves!" or "Oh, Lord, that you would slay those who are advancing evil in this world in defiance of Your great Name." Suddenly David's words don't seem so horrible when we hold them up against modern atrocities.

Listen, any assault on life is an affront to God, who is the Creator of life. We have both the right and the responsibility to be indignant when it comes to unchecked evils! Warren Wiersbe said, "We could use a little more holy anger today. Christians sometimes are too bland, too complacent, and too comfortable." And the apostle Peter wrote: "*This is commendable, if because of conscience toward God one endures grief, suffering wrongfully. For what credit is it if, when you are beaten for your faults, you take it patiently? But when you do good and suffer, if you take it patiently, this is commendable before God. For to this you were called, because Christ also suffered for us, leaving us an example, that you should follow His steps: 'Who committed no sin, nor was deceit found in His mouth;' who, when He was reviled, did not revile in return; when He suffered, He did not threaten, but committed Himself to Him who judges righteously; who Himself bore our sins in His own body on the tree, that we, having died to sins, might live for righteousness—by whose stripes you were healed*" (1 Pet 2:18-24).

There is so much contained in these verses, but let's highlight two things from them for now. Yes, we are to endure injustices in this world as Jesus did; and we are to commit ourselves to "Him who judges righteously." This reminds us that God is sovereign and that no sin goes unpunished. For those who have accepted Christ as Savior and Lord, Jesus bore the punishment for their sins; those who reject Him as Savior and Lord will be punished for theirs. No sin goes unpunished. That would be an injustice, and God is not unjust.

And to return to our mention yesterday of the "two Gods" concept in the Bible, check this out: "*I saw heaven opened, and behold, a white horse. And He who sat on him was called Faithful and True, and in righteousness He judges and makes war. His eyes were like a flame of fire, and on His head were many crowns. He had a name written that no one knew except Himself. He was clothed in a robe dipped in blood, and His name is called The Word of God. And the armies of heaven, clothed in fine linen, white and clean, followed Him on white horses. Now out of His mouth goes a sharp sword, that with it He should strike the nations. And He Himself will rule them with a rod of iron. He himself treads the winepress of the fierceness and wrath of Almighty God. And He has on His robe and on His thigh a name written: KING OF KINGS AND LORD OF LORDS*" (Rev 19:11-16). Judging and making war are acts of *righteousness* when the One doing so is God himself, or when we must defend the world from evils. The One judging and making war in righteousness during the Tribulation (the 70th week of Daniel) is the Word of God, which is Jesus.

So, "easy-breezy" Jesus and angry, wrathful Jehovah are false and heretical concepts of the sovereign God. Righteous indignation on our part must be benevolent toward our personal enemies, but indignant about those who are God's.

December 4

Is This Hate Talk?

> [21]Do not I hate them, O Lord, that hate thee? [22]I hate them with perfect hatred; I count them mine enemies. —*Psalm 139:21-22*

WE'VE HEARD people say that a loving God doesn't hate anyone, nor should we. They also say that Jesus never judged anyone, and we shouldn't either. In Malachi 1:1-4 we read the Lord's words through the prophet: " '*I have loved you,' says the Lord. Yet you say, "In what way have You loved us?" 'Was not Esau Jacob's brother?' says the Lord. 'Yet Jacob I have loved; but Esau I have hated, and laid waste his mountains and his heritage for the jackals of the wilderness. . . . They [are] the people against whom the Lord will have indignation forever.'*"

In Romans 9, Paul makes a case for the sovereignty of God. In Malachi, the Lord quoted the people's words, "In what way have You loved us?" He responds by contrasting His love for Jacob and His hatred of Esau. For those who believe that Jesus never judged anyone, consider His words to the Pharisees in John 8:44, telling them that their father is the devil. That sounds like judgment to me! It makes us ask, "How can a man (or a woman) after God's own heart, as was David, hate those who hate God and be justified in doing so?"

Could it be that "hate" isn't what we think it is? The Hebrew word means "to view as enemies or foes." David goes so far as to say, "I hate God's enemies with perfect [or complete] hatred and count God's enemies as my enemies." The apostle John wrote: "*Do not marvel, my brethren, if the world hates you. We know that we have passed from death to life, because we love the brethren. He who does not love his brother abides in death. Whoever hates his brother is a murderer, and you know that no murderer has eternal life abiding in him*" (1 John 3:13-15).

Let's consider these facts: We have God, who is love, yet the Bible says that He hated Esau. We also have David, the man after God's own heart, who said that He hated God's enemies and considered them as his own. Next we see John the beloved saying that he who hates his brother (fellow believer) is the same as an unregenerate murderer.

The only conclusion that we can draw in attempting to understand the sovereignty of God in both the Old and New Testaments, is this: Love and hate are *contrasting* divine attributes, not *conflicting* ones. Whom did David hate? Those who hated God! He loathed those who rose up against God. In our own lives, every time we pray, "Thy kingdom come, Thy will be done on earth as it is in heaven," we're asking that God's wrath be poured out upon the earth, which is how Jesus told us we're to pray—this is the same Jesus who also tells us to love our enemies.

In the Bible, we read that the Lord *hates* some things. Proverbs 6:16-19 reads, "*These six things the Lord hates, yes, seven are an abomination to Him: a proud look, a lying tongue, hands that shed innocent blood, a heart that devises wicked plans, feet that are swift in running to evil, a false witness who speaks lies, and one who sows discord among brethren.*" Isaiah, writing the Lord's words, penned, "*Your New Moons and your appointed feasts My soul hates: . . . I am weary of bearing them. . . . I will hide My eyes from you; even though you make many prayers, I will not hear. . . .*" (v. 1:14-15).

So we see that God, who "so loved the world that He gave His only begotten Son," hates sin and its consequences. Yet because of His justice, He can't let sin go unpunished. Unless they repent, those whom He loved enough to offer salvation will spend eternity in hell. God loves justice, and He hates sin and eternal separation from Him. These are not in conflict in light of the fact that He sent His own Son into a condemned world to die for them in order to save those who would have ears to hear. They have no excuse.

Just Look at Yourself!

23Search me, O God, and know my heart; Try me, and know my anxieties; 24and see if there is any wicked way in me, and lead me in the way everlasting. —Psalm 139:23-24

DAVID, THE AUTHOR of these verses, was a human being, just as we are. And yet, God called him to into some amazing situations in places where he never dreamed he would go. Remember Goliath? *"David spoke to the men who stood by him, saying, 'What shall be done for the man who kills this Philistine and takes away the reproach of Israel? For who is this uncircumcised Philistine, that he should defy the armies of the living God?'"* (1 Samuel 17:26). This young man stared into the face of a 9'6" tall giant and said, in essence, "I'm not afraid of you! You defied God and now you're going to fall on your face by my hand." This is the very same man who later let his eyes linger on his neighbor's wife and fell headlong into tragic sin. I'm quite sure that David, being a human like all of us, had at some point thought to himself, "Those things will never happen to me." Look at the apostle Peter, who swore to Jesus, *"Though all others forsake you, I won't. I'm ready to go to prison and death before I would deny You!"* (Luke 22:33). Remember the despair that Peter fell into after he did that exact thing not once but three times! We are such frail "heroes" at times.

In our verses today, David was saying, "Don't let me act like one of your enemies. If there is anything like that in me, please reveal it to me and rescue me! Lead me on Your path alone!" David was really on to something. In 2 Corinthians, Paul wrote, *"Examine yourselves as to whether you are in the faith. Test yourselves. Do you not know yourselves, that Jesus Christ is in you?—unless indeed you are disqualified"* (v. 13:5). Just as David asked the Lord to search him and reveal any hidden faults, so Paul tells us to constantly be on guard against our own penchant for sinning, reminding us that Jesus Christ is in us, so we have no excuse for not being "able to help it."

Look at your own self. Look at your own heart. In Matthew 7:3-5, Jesus himself said, *"Why do you look at speck in your brother's eye, but do not consider the plank in your own eye? Or how can you say to your brother, 'Let me remove the speck from your eye'; and look, a plank is in your own eye? Hypocrite! First remove the plank from your own eye, and then you will see clearly to remove the speck from your brother's eye."* Notice that Jesus didn't say that we're to help others to overcome their sins (removing their "plank") but that it's hypocritical for you to judge others for the same sins that you continue to commit! Repent of your own sin first, and then you may be more able to help others to repent of theirs.

December 6

Oh, That Deceitful Heart

[23]Search me, O God, and know my heart; try me, and know my anxieties; [24]and see if there is any wicked way in me, and lead me in the way everlasting. (Cont'd) *—Psalm 139:23-24*

WHAT WE'VE learned from this psalm is something that might cause us to sit up and take notice, but it should also help us to see what it really means: The sins that repulse us the most should be our own! David, in the closing verses of this psalm reminds us of the intimate relationship that the omniscient, omnipresent, omnipotent, and sovereign God desires to have with us. The underlying message in this psalm, as we noted earlier, is that you can't flee from God, you can't fight God, so you may as well follow God!

David had learned what Jeremiah would later write as the Lord gave it to him: *"The heart is deceitful above all things, and desperately wicked; who can know it? I, the Lord, search the heart, I test the mind, even to give to every man according to . . . the fruit of his doings"* (Jer 17:9-10). David writes what we all might share, "I've seen what I'm capable of in my heart, Lord, so search me and lead me, and change my thoughts before they become actions."

Friends, this is a perfect prayer for the perilous times in which we now live! God is love—and He hates sin. And so should we, especially our own. Yet some sins are so subtle or they lurk so secretly in our thoughts that they require the Lord to root them out that we may continue on the path of everlasting life. Back in Psalm 19:12, David wrote, *"Who can understand his errors? Cleanse me from secret faults."* Initially, David didn't know just what he was capable of, nor did Peter. Both were caught off guard, learning the hard way that sin lurked within them. Both knew the awful pain and suffering that were the consequences of having failed the Lord, and both also realized the blessings of God's mercy and grace.

God is sovereign over all. He loves His creation, but He hates the sin in it, and therefore, so should we. Righteous indignation is a built-in part of our new nature, not a negative element of our old. Love and hate are contrasting attributes, not conflicting ones. In order for there to be a place where righteousness dwells, where sin is banished, and only goodness exists, there must also be a place where only evil remains, being eternally separated from the kingdom of those made righteous by the blood of the Lamb. Heaven wouldn't be heaven if those who hated God were allowed in. We also saw that everyone does *not* go to heaven, despite the cries of the universalists. But never, ever forget that God loved *everyone* enough to reveal Himself to them all through His creation (see Romans 1). And clear back to the time of Adam and Eve, He told the *world* how to be saved (Gen 3).

The truth is, those who go to hell said "no" to heaven because they didn't like the terms and conditions of how to get there. They preferred to "live like hell" but think they'll still go to heaven. Their hearts are deceived. God can't ever accept such a proposition in light of the fact that *His own Son* died on the cross upon which His blood was shed in order to destroy the works of the devil and to free us from the awful grip of sin. John put it like this: "*He who believes in Him is not condemned; but he who does not believe is condemned already, because he has not believed in the name of the only begotten Son of God. And this is the condemnation, that the light has come into the world, and men loved darkness rather than light, because their deeds were evil*" (John 3:18-19).

Saints, a loving God who condemns men to eternal darkness because they hate Him, rejecting Christ's love, is not unfair. His love doesn't require the absence of a place like hell; it demands it. They have no excuse and are getting what they wanted. Our sovereign and loving Father has prepared a place for you, if you will submit to His tender words, "*Come to Me, all you who labor and are heavy laden, and I will give you rest*" (Mat 11:28)

December 7

The Outer Limits

Introduction

A Psalm of David—Psalm 143

OVER THE NEXT few days, we're going to take a close look at this psalm, which is one to which most of us can really relate. I encourage you to read it in your Bibles before we begin our study. In this psalm, David records his experience of being severely tested, feeling alone, and in desperate need of the Lord's deliverance. Even though he doesn't seem to hear from the Lord during the course of these verses, it appears that his faith is being strengthened with each cry that he makes to God.

Look at Psalm 31:13-16, another of David's psalms: "*For I hear the slander of many; fear is on every side; while they take counsel together against me, they scheme to take away my life. But as for me, I trust in You, O Lord . . . 'You are my God.' My times are in Your hand; deliver me from . . . my enemies, and from those who persecute me.*

Make Your face shine upon [me]; save me for Your mercies' sake." We can all relate to David's pain; can we relate also to His trust in the only One who can save him?

One thread runs throughout Scripture, and it is this: There's a definite line drawn between the righteous and the wicked, and although those who love the Lord will experience attacks, trials, and tribulations, God remains faithful to His children through them all. Over the next few days, we're going to be reminded that true faith is always going to be tested, but we can be encouraged by the book of James, in which he writes, *"Count it all joy when you fall into various trials, knowing that the testing of your faith produces patience. But let patience have its perfect work that you may be perfect and complete, lacking nothing"* (James 1:2-4).

It's been said that without *tests*, we have no *testi*mony, which comes from the Latin word for "witness." Faith can only be trusted once it's been tested. And the testing will leave us with a witness, a testimony, that will strengthen not only ourselves but those with whom we share it or who observe it firsthand in our lives.

So get ready! Our faith is going to be stretched to the *outer limits*. What outer limits? We'll be tested to the limit when it comes to our trust in God; tribulations may bring us to the outer limits of hope. When we walk strictly by faith in Him, we may feel that we're stretched to the outer limits of our peace and joy. But what we'll also be able to hold onto is that even in the outer limits the Lord is leading us.

Listen, friends, I understand what it's like to be stretched to the outer limits, where trials, traumas, and tribulations seem to assault us beyond what we think we can endure. But these verses will remind us that we've been neither forsaken nor forgotten by God, who purchased us with His own Son's blood. Does He understand? You know that He does. He supplied the greatest sacrifice ever, and He will stand beside us to encourage us, to hold us, and to help us through anything that He allows to come into our lives. And always keep in mind that life in the Outer Limits is only temporary. What He has prepared for us later on is glorious beyond compare!

Like a Walk in the Dark

¹Hear my prayer, O Lord, give ear to my supplications! In Your faithfulness answer me, and in Your righteousness. ²Do not enter into judgment with Your servant, for in Your sight no one living is righteous. ³For the enemy has persecuted my soul; he has crushed my life to the ground; he has made me dwell in darkness, like those who have long been dead. ⁴Therefore my spirit is overwhelmed within me; my heart within me is distressed. —*Psalm 143:1-4*

DAVID'S ANGUISH is evident in these opening verses. We sense his urgency in the midst of extreme difficulties. And yet he knows what he must do—cry out to the Lord, because only God can help. He prays that God won't judge him, acknowledging his own unrighteousness. David repeats what he has said elsewhere, that the enemy was persecuting his very soul, crushing him with a huge weight. This horrible walk in the dark leaves him feeling what it might be like to be dead and without the Lord.

Have you ever been there? Frightened, exhausted, weak, confused—wondering where God was? David had written a psalm with a different tone once. Listen to his confident words: "*The righteous cry out, and the Lord hears, and delivers them out of all their troubles. The Lord is near to those who have a broken heart, and saves such as have a contrite spirit. Many are the afflictions of the righteous, but the Lord delivers him out of them all. He guards all his bones; not one of them is broken. Evil shall slay the wicked, and those who hate the righteous shall be condemned. The Lord redeems the soul of His servants, and none of those who trust in Him shall be condemned*" (Ps 34:17-22).

Those verses stand in shining contrast not only to our psalm today but also to others that he had written along similar lines. David, the man after God's own heart, experienced the blessings and sorrows of life just like everyone else, yet he had been handpicked by the Lord to be the king of Israel! That may give us a little comfort. In Psalm 6:6-7 he had written, "*I am weary with my groaning; all night I make my bed swim; I drench my couch with my tears. My eye wastes away because of grief; it grows old because of all my enemies.*"

Friends, we all go through similar life experiences, even—and perhaps especially—if we're God's children. He does try us and test us in order to prove *to us* whether or not we truly trust Him. It seems that during these times, while we're way out in the outer limits, our minds wander into places where they shouldn't go, as in, *Maybe God's word isn't true. . . . Maybe I don't really belong to Him. . . . Why has God forsaken me in my time of deepest need?* Then Satan comes along and taunts us, "What kind of Christian *are* you? You're not one at all, and that's why you feel this way!"

The Bible gives examples of the devil's plots against God's people: Remember Adam and Eve? Or Pharaoh and Noah, with the children of Israel? Satan sent cruel "counselors" to Job, along with his own wife who encouraged him to just curse God and die. And Satan approached Jesus when He was in the wilderness, tempting him to forget about God and follow him, promising that he would give Him everything He could ever want! How stupid is Satan, to think that he could thwart God's hand in the lives of His children! The devil is the old accuser, who taunts us, "After what you did, do you really think that God wants to hear from you again?" Never forget during those times that we stand before God in His *mercy*, not on our own merit. David understood this, deep down, understanding that he needed to petition God based on *His* faithfulness and righteousness. And he did that, standing before the Father, just like every other unrighteous human being, still in the dark, but knowing that God was His only help.

December 9

"Fiery Trials"

[Cont'd] ¹Hear my prayer, O Lord, give ear to my supplications! In Your faithfulness answer me, and in Your righteousness. ²Do not enter into judgment with Your servant, for in Your sight no one living is righteous. ³For the enemy has persecuted my soul; he has crushed my life to the ground; he has made me dwell in darkness, like those who have long been dead. ⁴Therefore my spirit is overwhelmed within me; my heart within me is distressed. —Psalm 143:1-4

DAVID WAS experiencing overwhelming hardship, but he knew just where to turn. No matter how wretched a sinner he was, he knew that God is righteous and that He can be trusted always. So can we! Whether we've been pushed to the outer limits because of our sin, or whether simply by the normal tribulations that come from living on this planet, we can still rise up and stand before our merciful Father, pleading for help and forgiveness.

Ephesians 6 tells us that it's not with flesh and blood we wrestle during these dark times but with principalities and powers and rulers of darkness and hosts of wickedness who want to make things as hard on us as they possibly can. And even though as spirit beings they aren't flesh and blood themselves, they often use flesh-and-blood enemies of the Cross to persecute souls that have been made righteous in Christ, hoping to crush them to the ground, overwhelm their spirits, and make their hearts distressed within them.

The enemy may use other people to push us to the outer limits, but he also uses circumstances like broken-down cars, unexpected expenses, damaged relationships, exploited weaknesses, and anything else that he can muster in his efforts to cause you to believe that God has forsaken you or that you've lost your right to ask Him to rescue you.

I'll say it again: we don't stand before God on our own merit! It is only through Christ's mercy and by His grace that we stand before God in the righteousness of Christ! Our circumstances are not the barometer of His mercy. Hebrews 4:14-16 states, "*Seeing then that we have a great High Priest who has passed through the heavens, Jesus the Son of God, let us hold fast our confession. For we do not have a High Priest who cannot sympathize with our weaknesses, but was in all points tempted as we are, yet without sin. Let us therefore come boldly to the throne of grace, that we may obtain mercy and find grace to help in time of need.*"

The fact that we've been pushed to the outer limits doesn't mean that God doesn't love you or care about what you're going through. He is drawing you to Himself during this time! Come, and stand before Him, and tell Him that you need His help. Cry out! Plead your case before Him, even if you, yourself, are the cause of your current crisis!

Yes, God does discipline His children, but it is always for the purpose of restoration and repair of those things that are hindering our walk and that harm ourselves or others. But even then, the throne of grace is available to us. We need to arrive at the place where David did, when he said, essentially, "I'm no better than anyone else. No one living is righteous enough to stand before You in their own merit. So here I stand, with my doubts, fears, and failures."

We find comfort in knowing that others, even great men like David, have gone through their own outer-limits experiences and have found God faithful always. The writer of the hymn "How Firm a Foundation" expressed it well within those verses:

> When through fiery trials thy pathway shall lie,
> My grace all-sufficient, shall be thy supply.
> The flames shall not hurt thee, I only design
> Thy dross to consume, and thy gold to refine.

He is purifying us through these trials, and His grace is *always* sufficient to see us through anything He permits us to undergo.

What Are You Looking At?

⁵I remember the days of old; I meditate on all Your works; I muse on the work of Your hands. ⁶I spread out my hands to You; my soul longs for You like a thirsty land. Selah. ⁷Answer me speedily, O Lord; my spirit fails! Do not hide Your face from me, lest I be like those who go down into the pit. ⁸Cause me to hear Your lovingkindness in the morning, for in You do I trust; cause me to know the way in which I should walk, for I lift up my soul to You. *—Psalm 143:5-8*

AH, DAVID . . . Even as flawed as he was, what a love He had for the Lord! In all of the trials and joys of life, he ultimately turned to God in praise, in fear, in love, in need. And for our own lives, we can learn from what he describes here. His heart is overwhelmed and his spirit is crushed, and yet he remembers the days of old and the wonderful works of the Lord. He may have remembered the single rock that flew from his hands and, guided by the Lord, straight into the heart of one of the greatest enemy's that Israel faced. He may have thought about the parting of the Red Sea, or the crumbling walls of Jericho. Perhaps he even thought all the way back to the beginning, when God said, "Let there be light!" and there was light.

As David prays, he spreads out his hands to the Lord, longing for God's refreshing touch on him and on his desperate circumstances. In this situation, David was not unlike Gideon when he also was stretched to the outer limits: *"And the Angel of the Lord appeared to him, and said to him, 'The Lord is with you, you mighty man of valor!' Gideon said to Him, 'O my lord, if the Lord is with us, why then has all this happened to us? And where are all His miracles which our fathers told us about?' . . . . But now the Lord has forsaken us and delivered us into the hands of the Midianites"* (Judges 6:12-13).

I believe that every Christian has experienced these kinds of thoughts at one point or another. "Lord, where is all that stuff that we read about in the Bible?" or "Why does my present experience seem to be so different from what you promised?" or even, "How come You don't do the miracles in my life that I've seen you do for others?"

Saints, you may have experienced things that seem very at odds with what we expect as Christians. Why does it seem that the Lord delivers one believer from a situation and leaves another to deal with the circumstances seemingly on his own? Why must we have to endure actual harm done to us by others; maybe even had things said or done to us that was meant to ruin our reputation? Ever been there? Ever prayed something like, "How long, O Lord, before You expose these liars for what they are and repair the damage they've done?"

Beware, though, when you're thinking along those lines. You don't want to keep your focus on the evil being done but on the goodness and beauty of the Lord, who holds your very life in His hands. Even though what we're going through feels like it will never end, here's what we need to remember. We have a choice in how we respond! If we focus on the harm that someone has done or wonder why God helped somebody else out of a similar situation as ours, we'll only find despair. If we look for reasons to doubt and question God, we'll find them. But if we meditate on the mighty, majestic works of our Father and feed on His faithfulness, we'll find hope. If we look for His "lovingkindness in the morning" as David determines he will do, we'll find trust and an uplifted soul.

What is it that you're looking at? Keep this psalm in mind when you're tempted to wallow in the swamp of despair, and keep your focus on the One who holds your hand, who sustains your very breath, and look up. *"Oh, magnify the Lord with me, and let us exalt His name together. I sought the Lord, and He heard me, and delivered me from all my fears. . . . The angel of the Lord encamps all around those who fear Him, and delivers them"* (Psalm 34:3-6).

Testing, Testing . . .

[Cont'd] ⁷Answer me speedily, O Lord; my spirit fails! Do not hide Your face from me, lest I be like those who go down into the pit. ⁸Cause me to hear Your lovingkindness in the morning, for in You do I trust; cause me to know the way in which I should walk, for I lift up my soul to You.
—Psalm 143:7-8

AS WE LOOKED back yesterday at Psalm 34, in which David referred to himself as "this poor man," he described himself as distressed (same translation as "poor"). So what he said, in essence, was, "In my distress I cried out, and the Lord heard and saved me from all my troubles." It was to the *Lord* that he cried out, and it was there that he found what was needed.

The truth is, too often in times of trouble we find ourselves looking for what we want, which may not necessarily be what we need or what is best. The main thing we desire, however, is for the trial to end! What we don't usually stop to think about is that between the beginning and the end of trials there is the testing ground in the middle. And what do we know that we're supposed to do during those times of being tested? *"My brethren, count it all joy when you fall into various trials, knowing that the testing of your faith produces patience. But let patience have its perfect work, that you may be perfect and complete, lacking nothing"* (James 1:2-4).

Of course, there will be times when we're tempted to circumvent waiting, either by giving up or taking action to resolve the issue on our own. Sometimes when we land there, we find ourselves thinking things that we shouldn't. In my own life, during times of experiencing the effects of adversaries who had harmed me, it crossed my mind more than once to expose on social media what they had done, and do you know what I would get from that? *Nothing good!* No, I would end up looking like a bitter, unforgiving Christian. Does that in any way glorify the Lord?

Friends, the point is that in times of trouble and testing, we find ourselves looking for ways that God might want to fix things, when what we should be doing is just looking to God! To search and meditate on His Word and remember His righteousness and faithfulness is a balm to our souls. If we focus on what we think He should have done, we'll wind up in despair.

We need to remind ourselves that life in heaven will be far better than it is on earth. Everyone there will be perfect. There won't be any pride or envy, no backstabbing or slander, no trials of any kind. So while I'm enduring times of testing that seem unending, I determine to look forward to the precious promises of God that He is in me no matter what the trial is. Even in the outer limits, He is with me still and will be for all eternity.

December 12

Is It Time for a Change?

⁹Deliver me, O Lord, from my enemies; in You I take shelter. ¹⁰Teach me to do Your will, for You are my God; Your Spirit is good. Lead me in the land of uprightness. ¹¹Revive me, O Lord, for Your name's sake! For Your righteousness' sake bring my soul out of trouble. ¹²In Your mercy cut off my enemies, and destroy all those who afflict my soul; for I am Your servant. —*Psalm 143:9-12*

WE NOW SEE David actively requesting not only God's deliverance from his enemies but also their destruction. How are we, as New Testament believers, to pray? Paul wrote: "*The weapons of our warfare are not carnal but mighty in God for pulling down strongholds, casting down arguments and every high thing that exalts itself against the knowledge of God, bringing every thought into captivity to the obedience of Christ and being ready to punish all disobedience when your obedience is fulfilled*" (2 Cor 10:4-6).

The background of this was that the Corinthian Christians were being pushed to the outer limits and were attempting to fight a spiritual battle with carnal weapons. Paul said, "That's not the way we fight." Yes, we're told to pull down strongholds, but not through personal retaliation. We can and should cast down arguments and things that exalt themselves over Christ, but we have to bring our own thoughts into captivity and live in obedience to Christ. Once we're obedient, punishment can be enforced. How do we connect this idea with what David is writing? Remember that *righteous indignation is not carnal*, and David, as "a man after God's own heart," is experiencing righteous indignation.

Paul addresses a situation within the New Testament church where someone was committing grievous sin, and he tells the believers to judge that individual harshly, even putting him out of the church in the hope of his repentance. But in the same passages, he tells them that they are *not to judge* unbelievers. Why? Because it's up to God to judge them, not us. We're to try to help those within the church to repent and be made right, and we're to share the mercy and justice of God with those who aren't part of the body of Christ, trusting that He alone is able to truly judge those hearts (See 1 Cor 5:9-13).

Does David say, "Let me at 'em, Lord! I need to destroy them." No, he commits them to the hands of the Lord, who alone can judge hearts not only among His children but also His enemies. A takeaway from all of this is: *When God doesn't change our circumstances, He's probably changing us*. Ouch! Not always, because sometimes it's more a matter of His orchestrating things that affect more than just us that will all work out for our good and to His glory. But most often, I believe, He's perfecting us. He wants to change us into His likeness, ultimately, and to perfect us while we're still in this world. Paul declared that through it all he's learned to be content: "*I know how to be abased, and . . . how to abound. Everywhere and in all things I have learned both to be full and to be hungry, . . . to abound and to suffer need. I can do all things through Christ who strengthens me*" (Phil 4:10-13).

Wow! What a lesson! Many of us might sometimes think, "Well, I know how to be abased—and how to be abased! That 'abounding' part—not so much!" Remember that James said that the testing of our faith yields patience? Contentment must be *learned*. And God doesn't always change our circumstances, but He does change us through them, and it's for the best if we just let Him do it. We *will* spend hard times in the outer limits while the principalities, powers, and rulers of darkness seek to afflict our flesh and get us to react carnally. Instead of letting them to do that, walk in the Spirit, because then, even in the darkness, God can deliver, teach, lead, revive, and *change* us! As for our enemies? God is far more powerful than they. He can handle them just fine without our help, especially when we're in the outer limits.

Happiness, Help, and Hope

Introduction

¹Praise the Lord! Praise the Lord, O my soul!—Psalm 146

LET'S REMEMBER that the Book of Psalms is actually divided into five books. The first section contains psalms 1-41, the second, psalms 42-72, the third, psalms 73-89, the fourth, psalms 90-106, and the fifth opens with the psalms of ascent in chapters 120-134 continuing on to Psalm 150. Books one and two are Davidic psalms; Book three includes the psalms of Asaph and the sons of Korah; Books four and five are largely anonymous psalms, with a few of them attributed to King David.

Do you also recall that the Book of Psalms has often been called the Hymn Book of Israel? That's actually a bit of a misconception, because not all of the psalms are songs, nor are they limited by application to Israel alone. In fact, they're filled with information, counsel, and admonitions that relate to much that we go through in the Christian walk.

If there's one thing that we can glean from this Book is that in every book division in every type of psalm we're reminded and inspired again and again to praise the Lord. Paul, in the Book of Romans, wrote, "*Now I say that Jesus Christ has become a servant to the circumcision for the truth of God, to confirm the promises made to the fathers, and that the Gentiles might glorify God for His mercy, as it is written: 'For this reason I will confess to You among the Gentiles, and sing to Your name.' And again he says: 'Rejoice, O Gentiles, with His people!' And again: 'Praise the Lord, all you Gentiles! Laud Him, all you peoples!' And again, Isaiah says: 'There shall be a root of Jesse; and He who shall rise to reign over the Gentiles, in Him the Gentiles shall hope.' Now may the God of hope fill you with all joy and peace in believing, that you may abound in hope by the power of the Holy Spirit*" (Romans 15:8).

These quotes that Paul cites in Romans are from 2 Samuel 22:50, Psalm 18:49, Deuteronomy 32:43, Psalm 117:1, and Isaiah 11:10, respectively. They all remind us that saving the Gentiles has always been God's plan, and much that is written in the psalms and the Old Testament in general was written also for instruction within the church. These instructions would include the many reasons we have to praise the Lord. After all, the closing words of the psalms are: "*Let everything that has breath praise the Lord. Praise the Lord!*" (Psalm 150:6).

Do we do that? As long as there is breath in our bodies, do we praise Him? That would include during all of our life experiences, good and bad. We are also to praise Him in spirit and in truth, as opposed to with lip service and insincerity!

The psalm provides a sort of formula, if you will, for what everyone in the world is looking for but that can be found only in God. And what is that? It is Happiness, Help, and Hope?

Let us pray that the Lord will open our eyes to an even deeper understanding of the truth in the words of this psalm.

So we can be happy, or blessed, no matter what our circumstances are. "Poor in spirit" means "humble." Comfort comes to those who in mourning; the meek are blessed; a thirst for righteousness will bring satisfaction; those who are merciful will obtain mercy, and so on. Can this blessedness be found by doing what *seems* right or by going after whatever our heart desires? No! If you sow to the flesh, you'll reap the sorrows of the flesh; if you sow to the wind, you'll reap the whirlwind. Can blessedness be found by looking to the ways of the world? Don't trust in princes or in people. Trusting in God establishes hope. Happiness, help, and hope come from God. Why settle for less, when the Lord holds out to us the very best happiness that can be found?

December 14

If You're Happy, and You Know It . . .

[1]Praise the Lord! Praise the Lord, O my soul! [2]While I live I will praise the Lord; I will sing praises to my God while I have my being. [3]Do not put your trust in princes, nor in a son of man, in whom there is no help. [4]His spirit departs, he returns to his earth; in that very day his plans perish. —*Psalm 146:1-4*

HAPPINESS, HELP, and hope—let's look at each one of these terms individually, beginning with "happiness." Although anyone, believer or nonbeliever, can experience happiness, there's a type of happiness that's exclusive only to those who have the God of Jacob as their help and their hope. The word "happy" is the same word translated as "blessedness." Blessedness is reserved exclusively for God's people and does not require circumstances to create it. Happiness *without* God is circumstance-caused and circumstance related and therefore is temporary and fleeting at best.

"There is a way that seems right to a man, but its end is the way of death. Even in laughter the heart may sorrow, and the end of mirth may be grief. The backslider in heart will be filled with his own ways, but a good man will be satisfied from above" (Prov 14:12-14). And, *"By faith Moses, when he became of age, refused to be called the son of Pharaoh's daughter, choosing rather to suffer affliction with the people of God than to enjoy the passing pleasures of sin, esteeming the reproach of Christ greater riches than the treasures in Egypt; for he looked to the reward"* (Heb 11:24-26).

There is a pleasure-based happiness that comes from doing what you want, including the momentary pleasures of sin. But that "happiness" has an unhappy ending. The Bible calls it "the way of death, sorrow, and grief." On the other hand, the person who belongs to the Lord will be satisfied from the Father above. Moses (Heb. 11) made the correct if difficult decision to follow the Lord, and there was great blessing in that choice.

Our psalm today tells us, "Praise the Lord while you live and have your being, and do not put your trust in princes (or, in Moses' case, Pharaoh), or other people whose plans perish when they do." Don't allow the world to define success or happiness. If you want to be blessed and happy, live *above* the realm of inferior expectations and results.

Look at how Jesus opened his earthly teaching ministry with the keys to happiness in the Beatitudes of the Sermon on the Mount: "*Blessed are the poor in spirit, for theirs is the kingdom of heaven. Blessed are those who mourn, for they shall be comforted. Blessed are the meek, for they shall inherit the earth. Blessed are those who hunger and thirst for righteousness, for they shall be filled. Blessed are the merciful, for they shall obtain mercy. Blessed are the pure in heart, for they shall see God. Blessed are the peacemakers, for they shall be called sons of God. Blessed are those who are persecuted for righteousness' sake, for theirs is the kingdom of heaven. Blessed are you when they revile and persecute you, and say all kinds of evil against you falsely for My sake. Rejoice and be exceedingly glad, for great is your reward in heaven, for so they persecuted the prophets who were before you*" (Mat 5:1-12).

December 15

From Whence Cometh My Help

> [5]Happy is he who has the God of Jacob for his help, whose hope is in the Lord his God, [6]who made heaven and earth, the sea, and all that is in them; who keeps truth forever, . . . —*Psalm 146:5-6*

WE'LL BE LOOKING today at the "help" aspect of our title, and there's a subtlety here in the Old Testament that we don't want to miss, which is also present in the New Testament. Remember what happened in Genesis 32 when Jacob wrestled with God: "*He said to him, 'What is your name?' He said, 'Jacob.' And He said, 'Your name shall no longer be called Jacob, but Israel; for you have struggled with God and with men, and have prevailed'*" (Gen 32:27-28). Now, let's look at the New Testament: "[Jesus] *said to them, 'But who do you say that I am?' Simon Peter answered and said, 'You are the Christ, the Son of the living God.' Jesus answered and said to him, 'Blessed are you, Simon Bar-Jonah, for flesh and blood has not revealed this to you, but My Father who is in heaven. And I also say to you that you are Peter, and on this rock I will build My church, and the gates of Hades shall not prevail against it'"* (Mat 16:15-18).

Both men—Jacob (Israel) and Simon (Peter)—were made new men who still struggled with their old nature, yet both loved God intensely. And look at what the Lord says: "To him who overcomes I will give . . . him a white stone, and on the stone a ***new name*** written which no one knows except him who receives it" (Rev 2:17). Jacob, with his new name, still struggled to live up to the "Prince of God" title, and Simon, renamed Peter, struggled with being the immoveable rock that his name implied. Likewise, we have been given a new name as new creations in Christ, yet we also battle at times living as these new creatures. And even so, God remains our help.

Happiness, help, and hope are available even to people who struggle and fail, because the One who made the heavens and the earth, the sea, and all that is in them, and who keeps truth forever is the source of all. *God is for us, even though we fail Him!*

Verse 6 reminds us that those who hope in the Lord have the God of Jacob Himself to turn to. We'll be seeing that happiness, help, and hope are presented *before* we experience justice, provision, and redemption! In other words, our greatest needs are spiritual, not material. In the New Testament, when the disciples asked the Lord how to pray, He told them: *"In this manner, therefore, pray: Our Father in heaven, hallowed be Your name. Your kingdom come, Your will be done on earth as it is in heaven. Give us this day our daily bread. And forgive us our debts, as we forgive our debtors. And do not lead us into temptation, but deliver us from the evil one. For Yours is the kingdom and the power and the glory forever. Amen."* Most of this text deals with spiritual as opposed to material needs, which shows us where our emphasis should be. Our help in these areas will come from the Lord himself as we trust Him. We need to keep in mind that although God takes care of us materially, of greatest importance is the spiritual side of His help. You don't need a new car when your child is sick. You need His healing touch. You don't need more money to make the pain of losing a loved one lessen; you need God's comfort and strength from then on. Philippians 4:19: *"My God shall supply all your need according to His riches in glory by Christ Jesus."*

Think of it like this: The Lord often says "no" to material desires that we think are important. But have you ever cried out to Him for strength, comfort, mercy, grace, help, etc., and He said no? Oh, you may not have sensed His help immediately, but looking back, you'll see how He was always right beside you, leading you, holding your hand, and loving you. How much worse would the situation have been had He not been there? He knows what we need, and He'll provide all the help necessary at the proper time. That's His promise!

December 16

Hope for the Hopeless

[7] . . . Who executes justice for the oppressed, who gives food to the hungry. The Lord gives freedom to the prisoners. [8] The Lord opens the eyes of the blind; the Lord raises those who are bowed down; the Lord loves the righteous. [9] The Lord watches over the strangers; He relieves the fatherless and the widow; but the way of the wicked He turns upside down. [10] The Lord shall reign forever—your God, O Zion, to all generations. Praise the Lord! —*Psalm 146:7-10*

WE DON'T THINK about it too much, but hope is a very important element in our lives. God knows how necessary it is as well. In fact, the word "hope" occurs 143 times in Bible. In Lamentations 3:21-23 we read, *"This I recall to my mind, therefore I have hope. Through the Lord's mercies we are not consumed because His compassions fail not. They are new every morning. . . ."* And Romans 15:13: *"Now may the God of hope fill you with all joy and peace in believing, that you may abound in hope by the power of the Holy Spirit."*

Our opening verses this morning remind us of God's mercy, justice, and provision. He lifts up those who are downtrodden. He watches over those who see themselves as strangers and pilgrims in a foreign land. He cares for the orphan and the widow, but He defeats the ways of the wicked! Nothing is too difficult for our God (Jer 32:27)! Paul wrote in Ephesians, *"Now to Him who is able to do exceedingly abundantly above all that we ask or think, according to the power that works in us, to Him be glory in the church by Christ Jesus to all generations, forever and ever. Amen"* (3:20-21).

Do you believe that these verses are true for you? Is our God *able*? Here are some things we need to wrestle through: Does God physically heal everyone we pray for? Is He able to do so? Does He give sight to every blind person we pray for? Is He able to? Does He avert every injustice aimed at believers and at His church today? Could He? Does He protect every Christian in every country and age from being persecuted, even to death? No, He doesn't, in every case, but yes, He is able to!

Stop and think for a moment. Our flesh has a hard time with the idea that God allows people to die. But for the believer, death is a *victory*! It is deliverance, being set free, from this corrupt, anti-Christian, and perilous world that calls evil good and good evil and treats the wicked well but seeks to murder those whose hope is in the Lord. We need to remember that there will be eternal justice in the end. Jesus

Christ rose from the dead, conquering death and sin and hell! Our hope lies in the future. And the future for those who belong to Christ is beautiful beyond description. There is no injustice in heaven; there are no prisoners, no blindness; no one is downtrodden; there are no orphans or widows, no wickedness, no strangers, no sorrow, and no death!

God wants us to live with the *expectation* of eternity—and happiness, help, and hope are all based upon the understanding that eternal justice will someday prevail. The former things will pass away, and nothing will ever be able to hurt us again. Justice is coming, and relief is on the way! Until then, happiness, hope, and help are ours right now as we continue to love and praise our Savior who loved us first!

December 17

Psalm 146, Too!

Introduction—Psalm 146-II

YOU CAN'T HAVE too much of a good thing, and there's nothing better than digging into God's Word. I've often told young Bible teachers, and have even reminded some who've been at it for a while, that every text has a thousand sermons. Preach them one at a time, because a sermon that tries to go everywhere at once gets nowhere. With that in mind, I'd like to continue our look at Psalm 146 and glean further insights from the great nuggets of wisdom contained in these verses, which are especially relevant for the modern church.

Apart from the chemical and biological composition of the body, there are two things that the human frame can't live without—food and water. One may survive for a time without both, but it's the lack of water that will most quickly take the life of the person who is without it. Likewise, there are two things that the human soul can't live without—truth and hope. The two go together: truth, the most precious commodity in the universe, is essential to establishing hope. Hope that isn't based on truth is in vain.

In our day, truth has become "relative." It means one thing to one person and something entirely different to another. Ethics are considered "situational" and relative, and, in the minds of many, the concept of "moral absolutes" has no meaning. For many people, "truth" comes from any source except where from God has put it.

Think of it like this: when someone has been shipwrecked and is drifting around on the ocean, they're floating on a body of water that covers two-thirds of the world's surface, yet not *one drop* of it has any value for sustaining life. Many have died of thirst on the sea for want of fresh water. You simply can't drink salt water, brackish water, or water that has been contaminated by outside sources.

The same is true for the source of what is fed to the soul. Jeremiah, quoting the Lord, wrote, "*For My people have committed two evils: they have forsaken Me, the fountain of living waters, and they have hewn themselves . . . broken cisterns that can hold no water.*" This is why our world today is shrouded in hopelessness and despair. There are "truth sources" (i.e., broken cisterns) in every corner of the world, but none can sustain the life of the soul. People live in hopelessness, and souls are entering a black eternity around the world because of the lack of living water—truth—and the hope of life that it brings to the soul.

But there is hope, even in a dry land! Psalm 103:1-5 tells us to "*Bless the Lord, O my soul,*" because it is He who forgives our iniquities, heals our diseases, redeems our lives from destruction, crowns us with loving kindness and tender mercies, and satisfies our mouths with good things, giving us renewed life and hope. The world may be a mess, and yet, in the midst of it all, our psalm tells us that we can find the sufficiency of hope! Psalm 107:9 says, "*He satisfies the longing of the soul, and fills the hungry soul with goodness.*" If we feed on the world, we'll be filled with dissatisfaction, but if we feed on the Word, the longing in our souls will be satisfied.

Saints, we are the only salt and light on this planet, and it's only the work of the Holy Spirit that restrains utter lawlessness in our world today. We're here for a reason, and it's not just to get saved and then float on up to heaven! God has left us here to be salt and light in a dreary world, and that's not easy. But Isaiah tells us, "*You [God] will keep him in perfect peace, whose mind is stayed on You, because He trusts in You*" (Isaiah 26:3).

December 18

The Sufficiency of Hope

> [1]Praise the Lord! Praise the Lord, O my soul! [2]While I live I will praise the Lord; I will sing praises to my God while I have my being. [3]Do not put your trust in princes, nor in a son of man, in whom there is no help. [4]His spirit departs, he returns to his earth; in that very day his plans perish. —*Psalm 146:1-4*

THESE FIRST FEW verses establish for us the firm foundation for a lifetime of hope, which is through praise. We don't praise the Lord because things are good; we praise Him because *He* is good! This should be a regular part of lives, something that comes as naturally as breathing, because He's also the One who puts the breath in our lungs. When we praise the Lord, we're showing our trust in Him rather than the futility of putting our trust in men. Even if a man is a prince or the wealthiest man on earth or the most brilliant scientist, one day he'll perish and his body will return to the earth.

Do you remember the story of Balaam, a somewhat lapsed prophet, whom the wicked Moabite king Balak hired to put a curse on the people of Israel so they couldn't overthrow his people in battle? When Balaam got to the place where he was to curse the Israelites, the Lord put a word in his mouth and instead of cursing the Israelites, he issued a wonderful blessing on them! Balak was furious and told him to go and curse them from another spot. But the Lord himself spoke to Balaam, and told him, "*Go back to Balak, and thus you shall speak.*" So Balaam returned to Balak and said to them: "*God is not a man, that He should lie, nor the son of man, that He should repent. Has He said, and will He not do? Or has He spoken, and will He not make it good? Behold, I have received a command to bless; He has blessed and I cannot reverse it*" (Numbers 23:16-20).

God is not like men! His promises are yes and amen (2 Cor 1:20). He will never break them. Has He told us that His strength is sufficient for us in times of weakness? Then it is! Has He promised that we'll have all we need through the riches and glory that is in Christ? Then we will! What God has spoken, no man, no demon, no devil, can reverse! This means that the sufficiency of our hope is built on this truth: Our hope is in One who can be trusted through anything, whether through our trials, or in His always speaking the truth and performing His promises. He can be trusted with our children and our families. He is God. He is not a man who can lie. He is the way, the truth, and the life, and no one can reverse His commands—not even a prophet like Balaam.

How about this promise: "*Because you have kept My commandment to persevere, I also will keep you from the hour of trial which shall come upon the whole world, to test those who dwell on the earth*" (Rev 3:10)? This world is a mess, and we know that people in high places are going to let us down and break their promises, but *God is not like them*. People will lie to us to further their agendas or promote their ideologies, but *God is not like them*.

Where does our hope lie? It is in the only One who can be trusted through anything, including these last days. He has commanded us to persevere, and thus He will also provide the wherewithal for us to do that! I don't deserve it. I haven't earned it, and I've done things that should have caused me to lose it, but I fully expect to receive the end of my faith, the salvation of my soul, when my time comes to leave this world, whether through death or in the Rapture. I know that my soul, saved by the blood of Christ, will one day be housed in an immortal and incorruptible body in which I will live forever with the Lord! I have a satisfying hope because of the One who, unlike the princes, politicians, and other people of the world, can be trusted though every season of life. Along with that, I have the peace of knowing that my hope is not in vain, and in the end, I can cry, "It is well, it is well, with my soul"!

Where Does Your Hope Lie?

⁵Happy is he who has the God of Jacob for his help, whose hope is in the Lord his God, ⁶who made heaven and earth, the sea, and all that is in them; who keeps truth forever, ⁷who executes justice for the oppressed, who gives food to the hungry. The Lord gives freedom to the prisoners. ⁸The Lord opens the eyes of the blind; the Lord raises those who are bowed down; the Lord loves the righteous.
—*Psalm 146:5-8*

THE HEBREW word translated "hope" means expectation. In Greek, the word carries the same primary meaning but broadens it a bit, adding "to anticipate with pleasure." Thus we can see that happiness and hope go together. Sadly, most people today are not happy with themselves, with one another, or with their life circumstances. They don't like the way they look and they're not satisfied with the things they have, because someone else always looks or seems to have something better.

An interesting article in *Psychology Today* from November 6, 2015, carried an article reporting that not that long ago, people in their 60s and 70s were more content than any other age group. Recently, however, this is no longer true. Most people from all age groups reported being less happy in recent years than they had been in the past. Why? The article stated that "a prime suspect is our modern belief system that everyone should follow their dreams. . . . Reality shows lift ordinary people from obscurity and into the limelight. Nearly 60 percent of high school students . . . expect to earn a graduate or professional degree, even though the number who actually will has remained stuck at 10 percent. Seventy-eight percent of college students believe that their drive to achieve is above average. Yet . . . their SAT scores are lower. As other research has shown, *positive thinking doesn't automatically produce success* [emphasis added]. . . . Many of the Millennials interviewed were angry. 'No one told us it was going to be this hard,' they said."

That is very telling. People today go to greater extremes to make themselves happy—changing their bodies, their spouses, their careers—all in the hope of gaining that illusive happiness. But according to the One who made us, happiness doesn't come from within. It comes from placing our hope in God! *"Pride goes before destruction, and a haughty spirit before a fall. Better to be of a humble spirit with the lowly, than to divide the spoil with the proud. . . . Whoever trusts in the Lord, happy is he.... But the correction of fools is folly.... There is a way that seems right to a man, but its end is the way of death*" (Prov 16:18-25).

Many today are following that "way of death," which is "man's way." They don't find happiness because they look for it in places where God doesn't keep it! In contrast, happy is the one who has the God of Jacob as their help and the Lord God as their hope. The one who hopes in the Lord can expect to receive from the Lord the truth as it pertains to life and godliness. They can expect Him to be just and to look upon the oppressed with favor. They can expect the hungry to be fed, the captives set free, the eyes of the blind opened, and the humble exalted. The Lord loves the righteous, and blessed is the one who trusts in Him.

How's this for something to hold onto? The object of *our* hope is One of unlimited power! He can be trusted through anything. Is anything too difficult for Him? Our God is *God Almighty*! He is able, He is powerful, He is incomparable, and He is never intimidated by the things that intimidate us. In Jude 24-25 we read, "*Now to Him who is able to keep you from stumbling, and to present you faultless before the presence of His glory with exceeding joy, to God our Savior, who alone is wise, be glory and majesty, dominion and power, both now and forever. Amen.*"

December 20

Do You Have High Hopes?

[Cont'd] ⁵Happy is he who has the God of Jacob for his help, whose hope is in the Lord his God, ⁶who made heaven and earth, the sea, and all that is in them; who keeps truth forever, ⁷who executes justice for the oppressed, who gives food to the hungry. The Lord gives freedom to the prisoners. ⁸The Lord opens the eyes of the blind; the Lord raises those who are bowed down; the Lord loves the righteous. —*Psalm 146:5-8*

THE PURSUIT of happiness is one of the "rights" to which we're entitled from the United States Declaration of Independence, and people sometimes try to take it too far. Does it seem unattainable to you? What is it you're pursuing that you think will make you happy? Is it stuff? A better work situation? More money? A bigger house? World peace? In Psalm 20:7 the psalmist writes, "*Some trust in chariots and some in horses; but we will remember the name of the Lord our God.*" And Isaiah wrote: "*Woe to those who ... trust in chariots because they are many, and in horsemen because they are very strong, but who do not look to the Holy One of Israel, nor seek the Lord!*" (31:1).

It amazes me that we (and I include myself in this) trust God with our eternal destiny, but we struggle to trust Him with our todays and tomorrows. Saints, if we look to "Egypt," and pursue the things of the world in the hope of producing happiness, we won't get what we expect but will receive "woes" instead. I can't tell you how many parents wish their son or daughter had never stepped foot onto a college campus because the pursuit of success destroyed their child's faith, and, as a consequence, their hope. It's not true all the time, but it happens too frequently to ignore, and it is tragic.

"But how will they make it in this world without a degree?" some will ask. Well, who said they are supposed to "make it" in this world at all? According to God's Word, He will take care of the righteous. It's better to be a janitor in His house than to dwell in a house built by wickedness. If that upsets you, remember, I didn't write the Bible; God did. *"Better to be of a humble spirit with the lowly than to divide the spoil with the proud"* (Proverbs 16:19).

Our hope isn't in this world. It comes from looking to the Lord and believing His Word. This doesn't mean that we sit around waiting for God to shower us with blessings so that we don't have to lift a finger. It means that we're not to worry about how we're going to pay our bills, provide for our children, dress ourselves, etc. We're to work and also to help others. Second Thessalonians tells us, *"If anyone will not work, neither shall he eat"* (3:10). First Timothy 5:8 says, *"If anyone does not provide for his own, and especially for those of his household, he has denied the faith and is worse than an unbeliever."* So please don't misinterpret what is being said here. God has a role for us to play in our provision, but we are not to fear that He won't help us when we need assistance. Trust in the Lord!

Today, many are hopeless and miserable because the way they had thought their lives would turn out didn't work out that way at all. But the Bible says that *"Happy is the one who has the God of Jacob for his help, whose hope is in the Lord his God"* (Ps 146:5). Conversely, unhappy are those who look for it elsewhere!

Looking to the Lord for everything is not a weird or difficult thing to do. He is faithful. He will provide. He will direct our steps and lead us in the path in which we're to go, whether that be a new job, a ministry—whatever He has for us! Our place is to seek His face and then let Him direct our steps. *Lord, help me to follow wherever You lead, even when I don't understand what you are doing. Fill me with faith to trust You always.*

Got Hope?

⁹The Lord watches over the strangers; He relieves the fatherless and widow; but the way of the wicked He turns upside down. ¹⁰The Lord shall reign forever—your God, O Zion, to all generations. Praise the Lord! —*Psalm 146:9-10*

OUR GOD is so good! The word "strangers" means "sojourners" and would apply to the non-Jews living in Israel. Figuratively, it means "those without rights," or "the downtrodden." God also lifts up the orphans and the widows. Such is the loving heart of our Father. But He turns the ways of the wicked upside down! We see that the Lord has mercy on the weaker ones: the impaired, the helpless, the lonely, and the needy. "*The righteous cry out, and the Lord hears, and delivers them out of all their troubles. The Lord is near to those who have a broken heart, and saves such as have a contrite spirit. Many are the afflictions of the righteous, but the Lord delivers him out of them all*" (Ps 34:17-19).

Have you ever had to wait for something to be delivered to your house or for someone to arrive that you really wanted to see? Sometimes being delivered from our troubles and afflictions involves waiting, but the Lord is still near you during those times, surrounding you with His love and lifting you up. He hears our cries, and even though He is permitting us to go through this seemingly unending period of waiting, He wants us to be content in just knowing that our world isn't going to be turned upside down, even though sometimes we feel like that. What He promised, He will perform!

It's during those times when we feel left alone, having to wait and trust, that it's all the more crucial that we have hope! We can praise the Lord even in the middle of our distress or trial because, as verse 10 tells us, the Lord shall reign forever to all generations. You can praise Him, because He knows your struggle, and He always defends the righteous.

Isaiah 54:17 gives us the encouraging news that God is with us and watching over us: "*No weapon formed against you shall prosper, and every tongue which rises against you in judgment you shall condemn. This is the heritage of the servants of the Lord, and their righteousness is from Me, says the Lord.*"

As believers, God's imputed righteousness, meaning the righteous life of Christ, has been transferred into our account, so we have the expectation that God will always defend and provide for His children. Sometimes He defends our flesh, but *He always defends our souls*. This is our inheritance, and not because we earned it or deserve it, but because when God looks at us He sees us in Christ as new creations with all the old things having passed away and all things having been made new. This is what sufficient hope is.

Do you want to be happy? Happiness can be a vague, ethereal kind of thing. Rather than seeking happiness, put your hope in the God of Jacob. And *"Be anxious for nothing, but . . . let your requests be made known to God; and the peace of God, which surpasses all understanding, will guard your hearts and minds through Christ Jesus"* (Phil 4:6-7).

It's tragic, but there are an awful lot of Christians today who simply are not happy. And the reason? They act as if this world is our home and we have to get all we can out of it. They're seeking after something that God has not promised us. This is *not* our home, and although we're supposed to take care of the blessings the Lord has given to us, we're not to place our hope in this world. Tragedies can take that away in a moment. But if we place our hope in the Lord, nothing can rob us of our peace. Troubles only remind us that life is but a vapor, and the next one is long and wonderful and perfect. So how are you doing? Got hope? If yes, then praise the Lord! If you're weak in that area, ask God to help you shift your thinking over to His plan for you, and be at peace.

December 22

The Importance of Praise

Introduction

Praise ye the Lord! —Psalm 149

—

AS WE BEGIN this next-to-last psalm, which is one of the Hallel psalms, we'll see several elements in common with the other Hallel psalms, and we'll be reminded once again of the words of King David in Psalm 34:1: *"I will bless the Lord at all times; His praise shall continually be in my mouth."*

Some things that we've learned from previous Hallel psalms have reminded us that we don't praise the Lord because things are good. We praise the Lord because *He* is good. This means that we can, and should, praise Him at all times because He is always good!

Psalm 32:3 reads, *"When I kept silent, my bones grew old through my groaning all day long."* If we put this together with the psalm in the first paragraph, we realize that not only should we bless the Lord at all times, but if we grow silent in our praise, we suffer, being robbed of joy and peace, and we end up groaning rather than praising.

Of course, praising the Lord continually doesn't mean just obliviously, robotically, and insincerely mouthing "praise" words. Nor does it mean that there aren't appropriate times for sorrowful groaning.

What we'll be looking at over the next few days is the importance of corporate praise, personal praise, and public praise. Some beautiful words from the King James Version of the Bible are recorded in Psalm 22:3: "*But thou art holy, O thou that inhabitest the praises of Israel.*" You may recall that "Israel" means "governed by God," so the words are not limited to national Israel. God inhabits our praises as well! (By the way, the word "inhabits" means "enthroned," or "settled in," or even "married to.") As temples of the Holy Spirit, God is always with us. But the idea of God "inhabiting our praises" should tell us that God manifests Himself in a special way that is exclusive to our praising Him.

"*But let the righteous be glad; let them rejoice before God; yes, let them rejoice exceedingly. Sing to God, sing praises to His name; extol Him who rides on the clouds, by His name Yah, and rejoice before Him*" (Psalm 68:3-4).

We're instructed throughout the Bible to praise the Lord. But do we realize what a privilege it is to praise Him and to know that He actually hears what we're saying? A person may have great words to say to and about a famous individual whom they respect and admire, but the chances that one would ever have an opportunity to actually express that admiration even once to the individual would be pretty slim. Not so with our God! He not only hears us, but He loves us, and He loves to hear us speak to Him! This should cause us to joyfully say, "Blessed is he who comes in the name of the Lord with exceeding joy!" We can sing praises to His name corporately, privately, and publicly with more zeal and passion than ever before because we've come to understand not only the importance, but the privilege, of praising our God.

Don't let your "bones grow old" through your "groaning all day long." The Lord is with you and in you! He reads your heart and mind; He comprehends your path and your lying down and is "intimately acquainted" with all your ways (Psalm 139:3). And you can freely cast all your care upon Him, for He cares for you (1 Peter 5:7). Praise the Lord!

December 23

Singing in the Reign

¹Praise the Lord! Sing to the Lord a new song, and His praise in the assembly of saints. ²Let Israel rejoice in their Maker; let the children of Zion be joyful in their King. ³Let them praise His name with the dance; let them sing praises to Him with the timbrel and harp. *—Psalm 149:1-3*

A̲RE YOU getting this? *Sing to the Lord a new song*. There are reasons to praise Him every day—morning, noon, and night. Verse 2 states that we rejoice in our Maker, and verse 3 says that we're to strike up the band and praise Him with the dance!

Remember when David "danced before the Lord with all his might," rejoicing that the ark had returned at last to Jerusalem? David was delighting in the Lord with a full heart. But what did his wife, Saul's daughter, have to say? Let's read it, and notice God's response to her reaction: *"David returned to bless his household. And Michal the daughter of Saul came out to meet David, and said, 'How glorious was the king of Israel today, uncovering himself today in the eyes of the maids of his servants, as one of the base fellows shamelessly uncovers himself!' So David said to Michal, 'It was before the Lord, who chose me instead of your father . . . to appoint me ruler over the people of the Lord, over Israel. Therefore I will play music before the Lord. And I will be even more undignified than this, and will be humble in my own sight. . . .' [And] Michal . . . had no children to the day of her death"* (2 Sm 6:20-23).

Be very careful about criticizing styles of worship. Old hymns, as beautiful as some of them may be, are not necessarily more anointed or sacred than new ones. The Holy Spirit is still writing "new songs," as the Spirit inspired the author of this psalm to tell us, and God will inhabit the praises coming from sincere hearts, even if the style may not be according to your preference. What matters is the theology of worship behind the songs, not the style.

The first thing that's brought to our attention in the opening lines of this psalm is that the writer refers to corporate worship—i.e., in the assembly of the saints. It's a great puzzle to me why "praise and worship meetings" in fellowships are usually not well attended. I understand that people are busy with work, school, and families. And mid-week Bible studies can be difficult for some to work into their hectic schedules. But if you search your hearts, can you find justification to avoid a once-a-month-or-so evening of simply praising the Lord? God inhabits the praises of His people. Isn't that a beautiful image? Do you want to pass that up because you're too tired or the music style doesn't suit you?

Corporate praise strengthens our spiritual unity! The psalmist encourages the people to be joyful in their King and "praise Him with the dance." God is to be the focus of these gatherings, not just a gifted singer or a talented instrumentalist, although these are attributes that the Lord has blessed some with, just as He did in David's day! In 2 Chronicles 5:11-6:1a we read, *"When the priests came out of the most holy place . . . and the Levites who were singers, all those of Asaph and Heman and Jeduthun, with their sons and their brethren, stood at the east end of the altar, clothed in white linen, having cymbals, stringed instruments and harps, and with them one hundred and twenty priests sounding with trumpets . . . praising and thanking the Lord, and when they lifted up their voice with the instruments of music, and praised the Lord . . . the house of the Lord was filled with a cloud, so that the priests could not continue ministering because of the cloud; for the glory of the Lord filled the house of God."*

That's truly a worship service, with voices lifted along with the sounds of the instruments, honoring God! This is truly "singing in the Reign" of God, our Savior! And when He is honored, glory fills the place! Who would want to miss that? Praise unites God's people as the focus is centered on Him and on no one else. Glory to God! (Kind of makes you want to join David, singing and dancing before Him, doesn't it?)

December 24

When Life Isn't Good

⁴For the Lord takes pleasure in His people; He will beautify the humble with salvation. ⁵Let the saints be joyful in glory; let them sing aloud on their beds. —*Psalm 149:4-5*

WE'VE LOOKED at what the Lord desires from us in the way of offering our praises to Him, but look at the benefits we reap from doing so! We're reminded that the Lord loves His children and *takes pleasure* in them. Those of you who are parents might think of it this way: of course you love your children all the time, when they're naughty and when they're nice. But when they're *willingly* obedient to you, seeking to please you, aren't you blessed by that? Doesn't it make your heart glad? Don't you feel like you want to hold them close to you? This is similar to what the psalmist is expressing here.

Verse 4 says that God will *beautify* the humble with salvation. One of the meanings of "beautify" is to glorify. The word "humble" means depressed, whether in mind or in circumstances. This gives us the context of them being on their beds, whether an actual sickbed, or even just a picture of being in a state of loneliness or discouragement. But God will lift them up and comfort them as they praise Him.

Peter wrote: *"Therefore, humble yourselves under the mighty hand of God, that He may exalt you in due time, casting all your care upon Him, for He cares for you"* (1 Pt 5:6-7). Precious words, my friends! Sometimes, life doesn't go the way we want it to. For some, it may be because we aren't walking rightly with the Lord. For others, He may allow hard things to come into their lives to show them their need for His salvation if they would just humble themselves enough to ask for it! Everlasting life is the promised prize for simply acknowledging one's sin and need of a Savior. Even then, we're not quite finished. We look forward to that time when we will stand before Christ in person, face to face, and know that we have all of eternity to pursue the depths and riches of our heavenly Father!

But back to the present—until that day, we are "promised" trials, tribulations, and troubles. Life on the outside isn't always going to be pleasant, but it can always be beautiful. Jesus told us to *"be of good cheer, for I have overcome the world"* (John 16:33), and He stands beside us every moment—when life is good and when it isn't.

What did the apostle Paul write about the trials that we must go through? Listen to his testimony! *"And lest I should be exalted above measure by the abundance of the revelations, a thorn in the flesh was given to me, a messenger of Satan to buffet me, lest I be exalted above measure. Concerning this thing I pleaded with the Lord three times that it might depart from me. And He said to me, 'My grace is sufficient for you, for My strength is made perfect in weakness.' Therefore most gladly I will rather boast in my infirmities, that the power of Christ may rest upon me. Therefore I take pleasure in infirmities, in reproaches, in needs, in persecutions, in distresses, for Christ's sake. For when I am weak, then I am strong"* (2 Cor 12:7-10). Remember, this is *Paul*, the man who was 100 percent sold out for the Lord. Should we even question why the Lord allows *us* to go through trials?

What is our psalmist saying about the importance of praise? In short, personal praise is an expression of thanks and trust. Notice that our verse today doesn't tell us to "be joyful in glory and sing aloud from the mountain top or palace." We're told to be joyful in glory and sing aloud *because the Lord takes pleasure in His people and beautifies the lives of the humble with salvation*! This knowledge should make us want to sing right out loud, even from our sickbed!

Tomorrow, we'll dig a little deeper into these precious promises, but meanwhile, keep on singing praises to the One who always holds you by the hand, in good times and bad.

Does Your Face Shine?

[Cont'd] *⁴*For the Lord takes pleasure in His people; He will beautify the humble with salvation. *⁵*Let the saints be joyful in glory; let them sing aloud on their beds. *—Psalm 149:4-5*

IT'S DIFFICULT for some people to understand why believers have to go through hard times. As God's children, doesn't it seem like He'd make it so that we never have to face hard situations? After all, He's God! He could keep us from ever having to suffer, couldn't He? Oh, but God knows His children, and He knows that if we were able to skate through life unchallenged by difficulties and hard times, we'd never understand or appreciate the depths of what the Father and the Son went through to save us from eternal suffering. We just saw what Paul had to face, and he got the message. It's better to suffer here and remain humble, knowing that God is with us and loving us every second, than to always ride high without any trials to soften and change us.

Psalm 34:2-8 "*My soul shall make its boast in the Lord; the humble shall hear of it and be glad. O magnify the Lord with me, and let us exalt His name together. I sought the Lord, and He heard me, and delivered me from all my fears. . . . The angel of the Lord encamps around those who fear Him, and delivers them. O, taste and see that the Lord is good; blessed is the man who trusts in Him!*" These are the words that follow the first verse of Psalm 34: "*I will bless the Lord at all times; His praise shall continually be in my mouth.*" The result? The humble will hear this and rejoice. They will join in, singing and magnifying and exalting the name of the Lord together in corporate worship! And the joy of the Lord will shine on our faces as we rejoice in the One whom we are praising.

It's a lot easier to be joyful and to sing right out loud when things are going well, and we should. But remember what we learned before, that praising God has nothing to do with our circumstances and everything to do with where we're headed. Where is that? Eternity with God! Praise expresses thanks for our salvation and trust through our trials. We don't have to wait for *anything* or go anywhere to praise the Lord. We can be joyful that there is glory that awaits us, even if we feel like we're in the pit of despair.

"*Though the fig tree may not blossom, Nor fruit be on the vines; Though the labor of the olive may fail, And the fields yield no food; Though the flock may be cut off from the fold, And there be no herd in the stalls— Yet I will rejoice in the Lord, I will joy in the God of my salvation. The Lord God is my strength; He will make my feet like deer's feet, And He will make me walk on my high hills*" (Habakkuk 3:17-19). Having feet like deer's feet and walking on high hills is figurative for walking above the difficult circumstances of life with a heart of rejoicing in the God of our salvation. Life may not offer us much that seems praiseworthy at times, but salvation is always a cause for rejoicing, and personal praise is an expression of both thanks and trust. We can trust that God is good, even when life isn't, and we can give thanks that this life isn't all there is. Others will see our joy and want to know the reason.

All of these things are reasons why it's important for us to gather together with other believers in corporate praise, which strengthens our spiritual unity. It's also vital that we offer to the Lord our personal praise on a daily, even hourly, or moment-by-moment, basis for thanksgiving and that we have trust in our salvation.

Tomorrow, we'll take a look at public praise and the necessity of that, but as for today, do you understand the need to set aside a few moments to step away from your desk or the sink or the table (even if just in your heart) and offer to the Lord your heartfelt praise and thanksgiving for giving you life, now and forever? He's right there beside you, listening.

December 26

Victor or Victim?

> [6] Let the high praises of God be in their mouth, and a two-edged sword in their hand; [7] to execute vengeance on the nations, and punishments on the peoples; [8] to bind their kings with chains, and their nobles with fetters of iron; [9] to execute on them the written judgment—this honor have all his saints. Praise the Lord! —*Psalm 149:6-9*

AN INTERESTING shift takes place in the middle of verse six when the high praises in our mouths are accompanied by a two-edged sword in our hands. Verse 9 even speaks of executing vengeance on the nations, punishing people, binding kings with chains and their nobles with fetter of iron as being an honor for the saints of the Lord!

How do we interpret this? First of all, remember that as believers we're the *victors* in this life, not the *victims*. No matter what happens during our time on earth, we live always with the Lord beside us. Romans 8:35-39 reads, "*Who shall separate us from the love of Christ? Shall tribulation, or distress, or persecution, or famine, or nakedness, or peril, or sword? As it is written: 'For Your sake we are killed all day long; we are accounted as sheep for the slaughter.' Yet in all these things we are more than conquerors through Him who loved us. For I am persuaded that neither death nor life, nor angels nor principalities nor powers, nor things present nor things to come, nor height nor depth, nor any other created thing, shall be able to separate us from the love of God which is in Christ Jesus our Lord.*"

Notice that it says, "Who shall separate us from the love of Christ?" The verse then goes on to list all the things that the "whos" will try to use—but they won't succeed. The persecution of Christians around the world has never been higher and is growing worse by the day. Yet, we, the church, are "more than conquerors"? In what way? Because of the very simple truth that Jesus Christ conquered death, and thus death has lost its sting. As believers, we belong to the Lord forever, and we need have no fear of death!

Another thing to note is that, for Israel, the verses in psalm 149 had a literal meaning; for the church, the meaning is spiritual. Israel was commissioned by God to take the land of Canaan by force, executing vengeance on the nations who withstood them, binding their kings and nobles, and delivering them over to the judgment of God. Although the meaning for the church is spiritual, the battle is just as fierce. Paul wrote, "*For the weapons of our warfare are not carnal but mighty in God for pulling down strongholds, casting down arguments and every high thing that exalts itself against the knowledge of God, bringing every thought into captivity to the obedience of Christ, and being ready to punish all disobedience when your obedience is fulfilled*" (2 Corinthians 10:4-6). And in Ephesians we read: "*Finally, my brethren, be strong in the Lord and in the power of His might. Put on the whole armor of God, that you may be able to stand against the wiles of the devil. For we do not wrestle against flesh and blood, but against principalities, against powers, against the rulers of wickedness in the heavenly places. Therefore take up the whole armor of God, that you may be able to withstand in the evil day, and having done all, to stand*" (Ephesians 6:10-13).

To repeat, the weapons of our warfare are not carnal because the battle is spiritual, but it can be fierce. Our enemies, however, often *are* physical and are used against us in this spiritual battle. But verse 6 of our psalm today reminds us that we are to have the high praises of God in our mouths as we engage in these battles, and that would mean praising Him out loud in the hearing of our enemies! This is why *public praise* is so vital. It's our declaration of God's supreme power and authority. Will you allow the world to see that you're not afraid to give public praise to our Lord and Savior? "*I am not ashamed of the gospel of Christ, for it is the power of God to salvation for everyone who believes*" (Rom 1:16).

Going Public

[Cont'd] ⁶Let the high praises of God be in their mouth, and a two-edged sword in their hand; ⁷to execute vengeance on the nations, and punishments on the peoples; ⁸to bind their kings with chains, and their nobles with fetters of iron; ⁹to execute on them the written judgment—this honor have all his saints. Praise the Lord! —*Psalm 149:6-9*

"ANTIPAS" is a name that's relatively unknown to most, but the Lord knew who he was! "*And to the angel of the church in Pergamos write: 'These things says He who has the sharp two-edged sword: "I know your works, and where you dwell, where Satan's throne is. And you hold fast to My name, and did not deny My faith even in the days in which **Antipas** was My faithful martyr, who was killed among you, where Satan dwells"'"* (Rev. 2:12-13).

The term "martyr" means "witness," and it became a synonym for those killed for their faith in the first century. Tradition tells us that those assigned to execute this dear man, known for his love and kindness to others, pleaded with him to recant his belief in Jesus, saying to him, "But Antipas, the whole world is against you," to which Antipas replied without hesitation, "Then I am against the whole world."

This is the honor of the saints, including yours and mine. To praise God in the face of persecution and to declare His supreme power and authority is one of the greatest acts of love we can show to our Lord and before the lost. There is power in the very name of Jesus to break every chain. (See Acts 3:6; 16:18; 19:13; Rom 1:3-4, 1 Cor 5:4; etc.).

The importance of public praise is that power is innate within it to break not only chains, but to heal broken hearts, forgive sin, "restore the years eaten by the canker worm," grant hope, give peace that passes understanding, bring joy, destroy the fear of death, etc. The world needs to hear these things! They won't hear them in the classroom or on television. Unless they do some serious searching they won't run across these truths online. God has given us mouths to speak with, and He longs to fill those mouths with His words, because they alone contain life, healing, strength, and the love that passes understanding. First Chronicles tells us, "*Sing to the Lord, all the earth; proclaim the good news of His salvation from day to day. Declare His glory among the nations, His wonders among all peoples. For the Lord is great and greatly to be praised; He is also to be feared above all gods. For all the gods of the peoples are idols, but the Lord made the heavens. Honor and majesty are before Him; strength and gladness are in His place*" (16:23-27).

The Lord is great and worthy of all praise, and we must declare His glory by preaching and praising Him to all nations. Why? We're instructed to do so in many places in the Bible. For example, Peter wrote: *"But you are a chosen generation, a royal priesthood, a holy nation, His own special people, that you may proclaim the praises of Him who called you out of darkness into His marvelous light; who . . . now have obtained mercy"* (1 Peter 2:9-10).

Remember: *corporate* praise blesses God and strengthens our spiritual unity; in *personal* praise we express our thanks and trust in the Lord; *public* praise declares God's power and authority over all creation, even when much of that creation has turned against Him. It's vital that we praise our God because it blesses Him and strengthens us, drawing us closer to Him. How can we praise Him publicly? Tell a nonbeliever that God is good. Praise the Lord in the hearing of someone lost in his or her sin. Leave tracts behind you when you use a public restroom or on a table in a restaurant. Tuck one into the envelope before you send off that bill. Probably not many will be read, but *that's not up to you!* Our job is to spread the good news, praise the Lord, and seek to do His will. The rest is up to God. Your "going public" may be the very means that rescues someone from the jaws of hell.

December 28

The Person of Praise

Introduction

Praise the Lord! —Psalm 150

AS WE MOVE toward the end of this year that the Lord has given to us, let's review a little. We've been taking a serious look at the importance of praise. We learned not to be too critical of "new songs" with perhaps a different style than we're accustomed to as long as the content is glorifying to the Lord. The main thing is that we are to praise the Lord with our hearts, our minds, and our voices, in sincerity and truth.

Psalm 149:1, if you remember, read, *"Praise the Lord! Sing to the Lord a new song, and His praise in the assembly of the saints."* We can sing "new songs," but we can sing old songs. Regardless, we saw that corporate praise strengthens our spiritual unity; personal praise is an expression of thanks and trust, and public praise is a declaration of God's supreme power and authority. The primary key is that we are praising the Lord, who admonishes us again and again through His Word that we are to be people of praise.

Psalm 9:1-2 states, "*I will praise You O Lord, with my whole heart; I will tell of all your marvelous works. I will be glad and rejoice in You; I will sing praise to Your name, O Most High.*"

When we understand the importance of praise, our praise will come freely from hearts of gladness and rejoicing before the Most High, an act that indicates that we are on our way to becoming a person of praise.

As we continue through this short final psalm, we'll learn more about what it means to be a person of praise, and we'll see that one of the many reasons we have to praise the Lord is represented in the bread and cup, representing the Body and Blood of the Lord Jesus as we partake of communion with our fellow believers.

Let's go forward with joy as we seek for ways to please our Father and to be witnesses to the world of His goodness and love for us. He *alone* is worthy of all of our praise.

December 29

All That I Have

³Praise Him with the sound of the trumpet; praise Him with the lute and harp! ⁴Praise Him with the timbrel and dance; praise Him with stringed instruments and flutes! ⁵Praise Him with loud cymbals; praise Him with clashing cymbals! —Psalm 150:3-5

AS WE CONTINUE this look at our great and awesome God, who is worthy of all praise, we recall that the Scriptures tell us that He commands the seas to stay within their prescribed boundaries; He names and numbers the stars of the heaven! He keeps our tears in His bottle, saints, and He knows how many hairs are on our head. He guards and keeps us; nothing can separate us from His love, and certainly no one can snatch us from His hand!

Who is this King of Glory? Revelation describes Him: "*His eyes were like a flame of fire, and on His head were many crowns. He had a name written that no one knew except Himself. He was clothed with a robe dipped in blood, and His name is called the Word of God. And the armies in heaven, clothed in fine linen, white and clean, followed Him on white horses. Now out of His mouth goes a sharp sword, that with it He should strike the nations. And He Himself will rule them with a rod of iron. He Himself treads the winepress of the fierceness and wrath of Almighty God. And He has on His robe and on His thigh a name written: KING OF KINGS AND LORD OF LORDS*" (Rev 19:11-16).

This is the almighty God, who is worthy to be praised. Although singing isn't specifically mentioned in this psalm, it certainly isn't excluded based on other scriptures. Moses and the children of Israel sang, *"I will sing to the Lord, for He has triumphed gloriously! The horse and its rider He has thrown into the sea! The Lord is my strength and song, and He has become my salvation; He is my God, and I will praise Him . . ."* (Ex 15:1-2).

Does this mean that we all need to be musically adept if we want to praise the Lord? Not at all! The person of praise will use *everything* they are and have for God's glory. There's no denying that David was a person of praise. He understood that praise wasn't merely cheap words or an offering that cost him nothing. David wrote as a person of praise even in the depths of despair or on the heels of horrific sin in his life. Praise, worship, and offerings are to *always* be given to God with hearts of thanksgiving and praise. Whatever you've been gifted or blessed with, are you using those things as a means and an opportunity to bring glory to God? (See John 6:62-66: without the Holy Spirit's work, the flesh profits nothing.) A person of praise will have an elevated view of God and will use all that he or she is and has for His glory, for He alone has and is the Word of Life. Are we like David? Do we know and believe that bringing glory to God and worshiping Him is worthy of anything that it may cost us? Or do we only offer to Him that which costs us nothing? The heart of a person of praise wants to glorify God even on the heels of great sin in their own life! Sometimes that's the best way to begin to be set free not only from the bondage that sin can keep us in but also the horrible guilt that can follow us afterward. Praise, worship, and offerings are given to God with a heart of thanksgiving, a heart of praise. No matter what your gift is, are you using it as an opportunity to bring God the glory?

Do you fully comprehend the value of having Christ reigning in your life? Have you come to understand that once you've come to Jesus, there's nowhere else worthwhile to go? May our hearts be touched as we're reminded that all that we are and have is of Him and for His glory through us!

December 30

Are You Breathing?
Praise the Lord!

[6]Let everything that has breath praise the Lord.
Praise the Lord! —*Psalm 150:6*

WHO ARE THOSE who are told to praise the Lord in this verse? Everyone who has breath! A better way to read this (as not all who are breathing praise the Lord, although they should) is "Because you have breath, praise the Lord!" For what should we praise Him? The reasons are innumerable. Think on His mighty acts and

His excellent greatness. Think of the fact that He had the power to form you within the womb of your mother, hidden from sight, but wonderfully designed!

Our journey through the psalms has revealed to us, more than anything, that we must keep focused on the fact that God is higher and greater than anything in the universe. This should also help us to have an accurate perception of ourselves, which Jesus Himself revealed to us and is recorded in John 15:5: "*I am the vine, you are the branches. He who abides in Me, and I in him, bears much fruit; for without Me you can do nothing.*" And Paul wrote: "*For I say, through the grace given to me, to everyone who is among you, not to think more highly than he ought to think, but to think soberly, as God has dealt to each one a measure of faith*" (Romans 12:30). In fact, we're told that regardless of who we are, because we *do* have breath, praise the Lord!

Praise is warranted because of God's mighty acts and His excellent greatness, including the description of our beginning as having been fearfully and wonderfully designed. When we consider "the work of His fingers," it should be easy to have an elevated view of our God and an accurate perception of ourselves.

When Paul met with the "deep thinkers" at the Areopagus and the statue that had been erected there, which was dedicated to the "unknown God," he said, "*And He [God] has made from one blood every nation of men to dwell on all the face of the earth, and has determined their preappointed times and the boundaries of their dwellings, so that they should seek the Lord, in the hope that they might grope for Him and find Him, though He is not far from each one of us; for in Him we live and move and have our being, as also some of your own poets have said, 'For we are also His offspring.' Therefore, since we are the offspring of God, we ought not to think that the Divine Nature is like gold or silver or stone, something shaped by art and man's devising*" (Acts 17:26-29).

Did you catch that? "*In Him we live and move and have our being.*" For that very reason alone we ought to praise the Lord. Even those who don't know Him are given this gift of being sustained by Him, and they don't even recognize it. What a loving God! As for ourselves, we want to continue to be reminded that being a person of praise means that our total dependence is upon God.

Did you wake up this morning? Praise the Lord! Did you stay awake through the Sunday service? Praise the Lord! Are you still alive and able to crawl into bed at night? Praise the Lord! He is the one who allowed you to awaken, to attend church or work, to make it through the day, and to get under your covers at night. Do you understand that your salvation is secure because it's dependent upon Him? Praise the Lord! Are you covered by the shadow of His wings? The Bible says you are. Praise the Lord!

The prophet Isaiah wrote: "*The humble also shall increase their joy in the Lord, and the poor among men shall rejoice in the Holy One of Israel*" (Isaiah 29:19). To know the Lord God and His majesty and mighty works is to be humbled by His love for lowly man and amazed at His grace and mercy on us, for us, and in spite of us! If this is true of you, then you are well on your way to becoming a person of praise!

December 31

Alone No More!

Praise the Lord! —Psalm 150:3-5

NOW THAT we've come to understand the "who," "what," "where," "when," and "how" of praise and why we should bless the Lord at all times with that praise continually on our lips, praising Him should become a way of life, not just a part of a church service. Whether we realize it or not, we're dependent upon the Lord for everything. We just saw yesterday that we abide in Christ, the vine, who brings life and bears fruit. We can't save ourselves. We can't conquer death by ourselves. We can't be reconciled to God by ourselves. But most importantly, *we are not by ourselves!* Hallelujah! Isn't that wonderful?

We're able to abide because we're *in* Him. So, because we do have the breath of life in us, praise the Lord! What present reasons do we have to praise Him? There is none greater than that represented by the bread and the cup as we partake of communion.

There's an often-overlooked component of the Lord's table found in 1 Corinthians 11:23-26: "*For I received from the Lord that which I also delivered to you: that the Lord Jesus on the same night in which He was betrayed took bread; and when He had given thanks, He broke it and said, 'Take, eat; this is My body which is broken for you; do this in remembrance of Me.' In the same manner He also took the cup after supper, saying, 'This cup is the new covenant in My blood. This do, as often as you drink it, in remembrance of Me.' For as often as you eat this bread and drink this cup, you proclaim the Lord's death till He comes.*"

There's a lot to consider in these words of Paul, who describes himself as "one born out of due time" in 1 Corinthians 15:8. He meant that he wasn't among the original twelve apostles, nor was he present at the Last Supper. Yet even so, he received direct instruction from the Lord concerning communion that wasn't mentioned at that first event. One is "as often as you do this . . . " when Jesus spoke of the continuance of the taking of the bread and the cup. He wasn't saying, "Do this often," but "*when* you do this, do it in remembrance of the cross, My broken body, and My shed blood." He reminds us that not only do we remember the Lord's death at communion time and proclaim that His broken body and shed blood is the only means of salvation, but He adds, "Do this until I come."

Jesus also said, "*Let not your heart be troubled; you believe in God, believe also in Me. In My Father's house are many mansions; if it were not so, I would have told you. I go to prepare a place for you. And if I go and prepare a place for you, I will come again and receive you to Myself; that where I am, there you may be also. And where I go you know, and the way you know*" (John 14:1-4). These words Jesus spoke at the Last Supper and the institution of the New Covenant in His blood. At the communion table, not only do we remember Christ's coming to earth as a Man but that He has unfinished business on this earth. He is coming again! Among the mighty acts of God and His excellent greatness is the giving of His Son to die for our sins, the promise of His return, and the bodily resurrection of all who believe to everlasting life. When we partake at the table of the Lord, we should remember the unusual meshing of solemnity and celebration. We solemnly remember the Lord's death, but we also celebrate His soon return! He died on the cross as the Lamb of God who takes away the sins of the world, but He returns as the *Lion* of the tribe of Judah, ultimately conquering a Christ-rejecting and sinful world and ruling and reigning with a rod of iron.

Then begins the most glorious time, as we head into the promised eternity of joy, blessing, and union with our Lord and Savior, to whom we were meant to belong forever and ever! There will be no more sorrow, death, loneliness, or grief of any kind. We look forward to His coming, maybe in the year ahead! To God be the glory! Amen.